GW00792891

Sheldon and Fidler's
Practice and Law
of Banking

Other M & E books of interest:

Cases in Banking Law
Commercial Banking Law
A Dictionary of Banking
Practical Bank Management

Sheldon and Fidler's Practice and Law of Banking

P. J. M. Fidler, MA (Oxon)

Solicitor of the Supreme Court

assisted by

M. I. Freeman, BA (Oxon)

ELEVENTH EDITION

MACDONALD AND EVANS

Macdonald & Evans Ltd
Estover, Plymouth PL6 7PZ

First published 1920
Reprinted 1921, 1924 (twice)
Second edition 1925
Reprinted 1926
Third edition 1928
Reprinted 1929
Fourth edition 1930
Reprinted 1931, 1934
Fifth edition 1935
Reprinted 1937, 1939, 1941, 1942, 1944,
1945, 1946, 1947
Sixth edition 1949
Reprinted 1949, 1951
Seventh edition (with C. B. Drover) 1953
Reprinted 1955
Eighth edition 1958
Reprinted 1960, 1961
Ninth edition 1962
Reprinted 1963, 1965
Tenth edition 1972
Reprinted 1972, 1975, 1978
Eleventh edition 1982
Reprinted 1984

© Macdonald & Evans Ltd 1982

ISBN: 0 7121 1990 6 (Hardcased)
ISBN: 0 7121 1978 7 (Paperback)

*Filmset in Monophoto Times by
Northumberland Press Ltd, Gateshead
and printed in Great Britain by
Richard Clay (The Chaucer Press) Ltd, Bungay, Suffolk*

Preface to the First Edition

The object of this book is to provide, for the practical bank man and for the student of English banking law and practice, a manual sufficiently extensive in scope to meet present-day requirements.

The author wishes to acknowledge his indebtedness to the works of Sir John Paget and Dr Heber Hart, to *Questions on Banking Practice*, the *Journal of the Institute of Bankers*, and numerous other books, a list of which is given in the appendix as a bibliography. *Questions on Banking Practice* (referred to in the text as *QBP*), and the *Journal of the Institute of Bankers* contain a mine of information not to be found elsewhere, and they have rendered great service to banking in co-ordinating and establishing uniformity of practice among bankers.

Grateful thanks are also due to those friends who have freely given the benefit of their experience, particularly to Mr Ernest Sykes, and to the Publishers for the extra work entailed by the absence of the author on military service.

London, EC3   H.P.S.

August, 1920

Preface to the Eleventh Edition

It is now some sixty years since the first edition, and although Sheldon has always been a favourite with lawyers, accountants, bankers and students of banking, changing times and changing conditions have rendered both the style and the general approach somewhat out of date. The general plan of the book has accordingly been completely redesigned, and much of the material rewritten, although Sheldon's original emphasis on the practical aspects has been retained. The chapter on lending has been strengthened.

Among the most significant changes in the banking world since the last edition have been the expansion of the system of supervision of banks by the Bank of England, following the secondary banking crisis in 1973/4, and the introduction of control of deposit-taking institutions under the Banking Act 1979. The book now opens with an outline of the UK banking system, which includes new chapters on the Bank of England supervision and on the Banking Act. With the abolition of exchange control in 1979, the whole subject of exchange control has been deleted.

The Appendixes have been revised once again and now incorporate the Congenbill Bill of Lading (for permission to reproduce which I am indebted to the Baltic and International Maritime Conference), and specimen forms of many of the commoner types of security documentation and other documents used in connection with trade.

Since the text was completed, the whole of the 1980 Companies Act has come into force and the 1981 Companies Act has been passed and most of it has come into force. From the banker's point of view the most important provisions of the 1981 Act are: the contents and presentation of companies' annual accounts; the abolition of the Business Names Registry; the possibility for a company to purchase its own shares; the new formulation of the prohibition against financial assistance by a company in connection with the acquisition of its shares; and the amendment to the rules regarding the commencement of a voluntary winding up. Probably the most important of these are the last two.

Section 42 defines financial assistance, and permits assistance if a company's principal purpose in giving assistance is not to give it for the purpose of the acquisition (or to reduce or discharge a liability incurred for the purpose of the acquisition), or the giving of the assistance is only an incidental part of some larger purpose and the assistance is given in good faith in the interests of the company. It expressly permits certain transactions, such as the payment of lawful dividends, payments in the course of a winding up and the allotment of bonus shares. The old exceptions, where the lending of money was in the ordinary course of the business of the company, employee share schemes and loans to employees other than directors, still apply, but in the case of a public company only if the company has net assets which are not thereby reduced, or if they are, then the financial assistance must be provided out of distributable profits.

For private companies the restrictions are relaxed provided certain requirements are met; these include approval by special resolution of the company and the making and filing of a statutory declaration giving the required particulars.

With regard to the commencement of a creditors' winding up, at least seven days' notice must be given of the meeting of the company at which the resolution for winding up is to be proposed, and the meeting of creditors must be on the day of, or the day after, the members' meeting and notice of the creditors' meeting must be sent out at the same time as notice of the members' meeting. Failure to give the requisite notice of the meeting of the company will not affect the validity of any resolution passed at that meeting which would be valid but for the failure to give notice, but the fine for failure to comply with the requirements of s. 293 as amended has been increased by the 1980 Act.

The table of cases has been considerably expanded, as authorities have been cited more extensively than before in keeping with modern practice. The law is stated as at 31st August 1982, except where otherwise indicated.

Several new chapters have been added, dealing with the various specialist banking activities, and my thanks are due to Mr Nicholas Johnson, a director of Orion Bank, who wrote the chapter on The Underwriting and Syndication of Loans; to Mr David Wake-Walker, a Director of Kleinwort Benson, who wrote the chapters on Dealing in Foreign Exchange, Documentary Credits and Commercial Paper and Finance for Foreign Trade; to Mr Stuart Stradling, a partner in Rowe & Pitman, who wrote the chapter on Raising Money on The Stock Exchange; to Mr Frederick Salinger, a Director of Anglo Factoring Services, who wrote the chapter on Factoring; to Mr Alan Outten, a Director of Midland Montagu Leasing and Forward Trust Group, who wrote the chapter on Leasing; and to Mr Michael Cronin, Group Solicitor of Forward Trust, who wrote the chapter on Hire-Purchase.

My thanks are also due to Mr Bob Morrow of National Westminster Bank, who contributed many sections dealing with aspects of practical banking; to Mr Roger Barnes, of the Bank of England Supervision Department, who read the chapters concerning the role of the Bank of England, and Mr Gerry Weiss of Cork Gully, who read the chapters on Insolvency, and who both made many helpful suggestions; to Mr S. C. Veal, the Chief Inspector of the Bankers' Clearing House, who revised the chapter on the Clearing System; and to Mr Don Hughes of The Agricultural Mortgage Corporation who kindly revised the section concerning the AMC.

I have found *Questions on Banking Practice* a constant source of help, and gratefully acknowledge the permission I have received from the Institute of Bankers to reproduce material from it.

I am also grateful to Mrs Effie Ferrao and Mrs Christine Gilroy, who both gave much assistance in the typing, and in particular to

Mrs Carol O'Connor, who has processed every word of the work (many of them several times) on her magical word-processor.

In conclusion, I would like to express my warmest thanks to my friend Mr Michael Freeman, who suggested the revised layout of the book and gave me considerable assistance with the final drafts of several chapters, and to my senior partner, Mr David J. Freeman, without whose encouragement and advice this edition could not have been written.

43 Fetter Lane   P. J. M. Fidler
London EC4

1982

Contents

PART III   MONETARY INSTRUMENTS

payment; Banker presenting bill for payment; Payment of a
bill; Dishonour by non-acceptance or non-payment; Noting
and protest; Acceptance and payment for honour supra
protest; Bills drawn in a set; Effect of Limitation Act 1980
on bills; Conflict of laws; Promissory notes; Indorsement sans
recours

PART IV LENDING AND SECURITY

borrower's title; Local Land Charges Register; Land Charges
Register; Rights of pre-emption and options; Rights of
occupiers; Restrictions on owner's right to offer land as
security; Mortgages; Legal mortgages; Equitable mortgages;
Priority of mortgages; Unpaid vendor's lien; Mortgagor's
rights to redeem the mortgage; Rights of the mortgagee;
Second mortgages; Discharge of mortgages; Sub-mortgages;
Transfers of mortgage; Rates and taxes relating to mortgaged
land; Joint owners; Compulsory acquisition; Lending money
on leaseholds; Agreements for lease; Banker's inquiries where
registered land is offered as security; The Registers; Titles
capable of registration; Compulsory and voluntary registration; Borrower's title where registered land is offered as
security; Conveying registered land; Mortgages of registered
land; Rights and remedies; Second mortgages and sub-
mortgages of registered land; Rectification of register and
compensation

with charges, fixed and floating; Other conflicts; Bankruptcy
of the supplier; Liquidation of companies; Appointment of
a receiver by a floating chargee; Lending against security
distinguished

PART VII   THE BANKER AND INSOLVENCY

APPENDIXES

appointment of bankers by company; Resolution for appointment of bankers; Securities register

2. *Security Forms.* Guarantee; Charge by way of legal mortgage; Receipt on discharge of charge by way of legal mortgage;
Memorandum of deposit of title deeds; Memorandum of
deposit of shares by a customer to secure his own liability;
Stock transfer form; Debenture (floating charge); Mortgage
of insurance policy; Request for guarantee and counter-
indemnity; Form No. 47

3. *Documents Relating to Goods.* Bill of lading; Dock warrant;
Warehouse-keeper's certificate; Delivery order; General letter
of hypothecation; Trust receipt; Dock warrant

List of Illustrations

Table of Cases

Table of Statutes

PART I

THE UK BANKING SYSTEM

CHAPTER ONE

Banks in the United Kingdom

BANKS

Before the passing of the Banking Act 1979[1] any partnership or company or any individual could take money on deposit. To carry on a deposit-taking business no licence was needed, and no undertaking had to be given about the assets of the business or the way in which the business would be conducted.

Whether a particular deposit-taking business was a "bank" or not depended in the main on the nature of the privileges granted to it by the Bank of England and its reputation among the established members of the banking community.

If a deposit-taking business was not regarded as a bank by the elite of the banking community, it might nevertheless be "a bank" or "a banker" or "bona fide carrying on a banking business" for the purposes of a particular statute.

In all there were more than a dozen statutes which created a distinction between banking businesses and other deposit-taking businesses. In the case of some of the statutes lists of the businesses which were classified as banking businesses were published by the Department of Trade. The other statutes left it to the courts to decide whether a particular business was or was not a banking business for the purposes of the statute.

None of the statutes contained any formal definition of a bank, and it is probably true to say that in the whole of English law there is no accepted definition of the words "bank", "banker" or "banking". From time time to time the courts would attempt a definition, notably in the case of *United Dominions Trust* v. *Kirkwood*.[2]

In that case it was suggested in the Court of Appeal that for a

---

1. The Banking Act 1979 is discussed in detail in Chapter Three.
2. [1966] 1 Q.B. 431; [1966] 1 All E.R. 968.

deposit-taking business to be carrying on a banking business for the purposes of the dozen or so statutes mentioned above[3] it did not have to be engaged in making loans but, as Paget had written in the then current edition, it must

... accept money on current accounts, pay cheques drawn upon such account on demand and collect cheques for customers; that if such minimum services are afforded to all and sundry without restriction of any kind ..., the business is a banking business, whether or not other business is undertaken at the same time; that providing the banking business as so understood is not a mere facade for other business, the person or corporation is a banker or bank for the purposes of statutes relating to banking other than those where the sole criterion is the satisfaction of some government department.[4]

The Court of Appeal decided that although the suggested definition could not be applied to United Dominions Trust, it was nevertheless bona fide carrying on a banking business for the purposes of the Moneylenders Act because the banking community regarded it as doing so. The suggested definition was therefore not wholly acceptable, and the main point to consider in defining a banking business was the opinion of other banks.

There are also no formal definitions of such familiar banking terms as clearing bank and deposit bank; merchant bank; discount house; finance house; foreign bank and consortium bank; and so on. Such terms are merely terms of convenience and have no legal force. All the same, it is important to consider what they mean.

CLEARING BANKS AND DEPOSIT BANKS

The London clearing banks (or "clearers") are the Bank of England[5] and the proprietors of the London Bankers' Clearing House through which cheques are cleared and settled, namely the "Big Four" banks, Barclays, Lloyds, Midland and National Westminster, together with Coutts and Williams and Glyn's. The Co-operative Bank and the Central Trustee Savings Bank also have direct access to the Clearing House for clearing their cheques. The Scottish Clearing Banks, Bank of Scotland, Clydesdale Bank and Royal Bank of Scotland have their own clearing system in Scotland.

For many people the word "bank" is synonymous with the names of the Big Four, and in financial circles the term "clearing banks"

---

3. The statutes considered in the case were: Bills of Exchange Act 1882; Stamp Act 1891; Bankers' Books Evidence Act 1879; Moneylenders Acts 1900 to 1927; Finance (No. 2) Act 1915; Bank of England Act 1946; Companies Act 1948; Income Tax Act 1952; Cheques Act 1957; Protection of Depositors Act 1963.
4. This definition was suggested by Lord Denning M.R. and Diplock L.J. who were quoting from Paget's *Law of Banking* (7th Edn), p. 12.
5. The Bank of England is discussed in Chapter Two.

is sometimes loosely used to describe the Big Four banks alone. Between them, Barclays, Lloyds, Midland and National Westminster had over 11,000 branches in 1979, and in 1979 the total value of deposits with the Big Four and their subsidiaries was some £70 billion. In 1979 some 20 million people in the UK had personal bank accounts with the Big Four. All of the Big Four are public companies listed on the Stock Exchange and anyone can buy shares in them. The Big Four have substantial interests in other banks and financial institutions in the UK and abroad.

The presence of Coutts and Williams and Glyn's among the clearing banks is perhaps best explained as a historical accident. Neither bank is particularly large and today neither bank is independent. In 1979 Coutts had only 11 branches while Williams and Glyn's had 321 branches. Coutts is part of the National Westminster group. Williams and Glyn's is part of the group which includes the Royal Bank of Scotland.

The Co-operative Bank, admitted in 1975, is a newcomer to the London clearing system and is owned by the Co-operative Wholesale Society. In 1979 it had branches in 3,000 of the Co-op stores.

The Central Trustee Savings Bank was also admitted to the London clearing system in 1975. It was established in 1973 to provide banking services to all the Trustee Savings Banks (TSBs) and associated companies in the United Kingdom. The Trustee Savings Bank movement was founded in the nineteenth century to encourage savings among the poor; the TSBs are now governed by the Trustee Savings Banks Act 1981 and are subject to the supervision of the Trustee Savings Bank Central Board and the Registrar of Friendly Societies. Amalgamations in the wake of the Trustee Savings Banks Act 1976 had by 1979 reduced the number of regional TSBs to 17, operating a network of 1,640 branches for the benefit of some 8 million account holders with deposits of over £4.5 billion. The 1976 Act empowered the TSBs to provide a full banking service, removed the requirement that they invest deposits with the National Debt Commissioners, and provided that, with the approval of the Trustee Savings Bank Central Board, they might remunerate their trustees.[6] In 1978 the TSBs were given power to borrow money other than from depositors[7] and in 1979 they started to make loans to small businesses for a trial period.

The clearing banks are sometimes also referred to as "deposit banks", a name which is applied as well to certain other banks and which appears to signify that the bank in question has traditionally

6. Trustee Savings Banks Act 1978, ss. 9 and 12.
7. Ibid., s. 3. (*See now* the Act of 1981, s. 19.)

concentrated on the basic banking business of taking money on deposit and handling accounts, and has not specialised in providing other financial services such as those provided by the merchant banks. Among the banks which are sometimes referred to as deposit banks are the two big Northern Ireland banks, the Ulster Bank and the Northern Bank, which are owned by National Westminster and Midland respectively, and certain long-established but comparatively small banks such as C. Hoare & Co.

In recent years the distinction between a deposit bank and a merchant bank has become blurred as the deposit banks, the Big Four in particular, have expanded into some areas which were traditionally the prerogative of the merchant banks, and both the deposit banks and the merchant banks have expanded into new areas such as the Eurocurrency market[8] and leasing[9] as well as into areas such as trusts and investment advice which were traditionally the prerogative of the solicitor and the stockbroker. In addition, several new banks have emerged which are concentrating on deposits and accounts but would nevertheless not generally be referred to as deposit banks. As a result of these developments the term "deposit bank" has become too imprecise to be of much value and is now perhaps redundant.

Occasionally the clearing banks, or at any rate the Big Four, are referred to as "branch banks" or "High Street banks" or "joint stock banks". The first two terms are self-explanatory. The term "joint stock bank" was originally used to distinguish those banks which traded as companies with limited liability from those banks which traded as companies with unlimited liability or as partnerships. Since the overwhelming majority of banks today trade with limited liability, the term "joint stock bank" is no longer valuable.

MERCHANT BANKS

Merchant banks are, broadly speaking, banks which specialise in financial advice to businesses and the financing of trade, particularly international trade. Although most businesses have an account with a clearing bank, the largest businesses still tend to go to a merchant bank when they want to raise money on the Stock Exchange, or when they are involved in a merger or a takeover or a company reconstruction, or when they wish to obtain a long-term loan on the domestic or international money markets, or when they are looking for advice about foreign exchange transactions or investment

8. The Eurocurrency market is discussed in Chapter Twenty-Four.
9. *See* Chapter Twenty-Seven.

of their funds. Unlike the clearing banks, merchant banks have few private account holders and generally have only one or two branches in the UK, though they often have a number of branches overseas. Among the most important of the merchant banks are the seventeen "Accepting Houses",[10] so called because for a long time the principal device used by the merchant banks to finance trade was the acceptance credit.[11] Although the Accepting Houses are not necessarily the biggest or the most active of the merchant banks their position in the banking community is such that the term "merchant banks" is sometimes used to describe the Accepting Houses alone.

The Accepting Houses are all based in the City of London and include such illustrious banking names as Barings, Hambros, Lazards, Rothschilds and Warburgs. Their customers include many of the largest corporations in the world as well as many governments and public bodies.

Outside the ranks of the Accepting Houses there are perhaps twenty well-established banks which would generally be described in financial circles as merchant banks. Some of these banks, together with some of the Accepting Houses, are sometimes also referred to as "Issuing Houses" because at one time they specialised in raising money for companies by issuing shares on the Stock Exchange, a service now provided by most other merchant banks as well.

DISCOUNT HOUSES

Discount houses are highly specialised banks which take money on deposit from the banking sector and business sector and use the money deposited to make short-term loans to the Government, to public bodies and to businesses in return for such securities as Treasury bills, Government and local authority bonds, commercial bills and certificates of deposit. The Discount Houses thus act as a broker in the money market (or "discount market") between those who wish to lend short-term funds and those who wish to borrow short-term funds.

The term "discount houses" originated in the eighteenth century to describe those banks which specialised in lending money to businesses by discounting bills of exchange.[11] It is now generally used to describe the thirteen members of the London Discount Market

10. The full list of Accepting Houses is: Arbuthnot Latham & Co.; Baring Brothers & Co.; Brown, Shipley & Co.; Charterhouse Japhet; Antony Gibbs Holdings; Guinness Mahon & Co.; Hambros Bank; Hill Samuel & Co.; Kleinwort Benson; Lazard Brothers & Co.; Samuel Montagu & Co.; Morgan Grenfell & Co.; Rea Brothers; N. M. Rothschild & Sons; J. Henry Schroder Wagg & Co.; Singer & Friedlander; S. G. Warburg & Co.
11. This method of raising money is discussed in Chapter Nine.

Association,[12] the discount houses proper. The term is, however also used loosely to include the various "discount brokers", "money brokers" and "money trading banks" which have traditionally been active in the discount market. The largest of the discount houses is Union Discount which handles about a third of all discount market business.

FINANCE HOUSES

Finance houses specialise in the financing of hire-purchase transactions, particularly the financing of car purchases which accounts for nearly two-thirds of their business. With the growth of hire-purchase business after 1950 many finance houses expanded rapidly and diversified into new areas of activity, including a wide range of banking activities.

In 1979 about ninety per cent of all finance house business in the UK was carried on by the 84 members of the Finance Houses Association, the largest of which is United Dominions Trust.[13] Three of the leading finance houses, Lombard North Central, Mercantile Credit, and Forward Trust, are owned by National Westminster, Barclays, and Midland respectively.

FOREIGN AND CONSORTIUM BANKS

Over the last twenty years or so one of the most interesting banking developments in the UK has been the growth of the international money markets, particularly the Eurocurrency market, which, in the opinion of many commentators, has restored the City of London to its nineteenth-century position as the world's most important financial centre.[14]

To participate in these markets and to carry on general banking activities, a large number of foreign banks established offices in London. By the end of 1979 some 400 foreign banks had offices in London, including almost all the hundred largest banks in the world. The majority of the banks are not incorporated in the UK, but are nevertheless subject to the general supervision of the Bank of England.

12. The members of the London Discount Market Association are: Alexanders Discount Company; Allen, Harvey & Ross; Cater, Ryder & Co.; Clive Discount Company; Gerald Quin Cope & Co.; Page & Gwyther; Gerrard & National Discount Co.; Gillett Bros. Discount Company; Jessel, Toynbee & Co.; King & Shaxson; Secombe, Marshall & Campion; Smith, St. Aubyn & Co.; Union Discount Company of London.
13. A list of the members of the Finance Houses Association can be found in *The Bankers' Almanac and Year Book 1980–81*, Thomas Skinner Directories, p. G1403.
14. The international money markets are discussed in Chapter Twenty-Four.

The rise of the international money markets has also led to the appearance in the UK of a number of "consortium banks" (or "multinational banks") owned jointly by several major banks, usually from different countries and specialising in medium-term Eurocurrency loans. Among the most important of the consortium banks are Orion, in which National Westminster is a shareholder; Midland and International Banks (known affectionately as MAIBL), in which Midland is a shareholder; and Scandinavian Bank.

THE POST OFFICE NATIONAL GIROBANK

The Post Office National Girobank (formerly known as National Giro until 1978) was established in 1968 to provide a money transfer and current-account banking service, operating through most post offices in the UK. By 1979 the majority of public bodies and larger businesses were offering Giro payment facilities to customers as an alternative to payment by cheque, and international Giro facilities enabled Giro account holders to transfer money to other Giro account holders in most West European countries.

In 1976 personal and corporate overdrafts and loans were introduced, together with the Giro guarantee card, and in 1978 budget accounts, deposit accounts and bridging loans became available. By the end of 1979 the Girobank had about 880,000 account holders and deposits worth about £391 million.

OTHER DEPOSIT-TAKING OR LOAN-MAKING INSTITUTIONS

There are a number of other institutions which take deposits or make loans (or both) but which would not generally be regarded as banks. These include the building societies, credit unions, the various public sector bodies which make loans to industry, the Crown Agents, and (despite its name) the National Savings Bank.

All of these institutions are for most purposes outside the scope of this book.

CHAPTER TWO

Regulation of the UK Banking Sector

THE BANK OF ENGLAND

Banking in the UK is regulated by the Bank of England ("the Bank") which was founded in 1694 to provide finance for the Government and was brought into public ownership by the Bank of England Act 1946. In theory the Bank is subordinate to the Treasury,[1] but in practice the relationship is one of close cooperation rather than subordination.

The Bank is administered by the Court, composed of the Governor and Deputy Governor, four executive directors and twelve non-executive directors, who are all men with distinguished records in finance, industry or public life. The day-to-day management of the Bank is the responsibility of the Governors and executive directors (and associate directors) who are not permitted to hold positions outside the Bank.

The Bank prints, puts into circulation and withdraws from circulation all the paper currency in England and Wales and some of the notes in Scotland and Northern Ireland.[2] Until 1925 paper currency could be exchanged on demand for its face value in gold, but this is no longer possible.[3]

On behalf of the Treasury the Bank manages the Exchange Equalisation Account which holds Britain's official reserves of gold, foreign exchange and special drawing rights on the International Monetary Fund. The Exchange Equalisation Account is used to help stabilise the exchange rate.[4] As agent for the Treasury the Bank administered exchange control which came into force in 1939 to protect the country's reserves and was abolished in 1979.

1. Bank of England Act 1946, s. 4(1).
2. The principal rules relating to the issue and withdrawal of paper currency are contained in the Currency and Bank Notes Act 1954, s. 2; also the Bank Charter Act 1844, the Gold Standard Act 1925 and the Currency and Bank Notes Act 1928.
3. The right to exchange paper currency for gold on demand was extinguished by the Gold Standard Act 1925.
4. For an account of the way in which the Exchange Equalisation Account is used, see "The Exchange Equalisation Accounts—Its Origins and Development", Bank of England Quarterly Bulletin, December 1968.

In addition to the activities mentioned above the Bank acts as banker to the Government and to the banks.

THE REGULATION OF BANK LENDING

The Bank plays, like most other central banks, an important traditional role in regulating bank lending. It does this partly by laying down guidelines regarding the banks' employment of their funds, and partly by its control over base rate (formerly called) minimum lending rate (MLR). This is the rate of interest which the Bank charges, in its capacity as "lender of last resort", to a discount house which otherwise by 3.30 p.m. on any banking day would have insufficient deposits to cover all the loans that it has made. It is the rate which influences all other rates of interest throughout the economy and as such it has a profound influence upon the overall demand for loans.

The guidelines laid down by the Bank regarding the banks' employment of their funds have, broadly speaking, two main objects: first, to ensure that banks do not run into liquidity problems by lending too large a percentage of deposits for too long a time; and secondly, to control the size of the money supply in accordance with Government policy.

Under the system in operation until 1971 the clearing banks were supposed to keep about 8 per cent of deposits in cash or in their non-interest-bearing accounts with the Bank, and about 20 per cent of deposits in certain liquid investments which could be turned into cash at short notice. This 28 per cent of deposits was known as the "liquidity ratio". The remaining 72 per cent of deposits could in theory be lent without restriction but in practice a substantial proportion was usually invested in short-dated Government bonds. From time to time, when the money supply was considered too large, the Bank would call upon the clearing banks to make "special deposits" with the Bank at an interest rate very much lower than the rate they would have received if they had lent the money elsewhere.

This system also involved the imposition of limits on the permitted growth of lending by the clearing banks. The extensive reliance placed on such direct controls over the operations of clearing banks inhibited competition and the working of the price mechanism. In 1971 a new system was introduced, based on the Bank's paper "Competition and Credit Control".[5] Its object was to control bank lending to the private sector primarily by the interest rate. If the

5. "Competition and Credit Control", Bank of England 1971.

cost of the banks' funds was pushed up, it was thought, the banks would increase their interest charges, and there would be a reduction in borrowings.

Unlike the old system, which acted on clearing banks, but left other banks free of any such restrictions, under competition and credit control a $12\frac{1}{2}$ per cent minimum reserve asset ratio was introduced, and a 50 per cent public sector debt ratio was imposed on the discount houses.

Reserve assets must be at least $12\frac{1}{2}$ per cent of eligible liabilities. Reserve assets comprise balances with the Bank (other than special deposits), money at call with listed discount market institutions, money at call with listed brokers, UK and Northern Ireland Treasury Bills, UK local authority bills eligible for re-discount at the Bank and UK bank bills eligible for re-discount at the Bank (but commercial bills must not exceed 2 per cent of total eligible liabilities). Reserve assets must be in sterling; notes and coin are not reserve assets, unless deposited at the Bank.

Eligible liabilities ("ELs") comprise broadly sterling deposits drawn from outside the banking system, with an original maturity of two years or less, plus the bank's net foreign currency liability.[6]

To increase pressure on banks to raise interest rates the Bank also announced that it would intervene much less actively in the gilt-edged market to smooth out price fluctuations.

There have been problems under the new system. One early problem was that when interest rates rose the banks sought to retain customer goodwill by absorbing some of the increase by reducing the margin between borrowing and lending rates; so much so that at times the lending rates fell below the rates at which the banks were prepared to borrow money from their customers. A circular flow of money from banks to customers and banks developed, having the appearance of an explosion of bank lending to the private sector. To control this the Supplementary Special Deposits Scheme (later christened the "corset") was introduced in December 1973. This limited the ability of banks to increase their interest-bearing deposits by imposing penalties in the form of a requirement to lodge non-interest-bearing supplementary special deposits with the Bank.

The Scheme has not been wholly successful. Banks avoided the corset restrictions by bringing non-bank borrowers and lenders into direct contact with one another. This enabled funds to be made available for borrowing without breaking corset limits or appearing in the monetary aggregates. The banks also began to anticipate the

6. This abbreviated definition is taken from *Britain 1979*, published by HMSO, p. 343.

periodic imposition of the corset, brought in only when other monetary policy instruments have needed support and the monetary aggregates were at or near the top of their target range. A much more serious threat to the Scheme has been the abolition of exchange controls in October 1979, which has given UK banks freedom to borrow and lend sterling to UK residents through overseas offices and thus escape the control.[7]

At the time of writing the Scheme is still formally in operation, and new methods of monetary control are under consideration.

THE SUPERVISION OF BANK MANAGEMENT

As well as regulating bank lending the Bank of England has traditionally taken upon itself the supervision of bank management.[8] This function of the Bank was placed upon a statutory basis by the Banking Act 1979.

Until the banking crisis of 1973–74 the Bank's supervision of the banks was exercised through its Discount Office and extended for most purposes only to the clearing banks, the Accepting Houses and the Discount Houses. In the summer of 1974 the Discount Office was absorbed into a new Banking and Money Market Supervision Division and all banks registered in the United Kingdom, together with most non-bank deposit-taking businesses, began to submit quarterly returns on a voluntary basis.

Under the system in operation at the beginning of 1980 the basic return submitted by most UK banks is a quarterly balance sheet, accompanied by a number of other returns which break down the balance sheet in such a way as to show the liquidity of the bank, the maturity structure of its assets and liabilities, details of any large deposits and loans or other areas of concentration of risk and of any bad loan provisions, and, in the case of foreign loans, details of the countries to which they were made. These returns form the basis of regular interviews between the Bank of England and the managers of the banks. The purpose of the interviews and returns is to ensure that all UK banks are being capably managed according to sound banking priciples, without undue exposure of the depositors to the risk that their deposits may not be repaid on their due date.

For the supervision of the clearing banks and British overseas banks with large foreign branch networks the system is somewhat

7. For a detailed account of the way in which the Bank of England regulates bank lending, *see Monetary Control*, HMSO, March 1980, Cmnd No 7858.
8. This section is based on "The Supervision of Banks and Other Deposit-Taking Institutions", forming part of the evidence submitted by the Bank of England to the Committee to Review the Functioning of Financial Institutions (the Wilson Committee). The evidence was published in July 1978.

different though its purpose is the same. These banks are supervised on the basis of detailed annual returns and the interviews between the Bank and the managers of the banks each deal with a particular aspect of the bank's operations. In the case of these banks, with their great size and large number of branches, the Bank places particular emphasis on the examination of control systems and reporting and auditing procedures.

The returns submitted by the banks, together with additional weekly and monthly returns submitted by some of the larger banks, are aggregated and the statistics obtained are used for a variety of purposes, for example, national income and balance of payment statistics, flow of funds analyses and monetary policy as well as for prudential supervision.

CHAPTER THREE

The Banking Act 1979

PURPOSE OF THE ACT

The Banking Act 1979[1] is intended to give greater protection to depositors. To this end, the right to carry on a deposit-taking business has for the first time been restricted. It is now an offence for anyone except the Bank of England, the two classes of institution authorised under the Act and a few other institutions specified in Schedule 1[2] to carry on a deposit-taking business.[3] The two classes of institution authorised under the Act are called "recognised banks" and "licensed institutions". To be a recognised bank or licensed institution an institution must satisfy the Bank that it fulfils the minimum criteria listed in Schedule 2.[4]

For the further protection of depositors the Act has established a Deposit Protection Fund.[5] Generally speaking, all recognised banks and licensed institutions must contribute to the Fund which will be used to compensate depositors in a recognised bank or licensed institution that becomes insolvent. The Act also contains provisions aimed at the control of misleading advertisements and regulating the use of banking names and descriptions.[6] The Act is principally concerned with the business of taking deposits and is concerned only in passing with the business of making loans.[7] The Act was passed in accordance with a Banking Co-ordination Directive of the Council of Economic and Finance Ministers of the

1. The footnotes in this chapter refer to the Banking Act 1979 unless otherwise stated.
2. The institutions specified in Schedule 1 are the central banks of other EEC countries, the National Savings Bank, the Post Office, a trustee savings bank or penny savings bank, a municipal bank, a building society, a friendly society, a member of the Stock Exchange in the course of business as a stockbroker or stock-jobber, local authorities credit unions and certain other institutions. The Treasury may make alterations to this list.
3. Section 1(7).
4. The minimum criteria are discussed later in the chapter.
5. The Deposit Protection Fund is discussed later in the chapter.
6. These provisions are discussed later in the chapter.
7. The making of consumer credit loans is regulated by the Consumer Credit Act 1974. This Act, which does not affect unsecured overdrafts with banks, is discussed in Chapter Twelve.

EEC.[8] The Directive was intended as a first step towards the creation of a European supervisory law governing banking.

DEPOSIT-TAKING BUSINESSES

For the purposes of the Act a business is a deposit-taking business if it takes money on deposit in the normal course of business and uses the money deposited to make loans to others, or if it takes money on deposit and uses the money deposited (or the interest on the money) to finance its own activities.[9] A business is not, however, a deposit-taking business if it accepts deposits only on "particular occasions" unless the person carrying on the business holds himself out "to accept deposits on a day-to-day basis".[10]

A deposit is defined by the Act as "a sum of money paid on terms under which it will be repaid, with or without interest or a premium, on demand or in circumstances agreed" by the parties.[11] This definition is, however, heavily qualified so as to exclude a loan made by the Bank, a recognised bank, a licensed institution or an institution specified in Schedule 1; a loan made by any other person in the course of carrying on a business of lending money; a sum of money paid by a company to another company in the same group; a sum of money paid to any institution by its managers, directors or controllers or their immediate relatives;[12] and a sum of money paid on terms "referable to the provision of property or services or to the giving of security".[13]

Money is considered by the Act to be paid on terms referable to the provision of property or services if it is paid by way of advance or part payment for the sale, hire or other provision of property or services and repayable only in the event that the property or services are not in fact provided.[14] Money is considered by the Act to be paid on terms referable to the giving of security if it is paid by way of security for payment for the provision of property or services, or by way of security for the return of property.[14]

8. Directive of the Council of Economic and Finance Ministers of the EEC dated 12th December 1977 on the co-ordination of laws, regulations and administrative provisions relating to the taking up and pursuit of the business of credit institutions.
9. Section 1(2).
10. Section 1(3).
11. Section 1(4).
12. These terms are defined in s. 49.
13. Section 1(4),(5).
14. Section 1(4).

MINIMUM CRITERIA FOR A RECOGNISED BANK

To be a recognised bank an institution must fulfil the following minimum criteria.[15]

(a) The institution must enjoy (and must for a reasonable period have enjoyed) a "high reputation and standing in the financial community".

In the case of an institution which is not yet carrying on a deposit-taking business or has not yet carried on such a business long enough to have earned the reputation and standing referred to, this criterion may be taken to be fulfilled if control of the institution lies with "one or more other bodies of appropriate standing".

In its guidance to prospective applicants, the Bank has indicated that the reference to the financial community includes in particular the banking community, and that this embraces primarily the UK but that in appropriate cases, international reputation and standing are taken into account.

The Bank has regard to market opinion, and where appropriate takes soundings among other institutions. Relevant factors may also include the individual standing of members of the applicant's management, and the range and quality of its customers and counter-parties and of its correspondent relationships.

The reputation and standing should have been enjoyed for a reasonable period to establish that they are secure. Whilst no precise period can be specified, this would normally have to be measured in years rather than in months.

(b) The institution must provide in the United Kingdom "either a wide range of banking services or a highly specialised banking service".

In the case of an institution which is not yet carrying on a deposit-taking business in the United Kingdom, this criterion may be taken to be fulfilled if the institution will provide the services referred to when it begins to carry on a deposit-taking business in the United Kingdom.

An institution will not in general be regarded by the Bank as providing a wide range of banking services unless it provides the five banking services listed below.

(i) Current or deposit account facilities in sterling or foreign currency for members of the public or for bodies corporate or the acceptance of funds in sterling or foreign currency in the wholesale money markets.

15. Schedule 2.

(*ii*) Finance in the form of overdraft or loan facilities in sterling or foreign currency for members of the public or for bodies corporate or the lending of funds in sterling or foreign currency in the wholesale money markets.

(*iii*) Foreign exchange services for domestic and foreign customers.

(*iv*) Finance through the medium of bills of exchange and promissory notes together with finance for foreign trade and documentation in connection with foreign trade.

(*v*) Financial advice for members of the public and for bodies corporate or investment management services and facilities for arranging the purchase and sale of securities in sterling or foreign currency.

It is not in all cases necessary for all five services to be provided since the Bank has a discretion whether to regard an institution as providing a wide range of banking services if it provides the first two services and at least one of the others; the depth and strength of the services which are provided would be a material factor in the Bank's determination whether to waive the necessity for any which are not provided.

(*c*) The business of the institution must be carried on "with integrity and prudence and with those professional skills which are consistent with the range and scale" of the activities of the institution.

For evidence of this the Bank would look not only to maintenance of a satisfactory balance sheet, but also to management information and control systems which would highlight and limit exposure to particular risks or concentration of risks in particular countries or sectors.

In the case of an institution which is not yet carrying on a deposit-taking business, this criterion will be fulfilled if the business of the institution will be conducted in the manner described when the institution begins to carry on a deposit-taking business.

(*d*) The business of the institution must effectively be under the direction of at least two individuals. This requirement reflects the terms of the EEC Directive referred to above.

(*e*) The institution must at the time that recognition is granted have net assets[16] amounting to not less than £5,000,000 in the case of an institution having a wide range of banking services; and not

---

16. Net assets are defined as "paid-up capital and reserves".

less than £250,000 in the case of an institution providing a highly specialised banking service.[17]

(f) The institution must maintain net assets which, taken together with other financial resources considered appropriate by the Bank, are commensurate with the scale of its operations.

MINIMUM CRITERIA FOR A LICENSED INSTITUTION

The minimum criteria for a licensed institution are less stringent.[18]

(a) Every person who is a director, controller or manager of the institution must be a fit and proper person to hold that position. Relevant considerations would include the professional qualifications of such persons and observations made in any reports by Department of Trade Inspectors or by the Take-Over Panel or by any similar authorities abroad. It is unlikely that undischarged bankrupts, or persons with criminal records, especially in cases involving fraud, would be considered fit and proper.[19]

(b) The business of the institution must effectively be under the direction of at least two individuals. This reflects the terms of the EEC Directive referred to above.

(c) The institution must at the time that the licence is granted have net assets amounting to not less than £250,000.[20]

(d) The business of the institution must be carried on "in a prudent manner". In particular the institution must maintain adequate liquidity, make adequate provision for bad and doubtful debts and for contingent liabilities and maintain net assets which, taken together with other financial resources considered appropriate by the Bank of England, are sufficient to safeguard the interests of its depositors, taking into account the scale and nature of its liabilities, the sources and the amounts of deposits accepted by it, the nature of its assets and the degree of risk attached to them.

In the case of an institution which is not yet carrying on a deposit-

17. This criterion is without prejudice to the requirements under the sixth criterion. It does not apply to an institution which was carrying on a deposit-taking business in the United Kingdom on 9th November 1978 and which successfully applied for recognition within the six-month transitional period beginning on 1st October 1979.

18. Schedule 2.

19. By virtue of s. 43, s. 4(2) of the Rehabilitation of Offenders Act 1974, which would otherwise permit the non-disclosure of spent convictions, does not apply in this context.

20. There is provision for this sum to be increased by the Treasury after consultation with the Bank of England. This criterion does not apply to an institution which was carrying on a deposit-taking business in the UK on 9th November 1978, and successfully applied for a licence during the six-month transitional period, and it is without prejudice to the fourth criterion.

taking business, this criterion will be taken to be fulfilled if the business of the institution will be conducted in the manner described when the institution begins to carry on a deposit-taking business.

ROLE OF THE BANK OF ENGLAND

To become a recognised bank or licensed institution a deposit-taking business must apply to the Bank for recognition or a licence. Applications must be made in the manner specified by the Bank, and must be accompanied by whatever information the Bank reasonably requires.[21] The Bank will not grant recognition or a licence unless satisfied that the applicant fulfils the minimum criteria. Nor will it grant recognition or a licence to an applicant which is not a body corporate if the whole of the applicant's assets are owned by a single individual.[22] There are special provisions relating to applications by foreign institutions.[23]

If the Bank proposes to refuse an application, it must first notify the applicant in writing, giving its reasons and informing the applicant of the right to make written representations in reply.[24] Any such representations must be taken into account by the Bank before it comes to a decision.[25] Once a decision is made, the Bank must notify the applicant within specified time limits.[26]

A licensed institution may be granted either a full licence or a conditional licence. A conditional licence is granted on such conditions as are considered necessary by the Bank for the protection of depositors. Failure to comply with the conditions of the licence is an offence. A conditional licence may be surrendered and, unless revoked or surrendered, expires after a maximum of one year.[27]

The Bank may, in specified circumstances, revoke recognition or a licence, thereby terminating the right of a recognised bank or licensed institution to carry on a deposit-taking business, and on revocation may give such directions as it considers "advisable to safeguard the assets of the business".[28]

---

21. Section 5(1). The Bank has issued to prospective applicants a Handbook of Banking Supervision which contains a questionnaire for applicants and guidance on the application of the criteria. Some of the above comments on the respective criteria are derived from that Handbook. The Bank may where necessary seek any additional information it may reasonably require in order to reach a decision on any application.
22. Section 3(4).
23. Section 3(5).
24. Section 5(4).
25. Section 5(4).
26. Section 5(5).
27. Section 10.
28. Section 6(1); s. 8(1).

The Bank may promote a licensed institution to the status of recognised bank and may demote a recognised bank to the status of a licensed institution.[29]

The Act lays down an appeal procedure for those dissatisfied with any decision of the Bank relating to the grant or revocation of recognition or a licence. In the first instance appeal lies to the Chancellor of the Exchequer, who will refer the matter for a hearing to persons appointed for the purpose.[30] Appeal on a question of law from any decision of the Chancellor of the Exchequer lies to the High Court.[31] Appeal to the Court of Appeal may be made only with the leave of the High Court or the Court of Appeal.[32]

Where the Bank considers it desirable in the interests of depositors the Bank may appoint competent persons to investigate and to report on "the state and conduct of the business" of a recognised bank or licensed institution.[33] The Bank may compel any director, controller, manager or agent of a recognised bank or licensed institution to produce papers, attend hearings, or otherwise give assistance.[34]

The Bank may by notice in writing require a licensed institution to provide information about the nature and conduct of its business and its plans for future development, and may require an accountant to report on the information.[35] A licensed institution must give notice in writing to the Bank when any person becomes or ceases to be a director, controller or manager.[36]

Information obtained by the Bank about a recognised bank or licensed institution must be kept confidential and must not be disclosed except as permitted by the Act. Information may, for example, be disclosed with the consent of the person to whom the information relates, or to the extent that the information is or has previously been available to the public from other sources, or to an officer or employee of the Bank.[37]

The Bank of England may petition for the winding-up of a recognised bank or licensed institution if it is unable to pay sums due and payable to its depositors, or if it is able to pay such sums

29. Section 7; Sched. 4.
30. Section 11.
31. Section 13(1).
32. Section 13(3).
33. Section 17(1).
34. Section 17(3).
35. Section 16(1).
36. Section 14. A licensed institution is also required to keep a copy of its most recent audited accounts at each place in the UK at which it holds itself out to accept deposits (s. 15).
37. Section 19(1).

only by defaulting on its obligations to other creditors or if the value of its assets is less than the value of its liabilities.[38]

THE DEPOSIT PROTECTION FUND

The Deposit Protection Fund established by the Act[39] is managed by a Deposit Protection Board which has a duty to levy contributions to the Fund by written notice to "contributory institutions".[40] All recognised banks and licensed institutions are contributory institutions unless excluded by the Treasury.[41] Contributions are to consist of a percentage of the "deposit base" of each contributory institution. The deposit base is defined as the average value of sterling deposits with the UK offices of a contributory institution over a period selected by the Board, excluding secured deposits, deposits with an original term to maturity of more than five years and deposits in respect of which the institution has in the UK issued a sterling certificate of deposit.[42]

The fund is being set up with initial cash resources of between £5 million and £6 million. The minimum initial contribution payable is £2,500 and the maximum £300,000. There is provision for further contributions to increase the size of the fund, and special contributions if payments from the fund are expected to exhaust its cash resources before the end of the financial year. There is an overall cumulative limit on all contributions by any institution of 0.3 per cent of its deposit base.[43]

If at any time a contributory institution becomes insolvent, the Board must as soon as practicable make a payment out of the Fund to each depositor who has a "protected deposit" with the insolvent institution.[44] A protected deposit is the total liability of the insolvent institution to the depositor in respect of sterling deposits made with the UK offices of the institution, excluding interest and limited to a maximum sum of £10,000. The payment out of the Fund will be known as an "insolvency payment" and will be equal to 75 per cent of the depositor's protected deposit. The maximum insolvency payment that can be made to a protected depositor is therefore £7,500.

38. Section 18(1).
39. The part of the Act relating to the Deposit Protection Fund came into force on 1st April 1980.
40. Section 21.
41. Section 21.
42. Section 23.
43. The figures of £2,500 and £300,000, and the figure of £10,000 referred to below, are capable of alteration by statutory instrument, subject to an affirmative resolution of each House of Parliament (s. 27(5) and (6), and 29(3)).
44. Section 28(1).

To qualify for an insolvency payment a depositor will be required to lodge a proof of debt with the liquidator of the insolvent institution or have performed a corresponding act in the insolvency of the insolvent institution.[45] The Board has a discretion to refuse to make an insolvency payment to a depositor who, in the opinion of the Board, had any responsibility for (or in any way profited from) the circumstances which gave rise to the institution's financial difficulties.[46] After the Board has made an insolvency payment, it takes over all the rights of the protected depositor against the insolvent institution until it has recovered from the institution the full amount of the insolvency payment.[47]

ADVERTISEMENTS AND THE USE OF BANKING NAMES

The Act empowers the Treasury to make regulations concerning the issue, form and content of advertisements for deposits.[48]

The Act regulates the use of banking names. In general, only recognised banks and a number of specified institutions[49] will be allowed to use the words "bank", "banker", or "banking" in referring to themselves; but a licensed institution which is a wholly-owned subsidiary of a recognised bank or which has a wholly-owned subsidiary which is a recognised bank may use a name which includes the name of the recognised bank to indicate the connection between them.[50] An institution which is not normally allowed to use the words "bank", "banker" or "banking" in referring to itself may nevertheless make use of such words in order to comply with or take advantage of any or all of the dozen or so statutes mentioned in Chapter One.[51] There are special provisions concerning the representative offices of foreign institutions.[52]

The Act repeals the Protection of Depositors Act 1963.[53] Under that Act any deposit-taking business which was not classified as a "bank" had to comply with the regulations laid down by the Board (now the Department) of Trade when it advertised for deposits.[54]

45. Section 29. The rules of insolvency are discussed in detail in Chapter Twenty-nine.
46. Section 28(2).
47. Section 31.
48. Section 34(1).
49. For example, the Bank, central banks of other EEC member states, the Post Office National Bank, the National Savings Bank and Trustee Savings Bank.
50. Section 36(7).
51. Section 36(2).
52. Section 36(8) and (9).
53. Banking Act 1979, s. 51(2) and Sched. 7.
54. Protection of Depositors Act 1963, ss. 2 and 3.

FRAUDULENT INDUCEMENT TO MAKE DEPOSITS

The Act makes it an offence for any person by any statement, promise or forecast which he knows to be misleading, false or deceptive, or by any dishonest concealment of material facts, or by the reckless making (dishonestly or otherwise) of any statement, promise or forecast which is misleading, false or deceptive, to induce (or attempt to induce) another person to make (or agree to make or offer to agree to make) a deposit with him or with any third person.[55] There was a similar offence in the Protection of Depositors Act 1963.[56]

55. Section 39(1).
56. Ibid., s. 1.

PART II

ACCOUNTS OF CUSTOMERS

CHAPTER FOUR

The Banker's Relationship with his Customer

CUSTOMERS

There is no statutory definition of a customer. The Bills of Exchange Act 1882 and the Cheques Act 1957 both speak of customers but never define who they mean. The word "customer" has been considered by the courts in a number of cases, and it would appear that a person is not a customer unless he has "some sort of an account, either a deposit or a current account or some similar relation"[1] with a bank. It would appear too that any person may be a customer and that a person becomes a customer as soon as he opens an account.[2] A person might possibly be regarded as a customer even before he opened an account,[3] but this would probably only apply if it was his intention to open an account and he did subsequently open one.

CONTRACTUAL NATURE OF THE RELATIONSHIP

When a customer deposits money in a bank account, he does not, strictly speaking, "deposit" the money; he lends it to the banker. The relationship between the banker and his customer is therefore the contractual relationship of debtor and creditor, not, as might be thought, the very different relationship of trustee and beneficiary.

The debtor-creditor nature of the relationship was described by Lord Cottenham in *Foley* v. *Hill:*

Money in the custody of a banker is to all intents and purposes the money

1. *G. W. Railway Co.* v. *London and County Banking Co.* [1901] A.C. 414 per Lord Davey.
2. *Taxation Commissioners* v. *English, Scottish and Australian Bank* [1920] A.C. 683.
3. *Woods* v. *Martins Bank* [1959] 1 Q.B. 55.

of the banker, to do with it as he pleases; he is guilty of no breach of trust in employing it; he is not answerable to the [customer][4] if he puts it into jeopardy, if he engages in a hazardous speculation; he is not bound to keep it or deal with it as the property of his [customer]; but he is, or course, answerable for the amount because he has contracted, having received that money, to repay to the [customer], when demanded, a sum equivalent to that paid into his hands.[5]

The full terms of the contract between the banker and his customer are rarely reduced to writing. As a result the courts have frequently had to consider what terms, if any, should be implied. In *Joachimson* v. *Swiss Bank Corporation*, Atkin LJ considered that the following terms should be implied:

The bank undertakes to receive money and to collect bills for its customer's account. The proceeds so received are not to be held in trust for the customer but the bank borrows the proceeds and undertakes to repay them. The promise to repay is to repay at the branch of the bank where the account is kept and during banking hours. It includes a promise to repay any part of the money due against the written order of the customer addressed to the bank at the branch; and as such written orders may be outstanding in the ordinary course of business for two or three days, it is a term of the contract that the bank will not cease to do business with the customer except upon reasonable notice.

The customer on his part undertakes to exercise reasonable care in executing his written orders so as not to mislead the bank or to facilitate forgery. I think it is necessarily a term of such contract that the bank is not liable to pay the customer the full amount of his balance until he demands payment from the bank at the branch at which the current account is kept. Whether he must demand it in writing[6] it is not necessary now to determine.[7]

The implied rights and duties mentioned above, together with a number of other implied rights and duties which might be derived from them, are discussed in the following pages. It is important to remember that any of the implied rights and duties may be excluded or extended by express or implied agreement between the banker and his customer.

It is also important to remember that the relationship between the banker and his customer is a debtor-creditor relationship only as regards any money deposited by the customer with the banker and as regards any money lent to the customer by the banker. Where

4. The word actually used by Lord Cottenham was "principal". As he was talking about customers and went on to conclude that a customer is not in fact a principal, the word "principal" is misleading.
5. (1848) 2 H.L. Cas. 28.
6. An oral demand may be sufficient, per Parker J. in *Arab Bank* v. *Barclays Bank* (*DC&O*) [1952] 2 T.L.R. 920. This passage is unreported and is obiter.
7. [1921] All E.R. Rep. 92.

the customer gives the banker a mandate to do certain acts in connection with his account or to permit any other person to do such an act, the banker's relationship with his customer is not the contractual relationship of debtor and creditor, but the somewhat different contractual relationship of agent and principal.[8]

THE CUSTOMER'S RIGHTS

Right to repayment

As was stated in *Foley* v. *Hill*, it is an implied term of the contract between the banker and his customer that the banker promises to repay the customer "a sum equivalent to that paid into his hands". Money kept on current account is repayable to the customer on demand while money kept on deposit account is sometimes repayable on demand but is generally repayable either on a fixed date or at the end of a fixed period of notice.[9]

As was stated in *Joachimson's* case, the banker's promise to repay the customer is a promise to repay "at the branch of the bank where the account is kept and during banking hours". The customer is not entitled to repayment at any other branch.[10] The banker owes no duty to the public in the matter of banking hours; his only duty is to his customers and if a banker closes at a time when he has led his customers to believe that they may do business, he may be liable to them in breach of contract. In practice, changes in banking hours are authorised by the Committee of London Clearing Bankers, and notice of the changes is given in the press and in bank branches. It would appear that if adequate notice is given of any change, the banker cannot be liable to the customer in breach of contract. The banker is also permitted to deal with cheques within a reasonable margin of time after the advertised time of closing.[11]

Right to draw cheques

From the banker's implied promise to repay a current account customer on demand there derives first, the current account customer's implied right to draw cheques up to the amount of any credit balance on his account, and secondly, the banker's implied duty to honour any such cheques. These propositions follow from

8. The banker's mandate and the relationship of agent and principal are discussed in Chapter Five under "Agents".
9. Money on deposit due for payment on a Saturday or Sunday is payable on the next business day.
10. *Clare & Co.* v. *Dresdner Bank* [1915] 2 K.B. 576.
11. *Baines* v. *National Provincial Bank* (1927) 96 L.J.K.B. 801.

the fact that a cheque is in essence simply a written order from the customer to his banker to pay money on demand.[12]

Without the express or implied consent of the banker, the customer should not, strictly speaking, draw cheques on money paid into his account until the banker has been given reasonable time to make the necessary entries in his books.[13] If, however, a customer does draw a cheque before the necessary entries have been made, the banker often decides in practice to honour the cheque, especially when it is covered by a cash deposit; but if it is covered only by an uncleared[14] cheque, the banker may, in the absence of any express or implied agreement with the customer, refuse to honour the cheque and return it marked "Effects not cleared" even if, as is the usual banking practice, he has already credited the cheque as cash prior to its being cleared.[15]

The customer does not have a right to draw cheques in excess of the credit balance on his current account unless he has an overdraft arrangement or some other arrangement with his banker. Overdrafts are usually expressed to be repayable on demand but where an overdraft limit has been set for a fixed period, the banker may have difficulty in the absence of special circumstances if he seeks to cancel the overdraft limit and claim repayment on demand; in particular a customer might be entitled to redress if the banker dishonoured cheques drawn by the customer within the overdraft limit. Although most advances to customers are made by way of overdraft, bankers sometimes also advance money on "loan accounts", usually to business customers. The amount of the loan is credited to the customer's current account and the customer has the right to draw cheques against it.

It is not clear to what extent a customer has a right to draw cheques against money in a deposit account. Where money in a deposit account is not repayable on demand, it seems safe to say that a customer does not have the right to draw cheques against the account since a cheque is an order to pay money on demand. But where money in a deposit account is repayable on demand, the position is less clear. In *Hopkins* v. *Abbott*[16] Malins VC appeared to suggest that a customer does have the right to draw cheques against such an account; but according to the textbook writer, Paget, there is "probably not" any such right.[17] In practice, bankers do often honour cheques drawn against deposit accounts, and they also allow

12. For the full definition of a cheque, *see* Chapter Seven.
13. *Marzetti* v. *Williams* (1830) 1 B. & Ad. 415.
14. The clearing of cheques is discussed in Chapter Ten.
15. *See* Paget (8th Edn.), pp. 304–5.
16. (1875) L.R. 19 Eq. 222.
17. Paget (8th Edn.), p. 157.

customers to overdraw on current account, relying for their security on the banker's right of set-off between a customer's current and deposit accounts.[18]

Right to interest

The banker's promise to repay his customer does not include a promise to repay the customer with interest. Generally speaking, a current account customer whose account is in credit is not paid any interest by the banker. Deposit account customers, on the other hand, normally receive interest payments from the banker on the balance in their accounts and it seems certain that a deposit account customer has an implied right to such payments. The rate of interest paid to deposit account customers normally fluctuates in line with changes in prevailing market rates; but in the case of a special type of deposit account know as a "savings account" the customer normally receives a fixed rate of interest which tends to be lower than the rates paid on other deposit accounts.

Interest on money in a deposit account ceases to run on the date when the customer's notice of withdrawal expires. If the contract between the banker and his customer provides for notice of withdrawal and the banker allows withdrawal without notice, it is customary for the banker to deduct from the amount withdrawn by the customer an amount equal to the interest for the contractual period of notice.[19]

Under the Income and Corporation Taxes Act 1970, interest paid by a banker to his customer and chargeable to tax as income falling under Case III of Schedule D is paid gross to the customer if he is a UK resident. If, however, the customer is non-resident, interest is paid net to the customer after deduction by the banker of income tax at the basic rate unless the banker is recognised by the Inland Revenue as carrying on a bona fide banking business for the purposes of the Act, in which case interest is paid gross to the customer. Where interest is paid net to the customer by the banker, the banker must account to the Inland Revenue for the income tax deducted.[20]

CUSTOMER'S DUTIES

Duty of reasonable care in drawing cheques

It was stated in *Joachimson's* case that the customer had an implied duty "to exercise reasonable care in executing his written orders so

18. *See* later in the chapter.
19. *Q.B.P.*, No. 183.
20. Income and Corporation Taxes Act 1970, ss. 54(1) and (2).

as not to mislead the bank or facilitate forgery". This duty was further discussed in *London Joint Stock Bank* v. *Macmillan and Arthur*[21] when Lord Haldane said in the House of Lords that the customer contracts that "in drawing his cheques he will draw them in such a form as will enable the banker to fulfil his obligations and therefore in a form which is clear and free from ambiguity".

Lord Finlay said in the same case that:

... a cheque drawn by the customer is in point of law a mandate[22] to the banker to pay the amount according to the tenor of the cheque. It is beyond dispute that the customer is bound to exercise reasonable care to prevent the banker being misled. If he draws a cheque in a manner which facilitates fraud, he is guilty of a breach of duty between himself and the banker and he will be responsible to the banker for any loss sustained by the banker as a natural and direct consequence of this breach of duty.

Lord Haldane added that the banker "has a right to insist on having his mandate in a form which does not leave room for misgiving as to what he is called upon to do."

The facts of *Macmillan*'s case were as follows. The customer, a partnership, had a clerk who habitually prepared cheques for signature by one of the partners. On the occasion which gave rise to the case, the clerk prepared an uncrossed bearer cheque, entering the figure "2" in the middle of the space for figures and leaving blank the space for words. The clerk then presented the cheque for signature to one of the partners who was in a hurry and who signed the cheque without noticing anything unusual and without making any further inquiries after he was told by the clerk that the cheque was for petty cash and that two pounds would be sufficient. The clerk then added a "1" before and a "0" after the figure "2" and inserted the words "one hundred and twenty pounds" in the space for words. It was held that the customer had a duty to take reasonable and ordinary precautions against forgery and that the alterations made by the clerk were a direct result of a breach of this duty.

In *Slingsby* v. *District Bank*[23] the Court of Appeal considered that the customer did not have a duty to fill in any space after the payee's name. There seems no obvious reason for this decision and it is possible that another case on similar facts would be decided differently. In *Slingsby*'s case a cheque was signed in favour of AB. The clerk who had written out the cheque then added "per X and Y" after the name of the payee, endorsed the cheque and paid it into his own account.

21. [1918] A.C. 777.
22. The banker's mandate is discussed in Chapter Five.
23. [1932] 1 K.B. 544.

Duty to disclose forgeries

In *Greenwood* v. *Martins Bank*[24] it was established that the customer has an implied duty to inform the bank if he discovers that cheques purporting to have been signed by him have been forged. In *Greenwood*'s case the customer had an account with Martins Bank and his wife kept the cheque book and gave him cheques when he required them. In October 1929, when he wanted to draw a cheque, he was informed by his wife that there was no money in the account as she had drawn it all out to help her sister who was involved in legal proceedings. She begged him not to tell the bank and he promised not to do so.

There were no forgeries thereafter but in June 1930 the customer discovered that his wife's sister was not involved in any proceedings and that he had been deceived by his wife. He told his wife that he would have to inform the bank at once and his wife committed suicide. He then brought an action against the bank to recover the money paid out by the bank in respect of the cheques forged by his wife.

The Court of Appeal found against him, holding that a customer has a duty to disclose forgeries to his banker as soon as he discovers them. This view was upheld by the House of Lords which agreed with the Court of Appeal that in the circumstances of the case the bank was entitled to plead an "estoppel" against the customer and thereby prevent him recovering his money. In the House of Lords Lord Tomlin observed that a person cannot normally succeed with an estoppel unless he can show that he has suffered some detriment as a result of a representation (or conduct amounting to a representation) and mere silence does not normally amount to a representation; "but when there is a duty to disclose, deliberate silence may become significant and amount to representation."

In *Brown* v. *Westminster Bank*[25] the question of the customer's duty to disclose forgeries as soon as he discovers them was discussed further. In this case the bank had on several occasions drawn the attention of their customer, an old lady, to the number of cheques drawn on her account and payable to her servant. On the first occasion the customer said that she used to ask the servant to cash cheques for her at her club and on the other occasions she did not deny drawing the cheques.

Eventually the bank discussed the matter with the customer's son, following which the customer brought an action against the bank

24. [1933] A.C. 51.
25. [1964] 2 Lloyd's Rep. 187.

in respect of more than three hundred cheques alleged by the customer to have been forged by the servant. The court found against the customer, holding that the customer was estopped from setting up any of the forgeries against the bank, and could not even recover the money paid out by the bank in respect of those cheques forged by the servant before the first occasion on which the bank drew the matter to the customer's attention. This was on the grounds that the bank might have taken steps to recover from the servant all the money already obtained by him if the customer had not on that first occasion represented to the bank that the signatures on the cheques were genuine.

THE BANKER'S RIGHTS

Right to commission
A banker has an implied right to charge a customer a commission for keeping the customer's account and for other banking services. This right derives from the general legal right of any person to charge a reasonable sum for services rendered.[26] In practice, the amount of the commission is normally decided by express agreement or by an agreement implied from the usual course of dealings between the banker and his customer.[27]

In the past many banks charged no commission to private current account customers who kept their accounts in credit. Today most banks charge a commission (or "bank charges") for keeping such accounts except where the customer maintains his credit balance above a specified average or specified minimum level. The commission charged to the customer is normally a fixed fee per debit entry, though some banks make an allowance to the customer for notional interest on his money if the account is in credit. For business customers the banker's commission is normally decided by express agreement. Bankers do not normally charge customers a commission for keeping a deposit account.

Right to interest
It appears that a banker has no implied right to charge interest on money lent to a customer. The interest to be charged by the banker is normally decided by express agreement or by an agreement implied from the usual course of dealings between the banker and his customer.

---

26. *See* Cheshire & Fifoot, *The Law of Contract* (10th Edn.).
27. *Spencer* v. *Wakefield* (1887) 4 T.L.R. 194.

It is normal banking practice to charge the customer compound interest on loans, adding the interest to the principal debt every three months in the case of a clearing bank and sometimes every month in the case of other banks. Fixed sums of money lent to a customer on the security of land are, however, subject only to simple interest except where there is an express agreement to the contrary. The banker must therefore keep the customer's "mortgage account" separate from his current account. Today, however, most bankers' mortgage forms provide for interest on mortgage loans to be compounded, so it is not essential to keep the mortgage account and the current account separately. Where money is lent to a customer on the security of land to secure a fluctuating balance, the money is subject to compound interest and there is therefore no need for separate accounts.

If the banker and the customer have agreed expressly or impliedly that interest charges should be debited to the customer's account at certain dates,[28] the banker is not entitled, without due notice to the customer, to debit interest charges at any other dates in order, for example, to be able to dishonour a cheque drawn by the customer on the grounds that the customer's credit balance after interest had been debited was insufficient to cover the cheque. When a customer draws a cheque which takes his account into overdraft, the banker is entitled to charge interest on the overdrawn account from the date on which he honours the cheque, not from the date on which the cheque was drawn.

Right to set-off

As we have seen, the contract between the banker and his customer is a contract between a debtor and a creditor. The contract contains an implied promise by the banker to repay the money lent to him by the customer. Where, however, a customer has an account which is in credit but owes money to the banker in respect of another account, the banker may have the right to reduce his liability to repay the customer by the amount which the customer owes to him, or, if that is the case, to reduce the amount which the customer owes to him, by the credit balance in the customer's account. This is known as the banker's right of set-off or of combining accounts. The banker may exercise the right of set-off only when the money owed to him is a sum certain, which is due, and where there is no agreement, express or implied, to the contrary.

Suppose, for example, the customer has a No. 1 Account which

28. Interest on a loan account is normally debited on fixed dates to the customer's current account, and on overdraft accounts is usually debited either half-yearly or quarterly.

is £100 in credit, and a No. 2 Account with a debit balance of
£25. If the customer draws a cheque on the account for £100 the
bank may properly refuse to honour it (provided there is no
agreement for an overdraft).

It is sometimes also said that the banker has a "lien"[29] on the
customer's credit balance but as Lord Denning MR and Buckley
LJ pointed out in *Halesowen Presswork and Assemblies* v.
Westminster Bank,[30] a credit balance in favour of the customer is a
debt owed by the banker to the customer and "a debtor cannot
sensibly be said to have a lien on his own indebtedness to his
creditor".

The banker may only exercise the right of set-off when all the
relevant accounts are held "in the same right". If, for example, the
customer keeps his money for the sake of convenience in separate
accounts titled "Private Account" and "Household Account" or
"Current Account" and "Deposit Account" or "No. 1 Account" and
"No. 2 Account", the accounts are in the same right. If, on the other
hand, the customer keeps one account for his own money and
another for money which he holds as a trustee, the banker can have
no right to set off the customer's private account against the trust
account since he clearly has no right to take one man's money to pay
off another man's debt. Difficulty may arise where the title of the
account does not indicate clearly whether it contains trust moneys.
The heading "John Jones *re* Henry Smith" would not necessarily
indicate that John Jones holds the moneys in trust for Henry Smith.
It might as easily mean that Mr Jones opened the account to record
his business dealings with Mr Smith. In the latter case the banker
would have the right of set-off; in the former he would not. The
banker should, therefore, always be guided by his knowledge of the
circumstances, and should be cautious in exercising the right of set-
off in such cases. When the banker is given any indication by a
customer that an account contains trust moneys he should record this
information.

Professional men often maintain accounts specifically for clients'
money. Solicitors, indeed, are statutorily bound to keep clients'
money separate and to include the word "client" in the title to any
account in which it is kept. The banker has no right to set off the
moneys in such an account against any other account in the professional man's name.

Nor has the banker the right to set off the credit balance in a
customer's private account against the overdraft in his partnership

29. The banker's lien is discussed in Chapter Thirteen.
30. [1970] 3 All E.R. 473.

or joint account, or vice versa, without the agreement of all parties affected.

Where the banker's implied right of set-off applies, it is the right of a banker, not the customer. The customer has no right to draw a cheque where there are insufficient funds in the current account simply because there is a credit balance in another account. In practice, however, bankers sometimes do decide to honour such cheques, and in such cases the banker has implied authority to debit the other account with the amount required to meet the cheque.

The banker can exercise his right of set-off even if the customer's accounts are with different branches of the bank,[31] or if one is a current account and the other a deposit account. He cannot, without authority, exercise the right of set-off when one is a loan account.

When the banker advances a lump sum to a customer, debiting the amount to a loan account and crediting it to the customer's current account, he is not entitled to set off the two accounts without reasonable notice to the customer.[32]

The sums paid into the current account are appropriated by the customer to that account, and cannot be used by the bank in discharge of the loan account without the consent of the customer. No customer could have any security in drawing a cheque on his current account if he had a loan account greater than his credit balance on his current account. The debit balance on the loan account cannot be treated as discharged by subsequent payments into the current account.[33]

This principle will apply where what was a current account is frozen and is no longer capable of being treated in the ordinary way so that it in effect becomes a loan account.[34] Even when the banker has demanded repayment of the loan, he must honour all cheques within the credit balance drawn and put into circulation by the customer before receipt of the demand.

The implied right of set-off may be excluded by agreement, but the mere fact that the customer has opened two accounts does not constitute an agreement not to exercise the right to keep the two accounts separate. Where there is an agreement it ceases to be effective as soon as the relationship of banker and customer comes to an end, such as on the death or incapacity of the customer.[35] If a receiving order is made against a customer, or a company customer goes into insolvent liquidation, set-off must apply, since

31. *Garnett* v. *M'Kewan* (1872) L.R. 8 Exch. 10; [1861–73] All E.R. Rep. 686.
32. *Bradford Old Bank* v. *Sutcliffe* [1918] 2 K.B. 833.
33. Ibid., p. 847.
34. *Re (E.J.) Morel (1934) Ltd.* [1962] Ch. 21.
35. *National Westminster Bank* v. *Halesowen Presswork Assemblies* [1972] A.C. 785.

s. 31 of the Bankruptcy Act 1914[36] is mandatory, not optional.[35] When set-off applies compulsorily by virtue of s. 31 of the Bankruptcy Act, it embraces all debts and liabilities, whereas the implied right applies only to accrued and matured liabilities. It also covers some contingent liabilities, but apparently not all.[36] Thus if the customer wishes to withdraw his credit balance or a receiver is appointed by holders of a floating charge, the banker has no right to retain moneys against the customer's contingent liability on a maturing bill which the banker has discounted for the customer, or any other sum of money which is only to become due at a future time.[37] It could apply as against a debt which has already accrued due, even if it is not to be paid until some future time.

The implied right cannot be exercised until the relationship has terminated, or until bankruptcy or liquidation, unless the banker gives notice that he intends to exercise the right. Thus if the customer has one account in credit, and another overdrawn by more than the amount of the credit balance, but has a facility permitting him to overdraw on this account, then so long as the facility continues and the customer keeps within the agreed limit, the banker cannot simply refuse to honour cheques on the current account by purporting to combine the two accounts. He would first have to terminate the over-draft facility and give notice that he intended to exercise his right of set-off. Where notice is required before the right of set-off can be exercised, notice taking immediate effect is sufficient, for otherwise the customer could defeat the right by withdrawing the credit balance immediately; and even where immediate notice is given, the banker would be bound to honour outstanding cheques drawn in good faith before receipt of such notice. To avoid disputes as to whether the right of set-off does or does not apply in a particular case, and to extend it to contingent liabilities, it is becoming common these days for bankers to obtain a "letter of set-off" from any customer who has opened or is proposing to open two or more accounts, authorising the banker to combine them, without notice, at any time. Such letters of set-off usually expressly cover contingent and other liabilities which have not yet accrued or matured. An express right of set-off may be effective as against a "live" customer even in circumstances where there would be not set-off in respect of the particular contingent liability in the bankruptcy or liquidation of the customer.

If the banker had notice of an available act of bankruptcy at the time he gave credit to the customer, then he will not have the right of

---

36. *See* Chapter Thirty.
37. *Jeffryes* v. *Agra and Masterman's Bank* (1866) 35 L.J. Ch. 686; L.R. 2 Eq. 674; *Bown* v. *Foreign and Colonial Gas Co.* (1874) 22 W.R. 740.

set-off. Nor will a banker who has notice that an account contains money held by the customer on trust have the right to set-off the money against a debit balance on another account. In *Barclays Bank* v. *Quistclose Investments*[38] the company had been lent money for the specific purpose of paying a dividend that had been declared. The bank knew the purpose for which this money, which was paid into a special account, was intended. When the company went into liquidation before the dividend was paid, the House of Lords held that the bank was not entitled to set-off this money against the sum owed to it. As the dividend had not been paid, the money in the special account was impressed with a trust in favour of the lender.

The right of set-off is solely the right of the banker. The customer has no corresponding right. Thus, if the customer has a debit balance of £10 in one account and a credit balance of £100 in another account and then draws a cheque for £20 on the first account, he cannot demand that the banker should honour his cheque. If, however, the banker does decide to honour the cheque he has implied authority to debit the customer's second account to the extent that is necessary for him to do so.

THE BANKER'S DUTIES

Duty to receive money for his customer's account

As was stated in *Joachimson*'s case, "the bank undertakes to receive money and to collect bills for its customer's account". When a customer pays money into a current account, he or the person paying in the money on his behalf should ensure that the paying-in slip and the counterfoil are stamped and initialled by the receiving cashier. This stamping is an acknowledgment that the items on the paying-in slip will be credited to the customer's account provided that they are in order.

All paying-in slips should be dated and signed or initialled by the customer or the person paying in the money on his behalf though the slip does not have to be completed in the presence of the receiving cashier. The paying-in slip and the counterfoil should not be stamped by the receiving cashier unless the date on the paying-in slip is the same as the date on which the money is paid into the account. Current account customers normally receive from their bankers periodical details of their bank balance in the form of loose-leaf "bank statements".

When a customer pays money into a deposit account, he should ensure that the payment is acknowledged by an entry in the "pass-

38. [1968] 3 All E.R. 651.

book" supplied to him by the banker. The debit and credit entries in the pass-book enable a deposit account customer to know at any time the balance remaining in his account. Bankers sometimes acknowledge sums of money paid into deposit accounts not by entries in a pass-book but by the issue of "deposit receipts".

It is normal practice for bankers to credit uncleared cheques and other items as cash in their customer's account as soon as they are paid in. If such uncleared items are subsequently not honoured, the banker reserves the right to debit his customer's account accordingly. Where money is paid into a customer's account by a person other than the customer, that person does not have the right to withdraw the money without express authority from the customer. Bankers sometimes send statements to their customers, itemising any payments into the customer's account by persons other than the customer.

The banker's duty to collect cheques and bills on behalf of his customer is dealt with in Chapters Eight and Nine.

Duty to honour his customer's cheques

As we have seen, the banker has an implied duty to honour his customer's cheques provided that:

(*a*) they are drawn in the proper form;

(*b*) the account on which they are drawn is in credit to an amount sufficient to pay them, or arrangements have been made for an overdraft facility and the agreed overdraft limit will not be exceeded;

(*c*) there is no legal cause (e.g. service of a garnishee order nisi)[39] which makes the credit balance or the agreed overdraft limit unavailable;

(*d*) they are presented during banking hours (or within a reasonable time thereafter).[40]

The banker generally has until the close of business on the day of presentation to decide whether or not to meet a cheque, and if he decides not to meet it, he must immediately after the close of business (if not before) return it with some marking (called an "answer") on the cheque indicating why it has not been honoured.

If the banker wrongfully dishonours his customer's cheques, the customer may be able to sue him for damages in breach of contract. Where the customer is a trader,[41] he may be able to recover sub-

---

39. *See* later in the Chapter.
40. *Baines* v. *National Provincial Bank* (1927) 96 L.J.K.B. 801.
41. In English law, there is no relevant definition of a trader. In a New Zealand case, *Baker* v. *Australia and New Zealand Bank* [1958] N.Z.L.R. 907, a customer who was office manager of a company, as well as being a large shareholder and a director, was held not to be a trader.

stantial damages from the banker for injury to his commercial credit without having to prove any actual loss. In *Rolin* v. *Steward*,[42] for example, the customer recovered substantial damages without suffering any actual loss when three cheques and a bill were dishonoured in error even though they were honoured when presented again on the following day. If the customer is not a trader, he can recover substantial damages in breach of contract only if he can prove actual loss. In *Gibbons* v. *Westminster Bank*,[43] for example, the customer, who was not a trader and who suffered no actual loss, was awarded only nominal damages when a cheque was dishonoured by mistake after money paid in by the customer had been credited by the bank to another customer's account.

Whether he is or is not a trader, the customer may also be able to recover substantial damages without proving actual loss by bringing an action for libel[44] against a banker who wrongfully dishonours a cheque. To succeed in an action for libel the customer must prove, broadly speaking, that the words used by the banker in dishonouring the cheque would tend to lower the customer "in the estimation of right-thinking members of society generally".[45] For this reason a banker should make sure, whenever he refuses payment on a cheque, that the answer on the cheque should, so far as is consistent with the truth, be worded in a way calculated to cause as little damage as possible to the customer's reputation.

Some answers, based on irregularities on the face of the cheque, may safely be used by the banker. Examples include: "Requires confirmation", "Words and figures differ", "Indorsement irregular". Where none of these answers is appropriate, the safest course is probably "Refer to drawer" but even this answer is not entirely safe. In *Flach* v. *London and South Western Bank*[46] Scrutton J. held that the words "Refer to drawer" in their ordinary meaning meant no more than "we are not paying; go back to the drawer and ask why" or else "go back to the drawer and ask him to pay" and this view was followed in *Plunkett* v. *Barclays Bank*.[47] With the passing of time judicial opinion has altered with respect to the words "Refer to drawer". In 1930 these words were referred to the jury in *Jayson* v. *Midland Bank*[48] and considered to be libellous. In 1950,

42. (1854) 14 C.B. 595.
43. [1939] 2 K.B. 882.
44. For an introduction to the law of libel, *see* Winfield & Jolowicz, *On Tort* (11th Edn.).
45. Per Lord Atkin in *Sim* v. *Stretch* [1936] 2 All E.R. 1237 at 1240.
46. (1915) 31 T.L.R. 334.
47. [1936] 2 K.B. 107.
48. [1968] 1 Lloyd's Rep. 409.

in a Northern Ireland case,[49] the judge at first instance ruled that the words "Refer to drawer: present again" and even "Present again" were reasonably capable of defamatory meaning, and this ruling was upheld by the Court of Appeal.[50]

More recently the words "present again" were analysed by the Supreme Court of New Zealand in *Baker* v. *Australia & New Zealand Bank*.[51] A New Zealand case is, of course, not binding on English courts but the reasoning of the judge is well worth considering.

Whatever the answer "Present again" may imply as to the prospects of future or later payment, it surely imports the clear intimation that the maker of the cheque so answered has defaulted as to time for performance of the legal and ethical obligation to provide for payment by the bank on presentation of a cheque issued for immediate payment. Written words which convey such meaning must, to my mind, tend to lower a person in the estimation of right-minded members of society generally.

The judge therefore concluded that the answer "Present again" was as a matter of law reasonably capable of defamatory meaning.

The defamatory possibilities of various other answers have from time to time also been considered by the courts. In an English case in 1940[52] it was held, for example, that the words "Not sufficient" were libellous. The words "N/A" or "No account" would, unless true, be even more serious for they could lead to the inference that the customer was intentionally drawing cheques on a bank where he had no account, and drawing cheques with no expectation of their being met is a criminal offence.[53]

If a banker finds that he has dishonoured a cheque wrongfully, he should take immediate steps to minimise the damage. He should immediately contact the payee or his bankers by telephone and send a written apology to the payee. He should send a written apology to the customer, not only as a matter of courtesy but also because it may be relevant to the assessment of damages if the customer brings an action.

It has been suggested that before he dishonours a customer's cheque, a banker should take the following precautions.

(*a*) He should make sure that the customer's account has not been debited by mistake with any cheques drawn on other accounts.

49. *Pyke* v. *Hibernian Bank* [1950] I.R. 195.
50. The judges in the Court of Appeal were evenly divided. In Northern Ireland cases, this means that the decision of the judge at first instance is upheld.
51. [1958] N.Z.L.R. 907.
52. *Davidson* v. *Barclays Bank* [1940] 1 All E.R. 316.
53. *Smith* v. *Cox and Co.* [1923] *The Times*, 9th March.

(b) He should make sure that no post-dated cheque drawn by the customer has been prematurely debited.

(c) He should make sure that no regular credits, such as salary, are missing from the customer's account. If any such credits are missing, he should check to see whether they have been credited to another customer's account.

(d) He should make sure that the cheque which he proposes to dishonour is not backed by the customer's cheque guarantee card.[54]

Duty of secrecy

In most circumstances a banker has an implied duty to maintain secrecy about his customer's affairs. The banker's duty of secrecy is not confined merely to information about the state of the customer's account but extends to all information derived from the account. In *Tournier* v. *National Provincial Bank*[55] the court considered whether the banker's duty of secrecy also extended to information derived from sources other than the customer's account. The judges remained divided on the question and, in the absence of a definitive ruling, it is probably safest for a banker to assume that his duty of secrecy does extend to all such information. The court also considered whether the duty extended to information acquired by the banker before his relationship with the customer is first contemplated or after it has ended; again the judges were divided and again bankers would be well advised to adopt a cautious approach.

In *Tournier's* case it was established that the banker is entitled to disclose information about his customer's affairs in only four circumstances: first, when disclosure is compelled by law; secondly, when the banker owes a duty of disclosure to the public; thirdly, when disclosure is required in the interests of the bank; and fourthly, when the customer consents.

There are a number of other situations in which bankers may be compelled by law to disclose information about their customer's affairs. Bankers may, for example, be required to provide copies of entries in their books as evidence in judicial proceedings,[56] and may be required to disclose information in garnishee proceedings or where a writ of sequestration has been issued. Bankers may also be required to furnish information to inspectors appointed by the Department of Trade,[57] to produce books and papers to the Department of Trade[58]

---

54. *See* Milnes Holden, *The Law and Practice of Banking* (5th Edn.), Vol. 1, p. 88.

55. [1924] 1 K.B. 461.

56. Bankers' Books Evidence Act 1879.

57. Companies Act 1948, s. 167.

58. Companies Act 1967, ss. 109–16.

or to the court[59] or to a person named by the court,[60] or to give assistance to the Director of Public Prosecutions.[61] A banker may also be required to disclose to a company whose shares are listed on the Stock Exchange details of the beneficial ownership of any voting shares held by the banker or his nominee in a nominee capacity.[62] Under various sections of the Taxes Management Act 1970 and the Income and Corporation Taxes Act 1970 bankers may be required to disclose information to the Inland Revenue. In particular, the Inland Revenue may require a return of the names and addresses of all persons whose accounts have been credited with interest in excess of £15 in any year without deduction of tax, and may require returns of any amounts of interest in excess of £15 received by the bank on behalf of any person in respect of securities registered in the bank's name.[63]

Disclosure may also be ordered, under the court's developing power to order discovery of information at the earliest stages of an action, where to do so may assist a plaintiff to trace and recover property of which he claims to have been wrongfully or fraudulently deprived.[64] Such disclosure will be confined to the purposes of the action. In such cases the safest course for the bank is probably to agree to abide by whatever the court might rule.

It is rather more difficult to say with any degree of confidence when bankers owe a duty of disclosure to the public or when disclosure is required in the interests of the bank. In *Tournier*'s case, Bankes LJ considered the banker's duty of disclosure to the public and said that "many instances" of such a duty might be given, but did not actually give any. He did, however, refer to the words of a judge in another case who spoke of situations where "a higher duty than private duty is involved, as where dangers to the State or public duty may supersede the duty of the agent to his principal."[65]

Some disclosure of information about the customer's affairs will probably be necessary in the interests of the bank wherever there is litigation between the banker and his customer. As Bankes LJ said in *Tournier*'s case, "a simple instance is where the bank issues a writ claiming payment of an overdraft stating on the face of the writ the amount of the overdraft". Disclosure of information in the interests of the bank may also be necessary where there is litigation between

59. Companies Act 1948, s. 268.
60. Ibid., s. 441.
61. Ibid., s. 334.
62. Companies Act 1976, s. 34.
63. Taxes Management Act 1970, ss. 17 and 24. *See also* s. 13 of that Act; and Income and Corporation Taxes Act 1970, s. 481.
64. *Bankers Trust Company* v. *Shapira* [1980] 1 W.L.R. 1274. The basic principles were set out in *Norwich Pharmacal Co* v. *Customs and Excise Commissioners* [1974] A.C. 133.
65. Per Lord Finlay in *Weld-Blundell* v. *Stephens* [1920] A.C. 956 at 965.

the banker and a third party such as a guarantor. In *Sunderland* v. *Barclays Bank*,[66] disclosure in the interests of the bank was interpreted very generously in favour of the bank. In *Sunderland*'s case the bank disclosed to the husband of the customer that in view of the cheques which the customer had drawn in favour of her bookmaker, the bank was not prepared to grant the customer an overdraft. The customer sued the bank for breach of its duty of secrecy but it was held that disclosure of the information to the customer's husband was in the interests of the bank and therefore permissible.

As to the fourth exception, the customer's express or implied consent, two of the judges quoted as examples customers giving bankers' references, although the extent to which the disclosure of information is authorised must be a question to be determined from the facts of each case. Another example would be a customer authorising his banker to disclose his affairs in order to assist his accountant.

Since status inquiries are frequently received not from the customer but from the bankers of the third party requesting the information, there may be nothing in the form of the inquiry to reveal that it was in fact authorised. Any person who receives payment of any sum by cheque must know that the payer has an account at the bank on which the cheque is drawn, and could presumably initiate a request through his own bank without the customer's consent. It might be a wise precaution for bankers to include in their opening of account forms an authority to the banker to answer all inquiries relating to him and to his financial affairs which are, or appear to the banker to be, bona fide.

Duty with regard to garnishee orders

When a creditor seeks to recover money owed to him by someone who is himself owed money by a third person, he may be able to obtain a court order "attaching" money in the hands of the third person. The money attached by such an order cannot be released by the third person without the consent of the court. Such orders are known as garnishee orders and the third person is known as the garnishee. The person who obtains the order is the "judgment creditor" and the person who owes him money is "the judgment debtor". The amount of money owed by the judgment debtor to the judgment creditor is called "the judgment debt".

Since by definition a customer with a credit balance is owed money by his banker, garnishee orders are sometimes served on bankers by

---

66. [1938] *The Times*, 25th November, Five Legal Decisions Affecting Bankers, 163.

their customer's creditors. When a garnishee order is served on a banker, the banker has a duty not to release the money attached by the order until directed to do so by the court. This duty takes precedence over the banker's implied promise to repay his customer which was discussed earlier in this chapter.

Garnishee orders may be obtained either in the High Court or in the County Court. Before a garnishee order absolute can be obtained, the judgment creditor must obtain a garnishee order nisi, otherwise referred to as an "original order". A garnishee order nisi obtained in the High Court is known as an "order to show cause". A garnishee order nisi obtained in the County Court is known by the same name.

When an order to show cause is served on a banker, the banker, as garnishee, must appear before the High Court and must either state that he can satisfy the order or show cause why he cannot.[67] If the court decides that the order should be made absolute, the banker must then satisfy the judgment debt in the manner laid down in the order. The banker should not satisfy the judgment debt before the order has been made absolute or he will be liable to the customer for the money paid out of the customer's account. If the customer is made bankrupt, the banker will be liable to the customer's trustee in bankruptcy for any money paid out of the customer's account in satisfaction of the judgment debt, even if it was paid out after the order had been made absolute, unless the money was received by the judgment creditor before a receiving order was made against the customer, or before notice of the presentation of a bankruptcy petition, or before the commission of an available act of bankruptcy.[68]

When a County Court order is served on a banker, the effect is similar except that the banker has to appear before the County Court rather than the High Court and the banker has the option of paying into court a sum sufficient to satisfy the judgment debt and any costs before the date fixed for the County Court hearing.[69] If the banker intends to exercise this option, he should notify the customer and he will not then be liable to the customer for the money paid out of the account. Nor will he be liable for any further costs or be obliged to attend the hearing. If the money in the customer's account is insufficient to satisfy the judgment debt, the banker may still exercise his option by paying into court all the money that there is in the account.

When a garnishee order is served on the head office of a bank

67. Rules of the Supreme Court, Order 49, Rule 1.
68. Receiving orders, bankruptcy petitions and acts of bankruptcy are discussed in Chapter Thirty.
69. County Court Rules, Order 30, Rules 1 and 4.

against an account kept at one of the bank's branches, the order should be forwarded to the branch without delay. An account at a foreign branch outside the jurisdiction of the English courts cannot be attached by the English courts as the banker would be liable to his foreign customer for any money paid out of the customer's account in satisfaction of a judgment debt in England.

If a garnishee order does not correctly designate the account to be attached, the banker is entitled to ignore the order. This was established in Koch v. Mineral Ore Syndicate[70] where the bank had no account in the name designated on the garnishee order. The bank reported this fact to the judgment creditor's solicitors who designated another account which was, they alleged, the account of the judgment debtor and asked the bank to attach it. The bank refused and continued to allow its customer, the alleged judgment debtor, to draw cheques on his account. The judgment creditor meanwhile sought and obtained from the court an amended garnishee order, designating as the account to be attached the account designated by the judgment creditor's solicitors. When the amended garnishee order was served on the bank, the bank duly attached the account designated, and in a subsequent action the bank was not held liable to the judgment creditor for having paid cheques out of the account in the meantime.

On the basis of Koch's case, it would seem that a banker should refuse to give effect to a garnishee order if he has any reason to doubt that it applies to his customer. The banker should not, however, refuse to give effect to an order merely because of a technical error in the designation of the account to be attached, such as a wrong initial or the misspelling of a name. If there is any reasonable room for doubt, but the customer admits that the order applies to him, the banker should, for his own protection, obtain the admission in writing.

A garnishee order only attaches money which is owed by the banker to his customer at the date of the order.[71] According to the principles established in Joachimson's case, no money is owed by the banker to his customer until the customer demands repayment so it was necessary in that case to create a legal fiction whereby service of the garnishee order nisi is deemed to be a sufficient demand on the banker.[72] It seems that uncleared cheques credited as cash by the banker in the customer's account are not attached by a garnishee order since they do not represent money owed by the banker to his customer.[73] Money belonging to the customer but not yet paid into

70. (1910) 54 S.J. 600.
71. *Heppenstall* v. *Jackson and Barclays Bank, Garnishees* [1939] 1 K.B. 585.
72. [1921] 3 K.B. 110.
73. *Fern* v. *Bishop Burns and Lloyds Bank* (unreported; judgment 5th June 1980).

the hands of the banker is not attached by a garnishee order. This would apply, for example, to the proceeds from the sale of shares sold on the customer's instructions and not yet paid over by the stockbroker to the banker.

Garnishee orders may attach the customer's current account or his deposit account or both. Until the passing of the Administration of Justice Act 1956, a deposit account could not be attached by a garnishee order because money in a deposit account is not owed by the banker to his customer until the specified notice of withdrawal has been given by the customer or the pass-book or deposit receipt has been produced or some other specified procedure has been observed. Section 38 of the 1956 Act provided that, even if the specified conditions for withdrawal have not yet been observed, the money in a deposit account is regarded for the purpose of garnishee proceedings as a sum "due and accruing" and it may therefore be attached. These rules are now contained in the Supreme Court Act 1981, s. 40.

A joint account can be attached by a garnishee order but a garnishee order will not be granted to a creditor who is seeking to recover money owed to him by one of the parties to a joint account.[74] The reason for this is that the banker owes money collectively to the parties to a joint account but does not owe them any money individually. The fact that the party who owes money to the judgment creditor has authority from each of the other parties to draw cheques on the account will not make any difference. This point was established in *Hirschorn* v. *Evans*[75] where it was pointed out that a banker does not owe money to a person merely because that person has authority to draw money from an account.

An account containing trust money can be attached by a garnishee order but the rights of the beneficiaries as against the trustees are not affected by the order and the beneficiaries can apply to the court for the trust money to be excluded from the effects of the order. When an account containing trust money is attached, the banker has a duty to make the position known to the court.

When a judgment creditor seeks to garnishee bank accounts belonging to a solicitor he should ask the court specifically to exclude the solicitor's clients' account. If he does not do so, and the bank is served with a garnishee order nisi, it should inform the judgment creditor's solicitors, who will ask the court to draft the order in terms that exclude the clients' account.

In the past garnishee orders served on bankers usually attached the whole of the customer's account and not merely the amount of the

74. *Macdonald* v. *Tacquah Gold Mines Co.* (1884) 13 Q.B.D. 535.
75. [1938] 2 K.B. 801.

judgment debt. Today, however, it is more usual for a garnishee order to attach only a specified amount of money in the customer's account. The banker may safely regard the remainder of the money in the customer's account as being at the customer's disposal.

Where the whole of the customer's account is attached by a garnishee order, the account must remain dormant until the order is either satisfied or withdrawn. The banker is not permitted to make any payments out of the account even in respect of cheques which were drawn by the customer before the date of the order. In such cases it is the usual practice of the banker to inform the customer that the garnishee order has been served and to open a new account for the customer. Money paid in by the customer after the date of the garnishee order is credited to the new account.

If the new account becomes overdrawn the banker has the right to transfer to the new account any balance remaining in the old account after the garnishee order attaching the old account has been satisfied. If, however, the customer is made bankrupt before the ganishee order has been satisfied, the customer's trustee in bankruptcy is entitled to all of the money in the attached account. For this reason the banker should not allow the new account to become overdrawn if his only security is the balance which will be left in the old account after the garnishee order is satisfied.

Before he pays the money attached by a garnishee order to his customer's creditor or into court, the banker has a right to deduct from the sum attached the value of any debts owed to him by his customer at the date of the order. The banker is only entitled to deduct from the sum attached the value of any debts which have actually accrued. He is not entitled to deduct the value of any contingent debts owed to him by his customer. Thus he cannot, for example, deduct from the sum attached the value of a bill of exchange which he has discounted for his customer and which has not yet reached its term date.[76]

When calculating the value of the debts owed to him by his customer at the date of the garnishee order, the banker is entitled to set off against each other any of the customer's accounts which at the date of the order the banker had the right to combine without notice to the customer. If the attached account of the customer is overdrawn or if the accounts set off against each other by the banker show an aggregate debit balance, the customer is not owed any money by the banker. The garnishee order is therefore ineffective since there is no money in the customer's account which can be

76. *Bower* v. *Foreign & Colonial Gas Co., Metropolitan Bank, Garnishes* (1874) 22 W.R. 740.

attached by the order. This remains the case even if the the customer has not yet reached the agreed limit of his overdraft at the time that the garnishee order was served on the banker. Where the customer has a credit balance on his account (or accounts) but owes money to the banker in respect of a loan account, the banker has no right to set off the credit balance against the loan account in order to reduce the sum attached by the garnishee order unless the money owed by the customer to the banker in respect of the loan account has already become repayable.

APPROPRIATION OF PAYMENTS

When a customer pays in money to his banker, he has an implied right to demand that the money should be "appropriated" by the banker to a specified purpose, for example the payment of a specified debt owed by the customer. The customer enjoys this right, whether he owes money to the banker or the banker owes money to him.[77] Thus, if a customer whose account is overdrawn pays a cheque drawn in his favour into the account and demands payment in cash of the amount of the cheque, the banker must comply with the demand and is not entitled to appropriate the cheque to the reduction of the customer's overdraft.

If, however, the customer does not make a specific appropriation at the time that he pays in the money, the banker has the right to decide how the money will be appropriated.[78] The banker may appropriate the money to the payment of any debt owed by the customer and may even appropriate the money to a debt barred by the Limitation Act 1980 though such an appropriation will not have the effect of reviving the statute-barred debt.[79] The banker may not, however, appropriate the money to the payment of an illegal debt owed by the customer.[80] The banker need not make the appropriation as soon as he receives the money from the customer, but having once made it he cannot subsequently change his mind and appropriate the money to the payment of a different debt. This is an example of the general principle applying as between debtor and creditor.

77. *Farley* v. *Turner* (1857) 26 L.J. Ch. 710; *W. P. Greenalgh & Sons* v. *Union Bank of Manchester* [1924] 2 K.B. 153.
78. *Simson* v. *Ingham* (1823) 2 B. & C. 65.
79. *Mills* v. *Fowkes* (1839) 5 Bing. N.C. 455; *Williams* v. *Griffith* (1839) 5 M. & W. 300. Statute-barred debts are discussed in this chapter under "Effect of the Limitation Act 1980".
80. *Ex parte Randelson* (1833) 2 Deal. & Ch. 534; *Wright* v. *Laing* (1824) 3 B. & C. 165. Illegal debts are discussed in Cheshire & Fifoot, *The Law of Contract*, (10th edn.).

The person paying the money has the primary right of say to what account it shall be appropriated; the creditor, if the debtor makes no appropriation, has the right to appropriate; and if neither exercises the right of appropriation, one can look on the matter as a matter of account and see how the creditor has dealt with the payment in order to ascertain how in fact he did appropriate it. And if there is nothing more than a current account kept by the creditor or a particular account kept by the creditor and he carries the money to that particular account, then the court concludes that the appropriation has been made; and having been made, it is made once and for all, and it does not lie in the mouth of the creditor afterwards to seek to vary that appropriation.[81]

Where money is appropriated to a current account either expressly or impliedly without being appropriated to a particular debt, the money is appropriated by law to discharging or reducing the earliest debt recorded on the account. In other words, if there are two items on the debit side of the customer's current account, a debt of £10 on the third of the month and a debt of £2 on the sixth of the month and the customer pays in £5 on the twelfth of the month, the sum paid in will be appropriated, assuming that there is no other money on the credit side of the account, to reducing the earlier debt of £10 rather than to discharging the later debt of £2. This rule is known as the rule in *Clayton*'s case[82] and is often expressed by the formula "first in, first out". In other words the first sum of money paid into the account is deemed to repay the first item recorded on the debit side of the account.

Where the customer's current account contains money which the customer holds as a trustee, mixed with the customer's own money, the rule of first in, first out applies in the absence of any express appropriation, but subject to an important proviso. The first money used for the customer's own purposes is deemed to have been the customer's own money, and the money which the customer holds as a trustee is regarded as not having been used until the customer's own money has been exhausted. This is known as the rule in *Hallett*'s case[83] and is of great importance where there is a breach of trust by the trustee and the beneficiary wishes to make use of the remedy of "tracing".[84]

If, however, the customer mixes trust money with his own money in an account and draws upon the account to the extent that all of his own money and some or all of the trust money is used, a

81. *Deeley* v. *Lloyds Bank* [1912] A.C. 756 at pp. 783–4 per Lord Shaw of Dunfermline, adopting the statement by Eve J. at first instance.
82. *Devaynes* v. *Noble, Clayton*'s case (1816) 1 Mer. 529.
83. *Re Hallett's Estate, Knatchbull* v. *Hallett* (1880) 13 Ch. D. 696.
84. For breach of trust and the remedy of tracing, *see* Snell's *Principles of Equity* (28th Edn.).

subsequent payment of his own money into the account cannot be appropriated to replace the trust money used earlier.[85] Suppose, for example, that on the sixth of the month the customer's account contained £200 of trust money and £100 of the customer's own money. On that day the customer draws out £250 for his own purposes: this will be appropriated so that £100 of the customer's own money, and £150 of trust money is used. On the eighth of the month the customer pays in £150 of his own money. This cannot be appropriated to replace the £150 of trust money, so that the account will now contain £150 of the customer's own money and £50 of trust money.

The rules in *Clayton*'s case and *Hallett*'s case frequently cause bankers to insist, when dealing with a customer or a third party such as a guarantor, that if a specified event occurs, the banker should have the right to stop the customer's current account and open a new account instead. The reason for this may be illustrated by the following example. Suppose that the banker receives notice of the death, bankruptcy or mental disorder of a guarantor at a time when the customer whose current account he has guaranteed has a debit balance of £2,000. Suppose too that after this the customer pays in £2,000 and he later draws out £1,000.

If the customer's current account is not stopped after such notice and the customer carries out these two transactions on the account, the effect of the rule in *Clayton*'s case will be that the £2,000 paid in by the customer will be taken to have discharged the pre-existing debt of £2,000 which is secured by the guarantee, and the £1,000 drawn out subsequently will constitute a new debt which is not guaranteed because the guarantee determined when the banker received such notice.

If, on the other hand, the banker stops the customer's current account on receipt of such notice and opens a new account instead, no subsequent payment in will reduce the amount then owing on the old account. The £2,000 on that account will continue to be owed by the customer to the banker and will be secured by the guarantee. The £2,000 paid into the new account by the customer will more than cover the £1,000 which he subsequently draws out. In either eventuality, the customer will owe the banker £1,000; but if a new account is opened, the debt will be secured whereas if the old account is continued, the debt will be unsecured. If the banker does not insist on a new account being opened in the event that his security expires, he should at least insist that the customer maintains a credit balance until fresh security is provided.

85. *James Roscoe (Bolton)* v. *Winder* [1915] 1 Ch. 62.

If either the customer or the banker does decide to make an appropriation, it is important that his intention should be made clear in order to avoid the rules in *Clayton*'s case or *Hallett*'s case being invoked. When the right of appropriation lies with the banker, it was held in the case of *The Mecca*[86] that:

... it is always his intention, express or implied or presumed, and not any rigid rule of law that governs the application of the money. The presumed intention of the [banker] may no doubt be gathered from a statement of account or anything else which indicates an intention one way or another, and is communicated to the [customer], provided there are no circumstances pointing in an opposite direction.

STANDING ORDERS AND DIRECT DEBITS

Customers frequently give their bankers written orders to make periodical payments direct to payees. These are known as *standing orders* and can be used, for example, to pay club and charitable subscriptions, rent or hire purchase payments.

Conversely, the system of direct debiting enables the payee to claim payment through his bank not only of fixed amounts due at fixed intervals from a debtor, but also of amounts which vary from time to time and are due at irregular intervals. The payee, who is known as the creditor, must first execute an indemnity addressed to all the clearers and to the Scottish banks, which indemnifies them against all actions, claims, damages, costs and expenses arising out of such debiting, either directly or indirectly. The creditor authorises each bank to admit, compromise or reject any claim without reference to him. The creditor then obtains the agreement of any debtor whose account is to be debited, in the form of a standing order to that person's own bank to permit direct debiting in the creditor's favour to the agreed extent.

Thereafter the creditor can initiate payment to himself by delivering lists of direct debits with individual direct debit forms to his own bank for collection. His bank will credit his account with the sums due, and send the direct debit forms to the individual debtors' banks for collection. If, through lack of funds, any debt cannot be paid, it is returned to the creditor's bank, and will be debited by the bank to the creditor's account.

INCORRECT CREDIT AND DEBIT ENTRIES

As we have seen, a current account customer receives from his banker periodical bank statements, giving him details of his bank balance. A

86. [1895] P. 95; (1895) 71 L.T. 711.

deposit account customer is supplied with a pass-book in which payments into and out of the account are recorded. According to Paget, the "proper function" of the bank statement and the pass-book is:

... saving negligence or reckless disregard on the part of either the banker or the customer ... to constitute a conclusive, unquestionable record of the transactions between them ... After the full opportunity of examination on the part of the customer all entries, at least to his debit, ought to be final and not liable to be reopened later, at any rate to the detriment of the banker.[87]

If that was really the position, it would mean that an incorrect entry which was detrimental to the banker might be reopened at any time, subject to the Limitation Act 1980, whereas an incorrect entry which was detrimental to the customer could presumably only be reopened within a reasonable time after the customer had exhausted his "full opportunity" of examining the entries. Paget acknowledges, however, that the real position is rather different. The customer is in fact under no implied obligation to examine the entries in his bank statement or pass-book (though a prudent customer will obviously do so) and even if the customer does discover an incorrect entry, he is apparently under no obligation to report it to the banker within a reasonable time.[88] The customer therefore has as much right as the banker to have incorrect entries reopened.

Where an incorrect entry is made which is detrimental to the banker, the banker is entitled to reopen the entry and recover the money. He cannot, however, recover any part of the money which the customer has spent in good faith, relying upon the accuracy of the entry, if it would be inequitable to require the customer to repay the money. This principle was established in *Skyring* v. *Greenwood*[89] where the customer, an army officer, was credited with a salary in excess of that to which he was entitled. For several years the banker knew of the excess but never informed the customer who, it seems, had no reason to suspect that his bank statement was incorrect and had therefore drawn out the excess money and spent it.

The court considered that it was of great importance that people "should not be led to suppose that their annual income is greater than it really is. Every prudent man accommodates his mode of living to what he supposes to be his income; it, therefore, works a great prejudice to any man if, after having been allowed to draw on his

---

87. Paget (8th Edn.), p. 114.
88. But if the banker incorrectly debited to the customer's account a cheque that had been forged and the customer discovered the mistake, he would have a duty to report the mistake to the banker. *See* this Chapter ("The Customer's Duty to Disclose Forgeries").
89. (1825) 4 B. & C. 281; [1824–34] All E.R. Rep. 104.

agent on the faith that the sums belonged to him, he may be called to pay them back."[90] In the circumstances of the case the court decided that the customer did not have to repay the excess money to the banker.

The principle established in the *Skyring* case was discussed and followed in two other important cases. In *Holt* v. *Markham*,[91] another case involving excess pay credited to an army officer, one of the judges suggested that the principle applied not only to incorrect entries caused by a clerical mistake or a mistake of fact but also to those caused by a mistake of law. In *Lloyds Bank* v. *Brooks*,[92] where the bank erroneously credited to a lady customer income to which she was not entitled, the judge said that the bank had a duty to keep the customer correctly informed regarding her account and not to make excess credit entries on her bank statements and not to authorise or induce her by the representations contained in her bank statements to draw from her account money to which she was not entitled. In all three cases the customer was a private customer but it is difficult to see why the principle should not apply equally to business customers.

The *Skyring* principle only applies if the customer can show that he was induced by the incorrect entry on his bank statement to act, to his detriment, in a way which he would not otherwise have acted.[93] If, for example, the customer spent the excess money on a purchase which he would have made anyway, financing the difference by borrowing from a third party, he cannot estop the banker from recovering the money. This point was clearly made in *United Overseas Bank* v. *Jiwani*[94] where the banker received a telex message instructing him to credit his customer's account with a certain sum and then received a written confirmation of the message. The banker mistakenly believed that the second communication was not a confirmation of the first, but an instruction to credit a second identical sum to his customer's account. He therefore credited his customer's account with two sums of money instead of one, and the customer used the second sum to help finance a purchase which he would otherwise have financed by some other means. In the circumstances, it was held that the banker was entitled to recover from the customer the money which was incorrectly credited to the customer's account.

Where an incorrect entry is made which is detrimental to the customer, the customer is entitled to have the entry reopened unless

90. [1824–34] All E.R. Rep. 104 at p. 107.
91. [1923] 1 K.B. 504.
92. (1950) Six Legal Decisions Affecting Bankers, 161.
93. *British and North European Bank* v. *Zalstein* [1927] 2 K.B. 92.
94. [1976] 1 W.L.R. 964.

he has indicated by his conduct that he regards the account as "settled" or has been so negligent in his duties towards the banker that it would be inequitable for the banker to be required to reopen the entry.

If the customer had a duty to examine the entries in his bank statement or pass-book and to report any incorrect entries to the banker, it would follow, on this reasoning, that he would not be entitled to have an incorrect entry reopened if it could be shown that he had carried out the duty negligently. But in *Chatterton* v. *London County Bank*,[95] it was decided that no such duty could be implied into the contract between the banker and his customer. This decision was followed in *Kepitigalla Rubber Estates* v. *National Bank of India*[96] where the judge said that it would be absurd to regard an account as settled merely because the customer had withdrawn the pass-book from the bank and then returned it without comment. Both cases were decided in the days when current account customers, as well as deposit account customers, received pass-books as opposed to bank statements, but it is difficult to see why the principle established in both cases with regard to pass-books should not also apply to bank statements.

EFFECT OF THE LIMITATION ACT 1980

If the banker or the customer is in breach of any of the duties discussed in the preceding pages, he can be sued for breach of contract. Damages will be assessed on the principles that apply to breach of contract generally.[97] Under the Limitation Act 1980 an action for damages must normally be commenced within six years from the date that the right of action "accrues". But where a contract has been made under seal, the "limitation period" is twelve years rather than six.[98] If the injured party is a minor or a person of unsound mind or is under any other legal incapacity, the limitation period does not begin to run until the disability ceases or he dies.[99]

If the banker commits a breach of his implied duty to repay a customer's credit balance, the right of action accrues, as regards a current account, on the date that the customer demands repayment, not on the date that the banker refuses to comply with the demand. As regards a deposit account, the customer's right of action accrues on the date that the deposit becomes repayable; in the case of a

95. [1891] *The Times*, 21st January, but fully reported only in *The Miller* newspaper.
96. [1902] 2 K.B. 1010.
97. These principles are discussed in Cheshire & Fifoot, *The Law of Contract* (10th Edn.).
98. Limitation Act 1980, s. 8(1).
99. Ibid., s. 28.

fixed term deposit, this will be the expiry of the fixed term. Where a period of notice is required, it will be the date on which the customer's notice of withdrawal to the banker expires; if it is repayable on demand it will be the date of demand, or when the customer returns his pass-book or deposit receipt or fulfils any other agreed condition of repayment.

If the customer is in debit, it was held, in *Parr's Banking Co. v. Yates*[100] that, in respect of an overdrawn current account, the banker's right of action accrues as soon as each advance is made except where there is an agreement to the contrary. On the other hand, remarks made in *Joachimson*'s case suggest the banker's right of action does not accrue until the banker demands repayment. If the customer owes money to the banker in respect of a loan account and the loan is repayable in a single lump sum on an agreed date, the banker's right of action accrues on the date that the loan becomes repayable. If the loan is repayable in instalments, a separate right of action accrues in respect of each instalment; but if the whole loan becomes repayable, or the banker has the right to make the whole loan repayable, in the event that the customer defaults on an instalment, the right of action on the whole of the balance of the loan accrues on the date of any such default.[101]

An action to recover a loan secured by a mortgage of either real or personal property may only be brought within twelve years from the date when the right to receive the money accrued.[102] A foreclosure action in respect of mortgaged property may only be brought within twelve years from the date on which the right to foreclose accrues.[103] The creditor may sell the mortgaged property even after the debt is statute-barred, but if the value of the mortgaged property is less than the value of the debt, he cannot bring an action to recover the balance. If a loan is secured by a charge over a future interest, such as an insurance policy which has not yet matured or a reversionary interest in property, the right of action does not accure until the policy matures or the interest in property falls into possession.[104]

If a debtor makes a written acknowledgment of his debt or makes any payment to his creditor in respect of the debt, including a payment of interest, the limitation period begins anew from the date of

100. [1898] 2 Q.B. 460.
101. Once the right of action has accrued by virtue of one default, a subsequent default will not start time running again since the right of action has by then already accrued. *See Smith* v. *Craig* 1938 S.C. 620; *Wotherspoon* v. *M'Intosh* 1953 S.L.T. 50.
102. Limitation Act 1980, s. 20(1).
103. Ibid, s. 20(2). For the right to sell or foreclose mortgaged property, *see* Chapter Fifteen.
104. Act of 1980, s. 20(3).

the acknowledgment or payment.[105] In this way even a statute-barred debt may be "revived" though if the debtor makes a payment of interest only, the payment will revive the principal sum but will not revive any overdue interest payments which have become statute-barred.[105] When a person makes a written acknowledgment of his debt or makes part payment of a debt which has already become statute-barred, the new limitation period is binding only on the person making the payment or his personal representatives.[106] But when he acknowledges or makes part payment of a debt that is not yet statute-barred, the new limitation period is also binding on all persons liable.[106] A written acknowledgment will not cause the limitation period to begin anew unless it is made to the creditor or his agent and signed by the debtor or his agent.[107]

PURCHASE AND SALE OF AND ADVICE ON INVESTMENTS

Many banks these days offer their customers the service of advice on investment and financial matters generally, and handle the purchase and sale of Stock Exchange and certain other securities. Investment and financial advice is less likely to be found in country branches, but would almost invariably be available in London and other city centres. It would be unusual for banks to give advice on specific investments. They normally confine themselves to advising in general terms on the sort of investment which would be suitable for the customer, and when it comes to the selection of particular invest-ments in the desired category, bankers normally refer such matters to their brokers. They then pass the specific recommendations on to the customer, expressly disclaiming responsibility themselves.

In 1918, when it was not yet thought to be part of the ordinary buisness of a banker to give investment advice, Lord Finlay LC said, in *Banbury* v. *Bank of Montreal*,[108] that if a banker took it upon himself to give advice he must exercise reasonable care and skill, and would be liable if he was negligent. Today, the giving of advice is part of the ordinary business of a banker, and banks advertise this as one of the services they provide. The mere fact that they advertise this service does not on its own mean that a clearing bank is under a duty, in any particular case, to advise a customer on the prudence of making any particular borrowing, whether from the bank itself or a third party, or of using the money so borrowed in a particular

105. Limitation Act 1980, s. 29(5) and (6).
106. Ibid., s. 29(7).
107. Ibid., s. 30.
108. [1918] A.C. 626.

manner. A banker will only be under a duty to advise on such matters if the banker has agreed to take on the responsibility of advising a particular customer or has in fact assumed that responsibility so that the bank knows that the customer is relying on such advice.

If the banker does give advice on specific investments in such circumstances, he would be liable to the customer if that advice were negligent. The mere fact that a selected investment does not turn out well does not mean that the advice was negligent. But a banker should never in any circumstances take the risk of advising a customer to invest in a private company which is not listed on the Stock Exchange.[109]

Some banks, particularly merchant banks, go further, and offer an investment management service for investment portfolios with a certain minimum size. In such cases, the bank will charge a fee for management. The service may be on the basis that the customer must approve all purchases and sales, or the bank may be given discretionary management, without reference to the customer. In the latter case, the investments will certainly be registered in the name of the bank's nominee company, so that the bank may act speedily where it thinks necessary. In other cases, the customer may wish investments to be registered in the name of the bank's nominee company, so as to avoid being bothered with the necessity for signing share transfers and other documents.

When it comes to carrying out a customer's instructions for the purchase or sale of securities, whether or not following advice given by the banker, his instructions should be taken on the usual bank form, giving full particulars of the securities and stating the limit of price, if any. If the security is a registered one, the order to sell should be signed by all the registered holders, and if it is to bearer, by each person holding himself out to be the owner. When a purchase is intended, full particulars of the security required should be stated on the order, together with any limits of price, and in such cases it is preferable that a clause be added giving the banker authority to debit, if necessary, the customer's account with the cost.

The banker as his customer's agent must act with all diligence both in buying and selling, forwarding his principal's instructions to the brokers accurately and without variation, and when the transaction is completed he must get possession of the proper documents of title in a purchase and of the proceeds in a sale. If the banker negligently fails to secure a purchase or to effect a sale, he will be liable to

109. *Woods* v. *Martins Bank see* p. 23 [1959] 1 Q.B. 55; [1958] 3 All E.R. 166.

the customer for any loss that may ensue. So also will he be liable for any loss if he varies the instructions which the customer has sent him. The banker makes his profit on these transactions by dividing the commission with the broker. The fact that the commission is divided should be clearly stated on the broker's contract note.

The foregoing paragraphs deal with the matter of buying and selling stocks and shares on behalf of customers from the point of view of the branch bank. Many banks, however, have large and active executor and trustee departments and the banks in such cases have to carry the usual responsibility of trustees in regard to the investments of the trust funds under their care. As executor or trustee, the banker, fortified by what outside advice he deems necessary, must exercise his own judgment in the purchase and sale of the securities relating to the trusts. He will have to keep within the terms of the will or trust deed, or, in the absence of a discretionary clause, within those classes of investment authorised by the Trustee Investments Act 1961. Naturally, a very high standard of prudence and acumen will be expected of a banker-trustee. He will often have to hold the scales fairly between the tenant for life, who wants as high an income as possible, and the remainderman, who wants safety and appreciation of the capital funds. The subject of a banker as an executor or trustee is a very large one, and one that requires its own literature on the matter. It is outside the scope of this book.

VALUABLES FOR SAFE CUSTODY

The fact that the banker for his own protection has to provide himself with strong-rooms makes him peculiarly suitable as a medium for taking charge of such of his customer's valuables as can be conveniently stored in them. By taking charge of property in this way, the banker becomes a "bailee", i.e. a person to whom the goods are entrusted for a specific purpose. There are two kinds of bailee, gratuitous bailees and bailees for reward. Since the banker does not usually make a specific charge for taking care of his customer's property, it has been argued that he is a gratuitous bailee. On the other hand, some authorities contend that the practice of taking charge of customer's valuables is so general that it is as truly a consideration for the customer's opening or continuing his account as some of a banker's other services undoubtedly are. Therefore it is contended that the banker is a bailee for reward.

This distinction used to govern the extent of the bailee's duties. A gratuitous bailee, it was said, was only bound to take the same care of the property entrusted to him as a reasonably prudent and careful man might fairly be expected to take of his own property of the like description,[110] and so was liable only in case of "gross negligence". A paid bailee, on the other hand, was liable for loss through mere negligence and must safeguard the property by every means in his power and provide the most effective appliances possible to ensure this end.

Ormerod LJ said in *Houghland* v. *R.R. Low (Luxury Coaches)*[111] that drawing such distinctions was the wrong approach. What really matters in a particular case is whether the bailee has observed the standard of care required in that particular case, and whether a bailee is sued in conversion[112] or in negligence, the burden is on him to show that the care which he took of the goods was such that there was no negligence on his part.

With regard to bankers, it seems that the standard of care is such care as an ordinary efficient and prudent banker would take in similar circumstances. The banker is, however, certainly not an insurer of the goods, and unless he is guilty of failure to take the appropriate degree of care, he is not liable if the goods are stolen.

If the banker keeps the valuables in his strong-room and they are stolen from the strong-room, then unless the theft is itself due to some negligence (such as allowing one person alone unsupervised access to the strong-room) then the banker is most unlikely to be liable. However, keeping them outside the strong-room would itself be an indication of negligence on the part of the bank if they were then stolen. Similarly, failure to report a theft to the police, or to take other steps to recover the stolen property, would be negligence.

Some banks accept valuables for safe custody on the basis of the obligations imposed upon them by the ordinary law. Other banks, such as the trustee savings banks, have an express provision in the contract for their safe-custody service disclaiming liability for loss, and such an express disclaimer has been upheld in the courts.

Since the passing of the Unfair Contract Terms Act 1977, however, a banker may now only exclude or limit his liability by an express term to the extent that the term in question satisfies the requirement of reasonableness.[113] In the absence of cases on the Act, it is too soon to say how the courts will interpret this requirement of reasonableness, although Schedule 2 to the Act lays down certain "guidelines" in interpreting the test of reasonableness.

In any event it is wise for customers to insure valuables while

110. Per Lord Chelmsford in *Giblin* v. *McMullen* (1868) L.R. 2 P.C. 317; 5 Moo. P.C.C.N.S. 434.
111. [1962] 1 Q.B. 694.
112. By virtue of the Torts (Interference with Goods) Act 1977, s. 2, detinue has been abolished and an action for loss or destruction of goods whilst under the control of a bailee, which previously lay in detinue, now lies in conversion.
113. Unfair Contract Terms Act 1977, s. 2.

they are deposited with a bank for safe custody, and some house-holder's comprehensive policies include such cover.

If the bank wrongfully delivers any such valuables to a third party without the customer's authority, it would be liable to the customer in conversion,[114] even if the wrongful conversion was made bona fide and without negligence.

All articles left for safe custody must be entered in the safe-custody register, which may be signed by the bank official who receives the articles. The property concerned should preferably be deposited in a locked box or suitcase, with the customer retaining the key. If this is not possible, or in the case of items such as deeds, policies and other securities, they should be enclosed in an envelope or other form of packet which is sealed with sealing wax, with the customer's personal seal, if he has one, impressed on the wax. Alternatively, the customer should be asked to sign his name across all places where the envelope or packet is stuck down, and the signature should then be covered with the sort of sticky tape which will take the customer's signature with it if it is removed.

However, where items are left to which regular access is required, such as stock exchange certificates, and, in particular, which cannot be disposed of without the owner's written consent on the appropriate form, these may often be held on "open" safe custody, normally under the control of two authorised bank officers. Wills are often held in open envelopes, too, to facilitate reference to their provisions in the event of the testator's death.

When the things are given up, the book must be signed by the customer or his representative as a receipt, unless, as is sometimes done, a separate receipt is taken from the customer. Bankers sometimes give a receipt for valuables deposited with them. If the receipt contains the words "for safe custody", Paget does not consider that the phrase adds to his liability.[115] These or similar words do not make him an insurer of the goods, nor will the banker's liability for goods entrusted to him be affected by his knowledge or lack of knowledge of the nature of the goods.

Banks which issue customers with a form of receipt advise customers to bring the receipt with them when articles are withdrawn, but this is not a necessity. The customer should be asked to attend in person, if at all possible, to withdraw articles deposited. If a third party presents the customer's authority to inspect or to withdraw all or part of the articles deposited, the banker must satisfy himself that the third party does not act outside the scope of the customer's

114. For conversion, see under "Defect in customer's title" in Chapter Eight.
115. 8th Edn., p. 189.

authority. It is usual for a bank official to be present on occasions of inspection or withdrawal by a third party, in order to see that the customer's instructions are not exceeded.

Executors are not entitled to remove articles left in the banker's charge by a deceased customer until they produce probate of the will, and where there is more than one executor, it is the practice to obtain the authority of all before the articles are released. In practice a customer's will is often deposited with the banker for safe custody, and it is necessary to allow one or more of the interested parties to inspect it. This should be done under the strict supervision of the bank and while an inventory may be made of the contents of a box, only the will if found should be removed. The will should be handed to the solicitors acting for the estate or to the parties named as executors against their receipt. Where a will is deposited with a banker in a sealed envelope, he should ensure that the names of the executors are recorded on the outside of the envelope.

If articles are deposited by trustees or executors the banker should obtain the authority of all before parting with the articles. This course is essential in the case of trustees who have no power to delegate their authority, save in exceptional circumstances, even to one of themselves, but in the case of death authority vests in the survivors or survivor.

Articles deposited in the joint names of persons not being partners should not be released except on the authority of all the depositors, unless there is a mandate permitting withdrawal by less than all.

The bankruptcy of a person who has deposited articles for safe custody necessitates getting the permission of the Official Receiver or trustee in bankruptcy before the banker can safely release any of the articles left in his charge by the bankrupt.

A banker *in his capacity of bailee* has no lien on articles left in his charge merely for safe custody, but if the articles have been left with him in order that he may *deal with them* in his capacity of banker, he has a lien on them.[116]

BANK AS CUSTODIAN TRUSTEE

A custodian trustee is a trustee, appointed under s. 4 of the Public Trustee Act 1906, who has the custody, as distinct from the management, of the trust property. The only parties eligible for such an appointment are the public trustee, and a banking or insurance *company* or body corporate "entitled by rules made under this Act

116. *See* Chapter Thirteen.

to act as custodian trustee".[117] Since the Act expressly limits the appointment to banking *companies* and bodies corporate, it follows that private bankers are not eligible, though they are entitled to act as bankers of a trust. Banking companies appointed to the office have "power to charge and retain or pay out of the trust property fees not exceeding the fees chargeable by the Public Trustee as custodian trustee".[117] It is to be noted that a banking company which is the banker of a trust does not thereby become a custodian trustee and entitled to the fees of that office.

Where a custodian trustee is appointed, the trust property must be transferred to the custodian trustee as if he were sole trustee, and for that purpose vesting orders may, where necessary, be made under the Trustee Act 1925.[118] The management of the trust and the exercise of any power or discretion exercisable by the trustees under the trust remain vested in the trustees other than the custodian trustee (referred to as the managing trustees).[119] "Subject and without prejudice to the rights of any other person the custodian trustee has the custody of all securities and documents of title relating to the trust property, but the managing trustees shall have free access thereto and be entitled to take copies or extracts therefrom."[120]

All sums payable to or out of the income or capital of the trust property are to be paid to or by the custodian trustee, but the custodian trustee may allow the dividends and other income derived from the trust property to be paid to the managing trustees or to such other person as they direct, or into such bank to the credit of such person as they may direct, and in that case he is exonerated from seeing to the application thereof, and is not answerable for any loss or misapplication thereof.[121]

The custodian trustee must concur in and perform all acts necessary to enable the managing trustees to exercise their powers of management, unless the matter in which he is requested to concur is a breach of trust or involves a personal liability upon him in respect of calls or otherwise; unless he so concurs he is not liable for any act or default on the part of the managing trustees.[122] The custodian trustee, if he acts in good faith, is not liable if he accepts as correct and acts upon any *written documentation* drawn up by the managing trustees in connection with the trust property. Neither is he liable for acting upon legal advice obtained by the managing trustees

117. Public Trustee Act 1906, s. 4(3).
118. Ibid., s. 4(2)(*a*).
119. Ibid., s. 4(2)(*b*).
120. Ibid., s. 4(2)(*c*).
121. Ibid., s. 4(2)(*e*).
122. Ibid., s. 4(2)(*d*).

independently of himself, as, for example, advice obtained from a solicitor other than the custodian trustee's own solicitor.[123]

The power of appointing new trustees, when exercisable by the trustees, is exercisable by the managing trustees alone, but the custodian trustee has the same power of applying to the court for the appointment of a new trustee as any other trustee.[124]

In addition to acting as custodian trustee, a banking company, if duly authorised under its constitution, is a "trust corporation" and as such may act as executor, administrator or trustee, in the same way as the public trustee.

BANKER'S OPINIONS

A bank manager sometimes receives inquiries from another bank with regard to the financial position or business integrity of one of his customers. Usually this happens where his customer wishes to enter into some contractual relationship with a third party, and the third party asks the customer to supply a banker's reference. The customer gives the name of his bank to the third party, who passes this information on to his own bank, which then approaches the customer's bank "in confidence". The fact that the reply is given in confidence does not mean that the third party's bank is not authorised to disclose the information to the third party; indeed disclosure to the third party is the whole purpose of obtaining such a reference.

Some well-known trade protection societies address their inquiries direct to the customer's bankers. Such inquiries are usually answered direct, as if they had been made by banks; in other cases, if a bank receives inquiries direct, rather than through the third party's bankers, the proper course is either to request that the inquiry be sent through the third party's own bank, or if it replies at all, to reply to the third party's own bankers. Some banks, however, are willing to reply direct to certain other carefully chosen classes of inquirer.

The request for an opinion ought to give some indication of the amount of the liability concerned, whether this is a single amount, or a sum payable monthly or yearly.

Where the banker replies to such status inquiry, it should use such knowledge as it possesses concerning the customer's affairs; it is not under any duty to make outside inquiries before replying.[125] The reply, or banker's opinion, gives a general indication of the credit-worthiness of the customer. It should not give any details of the account itself. The usual form of favourable reply is "Respectable

123. Ibid., s. 4(2)(*h*).
124. Ibid., s. (2)(*f*).
125. *Parsons* v. *Barclay & Co.* (1910) 103 L.T. 196.

and trustworthy and considered good for your figures and purpose",
but if the banker wishes to be more cautious he may say something like "Respectable and trustworthy, but your figure is larger
than we are accustomed to see." He may then moderate this sentence,
if he wishes, by adding "However, we do not think he would enter
into an obligation he could not see his way to fulfil."

In the case of customers who have only recently opened an account,
the opinion might say "Considered respectable and trustworthy, but
has only recently opened an account with us, and we cannot speak
for your figures."

If the phrase "respectable and trustworthy" cannot be used no
doubt the bank manager will have given serious consideration to the
advisability of closing the account altogether.

The bank manager should be scrupulously careful when answering
such inquiries. If his report is too favourable, he may have to face an
action for misrepresentation or negligence brought by the inquirer,
and if he speaks too unfavourably, the customer may have a claim
against the bank either for libel or for damages for breach of duty,
although there do not appear to be any reported decisions on this
point.

If the opinion is too favourable, the position of the inquirer would
depend on whether the opinion was given negligently or fraudulently.

For the bank to be liable in negligence, it is not necessary for the
opinion to be in writing or signed by the banker.[126] This area of
law was explored extensively by the court in *Hedley Byrne & Co.*
v. *Heller & Partners.*[127] The banker does owe a duty of care to the
third party who originated the request for the reference, and may be
liable to the third party for any loss resulting to the third party from
relying on the opinion. In *Hedley Byrne*, the banker expressly stated
the opinion to be given "without responsibility", and because of that,
the bank was able to escape liability in that case. In view of the
provisions of the Unfair Contract Terms Act 1977, it is not certain
to what extent the banker can now exclude liability by such an
express disclaimer of responsibility. As mentioned above, such
disclaimer will be allowed only to the extent that it satisfies the test
of reasonableness.[128]

It should be noted that many banks are not licensed as credit
reference agencies within the terms of s. 145(8) of the Consumer
Credit Act 1974, and the content and source of their opinions need
not therefore be disclosed (unless of course in so far as some subsequent processing by a licensed agency may bring the opinion within

126. *Banbury* v. *Bank of Montreal* [1918] A.C. 626.
127. [1964] A.C. 465; [1963] 2 All E.R. 575.
128. *See* this chapter under "Valuables for Safe Custody".

the scope of that section). It follows that such a bank is not required to produce a copy of any file it maintains on any customer. It is usual to incorporate a sentence to this effect with the disclaimer.

If it is alleged that the opinion was given fraudulently, the position will be governed by the Statute of Frauds Amendment Act 1828 (known as Lord Tenterden's Act), s. 6 of which reads as follows.

No action shall be brought whereby to charge any person upon or by reason of any representation or assurance made or given concerning or relating to the character, conduct, credit, ability, trade or dealings of any other person to the intent or purpose that such other person may obtain credit, money or goods upon [such representation or assurance] unless such representation or assurance be made in writing signed by the party to be charged therewith.

The words interpolated are not in the original Act, but are inserted to make sense.

This section applies only in the case of fraudulent misrepresentation,[129] namely "... one which is made knowingly, or without belief in its truth, or recklessly, without caring whether it be true or false. A false statement, made through carelessness and without reasonable ground for believing it to be true, may be evidence of fraud, but does not necessarily amount to fraud".[130]

Thus if a misrepresentation is made innocently and without negligence, there is no cause of action. If it is made negligently there may (subject to any express disclaimer of responsibility, to the extent that such disclaimer is effective) be a cause of action whether the misrepresentation was in writing or not. If it was fraudulent, it would not be actionable unless in writing signed by the party to be charged.

The practice of bankers of giving information to one another for their mutual protection is well established, and is of very considerable value to the business community, whose credit facilities would be severely curtailed were the custom not in vogue. On the other hand, in *Tournier* v. *National Provincial Bank*[131] the implication was that even between bankers information concerning a customer should only be given at his request or with his express or implied consent.[132]

---

129. *Banbury* v. *Bank of Montreal, supra.*
130. *Derry* v. *Peek* (1889) 14 App. Cas. 337; [1890] All E.R. Rep. 1.
131. [1924] 1 K.B. 461; [1923] All E.R. Rep. 550.
132. *See also* this chapter "The banker's duties" under "Duty of secrecy".

CHAPTER FIVE

Accounts of Customers

PRELIMINARY INQUIRIES

Before opening an account for a customer who is not already known to him, a banker should make proper preliminary inquiries. In particular, he should obtain references from responsible persons with regard to the identity, integrity and reliability of the proposed customer.

If a banker does not act prudently and in accordance with current banking practice when obtaining references concerning a proposed customer, he may later have cause for regret. Suppose, for example, that a banker collects payment of a cheque for a customer and it later turns out that the customer is not the true owner of the cheque. The banker will be liable to the true owner unless he (the banker) collected the cheque for his customer "in good faith and without negligence".[1]

In *Ladbroke & Co.* v. *Todd*,[2] a thief opened an account with a stolen cheque, professing himself to be the payee. He was not introduced to the bank and no references were obtained. The cheque was specially cleared at the request of the thief, and he drew out the proceeds on the next day. The fraud was discovered soon afterwards. The drawers thereupon sent another cheque to the real payee and, taking an assignment of his rights in the stolen cheque brought, as holders of the cheque or alternatively as assignees, an action against the bank to recover the proceeds collected by the bank as money had and received to their use. Evidence was given that it was the general practice of bankers to obtain a satisfactory introduction or reference. It was held that failure to obtain a satisfactory introduction or reference constituted a breach of the duty to the true owner of a cheque, and so the bank had not acted "without negligence".

It is not possible to say how many references a banker should take up or how zealously he should pursue references; the answer will

1. Cheques Act 1957, s. 4; *see* Chapter Eight.
2. [1914–15] All E.R. Rep. 1134.

obviously vary from case to case. It would seem, however, that a banker may refrain from "making inquiries which it is improbable will lead to detection of the potential customer's purpose if he is dishonest and which are calculated to offend him and maybe drive away his custom if he is honest."[3]

In *Hampstead Guardians* v. *Barclays Bank*,[4] a person claimed his name to be Donald Stewart and opened an account with the bank. A reference was given and, in due course, a reply to the bank's inquiry was received which purported to be from the referee but was in fact a forgery. The day the reply was received the customer brought in two orders payable to D. Stewart and Co., saying that was his trading name. In fact the cheques had been stolen from the plaintiffs by a temporary employee. There was only one firm of the name of D. Stewart & Co. in London, at an address different from the one given by the prospective customer when the account was opened. It was held that the bank had been negligent in that case, since the reference would only have been good for the genuine Donald Stewart.

In *Lloyds Bank* v. *Savory*[5] two stockbroker's clerks, P and S, stole a series of cheques which were intended as payment to jobbers and were, in accordance with the then rules of the London Stock Exchange, made payable to bearer.[6] P and Mrs S had accounts at country branches of the bank. The bank's rules provided that no current account was to be opened without knowledge of or inquiry into the circumstances and character of the customer, and there was an unwritten rule which was nevertheless generally recognised that banks did not take payments in, without inquiry, of cheques drawn by a firm in favour of a third party and paid in by a person (other than the payee) who was or ought to be known to be an employee of the drawing firm.

The bank had received a satisfactory reference for P, and a reference for Mrs S which it took as being satisfactory, but it knew nothing of S's employment, and although it knew that P was a stockbroker's clerk, it did not ask the name of his employers. It was held by the House of Lords, by a majority, that the bank's practice was defective in that it did not make sufficient inquiries regarding P and Mrs S.

In several other cases bankers have been held negligent because they collected cheques which their customers, abusing their position as employees, partners, agents or trustees, had drawn in favour of

3. *Marfani & Co.* v. *Midland Bank* [1968] 2 All E.R. 573 at p. 582.
4. (1923) 39 T.L.R. 229.
5. [1933] A.C. 201.
6. *See* Chapter Seven for bearer cheques.

themselves. So, in addition to obtaining proper references, a banker should not open an account for a new customer without first taking reasonable steps to find out who the proposed customer is employed by, whether he is a partner in any firm and whether he is an agent or trustee for any person. Although a banker who fails to make such inquiries before opening an account may well be acting negligently, it would seem that a banker is not bound to keep himself up to date as to the identity of his customer's employer.[7]

When a new customer is a married woman, the banker should ask her for her maiden name and should check the name she gives against the name given on her marriage certificate. Otherwise the customer could fraudulently pay into her account a cheque made out to someone else by claiming that it was in fact made out to her in her maiden name. On the same principle, when an existing woman customer marries, the banker should check her married name.

OPENING AN ACCOUNT

When a new account is opened, the banker takes a "mandate" from his customer. In its simplest form a mandate will consist of a specimen signature of the customer, details of the customer's address and occupation, and details of any overdraft facilities or of any drawing rights at other branches of the bank. The specimen signature is recorded in the banker's "signature book" or on an individual ledger card, together with these details. The mandate will also contain details (including specimen signatures) of all persons other than the customer who will have authority to draw cheques or carry out other transactions on the account.

A more complex mandate will be required wherever there are two or more parties to the account, in whatever capacity. It should deal with the following matters.

(*a*) When new accounts are to be opened, whether this is to be on the instructions of any one, or more, or all, of the parties: in the absence of express agreement, instructions would have to be given by all the parties.

(*b*) Whether cheques and other instruments may be signed by, and instructions given by, any one, or more, or all, of the parties or indeed by any person who is not a party: this provision should be expressed to apply whether or not the account would become overdrawn or the overdraft increased. Again, in the absence of specific instructions in the mandate, all would have to sign. Each

---

7. *Orbit Mining & Trading Co.* v. *Westminster Bank* [1963] 1 Q.B. 794.

signatory ought also to give the bank a specimen signature to keep in its signature book or card index.

(c) Whether payment may be countermanded by any one or more: probably in the absence of anything to the contrary, any one party could countermand payment, but it is better to have the matter settled in the mandate.

(d) Whether loans or advances may be given at the request of any one, or more, or all, of the parties.

(e) Whether property deposited for safe custody or as security may be surrendered on request to any one, or more, or all of the parties.

(f) The liability of the parties should be made joint and several: in the absence of express agreement, the liability of the parties will be joint only.

(g) In the case of a partnership, the partners should undertake to procure that any incoming partner will assent to the mandate on his admission, that notice will be given to the bank of any other change in the constitution of the firm, and whether revocation in, or changes of, the mandate are to be on the signature of any one, or more, or all of the partners.

STOPPING AN ACCOUNT

When a banker ceases to permit money to be paid into or out of an account until further notice, the account is said to be "stopped". A banker should stop an account as soon as his mandate is revoked, expressly or impliedly. A banker must treat his mandate as impliedly revoked as soon as he has notice of any of the following events:[8]

(a) the death or mental incapacity of the customer;

(b) the bankruptcy of the customer (if the customer is an individual);

(c) a resolution for voluntary liquidation or the making of a winding-up order (if the customer is a company);

(d) a garnishee order or any other court order affecting the customer's account;

(e) an assignment of the credit balance in the account by the customer to a third party.

Once an account has been stopped, the banker should not honour any cheque or pay any standing order out of the account even if it was drawn or fell due before the date of the event which caused the

8. *See* Chapter Four.

banker to stop the account. Otherwise, the banker may be liable to the customer or to the person entitled to the money in the account. The banker is, however, entitled to debit the customer's account with the amount of any cheque or standing order which he had already paid before he received notice of the event which caused him to stop the account.

In most cases a banker would also be well advised to stop an account if the account is overdrawn and some event occurs which discharges the guarantor of the account from further liability. The reason for this is that the rule in *Clayton*'s case[9] will generally apply to a guarantee of an overdrawn account. Thus, if a guarantor is discharged when an account is £100 overdrawn, the guarantor will continue to be liable for the whole £100 if the banker stops the account. But if the banker does not stop the account, any money subsequently paid into the account by the customer will reduce the guarantor's liability to the banker.[10] So, if the customer paid £20 into his account after the discharge of the guarantor, the maximum possible liability of the guarantor would become £80 instead of £100.

An account which has been stopped is sometimes said to have been "suspended" or "broken" or "ruled off" or "frozen"; and from time to time an account which has been stopped is also referred to as a "closed" account. This last usage is both misleading and inaccurate because a stopped account and a closed account are actually not the same. Stopping an account should also be distinguished from stopping a cheque. When a customer stops a cheque, he merely countermands the banker's authority to pay that particular cheque when it is presented, but the account as a whole is not affected.

CLOSING AN ACCOUNT

Either the banker or the customer may take the initiative in closing an account. When an account has been closed, the banker has no further relationship with his customer. Any money owed by one party to the other has been paid or is treated by the party closing the account as no longer recoverable. Unlike a stopped account, an account which has been closed cannot later be reopened.

If the customer wishes to close an account, he does not have to give notice to the banker. However, a banker should not assume that the customer has closed the account merely because the customer has withdrawn the whole of the credit balance in the account, but

9. (1816) 1 Mer. 529; *see* Chapter Four.
10. *Bradford Old Bank* v. *Sutcliffe* [1918] 2 K.B. 833.

should ensure that the customer states in writing that he is in fact closing the account.

If the bank acts on the basis of a telephone conversation, which the customer then denies, and then credits to a different account (because the banker had closed the account in reliance on the telephone conversation) moneys paid in by the customer, the banker will be liable to the customer if the customer is believed and the banker wrongfully dishonours a cheque with the answer "No account".[11] The bank should invite the customer to provide for the payment of any outstanding cheques; otherwise it may dishonour cheques subsequently presented with the answer "Account closed". The bank should also ask the customer to return any unused cheque forms.

When the banker wishes to close the account, he should give the customer reasonable notice.[12] The period of notice must be long enough to allow the customer to make alternative banking arrangements, the period required varying from case to case. In *Prosperity* v. *Lloyds Bank* one month was held to be not long enough in the circumstances. If the banker does not give the customer reasonable notice or if he fails to honour cheques and standing orders until the notice expires, he will be liable to the customer in breach of contract. The banker should honour any cheque or standing order which is payable before the notice expires provided that it is within the customer's credit limit. When the notice expires, the banker should pay any remaining credit balance to the customer.

JOINT ACCOUNTS

This section deals with joint accounts other than trustee accounts (discussed later in this chapter) and partnership accounts (*see* Chapter Six). A joint account is an account where the customer is more than one person. The rights and duties of the banker and the customer are the same, whether an account is a joint account or an individual account. Where an account is a joint account it is, however, necessary for a banker to know the position with regard to the mandate and the liability of each of the parties to the account.

(*a*) On the opening of a joint account, the banker should obtain a written mandate signed by all parties to the account. The mandate must state which and how many of the parties (and which third parties, if any) have authority to sign cheques or carry out any other transactions in connection with the account. Without such a mandate

---

11. *Wilson* v. *Midland Bank* (1961) *The Reading Standard*, 13th October.
12. *Prosperity* v. *Lloyds Bank* (1923) 39 T.L.R. 372.

the banker is not safe in paying a cheque unless the cheque has been signed by all the parties to the account (*see* p. 67). Where the banker holds any valuables or securities on behalf of the joint account holders, he should only release them (or the proceeds of their sale) to all the account holders together unless the mandate specifies otherwise.

(*b*) Unless there is an agreement to the contrary, the mandate may be revoked at any time by any of the parties to the account, expressly or impliedly, wholly or in part. This means, for example, that one party to the account can stop a cheque drawn by another party to the account even though the cheque was drawn in accordance with the mandate. The mandate is revoked automatically by the death, bankruptcy or mental incapacity of any of the parties and the banker should therefore stop the account as soon as he has notice of any of those events.

(*c*) As soon as the banker learns of a bankruptcy petition against any of the parties, he should permit no further drawings from the account. Any cheque drawn by the party concerned presented to the bank for payment while the account is stopped should be returned with the answer "Refer to drawer". But a cheque drawn by any of the other parties must be returned with an answer calculated to cause as little damage as possible to their credit and reputation. A suitable answer in such a circumstance might be "Joint account customer X involved in bankruptcy proceedings".[13]

If the account is overdrawn, it should be stopped if the banker is to preserve his rights against the bankrupt's estate. The banker may prove in the bankrupt's estate for the whole debt, ignoring any liability of or security deposited by any other party; but security deposited by the bankrupt will be subject to the same rules as if the bankrupt was the only person liable.[14]

On the making of a receiving order, the new parties to the account will be all the old account holders who are still solvent, together with the trustee in bankruptcy of the bankrupt party, and any credit balance, or articles deposited for safe custody, may be withdrawn on their joint instructions.

(*d*) The position on mental incapacity of one of the parties is similar. The banker must refuse to allow withdrawals as soon as he learns of the mental incapacity of any party, and withdrawals can only be permitted on the joint instructions of the receiver (if and when one is appointed by the Court of Protection)[15] and the remaining parties.

13. *Q.B.P.*, No. 36.
14. *See* Chapter Thirty.
15. *See* below in this chapter.

(*e*) When a joint account is stopped because of the death of one of the parties, the doctrine of survivorship applies. This means that the balance in the account is transferred to the surviving parties. After he has been shown the death certificate of the deceased party, the banker may with safety allow money to be paid out of the account provided that he is authorised to do so by all of the surviving parties. A banker probably has implied authority to honour a cheque drawn before the death but presented after he received notice of the death if the cheque was signed by all of the surviving parties and not by the deceased party. Following the death of any of the parties to a joint account, the usual practice is for the banker to obtain authority from the survivors to close the old account and open a new account in the name of the surviving parties alone. It is advisable to obtain at the same time the instructions of the survivors with regard to all outstanding cheques. The fact that the balance is transferred to the survivors does not mean that it belongs beneficially to them; this is a matter to be resolved between the survivors and the personal representatives of the deceased party, and will depend upon the terms on which the account was held as between the deceased and the surviving parties. When valuables (other than documents of title) are deposited in joint names for safe custody and one of the parties dies, bankers normally obtain the consent of the personal representatives of the deceased party before handing over the valuables to the survivors, though the doctrine of survivorship means that it is not strictly necessary for a banker to do so.

(*f*) Since parties to a joint account are not automatically authorised to pledge each other's credit, a banker should not lend money to the parties of a joint account, either by means of an overdraft or in any other way, without obtaining from each of the parties an undertaking to be severally as well as jointly liable to repay the loan. The first reason for this is that when a party who is severally or jointly and severally liable dies, his personal representatives will be liable to repay the loan, whereas when a party who is only jointly liable dies, his personal representatives will not be liable at all because a joint liability, like a jointly owned asset, passes to the survivors alone. The second reason is that when a party is severally or jointly and severally liable, the banker has the right to set-off the credit balance on that party's personal account against the overdraft on the joint account, whereas when a party is only jointly liable, the banker has no rights of set-off except in respect of other joint accounts of the same parties.[16]

(*g*) If a banker does lend money to the parties to a joint account

---

16. *See* Chapter Four for the right of set-off.

and the loan is not repaid as agreed, time will run against the banker under the Limitation Act 1980 in the normal way.[17] This means that if one party to the joint account makes part payment of the debt before it has become statute-barred, time will begin to run anew against each of the parties. But if one party to the joint account makes part payment of the debt after it has become statute-barred or makes a written acknowledgement of the debt, time will only run anew against that party and any other party on whose behalf he was acting.[18]

AGENTS

When a customer authorises another person to draw cheques or carry out other transactions on his behalf in connection with his account, the customer is the "principal" and the person to whom he gives authority is his "agent".[19] The customer must give details of the agent to the banker as part of the banker's mandate and must define clearly for the banker the extent of the agent's authority. The banker must construe his mandate strictly. For example, an authority for an agent to draw, accept and indorse cheques does not imply authority to draw, accept and indorse other forms of bills of exchange and it does not imply authority to negotiate new overdraft facilities or to give or withdraw security. Except where the banker himself is appointed as an agent, he should obtain a specimen signature of the agent as part of his mandate.

Any person of sound mind may be appointed as an agent even if the person is a minor (or a bankrupt). This means that a person may legally be entitled to carry out certain transactions on his principal's behalf which he would not be able to carry out on his own behalf. But an agent cannot appoint another person to act in his place on his principal's behalf, except with the principal's express or implied consent. Consent may be implied from the conduct of the parties or the usage of the trade. Without such consent the principal would not be liable for the acts of the sub-agent, since there would be no privity of contract between the principal and the sub-agent.[20] Privity of contract arises only if the agent has clear authority to create such privity or his act in so doing is ratified.[21]

---

17. *See* Chapter Four.
18. Limitation Act 1980, s. 29(7).
19. For a general discussion of the law of agency, *see* Cheshire & Fifoot, *The Law of Contract* (10th Edn.).
20. For privity of contract *see* Cheshire & Fifoot, *The Law of Contract* (10th Edn.).
21. *De Bussche* v. *Alt* (1878) 8 Ch. D. 286; *Keay* v. *Fenwick* (1876) 1 C.P.D. 745; *New Zealand and Australian Land Co.* v. *Watson* (1881) 7 Q.B.D. 374.

An agent may sometimes quite honestly enter into a binding contract on behalf of his principal, and it may turn out afterwards that he had no power to do so. In these circumstances, though he cannot be sued as a principal on the contract, it has been held that he warrants his authority as an implied condition of the contract, and may, therefore, be sued for a breach of this warranty.[22] In *Richardson* v. *Williamson*,[23] directors of a building society borrowed on behalf of the society money which, it turned out, they had no power to borrow. It was held that the directors were personally liable, for "persons who induce others to act on the supposition that they have authority to enter into a binding contract on behalf of third persons, on it turning out that they have no such authority, may be sued for damages for a breach of an implied warrant of authority."[24] In another case, *Starkey* v. *Bank of England*,[25] a stockbroker, by virtue of a power of attorney forged by one of two joint holders of stock, but which the stockbroker believed to be genuine, instructed the bank to transfer stock, which they did, and the proceeds of the sale were applied by the forger of the power of attorney to his own use. The Bank was obliged to transfer a like amount of stock to the true owner; its claim to be indemnified by the stockbroker was allowed on the grounds that the stockbroker had given an implied warranty that he had authority.

However, to make the agent liable it must be shown that the want of authority was not known to the third parties. The bank would, of course, be put on inquiry if any such agent drew cheques in his own favour on the principal's account, or paid his own personal debts to third parties with cheques drawn on that account.[26]

The authority of an agent may be revoked by his principal as agreed between them. Most agency agreements provide for the agency to be revoked at the end of a fixed period, or on the occurrence of a specified event, or on the expiry of an agreed period of notice. Except where an agency is irrevocable, it is revoked automatically by the death, mental incapacity or bankruptcy of the principal[27] or the death of the agent.[28] An agency is irrevocable if it is expressed to be irrevocable and is given to secure a proprietary interest of

22. *Collen* v. *Wright* (1857) 8 E. & B. 647; [1843–60] All E.R. Rep. 146; *Firbanks Executors* v. *Humphreys* (1886) 18 Q.B.D. 54; *Chapleo* v. *Brunswick Permanent Benefit Building Society* (1881) 6 Q.B.D. 696.
23. (1871) L.R. 6 Q.B. 276.
24. At 279, per Cockburn CJ.
25. [1903] A.C. 114.
26. *Midland Bank* v. *Reckitt & Others* [1933] A.C. 1; *see also Reckitt* v. *Barnett, Pembroke & Slater* [1929] A.C. 176.
27. *Blades* v. *Free* (1829) B. & C. 167; *Drew* v. *Nunn* (1879) 4 Q.B.D. 661; *Yonge* v. *Toynbee* [1910] 1 K.B. 215.
28. *Friend* v. *Young* [1897] 2 Ch. 421.

the agent or the performance of an obligation owed by the principal to the agent.[29] This may happen, for example, if a banker lends money to his customer and, as security for the loan, the customer gives the banker authority to sell certain valuables in the event that the customer fails to repay the loan. An irrevocable agency given by way of security will end automatically when the customer repays the loan which the agency was intended to secure (or when any other obligation which it was given to secure has come to an end).

When engaging in a transaction on behalf of his principal, an agent should be careful not to give the impression that he is assuming any personal liability. If, for example, he is signing a cheque or any other document, he should add words to his signature indicating that he is signing on the customer's behalf or in a representative character; if he does so, he will not be personally liable on the document, but the mere addition of words describing him as agent or as filling a representative character does not exempt him from personal liability.[30] The agent should in no circumstances rely for his protection on the mere fact that he is described as an agent in the body of the document.

Where an agent signs *per procurationem* (*p.p.* or *per pro.*), the signature gives notice that the agent has only a limited authority to sign and the principal is bound by the signature only if the agent was acting within the actual limits of his authority in so signing.[31] If the agent signs a document or engages in any other transaction outside the limits of his authority, the principal will have no liability and the agent will be personally liable.

When a banker is asked to collect or pay a cheque or bill which the agent drew or endorsed on behalf of his principal in favour of himself, the banker must make proper inquiries in order to discover whether the agent does in fact have authority to draw or indorse such instruments on his principal's account in favour of himself. Where a banker collects or pays such an instrument without making proper inquiries, he may be liable to the principal or the true owner of the cheque if it turns out that the agent did not have the relevant authority.[32] If an agent borrows a sum of money from a banker on the security of documents belonging to his principal and the banker lends the money in good faith and without reason to suspect that there is any irregularity in the transaction, the banker will be entitled to hold the documents as security for the loan and the

29. *Smart* v. *Sanders* (1848) 5 C.B. 895 at p. 917.
30. Bills of Exchange Act 1882, s. 26(1).
31. Ibid., s. 25.
32. *Morrison* v. *London, County and Westminster Bank* [1914] 3 K.B. 356; *Reckitt* v. *Midland Bank* [1933] A.C. 1; *Underwood* v. *Bank of Liverpool and Martin's Bank* [1924] All E.R. Rep. 230, [1924] 1 K.B. 775.

principal will not be entitled to recover them even if the agent does not pay over to the principal any of the money which he has borrowed. The banker is not deemed to be acting in good faith "if there be anything which excites the suspicion that there is something wrong in the transaction" and if he then "shuts his eyes to the facts presented to him and puts the suspicions aside without further inquiry."[33]

Certain transactions, including any conveyance or legal mortgage of land, cannot validly be completed except by a "deed", i.e. a document under seal. An agent cannot have authority to execute a deed unless he has himself been appointed by deed.[34] Such a deed of appointment is known as a "power of attorney" and the agent is known as an "attorney". The law relating to powers of attorney is now largely contained in the Powers of Attorney Act 1971.[35] Under this Act a power of attorney must be signed and sealed by the donor of the power or by his direction and in his presence. If execution takes place by direction and in the presence of the donor, two other persons must be present as witnesses and must attest the instrument.[36] The Act abolishes the deposit or filing of powers of attorney at the central office of the Supreme Court or at the Land Registry.[37] The contents of a power of attorney may be proved by means of a photo, or other facsimile, copy containing a certificate at the end of each page signed by the donor of the power or by a stockbroker or solicitor that the copy is a true and complete copy of the original.[38]

Where a power of attorney is expressed to be irrevocable and is given to secure (a) a proprietary interest of the donee of the power, or (b) the performance of an obligation owed to the donee, then so long as the donee has that interest or the obligation remains undischarged, the power may not be revoked (i) by the donor without the consent of the donee, or (ii) by the death, incapacity or bankruptcy of the donor or, if the donor is a body corporate, by its winding up or dissolution.[39]

A donee who acts in pursuance of the power at a time when it has been revoked does not by reason of the revocation incur any liability either to the donor or to any other person, if at that time he did not know the power had been revoked.[40] Again, where a power of attorney has been revoked and a person without knowledge

33. *London Joint Stock Bank* v. *Simmons* [1892] A.C. 201.
34. *Berkeley* v. *Hardy* (1826) 5 B. & C. 355.
35. This repeals Law of Property Act 1925, ss. 123, 124, 125(1) and 126 to 129.
36. Powers of Attorney Act 1971, s. 1.
37. Ibid., s. 2(1).
38. Ibid., s. 3(1).
39. Ibid., s. 4.
40. Ibid., s. 5(1).

of the revocation deals with the donee, the transaction as between them shall be as valid as if the power had then been in existence.[41]

Where the power is expressed to be irrevocable in the instrument creating it and to be given by way of security then unless the person dealing with the donee knows that it was not in fact given by way of security, he is entitled to assume that the power is incapable of revocation, except by the donor acting with the consent of the donee.[42]

Where the interest of a purchaser is at issue, it will be conclusively presumed that a person dealing with the donee of a power did not know of the revocation of that power if:

(a) the transaction was completed within twelve months of the date on which the power came into operation; or

(b) the person dealing with the donee makes a statutory declaration within three months after the completion of the purchase that he did not at the material time know of the revocation of the power.[43]

Thus if an attorney sells property belonging to his principal after his authority has been revoked the purchaser will be protected provided he did not know of the revocation. If he then sells the property to a second purchaser, the interest of the second purchaser in the property cannot be overturned on the grounds that the first purchaser knew that the attorney's authority had been revoked:

(a) if the sale to the first purchaser was completed within twelve months after the date on which the power of attorney took effect; or

(b) if the first purchaser makes a statutory declaration within three months after the completion of the sale by the attorney, stating that he did not know the authority had been revoked at the time when the sale was completed.

The wording of powers of attorney is construed strictly by the courts. A power granted to a donee to manage certain property followed by general words giving the attorney full powers would not necessarily, for example, give the attorney power to indorse bills of exchange, for the indorsing of bills of exchange is not necessarily incidental to the management of property. But a power in the form set out in Schedule 1 to the Act, without restrictions, would give the attorney power to do anything which can lawfully be done by an attorney.[44] When signing as an attorney, it is normal to write

41. Powers of Attorney Act 1971, s. 5(2).
42. Ibid., s. 5(3).
43. Ibid., s. 5(4).
44. Ibid., s. 10.

the principal's name and then add such words as "By his attorney, John Smith".

If an attorney appointed by a power in the form in Schedule 1 wishes to carry out certain transactions on his principal's account and there is no mandate authorising him to do so, the attorney may execute a mandate in the name of his principal, stating on the mandate that he is acting as the principal's attorney.

MINORS

A person now attains "full age" at eighteen instead of twenty-one, and a person who is not of full age is now termed a "minor", not an "infant".[45] In several important respects the legal position of a minor is different from the position of a person of full age, and when dealing with a minor, a banker must not forget this is so. In particular, a banker must remember that a minor is not bound by certain agreements which would be binding on a person of full age.

The main rules relating to a minor's capacity to enter into binding contracts are as follows.

(a) A minor is bound to pay a reasonable price for any "necessary" goods or services.[46] If he agrees to pay more than a reasonable price for them, he will only be bound to pay a reasonable price and will not be bound to pay the agreed price. "Necessary" goods are defined by statute as meaning goods sold and delivered to him, suitable to his actual condition in life and to his actual requirements at the time of the sale and delivery.[47] What goods are in fact necessary will vary according to the minor's wealth and position in life, and whether he is already sufficiently provided with goods of the kind in question, even if this fact is not known to the seller.[48] No doubt the same principles would apply to necessary services. A minor is also bound by an agreement for his employment, but only if it is on balance for his benefit.[49]

(b) A minor is also bound by certain other types of agreement unless and until he repudiates or avoids them at any time during his minority or within a reasonable time after he attains full age. These "voidable" contracts include partnership agreements,[50] partly

---

45. Family Law Reform Act 1969, s. 1.
46. This is an old common law principle now enshrined, as regards goods, in the Sale of Goods Act 1979, s. 3(2).
47. Ibid., s. 3(3). *See Chapple* v. *Cowper* (1844) 13 M. & W. 252.
48. *Ryder* v. *Wombwell* (1868) L.R. 4 Exch. 32 at p. 38; *Nash* v. *Inman* [1908] 2 K.B. 1; *Barnes & Co.* v. *Toye* (1884) 13 Q.B.D. 410.
49. *See*, for example, *Clements* v. *London and North Western Rail Co.* [1894] 2 Q.B. 482; contrast *De Francesco* v. *Barnum* (1890) 45 Ch. D. 430.
50. *Goode* v. *Harrison* (1821) 5 B. & Ald. 147.

paid shares[51] and agreements for the renting by the minor of a building or other land.[52] A voidable contract is, however, valid unless and until avoided, and so by repudiating a contract, the minor does not escape liability for obligations incurred before the date of the repudiation; thus he will remain liable for any calls on shares made, or rent accruing due, before he repudiated the contract, and he cannot recover back any money he has actually paid.[53] If, however, a minor is a member of a partnership, he will not be liable for any debts of the partnership contracted during the period when he was a minor,[54] though he cannot prevent the other partners discharging the partnership debts out of the partnership property.

(c) Under s.1 of the Infants Relief Act 1874, a contract for the repayment of money lent or to be lent to a minor (and any security associated with the loan) is "absolutely void", as is a contract for the purchase by a minor of non-necessary goods or services. Although the words "absolutely void" seem very final, such contracts are not in fact wholly without effect. For example, the minor can sue on them, although he cannot be sued,[55] and no money paid by the minor under such contracts can be recovered by the minor unless the other party has given the minor no consideration under the contract.[56] A loan made to a minor will not become binding on the minor even if he makes a fresh promise to repay the loan after he attains full age, nor will he be bound if he ratifies any contract made during his minority, even if new consideration is given for the ratification.[57] So if he agrees after coming of age to pay any money which is in reality the old loan and not a new advance, the agreement and any instrument given for carrying it into effect is absolutely void, and if he ratifies some other contract, it will still be unenforceable.[58] A new contract to perform some obligation which is not a debt may, however, be enforceable.

(d) Repayment of a loan cannot be enforced against a minor, even if he obtained the advance by falsely representing that he was of full age,[59] and any security given by a minor for a loan to him is void.[60] Nevertheless, security is not always wholly ineffective. In *Nottingham Permanent Benefit Building Society* v. *Thurstan*[61] a

51. *Cork and Bandon Rail Co.* v. *Cazenove* (1841) 10 Q.B. 935.
52. *Davies* v. *Beynon-Harris* (1931) 47 T.L.R. 424.
53. *Steinberg* v. *Scala* (*Leeds*) [1923] 2 Ch. 452.
54. *Lovell and Christmas* v. *Beauchamp* [1894] A.C. 607 at p. 611.
55. *Warwick* v. *Bruce* (1813) 2 M. & S. 205.
56. *Valentini* v. *Canali* (1889) 24 Q.B.D. 166.
57. Infants Relief Act 1874, s. 2.
58. Betting and Loans (Infant) Act 1892, s. 5.
59. *Leslie* v. *Sheill* [1914] 3 K.B. 607.
60. Infants Relief Act 1874, s. 1.
61. [1903] A.C. 6.

minor borrowed money for the purchase of a house which she began to improve. The building society discovered that she was a minor and discontinued the advances, took possession of the property and completed the building works themselves. It was held that although the mortgage was void, the society was entitled to be subrogated to the position of the vendor, and was entitled to a lien for the purchase money and all expenses paid on completion of the purchase, together with interest. The lien did not, however, cover any of the advances made or the expenses incurred for the improvements, which there was no right to recover.

Since a minor is bound to pay a reasonable price for necessaries supplied to him, if a loan is made to a minor and he uses the loan to purchase necessaries, the lender is entitled to be subrogated to the seller's right to be paid a reasonable price for them.[62] It would, however, be rash for a banker to lend money in reliance on this.

(e) It is uncertain whether the relationship between the banker and a minor customer comes into the category of contracts for the benefit of the minor on balance, which are fully enforceable contracts, or whether it is a contract on which the minor can sue, but not be sued. At all events, it seems fairly safe to say that it is a contract on which the minor can sue the banker. In other respects, the law relating to the capacity of minors to contract affects bankers in two ways: first, as regards cheques and bills of exchange drawn or indorsed by a minor; secondly as regards loans made to a minor by a banker, whether by means of overdraft or in any other way.

With regard to cheques and bills of exchange, the Bills of Exchange Act 1882 provides that "capacity to incur liability as a party to a bill is co-extensive with capacity to contract".[63] This means, for example, that a minor who pays for necessary goods or services by cheque will not be liable on the cheque, even though he is liable to pay a reasonable price for the goods or services. In fact a minor who pays for anything by cheque will never be liable on the cheque. But if the money is in fact paid the holder is entitled to retain the payment.[64] Thus a banker who has a minor as a customer does not have to find out, when a cheque drawn by a minor is presented to him for payment, whether the cheque is in payment of an obligation binding on the minor. Provided that there is nothing suspicious on the face of the cheque and the minor has sufficient funds in his account to meet the cheque, the banker should honour the cheque. Otherwise, he may be liable to the minor in breach of contract, just

62. *Re National Permanent Benefit Building Society* (1869) 5 Ch. App. 309; *Lewis* v. *Alleyne* (1888) 4 T.L.R. 560. For an explanation of the concept of subrogation, *see* below in this section.
63. Bills of Exchange Act 1882, s. 22(1).
64. Ibid., s. 22(2).

as he might be to an adult customer. Where a minor signs a cheque, either as drawer or indorser, in circumstances where he himself is not liable on the cheque, the cheque may still be enforced by the holder in the normal way against any other person not under an incapacity who is a party to it.[64]

A prudent banker should not allow a minor to go into overdraft or to borrow money from him in any other way without first obtaining a satisfactory promise from an adult to indemnify the banker in full in the event that the minor fails to repay the loan. The promise must be phrased as an indemnity not as a guarantee because a person who gives an indemnity undertakes a *primary* liability, whereas a guarantee is a *secondary* liability which pre-supposes that some other person is primarily liable with the effect that the guarantor is only liable if the principal debtor (the minor) is liable.[65]

If a banker is foolish enough to lend money to a minor without obtaining an indemnity from an adult, he may nevertheless be able to recover at least part of the loan by virtue of the doctrine of subrogation. If, for example, a minor borrows money and uses it to pay for purchases from various persons, the banker will be "subrogated" to the rights of those persons. In other words, he will have the same right to sue the minor as each of the various persons would have had if the minor had not paid them. Suppose, for example, that the banker lent £100 to a minor, and that the minor spent £60 on necessary goods and £40 on non-necessary goods. As the banker would be subrogated to the rights of the persons who sold the goods to the minor, he would be able to recover a reasonable price for the necessary goods, but would have no right to recover any of the money spent on the non-necessary goods.

Although certain contracts made by a minor on his own behalf are, as we have seen, either void or voidable, the minor has full capacity to make any contract if he is acting as an agent or attorney. But if a minor enters into a contract which is outside the limits of his authority, he can only be personally liable if it is the sort of contract on which a minor can be personally liable, e.g. a contract for necessary goods or services.

(*f*) A minor may also be a partner and, like any other partner, he may make an agreement which is binding on the other members of the partnership provided that he is acting within his actual or ostensible authority.[66] But such an agreement will not be binding on the minor as a partner unless it is an agreement which would

65. *Coutts & Co.* v. *Browne-Lecky* [1947] K.B. 104 and *Yeoman Credit* v. *Latter* [1961] 2 All E.R. 294. *See also* Chapter Fourteen.
66. *See*, for example, *Re A and M* [1926] Ch. 274.

have been binding on him if he made it on his own. So, if a minor borrows money from a banker on behalf of a partnership, the loan will be binding on the other partners, though the minor will not himself be liable because a loan made to a minor is "absolutely void".

(g) A minor may be appointed an executor, but he cannot act in that capacity until he has attained full age. He may validly witness a signature provided that he is old enough to understand what he is doing and for his testimony to be relied on. But he cannot validly make a will unless he is a soldier or seaman on active service.[67] A minor is not entitled to hold a legal estate in land, either for his own benefit or as a trustee.[68]

(h) A minor may be declared bankrupt if he fails to pay debts which are binding on him or if he fails to pay his taxes.[69] But a minor cannot be declared bankrupt in respect of any trade debts he incurs because a trading contract entered into by a minor is neither a contract for his employment nor a contract for necessary goods or services and is therefore not binding on the minor. Where a minor is a member of a partnership, a receiving order cannot be made against the firm as a whole, but receiving orders may be made against the other partners individually or against the firm excluding the partner who is a minor.

(i) Under the Limitation Act 1980 time does not start to run against a minor until he comes of age or dies.[70] If, when he comes of age, he is under another disability (e.g. a mental disorder), time does not start to run until that disability ceases or he dies.[70]

MENTALLY DISORDERED PERSONS

At common law, a person making a contract was presumed to be of sound mind, and if mentally unsound he could avoid the contract only if he, or someone on his behalf, could prove that the other party knew his mental condition at the time the contract was made.[71] This rule must now be read subject to the provisions of the Mental Health Act 1959, which set up an office of the Supreme Court, called the Court of Protection, "for the protection and management ... of the property of persons under disability".[72]

If the Master of the Court of Protection is satisfied that a person

---

67. Wills Act 1837, s. 11; Wills (Soldiers and Sailors) Act 1918, s. 1.
68. Law of Property Act 1925, ss. 19 and 20.
69. *Re a Debtor* (*Re 564 of 1949*), *ex parte Commissioners of Customs & Excise* v. *Debtor* [1950] Ch. 282.
70. Limitation Act 1980, s. 28(1).
71. *Imperial Loan Co.* v. *Stone* [1892] 1 Q.B. 599.
72. Mental Health Act 1959, s. 100(2).

is incapable of managing and administering his property and affairs, he can make orders under the Act to ensure the maintenance or other benefit of the patient and members of his family;[73] he has, *inter alia*, power to appoint a receiver (usually a relative of the patient).

Unless a person is declared incapable under the Act, the common law rules continue to apply, but where such a declaration has been made, the patient cannot be bound by any agreement which he enters into, even if he entered into the agreement during a lucid interval.

As soon as a banker receives notice that a customer has been declared incapable, he should stop the customer's account. Where a customer has not been declared incapable, but the banker learns that the customer is suffering from mental incapacity, he should suspend all operations on the account until he either receives an order of the court or learns of the customer's recovery. The banker should immediately make proper inquiries to find out whether the customer is well enough to be capable of managing his own affairs. If the customer is in hospital, the inquiries should be addressed to the medical superintendent, and if the customer is at home, to his own doctor. If the reply is that the customer is capable, the account may be managed as before, but if he is not then the account must be stopped.

All cheques honoured by the banker before receipt of notice can be debited to the customer's account, but the banker may be liable for all cheques honoured after receipt of notice, and he should not thereafter make any payments to third parties under standing orders.

In *Re Beavan, Davies, Banks and Co.* v. *Beavan*[74] a customer had a paralytic seizure which rendered him incapable both physically and mentally of managing his affairs. For some two years thereafter, with the approval of other members of the family, the bank allowed the customer's eldest son to operate the account for the maintenance of the household. When the customer died, the account was overdrawn, and two of the executors resisted the bank's claim for repayment. It was held that since a person of unsound mind is bound to pay a reasonable price for necessaries[75] the bank was entitled, under the doctrine of subrogation, to recover all sums paid for the purchase of necessaries, but was not entitled to recover interest or banking charges.

Where a third party has been authorised to draw on the customer's account, that authority will cease when the customer becomes incapable of managing his or her affairs, since when a principal can

73. Mental Health Act 1959, s. 100(1).
74. [1912] 1 Ch. 196.
75. Sale of Goods Act 1979, s. 3(2) (then Sale of Goods Act 1893, s. 2). *See* previous section on "Minors" for a definition of "necessary".

no longer act for himself, his agent can no longer act for him.[76] Similarly, if one party to an account opened in joint names becomes mentally incapable of managing his or her affairs, neither party should be allowed to operate the account, since the joint authority is in effect an authority by each for the other to draw, and like any other authority, must be deemed to be determined when one of them becomes mentally incapable of managing his affairs.

If the customer is suffering from a temporary mental derangement, it may sometimes be practicable to allow the customer's spouse or next of kin to operate the account, provided that a certificate in the form of a statutory declaration from two medical men is obtained, and that satisfactory security is furnished indemnifying the banker against any claim that may afterwards be made by the customer to recover any amounts so withdrawn while he was incapable. In this connection a wife, save in certain circumstances which need not concern us, has power to pledge her husband's credit for necessaries (clearly being his actual or ostensible agent in a normal case), and the banker who has permitted drawings on the husband's account for such purposes would have a right of subrogation.

Although the bank may be willing to accommodate relatives for small amounts or for temporary purposes, there seems no reason why banks should incur unnecessary risks and if the customer is incapable of managing his or her affairs, the bank may quite properly refuse to pay out any money. This may well encourage the relatives to take the proper steps to have a receiver appointed.

A person found to be incapable of managing his own affairs cannot deal with his property (except to make a will during a lucid interval) until the order is discharged by the court. A patient can be adjudicated bankrupt under the direction of the court. On the death of the patient the jurisdiction of the Court of Protection ceases, and the receiver is automatically discharged.[77] The receiver can no longer draw on the receivership account, but in due course, on production of the grant of probate or letters of administration, he must pay the balance over to the personal representatives. On the death of a receiver, application is made, usually by a close relative of the patient, for the appointment of another receiver.[78]

For the purposes of the Limitation Act 1980, where a cause of action accrues (e.g. the due date of a bill is reached) during a period of incapacity, time does not begin to run until the patient is certified to have recovered, or dies without recovering.[79] If a cause of action

76. *Drew* v. *Nunn* (1879) 4 Q.B.D. 661.
77. Mental Health Act 1959, s. 105(2).
78. *Q.B.P.*, No. 157.
79. Limitation Act 1980, s. 28(1).

of action has accrued before the incapacity begins, however, time continues to run notwithstanding the incapacity.

TRUST ACCOUNTS

A person holding property may either own it for his own benefit or hold it on trust for the benefit of someone else. In the second case he holds the property as a "trustee" and the person or persons for whose benefit he holds the property are the "beneficiaries" of the trust.[80] A trust may be an express trust or an implied trust. An express trust is created by a "settlor" formally settling some of his property on trust for beneficiaries. An implied trust arises out of the nature of the relationship between two or more persons. If A transfers to B the title to A's property and it is apparent from the circumstances that A intends B to hold the property on trust and not as "beneficial owner", then an implied trust arises.

The significance for bankers of trust accounts is that the banker must not knowingly be a party to a breach of trust.[81] If a customer places money the banker knows to be trust money in his charge, the banker must not allow the customer to draw out the money for a purpose obviously inconsistent with the customer's duties as a trustee.

Whether or not the banker has notice of the trust will be a question of fact, depending on the circumstances of each case.

A trust can be created over a bank account without the use of any such words as "trust",[82] and sometimes the heading of the account on its own is ambiguous. For instance, the expression "Re" in an account headed "John Smith *re* James Jones" does not necessarily indicate a trust, nor would an account headed "John Smith A/c James Jones", but in both cases regard must be paid to the surrounding circumstances, particularly if the banker wishes to rely on any set-off. Thus where a county treasurer had an account headed "Police Account" this was held to constitute notice of the trust.[83]

The mere fact that a customer has more than one account does not necessarily affect the banker with notice that one of them may be a trust account. Many customers for convenience have various accounts distinguished as Account No. 1, Account No. 2; or House A/c and Farm A/c, etc. In none of such cases of separation is there *per se* any indication of a trust account, and in the absence of any

80. For a general introduction to the law of trusts, *see* Snell's *Principles of Equity* (28th Edn.).
81. *Re Gross, ex parte Kingston* (1871) 6 Ch. App. 632.
82. *Re Kayford* [1975] 1 All E.R. 604.
83. *Re Gross, ex parte Kingston* (1871) 6 Ch. App. 632.

such indication, or of any agreement to the contrary, the banker is entitled to regard the accounts as one account and to set off one against the other.

Notice of the existence of a trust may come from some fact other than the heading of the account, but there is no presumption of a trust merely on account of the profession of the customer.[84] Nor is the fact that the person opening the account occupies a position which renders it probable that he has moneys of other persons in his hands sufficient to put the banker on inquiry.[85]

Where the banker does not have notice of a trust, the fact that, unknown to him, the customer holds moneys in a fiduciary capacity does not in any way affect the banker's right to treat them as the absolute property of the customer.

Where the banker does have notice of a trust, he may be faced with two conflicting duties, namely the duty to his customer to honour cheques etc., and his duty not to permit a breach of trust. His main difficulty is to decide between those conflicting duties, and the decided cases do not give very exact guidance as to what his decision should be.

The high point in decisions against bankers is the case of *Foxton* v. *Manchester & Liverpool District Banking Co.*,[86] where two executors, who had opened an executorship account with the bank, also had private accounts which were overdrawn, and after pressure from the bank to reduce the overdraft, substantial sums were transferred from the executors' account to their private accounts.

Fry J. held:

It appears to be plain that the bank could not derive the benefit which they did from that payment, knowing it to be drawn from a trust fund, unless they were prepared to show that the payment was a legitimate and proper one, having reference to the terms of the trust. It is said that they did not know what the trust was at that time. That appears to me, I confess, to be immaterial, because those who know that a fund is a trust fund cannot take possession of that fund for their private benefit, except at the risk of being liable to refund it in the event of the trust being broken by the payment of the money.

This strict line was also followed in *Rowlandson* v. *National Westminster Bank*,[87] where money intended for four minors was paid into an account opened in the name of their two uncles "Re AB and others" and marked "Trust Account". Although the bank was

84. *Thomson* v. *Clydesdale Bank* [1893] A.C. 282.
85. *Thomson* v. *Clydesdale Bank, supra.*
86. (1881) 44 L.T. 406.
87. [1978] 1 W.L.R. 798.

not a constructive trustee[88] for the children before the money was paid in, it did become under a fiduciary duty to the children once the money was paid in. Consequently, when one of the uncles drew the money out for his own purposes the bank was liable to refund the money to the children, since the circumstances regarding the withdrawals established a dishonest design which the bank should have questioned or prevented.

In *Selangor United Rubber Estates* v. *Cradock & Others (No. 3),*[89] where an elaborate scheme was devised which enabled a company's own money to be used for the purchase of its shares in contravention of s. 54 of the Companies Act 1948,[90] the bankers of the company were held liable as being constructive trustees,[90] and not mere debtors, of the company.

The courts, however, have not always followed the strict line. *Gray* v. *Johnson* [91] is the leading authority for the moderate view of the banker's liability.

In order to hold a banker justified in refusing to pay a demand of his customer, the customer being an executor and drawing a cheque as an executor, there must in the first place be some misapplication, some breach of trust, intended by the executor, and there must in the second place ... be proof that the bankers are privy to the intent to make this misapplication of the trust funds; ... and if it be shown that any personal benefit to the bankers themselves is designed or stipulated for, that circumstance above all others will most rapidly establish the fact that the bankers are in privity with the breach of trust which is about to be committed.

In *Coleman* v. *Bucks. and Oxon. Union Bank,*[92] Byrne J. attempted to reconcile these decisions. In that case a customer, who had in fact no trust account with the bank, received moneys which he knew, but the bank did not know, to be trust moneys. The moneys were credited to his overdrawn private account and it was held that the mere fact that a trustee has transferred money from the trust account to his own private account in reduction of an overdraft, so that the banker has derived some "personal benefit", does not itself make the banker a party to the fraud, on the ground that the personal benefit was not "designed or stipulated for" by him. The banker is put on inquiry only if there are sufficient circumstances or the bank intend and design a benefit for themselves.

It may be as well to emphasise the fact here that the banker's primary duty is to honour his customer's cheques. The banker must

---

88. On constructive trusts, *see* Snell's *Principles of Equity* (28th Edn.).
89. [1968] 2 All E.R. 1073.
90. *See* "Companies" in Chapter Six. The section has been repealed and replaced.
91. (1868) L.R. 3 H.L. I.
92. [1897] 2 Ch. 243.

not act on mere suspicion. Before refusing to honour his customer's cheques, he must have substantial grounds for believing that a breach of trust is intended. The relationship between banker and customer would unquestionably be an impossible one if the banker was put upon inquiry every time his customer drew a cheque, even a cheque on a trust fund.

If, however, the banker makes a pressing demand on the trustee to reduce his overdraft, and in response the trustee transfers money from what the banker knows to be a trust fund to his private account, then probably it would be held that the "personal benefit" to the banker was "designed or stipulated for", and the banker would have to refund the money to the beneficiaries if it turned out that they had been defrauded.

Cheques drawn in favour of a trust, whether crossed or uncrossed, must not be credited to the trustee's (or executor's) private account, or the banker will make himself liable for any misappropriation on the ground of negligence.

The banker cannot exercise his right of set-off between the trust account and the trustee's private account, unless he is not aware that one of the accounts is a trust account. So far as subsequent transactions are concerned, he may no longer exercise it after receipt of notice that one of them is a trust account. As the customer is personally liable for any overdraft on the trust account, the banker can, however, subject to reasonable notice, exercise his right of set-off against the private account to cover advances on the trust account.

The banker is generally thought to be quite safe in opening an account for persons professing to be trustees, subject to obtaining satisfactory references, and is under no obligation to see the trust deed or other evidence of their appointment, but the Gilbart Lecturer, 1931, recommended that in all cases where the banker knows that an account is a trust account he should ascertain the terms of the trust and file a copy of the instrument creating it for reference as to the appointment of new trustees, borrowing powers, etc. It is certainly better to open the account as a trust account and treat it as such, than to open it as an ordinary joint account with an intention to avoid notice of trust, for once the banker has notice that the account is a trust account, he cannot avoid it by suppressing all reference to the trust in the heading. Accordingly, on opening the account full inquiries should be made and sufficient details, or a copy of the trust deed, will or other governing document, filed for reference.

The mandate should provide for the signature of cheques. Trustees of a charity usually have power to delegate the power of signing cheques drawn on their account to any of their number, not being less than two,[93] and generally do so. Trustees of a private trust, however, are personally responsible for the exercise of their own judgment and the performance of their duties, and are generally unable to escape responsibility by delegating performance to some other person, even one of their co-trustees.

Unlike executors, trustees have no individual powers. They must all act together, and they cannot delegate their authority to any other person, even to one of themselves, unless the trust instrument contains a power of delegation. Consequently all must join in the signing of cheques, save where it is expressly provided for in the trust deed that one may sign on behalf of the others. Beneficiaries are entitled to the safeguard of control by all the trustees,[94] and permitting one trustee to sign cheques on his own is equivalent to giving him sole control of the funds. The mandate ought, therefore, to provide for cheques to be signed by all the trustees.

If, however, the trustees are insistent on their wish to delegate the power of signing cheques, and the bank wishes to accommodate them, it has been suggested that there are certain safeguards which should be observed.

(a) At least two of the trustees should sign cheques together.

(b) The trustees should open both a capital and an income account, and delegation should be permitted only in relation to the latter account.

(c) An indemnity protecting the bank from possible loss should always be executed by the trustees themselves, and, ideally, by those beneficiaries who are of full age.

(d) All the trustees should be asked to verify the balances of the bank accounts at least every six months.

(e) This exceptional procedure should be permitted only in those cases where the trustees are of undoubted integrity.[95]

The mandate ought to provide for all the trustees to be jointly and severally liable and for articles delivered for safe custody to be delivered on the instructions of all the trustees.

When a trustee mixes trust money with his own money, he is taken

---

93. Charities Act 1960, s. 34.
94. *Clough* v. *Bond* (1838) 3 Myl. & Cr. 490; *Trutch* v. *Lamprell* (1855) 20 Beav. 116.
95. J. Milnes Holden, *The Law and Practice of Banking* (2nd Edn.), Vol. 1, p. 407.

to have drawn out his own money in preference to the money he holds as trustee, and therefore the rule in *Clayton*'s case[96] does not apply, but it does apply as between the several beneficiaries (where more than one), and the first trust money paid in is, therefore, taken to be the first trust money paid out.[97]

Countermand of payment of a cheque may be effectively made by any one of the trustees, and the banker is bound to take notice of such countermand.

There are some circumstances in which trustees are permitted to delegate. Trustees and personal representatives may employ an agent, whether a solicitor, banker, stockbroker or other person, to transact any necessary business incidental to the execution of the trust or administration of the estate; if so they will not be responsible for such agent's default.[98] This power does not authorise them to delegate to one or more of their number the power to draw cheques on the trust account;[99] they may only employ paid agents to do specific work. A trustee may also delegate by power of attorney his powers and discretions to any person or trust corporation for a period not exceeding twelve months.[100] He cannot, however, appoint as his attorney his only other co-trustee, unless the latter be a trust corporation.[101] The donor-trustee is responsible for his attorney's acts and defaults.

Somewhat wider powers to delegate functions such as the execution of deeds or instruments are given to trustees of public or charitable trusts, but care must be taken to see that the statutory requirements are observed.[102]

Trustees have generally no implied power to borrow for the purposes of the trust, and unless the trust deed gives them express powers to borrow and to pledge the trust property, they cannot as a rule give security. Moreover, trustees are personally jointly liable for all advances made to them. Trustees have no power to deposit trust property as security for their private accounts.

There is, however, some limited statutory power to borrow, and some protection is to be found for persons lending to trustees. Where

96. (1816) 1 Mer. 529.
97. *See* Chapter Four.
98. Trustee Act 1925, s. 23.
99. *See* above in this section.
100. Trustee Act 1925, s. 35, as amended by Powers of Attorney Act 1971, s. 9.
101. Ibid., s. 68(1) and (18) for definition of a trust corporation: the Public Trustee or a corporation either appointed by the court in any particular case to be a trustee or entitled by rules made under the Public Trustee Act 1906, s. 4(3), to act as a custodian trustee.
102. Charities Act 1960, s. 34.

trustees are authorised to pay or apply capital money for any purpose or in any manner, they have power to raise the money required by sale or mortgage of all or any part of the trust property[103] and no purchaser or mortgagee, paying or advancing money on a sale or mortgage purporting to be made under any trust or power vested in trustees, need be concerned to see that such money is wanted, or that no more than is wanted is raised, or otherwise as to the application of the money.[104]

A trustee may, if not prohibited by the trust, invest in authorised securities payable to bearer, provided, unless the trustee is a trust corporation,[101] the bonds and the collection of the income are entrusted to the bank.[105] The latter must not part with the bonds, except on the written authority of all the trustees. (A joint authority for withdrawal is always necessary for all valuables deposited in joint names.) Trustees have statutory protection against loss due to such a deposit.[106] They are also authorised to deposit trust moneys with a bank.[107] No trustee, unless expressly authorised by the trust deed, may carry on the testator's trade or business for a longer time (except in special circumstances) than is reasonably necessary in order to sell it as a going concern.

On the bankruptcy of a trustee, any property held on trust by him for the benefit of any other person is not divisible among his creditors.[108] This does not apply where the trustee has any beneficial interest in the property. Unless the trustee is a trustee in bankruptcy, the fact that a receiving order has been made against him does not necessarily involve the resignation of his office, but where a trustee becomes bankrupt a new trustee *may* be appointed in his stead.[109]

On the death of a trustee, the surviving trustee or trustees have power to act, but only if there is nothing to the contrary in the trust deed.[110] As in many cases the deed provides for the appointment of a new trustee, the banker would not be safe in allowing the remaining trustees to operate on the account, until he had satisfied himself by a perusal of the deed that they were empowered to continue without the co-operation of a new trustee.

Where a trustee dies, or desires to be released, or refuses to act,

103. Trustee Act 1925, s. 16.
104. Ibid., s. 17.
105. Ibid., s. 7.
106. Ibid., s. 7(2).
107. Ibid., s. 11.
108. Bankruptcy Act 1914, s. 38(1).
109. Trustee Act 1925, s. 41.
110. Ibid., s. 18.

or is unfit to act, the person or persons nominated in the deed, or, if there is none, then the remaining trustee or trustees or the personal representative of the last trustee, may in writing appoint a new trustee or trustees.[111] The High Court has power to appoint new trustees when they are not appointed as above.[112]

The public trustee has power to act as custodian trustee, ordinary trustee, administrator or executor, and in that capacity he may employ any banker etc., that he may consider necessary,[113] but in selecting the banker etc., to be employed, he may, subject to what he considers the interests of the trust, take into consideration the wishes of the creator of the trust and of the other trustees (if any) and of the beneficiaries.

ACCOUNTS OF PERSONAL REPRESENTATIVES

Notice of a customer's death determines the duty and authority of a banker to pay his customer's cheques,[114] and brings to an end the banker-customer relationship. Therefore, upon receipt of notice of a customer's death, all operations on the account should be suspended until production of probate if the deceased left a will, or of letters of administration if the deceased died intestate.

Cheques paid before receipt of notice can be debited to the account, and so also can any amount due to a stockbroker for purchases made by the banker on the customer's behalf, and similar liabilities incurred by the banker on the customer's instructions. Cheques presented on or after the day on which the banker receives notice of the death should be returned; bills accepted by the customer before his death should not be paid.

Any receipts after notice of death and before probate or letters of administration should be credited to a new account to be available to the personal representatives of the deceased in due course.

The term personal representatives (often known as PRs) is the generic term for executors and administrators. Executors are appointed by the will of the deceased to administer that person's estate though they cannot administer the estate until they have obtained a grant of probate from the Family Division or the Chancery Division of the High Court. Administrators are appointed

---

111. Ibid., s. 36.
112. Ibid., s. 41.
113. Public Trustee Act 1906, ss. 1, 6, 11(1).
114. Bills of Exchange Act 1882, s. 75(2).

by the High Court to administer any part of an estate of which the deceased died intestate (i.e. any part which was not left by the deceased's will) or for which there is no "proving executor" (i.e. an executor willing and able to obtain probate of the deceased's will).

The duties of executors and administrators are substantially the same; they differ mainly in their appointment. An executor derives his authority from the will, and although a grant of probate is essential if the estate comprises land, since only the PRs can convey a good title, and production of a grant may be necessary to establish the right to recover or receive any part of the personal estate and effects of the deceased,[115] there may be some cases where a grant is not necessary, such as if the whole of the estate is in the name of joint tenants. Administrators, however, derive their title solely from the grant of letters of administration, and are unable to exercise any powers until such a grant.

After exhibition of probate or letters of administration to the banker, the PRs should be allowed to close the account and deal with the deceased's securities.

Executors may open a bank account soon after the deceased's death, and should pay into that account any money found in the house. Administrators cannot, however, open an account until they have received a grant. In either case, unless they are personally known to the bank, the bank should make the same inquiries from them in order to establish their identity and integrity as it would with any other customer.

When the account is opened, the PRs should sign a mandate dealing with the signature and countermanding of cheques. Although PRs, like any other trustees, have the power to delegate certain functions, they may not delegate the signing of cheques to third parties. The signing of cheques may be delegated to one or more of their number, but it is preferable for them all to be required to sign in the early stages. It is also usual to provide for the PRs to be jointly and severally liable for any borrowing on the account.

If there is more than one PR, they are regarded as one person, having a joint interest in all the estate of the deceased, and an interest not capable of division. That is to say, the acts of one when administering the estate are, generally speaking, deemed to be the acts of all. For example, any PR, where there is more than one, can give a valid discharge for a debt due to the estate, or for a credit balance handed over to him by the banker, but one of several PRs cannot sell or transfer real property without the authority of the

115. Revenue Act 1884, s. 11.

court.[116] Generally, all the PRs must concur in any transfer of stocks and shares, but in certain cases one of several may validly effect a transfer. Where any probate or administration is revoked, any payment made bona fide to any executor or administrator prior to revocation is a legal discharge for all persons making such payments.[117]

Before delivering up any securities deposited by the testator, the banker should obtain the authority of all the executors. He must not deliver up any securities before a grant has been obtained, except, of course, for the deceased's will, which should be delivered to the executors named in it against their receipt. He can, and should, however, allow persons proposing to apply for a grant, or their solicitors, an opportunity of examining, under supervision, securities and articles in the bank's custody.

The banker cannot set off a debt due to him by the PRs against a debt due from him to the estate, and vice versa.[118] Set-off cannot be pleaded unless the debts are between the same parties and in the same right.

The PRs should in general pay off any debit balance on the deceased's account as soon as they are able to realise sufficient of the deceased's assets, but it is a question of arrangement between the banker and the PRs. If the deceased left a credit balance on his account, the banker should not release it until he has been shown the PRs' grant of probate or letters of administration, copies of which should generally be kept by the banker. It should then be drawn out by the PRs and transferred to the PRs' account either by cheque or by a form of instruction signed by all the PRs. This account would be opened either in the personal names of the personal representatives (without reference to executorship), or in the following form: "The Executors of John Smith, deceased, H. Brown and W. Robinson, Executors".

Once they have obtained probate or letters of administration, the duty of PRs is to pay off any debts owed by the deceased, including any funeral expenses and capital transfer tax, and then to distribute the remainder of the estate to the beneficiaries, according to the legacies laid down in the will, if there is one, or otherwise according to the rules of intestacy.[119] Bankers are frequently asked to lend money to persons who are applying for probate or administration so that they can pay the capital transfer tax due on the estate. Grants

116. Administration of Estates Act 1925, s. 2.
117. Ibid., s. 27.
118. *Rees* v. *Watts* (1885) 11 Exch. 410.
119. On administration of an estate, *see* generally Parry & Clark, *The Law of Succession* (7th Edn.).

of probate or letters of administration are not generally issued until the capital transfer tax has been paid. A banker who lends money for this purpose should check that the persons requesting the loan are entitled to apply for probate or administration. He should also require them to sign an undertaking, stating that they will pay the Inland Revenue the sum advanced and that they will be jointly and severally liable to repay the loan.

Since only those who have authorised the loan are responsible for it, the banker must get the written sanction of all the PRs before making the advance, and as an unsecured loan is the personal debt of the PRs, the banker cannot levy execution against the general assets of the estate. If security is required a specific charge is necessary. All the PRs must join in any charge over land of the deceased, and in any mortgage of shares registered in their joint names. It is advisable, even when not legally necessary, to get the signature of all the PRs to all mortgages and charges.

When a PR borrows money from a banker, he is personally liable to repay the loan, but he has a right to indemnify himself out of the assets of the estate if the loan was properly incurred for the purposes of administering the estate. Although the PR is personally liable on the loan, he can give security for the loan either out of estate assets or out of his personal assets. Where there are joint PRs, the normal rules for liability on a joint account will apply: i.e. the banker should obtain an undertaking from the PRs to be jointly and severally liable; otherwise, they will only be jointly liable.[120]

Executors have power to pledge specific assets before probate and the act will be valid if probate is granted to them, but if probate is declined difficulty may arise. Administrators cannot give such a charge before obtaining grant of administration. A banker cannot hold, against such advances, securities deposited by the deceased.[121] Nor can he retain such securities if the overdraft on the deceased's account is taken over by the PRs (which they are not bound to agree to), since in this case the liability will be theirs personally, and unless they re-charge securities deposited by the deceased or pledge other assets the banker will be unsecured.

As with trust accounts, a banker should take care when dealing with the accounts of PRs. If he makes possible a breach of duty by PRs, either by his acts or by his omissions, he may be liable to the beneficiaries of the estate. It is therefore important for the banker to know what duties were laid down by the deceased in his will. Except where the will specifies otherwise, the following rules will apply by law to every estate.

120. *See* above under "Joint Accounts".
121. *Farhall* v. *Farhall* (1871) 7 Ch. App. 123.

(*a*) Any person of full age may be a PR.[122] A trust corporation or a corporation sole may obtain a grant of probate but any other corporation can only obtain letters of administration.[123] The practice with respect to corporations aggregate which are not trust corporations is to grant administration to a nominee.[124] In issuing a grant of probate, the court will normally give effect to the wishes of the deceased. In issuing letters of administration, where there is no will, the order of preference is first the spouse of the deceased, then parents, then brothers and sisters, then more distant relatives.[125] Where there is a will, but no proving executor, the order of priority for administrators is different and rather more complicated.[126] Where no relatives or friends of the deceased obtain probate or administration, a creditor of the deceased may be appointed as an administrator.[127]

(*b*) Before he begins to act, a PR can decide to renounce his office.[128] An executor can retract his renunciation, but an administrator cannot.[128] After a PR has begun to act, he cannot renounce his office, but in certain circumstances probate or administration may be revoked by the court.[129] The doctrine of survivorship applies to PRs so that when one PR dies, the remaining PRs continue in office. When a last surviving executor dies, his office passes to his own executor, but would not pass to his own administrator.[130] When a last surviving administrator dies, his office will not pass to anyone and, if administration has not yet been completed, a new administrator will be appointed by the court.[131]

(*c*) Before obtaining probate or administration, a putative PR should not in theory do any act by way of administering the estate. In practice, however, a putative PR can safely take steps for the protection of the estate, though he cannot enter into transactions such as dispositions of land which require proof of his authority. Once he has obtained probate or administration, a PR must "get in" the estate, pay the deceased's debts "with all due diligence" and distribute the remainder of the estate to the beneficiaries. For the purpose of administering the estate, PRs may carry on the business

122. Parry & Clark, *The Law of Succession* (7th Edn.), p. 130.
123. 39; *Re Haynes* (1842) 3 Curt. 75; Parry & Clark, *The Law of Succession* (7th Edn.), p. 131; for trust corporations *see* footnote 101 above.
124. Non-Contentious Probate Rules 1954, R. 34(3).
125. Ibid., R. 21; Administration of Estates Act 1925, s. 46.
126. Non-Contentious Probate Rules 1954, R. 19.
127. Ibid., R. 21.
128. Ibid., R. 35.
129. Parry & Clark, *The Law of Succession* (7th Edn.), pp. 195–200.
130. Administration of Estates Act 1925, s. 7.
131. Parry & Clark, *The Law of Succession* (7th Edn.), pp. 171–2.

of the deceased; if they do so, they will be personally liable for any debts contracted in the course of the business with a right to indemnify themselves out of estate assets if they have acted properly. The rules relating to remuneration of PRs and delegation of PRs' office are the same as for trustees.[132]

(d) Where an estate is insolvent, the bankruptcy laws apply[133] and the assets available for payment of debts include certain assets disposed by the deceased before his death. Where an estate is solvent, certain classes of assets must be used before certain other classes of assets in the payment of debts.[134] After all the deceased's debts have been paid the PRs should distribute the remainder of the estate to the beneficiaries. Where there is enough money left to satisfy all the legacies left by the deceased the PRs may distribute the estate in any order. Where there is insufficient money remaining, however, the PRs must distribute it in the order laid down by statute. Where the deceased died wholly or partially intestate, the rules of intestacy will apply.[135] These rules lay down the order in which the surviving relatives of the deceased are entitled to benefit from his estate.

(e) A single PR has authority to deal with any trust assets on his own. Where there are two or more PRs, they must act jointly when dealing with land or company shares, but may deal jointly or severally with other assets of the deceased. After PRs have paid all the debts of the deceased, they hold the remainder of the deceased's estate as trustees and their account should then be treated by the banker as a trust account.

ASSOCIATIONS, COMMITTEES, SOCIETIES, ETC.

Accounts are often opened by persons in control of the funds of clubs, agricultural and other shows, subscription societies formed to promote some national object, and the like. The committee of management of such societies usually depute certain of their number to operate the account.

If the account is always in credit, the banker has no need to trouble himself about locating responsibility for debts incurred on behalf of the society, but if an overdraft is required, it is essential that he should be able to fix the liability for repayment of the loan upon some definite person or persons. These voluntary associations, being unincorporated, cannot be sued, and it is probable that the individual members who administer the funds could not be personally liable

132. *See* above, under "Trust Accounts".
133. Administration of Estates Act 1925, s. 34(1) and Sched. 1, Pt. I, para. 2.
134. Ibid., s. 34(3) and Sched. 1, Pt. II.
135. Ibid., s. 46, as amended by the Intestate Estates Act 1952, s. 1 and Sched. 1, and by the Family Provision Act 1966, s. 1.

for any overdraft, so long as the members of the committee or council deputed to operate the account clearly sign cheques in their representative capacity, and do not hold themselves out as having authority to overdraw. In other words, if an account of this nature was opened under the style of "The Excel Cricket Club, John Jones, Treasurer", and cheques were signed in that manner, in the general way neither John Jones nor the committee of the club would be personally responsible for any overdraft.

This view is, perhaps, now open to some doubt as a result of the case of *Bradley Egg Farm* v. *Clifford.*[136] It was held there that although persons dealing with a society and making a contract probably never thought about the question of who precisely the contract was with, the function of the law was to imply an intention to make a contract with the persons whom the law regards as responsible in the circumstances. In the case of a society with an executive committee, the law holds the members of the executive committee liable, since they are the persons entrusted with the function of directing the activities of the society and putting them into execution.

Where there is no such committee, it may well be that those members who have authorised the borrowing in question would be liable. In any event, if an advance is required, the banker should obtain security, bearing in mind, however, that the guarantee or document of charge must cover the incapacity of the borrowers.[137]

When an account of this nature is opened in the name of the society, which is the usual and correct method,[138] the banker should be given an authenticated copy of the resolution appointing the treasurer and appointing the bank as bankers of the society, with specimen signatures and detailed instructions as to how cheques are to be signed. This should all be embodied in a mandate, signed by the chairman of the meeting and countersigned by the secretary.[139]

Any change in the officials should be immediately notified to the banker. If the treasurer dies or vacates his office, the banker should immediately on receipt of notice stop the account, but should honour all cheques drawn before receipt of the notice of death or resignation but presented afterwards, unless such cheques are countermanded before payment by a duly authenticated resolution of the controlling committee. The executors of a deceased treasurer do not take over an account of this nature, and the account therefore must remain

---

136. [1943] 2 All E.R. 378.
137. *See* Clause 6 in the specimen form in Appendix 1.
138. *See Q.B.P.*, No. 99.
139. *See* Appendix I for specimen form.

dormant until the banker receives a duly authenticated copy of the resolution appointing a new treasurer.

If the account on behalf of such an association is opened in the following form "John Jones, A/c The Excel Cricket Club", then John Jones is personally liable for any overdraft created by the drawing of cheques on this account. When an account is opened in this form, the banker is entitled to consider it as a personal account of John Jones, and therefore does not need to see a copy of any resolution respecting the account. When an association's funds are vested in and banked in the names of trustees, it is necessary that the banker should see the trust deed and the rules of the association defining the powers of the trustees and stating how withdrawals from the fund are to be made. The banker should get a mandate signed, and provided that this conforms to the rules and provisions in the trust deed and is strictly adhered to, the banker will not incur any liability.

BUILDING SOCIETIES

Building societies are of two kinds, (a) incorporated, and (b) unincorporated. The incorporated societies are controlled by the Buildings Societies Act 1962 which basically consolidated the Acts of 1874 to 1960. No building society established under these Acts can lawfully begin operations without first obtaining a certificate of incorporation from the Chief Registrar of Friendly Societies. The few unincorporated building societies still in existence are regulated by the earlier Benefit Building Societies Act 1836 and by the Friendly Societies Act 1974. Incorporated building societies are sub-divided into (a) terminating, and (b) permanent building societies. A terminating building society is one that terminates at a fixed date or on the happening of an event specified in its rules. A permanent building society is one that has no fixed time of determination.

Since every building society is governed by its rules (registered with the Chief Registrar of Friendly Societies), the banker must obtain a copy of the rules in order to ascertain the regulations controlling the actions of the persons entitled to operate the account. The rules declare how cheques are to be signed, and the banker must see that these rules are strictly adhered to. A copy of the resolution appointing the bank as bankers to the society should be included in a mandate, together with specimen signatures and full instructions as to the signing of cheques. This mandate must be duly authenticated.[140]

Formerly, building societies had no power to borrow money unless the rules expressly authorised them to do so, but a power of

140. *See* Appendix 1 for specimen form.

borrowing, within statutory limitations, has been conferred upon all incorporated societies[141] and the rules must set forth whether the society intends to borrow money, and if so within what limits, not exceeding the statutory limits.[142] In a permanent building society the total amount to be received on loan or deposit must not at any time exceed two-thirds of the amount for the time being secured by mortgages from its members.[143] In a terminating building society the amount so received may be either two-thirds of the amount lent on mortgage, or a sum not exceeding twelve months' subscriptions on the members' shares for the time being in force.[144] In ascertaining the amount secured on mortgages, mortgages twelve months or more in arrears, or where the society has been in possession for twelve months, must not be included.[145]

From what has been said, it can be seen how necessary it is that a banker making an advance to a building society should be thoroughly conversant with the rules and the Acts governing the society's method of procedure. This is necessary since as Brett L. J. said in *Chapleo* v. *Brunswick Permanent Benefit Building Society*,[146] "Where a society or a company has upon the face of its constitution, that is, either by the statute or statutory rules under which it is constituted, only a limited authority to borrow, then it seems to me that a person dealing with such a society or company must either inquire or run the risk"—the risk, that is, of being debarred from recovering from the society money borrowed in excess of the limits imposed either by statute or by the rules of the society.

Accordingly, the banker before making an advance must know whether the society has power by its rules to borrow and to pledge or mortgage its assets as security, for power to borrow does not necessarily imply power to give mortgages. An advance made to a building society should be on a loan account, so as to keep it distinct from the current account; this enables a check to be more easily kept on the total advance, and if the borrowing was within the limit when made, other later borrowings will not prejudice the bank.

Since the total amount that the society is permitted to borrow must always be *less* than the amount out on mortgage to its members, it follows that, although at the time of the banker's advance to the society, the total amount borrowed may be within the statutory limit, at some other time during the continuance of the loan, the statutory amount may be exceeded owing to the falling in of mortgages.

141. Building Societies Act 1962, s. 39.
142. Ibid., s. 4(1).
143. Ibid., s. 39(2).
144. Ibid., s. 39(3).
145. Ibid., s. 39(4).
146. (1881) 6 Q.B.D. 696.

If a building society receives loans or deposits in excess of the limits prescribed by the Act, the directors of the society are personally liable for the amount of the excess.[147] Apart from the personal liability of the directors, the banker has another remedy by virtue of the doctrine of subrogation, i.e. when a person borrows without authority or in excess of his authority and applies the borrowed money in payment of legal debts and liabilities, the lender's claim becomes valid to the extent such legal debts and liabilities are so reduced.

Before making an advance to a building society, it is desirable to take a declaration setting out all the facts necessary to ascertain the present borrowing and the unexhausted powers. The most usual form of security for a loan to a building society is a sub-mortgage on properties mortgaged to the building society.

The few unincorporated societies not yet registered under the 1962 Act or its predecessors have no power to borrow, except in so far as they are expressly authorised by their rules.

If a banker is offered building society shares or deposits as security, he should consult the rules and give notice of lien to the society. Some societies, however, refuse to accept any notice of charge. A form of charge should be taken and the certificate or deposit book retained.

The surplus funds of a building society which are not invested or kept in cash are required to be kept on current account with, or otherwise on loan to, a bank which is for the time being authorised to hold funds of building societies.[148] The Chief Registrar of Friendly Societies designates the banks which are so authorised by order made with the consent of the Treasury.

FRIENDLY SOCIETIES

Friendly societies are societies formed for mutual benefit, assistance, thrift and so on. They may be registered or unregistered. Various purposes for which such societies may be registered are listed in s. 7 of the Friendly Societies Act 1974, a consolidating Act. There is a Chief Registrar of Friendly Societies and a Central Office.[149] A society may not be registered unless it consists of seven persons at least, and in order to register an application form signed by seven members of the society and the secretary, copies of the rules, and the names of the secretary and of every trustee or other officer must

---

147. Building Societies Act 1962, s. 40.
148. Ibid., s. 59.
149. Friendly Societies Act 1974, s. 1.

be filed with the registrar.[150] The rules of a registered society must provide *inter alia* for the investment of its funds.[151] The trustees of a registered society may with the consent of the committee or a majority of the members present invest the funds of the society in *inter alia* the National Savings Bank, in any certified trustee savings banks, in public funds or in authorised trustee investments.[152] It appears that payment into an account at any other bank of money required for current business would not be deemed an investment and would therefore be permissible.[153]

The only statutory power of a registered society to borrow is to borrow on mortgage if its rules give it power to hold land. "It would seem however that a registered society or branch can take power by its rules to borrow for the purpose of the conduct of its business to the extent to which it is necessary for the purpose of carrying out its objects."[154] Certain specially authorised societies have power to receive deposits and borrow money, if their rules so provide.[155]

Unregistered friendly societies are unincorporated associations or clubs and should be treated as such. The Friendly Societies Act does not apply to them.

INDUSTRIAL AND PROVIDENT SOCIETIES (CO-OPERATIVE SOCIETIES)

Industrial and Provident Societies are societies incorporated by registration under the Industrial and Provident Societies Acts 1965 to 1968. The earlier Acts were all repealed by the Act of 1965 which is now the principal Act.

There is no statutory definition of a co-operative society except that s. 1(3) provides that a co-operative society does not include a society which carries on, or intends to carry on, business with the object of making profits mainly for the payment of interest, dividends or bonuses on money invested or deposited with or lent to the society or any other person. Halsbury suggests that "a society is co-operative if its main purpose is the mutual benefit of its members, and the benefit enjoyed by a member depends upon the use which he makes of the facilities provided by the society and not upon the amount which he invests in the society."[156] A society cannot be registered under these Acts unless (*a*) it is a bona fide

150. Ibid., s. 7(1) and Sched. 1.
151. Ibid., s. 7(2) and Sched. 2.
152. Ibid., s. 46.
153. *Halsbury's Laws of England* (4th Edn.), Vol. 19, para. 243.
154. Ibid., para. 248.
155. Friendly Societies Act 1974, s. 23.
156. *Halsbury's Laws of England* (3rd Edn.), Vol. 21, p. 9.

co-operative society; or (b) in view of the fact that the business of the society is conducted for the benefit of the community, there are special reasons why the society should be registered under these Acts instead of being incorporated under the Companies Acts.[157] The word "society" is used in this section to mean a registered society.

In order to effect registration an application signed by at least seven members and the secretary of the society must be sent with two printed copies of the society's rules to the appropriate registrar.[158] For societies whose registered office is in England, Wales or the Channel Islands the appropriate registrar is the Central Office of Friendly Societies. For Scotland the appropriate registrar is the assistant registrar for Scotland.[159]

A society is by virtue of its registration a body corporate known by its registered name, by which it may sue and be sued, with perpetual succession and a common seal and with limited liability.[160] The word "limited" must be the last word in the name of any society, but if the objects of a society are wholly charitable or benevolent, the appropriate registrar may authorise the word "limited" to be dispensed with.[161]

Schedule 1 to the 1965 Act contains the matters which must be included in a society's rules, and among these is the appointment and removal of a committee, by whatever name, and of managers or other officers with their respective powers and remuneration. The rules must provide whether the society may contract loans or receive moneys on deposit and, if so, under what conditions, under what security and to what limits of amount. The rules must further provide whether and, if so, by what authority and in what manner any part of the society's funds may be invested.

A promissory note or bill of exchange is deemed to have been made, accepted or indorsed on behalf of any society if made, accepted or indorsed in the name of the society, or by or on behalf or account of the society, by any person acting under the authority of the society.[162]

A society, unless its rules otherwise provide, may hold and mortgage land.[163]

Under the 1967 Act (which does not extend to Scotland or Northern Ireland) an instrument executed by a society which creates or is evidence of a fixed or floating charge over the society's assets

157. Industrial and Provident Societies Act 1965, s. 1(2).
158. Ibid., s. 2.
159. Ibid., s. 73(1)(c).
160. Ibid., s. 3.
161. Ibid., s. 5.
162. Ibid., s. 28.
163. Ibid., s. 30.

is not a bill of sale and registrable and such, but is registrable at the Central Office of Friendly Societies within fourteen days of the execution of the instrument. A copy of the instrument must be filed and available for inspection by the public.[164] A society may issue a debenture in favour of a bank creating a floating charge on agricultural stock. Such a charge is registrable at the Land Registry and notice must be sent to the Chief Registrar of Friendly Societies.[165]

A society may invest its funds in any security of a local authority, in the shares or on the security of any other registered society and in any security authorised by s. 1 to 6 of the Trustee Investments Act 1961.[166]

The winding-up provisions of the Companies Act 1948 apply to societies and a society may also be dissolved by an instrument of dissolution signed by not less than three-fourths of the society's members.[167]

The very large majority, if not all, of the societies with the word "Co-operative" in their names, including the Co-operative Wholesale Society Limited, are incorporated under the Acts. There are also numerous housing associations, societies engaged in providing and working allotments, agricultural, horticultural and forestry societies and so on. Indeed societies exist for a wide range of purposes.

If a bank is requested to open an account for a society it should require to see the society's "acknowledgment of registration" and the society's rules. It should also obtain a certified true copy of the resolution of the committee, directors or other governing body, signed by the chairman and secretary, and specimen signatures of the authorised signatories.

A society may borrow money for the purposes of its business as permitted by its rules and may charge as security any assets which may be charged by its rules.

TRUSTEES IN BANKRUPTCY, LIQUIDATORS OF COMPANIES, RECEIVERS, ETC.

Trustees in bankruptcy must pay all moneys received in their official capacity into the Insolvency Services Account at the Bank of England, but the Department of Trade, on application by the committee of inspection, may give permission for accounts to be opened with any other bank, if the committee of inspection considers

---

164. Industrial and Provident Societies Act 1967, s. 1.
165. Agricultural Credits Act 1928, ss. 9 and 14.
166. Industrial and Provident Societies Act 1965, s. 31.
167. Ibid., s. 55.

it of advantage to the creditors for the purpose of carrying on the debtor's business or because of the probable amount of the cash balance or for any other reason.[168]

Permission will not be given merely to enable interest to be earned with another bank since the interest earned on the account at the Bank of England is applicable to defray costs of the Department. To qualify, the "advantage" to the creditors must be administrative rather than financial.[169]

Under the Insolvency Act 1976 there is provision for funds in the Insolvency Services Account surplus to current requirements to be transferred to an Insolvency Services Investment Account.[170]

No trustee in a bankruptcy or under any composition or scheme of arrangement may pay any sums received by him as trustee into his private banking account.[171] Where the trustee is authorised to have an account at a local bank, the account must be kept in the name of the debtor's estate. All payments out must be made by cheque payable to order; every cheque must bear the name of the estate and must be signed by the trustee and countersigned, where there is a committee of inspection, by at least one member, and by such other person, if any, as the creditors or committee of inspection may appoint, and where there is no committee by such person if any as the Department of Trade may direct.[172] In practice, however, bankers do not usually require the cheques to be countersigned by one of the members of the committee of inspection unless special instructions to this effect are given at the time the account is opened. It has not been decided whether or not the banker incurs any liability by his omission to see that the rule is followed.

There are similar provisions regarding the use of the Insolvency Services Account in the winding-up of companies.[173] Where there is more than one liquidator, the court in the case of a compulsory liquidation or the appointment in a voluntary liquidation declares whether the signing of cheques, or any other act required to be done by the liquidator, shall be done by one or by more than one or by all. There is considerable doubt whether joint liquidators have any power to delegate their authority even to one of themselves.

Before opening an account with these official persons, the banker should see that the requisite authority, where applicable, has been given for the account to be opened with his bank. He should also

---

168. Bankruptcy Act 1914, s. 89, as amended by the Insolvency Act 1976, s. 3.
169. *Re Walker Decd. (in bankruptcy)* [1974] 1 All E.R. 551.
170. Insolvency Act 1976, s. 3(4) and (5).
171. Bankruptcy Act 1914, s. 88.
172. Ibid., s. 89(3), and Bankruptcy Rules 1952, Rule 346.
173. Companies Act 1948, s. 248, as amended by the Insolvency Act 1976, s. 3, and the Companies (Winding-up) Rules 1949, Rule 170.

inspect the order or appointment under which the parties derive their authority. In the case of a compulsory liquidation, this will be a court order. In a voluntary liquidation, the authority will generally be a resolution of the members; in a creditors' voluntary liquidation, a resolution passed by the creditors may in some circumstances overrule the appointment by the members.[174] The banker should always see a certified copy of the members' resolution, and in a creditors' voluntary liquidation he should at least seek confirmation from a responsible source that the appointment was not overruled by the creditors. The banker should see if there are any special directions to be observed by the parties.

In regard to borrowing, trustees in bankruptcy may, with the permission of the committee of inspection (or the Department of Trade), mortgage or pledge any part of the bankrupt's property to raise money for the payment of his debts.[175] Liquidators appointed under a winding up by the court have power to raise on the security of the assets of the company any money requisite without sanction of the court, the committee of inspection or Department of Trade.[176] The exercise of this power, however, is subject to the control of the court to which any creditor may apply with respect to the liquidator's exercise or proposed exercise thereof. A liquidator in a voluntary winding-up, whether members' or creditors', and in a winding-up under the supervision of the court, may exercise borrowing powers without sanction.[177] Normally a liquidator is merely an agent of the company, so that he does not incur any personal responsibility for advances made to the company.

A receiver may be appointed in a variety of cases, e.g. by the court to take charge of property in dispute, by a mortgagee or by debenture holders. If there is a business to be carried on, a receiver and manager is appointed provided that the debenture contains a power to appoint a receiver and manager, and not just a receiver.[178] All correspondence etc., on which the company's name appears, must contain a statement that a receiver or manager has been appointed. Power to borrow depends on the appointment and the debenture, and care must be taken as to the requisite authority and security. A receiver or manager is personally liable on any contract entered into by him, except in so far as the contract otherwise provides, and is entitled to be indemnified out of the assets.[179] Nevertheless, if it is desired to rely on his personal responsibility,

174. *See* Chapter Twenty-Nine.
175. Bankruptcy Act 1914, s. 56(5).
176. Companies Act 1948, s. 245(2)(*e*).
177. Ibid., ss. 303 and 315.
178. *See also* Chapter Seventeen.
179. Companies Act 1948, s. 369.

the fact should be made abundantly clear by his definite acceptance of the liability.

LOCAL AUTHORITIES

The whole of England, except Greater London, is split up into counties and in the counties are areas known as districts.[180] Some of the very large counties are known as metropolitan counties and the districts in them as metropolitan districts. Wales is also divided into counties and districts.[181]

In both England and Wales, each county and each district is a body corporate, administered by a council consisting of a chairman and councillors.[182] In England there are also parishes with parish councils and parish meetings.[183] Wales has instead communities, with community councils and community meetings.[184]

Greater London is covered by the London Government Act 1963. Greater London consists of the City of London, the Inner and Middle Temples, and thirty-two London Boroughs. The whole area is covered by the Greater London Council.

All local authorities are required to make arrangements for the proper administration of their financial affairs and to secure that one of their officers has responsibility for the administration of those affairs.[185] The person so chosen will supervise the local authority's banking accounts.

All bank accounts of a local authority should be opened in the name of the authority. If a subsidiary account is opened on the express instructions of the authority in the name of an officer it should be designated as an account of the officer of the council, and not as an account of the individual.[186]

The council should pass a resolution authorising the opening of the bank account, and containing precise instructions for its operation; the bank should obtain a copy of the resolution, certified by the chairman and countersigned by the clerk to the council. When a new treasurer or chief financial officer is appointed by the local authority, a copy of the resolution of the council appointing him should be sent to the bank, certified by the chairman and countersigned by the clerk as before. If changes are made in the other signing officers, written advice signed by the full-time treasurer or the chief

180. Local Government Act 1972, s. 1(1).
181. Ibid., s. 20(1).
182. Ibid., ss. 2 and 21.
183. Ibid., s. 9.
184. Ibid., s. 27.
185. Ibid., s. 151.
186. *Q.B.P.*, No. 88.

financial officer will suffice,[187] though this practice should be expressly authorised by the original council resolution.

The number and nature of separate banking accounts to be maintained by a local authority rests with the officer responsible, but it is usual for separate accounts to be kept for:

(a) any trading undertakings carried on under special local Acts or orders which restrict the application of surplus revenue to certain specified purposes; and

(b) the loan fund, if it exists.

Where separate banking accounts are kept for purposes other than those mentioned above, a local authority may consent by resolution to a set-off between credit and debit balances on such other accounts. It is usual to operate the accounts of a local authority (other than the exceptions stated above) on a group basis to show daily the net amount due to or from the bank.[188]

As a general rule, no authority has any legal power to borrow unless it can point to some statutory provision expressly or impliedly authorising it to do so. Again, generally speaking, a local authority, having statutory power to borrow, can only do so in the manner authorised by statute.[189]

It will be seen that before lending any money, the banker should ascertain:

(a) whether the local authority has statutory power to borrow;

(b) what are the limits of the power;

(c) what form of borrowing is authorised and what security must be offered;

(d) what government sanction is necessary before the power can be exercised.

The essential thing for the banker to keep in mind when dealing with local authorities is that they are statutory bodies controlled absolutely by statute. Whatever the statute creating the authority does not expressly or impliedly authorise it to do is "to be taken to be prohibited".[190] That is to say, any act done without or in excess of statutory authority, express or implied, is *ultra vires* and therefore null and void. Furthermore, all persons dealing with local authorities are presumed to know the authority's statutory powers and limitations.[191] A local authority has therefore, generally, no

187. *Q.B.P.*, No. 91.
188. *Q.B.P.*, No. 89.
189. *R.* v. *Reed* (1880) 5 Q.B.D. 483.
190. *Attorney-General* v. *Great Eastern Railway Co.* (1879) 11 Ch.D. 449.
191. *Chapleo* v. *Brunswick Permanent Benefit Building Society* (1881) 6 Q.B.D. 696.

implied powers, and the statutes and rules governing it must be followed precisely.

Instead of being compelled (in the absence of special Treasury sanction) to borrow direct from the Public Works Loans Commissioners, local authorities may now borrow from other sources. Local authorities' borrowing powers are now governed by the Local Government Act 1972. They may borrow for purposes authorised by Sched. 13 of the Act, or for any other purpose or class of purpose approved by the Secretary of State, and borrowing may be by mortgage, the issue of stock or debentures or bonds or in other manner set out in Sched. 13.

They may also borrow by way of temporary loan or overdraft from a bank or otherwise, without the approval of the Secretary of State, sums which they may temporarily require to defray expenses pending receipt of revenues or, pending the raising of an authorised loan, to defray expenses intended to be defrayed by means of the loan.[192]

All moneys borrowed by a local authority are charged indifferently on all revenues of the local authority, and all securities created by the authority rank equally without any priority.[193] The exceptions to this general provision are mortgages on sewage works and housing bonds.

If a local authority borrows *ultra vires*, then repayment of the loan is also *ultra vires*. In other words, no debts can be created by an illegal borrowing. The banker therefore who lends to an authority acting *ultra vires* when borrowing, may be forced to refund any moneys repaid to him by the authority and also any interest charged on the unauthorised loan.[194]

Some amelioration of the position may now be found in that

... a person lending money to a local authority shall not be bound to inquire whether the borrowing of the money is or was legal and regular, or whether the money raised was properly applied, and shall not be prejudiced by any illegality or irregularity in the matters aforesaid or by the misapplication or non-application of such money.[195]

This frees the lender from the necessity of inquiring into these matters, but it does not mean that he can ignore facts pointing to the contrary which may come to his knowledge without inquiry.

---

192. Local Government Act 1972, Sched. 13, para. 10.
193. Ibid., para. 11.
194. *Attorney-General* v. *Tottenham Urban District Council* (1909) 73 J.P. 437.
195. Local Government Act 1972, Sched. 13, para. 20.

PAROCHIAL CHURCH COUNCILS

By the Parochial Church Councils (Powers) Measure 1956 the council is made a body corporate by the name of the Parochial Church Council of the parish for which it was appointed, and with perpetual succession.[196] That is to say, the council has a corporate existence independent of the personnel comprised in it. The measure does not extend to Scotland or Northern Ireland or to such portions of Wales and Monmouthshire as are subject to the provisions of the Welsh Church Act 1914.

Any act of a parochial church council may be signified by an instrument executed pursuant to a resolution of the council and under the hands (or, if an instrument under seal is required, under the hands and seals) of the chairman presiding and two other members of the council present at the meeting at which such resolution is passed.[197] Among the powers and duties of a parochial church council are those relating to the financial affairs of the church, including the collection and administration of all money raised for church purposes and the keeping of accounts in relation to such affairs and money. The council may appoint one or more of its number to act as treasurer, solely or jointly, without remuneration.[198] Failing such appointment, the churchwardens, if members of the council, will act jointly as treasurers.

The banker should be furnished with a duly certified copy of the resolution of the council appointing the treasurer or treasurers and indicating how cheques are to be signed. The account should be opened in the name of "The Parochial Church Council of ... Parish".[199]

A parochial church council has power to borrow for such purposes as come within its province.[200] If security on church property, real or personal, is required, rather than the personal guarantees of parishioners, approval is required from the diocesan authorities. The 1956 measure provides that any interest in land (other than a short lease), or in personal property to be held on permanent trusts, acquired by a council must be vested in the diocesan authority, and where such property is so vested it cannot be charged without the consent of the diocesan authority.[201]

---

196. Parochial Church Councils (Powers) Measure 1956, s. 9.
197. Ibid., s. 3.
198. Ibid., s. 4.
199. Q.B.P., No. 96.
200. See Re St. Peter, Roydon [1969] 2 All E.R. 1233.
201. Parochial Church Councils (Powers) Measure 1956, s. 6.

NONCONFORMIST CHURCHES

These bodies make their own rules and in some senses are less restricted than the Church of England, but they have no such legislation as the Measure of 1956 which enables a parochial church council to be a legal entity in itself. Any dealings, therefore, must be supported by a resolution of a properly convened meeting of the trustees. If there is any question of borrowing, the church generally may be pledged as security subject to approval by the appropriate authorities. The Methodist Church, for example, is administered both locally and nationally. Hence an advance will require resolutions from the local trustees, supported by the recommendation of the Circuit and District Committees as well as the final authority on behalf of the whole Church. It is the usual position for the local trustees to give their joint and several guarantee. Bankers will occasionally encounter specialised legislation in the course of making proper inquiries (e.g. the United Reformed Church Act 1972 (c. xviii)).

The accounts of Roman Catholic churches are usually kept in the personal names of the priests or of the superiors of the various Orders concerned. If there is any question of borrowing, the Diocesan Bishop's sanction is required and his guarantee obtained.

ARMY (REGULAR OR TERRITORIAL) OR ROYAL AIR FORCE

The account of a regiment, battery, battalion or Royal Air Force squadron, should in the first instance be opened by the commanding officer, who should designate the officers having authority to sign cheques on the accounts and should supply specimens of their signatures. Subsequent changes should be notified by the commanding officer or by the adjutant acting on his behalf. Accounts may also be opened such as "Officers' Mess", "President of Regimental Institutes", "Bank Fund", and so on.[202]

202. *Q.B.P.*, No. 99.

CHAPTER SIX

Accounts of Companies and Partnerships

1. COMPANIES

THE COMPANIES ACTS

The word "company" means a company controlled and regulated by the Companies Acts 1948 to 1981. The 1948 Act, which is the principal Act, came into force on 1st July 1948, and applies to all companies registered in Great Britain under that Act, and, in the case of existing companies, to all those formed and registered under the various Joint Stock Companies Acts and Companies Acts prior to that date. It does not, however, include companies registered under those Acts in Northern Ireland or Eire. The latter, if they establish themselves within Great Britain, and any companies registered in the Channel Islands and the Isle of Man, have to comply with the regulations laid down for foreign companies which have established a place of business within Great Britain. These are dealt with later. Assurance companies are controlled by the Insurance Companies Act 1974.

Companies registered under the Companies Acts comprise a large and important section of a banker's customers, while the majority of the banks themselves (including overseas banks)[1] come within their scope. The Acts are long and comprehensive measures, with several lengthy schedules. It is hardly appropriate to deal with them in this book other than from the banker's point of view. Nevertheless, some discretion has been exercised in this regard and a somewhat wider view taken, with numerous references to the Acts, in the hope that they may serve to assist readers should they wish to refer direct to the Acts, copies of which should be on the banker's bookshelf.

TYPES OF COMPANIES

Unlike a partnership, a company is a legal person distinct from

1. *See* final section of this chapter.

its members. There are four main types of company: companies limited by shares, companies limited by guarantee, unlimited companies and chartered companies.

By far the commonest of these is the company limited by shares, of which the distinguishing feature is that the liability of the members to contribute to the assets of the company in the event of its being wound up is limited to any amount unpaid on the shares.[2] In the case of a company limited by guarantee the liability of the members is limited to the amount they have undertaken to contribute to the assets of the company in the event of its being wound up.[3] This is usually a small amount, £1 or £5 per member.

In the case of an unlimited company, the liability of the members for the debts and obligations of the company is unlimited. Such companies are rare; where they are found, the reason is usually either that they have been incorporated by professional men or by others who are not permitted to limit their liability, or alternatively, the desire to avoid the requirement to file annual accounts with the Registrar of Companies. One or two banking companies, such as Coutts and Co, are still unlimited companies.

Chartered companies are companies which have been granted a charter by the Crown. Royal charters were formerly given to some trading concerns, such as the Hudson's Bay Company; this is no longer done today, though there are some twenty chartered companies still trading, mostly banks and insurance companies. Charters are obtained today by petition to the Crown, through the office of the Lord President of the Council. If the petition is granted, the promoters and their successors become a body corporate with perpetual succession and a common seal.

As well as being limited or unlimited, a company may be a public company or a private company. In everyday parlance, a public company means a company whose shares are listed on the Stock Exchange but in the terminology of the Companies Acts, the term "public company" has a much broader meaning. Before the Companies Act 1980 came into force, a public company was any company which was not a private company. A private company was a company which satisfied the following conditions: it had fewer than fifty members; it restricted transfers of its shares; and it could not offer its shares to be subscribed for by the public.[4] The Companies Act 1980 reverses the technique, so that any company

---

2. Companies Act 1948, s. 1(2)(*a*).
3. Ibid., s. 1(2)(*b*).
4. Ibid., s. 28 (now repealed).

which is not a public company is a private company.[5] Under the 1980 Act a public company is defined as follows:

(a) it must have a minimum authorised and allotted share capital of £50,000 (the figure can be varied by statutory instrument);
(b) its memorandum must state that the company is a public company;
(c) the memorandum must include as the last part of its name, instead of "limited", the words "public limited company" or the abbreviation "plc" (or the Welsh equivalent for companies with a registered office in Wales);
(d) the minimum number of members is two, instead of seven as under the 1948 Act.

These provisions of the 1980 Act came into force in December 1980, with a transitional period of 15 months for companies which were public under the 1948 Act classification ("old public companies") to re-register as public companies under the 1980 Act.

The chief differences between a public company and a private company are as follows.

(a) A public company, registered after 31st October 1929, must have at least two directors, whereas a private company need only have one,[6] but a sole director cannot also be the secretary.[7]
(b) A public company may not, unless the articles expressly permit this, appoint directors over the age of 70.[8]
(c) The provisions regarding the Registrar's certificate before the company is entitled to commence business do not apply to private companies.[9]
(d) A proxy in a public company cannot speak at a meeting, or vote, except on a poll, unless the articles specifically permit this.[10]

CONSTITUTION OF THE COMPANY

The internal management of a company is governed by its articles of association, while its external activities are controlled by its memorandum of association. An up-to-date copy of each of these documents is therefore necessary to a banker who proposes to have dealings with the company.

"The Memorandum of Association is . . . a company's fundamental

5. Companies Act 1980, ss. 1–8.
6. Companies Act 1948, s. 176.
7. Ibid., s. 177(1).
8. Ibid., s. 185.
9. Companies Act 1980, s. 4.
10. Companies Act 1948, s. 136.

and, except in certain particulars, its unalterable law."[11] In the memorandum are set forth the objects for which the company was established, and the powers with which those in charge of its operation are invested. The objects may be altered by special resolution of the company for certain specified purposes.[12] No confirmation is required by the court unless an application is made to it for the cancellation of an alteration. This may be done by the required number of share or debenture holders within the time stipulated.[12]

Any act done or contract entered into by the company which is outside the scope of the memorandum is *ultra vires* (i.e. beyond the powers of the company), and not binding upon the company; this is so even if the directors acted in good faith and their action is indorsed by unanimous consent of all the shareholders, or the memorandum is subsequently altered in such a way that if the act had been done or the contract made after the alteration it would have been valid. The reason is that if an act is *ultra vires* it is void in its inception.[13] The doctrine ought, however, to be understood and applied reasonably and not unreasonably, and whatever may fairly be regarded as incidental to, or consequential upon, what is authorised by the memorandum ought not to be held to be *ultra vires*.[14]

The articles of association contain the regulations controlling the internal management of the company. The articles together with the memorandum must be registered with the Registrar of Companies. Subject to the provisions of the Companies Acts and to the conditions contained in its memorandum, a company may by special resolution alter or add to its articles.[15]

Every person dealing with a company is taken to know the provisions of the memorandum and articles, so far as they relate to the company's dealings with persons outside the company.[16] Both the documents can be inspected by any person at the Companies Registration Office upon payment of a fee.[17] For English companies the registers are kept both at Companies House, 55–61 City Road, London EC1 and at Companies House, Crown Way, Maindy, Cardiff. The main register is kept in Cardiff, but the London office

11. Per Lord Selbourne in *Ashbury Railway Carriage & Iron Co.* v. *Riche* (1875) L.R. 7 H.L. 653.
12. Companies Act 1948, s. 5.
13. *Ashbury Railway Carriage & Iron Co.* v. *Riche, supra.*
14. *Attorney-General* v. *Great Eastern Railway Co.* (1880) 5 App. Cas. 473.
15. Companies Act 1948, s. 10.
16. *Mahony* v. *East Holyford Mining Co.* (1875) L.R. 7 H.L. 869.
17. This is currently £1: *see* the Companies Act 1948, s. 426 and the Companies (Fees) (Amendment) Regulations 1980, S.I. 1980 No. 1980.

will be kept open for microfiche searches. For Scottish companies the register is kept in Edinburgh. The banker, therefore, before dealing with a company, must get to know the powers of the directors as prescribed in the two documents, more particularly their borrowing powers and their powers to mortgage the company's assets, and the regulations controlling the signing and indorsing of bills and cheques. But the banker is not taken to know anything relating to the internal management of the company.[18]

When a new company is formed, the memorandum of association, the articles (unless it is proposed to adopt Table A),[19] and certain other documents[20] are submitted to the Registrar of Companies, and provided these are in order the Registrar issues a certificate of incorporation.[21] The registrar's certificate is conclusive evidence that the statutory requirements as to registration have been complied with, that the company is duly registered,[22] and that the company is a body corporate by the name contained in the memorandum as from the date of incorporation mentioned in the certificate.[23]

As a general rule, and subject to what has been said above about public companies, any company limited by shares or by guarantee must have the words "public limited company" as the last part of its name.[24] Where, however, it is proved to the satisfaction of the Department of Trade that the objects of a limited company are the promotion of com-merce, art, science, religion, charity or some profession, and that it intends to apply its profits, if any, or other income in promoting its objects, and to prohibit the payment of any dividends to its members, the company may, in the case of a company about to be formed, be registered with limited liability, without adding the words "public limited company" to its name, and if already formed may omit them.[25] It is extremely unlikely that any such company would be a public company under the 1980 Act classification.

DIRECTORS AND SECRETARY

The directors are persons appointed by the shareholders to manage the business of the company in their interests. They are the agents

---

18. *Royal British Bank* v. *Turquand* (1856) 6 E. & B. 327. *See also* European Communities Act 1972, s. 9.
19. Companies Act 1948, s. 8(2).
20. *See* Companies Act 1980. ss. 3 and 4.
21. Companies Act 1948, s. 13.
22. *See* Companies Act 1980, s. 3.
23. Companies Act 1948, s. 13.
24. Companies Act 1980, s. 2(2).
25. *See* Companies Act 1981, s. 25.

of the company in its dealings with outside persons, and they occupy a fiduciary position in which they are in some respects like trustees, though their position differs considerably from ordinary trustees.[26] Their powers are strictly defined by the memorandum and articles. If they go beyond the powers conferred upon them by these documents, they may be personally liable to the company, and also to the party with whom they have contracted provided he had no notice that they were going beyond their powers. For example, if they borrow from a banker without authority or in excess thereof, they may be personally liable to the banker, as having committed a breach of warranty of authority,[27] provided that the banker when advancing the money was acting in good faith and without knowledge of the lack of authority, and that a scrutiny of the memorandum and articles would not have revealed the lack of authority.

If directors act within the scope of their authority with such care as may reasonably be expected from them, having regard to their knowledge and experience, and if they act honestly and for the benefit of the company, they "discharge both their equitable as well as their legal duty to the company".[28] They are not liable for mistakes made honestly or for not exercising due care in the administration of the company, but if the lack of care is of such a gross nature that no reasonable businessman could justify it, then they are liable.[29]

A public company must have at least two directors, while a private company must have not less than one director.[30] Every company must have a secretary and a sole director cannot hold both offices.[31]

Except in the case of companies registered before 23rd November 1916, all trade catalogues and circulars, business letters and the like on which the company's name appears must give the names of each director, disclosing any former Christian name or surname and nationality, if not British or a resident of any of the EEC countries.[32]

26. See *York and North Midland Railway* v. *Hudson* (1853) 16 Bear. 485; *Great Eastern Railway* v. *Turner* (1872) L.R. 8 Ch. 149; *Re Forest of Dean etc. Co.* (1878) 10 Ch. D. 450; *Joint Stock Discount Co.* v. *Brown* (1869) L.R. 8 Eq. 376; *Jacobus Marler Estates* v. *Marler* (1916) 85 L.J.P.C. 167; *Percival* v. *Wright* [1902] 2 Ch. 421.
27. See *Collen* v. *Wright* (1857) 8 E. & B. 647; [1843–60] All E.R. Rep. 146; *Firbanks Executors* v. *Humphreys* (1886) 18 Q.B.D. 54; *Chapleo* v. *Brunswick Permanent Benefit Building Society* (1881) 6 Q.B.D. 696; *Richardson* v. *Williamson* (1871) L.R. 6 Q.B. 276.
28. Per Lindley M.R. in *Lagunas Nitrate Co.* v. *Lagunas Syndicate* [1899] 1 Ch. 392.
29. See especially the discussion of this by Romer J. in *Re City Equitable Fire Insurance Co.* [1925] Ch. 407 at 427.
30. Companies Act 1948, s. 176.
31. Ibid., s. 177(1).
32. Ibid., s. 201 and the Companies (Disclosure of Directors' Nationalities) (Exemption) Order 1974.

The secretary's position depends upon the authority with which he is clothed. His duties were formerly regarded as those of a mere scribe, deputed to record and carry out the instructions of the directors. But the tendency today is for his powers to be greater than these and if they are, and the persons dealing with him know it, then his actions within the scope of the authority conferred upon him are binding both on the directors and the company. His increased responsibility is now recognised by the requirement in the Companies Act 1980 that the secretary of a public company "must have the requisite knowledge and experience to discharge the functions." If he did not hold the position of secretary of the company on the appointed day he must have been secretary of a public company for at least three years or hold an appropriate professional qualification.[33]

Neither the directors nor the secretary should be allowed to put cheques payable to the company into their private accounts. The danger of allowing a director or other agent to place cheques payable to the company or to his principal to the credit of his own account was emphasised in the case of *Underwood* v. *Bank of Liverpool*.[34] Underwood converted his business into a private limited company in which he held all the shares except one. By the articles he was appointed sole director. A debenture was issued creating a floating charge over all the assets of the company to secure its banking account. Soon after the formation of the company, Underwood commenced to pay into his own private account cheques in favour of the company duly indorsed by himself as sole director. In an action brought by the receiver for the debentureholders, it was held that Underwood's bankers had been guilty of negligence, and they had to refund all amounts so received.

Although Underwood was for practical purposes the sole proprietor of the company, his action was undoubtedly a fraud on the company's creditors, since even in the case of a "one-man" company, the company is an entity of itself quite apart from that of its chief proprietor. The collecting banker was, therefore, guilty of negligence. A banker should not allow any director, or other agent, or a partner, to put to his own account cheques drawn payable to the company, his principal or his firm.

33. Companies Act 1980, s. 79. The appointed day, when this provision came into force, was 22nd December 1980. Section 79 contains a list of appropriate professional bodies.
34. [1924] 1 K.B. 775; [1924] All E.R. Rep. 230. *See* Chapter Eight.

OPENING AND OPERATING THE ACCOUNT

Whenever a company proposes to open an account, the banker should, unless the directors are well known to the bank, take up the same references for the company and the directors as he would with any other new customer. The banker should also see its certificate of incorporation and memorandum and articles of association. In the case of public companies the banker should also see the certificate issued by the Registrar certifying that the company's allotted share capital is not less than the authorised minimum. After December 1980, no public company can begin business operations or borrow money until this has been issued. It seems that if the company enters into any transaction before this certificate is issued, the transaction is binding on the company, but the company and any officer in default will be liable to a fine. Moreover if the company does not meet its obligations the directors will now be jointly and severally liable to indemnify the other party to the transaction against any loss due to such non-compliance.[35]

There is no objection to a banker receiving funds paid in by a company prior to the production of its certificate of incorporation and (in the case of a public company) its "business certificate", but no withdrawals must be allowed until these documents are produced, except debentures when no allotment has been made by the directors.

New issues

All application money received by a company making an issue of shares or debentures must be placed in a separate banking account and it should not be withdrawn by the company until all the formalities connected with the issue have been satisfactorily completed.[36] Where a prospectus states that application has been made or will be made for permission for the shares or debentures to be dealt in on any stock exchange, any allotment made on an application in pursuance of the prospectus is void if the permission has not been applied for before the third day (Saturdays, Sundays and Bank Holidays excluded) after the first issue of the prospectus, or if the permission has been refused before the expiration of three weeks from the date of closing the subscription lists or such longer period not exceeding six weeks as may, within the said three weeks, be notified by the stock exchange whose permission is sought.[37] Where

35. Companies Act 1980, s. 4. This section came into force on 22nd December 1980, and applied only to public companies under the new classification— there was, as noted above, a transitional period of 15 months during which old public companies might re-register as new public companies.
36. Companies Act 1948, s. 51(3).
37. Ibid., s. 51(1).

permission has not been so applied for or has been refused, the company must forthwith repay all the relative application moneys. If this is not done within eight days, the directors responsible become jointly and severally liable for the amount, together with interest at 5 per cent per annum.[38]

Every prospectus must state the minimum sum which must be raised to enable the company to carry out its objects and provide working capital. If the issue does not raise this sum, all application money must be repaid on the expiration of forty days after the first issue of the prospectus. If it is not repaid within the following eight days, the directors incur the same liability as above.[39]

It will be seen that there are a number of important points to be satisfied before a company is entitled to draw off the funds standing to the credit of a new issues account. The banker, in the interests of his customer, the company, and in the public interest, should see that they have all been complied with.

In this connection, it should be noted that banks are rightly very jealous of the use of their names in any prospectus (or offer for sale) and that it is the practice for banks to insist on the prior submission of the prospectus (or offer for sale) for their approval of the mention of their names, even though their responsibility in the matter is limited to the receiving of the subscriptions.

Mandate

A duly certified copy of the board resolution appointing the bank as bankers to the company should be included in a mandate giving all the necessary particulars of the way in which the moneys of the company may be drawn out for the purposes of the company, including specimen signatures.[40] This mandate, duly signed by the chairman and countersigned by the secretary, forms the banker's authority for transacting business with the company, and this authority, provided it is consonant with the provisions of the memorandum and articles, will hold good even though as a matter of fact the resolution may have assigned powers to persons not properly appointed for such functions. The acts of a director or manager are valid, notwithstanding any defect which may afterwards be discovered in his appointment or qualification.[41]

While the standard form of mandate will suit the needs of the majority of companies, some transactions, such as the giving of guarantees and indemnities by the bank and the signing by the

38. Ibid., s. 51(2).
39. Ibid., s. 47.
40. *See* Appendix I for specimen form.
41. Companies Act 1948, s. 180.

company of the relative counter-indemnities, the deposit and withdrawal of securities and other articles, the signing of requisition forms for bank drafts, and the establishment of credits, etc., should be dealt with by separate, specific, applications by the customer.

As with any other customer, the question of who is authorised to draw cheques on the company's account will be determined by the terms of the mandate which must be faithfully observed. The mandate may authorise designated officials to sign cheques, in which case, where changes are made in the relevant appointments, the banker should obtain satisfactory evidence of the change in the appointment, such as a copy of the broad resolution, certified by the chairman. It is, however, preferable for it to authorise named persons, in which case certified copies of the board resolutions removing, adding or substituting names on the list will suffice. In all cases, the banker should obtain specimen signatures.

Where a facsimile signature is used, it will be valid only if impressed by authority. The resolution conferring authority should cover all cheques bearing facsimile signatures, whoever affixes them, and if any form of authentication is required by such resolution, the banker should check the authentication.[42]

Every limited company must have its name mentioned in legible characters in all business letters of the company and in all notices and other official publications of the company, and in all bills of exchange, promissory notes, indorsements, cheques and orders for money or goods purporting to be signed by or on behalf of the company.[43] The signing of bills, cheques and promissory notes may be done in one of two ways: (a) by a duly authorised agent signing the name of the company only, or (b) by a duly authorised agent signing by or on behalf of or on account of the company, followed by the agent's signature. Both forms of signature will be binding on the company.[44] Which form is used will be governed by the mandate.

If the true name of the company does not appear on the documents mentioned above, or if any official signing does not have the requisite authority, he may incur personal liability on the instruments, unless the same are duly paid by the company, and is also liable to a fine.[45]

If the authorised directors sign simply in their own name, rather than "for and on behalf of" the company, the directors so signing would be liable and not the company, unless the mandate authorised the bank to honour signatures in this form. The effect of this rule,

42. *Q.B.P.*, No. 62.
43. Companies Act 1948, s. 108(1).
44. Ibid., s. 33.
45. Ibid., s. 108(4). For the maximum fine, *see* Companies Act 1980, ss. 80, 87(1), and Sched. 2.

however, is somewhat diminished now that banks print the title of the account on cheques they issue.

Where moneys are to be transferred from one account of the company to another, e.g. the balance on the dividend account to the current account, provided the general mandate is drawn widely enough to cover the dividend account and the cheque is signed in the manner authorised by the mandate, no special board resolution is required.[46] However, where the secretary indorses a bill which is to be discounted and the proceeds credited to the company's account, unless there is a minute from the directors authorising this or the transactions are covered by the express terms of the mandate, the only safe course is to obtain specific authority from a board resolution.[47]

Where a cheque, signed in the way contemplated by the mandate, is presented for an amount in excess of the credit balance on the company's account, then provided that the signatories are directors who have borrowing powers, that the purpose of the borrowing is authorised by the memorandum, and that either the memorandum contains express borrowing powers or the company is a trading company,[48] the bank may honour the cheque. The mandate should expressly authorise the bank to honour cheques whether or not the account is in credit, but a trading company has implied power to borrow for the purposes authorised by its memorandum, and borrowing powers are generally exercisable by the directors.

Before opening an account for a company, the banker should check that there are sufficient directors to satisfy the minimum number prescribed by the articles. The well-known rule in *Royal British Bank* v. *Turquand*,[49] which allows an outsider to assume that the internal management of the company has been properly carried out, does not apply where the person dealing with the the company has notice that it has not. For this purpose a person is taken as having constructive notice of anything in the publicly filed documents which indicates some irregularity. For example, the minimum number of directors is a matter for the articles, and as particulars of the appointment of directors are also filed with the Registrar of Companies, if there are fewer than the minimum number of directors appointed when the mandate is given, the banker has notice of the irregularity and cannot rely on the rule for protection.

46. *Q.B.P.*, No. 68.
47. *Q.B.P.*, No. 66.
48. *Q.B.P.*, No. 70.
49. (1856) 6 E. & B. 327.

BORROWING POWERS

When a company requires an advance it is essential for the bank to know whether the company has or has not the power to borrow money, and to mortgage its assets, and any limit thereto. These powers, with or without restrictions, are contained in the memorandum and articles. These documents may give power to borrow money but not to pledge the company's property as security, or the power to borrow and give security may only be exercisable by the company in general meeting and not merely by resolution of the directors. It is well to remember that although the powers are to be construed reasonably, a liquidator will interpret them strictly.

A trading company has implied powers of borrowing and mortgaging; a non-trading company has no implied powers of borrowing and mortgaging, and if such powers are not mentioned it has no power to do these things except to such extent as is reasonable and necessary for the carrying out of its declared objects.[50] Where the company is a non-trading company, any power to borrow and mortgage must be included in its memorandum; no such power otherwise exists, and it cannot even discount bills of exchange.

The fact that a company has express (or implied) power to borrow does not mean that a banker can safely lend for any purpose. In *Introductions* v. *National Provincial Bank*[51] a company formed for one purpose changed its business after a change of ownership and was engaged in pig-breeding, an activity not authorised by its memorandum, and obtained a bank overdraft while doing so. The company was not carrying on the business of borrowing money as a separate activity (and this is a good example of the necessity of distinguishing between the objects, which are the primary purposes, and the powers, which are merely ancillary to the objects), and since the borrowing was for an *ultra vires* purpose and was known to be so by the bank, the borrowing was *ultra vires* and a debenture given as security was therefore invalid. This does not mean that a lender must follow up the use of every penny lent to ensure that his loan will not be *ultra vires*. The banker should ask, however, what the loan is required for and should inquire what business the company is carrying on; if these fall within the objects of the company the loan will not be *ultra vires* the company.

Even though s. 9 of the European Communities Act 1972 seems

---

50. *Attorney-General* v. *Great Eastern Railway Co.* (1880) 5 App. Cas. 473.
51. [1969] 1 All E.R. 887.

to offer some protection, it is considered that this will not avail the banker, should he lend money to a company for an *ultra vires* purpose, on the grounds that it is established English banking practice to require production of a company's memorandum and articles, and that the bank therefore has notice of their contents.[52]

Even if the borrowing is *intra vires* the company (i.e. is within the objects of the company), the banker should check that it is not *ultra vires* the directors, either by its manner or because of limited powers. The articles usually provide that the powers of a company are exercisable by the directors, but sometimes the amount that may be borrowed by the directors, either at all or without authority from the company in general meeting, is limited either to a stated figure or to some formula (usually related to paid-up capital and reserves).

Table A limits the directors' powers in this respect to an amount equal to the nominal value of the issued share capital,[53] and although it is usual to remove this limit in newly formed private companies, the Stock Exchange requirements are such that in the case of listed companies there must be some limit on the directors' powers.[54]

The banker should, before lending, take steps to ascertain that the proposed borrowing will not exceed such limits. To arrive at the total borrowings, there should be included outstanding mortgages and debentures (other than those which are purely security for third party borrowings), overdrafts, loans and deposits from directors, staff and others, and the like. The articles must be examined closely, however, since although it is established that moneys raised by the discounting of trade bills of exchange would not be a "borrowing",[55] the form of article commonly adopted by listed companies requires moneys outstanding under acceptances of such bills to be treated as "moneys borrowed".

If any such limit on borrowing is expressed in the memorandum, any borrowing in excess of the limit will be *ultra vires* the company and void; if it is in the articles, any borrowing in excess may be approved by the company in advance (or the articles may be altered by special resolution); it may also be ratified afterwards as it will only be *ultra vires* the directors and not *ultra vires* the company.[56]

If the directors have exceeded their powers, and their acts are not ratified by the company, they may be liable to the company. While the members of a closely-held company will probably be, or be related to, the directors, and so would be unlikely to enforce this,

52. *Q.B.P.*, No. 72. *See also* Chapter Fourteen.
53. Proviso to Regulation 79 in Table A in the First Schedule to the 1948 Act.
54. Rule 159(2) and Appendix 34, Schedule VII.
55. *I.R.C.* v. *Rowntree* [1948] 1 All E.R. 482.
56. *Grant* v. *United Kingdom Switchback Railways Co.* (1888) 40 Ch. D. 135; *Irvine* v. *Union Bank of Australia* (1877) 2 App. Cas. 366.

a liquidator might feel obliged to do so unless their acts had been sanctioned by the shareholders). If the lender knows that the powers of the directors have been exceeded or used for an improper purpose he will be unable to enforce the loan against the company. A banker should, therefore, always ask for a certificate that the proposed borrowing is within the unexhausted borrowing powers of the directors or the company. Sometimes the article states that no lender is concerned to see whether or not the limit is exceeded. In such case the restriction is intended to operate solely as between the company and its directors, unless the lender actually knows that they are exceeding their powers (e.g. if their powers are limited to £1 million and the proposed loan is for £1.5 million).

A banker unable to enforce against the company a loan which was *intra vires* the company but exceeded the powers of the directors may be able to sue the directors personally for breach of a warranty that they possessed the necessary power, if they gave such a warranty, express or implied.[57] If, however, the loan was *ultra vires* the company, the lender may be able to follow the money, if the company still has it; if not, he can only look to a right of subrogation, i.e. if the loan is used to repay enforceable debts and liabilities the lender is subrogated to the rights of the persons whose debts or liabilities were repaid or reduced to the extent of such repayment or reduction.[58] This does not, however, extend to securities belonging to, or the priorities of, such creditors.[59] In other words, he will be able to recover the money, but only as an ordinary unsecured creditor.

Under s. 54 of the Companies Act 1948[59A] it was not lawful for a company to give, whether directly or indirectly, and whether by means of a loan, guarantee, the provision of security or otherwise, any financial assistance for the purpose of or in connection with a purchase or subscription made or to be made by any person of or for any shares in the company or, where the company is a subsidiary company, in its holding company. This prohibition, however, did not apply where the lending of money was part of the ordinary business of a company and the proposed loan was of the sort which it is part of the company's business to make (e.g. on the same sort of scale as its other lending), and a bank could therefore make advances

57. *See Collen* v. *Wright* (1857) 8 E. & B. 647; [1843–60] All E.R. Rep. 146; *Firbanks Executors* v. *Humphreys* (1886) 18 Q.B.D. 54; *Chapleo* v. *Brunswick Permanent Benefit Building Society* (1881) 6 Q.B.D. 696; *Richardson* v. *Williamson* (1871) L.R. 6 Q.B. 276.

58. *Blackburn Building Society* v. *Cunliffe, Brooks & Co.* (1883) 22 Ch. D. 61; 9 App. Cas. 857; *Baroness Wenlock* v. *River Dee (No. 2)* (1887) 19 Q.B.D. 155; *Re Harris Calculating Machine Co.* [1914] 1 Ch. 920; *Sinclair* v. *Brougham* [1914] A.C. 398; *Re Airedale Co-operative Society* [1933] Ch. 639.

59. *Re Wrexham, Mold & Connah's Quay Railway* [1899] 1 Ch. 440.

59A. This section has now been replaced by s. 42 of the Companies Act 1981, for details see the Preface to this edition.

where the money was to be used for the purchase of its own shares. Advances to enable employees to purchase fully paid shares in the company were also excepted, but the aggregate amounts of any outstanding loans made in this connection had to be shown in the company's annual balance sheet. As any other advances of this nature were illegal and *ultra vires*, great care had to be exercised if the banker had any reason to suspect that any proposed advance might be intended for this purpose, and the matter had to be fully investigated. If the bank was on notice that the loan might ultimately be intended for this purpose, it could be liable in damages to the company (or its liquidator) for negligence, or liable as constructive trustee of funds which have been used in contravention of the section.[60]

Subject to certain exceptions, no company could make a loan, or enter into any guarantee or provide any security in connection with any loan made by any person, to a director of the company or of its holding company. In addition, public companies or member companies of public groups were prohibited from:

(*a*) making a "quasi-loan" (defined as a payment of, or an undertaking to pay, an amount on behalf of another person which was to be refunded by that person) to a director of the company or its holding company;

(*b*) making a loan or quasi-loan to a person connected with such a director;

(*c*) entering into a guarantee or providing any security in connection with a loan or quasi-loan made by any other person on behalf of such director or connected person;

(*d*) entering into a "credit transaction"[61] as creditor or on behalf of such director or connected person;

(*e*) entering into any guarantee or providing any security in connection with a credit transaction made by any other person for such director or connected person.[62]

The general prohibition on loans also covered indirect arrangements which might otherwise have enabled the company to avoid the restrictions.

There were, however, certain exceptions to the general prohibition.

(*a*) Where a director of a company (being a public company or

---

60. *Selangor United Rubber Estates* v. *Cradock* (*No. 3*) [1968] 1 All E.R. 1073; see also *Karak Rubber Co.* v. *Burden & Others* (*No. 2*) [1972] 1 All E.R. 1210. For an explanation of the term "constructive trustee" *see* Snell's *Principles of Equity* (28th Edn.).
61. Defined as meaning a sale on deferred payment terms, conditional sale, hire-purchase, hire or leasing: Companies Act 1980, s. 65(3).
62. Companies Act 1980, s. 49(1) and (2).

a member company of a public group) or of its holding company was associated with a subsidiary of either company, the company was not prohibited by reason only of that fact from: (*i*) making a loan or quasi-loan to that subsidiary; or (*ii*) entering into a guarantee or providing any security in connection with a loan or quasi-loan to that subsidiary.

(*b*) A company was not prohibited from making a quasi-loan to one of its directors or to a director of its holding company if the company was to be reimbursed within two months and the total amount involved did not exceed £1,000.

(*c*) A company was not prohibited from entering into a credit transaction where the aggregate did not exceed £5,000, or where the company entered into the transaction in the ordinary course of its business and its value was no greater and the terms no more favourable than would be offered to someone of the same standing who was not connected with the company.

(*d*) Any company could make a loan or quasi-loan or enter into a credit transaction or similar facility to or with its holding company.

(*e*) A company could provide a director with funds to meet expenditure incurred or to be incurred by him for the purposes of the company or to enable him to perform his duties as an officer of the company or which would enable him to avoid incurring the expenditure.

(*f*) A moneylending company[63] could make a loan or quasi-loan or guarantee a loan in the ordinary course of its business if the amount was no greater and the terms no more favourable than would be offered to someone of the same standing who is not connected with the company, and provided that, unless the company was a recognised bank, [64] the amount did not exceed £50,000.[65]

The issue of company debentures as security and the requirements as to registration contained in s. 95 of the Companies Act 1948 are dealt with in Chapter Seventeen.

In connection with borrowing by limited companies, it is a common practice for the banker to insist on the personal guarantees of the directors. If no security is offered, it is not unreasonable for the banker to ask the directors to show their own faith in their company. The practice has much to commend it. However, care should be exercised if the directors decided to issue a debenture or

63. Defined as meaning a company the ordinary course of business of which includes the making of loans or quasi-loans or the giving of guarantees in connection with loans and quasi-loans.
64. *See* Chapter Three.
65. Companies Act 1980, s. 50. The provisions are now (virtually) repeated in the Companies Act 1981, s. 22; special relaxations in favour of private companies appear in ibid. ss. 43 and 44.

charge on some asset of the company to cover the guaranteed debt. As a general rule, directors, being in a fiduciary position,[66] are not qualified to vote on, or form part of a quorum in relation to, any matter in which they are personally interested, except to the extent that the articles expressly permit them to do so. This is an example of a case where the directors, by reason of their liability under their guarantee, are personally interested in the question of the giving of security, and if the matter is not approved by a sufficient number of disinterested directors to form a quorum, there is a possibility of the security being upset on a liquidation.[67] Unless, therefore, the debenture or other security is created before the guarantee is given or even contemplated, or the articles expressly permit interested directors to vote,[68] it is desirable to have the authorising resolution passed by the company in general meeting.[69] If an interested director happens also to be a shareholder he can vote at a general meeting without declaring his interest and such vote would be validly cast. The form of notice to shareholders calling the meeting and setting out the terms of the proposed resolution should be approved by the bank.

Another danger which may arise in connection with a company's account covered by a director's guarantee where he has also deposited security was illustrated in *Re M. Kushler*.[70] A director, being alive to his responsibility under the guarantee, so conducted the company's business that he realised sufficient to repay the overdraft. On the subsequent liquidation of the company, the court upheld the liquidator's contention that the procedure was a fraudulent preference and the bank had to refund certain of the payments-in, and moreover was not allowed credit for items paid out during the period starting from the time it was deemed the preference of the bank had commenced.[71]

COMPANIES INCORPORATED OUTSIDE GREAT BRITAIN CARRYING ON BUSINESS WITHIN GREAT BRITAIN

Part X (ss. 406–23) of the Companies Act 1948 is devoted to these companies. In addition to foreign companies, companies incorporated in Northern Ireland, Eire, the Channel Islands and the

66. *See* above in this chapter.
67. *Victors* v. *Lingard* [1927] 1 Ch. 323.
68. Table A, Regulation 84(2), permits interested directors to vote on such an issue.
69. Alternatively, the articles may be altered by special resolution so as to permit this.
70. [1943] Ch. 248; [1943] 2 All E.R. 22.
71. The subject of fraudulent preference is more fully explained in chapters Twenty-Nine and Thirty.

Isle of Man are subject thereto. A certified copy of the charter, statutes or memorandum and articles, or other instrument defining the constitution of the company, with the names of the directors and secretary (including former names) and their addresses, and the names and addresses of one or more persons resident in Great Britain authorised to accept service of process and any notices, must be filed with the Registrar of Companies within one month of a place of business being established within Great Britain.[72] In the case of the directors, their nationality, business occupations and other directorships must also be filed.[73] All changes must be similarly notified.[74]

Accounts must be made out each year and published.[75] The company must conspicuously exhibit on every place where it carries on business in Great Britain the name of the company, the country where incorporated, and whether the liability of the members is limited. Similar information must be given in any prospectus, and on all billheads, letter paper, notices and advertisements, etc.[76]

The provisions of the Act in regard to the registration of charges extends, as regards charges on property in England, to all companies incorporated outside England (including companies incorporated in Scotland) which have an established place of business in England.[77]

A bank in England with which such a company opens an account cannot easily inquire whether the requirements of the law of the country in which the company is incorporated have been complied with, or whether the account is conducted in accordance with that law. It should, however, as a matter of prudence check that the persons with whom it is dealing are properly authorised to act for the company by that law, and by the statutes and bye-laws of the company.

2. PARTNERSHIPS

NATURE OF PARTNERSHIP

Partnership is defined as "the relation which subsists between persons carrying on a business in common with a view of profit".[78]

---

72. Companies Act 1948, s. 407(1).
73. Ibid., s. 407(2).
74. Ibid., s. 409.
75. *See* the Companies Act 1976, Pt. I and the Companies Act 1981, Pt. I.
76. Companies Act 1948, s. 411.
77. Ibid., s. 106.
78. Partnership Act 1890, s. 1.

Unlike a company, a partnership (or "a firm" as it is called in the Partnership Act 1890) is not a separate legal person distinct from the persons who are partners in the firm,[79] though a firm may sue and be sued in the firm name.[80] Partners almost always have un-limited liability for the debts of their firm, though a few limited partnerships exist, governed by the Limited Partnership Act 1907.[81] A partnership cannot have the word "Limited" as part of its name.[82]

There is a limited form of civil disability imposed on persons who are in breach of the disclosure provisions relating to persons who have been using business names; there are also certain criminal sanctions linked with the rules about disclosure of the persons who are involved with the business in question. Under the Companies Act 1981[83] it is required that when persons are trading under any name other than their own (and in the case of a partnership, this will mean the names of all the partners) they must give appropriate details of the persons involved in the business on all stationery, together with an address for each person where he may be served with any proper papers (this usually being the business address), and the like details are required to be displayed on the business premises. The consequence of non-compliance with the requirement to disclose the statutory details is as follows: if proceedings are brought to enforce any contract made at a time when there was some breach of the provisions of the Act and the defendant complains of that non-compliance, the case is automatically dismissed; the court has, however, a discretion to allow the case to continue if it thinks it right to allow the (defaulting) plaintiff to pursue his claim.[83]

Any person may be a partner, including a minor[84] or a mentally disordered person.[85] For most firms the maximum permitted number of partners is twenty;[86] but there is no maximum number for firms

---

79. *Re Sawers, ex parte Blain* (1879) 12 Ch. D. 522.
80. Rules of the Supreme Court, Order 81, Rule 1.
81. The feature of limited partnerships is that some partners, known as "limited partners", contribute capital but take no part in the management of the firm; their liability is limited to their capital contributions. The other partners, known as "general partners", do take part in the management of the firm and their liability is unlimited.
82. Companies Act 1948, s. 439.
83. Companies Act 1981, ss. 28–30.
84. *Goode* v. *Harrison* (1821) 5.B. & Ald. 147.
85. A partnership is not dissolved by one of its members becoming subject to mental disorder: *Jones* v. *Noy* (1833) 2 M. & K. 125; but if he enters into a partnership agreement while suffering from mental disorder and the other partners know of the disorder, the agreement would not be binding: *Imperial Loan Co.* v. *Stone* [1892] 1 Q.B. 599, nor would it be binding if a receiver had already been appointed under the Mental Health Act 1959 (*see* under "Mentally disordered persons" in Chapter Five).
86. Companies Act 1948, s. 434.

of solicitors, accountants, stockbrokers and jobbers, and the Department of Trade may extend the list to other kinds of partnership. So far it has been extended to patent agents, surveyors and other related professions, actuaries, consulting engineers and building engineers, provided that each of them (or in the case of surveyors etc. three-quarters of them, or in the case of consulting engineers, a majority of them) is recognised by the appropriate professional body.[87]

HANDLING THE PARTNERSHIP ACCOUNT

When opening an account for a firm, a banker should obtain a mandate, as he would when opening any other type of joint account. When dealing with a firm, however, a banker must be aware that the provisions of the Partnership Act 1890 will automatically apply unless they are specifically excluded by the terms of the partnership agreement. A banker must therefore be familiar with the main rules of the Partnership Act, which are summarised below, and must be sure to request a copy of the partnership agreement when he opens the account.

Every partner has authority in the normal course of business of the firm to enter into contracts which will be binding not only on himself, but also on all the other partners. This is by virtue of s. 5 of the Partnership Act 1890, which provides as follows.

Every partner is an agent of the firm and his other partners for the purpose of the business of the partnership; and the acts of every partner who does any act for carrying on in the usual way business of the kind carried on by the firm of which he is a member binds the firm and his partners, unless the partner so acting has in fact no authority to act for the firm in the particular matter, and the person with whom he is dealing either knows that he has no authority, or does not know or believe him to be a partner.

Every person who by words spoken or written, or by conduct, represents himself or who knowingly suffers himself to be represented as a partner in a particular firm, is liable as a partner to any one who has, on the faith of any such representation, given credit to the firm.[88] In short, any person holding himself out to be a partner may be estopped from denying that he is a partner.

A partner in a trading partnership (as opposed to a non-trading

---

87. Companies Act 1967, s. 120 and various Partnership (Unrestricted Size) Regulations (S.I. 1968, No. 1222; S.I. 1970, Nos. 835, 992 and 1319).
88. Partnership Act 1890, s. 14(1).

partnership, e.g. a firm of solicitors or accountants[89]) has certain implied powers. He has an implied power to bind his partners by the drawing and indorsing of cheques, the drawing, accepting and indorsing of bills of exchange, and the making and indorsing of promissory notes. A partner in a non-trading firm has no such implied powers, except possibly in the drawing and indorsing of cheques. A partner in a trading partnership also has an implied power to borrow money on behalf of the firm, but only for those transactions incidental to the firm's ordinary course of business. He has no power to bind his partners by accepting a bill of exchange in blank, or by accepting an accommodation bill, except as regards a holder for value who took the instrument without notice of the blank acceptance, or that the firm was an accommodation party.[90] He has no power to bind the firm, unless specially authorised by the other partners, for a purpose apparently outside the objects of the partnership business,[91] but is himself personally liable for the consequences of any such act.

It would appear that a partner in a trading partnership has an implied authority to open an account in the firm's name, but it has been held that he has no implied power to open a partnership account in his own name so as to make his partners liable for any debit balance on the account.[92] If it can be shown, however, that the other partners had expressly authorised the partner to open a partnership account in his own name, then the firm would be bound by the act of the partner. It has also been held that where a bank has transferred its business to or amalgamated with another bank, any partner may bind his partners by assenting to a transfer of the account to the new bank.[93]

Any partner in a trading partnership has implied power to sell or pledge any of the partnership property, but a banker should get any memorandum of deposit taken by him signed by all the partners. Any partner can even mortgage real property belonging to the firm, but the mortgage thus created would only be an equitable one, even though the partner had executed a legal mortgage, for a partner has no implied power to bind his partners by deed. This is a consequence of the general principle that authority to execute a deed

---

89. The reason for the distinction between trading and non-trading firms is an historical one. In former times it was thought likely that partners in commercial firms might be required to act quickly by the emergencies of the trade, without there being time to obtain the concurrence of all the partners.
90. See J.I.B., Vol. 33, Jan. 1912, pp. 24–5.
91. Partnership Act 1890, s. 7.
92. Alliance Bank v. Kearsley (1871) L.R. 6 C.P. 433.
93. Beale v. Caddick (1857) 2 H. & N. 326.

may be conferred only by deed.[94] To obtain a legal mortgage over freehold or leasehold property belonging to the partnership, the concurrence of all the partners is necessary, either in the mortgage deed itself, or in a deed authorising the partner to execute the mortgage on behalf of himself and his partners.

No partner can bind his partners by giving a guarantee on behalf of the firm, unless it is customary for that particular firm or usual in that particular trade to give guarantees.[95] Consequently either the guarantee or an express authority for the giving of the guarantee should be executed by all the partners.[96] Nor does a partner have implied authority to submit a dispute to arbitration, or to commit his partners to being partners in another firm.

As every partner has implied authority in certain circumstances to enter into contracts binding on the other partners, a partner who is a minor or mentally incapable can enter into a contract on behalf of the other partners which will be binding on the other partners even though it will not be binding on himself.

Every partner in a firm is jointly liable with the other partners for all debts and obligations of the firm incurred while he is a partner. After his death, by way of exception to the usual rule relating to joint debtors, his estate is also severally liable in the due course of administration for such debts as remain unpaid, but subject to the prior payment of his private debts.[97] A joint liability is not individual but collective; it is the liability of all together. Hence, though each partner is liable for all the debts contracted by the firm from the moment he became a partner and all the time he continues to be a partner, and the creditor is entitled to sue any partner or all of them, only one action can be brought. Judgment obtained against all the partners gives the creditor power to enforce it not only against the partnership property, but also against the private estates of the partners. If some and not all the partners are sued, and judgment is obtained against them, those not sued are no longer discharged from liability if, for some reason, the judgment is unsatisfied.

There has been a change in the position, for statute[98] now provides that judgment recovered against any person liable in respect of any *debt* or damage shall no longer be a bar to an action or to the continuance of an action, against any other person who is (apart from any such bar) jointly liable with him in respect of the same debt or

---

94. *Berkeley* v. *Hardy* (1926) 5 B. & C. 355.
95. *Brettel* v. *Williams* (1849) 4 Exch. 623.
96. *See* Chapter Fourteen.
97. Partnership Act 1890, s. 9.
98. *See* the Civil Liability (Contribution) Act 1978, s. 3.

damage. The consequences have yet to be made clear by decisions from the courts.

Where the cause of action is a breach of trust or a tort by a partner in the ordinary course of his business, a judgment obtained against one partner does not discharge his partners, since for such wrongful action or omission on the part of their colleague, all the partners are jointly and severally liable.[99] If a partner is a trustee, however, and improperly employs trust property in the business or on account of the partnership, no other partner is liable for the trust property to the beneficiaries, except any other partners who were privy to the breach of trust. Such misapplied trust money may, however, be followed and recovered from the firm if still in its possession and under its control.[100]

When a banker lends money to a firm and takes security from a partner, he should take steps to discover whether the security is partnership property or the property of the individual partner concerned. If the security which is offered is partnership property, the banker should make sure that the partner with whom he is dealing has authority to pledge the property. It is not always clear which property is partnership property. An asset is partnership property if it is "brought into the partnership stock or acquired, whether by purchase or otherwise, on account of the firm or for the purposes and in the course of the partnership business."[101] Property bought with the money belonging to the firm is deemed to have been bought on account of the firm.[101]

If a partner draws a cheque on the firm's account in favour of himself, a banker would probably be acting negligently if he collected or paid the cheque without making proper inquiries in order to discover whether the partner had the necessary authority. Similarly, a banker should make proper inquiries if he is asked to collect or pay a cheque drawn in favour of the firm and subsequently indorsed by one of the partners in favour of himself.[102]

DISSOLUTION: DEATH, BANKRUPTCY OR RETIREMENT OF A PARTNER

Where there is a partnership agreement, it will generally contain express provisions regarding dissolution. The Partnership Act 1890 sets out certain events which will, subject to express agreement to

99. *Blyth* v. *Fladgate* [1891] 1 Ch. 337, and Partnership Act 1890, ss. 10, 12.
100. Partnership Act 1890, s. 13.
101. Ibid., s. 20.
102. *See Baker* v. *Barclays Bank* [1955] 2 All E.R. 571; *Midland Bank* v. *Reckitt* [1933] A.C. 1; [1932] All E.R. Rep. 90; *Morison* v. *London County and Westminster Bank* [1914] 3 K.B. 356; [1914–15] All E.R. Rep. 853 and Chapter Eight.

the contrary, dissolve the partnership, other events in which it may be dissolved, and one event in which it must be dissolved.

The only circumstance in which the partnership must be dissolved in any event is if it becomes unlawful for the business of the firm to be carried on, or for the members of the firm to carry it on in partnership.[103] An example of this would be where a partner is a foreigner and he becomes an alien enemy on account of the outbreak of war.[104]

There are other circumstances in which the partnership may, subject to express agreement, be dissolved.[105] These are if any fixed term or single enterprise for which the partnership was formed has expired or been fulfilled, or if, in the case of a partnership at will, notice to determine is given by any of the partners.

The court has power to order the dissolution of a partnership in certain events.[106] These are:

(a) a partner becoming of permanently unsound mind or otherwise permanently incapable of performing his part of the agreement;

(b) a party being guilty of conduct prejudicially affecting the carrying on of the business of the firm;

(c) a partner being guilty of wilful misconduct;

(d) when the business can only be carried on at a loss;

(e) when circumstances have arisen which render it just and equitable that the partnership should be dissolved.

On the death or bankruptcy of a partner, the partnership will be dissolved, subject to express agreement.[107] It is usual to provide in the agreement for the partnership to continue, and in such a case the partnership agreement is likely to contain provisions regarding the purchase by the remaining partners of the deceased or bankrupt partner's share. The estate of a partner who dies or becomes bankrupt is not liable for partnership debts contracted after his death or bankruptcy, whether or not the creditor knew of the death or bankruptcy.[108] Somewhat similar considerations apply on the retirement of the partner.[109]

When the partnership is dissolved by the death, bankruptcy or retirement of a partner, the banker should stop the account at once if he intends to retain his recourse against the deceased, bankrupt or retiring partner's estate. If this is not done, the rule in *Clayton's*

103. Partership Act 1890, s. 34.
104. *R.* v. *Kupfer* [1915] 2 K.B. 321; *Hugh Stevenson and Sons* v. *Aktiengesellschaft für Cartonnagen-Industrie* [1919] A.C. 239.
105. Partnership Act 1890, s. 32.
106. Ibid., s. 35.
107. Ibid., s. 33.
108. Ibid., s. 36.
109. *See* below for position of a retiring partner.

case[110] will operate. The continuing partners should be asked to open a new account for future use. Appointment by the court of a receiver of the firm is sufficient ground for a banker to refuse any further operations on the partnership account. The receiver is then the only person who has power to deal with the partnership property.

If on the retirement of a partner the continuing partners notify the bank and sign a fresh mandate, but a cheque drawn by the retired partner before his retirement is presented after the fresh mandate is signed, the cheque should be paid, because when he drew it the retired partner was entitled to act as agent for the firm. If the continuing partners do not want it to be paid they can stop payment of it.

On the death of a partner, the other partners are entitled by the right of survivorship to any balance remaining on the partnership account, and can give the banker a valid discharge for it. The deceased partner's executors, or the trustee in bankruptcy of a bankrupt partner, have no power to bind the firm. In the matter of cheques issued before the deceased partner's death, since the death of a partner dissolves the partnership and automatically revokes any authority for signing on the account, the banker would be entitled to return any cheques presented after the death marked "Partner deceased". This applies whether or not they were signed by the deceased partner.

The banker will need to follow this course and stop the account if the account is overdrawn and he wishes to preserve his recourse to the deceased partner's estate. On the other hand, the surviving partners have power to bind the firm for the purpose of winding it up, and save in the circumstances indicated above it is usual to continue to pay the firm's cheques, getting their confirmation if deemed necessary.

After the dissolution of a partnership, the authority of each partner to bind the firm continues, notwithstanding the dissolution, so far as may be necessary to wind up the partnership business and to complete transactions begun but unfinished at the time of the dissolution, but not otherwise. In no case, however, is the firm bound by the acts of a partner who has become bankrupt.[111] That is to say, the remaining partners can sell or pledge the partnership assets, whether real estate or personal estate,[112] for the purpose of completing a transaction already begun or of securing an overdraft

110. (1816) 1 Mer. 529. *See* Chapter Four.
111. Partnership Act 1890, s. 38.
112. *Butchart* v. *Dresser* (1853) 4 De G.M. & G. 542, and *Re Bourne, Bourne* v. *Bourne* [1906] 2 Ch. 427.

already granted, and the banker is entitled to assume, in the absence of evidence to the contrary, that the remaining partners were, by so pledging the assets, engaged in the business of winding up the partnership affairs. The banker's mortgage would therefore take priority over any claim of a deceased partner's executors or a bankrupt partner's trustee for his share in the partnership assets. From the case of *Re Bourne*,[113] it would appear that a mortgage of partnership real property made by a surviving partner who is carrying on the business of the old firm is good as against the deceased partner's estate and that a mortgagee is safe unless he knows the money is not to be used for the proper business of the old partnership.

As already stated, a firm is in no case bound by the acts of a partner who has become bankrupt, and therefore, if a cheque drawn by a partner who is the subject of bankruptcy proceedings is presented, the banker should not pay it without getting it confirmed by the other partners. The partnership estate is wound up by the remaining partners without the intervention of the bankrupt's trustee. The bankrupt's share in the assets passes to his trustee, who cannot bind the firm but may be authorised by the court to bring an action in the names of the trustee and the other partners, notwithstanding that the other partners may have released the debtor or other person against whom an action has been brought. This release will be void.[114] If a firm is made bankrupt, it involves the bankruptcy of every member of the firm, and the banker must not permit operations on any accounts standing in the partner's names. Security deposited by an individual partner to cover the firm's account can be treated by the banker as a collateral security, and he may therefore prove against the partnership estate for the whole debt. If the firm gives security to cover an individual partner's debt, the banker can also prove against the individual partner's estate without taking the security into account. If a security is deposited to cover both the partnership and a partner's account, the banker would as a rule put the security against whatever debt it is collateral to, so as to secure his right of proof for the whole debt on the remaining estate.

The partnership assets are applicable in the first instance in payment of the joint, i.e. the partnership, debts, and the separate, i.e. the private, estate of each partner is applicable in the first instance to the payment of his private debts.[115] Any surplus on the separate estates is to be dealt with as part of the joint estate, and any surplus on the partnership estate is to be dealt with as part of the respective

113. [1906] 2 Ch. 427.
114. Bankruptcy Act 1914, s. 117.
115. Ibid., s. 33(6).

private estates, in proportion to the right and interest of each partner in the partnership estate. It follows from this that the partnership and private creditors cannot prove in competition with each other, the partnership creditors proving in the firm's estate, and the private creditors in each partner's private estate. The partners are bound to submit a statement of the partnership affairs, and each partner a separate statement of his private affairs.[116] If, however, there is no partnership estate and no solvent partner, the firm's creditors rank *pari passu* with the private creditors, and if an individual partner fradulently converts partnership moneys to his own use, the firm's creditors are entitled to prove against the private estate of the fraudulent partner in competition with his private creditors.

The disposal of the residue after all the outside creditors have been satisfied is (subject to any agreement to the contrary) as follows:

(*a*) paying to each partner *pro rata* what is due to him for loans advanced to the firm;

(*b*) paying to each partner *pro rata* what is due to him in respect of capital;

(*c*) any surplus to be divided in the proportion in which the profits are divisible.[117]

Where a person deals with a firm after a change in its constitution e.g. the retirement of a partner, he is entitled to treat all apparent members of the old firm as still being members of the firm, until he has had notice of the change.[118] Where there have been no previous dealings between the parties a notice in the *London Gazette* is sufficient.[119] Where there have been previous dealings, actual notice must be given, but may be given in any way. Once notice has been sent out and received, the retiring partner is no longer liable for debts incurred thereafter by his former partners. When a partner retires, the banker should, if the account is overdrawn and he wishes to retain the liability of the retiring partner, stop the account and request the continuing partners to open a new account.

A person who is admitted as a partner into an existing firm does not thereby become liable to the creditors of the firm for anything done before he became a partner.[120] This is true even when the incoming partner has agreed with the old partner to make himself liable for debts incurred before he joined the partnership. Where, however, there has been a novation of the debt, i.e. where the parties have agreed to substitute the liability of the new firm for that of

116. Bankruptcy Rules 1952, R. 287.
117. Partnership Act 1890, s. 44.
118. Ibid., s. 36(1).
119. Ibid., s. 36(2).
120. Ibid., s. 17(1).

the old, then the incoming partner will be liable. When a new partner comes into a firm, it is necessary for the banker to stop the account and get the partners of the old firm to sign a cheque transferring the balance to a new account, and also a letter signed by the partners of the new firm authorising the banker to debit to the new account all outstanding cheques and all articles dishonoured.

Any alteration in the constitution of a firm, whether by the death, bankruptcy or retirement of a partner, or by the admission of a new partner, will affect any charge which may have been given on the partnership property. A new mortgage or memorandum of deposit should therefore be taken, signed by all the new and continuing partners. A continuing guarantee in respect of the transactions of a firm is, in the absence of an agreement to the contrary, revoked as a future transactions by any change in the constitution of the firm.[121] The position is the same in the case of any other security given by a third party. The necessity of stopping the account when any change takes place in the constitution of a firm, in order to prevent the application of the rule in *Clayton*'s case, has already been emphasised. When all the securities are in order, the balance standing on the old account should be paid off by a cheque signed by all the partners of the new firm.

When any alteration takes place in the constitution of a firm, it is of great importance to the banker, if the firm is likely to require or continue an overdraft, to know how the capital of the firm is going to be affected. For example, retirement of a partner may involve either the immediate withdrawal of his capital or its retention by the firm as a loan, bearing interest. In neither case may it any longer be reckoned as part of the firm's surplus, and in the second case it would rank *pari passu* with the other creditors of the firm.

121. Partnership Act 1890, s. 18.

MONETARY INSTRUMENTS

CHAPTER SEVEN

Drawing and Negotiation of Cheques

LEGAL DEFINITION OF A CHEQUE

The law relating to cheques is mostly contained in two statutes, the Bills of Exchange Act 1882 and the Cheques Act 1957.[1] These statutes are of great importance to every banker and should always be readily available.[2] Where a particular point relating to cheques is not dealt with in either of these statutes, the rules of common law apply; these include the law of contract, the law of torts and the law merchant, this last being the customary practice of merchants and includes banking practice.[3]

Most of the provisions of the Bills of Exchange Act 1882 apply both to cheques and to other types of bill of exchange. Some provisions, however, apply only to cheques and some apply only to other types of bill. The provisions of the Cheques Act 1957 apply only to cheques and certain other classes of instrument but not to other types of bill. Although a cheque is a type of bill of exchange, the term "bill of exchange" is normally used in everyday speech to describe only those bills of exchange which are not cheques. In this and in the next two chapters, the everyday usage will be employed; any reference to a bill is a reference to a bill of exchange other than a cheque. This chapter deals with the drawing and negotiation of cheques and the next chapter deals with the presentation and payment of cheques. Chapter Nine deals with bills of exchange and with promissory notes, which are in some respects similar to, but nevertheless distinct from, bills of exchange.

Section 73 of the Bills of Exchange Act 1882 defines a cheque

1. The Cheques Act 1957 is to be construed as one with the Bills of Exchange Act 1882, Cheques Act 1957, s. 6(1).
2. Despite constant scrutiny in court, the Acts have been only slightly amended.
3. Bills of Exchange Act 1882, s. 97.

as a "bill of exchange drawn on a banker payable on demand".
Section 3 of the Bills of Exchange Act 1882 defines a bill of exchange
as "an unconditional order in writing, addressed by one person to
another, signed by the person giving it, requiring the person to whom
it is addressed to pay on demand or at a fixed or determinable future
time a sum certain in money to or to the order of a specified person,
or to bearer." By combining the definition contained in s. 3 with
the definition contained in s. 73, it can be seen that a cheque must
satisfy the following conditions:

(a) it must be an unconditional order in writing;
(b) it must be signed by the drawer (the person giving it);
(c) it must be drawn on a banker (the drawee);
(d) it must order the banker to pay a sum certain in money on
demand;
(e) it must be drawn in favour of a specified person (the payee)
or to his order or in favour of the bearer.

An order to a banker is not unconditional, and therefore cannot
be a cheque, if it orders "any act to be done in addition to the payment
of money"[4] or if it is an order "to pay out of a particular fund".[5]
But an order can be unconditional if it is an "unqualified order to
pay, coupled with an indication of a particular fund out of which
the drawee is to reimburse himself or a particular account to be
debited"; an order can also be unconditional if it is "an unqualified
order to pay, coupled with . . . a statement of the transaction which
gives rise" to the order.[5]

The cases on this point concern bills of exchange. An order in the
form "Please pay to X or order £600 on account of moneys advanced
by me for the S and F Co." has been held to be a valid bill.[6] An
order such as "Pay AB or order £100 out of proceeds of 50 bales
of cotton shipped per S.S. Swallow" is not unconditional, and so
is not a valid bill; had it been worded "Pay AB or order £100 against
50 bales of cotton shipped per S.S. Swallow" it would have been
a valid bill.

An order will not be unconditional if the drawer orders the banker
not to pay the specified sum without obtaining a receipt.[7] Orders
in this form are still commonly issued by insurance companies when
settling claims under policies. The order might be unconditional if
the direction or note concerning the receipt is addressed to the person
claiming payment of the cheque, not to the banker on whom the

4. Bills of Exchange Act 1882, s. 3(2).
5. Ibid., s. 3(3).
6. *Griffin* v. *Weatherby* (1868) L.R. 3 Q.B. 753.
7. *Bavins Jnr. & Sims* v. *London & South Western Bank* [1900] 1 Q.B. 270; *Capital and Counties Bank* v. *Gordon* [1903] A.C. 240.

cheque is drawn.[8] If a customer wants to draw cheques which the banker cannot pay without first obtaining a receipt, he must make sure that the receipt form is limited to a mere acknowledgment of receipt of the money and that the face of the cheque bears the letter "R" (for "receipt") in bold print at least half an inch high as near as possible to the pound sign (£) in the box on his printed cheque form.[9] The banker should obtain a special mandate to that effect, together with a promise from the customer to indemnify the banker in the event that the banker suffers any loss by doing as the customer requests.

An order can be unconditional, and can therefore be a cheque, if it is drawn payable to "bill attached" or "documents attached". In such cases it is considered that the banker should see that a bill is, or that documents are, attached to the cheque but that he has no further responsibility.[10]

A cheque must be in writing and should ideally be written in ink or typewritten, but a cheque written in pencil may be acceptable. If a cheque is written in pencil and the drawee banker has reason to suspect that it has been materially altered, he should not pay the cheque until the drawer has confirmed that the cheque should be paid. A cheque may be written anywhere and on anything. Recently, one Mrs Paddick of Felixstowe, resenting having to pay drainage rates at a time of flooding, wrote out her cheque on the side of an old freezer and the cheque was duly paid.[11] Now that cheques tend to be cleared by computers, bankers may not be willing to handle cheques drawn by their customers unless they are drawn on printed cheque forms. If, however, a banker intends to refuse to honour cheques which are not drawn on printed cheque forms, he should give reasonable notice of his intention to his customers; otherwise, he would probably be liable to his customers for breach of the banker's duty to honour his customer's cheques.[12]

While any form of cheque other than the usual printed form should be discouraged, a cheque, for example, drawn "I, James Smith, request you to pay ..." would be valid if written by or under the authority of James Smith. Such variations from the normal formula-

8. *Nathan* v. *Ogdens* (1905) 94 L.T. 126; *Thairlwall* v. *Great Northern Railway Co.* [1910] 2 K.B. 509; *Roberts & Co.* v. *March* [1915] 1 K.B. 42.
9. *See Q.B.P.*, No. 472, and the Committee of London Clearing Banks Circular dated 2nd September 1957.
10. *Q.B.P.*, No. 475.
11. *Daily Telegraph*, 18th March 1979. In this she doubtless had in mind the legendary Farmer Haddock, in A.P. Herbert's *More Misleading Cases*, who attempted to pay his income tax by drawing his cheque on the side of a cow.
12. *See* Chapter Four. *See also* the discussion of *Burnett* v. *Westminster Bank* [1966] 1 Q.B. 742; [1965] 3 All E.R. 81 in Chapter Eight.

tion are, however, very undesirable, and bankers would be justified in returning them, marked "Irregularly drawn".

SIGNATURE OF DRAWER

A cheque must be signed by the drawer, either personally or by someone authorised to sign on his behalf.[13] The signature may be in ink or, possibly, in pencil, and may be made mechanically or with a rubber stamp, but a typewritten signature would not normally be acceptable. The signature need not be in the customer's own name or that of his agent; a signature may, for example, be given in a fictitious name or in a trade name. When a cheque is drawn by a company, it may be signed by the officers or agents of the company or sealed with the company's seal.[14]

When a customer opens an account with the banker, he gives the banker a specimen of the form of signature which is to appear on all his cheques. It is not necessary that the drawer should sign his own name. Where a drawer signs a cheque in a trade or assumed name, he is liable on the cheque as if he had signed it in his own name.[15] For example, he may be trading under such a name as "The Sahara Cycle Company" and in that case could arrange so to sign his cheques, without the addition of his personal signature. Such a form of signature, however, has drawbacks, and should generally be discouraged. Where a cheque is signed in the name of a partnership, each partner is liable on the cheque as if he had signed the cheque personally.[16]

However the signature is made, it should conform with the specimen signature of the customer (or his agent) given to the banker in the mandate. If the signature on the cheque does not conform with the specimen signature, the banker should either refer the signature to the drawer for confirmation or return it marked "Signature differs".

If the drawer of a cheque is illiterate, he may sign by his mark, but the mark should be witnessed in the presence of the banker by a reliable witness known to the banker. The witness should sign as a witness and write his address. A witness unconnected with the bank is preferable, but if none is available, some bankers insist upon two bank officials acting as witnesses.[17] If a customer is too ill to sign a cheque except by a mark, the banker should insist that the mark is witnessed by the customer's doctor and another witness,

13. Bills of Exchange Act 1882, s. 91(1).
14. Ibid., s. 91(2).
15. Ibid., s. 23(1).
16. Ibid., s. 23(2).
17. *See also* *Q.B.P.*, No. 536.

and should obtain from the doctor a certificate stating that the customer could not sign except by a mark and was in full possession of his faculties at the time that the mark was made. Pencil signatures, though legally valid, should be discouraged. Facsimile signatures impressed on the cheque by means of a rubber or other stamp should not be permitted unless authorised in each case; a general authority may be sufficient, or the authority may call for each use to be authenticated, in which case the banker must check that it is so authenticated.[18] A banker usually requires an indemnity in such cases. It is not necessary that the drawer should sign the cheque with his own hand, but if otherwise signed, it must be done by or under the drawer's authority.[19] Obviously, where a stamp is used, the banker has no means of knowing whether the stamp has been impressed by the drawer's authority. The banker, therefore, is entitled to satisfactory proof of authority on each occasion when such a stamp is used for signing.

If the drawer's signature or the signature authorised by him is forged, then the banker, should he pay the cheque, cannot usually debit the drawer with the amount. If, however, the drawer does not disclaim a forged signature as soon as the forgery comes to his knowledge, so that he thereby prevents or prejudices the banker's chances of recovering the money from the forger, then the banker may be entitled to debit the drawer with the amount.[20]

DRAWEE OF A CHEQUE

A cheque must be drawn on a banker. As was stated in Chapter One, it is not always clear whether a person is or is not a banker for the purposes of a particular statute. Some statutes provide that recognition by some authority is to be conclusive as to the persons who are to be regarded as bankers for the purposes of the statute, but the Bills of Exchange Act 1882 contains no such provision. It merely says, rather unhelpfully, that for the purpose of the Act a banker "includes a body of persons, whether incorporated or not, who carry on the business of banking."[21] Following the passing of the Banking Act 1979, which restricts the right to carry on a deposit-taking business and provides for a system of recognition of certain institutions as banks, it is probable that an institution will only be regarded as a banker for the purpose of the Bills of Exchange Act

18. *Q.B.P.*, No. 62.
19. Bills of Exchange Act 1882, s. 91.
20. *Greenwood* v. *Martins Bank* [1933] A.C. 51; *Brown* v. *Westminster Bank* [1964] 2 Lloyd's Rep. 187. *See* Chapter Four.
21. Bills of Exchange Act 1882, s. 2.

1882 if it has been recognised as a bank under the Banking Act 1979.

Section 6 of the Bills of Exchange Act 1882 provides that the drawee must be named or otherwise indicated with reasonable certainty. In practice, this is unlikely to raise any problems with cheques because today the great majority of cheques are drawn on printed cheque forms with the name of the drawee banker clearly indicated at the top of the cheque. Section 6 also provides that a cheque can be drawn on more than one drawee (though this is far more likely with a bill of exchange), but it cannot be drawn on alternative or successive drawees.

One of the great differences between a cheque and a bill is that the drawee of a cheque, unlike the drawee of a bill, does not undertake liability on a cheque by adding his signature to the cheque as an "acceptor".[22]

AMOUNT OF CHEQUE

A cheque must be for a sum certain in money. The sum may be expressed in words or in both words and figures. Where the amount of a cheque is expressed in both words and figures and there is a discrepancy between the two, the Act provides that the amount in words is the amount payable,[23] but in such cases the usual practice of bankers is to return the cheque for confirmation by the drawer, particularly if a large amount of money is involved.[24] Although the Bills of Exchange Act 1882 does not stipulate that the amount of the cheque must be in words, if the amount is in figures only, it is customary, in the absence of special arrangements with the drawer, to return such cheques marked "Amount required in words";[25] if the amount is in words only, the banker must pay the cheque, for though unusual in form it is not incomplete, and the banker would probably be liable to his customer for any damage or loss incurred through refusal.[26]

The amount of a cheque may be expressed in sterling or in foreign currency. Where the amount is expressed in sterling, it must be expressed in decimal currency.[27] For the purposes of the Bills of

---

22. A banker may be liable on a cheque, but not in the same sense as the acceptor is liable on a bill or the drawer is liable on a cheque. If a banker is liable, he is liable to the customer under the banker's duty to pay his customer's cheques; see Chapters Four and Eight.
23. Bills of Exchange Act 1882, s. 9(2).
24. *Q.B.P.*, No. 417.
25. *Q.B.P.*, No. 421.
26. *Q.B.P.*, No. 420.
27. Decimal Currency Act 1969, s. 2(1).

Exchange Act 1882, the amount of a cheque may be a sum certain even if the drawer provides for payment with interest or in instalments or at a specified rate of exchange.[28] Cheques drawn in the United Kingdom are rarely expressed in foreign currency, but where a cheque is drawn in foreign currency outside the United Kingdom, the amount is normally payable in sterling at the rate of exchange for banker's sight drafts at the place of payment on the day payment is made.[29] If the person receiving payment objects to the rate of exchange, the drawee will normally arrange for the payment to be made in foreign currency and will debit the drawer's sterling account accordingly.

The old rule that the English courts cannot give judgment for a sum of money expressed in a foreign currency no longer applies. The House of Lords has ruled[30] that an English court is entitled to give judgment for a sum of money expressed in a foreign currency in the case of obligations of a money character to pay foreign currency under a contract. That judgment was limited to cases where the proper law is that of a foreign country, and when the money of account is of that country, or possibly some other foreign country, but deliberately left the position open in other cases. The principle has now been extended to cases where the proper law is English law,[31] and in *Barclays Bank International* v. *Levin Brothers (Bradford)*[32] the courts considered s. 72(4) of the Act for the first time since the *Miliangos* case. It was held that that sub-section applied only where the acceptor of a bill paid on the date the bill matured, and chose to pay in sterling; if the bill was dishonoured the holder could sue for the amount due, and recover judgment, in the currency expressed in the bill. It is submitted that the same would apply to a dishonoured cheque.

To limit the effect of a fraudulent alteration to a cheque, the drawer will sometimes mark a cheque with words such as "Under one hundred pounds" or "Not exceeding one hundred pounds". The banker should not pay a cheque for an amount greater than the limit so prescribed, but should return the cheque for confirmation by the drawer or he might incur liability.[33]

28. Bills of Exchange Act 1882, s. 9(1).
29. *See* ibid., s. 72(4). The practice continues despite the repeal of this provision by the Administration of Justice Act 1977, s. 4.
30. *Miliangos* v. *Frank (Textiles)* [1976] A.C. 443.
31. *See*, for example, *Services Europe Atlantique Sud* v. *Stockholms Rederiaktiebolag, The Folias* [1979] 1 All E.R. 421, where it was held in the House of Lords that "the plaintiff should be compensated for the expense or loss in the currency which most truly expresses his loss"; one must find which currency appropriately or justly reflects the recoverable loss.
32. [1977] Q.B. 270. For the repeal of s. 72(4), *see* footnote 29 above.
33. *Q.B.P.*, No. 419.

PAYMENT ON DEMAND

A cheque must be payable on demand. It is not necessary for the cheque to include the words "on demand". Words such as "at sight" or "on presentation" will do equally well and a cheque will be deemed payable on demand if (as is the case with most printed cheque forms) no time for payment is expressed.[34] A banker's duty to honour his customer's cheques on demand does not oblige him to honour his customer's cheques at any time of day or night, but only during banking hours or within a reasonable time thereafter.[35]

ORDER CHEQUES AND BEARER CHEQUES

A cheque must be drawn to or to the order of a specified person or to bearer. A cheque drawn to or to the order of a specified person ("the payee"), using words such as "Pay John Smith or order" is known as an order cheque. A cheque drawn in favour of the person for the time being in possession of the cheque using words such as "Pay bearer", is known as a bearer cheque.

An order cheque may be drawn in favour of any person, including the drawer or the drawee,[36] and may be drawn in favour of one payee or any number of payees or to the holder of an office for the time being.[37] If an order cheque is drawn in favour of a number of payees, the drawer may provide for payment to be made to any of the payees or to some of the payees or to all the payees jointly.[37] Whether there is one payee or a number of payees, the payee of an order cheque must be "named or indicated ... with reasonable certainty".[38] Otherwise, the drawee should obtain the confirmation of the drawer before honouring the cheque. The drawee banker does not, however, have to return a cheque for confirmation merely because the name of the payee was misspelt by the drawer.

If a cheque is drawn in favour of a "fictitious or non-existing" person, the cheque may be treated as a bearer cheque.[39] "Fictitious" does not mean the same as "non-existent", though clearly where the cheque is drawn in favour of a person who does not exist, the payee will be a fictitious person.[40] In *Bank of England* v. *Vagliano Bros.*,[41] a trader's clerk who dealt with foreign correspondents forged

34. Bills of Exchange Act 1882, s. 10(1).
35. *See* Chapter Four.
36. Bills of Exchange Act 1882, s. 5(1).
37. Ibid., s. 7(2).
38. Ibid., s. 7(1).
39. Ibid., s. 7(3).
40. *Clutton* v. *Attenborough* [1897] A.C. 90.
41. [1891] A.C. 107.

the signature of a foreign correspondent as the drawer of a number of bills drawn in favour of another firm in whose favour that correspondent had drawn genuine bills. Other documents from the correspondent were also forged. When the trader claimed back from the Bank of England the amount of the bills, which had been paid and debited to his account, the Bank pleaded that the bills were payable to fictitious persons, and were therefore payable to bearer, and they were upheld by the House of Lords.

I think the proper meaning of the word is "feigned" or "counterfeit". It seems to me that the C. Petridi & Co named as payees on these pretended bills were, strictly speaking, fictitious persons. When the bills came before Vagliano for acceptance they were fictitious from beginning to end. The drawer was fictitious, the payee was fictitious, the person indicated as agent for presentation was fictitious. One and all they were feigned or counterfeit persons put forward as real persons, each in a several and distinct capacity; whereas, in truth, they were make-believes for the persons whose names appeared on the instrument. They were not, I think, the less fictitious because there were in existence real persons for whom these names were intended to pass muster.

The importance of this case has been somewhat diminished by two later cases, where traders were fraudulently induced by their clerks to draw cheques in favour of existing persons, whose indorsements were then forged. In such cases it was held that the payee was an existing person, and the drawer, although misled by the fraud, did intend the payee to receive the money, whereas in *Vagliano*'s case the drawer did not intend the payee to receive the proceeds of the bill.[42]

If, on the other hand, a cheque is not drawn in favour of a person at all, it is neither an order cheque nor a bearer cheque. It is simply not a cheque. If such an order is presented to a banker for payment, he should return it marked "Payee's name omitted". An obvious example of such an order is "Pay five pounds or order" because five pounds is not a person. In some cases, however, the position is less clear. It has been held, for example, that "Pay to ... order" means "Pay to my order" and can be treated as a cheque,[43] whereas "Pay ... or order" is not a cheque because it does not indicate the payee with reasonable certainty; it must therefore be returned marked "Payee's name omitted".[44]

Strictly speaking "Pay cash or order" is analogous to "Pay five pounds or order" and is therefore not a cheque so not payable to

42. *Vinden* v. *Hughes* [1905] 1 K.B. 795; *North & South Wales Bank* v. *Macbeth* [1908] A.C. 137.
43. *Chamberlain* v. *Young & Tower* [1893] 2 Q.B. 206.
44. *Q.B.P.*, No. 482.

bearer, though for some purposes the practical effect is the same as if it were.[45] The *Journal of the Institute of Bankers* has given the following advice on how to deal with such documents.[46]

The following rules may, perhaps, be taken as a guide in dealing with an instrument drawn "Pay cash or order" (which is assumed to be otherwise in order):

(a) if uncrossed it may safely be paid over the counter only to the drawer or his known agent and whether indorsed or not (the indorsement of the drawer does not make the instrument transferable);

(b) if crossed and bearing no sign of having been transferred, it may be paid through the clearing or over the counter to another bank without question, whether indorsed by the drawer or not;

(c) it should not be collected, if uncrossed, except for a responsible customer, who, anyhow, should be asked to cross it.

ISSUE OF A CHEQUE

A cheque is said to be "issued" (or to "enter into circulation") at the time of its first delivery, complete in form, to a person who takes it as a holder.[47] Thus, there are two conditions which have to be fulfilled before a cheque is issued: the cheque must be complete in form and, when complete in form, it must be delivered to a holder. Until a cheque has been issued, or the drawer is precluded from denying its issue, no one can be liable on it.

There is no definition in the Act of when a cheque is complete in form. For guidance in this, one must look at the cases on alterations[48] and on "holder in due course".[49] It must not be wanting in any material particular (or, in the case of a bill of exchange, have a blank acceptance). All the items constituting the formal definition of a cheque must be presented, and it must be dated (though it may be post-dated).

A cheque is duly issued even though the drawer was induced by fraud to issue it. Suppose, however, the drawer writes out a cheque which he leaves lying about, and it is stolen and negotiated to a holder for value. Can the latter, if it is a bearer cheque and there is, therefore, no question of a forged indorsement, enforce or retain payment? If a cheque has come into the hands of a holder in due

45. *North and South Insurance Corporation* v. *National Provincial Bank* [1936] 1 K.B. 328; [1935] All E.R. Rep. 640; *Cole* v. *Milsome* [1951] 1 All E.R. 311; *Orbit Mining & Trading Co.* v. *Westminster Bank* [1963] 1 Q.B. 794; [1962] 3 All E.R. 565.
46. (1951) 72 J.I.B. 200. *See also Q.B.P.*, No. 344.
47. Bills of Exchange Act 1882, s. 2.
48. *See* Chapter Eight.
49. *See* below in this chapter for definition of "holder in due course".

course a valid delivery of the cheque by all parties prior to him, so as to make them liable to him, is conclusively presumed.[50] Clearly therefore a holder in due course could enforce payment against the drawer.

Once a cheque is complete in form, it will be issued at the time of its first delivery to a person who takes it as a holder. In the language of the Bills of Exchange Act 1882, "delivery" is a very general term, meaning "transfer of possessions, actual or constructive from one person to another".[51] Any transfer of possession of a cheque is a delivery even if the transferee stole the cheque or found it lying in the gutter.

In determining whether a cheque has been issued (which in turn will determine whether anyone can be liable on the cheque), it is therefore not enough to establish that a delivery has taken place. What matters is whether the delivery was or was not to a "holder". If the cheque is a bearer cheque, no problem arises. The person in possession of a bearer cheque is always the "holder" of the cheque.[51] Thus, where a bearer cheque is concerned, every delivery and every transfer of possession is to a holder. For this reason, a person who draws or takes a bearer cheque should take great care lest it be stolen or mislaid for as soon as a bearer cheque falls, complete in form, into the possession of a person other than the drawer, there is delivery to a holder and the cheque has been issued.

If, on the other hand, the cheque is an order cheque, the person in possession of the cheque is not necessarily a holder. The payee of an order cheque is the holder of it, for as long as he is in possession of it. If the payee transfers the cheque by "indorsement" and delivery to another person (the indorsee), the indorsee becomes the holder of the cheque for as long as he is in possession of it. If the indorsee in turn transfers the cheque to a subsequent indorsee by indorsement and delivery, the subsequent indorsee becomes the holder of the cheque for as long as he is in possession. Each time that cheque is indorsed and delivered by an indorsee to a subsequent indorsee, the latter will be the holder for as long as he is in possession. Since by definition only a payee or indorsee in possession can be the holder of an order cheque,[51] if an order cheque falls into the possession of someone else, that person will not become a holder.

An understanding of the words "delivery" and "holder" is central to any understanding of the law relating to cheques. In particular, it must be understood that the person currently in possession of a bearer cheque is always the holder of the cheque, whereas a person

50. Bills of Exchange Act 1882, s. 31(2).
51. Ibid., s. 2.

cannot be the holder of an order cheque unless he is the payee or an indorsee and is currently in possession.

The holder of a cheque has certain rights acquired by negotiation. He may sue on the cheque in his own name.[52] Where he is a holder in due course, he holds the cheque free from any defect of title of prior parties, as well as from mere personal defences available to prior parties among themselves, and may enforce payment against all parties liable on the cheque.[53]

Where his title is defective (a) if he negotiates the cheque to a holder in due course that holder obtains a good and complete title to the cheque, and (b) if he obtains payment of the cheque the person who pays him in due course gets a valid discharge for the cheque.[54]

DATE

A cheque is not invalid by reason that it is not dated.[55] Where a cheque is dated, it can be ante-dated, post-dated or dated on a Sunday.[56] An ante-dated cheque is one that bears a date before the date of issue; a post-dated cheque is one dated later than the date of issue.

Where a cheque is wanting in any material particular (which would include a date) the person in possession of it has a prima facie authority to fill up the omission in any way he thinks fit.[57] This prima facie authority must be exercised within a reasonable time. Where an undated cheque was given to the payee in August 1931 and dated 20th February 1933 by him in February 1933, and the cheque was dishonoured, the payee failed in an action on the cheque. It was held that while the payee had authority to fill in the date, such authority would expire after a reasonable time had elapsed and in this case the judge held that "a reasonable time had long since elapsed."[58]

If the cheque had been negotiated to a third party the position might have been different, since if an incomplete instrument is negotiated to a holder in due course after being completed it is valid and effectual for all purposes in his hands, and he may enforce it as if it had been filled up within a reasonable time.[59]

A cheque dated on a Saturday or a Sunday should not be paid

52. Bills of Exchange Act 1882, s. 38(1).
53. Ibid., s. 38(2).
54. Ibid., s. 38(3).
55. Ibid., s. 3(4).
56. Ibid., s. 13(2).
57. Ibid., s. 20(1).
58. *Griffiths* v. *Dalton* [1940] 2 K.B. 264.
59. Bills of Exchange Act 1882, s. 20(2).

until the following business day. If presented for payment on the Friday previous it should be returned marked "Post-dated". A cheque which bears a date not in the calendar, e.g. 31st November, should be paid on or after 30th November.[60] Although a cheque can be post-dated, it must be payable on demand.

A post-dated cheque is an exceptional instrument, though, as stated above, a cheque so dated is valid. Its negotiability is not impaired because it is post-dated. For example, A gives B a post-dated cheque, and B before the due date gives it to C in payment of a debt. C takes the cheque without notice of any dispute between A and B. A stops payment because B has not fulfilled his contract. Nevertheless, C acquires a good title to the cheque, and when the due date arrives, can sue A for the amount of the cheque.

A banker will lose his statutory protection if he pays a post-dated cheque before it is due for payment, and must bear any loss that arises out of his action. For example, if a person found a post-dated cheque, and was able to get it cashed by the drawee banker before the date written on the cheque, the banker would be liable to the drawer for the amount. Moreover, if a banker pays a post-dated cheque and dishonours other cheques which would otherwise have been paid, he will be liable to his customer for damage to the customer's credit. If he holds such a cheque pending the arrival of the due date, the customer may fail in the meantime. The banker cannot debit his customer's account with a post-dated cheque on arrival of its due date if the customer stops payment of it before such date. The view has been expressed that "a banker who pays a post-dated cheque before the ostensible date stands a very poor chance of being able to debit his customer with it in any conceivable circumstances if the customer chooses to object to be so debited."[61] In such a case the banker has disobeyed his customer's mandate and authority.

BLANK CHEQUES

If a person signs a printed cheque form (or anything else) with the intention that it should be "converted" into a cheque, but leaves out any "material particular" of a cheque (e.g. the amount or the name of the payee), the instrument is known as a blank cheque or, in the language of the Bills of Exchange Act 1882, any person in possession of a blank cheque has "a prima facie authority to fill up the omission in any way he thinks fit".

60. *Q.B.P.*, No. 403.
61. Sir John Paget in the Gilbart Lectures, 1917.

The person in possession must fill up the omission within a "reasonable time" and strictly in accordance with the authority given him or he will lose the right to enforce the cheque.[62] Nevertheless, the cheque might still be enforceable by a subsequent holder in due course.[63] Because a blank cheque can be filled in by the person in possession as he thinks fit, blank cheques should only be drawn in exceptional circumstances. Where the drawer does not fill in the amount of the cheque, he should write a maximum amount at the top of the cheque or along the crossing in order to protect himself.

NEGOTIATION OF A CHEQUE

A cheque is a negotiable instrument. The principal characteristics of a negotiable instrument are as follows.

(a) It can be transferred from one holder to another without either the old holder or the new holder having to give notice to the drawer or to anyone else who is liable on it.

(b) The transferee may sue in his own name any person who is liable on the instrument.[64]

(c) A holder in due course, or his equivalent for other sorts of instrument, can obtain a better title to the instrument than a previous holder if the previous holder's title was defective, and will take free of any "equities" which could have been pleaded against a previous holder.[65] This is one of the exceptions to the general rule *nemo dat quod non habet* (equivalent to: nobody can confer a better title than he has himself) and is the most important characteristic of a negotiable instrument.

A cheque is negotiated when it is transferred from one person to another in such a manner as to constitute the transferee the holder of the cheque.[66] As we have already seen, a bearer cheque can be negotiated by simple delivery (i.e. every transfer of possession of a bearer cheque constitutes the transferee the holder of the cheque).[67] An order cheque is negotiated by "the indorsement of the holder completed by delivery".[68] If the holder of an order cheque transfers the cheque for value without indorsing it, the transferee nevertheless acquires all the rights of the transferor, together with the right to have the transferor indorse the cheque.[69]

62. Bills of Exchange Act 1882, s. 20(2).
63. Ibid., s. 20(2) proviso. *See* Chapter Eight.
64. Bills of Exchange Act 1882, s. 38(1).
65. For holder in due course, *see* below in this chapter.
66. Bills of Exchange Act 1882, s. 31(1).
67. Ibid., s. 31(2).
68. Ibid., s. 31(3).
69. Ibid., s. 31(4).

All cheques are negotiable unless they have become overdue or have been marked in a way which indicates that they are not transferable. An order cheque is negotiable even if the words ". . . or order", which appear on most printed cheque forms, are omitted. A cheque is marked in a way which indicates that it is not transferable when it has been marked with words such as "Not transferable" by the drawer or when it has been restrictively indorsed.[70]

A cheque which is marked "Not transferable" should be distinguished from a cheque which has been crossed "Not negotiable".[71] A cheque marked "Not transferable", or one which has been restrictively indorsed, cannot be transferred at all in such a manner as to constitute the transferee a holder of the cheque. A cheque crossed "Not negotiable" or one which has become overdue can still be transferred but cannot be transferred as a negotiable instrument. The transferee of such a cheque, therefore, takes it subject to equities, i.e. he cannot "acquire or give a better title than that which the person from whom he took it had".[72] Thus any defect in title is perpetuated.

A cheque is overdue, or, as it is called, "stale", when it appears on the face of it to have been in circulation for an unreasonable length of time.[73] But what is "an unreasonable time" has never been legally defined. Paget considers that "in the absence of special circumstances", a cheque would probably be deemed stale, so far as its negotiability was concerned, if it had been issued "ten days or so" before negotiation.[74] The question is one of fact, and each case depends upon its circumstances.

It is necessary to distinguish between cheques deemed "out of date" in law for purposes of negotiation and those termed "out of date" by bankers' custom. As regards the latter, most bankers return cheques presented six or more months after date, marked "Out of date", and require the drawer's confirmation before payment.[75] Some banks fix the limit at twelve months.

This practice does not affect the drawer's liability to the holder of the cheque, which remains alive until barred by the Limitation Act 1980. This means that the holder can sue the drawer at any time within six years of the date of the cheque or the date of its issue (whichever is the later) unless the drawer has suffered actual damage through the delay in presentment, or unless the person in possession

70. Bills of Exchange Act 1882, s. 35(1). Examples would be "Pay D only" or "Pay D for the account of X". *See* below under "Valid indorsements".
71. For crossings on cheques, *see* Chapter Eight.
72. Bills of Exchange Act 1882, s. 36(2).
73. Ibid., s. 36(3).
74. Paget (8th Edn.), p. 303.
75. *Q.B.P.*, No. 407.

of the cheque, negotiated when overdue, is unable to acquire a title owing to a defect in the title of the person for whom he negotiated it. For example, if, between the date of issue and the latest date deemed reasonable for presentment, the banker failed, and the drawer lost the money standing to his credit, it is obvious that he would lose more than he would have done if the holder had presented the cheque promptly. Hence, if the drawer had a sufficient balance to meet the cheque, he is discharged to the extent of his loss, but no further.[76]

DEFECTS OF TITLE

A holder of a cheque has a defective title if he obtains it "by fraud, duress, force or fear, or other unlawful means, or for an illegal consideration, or when he negotiates it in breach of faith or under such circumstances as amount to a fraud".[77] A title which is defective is liable to be overturned by a person entitled to avoid the contract, whether the contract be the drawing and issue or the negotiation of the cheque. Thus, if X draws a cheque in favour of Y and Y indorses it to Z under duress, the title of Z is defective and liable to be overturned in favour of the claims of Y, who can avoid the contract of the negotiation to Z. Any holder who takes a cheque subsequent to a holder with a defective title will take subject to the same defect unless the subsequent holder is a "holder in due course", in which case he will have a good title to the cheque.[78] This is what is meant by saying that a holder in due course of a cheque can obtain a better title than a previous holder, and is one of the main characteristics of a negotiable instrument.

HOLDER IN DUE COURSE

A holder is a holder in due course if he satisfies the following conditions at the time that he takes the cheque.[79]

(a) The cheque must be "complete and regular on the face of it". This means, *inter alia*, that the cheque must have been complete in form and that it should not be wanting in any material particulars. Any indorsements must have been regular indorsements,

---

76. Bills of Exchange Act 1882, s. 74(1) and (2).
77. Ibid., s. 29(2).
78. Unless it was overdue, or marked not negotiable or not transferable—*see* above.
79. Bills of Exchange Act 1882, s. 29(1).

and it should not have been torn and pasted together, at least if the tear appears to show an intention to cancel it.[80]

(b) The cheque must not be overdue.[81]

(c) He must not be aware that the cheque has previously been presented for payment and dishonoured if that was, in fact, the case.

(d) He must take the cheque in good faith. This means that he must act honestly, even though he may be acting negligently.[82]

(e) He must not be aware of any defect of title in the person who negotiated the cheque to him.

(f) He must take the cheque for value. The meaning of value for a cheque is discussed in the next section.

If a holder satisfies these six conditions, he is a holder in due course and any subsequent holder (even if he could not satisfy these six conditions) has all the rights of that holder in due course against all parties prior to the holder in due course unless he himself is a party to any fraud or illegality affecting the cheque.[83] There is a prima facie presumption that every holder of a cheque is a holder in due course unless it is proved that the issue or negotiation of the cheque was affected by fraud, duress, force or illegality, in which case every holder is presumed not to be a holder in due course unless it can be shown that, subsequent to the alleged fraud or illegality, value was in good faith given for the cheque.[84]

In *Jones* v. *Waring & Gillow*[85] it was decided by the House of Lords that the original payee of a bill or cheque is not a "holder in due course". Before a person can be a holder in due course, the bill or cheque must have been negotiated to him; the original delivery of the instrument is not such a negotiation. The original payee or subsequent holder in due course is the "true owner".

In *Arab Bank* v. *Ross*[86] the Court of Appeal held that a promissory note (and semble also a bill of exchange or cheque) is not "complete and regular on the face of it" unless the indorsement purports to be the indorsement of the payee or indorsee. In that case, promissory notes payable to A & BC Co. bore indorsements in the form "A & BC". It was held that the indorsements were irregular. In his judgment, Denning LJ distinguished regularity from both validity and liability.

80. *Ingham* v. *Primrose* (1859) 7 C.B.N.S. 82; *see also* under "Cancellation and mutilation of a cheque" in Chapter Eight.
81. *See* above for definition of "overdue".
82. Bills of Exchange Act 1882, s. 90.
83. Ibid., s. 29(3).
84. Ibid., s. 30(2).
85. [1926] A.C. 670, [1926] All E.R. Rep. 36.
86. [1952] 2 Q.B. 216; [1952] 1 All E.R. 709.

VALUE FOR A CHEQUE

In the normal law of contract, a party can only enforce a contract if he himself has given "valuable consideration" or, in other words, if he has performed some act, undertaken some liability or given some promise as his part of the bargain.[87] He cannot enforce a contract in reliance on consideration given by someone else, and he cannot enforce a contract in reliance on "past consideration" (i.e. an act performed or a promise given prior to and unrelated to the contract which he now seeks to enforce).

Section 27 of the Bills of Exchange Act 1882 provides, however, that past consideration ("an antecedent debt or liability") does constitute valuable consideration for the purpose of enforcing a cheque and any holder will be deemed to have given value provided that valuable consideration had been given by any previous holder. Section 27 also provides that a holder who has a lien over a cheque (as a banker often does) is deemed to have given value for the cheque to the extent of the sum for which he has a lien.

VALID INDORSEMENTS

The first condition for a valid indorsement is that it must be written on the cheque itself and signed by the indorser.[88] The simple signature of the indorser on the cheque, without additional words, is sufficient.[88] Despite the original meaning of the word "indorsement",[89] an indorsement does not have to be written on the back of the cheque, but may be written anywhere on the cheque. An indorsement is deemed to be written on the cheque itself if it is written on an "allonge", a strip of paper attached to the cheque or on a "copy" of a cheque issued or negotiated in a country where copies are recognised.[90] If there are joint holders of a cheque and they are not partners, all the joint holders must indorse the cheque unless those who so indorse have authority to indorse on behalf of the others.[91]

The second condition for a valid indorsement is that it must be an indorsement of the entire cheque.[92] A partial indorsement, that is to say, an indorsement which purports to transfer to the indorsee a part only of the amount payable, or which purports to transfer

---

87. For a discussion of consideration, *see* Cheshire & Fifoot, *The Law of Contract* (10th Edn.).
88. Bills of Exchange Act 1882, s. 32(1).
89. From the Latin *in*, meaning "on", and *dorsum*, meaning "back".
90. Bills of Exchange Act 1882, s. 32(1).
91. Ibid., s. 32(3).
92. Ibid., s. 32(2).

the cheque to two or more indorsees severally, does not operate as a negotiation of the cheque.[92]

If the indorser indorses the cheque with his signature alone without naming or indicating the indorsee, the indorsement is known as an "indorsement in blank".[93] If, on the other hand, the indorser does name or indicate the indorsee, the indorsement is known as a "special indorsement".[94] A bearer cheque which has been specially indorsed is automatically converted into an order cheque, while an order cheque which has been indorsed in blank is automatically converted into a bearer cheque.[95]

If an indorsement prohibits the further negotiation of a cheque—or expresses that it is a mere authority to deal with the cheque as the indorsement directs and not a transfer of ownership of the cheque —it is known as a "restrictive indorsement".[96] A cheque would, for example, be indorsed restrictively if the indorser wrote "Pay X only" or "Pay X for the account of Y" or "Pay X or order for collection". If a restrictive indorsement does authorise future transfers, any subsequent indorsee must take the cheque subject to the restrictions imposed on the first indorsee under the restrictive indorsement.[96]

If an indorser indorses a cheque conditionally in favour of the indorsee, the indorsement is known as a "conditional indorsement".[97] The condition may be disregarded by the drawee (or whoever else pays the cheque) and the amount of the cheque may validly be paid to the indorsee even if the condition has not yet been fulfilled;[98] until the condition is fulfilled, however, the indorsee will hold the money as trustee for the indorser. If the indorsee himself negotiates the cheque before the condition is fulfilled, the new indorsee will hold the cheque subject to the condition.

REGULAR INDORSEMENTS

Whether an indorsement is valid, and genuine, is a question which it is often impossible for a banker to decide. The indorsers will frequently be parties unknown to him. He is, therefore, not in general

---

93. Ibid., s. 34(1).
94. Ibid., s. 34(2).
95. Ibid., ss. 8(3), 34(1) and 34(4). But where a cheque which has been indorsed in blank is specially indorsed by the holder, the holder does not thereby become liable as an indorser, *Vincent* v. *Horlock* (1808) 1 Camp. 442; 170 E.R. 1015.
96. Bills of Exchange Act 1882, s. 35.
97. An example would be "Pay to the order of X on arrival of the S.S. Swallow at Liverpool".
98. Bills of Exchange Act 1882, s. 33.

required to see that an indorsement is valid; that is a matter for the parties to the instrument. He can, however, tell whether an indorsement is regular. The meaning of this term was explained by Denning LJ in *Arab Bank* v. *Ross*.[99] An indorsement is irregular whenever it is such as to give rise to doubt whether it is the indorsement of the named payee. The question of when an indorsement is such as to give rise to doubt is one which can better be answered by a banker than by a lawyer, since bankers have to consider the regularity of indorsements many times every day, whereas the question rarely comes before the courts. The answer is to be found by following the custom of bankers in the City of London. They have for over 150 years insisted on strict conformity, in their own interests and in those of their customers, as some safeguard against dishonesty, and were doing so before the enactment of any provisions corresponding to ss. 60, 79, 80 and 82 of the 1882 Act.

Since the passing of the Cheques Act 1957, the rules have diminished in importance because bankers who pay and collect cheques for their customers can no longer incur liability by reason only of an absence of, or irregularity in, indorsements on a cheque.[100] Nevertheless, the rules still apply to bills of exchange and certain other instruments and should therefore be studied carefully. The rules are also of importance in determining whether the holder of a cheque is a holder in due course, for, as we have seen, a holder cannot be a holder in due course unless he took the cheque "complete and *regular* on the face of it".[101]

99. [1952] 2 Q.B. 216.
100. Cheques Act 1957, ss. 1(1) and 4(3).
101. Bills of Exchange Act 1882, s. 29(1).

CHAPTER EIGHT

Presentation and Payment of Cheques

LIABILITY ON A CHEQUE

The rules which govern liability on a cheque are as follows.

(*a*) A person cannot be liable on a cheque until it has been issued and until some holder has given value for it.[1] A person can only be liable on the cheque if he has signed the cheque as a drawer or an indorser.[2] A person signing as a drawer or indorser does not have to sign in his own name and an agent may sign on his behalf.[3] An agent who signs a cheque as a drawer or indorser will not be personally liable on the cheque provided that he is acting within the actual limits of his authority and provided that he adds words to his signature indicating that he signs for and on behalf of a principal or in a representative character; the mere addition, however, to his signature of words describing him as an agent or as filling a representative character does not exempt him from personal liability.[4] But if any person signs a cheque (or bill of exchange, promissory note or indorsement) on behalf of a company, or authorises it to be so signed, and the correct name of the company is not stated on the instrument, he is personally liable to the holder of the instrument unless it is paid by the company (as well as being liable to a fine).[5]

A person may sign a cheque in a trade name or an assumed name, but will be liable on the cheque as if he had signed it in his own name.[6] The signature of the name of a firm is equivalent to the signature by the person so signing of the names of all persons liable as partners in that firm.[7] A corporation can incur liability on a cheque by sealing the cheque with its corporate seal or by adding

1. *See* Chapter Seven.
2. Bills of Exchange Act 1882, s. 23.
3. Ibid., s. 91(1).
4. Ibid., s. 26(1).
5. Companies Act 1948, s. 108(4). *See also* Companies Act 1980, ss. 80 and 87(1) and Sched. 2.
6. Bills of Exchange Act 1882, s. 23(1).
7. Ibid., s. 23(2).

its name to the cheque in any other way permitted by its articles or rules.[8]

(b) The drawer of a cheque engages that, on due presentment, the cheque will be paid "according to its tenor" (i.e. in accordance with the instructions as to amount, date, etc., drawn on the cheque).[9] If the cheque is dishonoured, the drawer engages that he will compensate the holder or any indorser who is compelled to pay it provided that the requisite proceedings on dishonour are duly taken.[10] The drawer is precluded from denying to a holder in due course the existence of the payee and his then capacity to indorse.[9]

(c) An indorser of a cheque engages that on due presentment it will be paid according to its tenor.[11] If it is dishonoured, he engages to compensate the holder or a subsequent indorser who is compelled to pay it provided that the requisite proceedings on dishonour are duly taken. An indorser is precluded from denying to a holder in due course the genuineness and regularity in all respects of the drawer's signature and all previous indorsements. An indorser is also precluded from denying to his immediate or a subsequent indorsee that the cheque was at the time of his indorsement a valid and subsisting cheque and that he had then a good title to it.[11]

(d) Any person who signs a cheque as a drawer or indorser without requiring value and for the purpose of lending his name to some other person is liable on the cheque to any holder for value.[12] Such a person is known as an "accommodation party". Any person who signs a cheque except as a drawer incurs the liabilities of an indorser to a holder in due course even if the person so signing was never himself a holder of the cheque.[13]

(e) Because a person cannot be liable on a cheque unless he has signed it, the drawee of a cheque, unlike the drawee of a bill, cannot be liable on the cheque unless he has signed it *qua* indorser in which case he will be liable *qua* indorser. The drawee of a cheque must always be a banker, by definition. He might be bound to pay the cheque by virtue of the banker's duty to pay his customer's cheques,[14] but if he is liable in this way, the duty will be owed not to the holder but to his customer, the drawer. It also follows that a holder of a bearer cheque who transfers a cheque to a subsequent holder by simple delivery would not normally be liable as an indorser,

8. Bills of Exchange Act 1882, s. 91(2).
9. Ibid., s. 55(1).
10. The drawer of a cheque will rarely be in a position to object if notice of dishonour is not given; *see* below in this chapter.
11. Ibid., s. 55(2).
12. Ibid., s. 28.
13. Ibid., s. 56.
14. *See* Chapter Four.

but if he signed the cheque he would be liable as an indorser. The holder of a bearer cheque who transfers a cheque without signing it is known as a "transferor by delivery".[15] Although a transferor by delivery is not liable as an indorser, he nevertheless warrants to his immediate transferee that the cheque is what it purports to be, that he has a right to transfer it and that at the time of the transfer he is not aware of any fact which renders it valueless. This warranty is, however, only implied if the immediate transferee is a holder for value.[15]

(*f*) The drawer of a cheque is primarily liable on the cheque. Where there are two or more indorsements on a cheque, each indorsement is deemed to have been made in the order in which it appears on the cheque until the contrary is proved.[16] This rule may best be illustrated by reference to bills of exchange. Suppose, for example, that a third party indorses a bill which has been drawn to the order of the drawer, and accepted, with the intention of making himself liable if the acceptor does not pay. If the drawer indorses it to complete it, and to make it enforceable against the third party, but his signature is placed below that of the third party, the drawer will nevertheless be able to recover from the third party if his signature was placed below the third party's through inadvertence which does not nullify the intentions or rights of the parties.[17]

(*g*) Any indorser of a cheque may, when signing his name, add an express stipulation which negatives or limits his liability to the holder of the cheque.[18] The drawer or any indorser may also waive all or any of the holder's duties, at least as regards himself;[19] the principal duties of the holder are concerned with due payment and proceedings on dishonour, both of which topics are discussed later in this chapter. A person who is under an obligation to indorse a cheque in a representative capacity may indorse the cheque in such terms as to negative personal liability.[20]

(*h*) A person who draws or indorses a cheque while under an incapacity is not liable on the cheque, though in the case of a minor or a corporation which has no capacity to incur liability on a cheque, the cheque may nevertheless be enforced against any person not

15. Bills of Exchange Act 1882, s. 58.
16. Ibid., s. 32(5).
17. *See National Sales Corporation* v. *Bernardi* [1931] 2 K.B. 188; *Yeoman Credit* v. *Gregory* [1963] 1 All E.R. 245.
18. Bills of Exchange Act 1882, s. 16(1). This applies also to the drawer of a bill of exchange, but not to the drawer of a cheque, who is the person primarily liable on it. *See* under "Indorsement sans recours" in Chapter Nine.
19. Bills of Exchange Act 1882, s. 16(2).
20. Ibid., s. 31(5).

under an incapacity who has signed the cheque, and if the cheque is actually paid, the holder may retain the money paid.[21]

(*i*) A forged or unauthorised signature on a cheque is wholly inoperative.[22] This means that any person in possession of the cheque after the forged or unauthorised signature cannot enforce or retain the cheque. The cheque remains the property of the person who was the holder of the cheque at the time that the forged or unauthorised signature was added to the cheque. An unauthorised (but not a forged) signature will, however, be operative if it is later ratified by the party on whose behalf it was made; a forged signature cannot be ratified. A forged or unauthorised signature will also be operative if the party against whom it is sought to retain or enforce the cheque is precluded from setting up the forgery or want of authority.[23]

(*j*) A person who is liable on a cheque as a drawer or indorser may be discharged from liability in the following circumstances: if the cheque is materially altered; if the cheque is cancelled; if there is delay in completing a blank cheque. An indorser may be discharged if the cheque is paid or if the cheque is dishonoured and the appropriate proceedings on dishonour are not taken. A person who is liable on a cheque is not, however, discharged from liability by reason only of the cheque being "stopped". Stopping a cheque (or "countermanding payment" of it) merely determines the banker's duty to pay the cheque.[24] These points will be discussed in the next few sections of this chapter.

MATERIAL ALTERATION OF A CHEQUE

Where a cheque has been "materially altered", any person who was liable before the alteration was made ceases to be liable unless he made, authorised or assented to the alteration. The cheque will, however, remain valid and may be enforced, as altered, against any holder who indorses it after the alteration is made.[25] If a material alteration is "not apparent", a holder in due course may enforce it as if it had not been altered, according to its original tenor.[25]

The Bills of Exchange Act 1882 specifies that the following alterations are material, namely any alteration of the date on the cheque or the amount of the cheque, and although cheques, unlike bills, rarely specify a place of payment, if a place of payment is specified,

21. Bills of Exchange Act 1882, s. 22.
22. Ibid., s. 24.
23. Ibid. *See Brown* v. *Westminster Bank* [1964] 2 Lloyd's Rep. 187, referred to in Chapter Four.
24. Bills of Exchange Act 1882, s. 75(1).
25. Ibid., s. 64(1).

any alteration is a material alteration.[26] Other alterations which have
been held to be material are the addition or alteration of a rate of
interest,[27] the insertion of a particular rate of exchange,[28] and, in the
case of bills of exchange, the alteration of the place of drawing if it
converts it from an inland to a foreign bill, but not if it remains an
inland bill.[29]

Whenever a material alteration is made, the full signature is
preferable to initials, for the reason that initials are easier to forge
than the full signature. Even in the latter case, however, careful
scrutiny is necessary, as a genuine signature will already be on the
cheque and may be copied.

If the banker pays a cheque which has been materially altered
without the drawer's consent, he does so at his own risk, for he
cannot, generally, debit his customer with money which he has paid
out without his customer's authority. But if the drawer by his own
act has facilitated or given opportunity for the material alteration
to be made, he may be precluded from asserting that the alteration
was made without his authority. This certainly applies where the
material alteration is one of amount.[30]

CANCELLATION AND MUTILATION OF A CHEQUE

If any holder of a cheque or his agent, acting within his authority,
intentionally cancels the cheque and the cancellation is apparent on
the face of the cheque, then the drawer and every other person who
is liable on the cheque is discharged from liability.[31] A cancellation
would be apparent if, for example, the cheque was torn in half
(except accidentally) or if the word "Cancelled" was written clearly
across the face of the cheque.

By cancelling one of the signatures on a cheque, a holder or his
agent may cancel the liability of the person whose signature is cancelled. The cancellation of the signature of one indorser does not
merely cancel the liability of that indorser. It also cancels the liability
of any subsequent indorsers,[32] but the drawer and any prior indorsers will remain liable.

A cancellation made unintentionally, or under a mistake, or

26. Ibid., s. 64(2).
27. *Warrington* v. *Early* (1853) 23 L.J.Q.B. 47; *Sutton* v. *Toomer* (1827) 7 B. & C.
416.
28. *Hirschfield* v. *Smith* (1866) L.R. 1 C.P. 34 D.
29. *Koch* v. *Dicks* [1933] 1 K.B. 307; contrast *Foster* v. *Driscoll* [1929] 1 K.B. 470.
30. *London Joint Stock Bank* v. *Macmillan and Arthur* [1918] A.C. 777; [1918–19]
All E.R. Rep. 30. *See* Chapter Four.
31. Bills of Exchange Act 1882, s. 63(1).
32. Ibid., s. 63(2).

without the authority of the holder, is inoperative.[33] Where, however, a cheque or any signature on the cheque appears to have been cancelled, the burden of proof lies with the party alleging that the cancellation is inoperative.[33]

If a drawer tears a cheque across in such a way that its condition affords sufficient evidence that he intended to cancel it and the banker pays it to a person who has pasted the pieces together and presented the cheque, the banker must suffer any loss that may be incurred by his paying it. If the payee accidentally tears it in two before presentation, he must get the drawer's confirmation, or the collecting banker's guarantee, before the drawee-banker will pay it. The general form is "Accidentally torn by us", followed by the banker's signature; it is the practice to pay such a cheque on the basis that among bankers such a confirmation is understood to imply an undertaking of indemnity.[34] If the drawer's confirmation or the collecting banker's guarantee is not obtainable, the cheque should be returned by the banker on whom it is drawn, marked "Mutilated cheque". A cheque torn, but not quite in two, would usually be paid, but the banker would be quite justified in returning it, marked as above, and in all cases of doubt this is the safer course to follow.[35]

EFFECTS OF DELAY

There are two circumstances in which the persons liable on a cheque might be discharged by delay. The first is when a blank cheque is not filled in by the person in possession within a reasonable time and strictly in accordance with the authority given.[36] Such an instrument could not be enforced by the person who fills it in, though it could still be enforced by a subsequent holder in due course.[37] For this purpose, "reasonable time" is a question of fact. In one case, the blank cheque was given to the payee in August 1931 and the cheque was completed in February 1933. It was held that "a reasonable time had long since elapsed."[38]

The second circumstance in which delay might affect liability is where there is delay in the presentation of a cheque for payment. If a cheque is not duly presented for payment within a reasonable time of an indorser signing the cheque, that indorser will be discharged. In determining what is a reasonable time, regard will be had to the usage of the trade with respect to similar cheques and

33. Bills of Exchange Act 1882, s. 63(3).
34. *Q.B.P.*, No. 432.
35. *Q.B.P.*, No. 431.
36. Bills of Exchange Act 1882, s. 20(2).
37. Ibid., proviso.
38. *Griffiths* v. *Dalton* [1940] 2 K.B. 264.

the facts of the particular case.[39] The drawer of a cheque will not, however, be discharged unless he suffers damage by the delay, in which case he will be discharged only to the extent of the damage suffered.[40] He will only suffer damage, and so be discharged, if the banker has become insolvent after a reasonable time for presenting the cheque, and if he had funds with the banker sufficient to meet the cheque at the time the banker became insolvent. The drawer is then discharged except to the extent of the dividends received.

Where a drawer or an indorser has expressly waived the holder's duties with regard to filling in a blank cheque or presenting a cheque, he will not be discharged by any delay in carrying out those duties.[41] Delay in making presentment for payment is excused when the delay is caused by circumstances beyond the control of the holder and not imputable to his default, misconduct or negligence; when the cause of delay ceases to operate, presentment must be made with reasonable diligence.[42]

DUE PRESENTMENT OF A CHEQUE

A cheque is duly presented if the following conditions are satisfied.

(a) The cheque must be presented within a reasonable time after its issue.[43]

(b) The cheque must be presented by the holder or by some person authorised to receive payment on his behalf.[44]

(c) The cheque must be presented at a reasonable hour on a business day.[44]

(d) The cheque must be presented at the place of business of the drawee (or other person authorised to pay on his behalf) unless some other place is stipulated on the cheque, in which case it must be presented there.[45] In the case of cheques, unlike bills of exchange, it will be very rare for the place to be anywhere other than the branch of the bank on which the cheque is drawn.

(e) Presentment for payment is dispensed with if, after the exercise of reasonable diligence, presentment cannot be effected. Presentment is not dispensed with merely because the holder has reason to believe that the bill would be dishonoured on presentment; but the drawer and, in some circumstances, an indorser cannot plead non-present-

---

39. Bills of Exchange Act 1882, s. 45(2).
40. Ibid., s. 74.
41. Ibid., s. 16(2).
42. Ibid., s. 46(1).
43. Ibid., s. 45(2).
44. Ibid., s. 45(3).
45. Ibid., ss. 45(3) and (4).

ment to avoid liability if he himself has no reason to believe that the bill would be paid if presented.[46]

In general presentment for payment is not necessary in order to charge the person primarily liable on the cheque (i.e. the drawer— in the case of a bill of exchange, the acceptor); but there is the practical problem that a cheque cannot be paid until it is presented for payment, and in any event presentment for payment is necessary in order to obtain a right of recourse against any indorser. Even as against the drawer, presentment is prudent, to fix the time from which interest is to be calculated, and the plaintiff risks being required to pay the costs if an action is commenced without presentment for payment.[47]

A banker who takes an unreasonable time in presenting a cheque paid in by his customer is liable to the customer for any loss which results from the delay.[48]

CROSSED CHEQUES

Today, most cheques are crossed cheques and will only be paid by the drawee ("the paying banker") if they are presented for payment by a banker ("the collecting banker") or by another banker, acting as an agent for the collecting banker ("an agent for collection"). If a crossed cheque is presented by the holder himself for payment "over the counter" the paying banker should refuse payment unless the drawer has given clear instructions to the contrary. A crossed cheque in favour of the drawer (e.g. a cheque drawn "Pay self" or, less acceptably, "Pay cash") may, however, safely be paid over the counter to the drawer or his known agent, provided the crossing is opened and the full signature of the drawer is appended to the opening of the crossing.[49]

A cheque is a crossed cheque if two transverse parallel lines are drawn on the cheque. The words "and company" or any abbreviation thereof, and the words "Not negotiable" may be added, but a cheque bearing the parallel lines is a crossed cheque whether or not either of these expressions is used. A cheque is also a crossed cheque if a banker is named in writing on the face of the cheque other than as drawer, drawee, payee or indorser of the cheque. In the first case, the crossing is a "general crossing", and the cheque can only be paid to a banker and cannot be paid over the counter.[50] In the second

46. Bills of Exchange Act 1882, s. 46(2).
47. *Macintosh* v. *Hayden* (1826) Ry. & M. 362.
48. *Hare* v. *Henty* (1861) 30 L.J.C.P. 302.
49. *See* under "Order cheques and bearer cheques" in Chapter Seven.
50. Bills of Exchange Act 1882, s. 76(1).

case, the crossing is a "special crossing", and the cheque can only be paid to the banker named on the face of the cheque.[51]

Most printed cheque forms are crossed generally, with the two parallel lines situated slightly to the left of the box where the amount of the cheque in figures is to be filled in. They now usually run vertically, but formerly used to run diagonally. It is not necessary for the two parallel lines to be situated in this position. It would seem that they may be situated anywhere on the face of the cheque. It is preferable for them to be situated near the middle of the cheque and, judging from most printed cheque forms, the lines should be long enough to overlap the name of the payee, the amount in words and figures, and the drawer's signature. The lines do not have to be continuous; dotted lines are sufficient.

The addition of the words "Not negotiable" to a crossed cheque does not prevent the cheque being transferred; but a person who takes a cheque marked "Not negotiable" does not acquire and cannot give a better title to the cheque than the person from whom he takes the cheque.[52] Thus any defect in title will be perpetuated.

The words "Account payee" and variants such as "Payee's A/C", "Account A.B.", etc., are often added to the crossing of a cheque. Such expressions have no statutory significance, since they are not sanctioned by the Bills of Exchange Act 1882 or any other Act. If added, as they frequently are in practice, to order or bearer cheques, they do not in any way affect their negotiability.

When the paying banker has fulfilled his duty of paying the cheque in good faith and without negligence, his responsibility ceases, and he cannot be expected to follow the money after it has reached the collecting banker, and insist upon the collecting banker paying it into the proper account. The collecting banker, however, is in a different position. These words are in the nature of a direction to him, and if he places the money received to an account other than that of the specified payee, he stands to lose his statutory protection on the ground of negligence.[53] Thus bankers do not collect such cheques for third parties unless either the standing of the customers is undoubted or a satisfactory explanation is forthcoming.[54]

Another variant is "A/c payee only", sometimes strengthened by "Not transferable". If such a cheque is not accompanied by the transverse lines or the name of a banker, it is not a crossed cheque, but it is in so ambiguous and contradictory a form that if one were presented across the counter by a stranger, the paying banker would

51. Ibid., s. 76(2).
52. Ibid., s. 81. *See* Chapter Seven.
53. *See* below in this chapter.
54. *Q.B.P.*, No. 469.

be justified in refusing payment, and the best answer would be "Form of cheque irregular".[55]

Section 77 of the Bills of Exchange Act 1882 provides that where a cheque is uncrossed, any holder of the cheque may cross it generally or specially[56] and where a cheque has already been crossed, any holder may add the words "Not negotiable".[57] A holder may convert a general crossing into a special crossing, but not vice versa.[58] When a holder presents a cheque to his banker and asks him to collect payment of the cheque from the drawee, the holder's banker can cross the cheque specially to himself and once the cheque has been crossed specially to himself,[59] he can cross it specially to another banker as his agent for collection by writing the other banker's name on the cheque.[60]

A crossing authorised by the Bills of Exchange Act 1882 is a material part of the cheque; section 78 of the Act provides that it is not lawful for any person to add to or alter a crossing except as permitted by s. 77 and that in no circumstances may a crossing be obliterated.[61] Where the crossing has been materially altered—if, for instance, the words "Not negotiable" are ruled through and the deletion is not confirmed by the drawer—the banker on whom the cheque is drawn should refuse payment pending confirmation.[62] This means that once a crossing has been marked on a cheque, it is, strictly speaking, impossible to provide that the paying banker should pay the cheque directly to the holder instead of to the collecting banker. Nevertheless, bankers do sometimes permit their customers to obliterate the general crossing printed on their cheque forms so that they may pay money by cheque to payees who have no bank account.

If a banker does permit this dangerous practice, which is known as "opening a crossing", he should probably refuse to pay the cheque to anyone except the payee or his known agent and should take care to ensure that the payee is the "true owner" of the cheque. A banker who pays over the counter a crossed cheque which has been opened is deemed to have paid in contravention of the crossing; and a banker who pays a cheque in contravention of the crossing to a person other than the true owner is liable to the true owner for any loss that he suffers.[63]

55. *Q.B.P.*, No. 477.
56. Bills of Exchange Act 1882, s. 77(2).
57. Ibid., s. 77(4).
58. Ibid., s. 77(3).
59. Ibid., s. 77(6).
60. Ibid., s. 77(5).
61. Ibid., s. 78.
62. *Q.B.P.*, No. 429.
63. Bills of Exchange Act 1882, s. 79(2).

Duties of paying banker as to crossed cheques

Section 79 sets forth the duties of the paying banker as follows. Where a cheque is crossed specially to more than one banker, except when crossed to an agent for collection being a banker, the banker on whom it is drawn must refuse payment thereof.[64] Where there is a double crossing the banker, before paying the cheque, should make certain that the second banker is the agent of the first. A cheque crossed by two branches of the same bank is not crossed to two bankers.

Where the banker on whom a cheque is drawn which is so crossed nevertheless pays the same, or pays a cheque crossed generally otherwise than to a banker, or if crossed specially otherwise than to the banker to whom it is crossed, or his agent for collection being a banker, he is liable to the true owner of the cheque for any loss he may sustain owing to the cheque having been so paid.[65]

A banker is not justified in paying a cheque in a manner inconsistent with the directions contained in the crossing. If he does do so, and any loss ensues, he cannot debit the drawer's account with the cheque because of his negligence.

Since a banker must not pay a cheque contrary to the crossing, it follows that if the crossing is such that the banker is left in doubt what to do he should return the cheque. If the cheque is crossed to two bankers one of which is not the agent of the other, it is the practice to pay the cheque provided that the banker who receives the proceeds will give an indemnity to the paying banker. If a cheque is crossed to two branches of the same bank, as may happen when a cheque is transmitted from one branch to another for collection, the cheque may be paid since, if the two branches are only one bank,[66] the cheque is crossed to only one banker, and if the branches are treated as two banks, one would be a "banker for collection".[67]

The crossing of a cheque is not nullified by its being returned unpaid, and, if re-presented, it should be paid to the banker to whom it is crossed.

A crossed cheque drawn by one customer in favour of another customer of the same bank should be passed through the payee's account. Normal banking practice would be to insist that the cheque be presented through a banker, or paid into the payee's account. But if the banker personally knows the payee, it is not considered that he would generally be at risk because he is paying the true owner,

---

64. Bills of Exchange Act 1882, s. 79(1).
65. Ibid., s. 79(2).
66. *Prince* v. *Oriental Bank Corporation* (1878) 3 App. Cas. 325; [1874–80] All E.R. Rep. 769.
67. *See* Bills of Exchange Act 1882, s. 77(5) above, and Paget (8th Edn.), p. 261.

to whom alone he would be liable.[68] If the payee has acquired the cheque by fraud, however, the drawer would not have received the benefit of the payment and the banker could not debit his account.[69] Where a cheque is presented for payment which does not at the time of presentment appear to be crossed, or to have had a crossing which has been obliterated, or to have been added to or altered otherwise than as authorised by the Bills of Exchange Act 1882, the banker paying the cheque in good faith and without negligence is not responsible and does not incur any liability, nor may the payment be questioned by reason of the cheque having been crossed, or of the crossing having been obliterated or having been added to or altered otherwise than as authorised by the Act, and of payment having been made otherwise than to a banker or to the banker to whom the cheque is or was crossed, or to his agent for collection being a banker, as the case may be.[70]

DISCHARGE OF A CHEQUE

A cheque is discharged by "payment in due course" by the paying banker. Payment is made in due course if it is made on or after the date of the cheque and if the paying banker pays the cheque to the holder in good faith and without notice of any defect in the holder's title to the cheque.[71] If a cheque is paid by an indorser, it is not discharged because the indorser then has the right to enforce the cheque against the drawer and any prior indorser.[72]

The banker cannot be certain that he is making payment to the holder in due course, but the banker is under a duty to pay the customer's cheques,[73] and payment to anyone other than the true owner is not payment in due course. To meet this dilemma s. 60 of the Bills of Exchange Act 1882, which is referred to later in this chapter, affords the banker protection if in good faith and in the ordinary course of business he pays a cheque bearing a forged or unauthorised indorsement; in such cases the bank is deemed to have paid the cheque in due course, notwithstanding the forged or unauthorised indorsement.

LIABILITY OF A PAYING BANKER

A banker has a general duty to honour his customer's cheques when

68. Bills of Exchange Act 1882, s. 79(2).
69. Q.B.P., No. 343.
70. Bills of Exchange Act 1882, s. 79(2) proviso.
71. Ibid., s. 59(1).
72. Ibid., s. 59(2).
73. See the next section of this chapter.

they are presented for payment, provided they are in proper form.[74] The banker is not bound to pay the cheque in any of the following circumstances:

(*a*) if the banker has notice that the customer has died[75] or been declared bankrupt or mentally incapable,[74] or, if the customer is a company, that a receiver has been appointed, or if the contractual relationship of banker and customer has been terminated or suspended in some other way;

(*b*) if the customer has stopped, or "countermanded payment of", the cheque;[76]

(*c*) if the customer does not have sufficient funds in his account to meet the cheque, having regard to any right of set-off[74] which the banker is entitled to exercise, or the amount of the cheque is not within any overdraft facilities available to the customer and the banker is not willing to allow him an overdraft or an increased overdraft;

(*d*) if there is a legal bar to payment (e.g. a garnishee order[74] attaching the balance on the customer's account, or a claim has been laid thereto by the third party);

(*e*) if the banker has knowledge that payment of the cheque would amount to a breach of trust[77] or has notice that the person presenting the cheque has no title thereto.

These circumstances are all discussed in Chapters Four and Five. Countermand of payment and the sufficiency of the customer's balance are discussed further below.

When a cheque is presented for payment, the paying banker should also check, before paying it, that it is complete in form, that the date on the cheque has arrived and that the cheque has been signed by the drawer or by his authority and that the signature conforms with the signature in the mandate, that the sum to be paid is expressed in words, or in words and figures, which should agree, and if the cheque requires indorsement, that it purports to have been regularly indorsed.[78] He should also make sure that there is no material alteration apparent on the cheque and no sign that the cheque has been cancelled. If the paying banker has any reason to be suspicious on any of these scores, he should do what he considers to be in the best interests of his customer, which in practice means that he should return the cheque or obtain confirmation from the drawer that the cheque may be paid.

74. *See* Chapter Four.
75. Bills of Exchange Act 1882, s. 75(2).
76. Bills of Exchange Act 1882, s. 75(1).
77. *See* "Trust accounts" in Chapter Five.
78. *See* Chapter Seven.

Countermand of payment

When a cheque is lost or destroyed, the drawer should, as we have seen, refuse to issue a duplicate to the holder until the holder gives security to indemnify him. As an additional precaution, the drawer may "stop" (or "countermand payment" of) the original cheque. A drawer may also wish to stop a cheque if he believes that the payee is unwilling or unable to fulfil the contract in respect of which the drawer issued the cheque. When the drawer stops a cheque, the duty and authority of the paying banker to pay the cheque are terminated.[76] The stopping of a cheque does not, however, terminate the liability of the drawer or any indorser, and they will remain liable on it to any holder in due course.

To be effective, the notice of countermand must reach the banker. There is no such thing as constructive countermand. The countermand must actually be brought to his notice. It may be either by word of mouth or in writing but a bank is not bound to accept an unauthenticated telegram as sufficient authority for the serious step of refusing to pay a cheque.[79] The instruction must be un-ambiguous. In one case, the drawer gave details of the payee and the amount to his banker, but gave the banker the wrong cheque number; the banker paid the cheque and it was held that he had not acted negligently and was therefore not liable to the drawer.[80]

In another case the drawer, who had two accounts at different branches, altered in ink the account number on which the cheque was drawn, so as to make it payable at the other branch, which was not automated. He later stopped the cheque, giving notice to the non-automated branch of the bank and quoting the account number, as altered. The cheque was presented for payment, was passed through the bank's computer and the magnetic ink coding took the cheque to the automated branch, where it was paid, no one noticing the handwritten alteration. The bank was held liable to the drawer because it should have informed him that ink alterations could not be detected by the computer. The warning that cheques in the books which bore magnetic ink characters would "be applied to the account for which they have been prepared. Customers must not, therefore, permit their use on any other account" was not adequate to alter the pre-existing contractual relationship, as the bank could not show that the customer had read the warning, or had agreed to it in writing.[81]

Immediately on receiving notice the banker should attach full par-

79. *Curtice* v. *London City & Midland Bank* [1908] 1 K.B. 293.
80. *Westminster Bank* v. *Hilton* (1926) 43 T.L.T. 124.
81. *Burnett* v. *Westminster Bank* [1965] 3 All E.R. 81; [1966] 1 Q.B. 742.

ticulars of the stop to the customer's ledger account, and add the notice to the general list of such orders. If the cheque is drawn "Pay self", notice of the stop should also be sent to each branch or bank where a standing order to cash the customer's cheques is in force. If the drawer sends notice of a stop which is duly received, then the banker will have to bear any loss that may ensue should he pay the stopped cheque, though he may in some circumstances be able to recover the money paid from the payee if he pays the cheque through inadvertently overlooking the countermand.[82]

The best answer on stopped cheques is "Orders not to pay". If the customer sends a telegram or cable to his banker to stop payment of a cheque, the banker should at once communicate with his customer, requesting confirmation. If the cheque is presented before such a confirmation is received, the banker should postpone payment, taking care not to say or do anything that could be construed as damage to his customer's credit. A suitable answer would be "Payment countermanded by telegram; payment postponed pending confirmation; present again." A stop by telephone would justify the same cautious attitude, unless the banker were satisfied that the telephone message was actually delivered by the customer himself, or by someone acting with his authority.

Countermand of payment can only be effectively made by the drawer,[83] so that when a banker is advised by a holder that he has lost a cheque, he should request the holder at once to communicate with the drawer, and obtain the latter's written instructions. Should the cheque be presented in the meantime, the banker should make careful inquiries into the title of the presenter before paying the cheque, or, alternatively, he may postpone payment as in the case of a stop by telegram. If the cheque requires an indorsement before payment, and the holder, having lost it, informs the banker that he has not indorsed it, and that, therefore, any indorsement purporting to be his must be a forgery, the banker, if he pays the cheque to a party other than the alleged holder, might not be entitled to debit his customer's account with it, on the ground that the cheque had not been paid in good faith and in the ordinary course of business.[84]

Any one of several partners, trustees, executors, or joint account holders, may countermand the payment of a cheque drawn by any or all of them.[85] This rule is, of course, subject to any contrary instruction given by all the parties when the account is opened. To

82. *See* under "Recovering money paid by mistake" later in this chapter.
83. Except as mentioned in the next paragraph.
84. *See* Bills of Exchange Act 1882, s. 60.
85. *See* Chapter Five.

remove a stop the bank should require the instructions of all the signatories, or alternatively should require the issue of a new cheque.[86] While the above sets out the position as between banker and customer, it may be well to mention that the drawer may not be able to avoid liability to a third party, who may have become possessed of the cheque in such circumstances that he can claim to be a holder in due course. The drawer's safeguard is to see that he crosses his cheques and adds the words "Not negotiable".

Customer's balance

The banker, before taking such a serious step as dishonouring a cheque for lack of funds, must make absolutely certain that the state of the account justifies him in so doing. Substantial damages would usually be awarded against a banker who had improperly dishonoured a cheque and thereby injured the credit of a trader. In the case of a non-trading customer, only nominal damages would be awarded unless special damage was proved or unless the action by the customer could be framed in defamation.[87]

When computing the customer's balance available for drawing, the banker need not take cognisance of any credit balance the customer may have at some other branch of the same bank, and would not be liable if he dishonoured a cheque for the reason that there were not sufficient funds to pay the cheque at the branch on which it was drawn. But if the customer has a debit balance at another branch, the banker may, unless there is an agreement express or implied to the contrary, combine the two accounts, and dishonour a cheque drawn on the branch with the credit balance, should the combined accounts show a debit or an insufficient credit balance.[88] As, however, his right depends on there being no implied agreement or course of business to keep the accounts separate, it is desirable to give notice to the customer before combining the accounts and dishonouring a cheque, or, better still, to take a definite agreement permitting combination without notice. If a customer has an account with a banker at one branch, and usually pays his credits into another branch, the banker is not bound, before dishonouring a cheque, to take cognisance of any credits which may have been paid in at the other branch, but not actually received by him. Neither is the banker bound to take into account money placed on deposit by a customer when deciding whether or not to honour a cheque drawn on the current account, but naturally the banker would usually do so.

86. *Q.B.P.*, No. 373.
87. *See* Chapter Four.
88. *Garnett* v. *M'Kewan* (1872) L.R. 8 Ex. 10.

In computing the balance available for drawing against, the banker is not justified in reserving money to meet bank charges accruing, but not actually debited, or (except in the event of the customer's bankruptcy) to meet a possible liability on bills discounted by him for the customer and not yet matured, unless the customer has otherwise agreed.

If the customer directs that certain moneys being or to be paid in are to be allocated to meet a particular cheque, the banker must obey his customer's instructions, irrespective of the state of the account between him and his customer.[89]

If the customer's balance is not sufficient to meet a cheque, the banker may nevertheless elect to pay the cheque, and can debit his customer with the amount. The drawing of a cheque when the funds are insufficient to meet it is equivalent to asking the banker for an overdraft.[90]

If the banker has followed the usual practice of crediting cheques as cash before clearance, he can, nevertheless, return cheques drawn against such uncleared credits, marked "Effects not cleared", unless there is an agreement, express or implied, permitting the customer to draw against such items.[91] Some banks have a notice printed in their pass books and on their paying-in slips reserving the right at the bank's discretion not to honour cheques drawn against uncleared items to credit. In the case of a weak customer the safer course is to put the matter beyond dispute by advising him that cheques must not be drawn against until cleared. In this connection, the banker should keep in mind the possibility of uncleared effects when computing his customer's balance in the event of bankruptcy, garnishee order, notice of a second charge on the security and the like.

If the banker has agreed to allow his customer an overdraft, with or without security, he cannot, without due notice to his customer, refuse cheques within the limit of the overdraft, and issued prior to receipt of his notice.[92]

If the paying banker decides to return the cheque, either because his duty to honour the cheque had been terminated or because there is something unsatisfactory on the face of the cheque, he should mark the cheque with an answer calculated to cause as little damage as possible to his customer's credit and reputation. If the paying banker refuses to honour a cheque without good reason or marks

89. *Farley* v. *Turner* (1857) 36 L.J. Ch. 710; *W.P. Greenhalgh & Sons* v. *Union Bank of Manchester* [1924] 2 K.B. 153.
90. This might constitute a regulated agreement for the purposes of the Consumer Credit Act 1974; *see* Chapter Twelve.
91. *Underwood* v. *Barclays Bank* [1924] 1 K.B. 775.
92. *See* Chapter Four.

a cheque with an incautious answer, he may be liable to his customer for any damage resulting from his actions.[92]

A paying banker may also be liable to his customer in damages if he does pay a cheque without authority, if, for example, the signature is not in accordance with the mandate, or forged. But if he pays a cheque on which his customer's signature has been forged or a cheque bearing an unauthorised material alteration, he may be able to avoid, or at any rate reduce, his liability to his customer if it can be shown that the customer had failed in his duty to draw cheques in such a way as to prevent forgery or unauthorised material alterations, or that the customer is estopped from setting up the forgery or want of authority or irregular signature.[93]

If a paying banker pays in good faith and in the ordinary course of business a cheque which is not indorsed or is irregularly indorsed, he is deemed to have paid it in due course even though it bears a forged or unauthorised indorsement or an indorsement is missing or irregular.[94] Because payment is deemed to be in due course, the cheque is discharged and no one can have any further liability on it.[95] A cheque is paid in the ordinary course of business if it is paid in accordance with the current practice of bankers.

If a banker pays a crossed cheque according to the crossing in good faith and without negligence, he is not liable even if the payment was not made to the true owner.[96] It seems likely that a paying banker is not acting negligently if he acts in accordance with current banking practice. A paying banker would be negligent if he paid without confirmation a cheque which showed signs of material alteration or cancellation. He would be acting in breach of the mandate if he paid a cheque which was not signed, and would be unable to debit the customer's account; if he paid a post-dated cheque before its date, he would run the risk of being unable to debit the account if anything happened in the meantime.[97]

Once a cheque has been presented, the paying banker must decide, probably within one day, whether he intends to pay the cheque or to refuse payment. If he decides to refuse payment, he must return the cheque to the collecting banker, marked with an answer calculated to cause the least possible damage to his client's credit and reputation.[98] The normal practice is to pay cheques strictly in the order in which they are presented but the banker has complete

93. *London Joint Stock Bank* v. *Macmillan and Arthur* [1918] A.C. 777; *Brown* v. *Westminster Bank* [1964] 2 Lloyd's Rep. 187. *See* Chapter Four.
94. Cheques Act 1957, s. 1(1).
95. Bills of Exchange Act 1882, s. 59.
96. Ibid., s. 80.
97. *See* Chapter Seven.
98. *See* Chapter Four.

freedom to decide which cheque may be paid when two or more are presented at the same time.[99] If the drawer's current account has a credit balance of £100 and two cheques are presented, the earlier for £200 and the later for £50, the paying banker could refuse to honour the earlier cheque and could honour the later cheque.

At the request of the holder, the collecting banker may ask the paying banker to "advise fate" by telephone (i.e. to state whether the cheque will or will not be honoured). The paying banker should take great care when advising fate for, if he advises that the cheque will be paid and then discovers that the drawer had insufficient funds to meet the cheque, he (the paying banker) will be bound to pay the cheque, even if by the time the cheque is presented the customer has stopped payment of the cheque, died, become bankrupt or withdrawn his balance. If the inquiry has been answered by saying that the cheque will be paid "if in order", he will be bound to pay it, if it is in order when presented, even though in the first three of those cases he will be unable to debit the customer's account, and in the fourth case his only redress will be that he can sue the customer on the resulting overdraft.

A more prudent reply would be "If in our hands and in order, it would be paid". In this case there is no commitment to pay; the banker has only stated it would be paid at the time of the inquiry.[100] If the paying banker advises that the cheque will not be paid and then pays the cheque, he might be liable to the drawer for any damage caused to the reputation of the drawer as a result of the incorrect advice.

There is no specific provision in the Bills of Exchange Act 1882 specifying what period of time is available to the banker for deciding whether or not to pay a cheque. Nevertheless if the cheque is presented through the London Clearing House, the rules of the London Clearing House should be observed, and objection could be taken if they were not. If they are presented otherwise than through the London Clearing House or a local clearing, the following rules should be observed.

(a) If an open cheque is presented over the counter, the drawee bank must decide promptly whether or not to pay. The question cannot be postponed until the close of business. If payment is made, it is final and irrevocable as soon as the money is placed on the counter and the banker cannot thereafter change his mind and ask for the money to be returned, even if he discovered that

99. *Q.B.P.*, No. 327.
100. *Q.B.P.*, No. 366.

the customer has insufficient funds in his account before the payee leaves the bank's premises. In *Chambers* v. *Miller*,[101] a clerk was sent by his employer to the bank to cash a third party's cheque. The cashier handed him notes, and while he was checking the notes the cashier discovered that the account on which the cheque was drawn had become overdrawn, and attempted to recover the cash from the clerk. It was held that when the money passed over the counter the property in it had passed too.

(b) If payment is made over the counter within a reasonable time of the advertised time for closing, this is final and irrevocable, and the customer cannot thereafter countermand payment.[102]

(c) If a cheque is drawn by one customer and is paid in for collection by another customer at the same branch of the same bank, there is authority for the view that the bank need not decide whether to pay or return the cheque until the next succeeding business day.[103] In practice, the bank usually decides on the same day whether to pay it or return it. If the customer paying in the cheque asks whether it is paid and is told that it is, such payment is final and irrevocable.

(d) If a cheque is specially presented for payment by one bank to another, the drawee bank will pay or dishonour it immediately and will, if telephoned, advise fate on receipt. If the payee sends a cheque direct to the drawee bank, the drawee bank has until the close of business on the day of receipt to decide whether to pay it or not, and anyone inquiring as to its fate should be told that no answer can be given until after the close of business.[104]

PROTECTION AFFORDED TO PAYING BANKER

A cheque is discharged by payment in due course, and, as noted above, "payment in due course" means payment to the holder in good faith and without notice that his title to the cheque is defective. If the drawee bank pays to someone other than the holder, this will not amount to payment in due course, but the bank cannot be certain that it is making payment to the holder. In particular, it cannot be expected to know the signatures of any indorsers. Protection is, therefore, to be found for the bank in s. 60 of the Bills of Exchange Act 1882, which provides that where the drawee banker pays an order cheque in good faith and in the ordinary course of business, even if it bears a forged or unauthorised indorsement, the

101. (1862) 13 C.B.N.S. 125.
102. *Baines* v. *National Provincial Bank* (1927) 32 Com. Cas. 216.
103. *Boyd* v. *Emmerson* (1834) 2 A. & E. 184.
104. *Q.B.P.*, No. 391.

bank is deemed to have paid the cheque in due course, in spite of the forged or unauthorised indorsement.

The drawer is also protected if a crossed cheque has come into the hands of the payee; in such cases the payee has to stand the loss if the cheque is lost or stolen and ultimately paid to someone else.

A thing is deemed to be done in good faith within the meaning of the Bills of Exchange Act 1882, where it is in fact done honestly, whether it is done negligently or not.[105] Good faith may be presumed on the part of bankers. Although there is no statutory definition of "in the ordinary course of business", it is clear that if the cheque was in order and none of the reasons mentioned above as making him no longer bound to pay the cheque applied, he would[106] be taken to have paid it in the ordinary course of business.

It seems unlikely that a bank could claim the protection of s. 60 if it had acted negligently. In the *Carpenters' Company*[107] case, the contrary view was expressed by two of their Lordships in the Court of Appeal, but this view has been criticised and the better view seems to be that of the third Lord Justice, who did not consider that a thing done negligently could be done in the ordinary course of business.[108]

The banker may also be protected by s. 80,[109] which is to be read in conjunction with s. 79 and sets out the duties of bankers with regard to the payment of crossed cheques. Where the banker on whom a crossed cheque is drawn pays it in good faith and without negligence to a banker, if it is crossed generally, or to the banker on whom it is crossed or his agent for a collection being a banker if it is crossed specially, the banker is entitled to the same rights and is placed in the same position as if payment of the cheque had been made to the true owner; the drawer is entitled to the same protection if the cheque has come into the hands of the payee. The provisions of s. 80 have been extended by ss. 4(2) and 5 of the Cheques Act 1957 to certain other instruments.[110]

There is some overlap between the two sections. Thus s. 60 applies to all cheques payable to order, whether crossed or not, but s. 80 applies only to crossed cheques.

105. Bills of Exchange Act 1882, s. 90.
106. Except as mentioned below in the case of unindorsed cheques.
107. *Carpenters Company* v. *British Mutual Banking Co.* [1938] 1 K.B. 511.
108. [1938] 1 K.B. 532.
109. There is some overlap between s. 80 and s. 60 for historical reasons. Section 76 to 82 re-enact certain provisions from the Crossed Cheques Act 1876, which was concerned exclusively with crossed cheques.
110. *See* final section of this chapter for the instruments in question.

Under s. 80, payment must be made without negligence, whereas s. 60 specifies only that the payment should be made in good faith and in the ordinary course of business; but if what seems to be the better view in relation to negligence[111] is correct, a bank would not be entitled to the protection of s. 60 if it had acted negligently.

Neither section applies to an order cheque which bears no indorsement or an irregular indorsement, but the Cheques Act 1957 abolished the necessity for indorsement in many cases. This was effected by s. 1(1), which provides that where a banker in good faith and in the ordinary course of business pays a cheque drawn on him which is not indorsed or is irregularly indorsed, he does not, in doing so, incur any liability by reason only of the absence of, or irregularity in, indorsement, and he is deemed to have paid it in due course.

Neither s. 60 or s. 80 of the Bills of Exchange Act 1882 was repealed, so that drawee banks may still rely upon those sections where cheques are paid which bear indorsements which appear to be regular but have in fact been forged, and they may rely on s. 1(1) of the Cheques Act 1957 where they have paid cheques bearing no indorsement or an irregular indorsement.

PROCEEDINGS ON DISHONOUR

If a paying banker dishonours a cheque when it is presented for payment, the position is as follows.

(a) The holder has an immediate right of recourse against the drawer and any indorsers. To protect this right the holder should give them each "notice of dishonour". If the drawer or an indorser is not given notice of dishonour, he will be discharged from liability unless the need to give him notice has been dispensed with (but see (g) below).[113] Notice of dishonour may be given in writing or by personal communication and may be given in any terms which sufficiently identify the cheque and intimate that the cheque has been dishonoured by non-payment.[113] The return of a dishonoured cheque to the drawer or an indorser is deemed a sufficient notice of dishonour,[114] but this would be an unwise step to take since the holder will need to retain the unpaid cheque in order to sue on it. A written notice need not be signed and an insufficient written notice may be supplemented and validated by oral communi-

---

111. *See Carpenters' Company's* case referred to in footnote 107.
112. Bills of Exchange Act 1882, s. 48.
113. Ibid., s. 49(5).
114. Ibid., s. 49(6).

cation. A misdescription of the dishonoured cheque does not vitiate the notice unless the party to whom the notice is given is in fact misled by the misdescription.[115]

(b) Notice of dishonour may be given as soon as the cheque is dishonoured and must be given within a reasonable time thereafter.[116] Where the person giving the notice and the person receiving the notice reside in the same place (i.e. town) notice is given in reasonable time if it is given or sent off in time to reach the recipient on the day after the dishonour. Where they reside in different places, notice is given in reasonable time if it is sent off on the day after the dishonour if there is a post at a convenient hour on that day or, if there is no such post, then by the next post thereafter.[116] Where notice of dishonour is duly addressed and posted, the sender is deemed to have given due notice of dishonour, notwithstanding any miscarriage by the post office.[117]

(c) Where notice of dishonour is required to be given to any person, it may be given to that person or to his agent.[118] If the person to whom notice is to be given has died and the person giving notice knows it, notice must be given to a personal representative of the deceased if there is one and he can be found with reasonable diligence.[119] If the person to whom notice is to be given is bankrupt, notice of dishonour may be given either to him or to his trustee in bankruptcy.[120] If two or more parties are liable jointly notice must be given to each of them, unless they are partners or one of them has authority to receive notice of dishonour on behalf of the others.[121]

(d) In order to protect his own position, an indorser of a cheque can himself give notice of dishonour to the drawer and any prior indorsers.[122] An indorser can give notice of dishonour as soon as the cheque is dishonoured and does not have to wait until he receives notice from the holder or a subsequent indorser.[123] Once an indorser has received notice of dishonour, he must give notice of dishonour within the same amount of time as is available to the holder following the dishonour.[124]

(e) Notice of dishonour may be given by an agent on behalf

---

115. Ibid., s. 49(7).
116. Ibid., s. 49(12).
117. Ibid., s. 49(15).
118. Ibid., s. 49(8).
119. Ibid., s. 49(9).
120. Ibid., s. 49(10).
121. Ibid., s. 49(11).
122. Ibid., s. 49(1).
123. Ibid., s. 49(12).
124. Ibid., s. 49(14).

of either the holder or an indorser.[125] Where a cheque is in the hands of an agent when it is dishonoured, he may either give notice of dishonour to the drawer and the indorsers or he may give notice to his principal. If he gives notice to his principal, he must do so within the same amount of time as if he (the agent) was the holder, and the principal must then give notice of dishonour to the drawer and the indorsers within the same amount of time as if he (the principal) was an indorser.[126]

(*f*) Delay in giving notice of dishonour is excused where the delay is caused by circumstances beyond the control of the party giving notice and not imputable to his default, misconduct or negligence. When the cause of delay ceases to operate, the notice must be given with reasonable diligence.[127]

(*g*) Notice of dishonour is dispensed with if, after the exercise of reasonable diligence, it cannot be given or does not reach the person to whom it is meant to be given.[128] Notice of dishonour does not have to be given to the drawer if the drawee (i.e. the banker) is under no obligation to pay the cheque[128] (e.g. because the drawer stopped the cheque or had insufficient funds in his account to meet the cheque or had died or become bankrupt).[129] Since these are the most frequent reasons why cheques are dishonoured, it is rare for a drawer to be able to plead as a defence that notice of dishonour was not given to him. The drawer or any indorser can waive, as regards himself, the need for notice to be given.[130]

(*h*) A notice given by or on behalf of the holder is deemed to be given on behalf of all subsequent holders (i.e. persons who become holders after the notice is given) and all indorsers prior to the holder but subsequent to the person to whom the notice is given.[131] A notice given by or on behalf of an indorser is deemed to be given on behalf of the holder and all indorsers subsequent to the person to whom the notice is given.[132]

The importance of giving notice of dishonour promptly is illustrated by *Yeoman Credit* v. *Gregory*.[133] The holders of certain bills sent them to Martins Bank, their agents, on 27th January 1960 with a letter saying: "You will notice that the bills are accepted

125. Bills of Exchange Act 1882, s. 49(1).
126. Ibid., s. 49(13).
127. Ibid., s. 50(1).
128. Ibid., s. 50(2).
129. *See* Chapter Four.
130. Bills of Exchange Act 1882, ss. 50(2) and 16(2).
131. Ibid., s. 49(3).
132. Ibid., s. 49(4).
133. [1963] 1 All E.R. 245; [1963] 1 W.L.R. 343.

payable at the National Provincial Bank, Piccadilly. We suggest that you present the bills accordingly, although we know they will be returned as the account has been moved to Midland Bank, Golden Square. We would like you to send the bills direct by post and when you receive them back, send them direct by post to Midland Bank." Payment was refused by National Provincial Bank; they were then sent to Midland Bank which also refused payment. On 28th January the holder knew that National Provincial Bank had refused payment, and on 30th January (a Saturday) he knew that Midland also had refused payment. The defendant was given oral notice of dishonour at a meeting on 30th January.

The person giving and the person to receive notice resided in the same place within the meaning of those words for the purposes of the rule,[134] but the notice was not given until the second day after the plaintiffs knew of the dishonour at National Provincial Bank (the only relevant dishonour). As there were no special circumstances to justify an extension of time, the notice of dishonour was out of time against the defendant as indorser (it was not necessary against the acceptor).

DAMAGES ON DISHONOUR

Where a cheque has been dishonoured, the holder may recover from the drawer, or from any indorser to whom notice of dishonour has been duly given, the amount of the cheque, together with such interest on that amount from the date of presentment as justice may require[135] If the holder recovers payment from any indorser, he may in turn recover payment of the same amounts from any prior indorser or the drawer.[136] Any indorser who pays the amount of the cheque, whether to the holder or to a subsequent indorser, has the right to recover payment against the drawer or a prior indorser unless, of course, they are for any reason (e.g. incapacity, material alteration) not liable on the cheque.

LIABILITY OF A COLLECTING BANKER

One of the principal functions of a banker is to receive instruments from his customer in order to collect the proceeds and credit them to his customer's account. When acting in this capacity he is called a "collecting banker". In the collection of some instruments he has statutory protection against the true owner; in the collection of

134. Bills of Exchange Act 1882, s. 49(12)(a).
135. Ibid., ss. 57(1) and (3).
136. Ibid., s. 57(1).

others he is liable to the true owner for conversion. When the banker had handled a cheque to which his customer has a defective or no title, a distinction must be made between a banker who is a mere agent for collection and one who is collecting a cheque for which he has already given cash, or against which he has permitted his customer to draw before clearance. In the latter case, in addition to being an agent for collection the banker will also be a holder for value and may also be a holder in due course.

In acting as his customer's agent in the collection of cheques, a banker will be expected to bring reasonable care and diligence to bear in presenting the effects for payment, in obtaining payment and in crediting his customer's account. If the customer suffers any loss through the negligence of the banker in any of these matters, such as, for example, through delay in presenting a cheque for payment, the banker will be liable to the customer to the extent of the loss.[137]

Under the 1882 Act one of the most important duties of the collecting banker was to examine the indorsements on all instruments to see that they were regular, i.e. that they purported to be in order,[138] and, except where the instrument was a crossed cheque, he was liable if the indorsements were forged. Failure to notice that the indorsement on a crossed cheque sent to him for collection was not a correct indorsement has been held to be negligence sufficient to deprive him of his statutory protection.[139] Now, however, by virtue of the Cheques Act 1957, which had as its primary objective the abolition of the need to indorse cheques paid direct into the accounts of the ostensible payees, the collecting banker need no longer concern himself with indorsements unless the cheque has been negotiated, in which case indorsement is still required. This is so whether the account is kept at the branch where the cheque is paid in or at another branch of the same bank or at another bank.

In practice, nevertheless, it will be realised that a greater measure of responsibility has been thrown on the collecting banker, since the paying banker will not normally examine indorsements at all on instruments other than those combined cheque and receipt forms marked "R".[140] Any negligence on the part of the collecting banker may forfeit his protection under s. 4, which is explained later.

The collecting banker must present with all diligence cheques sent to him for collection. Legally, he has until the day following receipt to present cheques payable to another banker in the same town,

---

137. *Hare* v. *Henty* (1861) 30 L.J.C.P. 302.
138. *See Arab Bank* v. *Ross* [1952] 2 Q.B. 216 for a discussion of the meaning of "regular" in this context.
139. *Bavins Junr. & Sims* v. *London and South Western Bank* [1900] 1 Q.B. 270.
140. *See* Chapter Seven for such instruments.

or to send them off where the cheque is drawn on another town. If presentment is made through an agent, that agent can legally hold the cheque until the day following receipt by him. Nevertheless, the practice of bankers is to forward on the day of receipt cheques required to be sent by post.[141]

Cheques payable alternatively, either at a country branch or in London, should be treated as London cheques unless time is saved by presenting them at the country branch. When, for any reason, knowledge of the fate of a cheque is urgently required, it is sent direct to the drawee-bank with the request to advise fate by return of post or to telephone fate. If a telephone call is asked for, the cost of it should be enclosed with the cheque. Cheques received by post in this way may legally be held until the day after receipt, but, as a matter of courtesy, it is usual for the receiving banker to advise the presenting banker if he is holding the cheque over.

When the drawer of a cheque and the person paying it in are both customers of the same banker, the banker is considered to be the collecting agent of the customer who pays in the cheque. He is, therefore, entitled to receive it without comment, although he may know that the drawer has insufficient funds to meet it, and he may legally hold the cheque until next day before returning it unpaid to the customer who has paid it in. If the banker acknowledges the receipt of such a cheque the acknowledgment cannot be taken by the customer to mean that the cheque has been paid. The usual practice of bankers, however, is to return unpaid cheques drawn on themselves on the day of receipt, or to send an advice that they are being held over. Cheques, crossed or uncrossed, drawn by one customer, and paid in by another customer, are within the scope of s. 4, and the banker is entitled to the statutory protection when dealing with such cheques. However, when a banker acts in the dual capacities of collecting and paying banker in this way, he must, to escape ultimate liability to the true owner, bring himself within the scope of the statutory protection afforded to both the paying and the collecting banker.[142]

In the matter of presentation or of giving notice of dishonour the branches of a bank are entitled to the same time as if they were separate banks.

The banker is entitled, on the ground of banking custom, to debit a dishonoured cheque to his customer's account, despite the fact that he may have allowed the customer to draw against the cheque

---

141. *Q.B.P.*, No. 384. Local clearings have to all intents and purposes been discontinued as from October 1969.

142. *Carpenters' Co.* v. *British Mutual Banking Co* [1938] 1 K.B. 511; [1937] 3 All E.R. 811.

before clearance, and even though the cheque may not bear the customer's indorsement. The position is different as regards a bill discounted by the banker for his customer. Unless the customer has indorsed the bill, he is not liable should it be dishonoured on maturity. It is imperative, therefore, that all bills tendered for discount should bear the customer's indorsement.

If a bill or cheque is dishonoured on presentation, but then reclaimed and paid before the presenting banker has had time to return it to his customer, the banker should, nevertheless, inform his customer what has happened. It is in the customer's interest to know that the drawer or acceptor is not perhaps so strong financially as he was supposed to be. If a cheque is returned for some technical reason which the collecting banker can rectify, he should nevertheless inform his customer in case the cheque, on re-presentation, is returned unpaid, in which case his customer might contend that in the absence of notice of dishonour he had assumed the cheque had been duly met.

When the holder of a cheque pays it in, the collecting banker must present it to the paying banker by the next day if the paying banker is in the same town. If the paying banker is in a different town, the collecting banker must send the cheque off to him by the next day. If the collecting banker presents a cheque to the paying banker via an agent for collection, the collecting banker must let the agent have the cheque within one day and the agent must present the cheque or send it off to the paying banker within one day after that. Most cheques are today drawn on the clearing banks and are collected and cleared through the London Clearing House system which is described in Chapter Ten. Since the passing of the Cheques Act 1957, the holder of a cheque does not have to indorse a cheque when he pays it in to his own account;[143] previously cheques were indorsed in blank before being paid in.

In general, the holder of a cheque has no guarantee that a cheque will be honoured since, as mentioned above, a cheque does not operate as an assignment of funds; nor is it possible to get round this problem, by getting the paying banker to "mark" (or "certify") the cheque as good for payment. The Committee of London Clearing Bankers have agreed that cheques are not to be presented for marking. If the fate of a cheque is desired to be known, it should be presented specially so that it can be paid or returned.[144]

---

143. Cheques Act 1957, s. 2.
144. *Q.B.P.*, No. 430. For cheque cards and similar "guarantee" systems *see* Chapter Eleven.

DEFECT IN CUSTOMER'S TITLE

A collecting banker's right to retain the proceeds of an instrument paid in by his customer depends on the customer's title. If the customer's title is defective, prima facie the banker is liable to the true owner of the instrument for conversion or alternatively for money had and received for his use, or, at least if the proceeds of the cheque are still credited to the customer's account, for the recovery of money paid under a mistake of fact.[145] An action for money had and received to the use of another is a technical action in the field of what is known as quasi-contract. It is sometimes pleaded as an alternative to conversion, but by and large the banker's defences are the same as in an action for conversion. "A conversion is an action ... of wilful interference, without lawful justification, with any chattel in a manner inconsistent with the right of another, whereby that other is deprived of the use and possession of it."[146] It is "an unauthorised act which deprives another of his property permanently, or for an indefinite time".[147]

The fact that an act is innocent or carried out without negligence will not excuse a converter though, as will be seen later, negligence is an important element in determining whether or not a banker is entitled to statutory protection. Nor is it a defence for the converter to maintain that he did not benefit by the transaction. The measure of damages is the value of the goods at the date of the conversion[148] and the liability normally continues for six years after the act of conversion.[149] In the case of a cheque or other instrument, the piece of paper forming the instrument is deemed to be "goods" and its value is deemed to be the face value of the instrument.[150]

But though the banker may be sued for conversion, or for money had and received, he can claim to be indemnified by his customer and is entitled to debit him with the amount he has had to pay to the true owner. The bank is acting as the customer's agent in collecting the cheque and an agent is normally entitled to be indemnified by his principal against all liabilities incurred in the reasonable

145. See National Westminster Bank v. Barclays Bank International [1975] Q.B. 654; [1974] 3 All E.R. 834 referred to below in this chapter.
146. Salmond, Torts (15th Edn.), p. 125.
147. Hiort v. Bott (1874) L.R. 9 Exch. 86.
148. Mercer v. Jones (1813) 3 Camp. 477; Caxton Publishing Co v. Sutherland Publishing Co. [1939] A.C. 178 at pp. 192, 203.
149. Limitation Act 1980, s. 2.
150. See Morrison v. London County and Westminster Bank [1914] 3 K.B. 356 at pp. 365 and 379; Bobbett v. Pinkett (1876) 1 Ex. D. 368; Fine Art Society v. Union Bank of London (1886) 17 Q.B.D. 705; Bavins Jnr. & Sims v. London and South Western Bank [1900] 1 Q.B. 270; Macbeth v. North and South Wales Bank [1908] 1 K.B. 13.

performance of the agency.[151] In most cases, a banker who admits liability or is held by the courts to be liable will be entitled to such an indemnity from its customer. Unfortunately, however, this remedy is in practice rarely available to the banker, since where a banker gets involved in a conversion claim, there has usually been fraud and the customer is rarely in a position to reimburse the banker.

DEFENCES AVAILABLE TO THE COLLECTING BANKER

The first and main defence to the collecting banker is the statutory protection which is conferred upon him by s. 4 of the Cheques Act 1957, which re-enacts and extends s. 82 of the Bills of Exchange Act 1882. It provides that where a banker, in good faith and without negligence, receives payment for a customer of a cheque, or, having credited a customer's account with the amount of the cheque, receives payment thereof for himself, and the customer has no title or a defective title to the cheque, the banker does not incur any liability to the true owner of the instrument by reason only of having received payment thereof. A banker is not to be treated for the purposes of s. 4 as having been negligent by reason only of his failure to concern himself with the absence of, or irregularity in, indorsement of an instrument.

The collecting banker's statutory protection applies to both crossed and open cheques and the banker, therefore, need no longer concern himself with the absence of or irregularity in an indorsement on cheques. Unfortunately this does not mean that the collecting banker can ignore indorsements entirely.[152]

A thing is deemed to be done in good faith where it is in fact done honestly, whether it is done negligently or not.[153] A banker can be expected to act honestly at all times, and nothing further need be said on this point.

Negligence means negligence towards the true owner. There can be no negligence unless there is a duty and the collecting banker's normal duty is towards his customer. In this case, however, the collecting banker's duty is owed to the true owner. The duty to the true owner has been held to be (a) to exercise the same care and forethought with regard to the cheque as a reasonable man would bring to bear on similar business of his own, and (b)

---

151. *Adamson* v. *Jarvis* (1827) 4 Bing. 66; *Frixione* v. *Tagliaferro & Sons* (1856) 10 Moo. P.C.C. 175.
152. *See* the final section of this chapter.
153. Bills of Exchange Act 1882, s. 90.

to provide a reasonable and competent staff to carry out this duty.[154]

The difficulty that faces practising bankers is that there is no certain test as to what would constitute negligence. As Paget says: "It would be futile to try and formulate particular conditions or circumstances which might or might not establish negligence . . ."[155] Whether or not a particular act or omission constitutes negligence in the light of all the surrounding circumstances is a question of fact and judges are not necessarily consistent in their approach to the matter. Indeed, in *Marfani & Co.* v. *Midland Bank*[156] Diplock LJ said: "Cases decided thirty years ago, when the use by the general public of banking facilities was much less widespread, may not be a reliable guide as to what the duty of a careful banker, in relation to inquiries and as to facts which should give rise to suspicion, is today." If one adds that the burden of proof is on the banker to show that he has not been negligent it is apparent that despite his statutory protection, the collecting banker's position is not an enviable one.

Probably the best test to apply is that set out in the Privy Council case of *Commissioners of Taxation* v. *English, Scottish and Australian Bank*,[157] where Lord Dunedin said: "The test of negligence is whether the transaction of paying in any given cheque coupled with the circumstances antecedent and present, were so out of the ordinary course that it ought to have aroused doubt in the bankers' minds, and caused them to make inquiry."

This does not mean that a bank has to subject the account to microscopic examination or that bank officials have to be amateur detectives[158] but they are expected to apply the same standards of care as a reasonable business man would apply in his own affairs. They are expected to carry on the bank's affairs in such a way as may be expected to protect not only themselves but the true owner against fraud.

The following examples may give some guidance.

(*a*) It would probably be negligence for a collecting banker to collect a cheque or other instrument having no indorsement or an irregular indorsement in those cases where indorsement is required

---

154. Per Sankey LJ in *Lloyds Bank* v. *Chartered Bank of India, Australia and China* [1929] 1 K.B. 40 at p. 69.
155. Paget (8th Edn.), p. 393.
156. [1968] 2 All E.R. 573 at p. 579. *See also* Chapter Five.
157. [1920] A.C. 683.
158. Per Sankey LJ in *Lloyds Bank* v. *Chartered Bank of India, Australia and China* [1929] 1 K.B. 40 at p. 73.

or it is the practice of bankers to require indorsement.[159] It is, however, to be noted that a banker can in certain circumstances be a holder in due course of a third party cheque which has not been indorsed by the payee.[160]

(b) It would be negligence to collect without inquiry a cheque or other instrument for a private person which bears on its face evidence that the moneys belong to someone other than the customer in question.

(c) It would be negligent to collect without inquiry for a private account a cheque drawn in favour of a public official and endorsed by the public official, such as the Collector of Taxes.[161]

(d) It would be negligent to collect without inquiry a cheque payable to a partnership for the private account of one of the partners[162]

(e) It would be negligent to collect without inquiry a cheque drawn in favour of a firm or limited company and indorsed by the customer in his own favour on behalf of the firm or limited company.[163]

(f) It would be negligent to collect without inquiry a cheque drawn by the customer as agent of a third party in his own favour. In *Midland Bank* v. *Reckitt*[164] the cheques were drawn by Reckitt's attorney in the attorney's own favour; in *Morison*'s case some of the cheques were drawn by the manager in his own favour on the firm's account, acting as agent of the firm.

(g) It would be negligent to collect without inquiry bearer cheques drawn by the customer's (or the customer's husband's) employer.[165]

(h) It would be negligent to collect without inquiry cheques drawn in favour of any third party if the customer's circumstances were such as to put the bank on inquiry.[166] In the *Motor Traders Guarantee Corporation* case, it was the unsatisfactory conduct of the customer's account; in the *Nu-Stilo Footwear* case, the customer said he was working as a freelance agent but "the receipt by him of large

---

159. See *Bavins Jnr. and Sims* v. *London and South Western Bank* [1900] 1 Q.B. 270. 663. For cases where indorsement is required, *see* final section of this chapter.
160. See *Westminster Bank* v. *Zang* [1966] 1 All E.R. 114 referred to below.
161. *Ross* v. *London County Westminster and Parr's Bank* [1919] 1 K.B. 678.
162. Compare *Re Riches and Marshall's Trust Deed, ex parte Darlington District Joint Stock Banking Co.* (1856) 4 De G.J. & Sm. 581; *Bevan* v. *National Bank* (1906) 23 T.L.R. 65. *See also Baker* v. *Barclays Bank* [1955] 2 All E.R. 571.
163. *Underwood* v. *Martins Bank* [1924] 1 K.B. 775; *Morison* v. *London County and Westminster Bank* [1914] 3 K.B. 356; [1914–15] All E.R. Rep. 853.
164. [1933] A.C. 1; [1932] All E.R. Rep. 90.
165. *Lloyds Bank* v. *E.B. Savory & Co.* [1933] A.C. 201.
166. *Motor Traders Guarantee Corporation* v. *Midland Bank* [1937] 4 All E.R. 90, and *Nu-Stilo Footwear* v. *Lloyds Bank* (1956) 7 L.D.B. 121.

sums was quite out of harmony with the description of his trade or prospects as revealed by him to the bank".[167]

(*i*) It would be negligent to collect cheques or other instruments for a new customer where sufficient inquiries had not been made on the opening of the account.[168] In *Marfani & Co.* v. *Midland Bank*,[169] where the bank did not probe a reference given by one of the bank's own customers of some years' standing and relied on only one reference (the second referee did not reply to the bank's inquiry), the bank narrowly escaped liability. In the circumstances it was held that the bank was not negligent.

(*j*) It would probably be negligent to collect a cheque or other instrument marked "Account payee only" for anyone other than the named payee.[170]

(*k*) It seems that it would not be negligent merely to collect a cheque crossed "Not negotiable" for someone other than the payee. Paget[171] is of the opinion that "the 'Not negotiable' crossing has nothing to do with the collecting banker or he with it."

In *Lloyds Bank* v. *E. B. Savory & Co.*[172] the bank collected bearer cheques drawn by the stockbrokers E. B. Savory & Co. for customers who they knew or should have known were employees (or wives of employees) of the stockbrokers. The cheques were paid in at branches other than the customer's own branches, and the bank's system then in force was such that the collecting branch did not know who were the drawers of the cheques. In some alleviation of this, Harman LJ in *Orbit Mining & Trading Co.* v. *Westminster Bank*[173] said: "It cannot at any rate be the duty of a bank continually to keep itself up to date as to the identity of a customer's employer," though presumably a bank is still required to know the identity of the customer's employer when he first becomes a customer.

The essence of all these cases is that there must have been something about the circumstances to arouse doubts in the bank and cause them to make inquiry. Such circumstances might relate to the drawer or, more usually, the payee of the cheque. Negligence may

167. (1956) 7 L.D.B. 121 at p. 127.
168. *Lloyds Bank* v. *E.B. Savory & Co. supra. See* Chapter Four.
169. [1968] 2 All E.R. 573.
170. *House Property Co. of London* v. *London County and Westminster Bank* (1915) 84 L.J.K.B. 1846 approved by Scrutton L.J. in *Underwood* v. *Martins Bank* [1924] 1 K.B. 775 at pp. 793–4. *See also* Bevan v. *National Bank* (1906) 23 T.L.R. 65, and *Ross* v. *London County Westminster and Parr's Bank* [1919] 1 K.B. 678.
171. 8th Edn., p. 417.
172. [1933] A.C. 201.
173. [1963] 1 Q.B. 794; [1962] 3 All E.R. 565.

consist of failing to make inquiries as to a customer on opening the account[174] or in not noticing the account from time to time and considering whether it is a proper one or a suspicious one.[175] Some of the above examples are so obvious as not to need comment. Thus in *Morison*'s case Lord Reading CJ said[176] that "for a firm to pay salary or commission or any debt to a manager by cheques made payable to the firm or order, and for a manager to pay cheques so drawn to his own private banking account after himself indorsing them as agent for the payees appear to me transactions so out of the ordinary course that they should have aroused doubts in the bank's mind and caused them to make inquiry."

In *Underwood* v. *Bank of Liverpool & Martins*,[177] it was held that for an agent to pay his principal's cheque into his own account was so unusual as to put the bank on inquiry. They should have inquired whether the company had its own account, and if so, why the cheques were not paid into it. Failure to inquire amounted to negligence.

In one case the judge did not accept that the bank was put on inquiry in all cases where the payee is a limited company and the cheque is indorsed in favour of a private person. Paget,[178] however, says that banks have "contributed to their own discomfiture in this connection by forbidding their staffs to accept for the credit of private accounts cheques drawn in favour of limited companies", and circumstances may be such, especially in the case of recently opened accounts, that the collection of any third party cheques without inquiry would be negligence.[179]

In *Motor Traders Guarantee Corporation*,[180] it was the unsatisfactory conduct of the customer's own account which should have put the bank on inquiry. The plaintiffs had issued a cheque in favour of a firm of motor dealers and handed it to one Turner who was to use the cheque to purchase a car for himself which the plaintiffs were financing under a hire-purchase agreement. The payee's signature was forged and the cheque paid into Turner's own account. The bank's regulations required such a cheque to be dealt with by the branch manager, not the cashier. This was not complied with, nor did the cashier discover that many cheques drawn by

---

174. *Ladbroke* v. *Todd* (1914) 19 Com. Cas. 256; *Commissioners of Taxation* v. *English, Scottish and Australian Bank* [1920] A.C. 683.
175. *Morison* v. *London County & Westminster Bank* [1914] 3 K.B. 356.
176. At pp. 356–7.
177. [1924] 1 K.B. 775.
178. 8th Edn., p. 409.
179. *See Baker* v. *Barclays Bank* [1955] 2 All E.R. 571, and *Nu-Stilo Footwear* v. *Lloyds Bank* (1956) 7 L.D.B. 121.
180. [1937] 4 All E.R. 90.

Turner on his own account had been dishonoured, or paid only after re-presentation. It was held that although a breach of the bank's own regulations was not conclusive proof that insufficient inquiry had been made, Turner's past banking history was such that the bank should have made further inquiry, possibly by reference to the drawer or payee of the cheque, and that the bank was guilty of negligence. Commenting on this case, Paget[181] says that "there is scarcely any protection left in the section save in the case of conversion arising from the collection for an individual of a cheque to which he has no, or only a defective, title, payable to another individual.... The banker is required to exercise a degree of care which cannot be reasonably expected of him, in view of the conditions in which he transacts his business."

Finally, it can be said that the current practice of bankers is all important. If the collecting banker complies with such practice implicitly, he will probably not be negligent. The difficulty for a banker may be to know what such practice is, since it is a question of fact which must be proved by the evidence of bankers. It can, however, be said that as the law now stands mere compliance with a bank's own standing instructions will not necessarily exonerate a banker from negligence, though as a practical matter a bank manager would presumably be exculpated from personal blame if he complied with internal instructions which nevertheless displayed an unsafe system of procedure. It now also seems that merely to refrain from making inquiries which, even if they had been made, would have been unlikely to detect a customer's dishonest purpose, is not lack of reasonable care, especially if such inquiries might be such as to offend an honest customer.[182] There would, however, be a heavy burden of proof on the bank to show that the inquiries would have been unavailing.

To obtain the protection of s. 4 the banker must receive payment for a customer of an instrument which is within the section, or if the banker receives payment for himself it must be as a corollary to his having first credited a customer with the amount of the instrument. If a banker collects such instruments for a stranger, he will not be entitled to the protection of s. 4.[183] Even if a banker collects for a customer, he may still lose the protection of s. 4 if he has been negligent by failing to make sufficient inquiries on the opening of the customer's account.[184]

A collecting banker who had acted negligently might, however,

181. 8th Edn., p. 409.
182. *Marfani* v. *Midland Bank* [1968] 1 All E.R. 573 at p. 582.
183. For who is a "customer", *see* Chapter Four.
184. *See* Chapter Five.

be able to escape liability to the true owner by pleading an estoppel by way of defence. An estoppel arises where one person either by his words or conduct induces another person to a course of action and that other person thereby suffers some detriment.[185] The banker would have to show that he had collected the cheque for his customer in reliance upon some indication that he might do so, given by or on behalf of the true owner. The defence of estoppel has never been raised successfully by a collecting banker in this country and is therefore somewhat theoretical.

Another defence is the defence of contributory negligence by the true owner, which might reduce the liability of the collecting banker to the true owner.[186] This defence was first established as a defence in tort cases in 1940, and is now enshrined in statute (Law Reform (Contributory Negligence) Act 1945, ss. 1, 4). The essence of the defence is that the damage suffered is partly as a result of the plaintiff's own fault and partly the fault of some other person. In such cases, the claim is not defeated altogether, but the damages are reduced to such extent as the court thinks just and equitable having regard to the plaintiff's share in the responsibility for the damages.

In *Lumsden & Co.* v. *London Trustee Savings Bank*[187] where a bank was sued for damages for conversion of cheques which it had collected for a customer the bank had been guilty of negligence, and so was not entitled to the protection of s. 4 of the Cheques Act 1957. Nevertheless the plaintiffs had also been negligent and the bank was therefore entitled to plead contributory negligence and the damages were reduced by 10 per cent.

Until the passing of the Cheques Act 1957, a banker who collected a cheque for a customer who was not the true owner was negligent if any indorsement was missing or irregular, but since 1957 a collecting banker is not treated as having been negligent by reason only of his failure to concern himself with absence of, or irregularity in, indorsements on a cheque.[188] This has greatly reduced the importance of the rules relating to regular and irregular indorsements, though a banker still has to concern himself with indorsements when collecting bills of exchange and certain other instruments for his customers.[189]

Another defence the banker might plead is that he has himself acquired a good title to the cheque as holder in due course.[190]

185. *See* Chapter Sixteen.
186. This defence was, perhaps inadvertently, removed by the Torts (Interference with Goods) Act 1977, s. 11(1) and restored by the Banking Act 1979, s. 47.
187. [1971] 1 Lloyd's Rep. 114.
188. Cheques Act 1957, s. 4(3).
189. *See* Chapter Nine and final section of this chapter.
190. *See* Chapter Seven.

"Holder" is defined as "the payee or indorsee of a (cheque) who is in possession of it, or the bearer thereof".[191] The difficulty which a banker generally has to face here is that he is not normally a holder because cheques are generally unindorsed, and he must therefore prove, in the case of unindorsed cheques, that he has given value for the cheque or has a lien on it if he is to have the benefit of s. 2 of the Cheques Act 1957. That section provides that a banker who gives value for, or has a lien on, a cheque payable to order which the holder delivers to him for collection without indorsing it, has such (if any) rights as he would have had if, upon delivery, the holder had indorsed it in blank. It is to be stressed that s. 2 of the Cheques Act 1957 applies only to cheques and does not apply to the other instruments to which s. 1 applies. If the issue or subsequent negotiation of a cheque is affected with fraud, duress or force and fear or illegality, the banker must prove that value has in good faith been given for the bill after the alleged fraud etc.[192]

The advantage of a banker being a holder in due course of a cheque is that, as a cheque is normally a negotiable instrument, the banker has an unassailable title against the whole world. Negligence is irrelevant. If a banker is merely an agent for collection he can always be challenged by a claim for conversion by the true owner, but if he is a holder in due course in his own right, there can be no claim against him for conversion or money had and received.

The question then arises as to what are the circumstances in which a collecting banker can be deemed to have given value for a cheque. These can be set out as follows.

(a) Clearly a banker has given value for a cheque if he has cashed it for a customer. In that event he would be collecting the cheque for himself and as s. 2 of the Cheques Act 1957 would not apply, it would be necessary for the banker to obtain the customer's indorsement on the cheque.

(b) A banker gives value if in fact he allows the customer to draw against a cheque paid in for collection, in anticipation of the proceeds being received. The banker then has a lien on the cheque to the value of the amount so drawn and when the holder of a bill has a lien on it, he is deemed to be a holder for value to the extent that he has a lien.[193] If therefore the cheque is returned unpaid, the banker could himself sue the drawer or a prior indorser, and this would be so, even if he has debited his customer's account with the amount of the returned cheque.[194] The more usual course is

191. Bills of Exchange Act 1882, s. 2.
192. Bills of Exchange Act 1882, s. 30.
193. Ibid., s. 27(3).
194. *Royal Bank of Scotland* v. *Tottenham* [1894] 2 Q.B. 715.

to debit the amount of the cheque to a suspense account or to an unpaid bills account.

In *Westminster Bank* v. *Zang*[195] one Tilley gave one Zang cash for £1,000 in exchange for a cheque drawn by Zang in favour of Tilley. The cash belonged to Tilley's company, namely, Tilley Autos Limited. Tilley paid in the cheque for the credit of Tilley Autos Limited, but did not indorse it. Although judgment was given against the bank in this case, the bank could have been the holder, and so protected by s. 2.

The banker should not however part with the cheque, for if possession is given up the lien is lost, and does not revive if the cheque is subsequently returned to the banker. In the case of *Westminster Bank* v. *Zang* referred to above, the bank returned the unpaid cheque to Tilley to enable him to sue Zang. Tilley's action did not proceed and on regaining possession of the cheque the bank sued Zang as holder in due course. The bank failed in the action because, having once parted with the cheque, it had lost its lien over the cheque[196], and on the facts it had not given value for the cheque so was not a holder in due course.

A banker does not give value for a cheque merely by crediting it to a customer's account (even if the account is overdrawn); it seems that there would have to be some express or implied agreement that the customer could draw against the cheque before the proceeds were received for the banker to have given value.[197] Normally when banks collect cheques they reserve the right not to allow customers to draw against uncleared effects.[197]

(c) A banker gives value if he credits a cheque to a customer's account in specific reduction or discharge of an overdraft. The banker is theoretically forbearing to sue the customer on his overdraft in consideration of the payment in of the cheque.[198] Alternatively, he is taking the cheque in reduction or discharge of an already existing debt and an antecedent debt or liability can constitute valuable consideration for a bill.[199] (This is an exception to the normal contractual rule.)

As already indicated, if a banker is a holder in due course this would be a complete defence to an action for conversion, whether there has been negligence or not; of course if the banker had notice of any defect in his customer's title or if the cheque was not complete and regular on the face of it he could not be a holder in due

195. [1966] A.C. 182; [1966] 1 All E.R. 114.
196. [1965] 1 All E.R. 1023 at p. 1029 (in the Court of Appeal).
197. *Underwood* v. *Barclays Bank* [1924] 1 K.B. 775.
198. *M'Lean* v. *Clydesdale Bank Co.* (1883) 9 App. Cas. 95.
199. Bills of Exchange Act 1882, s. 27(2).

course. Oddly enough there is no reported conversion case where this has been successfully pleaded as a defence. The defence of being a holder in due course was pleaded in *Baker* v. *Barclays Bank*[200] but failed because the bank knew the customer was collecting the cheques in question for a friend, and so the bank could not claim to have taken the cheques in satisfaction of the customer's debt. But in principle there does not seem to be any reason why the defence should not succeed in a proper case. In this connection it should be noted that if the cheque is crossed "Not negotiable", the bank cannot obtain any better title to it than the customer possessed.[201] But when a banker is a holder in due course he is in a position to take the initiative and sue the drawer of the cheque or a prior indorser, if there is one.[202]

CASHING OR EXCHANGING CHEQUES

A banker, if he cares to do so, is quite justified in cashing or exchanging cheques drawn on another banker, but in any transaction of the kind he is quite outside the protective sections. His chief danger lies in his liability to the true owner, who is entitled to sue him should the indorsement prove to be forged or unauthorised, as in such cases the banker cannot get a good title. Also, if the cheque is a "Not negotiable" crossed cheque, a defect in the title of any previous holder would render the banker liable to the true owner. Provided there is no question of a forged or unauthorised indorsement, or of the cheque being overdue, or of a "Not negotiable" crossing, the position of a banker who has taken the instrument in good faith is that of a holder in due course. Unless a cheque is marked "Not negotiable" as well as being crossed, it makes no difference to the banker's risk whether the cheque is crossed or uncrossed. If the cheque is a bearer one, the risk is less, since no question of a forged or unauthorised indorsement can arise.

It is immaterial whether the cashing is done for a customer or a stranger. In either case the banker is outside the statutory protection, and must fall back on his rights, if any, as a holder in due course. If the cashed or exchanged cheque bears the indorsement of the person who received the money, or if the banker holds the receiver's written request for its encashment, then the banker has recourse against him; otherwise, the receiver would probably not be liable on the instrument except in the case of a forgery. But the

---

200. [1955] 2 All E.R. 571.
201. Bills of Exchange Act 1882, s. 81.
202. For recent examples of successful actions by banks claiming to be holders in due course, *see Midland Bank* v. *R.V. Harris* [1963] 2 All E.R. 685, and *Barclays Bank* v. *Astley Industrial Trust* [1970] 1 Q.B. 527; [1970] 1 All E.R. 719.

banker's rights against the receiver of the money do not affect his liability to the true owner. Moreover, there is the further risk that the cheque may be dishonoured for lack of funds, or the drawer may stop payment. In both cases, provided the indorsements are genuine, the banker could sue the drawer. He would, however, lose his right to sue the drawer if the cheque was crossed "Not negotiable" and he had cashed it for a person whose title was defective or non-existent.

This is an appropriate place to mention the arrangement by the British Bankers' Association in 1945 to limit the facilities for the cashing or exchanging of cheques, etc., which would have the effect of avoiding a complete record of the transaction in the banker's books or the customer's account. In the terms of the arrangement, no member bank will, at any of its branches in Great Britain or Northern Ireland, cash or exchange any cheque, payable order, or draft (or part thereof) without credit to the banking account of the presenter, unless:

(a) it is uncrossed and drawn on the branch at which it is presented; or

(b) it is presented by the drawer or his known agent; or

(c) it is payable under a credit established on behalf of the drawer; or

(d) it is drawn for a sum not exceeding £10 in which case it may, at the discretion of the manager, on exceptional and isolated occasions, be encashed or exchanged.

Items which cannot be included in any of these categories must be paid in full into a banking account.[203]

RECOVERING MONEY PAID BY MISTAKE

When a paying banker pays a cheque to the wrong person by mistake, he may in certain circumstance be able to recover the money. This is an example of the general rule that money paid under a mistake of fact, but not a mistake of law, is recoverable.[204] The law was reviewed by Kerr J in *National Westminster Bank* v. *Barclays Bank International*[205] where in order to get cash out of Nigeria in breach of its strict exchange control regulations Mr Ismail, a Nigerian, bought, at a premium, a cheque for £8,000, but before paying for it he arranged for it to be specially presented. This was done and it was paid. It then transpired that the cheque had been

203. *See J.I.B.*, Vol. 66, 1945, p. 108.
204. *Holt* v. *Markham* [1923] 1 K.B. 504.
205. [1975] Q.B. 654.

stolen from the owner's cheque book, and the signature forged. The paying bank sued the collecting bank, Barclays, for recovery of the money, which was still credited to Mr Ismail's account at Barclays and had not been drawn out. Barclays took no part in the action, but Mr Ismail resisted. It was held that the paying bank was entitled to recover the money. Payment of the cheque, even on special clearance, did not amount to a representation that the cheque was genuine, in view of the suspicious circumstances in which the cheque was obtained which were not disclosed to the paying bank. It was further held that the paying bank did not owe any duty of care to the payee in deciding to honour a customer's cheque, at any rate when the cheque appeared regular on its face. It was further held that the mere fact that the defendant has acted to his detriment by spending or paying away the money in reliance on having received payment is not of itself a bar to recovery; detriment is relevant only as an exception to the general rule. If the forgery or other true circumstances are not discovered promptly, the right to recovery will clearly depend on the circumstances of the individual case.

Where a paying banker pays a cheque over the counter, the payment is deemed to be made as soon as the recipient puts his hands on the money. The paying banker cannot, therefore, demand that the money be given back even if he discovers before the recipient leaves the bank that the cheque should not have been paid because, for example, the drawer had insufficient funds in his account to meet the cheque.[206]

In a recent case the drawer of a cheque stopped the cheque by telephone on learning that the payee was insolvent. The payee had the cheque specially cleared, and although the drawee bank's computer had been programmed to stop the cheque, the branch manager overlooked the stop instruction and the cheque was paid before the computer rejected it. But for the bank's mistake in paying the cheque contrary to the stop, the real dispute would have been whether the drawer was entitled to stop the cheque. The funds were still credited to the payee's account at his bank, and the paying bank was held to be entitled to recover the money paid, leaving the drawer and payee, who were the real parties to the dispute, to resolve matters between themselves.[207]

LOST CHEQUES

If a cheque is lost or destroyed after it has been issued, the holder

---

206. *Q.B.P.*, No 438. *Chambers* v. *Miller* (1862) 13 C.B.N.S. 125.
207. *Barclays Bank* v. *W.J. Simms and Cooke (Southern)* [1979] 3 All E.R. 522.

may apply to the drawer for a "duplicate" of the cheque. The drawer has a duty to issue a duplicate, provided the holder gives him security, if required, to indemnify him in the event that someone else obtains payment of the original cheque.[208] If the holder brings an action to enforce payment of a cheque which has been lost or destroyed the court may order that the loss of the cheque shall not be pleaded as a defence against the holder's claims provided that an indemnity is given to the satisfaction of the court or judge against the claims of any other person upon the lost cheque.[209]

If a cheque is sent through the post and is lost or delayed in transit, the Post Office will generally not be liable.[210] If the cheque was in a registered inland packet, however, the Post Office will be liable for the loss unless it can be shown that the Post Office was not at fault and even then liability will be limited to the market value of the packet.[211] The drawer will be liable for any damage suffered by the payee as a result of the loss or delay if it can be shown that the Post Office was acting as his agent and not as the agent of the payee.

There is a rebuttable presumption that the Post Office is the agent of the drawer, not the payee, but this presumption will be rebutted if it can be shown that the payee expressly asked the drawer to send him the cheque by post. The presumption cannot be rebutted, however, merely by proof that the normal course of dealing between the drawer and the payee was for the drawer to send cheques by post, and even then, the drawer must show that he acted strictly in accordance with the payee's request. At law the debtor must seek out his creditor and pay him, and the courts are reluctant to find that the creditor has constituted the Post Office his agent, as opposed to the payer's. If the lost cheque turns up and it can be shown that the cheque was not drawn or sent by the drawer exactly in accordance with the instructions of the payee, it will no longer be necessary to decide whether the Post Office was the agent of the drawer or the payee because the drawer will automatically be liable to the payee for the delay.

PAYMENTS BY CHEQUE

Cheques rank with cash and credit cards as the most widely used means of payment in a modern economy. Nevertheless, cheques, unlike cash, are not legal tender,[212] which means that no one is

208. Bills of Exchange Act 1882, s. 69.
209. Ibid., s. 70.
210. Post Office Act 1969, s. 29.
211. Ibid., s. 30.
212. For legal tender, *see* Chapter Eleven.

obliged to accept a cheque in payment of a debt unless the terms
of a particular contract provide that he must do so. If a person
does decide to accept a cheque in payment of a debt, he is deemed
to have received "conditional payment" or, in other words, payment
conditional on the cheque being duly honoured upon presentation.
So a creditor who accepts a cheque cannot bring an action in respect
of the debt unless and until the cheque has been duly presented for
payment and payment has been refused. Where, however, the debtor
becomes bankrupt before the cheque is paid, the original debt revives
at once and the creditor can immediately take steps to recover the
money owed to him.

When a payment is made by cheque, it is not entirely clear at
what date the payment is, legally speaking, deemed to be made. In
Re Hone, ex parte the Trustee v. *Kensington Borough Council,*[213]
Harman J took what seems to be the commonsense view, namely
that "I cannot think that here the council did receive payment when
the piece of paper passed to them. They received the money when
they were the richer by £55." Nevertheless, the decision in *Re Hone*
has been criticised, and it would appear from the unanimous remarks
of the Court of Appeal, albeit in obiter dicta, in *The Brimnes*[214]
that the courts may be about to revert to the nineteenth century
view[215] that, once a cheque has been honoured, the payment is
deemed to have taken place on the date that the cheque was given
to the creditor, not on the date that the cheque was honoured. This
distinction may appear academic, but it can be of great practical
importance, for example in the law of bankruptcy where payments
made after a certain date are void.[216]

If a creditor who has accepted a negotiable instrument in payment
of a debt fails, through his negligence, in obtaining payment of the
instrument, then the debtor is discharged from his debt, at least to
the extent of his loss arising from the negligence. For instance, a
debtor may indorse a bill to his creditor, and if the creditor does
not present the bill on the due date, or, after presenting it, omits
to give the requisite notices of dishonour to the drawer and all indorsers, the debtor, as indorser, may be discharged. To preserve his
remedy on the original consideration, the creditor must present a
cheque for payment within a reasonable time, but delay in presentment does not discharge the drawer of a cheque, who is liable on

213. [1951] 1 Ch. 85 at p. 89.
214. *The Brimnes: Tenax Steamship Co.* v. *The Brimnes* (*owners*) [1974] 3 All E.R.
88.
215. *See*, for example, *Felix Hadley & Co.* v. *Hadley* [1898] 2 Ch. 680; *Re Owen
decd., Owen* v. *I.R.C.* [1949] 1 All E.R. 901.
216. *See* Chapter Thirty.

the cheque for six years from its date, except to the extent of any damage he may have suffered through the delay.

If the cheque is accepted as absolute payment the creditor loses his right to sue for the original debt and can only sue on the cheque.

When a crossed cheque sent by a debtor in payment of a debt has come into the possession of the creditor, and has been paid by the drawee-banker "in due course", then the debtor is fully discharged from his debt.[217] This is true, even if the creditor himself has lost the cheque, and even if payment has been made to a person other than the creditor. But the drawee-banker must have paid the cheque "in due course", or he will not be able to debit the debtor with the cheque, and is liable to the true owner, i.e. the creditor. "Payment in due course" of a cheque means payment to the holder thereof in good faith and without notice that his title to the cheque is defective.[218]

An unindorsed cheque which appears to have been paid by the banker on whom it is drawn is evidence of the receipt by the payee of the sum payable by the cheque.[219] A paid indorsed cheque has always been evidence of the receipt by the payee of the sum named in the cheque. Presumably an irregularly indorsed cheque would fall within the common law rule as if it were a paid indorsed cheque. It is to be noted that this applies only to cheques and not to other analogous instruments.

By the Payment of Wages Act 1960, the Truck Acts have been relaxed, so that the wages of a manual worker may now (if he makes a written request and his employer agrees) be paid direct to his own account or his joint account at a bank, or by postal order, or by money order, or by cheque.

A cheque remains the property of the holder until it is paid, when the property in it reverts to the drawer. The banker, however, is entitled to the possession of a paid cheque as a voucher, until such time as the account between him and his customer is a settled account. After this, the drawer is entitled to the cheque as a voucher between him and the payee. The British Bankers' Association has emphasised the desirability of stamping all paid debit vouchers with the word "Paid" incorporated with the date of payment. It is now the almost universal practice of banks to retain cheques with the authority of the customer.

217. Bills of Exchange Act 1882, s. 80.
218. *See* earlier in this chapter.
219. Cheques Act 1957, s. 3.

OTHER INSTRUMENTS TO WHICH THE CHEQUES ACT 1957 APPLIES

Mention has already been made of the protection conferred by s. 4 of the Cheques Act 1957 on the collecting banker when collecting cheques. The section also applies to the following instruments:

(a) any document issued by a customer of a banker which, though not a bill of exchange, is intended to enable a person to obtain payment from that banker of the sum mentioned in the document—this would include dividend and interest warrants (if and to the extent that such instruments do not count as cheques);

(b) any document issued by a public officer which is intended to enable a person to obtain payment from the Paymaster General or the Queen's and Lord Treasurer's Remembrancer of the sum mentioned in the document but is not a bill of exchange;

(c) any draft payable on demand drawn by a banker upon himself, whether payable at the head office or some other office of his bank.

The Cheques Act 1957 does not, however, make negotiable any instrument which, apart from that Act, would not be negotiable.[220]

The detailed position is set out in a circular dated 23rd September 1957 issued by the Committee of London Clearing Bankers and is as follows.

(a) Cheques and other instruments collected for account of the ostensible payee, will not require examination for indorsement, or in the case of dividend and interest warrants for discharge except:

(i)   combined cheque and receipt forms marked "R";
(ii)   bills of exchange (other than cheques);
(iii) promissory notes;
(iv)   drafts drawn on the Crown Agents, and certain other paying agents;
(v)   travellers' cheques;
(vi)   instruments payable by banks abroad.

These will all require indorsement.

(b) Cheques and other instruments payable to a bank to be applied after collection for the credit of a customer's account, e.g. when dividends are mandated to a bank, they will not require indorsement or discharge by the payee bank.

(c) Indorsement and discharge will be required if an instrument is tendered for the credit of an account other than that of the

220. Ibid., s. 6(2). *See* Chapter Eleven.

ostensible payee. If a cheque is specially indorsed to the customer for whose account it is tendered for collection, no further indorsement will be necessary.

(*d*) Banks will not be concerned with the completion of the discharge at the foot of a dividend or interest redemption warrant unless the instrument is being collected for the account of a third party.

(*e*) If the payee's name is mis-spelt or he is incorrectly designated, the instrument may be accepted for collection without indorsement or discharge unless there are circumstances to suggest that the customer is not the person to whom payment is intended to be made.

(*f*) Instruments payable to one or more of a number of joint holders may be collected for the credit of the joint account without indorsement or discharge. For this purpose, joint accounts include accounts of partners, trustees and so on.

(*g*) Instruments payable to joint payees will require indorsement or discharge if tendered for the credit of an account to which all are not parties.

(*h*) The above sub-paragraphs also apply when the account is domiciled with another branch of the collecting bank or with another bank.

(*i*) Where clearing banks act as collecting agents for non-clearing banks, the National Savings or Trustee Savings Banks instruments received need not be examined for indorsement or discharge. It may be assumed that any requisite indorsement will have been seen to by the non-clearing bank, the National Savings or Trustee Savings Bank as the case may be, to whom the collecting bank will be entitled to have recourse.

From the paying banker's point of view, the crossed cheque provisions of the Bills of Exchange Act 1882 apply to dividend warrants,[221] and to the instruments mentioned in s. 4 of the Cheques Act 1957.[222]

---

221. Bills of Exchange Act 1882, s. 95; *see also* Chapter Eleven.
222. Cheques Act 1957, ss. 4(2) and 5.

CHAPTER NINE

Bills of Exchange and Promissory Notes

The last two chapters were concerned with the handling of cheques which are bills of exchange drawn on a banker and payable on demand. This chapter is concerned with those bills of exchange which are not cheques either because they are not drawn on a banker or because they are not payable on demand (or both). Although cheques are a type of bill of exchange, the term "bill of exchange" (or "bill") is usually applied only to those bills of exchange which are not cheques and this everyday usage will be employed in this chapter. The bulk of this chapter is devoted to the handling of bills, but there is also a short section at the end of the chapter on the subject of promissory notes which are in many ways similar to bills.

DRAWING A BILL OF EXCHANGE

Section 3 of the Bills of Exchange Act 1882 defines a bill of exchange as an "unconditional order in writing, addressed by one person to another, signed by the person giving it, requiring the person to whom it is addressed to pay on demand or at a fixed or determinable future time a sum certain in money to or to the order of a specified person or to bearer". The person who gives the order is known as "the drawer", the person to whom the order is addressed is the "drawee", and where a bill is drawn to or to the order of a specified person, that person is "the payee" and the bill is a bill payable to order; where the bill is drawn in favour of the bearer, it is a bill payable to bearer. A bill is "issued" at the time of its first delivery, complete in form, to a person who takes it as a holder. When a bill is signed by the drawer, but is not yet complete in form, it is an "inchoate instrument" and is subject to the same rules as blank cheques.

Figure 1 gives two examples of bills of exchange.

Most of the components of the definition contained in s. 3 of the Bills of Exchange Act 1882 are discussed in the first six sections of Chapter Seven, and the rules given there apply equally to bills. Those sections do not, however, discuss bills drawn payable "at a fixed

---

Bristol,
                                                              1*st May,* 1968.

£50

On presentation pay Bearer the sum of Fifty pounds.

                                                              JOHN JONES.

To A.C. Davis, Esq.,
   Newport.

London,
                                                              1*st April,* 1968.

£100

One month after date pay to the order of The Southland Cycle Co.,
Ltd., the sum of One Hundred pounds for value received.

                                                              JOHN TAYLOR & CO.

To Mr. John Stevens,
   Gravesend.

Fig. 1   *Examples of a bill of exchange.*

or determinable future time" because those words do not apply to cheques which are, by definition, payable on demand. The meaning of those words is discussed in this chapter under the heading "Time for payment of a bill". Nor is there any discussion in that chapter of the drawee as "acceptor" because the drawee of a cheque, unlike the drawee of a bill, cannot be an acceptor. The subject of acceptance is discussed in detail in the next three sections of this chapter and will recur frequently throughout this chapter.

The definition of a bill contained in s. 3 does not require a place of payment to be named on the bill. It is unusual for a cheque to specify the place of payment, but it is fairly common for bills to be drawn with a place of payment specified. The place is frequently the drawee's bank. Where a place of payment is specified, any alteration of the place of payment is a material alteration and any person who is liable on the bill at the time of the alteration is discharged from liability unless he assented to the alteration expressly or impliedly.[1]

The other important rule to be remembered in connection with the drawing of bills is that the rules which apply to crossed cheques do not apply to bills.[2] This means that the holder of a bill can seek payment directly from the drawee without having to present the bill through the medium of a collecting banker. Nevertheless, bankers

1. Bills of Exchange Act 1882, s. 64.
2. *See* Chapter Eight.

do frequently collect bills as well as cheques on behalf of their customers.[3]

ACCEPTANCE OF A BILL

The drawee of a bill becomes liable on the bill if he "accepts" it or, in other words, if he signifies his assent to the order of the drawer by signing the bill.[4] Like the signature of a drawer or an indorser, the signature of a drawee can be given by the drawee himself or by an agent acting on his behalf.[5] The drawee (or his agent) can sign in an assumed name or a trade name, but the drawee will be liable as if he had signed in his own name.[6] If the drawee is a trading partnership and one partner in the firm accepts a bill in the firm's name, each partner in the firm will be liable as if he had signed in his own name.[7] In the case of a non-trading partnership, only the partner who accepts will be personally liable, unless his partners have authorised him to accept bills on their behalf. If the drawee is a corporation, it may accept a bill either by attaching the corporation's seal to the bill or in any other way permitted by the rules or articles of the corporation.[8]

Bills are normally accepted by the drawee after they have been issued, but they may be accepted even before they have been signed by the drawer or while they are otherwise incomplete.[9] Bills may also be accepted when they are overdue[10] or after they have been dishonoured by a previous refusal to accept or by non-payment.[11]

When a drawee accepts a bill, he does not become completely and irrevocably liable on the bill until he has either delivered it to the person entitled to the bill or given notice to (or according to the directions of) that person.[12] When a bill is no longer in the possession of its acceptor, he is presumed to have delivered it, and when the holder of the bill is a holder in due course, that presumption is conclusive.[13]

An acceptance may be either "general" or "qualified". A general acceptance assents without qualification to the order of the drawer. Examples of general acceptances are: "Accepted, John Smith";

3. *See* below in this chapter.
4. Bills of Exchange Act 1882, s. 17(1).
5. Ibid., s. 91(1).
6. Ibid., s. 23(1).
7. Ibid., s. 23(2).
8. Ibid., s. 91(2).
9. Ibid., s. 18(1).
10. For the meaning of "overdue", *see* below under "Date of a bill".
11. Bills of Exchange Act 1882, s. 18(2).
12. Ibid., s. 21(1).
13. Ibid., s. 21(2) and (3).

"Accepted at 3 Commercial Street, Northtown, John Smith";
"Accepted payable at Bullion Bank Ltd., Northtown, John Smith";
"John Smith".
A qualified acceptance varies the effect of the bill as drawn.[14] In
particular, a qualified acceptance may be:

(a) "conditional" (i.e. payment by the acceptor is made conditional
on a condition stated by the acceptor on the bill), e.g. "Accepted
payable on condition of one month's renewal, John Smith";

(b) "partial" (i.e. the acceptor agrees to pay only part of the
amount of the bill), e.g. on a bill for £100, "Accepted for £50 only,
John Smith";

(c) "local" (i.e. the acceptor agrees to pay only at a particular
place specified on the bill), e.g. "Accepted payable at Bullion Bank
Ltd., Northtown *and there only*, John Smith";

(d) qualified as to time, e.g. on a bill drawn payable one month
after date, "Accepted payable three months after date, John Smith";
or

(e) the acceptance of one or more of the drawees, but not of
all, e.g. on a bill drawn on John Smith and John Brown, acceptance
by one only, "Accepted, John Smith".[14]

By accepting a bill, the drawee engages that he will pay it according
to the terms of his acceptance.[15] In other words, he engages to pay
the bill as drawee if his acceptance is general, and he engages to
pay the bill as qualified if his acceptance is qualified. When a bill
is in the hands of a holder in due course, the acceptor cannot deny
the existence of the drawer, the genuineness of the drawer's signature
or the capacity and authority of the drawer to draw the bill.[16] This
means that the acceptor will be liable on the bill to a holder in due
course even if the drawer does not exist or if the drawer's signature
was forged or if the drawer did not have capacity and authority to
draw the bill. For this reason, a drawee should not accept a bill unless
he is satisfied that it is properly and legitimately drawn. Where a
bill is drawn payable to order, the acceptor is also precluded from
denying to a holder in due course the existence of the payee and
his then capacity to indorse, but the acceptor can deny that the
indorsement of the payee is genuine or valid.[16]

An acceptance must be written on the bill and be signed by the
drawee. The mere signature of the drawee without additional words
is sufficient.[17] An acceptance will, however, be invalid if the drawee
expressly states that he will perform his promise to pay the bill by

14. Bills of Exchange Act 1882, s. 19(2).
15. Ibid., s. 54(1).
16. Ibid., s. 54(2).

some means other than the payment of money.[17] Once a bill has been validly accepted and the acceptor has delivered it or given notice of acceptance to the person entitled, the acceptor becomes liable and (unless the terms of a qualified acceptance provide otherwise) he will remain liable even if the bill is not presented to him for payment and even if the appropriate proceedings on dishonour are not taken.[18]

In certain circumstances, however, an acceptor, like a drawer or an indorser, may escape liability. An acceptor will, for example, not be liable if he accepts a bill while under an incapacity[19] or if his signature on a bill is forged or unauthorised.[20] An acceptor will be discharged from liability if a bill is materially altered without his assent[21] or if a bill (or his signature on a bill) is cancelled.[22] An acceptor will be discharged from liability, except to a holder in due course, if an inchoate instrument is not filled up within a reasonable time and strictly according to the authority given[23]; but, unlike a drawer or an indorser, an acceptor will not be discharged from liability if a bill is not duly presented for payment.[24]

In the history of commerce, the importance of acceptances has been enormous. Without acceptances, it is doubtful that world trade could have expanded so rapidly over the last five centuries. Although acceptances are not quite as important as they used to be, they are still probably the most common method of financing international trade and every banker must be familiar with the rules which govern them. For an explanation of how acceptances are in practice used today the reader is referred to Chapter Twenty-Three.

PRESENTMENT FOR ACCEPTANCE

A bill must be presented to the drawee for acceptance if it is payable after sight or, in other words, if it is not payable on demand.[25] In such cases acceptance is necessary in order to fix the maturity of the instrument, i.e. if a bill is drawn payable at three months, it will mature (become payable) three months after the date of its acceptance. It should be presented for acceptance as soon as possible, for until the drawee has accepted it, he is not liable on it. Refusal to

17. Ibid., s. 17(2).
18. Ibid., ss. 45(1) and 48.
19. Ibid., s. 22. *See* Chapter Eight.
20. Bills of Exchange Act 1882, s. 24.
21. Ibid., s. 64.
22. Ibid., s. 63.
23. Ibid., s. 20.
24. Ibid., s. 45.
25. Ibid., s. 40(1).

accept gives the holder an immediate right of recourse against the drawer and any indorser.

Any other bill does not have to be presented for acceptance before it can be presented for payment, and the holder may await the mailing of the bill and then present it for payment, unless the bill either expressly stipulates that it must be or is drawn payable elsewhere than at the residence or place of business of the drawee.[26] If he does not present it for acceptance, however, he loses the opportunity of securing either the liability of the drawee, if he accepts (and this will enable the holder to discount it if he wishes), or the immediate right of recourse against prior parties if he refuses.

The holder of a bill drawn payable after sight must either present it for acceptance or negotiate it within a reasonable time. If he does not do so, the drawer and all indorsers prior to that holder are discharged from liability on the bill.[27] In determining what is a reasonable time for this purpose, regard must be had to the nature of the bill, the usage of trade with respect to similar bills and the facts of the particular case.[28]

A bill is duly presented for acceptance when it is presented by or on behalf of the holder to the drawee or to some person authorised to accept or refuse acceptance on his behalf.[29] Presentment must be made at a reasonable hour on a business day and before the bill is overdue.[29] Where the holder of a bill, drawn payable elsewhere than at the place of business or residence of the drawee, does not have time, with the exercise of reasonable diligence, to present the bill for acceptance before presenting it for payment on the day that it falls due, the delay caused by presenting the bill for acceptance before presenting it for payment is excused and does not discharge the drawer and indorsers.[30]

The holder of a bill may refuse to take a qualified acceptance, and if he does not obtain an unqualified acceptance may treat the bill as dishonoured by non-acceptance.[31] If a qualified acceptance is taken without the authorisation or subsequent consent of the drawer or an indorser, such drawer or indorser is discharged from his liability on the bill, but this rule does not apply to a partial acceptance provided due notice has been given. Where a foreign bill has been accepted as to part, it must be protested as to the balance.[32] A drawer or indorser receiving notice of a qualified acceptance is

26. Bills of Exchange Act 1882, s. 39(2) and (3).
27. Ibid., s. 40(1) and (2).
28. Ibid., s. 40(3).
29. Ibid., s. 41(1).
30. Ibid., s. 39(4).
31. Ibid., s. 44(1).
32. Ibid., s. 44(2).

deemed to have assented thereto unless he expresses his dissent to the holder within a reasonable time.[33]

Presentment for acceptance is also excused where the drawee is dead or bankrupt or is a fictitious[34] person or a person not having capacity to contract on a bill; where, after the exercise of reasonable diligence, presentment for acceptance cannot be duly made, or where, although the presentment was irregular, acceptance has been refused on some other ground.[35] The fact that the holder has reason to believe that the bill will not be accepted does not excuse him from presenting the bill for acceptance.[36]

Where presentment for acceptance is so excused, a bill may be treated as dishonoured by non-acceptance;[37] a bill must be treated as dishonoured by non-acceptance if it is duly presented for acceptance, but not validly accepted within the customary time.[38] A bill may also be treated as dishonoured by non-acceptance if the holder refuses to take a qualified acceptance.[39] Where a qualified acceptance is taken, the drawer and any indorsers will be discharged from liability unless they have expressly or impliedly authorised a qualified acceptance or subsequently given their assent to it;[40] where, however, the acceptance is partial (i.e. an engagement by the drawee to pay part of the amount of the bill), the drawer and indorsers will be liable provided that due notice of the partial acceptance is given to them.[40]

Once a bill has been dishonoured by non-acceptance, the holder has an immediate right of recourse against the drawer and indorsers and no presentment for payment is necessary.[41] To preserve that right, he must give them notice of dishonour in the manner laid down in the Bills of Exchange Act 1882.[42] The rules relating to notice of dishonour are almost identical to the rules relating to notice of dishonour on non-payment.[43] There are, however, two important differences:

(a) where a bill is dishonoured by non-acceptance and notice of dishonour is *not* given, the rights of a person who becomes a holder

33. Ibid., s. 44(3).
34. *See* Chapter Seven for discussion of "fictitious person".
35. Bills of Exchange Act 1882, s. 41(2).
36. Ibid., s. 41(3).
37. Ibid., s. 41(2).
38. Ibid., s. 43(1).
39. Ibid., s. 44(1).
40. Ibid., s. 44(2).
41. Ibid., s. 43(2).
42. Ibid., s. 48.
43. For these rules *see* Chapter Eight.

in due course subsequent to the omission are not prejudiced by the omission;[44] and

(b) where a bill is dishonoured by non-acceptance and due notice of dishonour *is* given, it is not necessary to give notice of a subsequent dishonour by non-payment unless the bill has in the meantime been accepted.[45]

BANKER PRESENTING BILL FOR ACCEPTANCE

Where a banker holds an unaccepted bill on his own behalf, he will, in his own interests, present it for acceptance as early as possible, because on acceptance he obtains additional security in the acceptor's liability; if acceptance is refused, he can take action at once against the other parties. The same considerations arise when a banker receives an unaccepted bill for presentation on behalf of a customer, and although in certain cases presentment for acceptance is not legally necessary in order to retain recourse against the drawer and indorsers, the banker must act in a manner most beneficial to his customer's interests, irrespective of any latitude the law allows him.

As his customer's agent, the banker must exercise skill and diligence in serving his customer's interest. Since early presentment is very advantageous, the banker must make early presentment; if he fails to do so, and loss ensues to his customer, the banker will be responsible.

As a rule, when a banker receives an unaccepted bill for presentment, he would present it on the day of receipt. If, however, the bill has only two or three days to run, presentment for acceptance is sometimes delayed until the due date, when it is presented both for acceptance and payment. There is, however, an element of risk even in a brief delay like this.

When a bill is presented to the drawee for acceptance he is entitled to possession of it and may retain it for twenty-four hours. Hence, if the drawee does not accept or refuse at once, the banker is quite justified in leaving the bill with him, but it should be called for the next day. In calculating the twenty-four hours, non-business days are excluded. Should the drawee refuse to deliver up the bill, accepted or unaccepted, after the expiration of this period, or destroy it, he is liable in an action for damages.

When a bill has to be presented in a place not within the bank's area of call, the banker sends it to his agent for presentment by him, or if there is no banker near, the bill may be sent by post to the

---

44. Bills of Exchange Act 1882, s. 48(1).
45. Ibid., s. 48(2).

drawee, a stamped addressed envelope being enclosed for its return. When any of the circumstances is out of the ordinary and the banker is unable to effect prompt presentment for acceptance he should always advise his customer or correspondent of the circumstances. This should be done as a matter of courtesy, even if it is not legally necessary.

If the work which the banker has undertaken to do, whether by express agreement or by implication, is delegated to an agent or correspondent, the banker will be held responsible for the acts of the agent or correspondent, and is liable for any loss sustained by the customer through the negligence of the agent or correspondent.

A banker must not take a qualified acceptance without the consent of his principal. If he is offered a qualified acceptance he should communicate at once with his customer or correspondent asking for instructions. A banker should not take the drawee's cheque and surrender the bill, because this would release the drawer and indorsers of the bill, and if the cheque is dishonoured, the drawer and indorsers of the bill, not being parties to the cheque, are not liable on the cheque. Before taking a cheque, therefore, the banker must obtain the principal's consent and if a cheque is taken the bill must not be given up. It should be noted, however, that by taking a cheque the banker secures an instrument on which the drawee is liable, whereas if he has not accepted the bill he is not liable as drawee of the bill.

If no place of payment is specified in the bill, the banker cannot insist on the drawee making it payable in the banker's own town, and, as the addition of a place of payment is a material alteration, the banker cannot add one without the acceptor's consent.

The only person competent to accept a bill is the drawee or his authorised agent, and if a bill is drawn on one party and accepted by another, the latter is not liable on the instrument as an acceptor.

If a bill is addressed to a trading partnership any partner can bind the firm by signing the firm's name. Where the partnership is a non-trading one the position is different, and only the partner who accepts will be personally liable, unless his partners have authorised him to accept bills on their behalf.

Where a bill is drawn on two or more drawees who are not partners, each of the drawees must accept, unless one is specially authorised to accept on behalf of all. If all do not accept, those who do accept are liable, but the acceptance would be a qualified one. A banker who receives a bill of this nature for presentment for acceptance should present it to each of the drawees, unless one drawee has proper authority to accept for all.

A minor is not liable on an acceptance given in his personal capacity,[46] but if he is an agent and is acting within the scope of his authority he can bind his principal.

TIME FOR PAYMENT OF A BILL

A bill is payable at a fixed or determinable future time if it is expressed to be payable at a fixed period after date or after sight or at a fixed period after the occurrence of a specified event which is certain to happen.[47] Where an instrument is expressed to be payable at a fixed period after the occurrence of an event which is *not* certain to happen, the instrument is not a bill because it is not payable "on demand or at a fixed or determinable future time", and the happening of the event does not cure the defect.[48]

Where a bill is drawn payable at a fixed period after sight, time begins to run from the date on which the bill is accepted, if it is accepted, or from the date of noting or protest if it is protested for non-acceptance or non-delivery.[49]

Where a bill expressed to be payable at a fixed period after date is issued undated, or where the acceptance of a bill payable at a fixed period after sight is undated, any holder may insert therein the true date of issue or acceptance, and the bill is payable accordingly, provided that (*a*) where the holder in good faith and by a mistake inserts a wrong date, and (*b*) in every case where a wrong date is inserted, if the bill subsequently comes into the hands of a holder in due course the bill will not be avoided thereby, but operates and is payable as if the date so inserted had been the true date.[50]

Where a bill or an acceptance or any indorsement on a bill is dated, the date will, unless the contrary be proved, be deemed to be the true date of the drawing, acceptance, or indorsement, as the case may be.[51] A bill is not invalid by reason only that it is ante-dated or post-dated, or that it bears date on a Sunday.[52]

Where a bill is not payable on demand the day on which it falls due is determined as follows:

(*a*) The bill is due and payable in all cases on the last day of the time of payment as fixed by the bill or, if that is a non-business day, on the succeeding business day.

46. Bills of Exchange Act 1882, s. 22.
47. Ibid., s. 11(1) and (2).
48. Ibid., s. 11(2).
49. Ibid., s. 14(3); *see also* below under "Noting and protest".
50. Bills of Exchange Act 1882, s. 12.
51. Ibid., s. 13(1).
52. Ibid., s. 13(2).

(*b*) Where a bill is payable at a fixed period after date, after sight, or after the happening of a specified event, the time of payment is determined by excluding the day from which the time is to begin to run and by including the day of payment.

(*c*) Where a bill is payable at a fixed period after sight, the time begins to run from the date of the acceptance if the bill be accepted, and from the date of noting or protest if the bill be noted or protested for non-acceptance or non-delivery.

(*d*) The term "month" in a bill means calendar month.[53]

Formerly, where a bill was not payable on demand three days of grace were, unless the bill otherwise provided, added to the time of payment as fixed by the bill, and the bill was payable on the last day of grace.[54] Days of grace have now been abolished and where a bill is not payable on demand it is due and payable in all cases on the last day of the time of payment as fixed by the bill or, if that is a non-business day, on the succeeding business day.[55]

A bill is current during the period between the date of issue and the date of maturity. The day after it is due to be paid the bill is no longer current. When a bill is payable so many months after date, the due date is calculated by counting the required number of months from the date of the bill.

As noted above, the term "month" means a calendar month.[56] This does not mean that a bill dated, say, 30th April at one month after date falls due on 31st May. Such a bill falls due on 30th May. The term "calendar month" in the Bills of Exchange Act 1882 is probably used to distinguish a "bill" month from a lunar month of four weeks.

At all events by the universal custom of bankers a bill dated on, say, 30th September at three months after date falls due on 30th December not on 31st December. Where a bill is payable at a fixed period after date, after sight, or after the happening of a specified event, the time of payment is determined by excluding the day from which the time is to begin to run and by including the day of payment.[57] No account must be taken of "lacking" days, so that a bill dated 31st March at one month after date falls due on 30th April.

When a bill is payable after sight, the time begins to run from the date of acceptance, if the bill be accepted.[58] If the sighting date

53. Ibid., s. 14 as amended by the Banking and Financial Dealings Act 1971, s. 3(2).
54. Bills of Exchange Act 1882, s. 14(1).
55. Banking and Financial Dealings Act 1971, s. 3(2).
56. Bills of Exchange Act 1882, s. 14(4).
57. Ibid., s. 14(2).
58. Ibid., s. 14(3).

does not coincide with the date of acceptance, the due date is calculated from the sighting date. Thus if a bill is accepted "Sighted 1st May, accepted 2nd May", the period runs from the sighting date, not from the date of acceptance. If a bill has been noted or protested for non-acceptance or non-delivery the period runs from the date of noting or protest.[58]

Where a bill payable after sight is accepted for honour,[59] its maturity is calculated from the date of the noting for non-acceptance and not from the date of acceptance for honour.[60] Where bills drawn abroad are payable "middle of January", "middle of February", and so on, such bills are generally considered to fall due on the 15th of the month. Where a bill is drawn in one country and is payable in another the due date thereof is determined according to the law of the place where it is payable.[61]

When the day of payment falls on a non-business day, i.e.

(a) Saturday, Sunday, Good Friday or Christmas Day;

(b) a bank holiday under the Banking and Financial Dealings Act 1971;

(c) a day appointed by Royal proclamation as a public fast or thanksgiving day; or

(d) a day declared by an order under s. 2 of the Banking and Financial Dealings Act 1971 to be a non-business day,

the bill is due and payable on the succeeding business day.[62]

A bill is payable on demand if it is expressed to be payable on demand or at sight or on presentation or if no time for payment is expressed.[63] A bill is deemed to be payable on demand as against any person who accepts it or indorses it after it has become overdue.[64]

Where a bill or any acceptance or indorsement is dated, the date is presumed to be the true date unless the contrary is proved.[65] Where there is no date of issue or acceptance on a bill drawn payable at a fixed period after date or after sight any holder may insert the true date of issue or acceptance and the bill will be payable accordingly.[66] If a holder inserts a wrong date in good faith and by mistake, the bill will be payable as if the true date had been inserted; in any

---

59. *See* below in this chapter for the meaning of this term.
60. Bills of Exchange Act 1882, s. 65(5).
61. Ibid., s. 72(5).
62. Ibid., ss. 14(1) and 92 as amended by the Banking and Financial Dealings Act 1971, s. 3.
63. Bills of Exchange Act 1882, s. 10(1).
64. Ibid., s. 10(2).
65. Ibid., s. 13(1).
66. Ibid., s. 12.

other case where a wrong date is inserted, if it subsequently comes into the hands of a holder in due course, he will enjoy the same protection.[67]

When a bill payable after sight is dishonoured by non-acceptance and the drawee subsequently accepts it, the holder is entitled to have it accepted as of the date of the first presentment for acceptance unless there is an agreement to the contrary.[68]

A bill drawn payable at a fixed or determinable future time is "overdue" if it is not paid on the first due date. A bill drawn payable on demand is deemed to be overdue for the purposes of s. 36 if it appears, on the face of it, to have been in circulation for an unreasonable length of time.[69] Where a bill is, or is so deemed to be overdue, it can no longer be treated as a negotiable instrument in the sense that it can no longer be negotiated free of any defects in title. No person can acquire a better title than the person from whom he took it.[70] It may still be transferred, and so long as there is then no defect, and no defect arises thereafter, all is well. But once a defect arises, if one then subsists, it can never be cured.

NEGOTIATION OF A BILL

The rules which govern the negotiation of a cheque also apply to bills.[71] As with cheques, a bill payable to bearer can be negotiated by delivery alone, whereas a bill payable to order can only be negotiated by indorsement and delivery. Like a cheque, a bill is negotiable unless there are words, such as "Not transferable" or "Pay John Smith only", which prevent negotiation. As with a cheque, a subsequent holder can obtain a better title to a bill than a prior holder, provided that the subsequent holder is a holder in due course.[71] The rules relating to regular and irregular indorsements, which have diminished in importance where cheques are concerned, are still of great importance as regards bills because a banker who pays a bill or collects a bill for a customer does not have the protection of s. 1 or s. 4 of the Cheques Act 1957.[72]

PRESENTMENT FOR PAYMENT

Like a cheque, a bill must be duly presented for payment if the drawer and indorsers are to remain liable (unless, of course, presentment

67. Ibid., s. 12 provisos.
68. Ibid., s. 18(3).
69. Ibid., s. 36(3).
70. Ibid., s. 36(2).
71. *See* Chapter Seven.
72. *See* Chapter Eight.

for payment is excused or dispensed with).[73] The acceptor of a bill is not, however, discharged by failure to present the bill for payment,[74] and if, by the terms of a qualified acceptance, presentment for payment is required, the acceptor, in the absence of express stipulation to that effect, is not discharged by the omission to present the bill for payment on the due date.[75]

The rules which govern presentment for payment of a bill are effectively the same as the rules for presentment of a cheque, with a few additions which apply only to bills as a result of the differences between bills and cheques. Where, for example, a bill is payable after sight, it is provided that presentment must be made on the day that the bill falls due.[76]

Where no place of payment is specified, a bill may be presented at the drawee's or acceptor's residence if his place of business is not known.[77] Where a bill is drawn on, or accepted by, two or more persons who are not partners and no place of presentment is specified, presentment must be made to them all.[78] Where the drawee or acceptor of a bill is dead and no place of payment is specified, presentment must be made to a personal representative of the deceased, if there is one, and he can be found with reasonable diligence.[79] Where the drawee of a bill is a fictitious person (as opposed to an existing person, using a trade or assumed name), presentment for payment is dispensed with.[80]

Where authorised by agreement or usage, presentment through the Post Office is sufficient.[81] Where the holder presents a bill for payment, he should exhibit it to the payer, and, on payment, deliver it up to him.[82]

Because bills are not subject to the rules relating to crossed cheques, they can be presented by their holder direct to the drawee. They do not have to be presented to the drawee through the medium of a collecting banker. Nevertheless, bankers do frequently collect bills for their customers. A banker who collects bills for his customers should take great care because the protection of s. 4 of the Cheques Act 1957 does not extend to a banker collecting bills. Under s. 4 of the Cheques Act 1957 a banker who collects a cheque for a customer who is not the true owner of the cheque will not be liable

73. Bills of Exchange Act 1882, s. 45.
74. Ibid., s. 52(1).
75. Ibid., s. 52(2).
76. Ibid., s. 45(1); *see* above for the date a when a bill falls due.
77. Bills of Exchange Act 1882, s. 45(4).
78. Ibid., s. 45(6).
79. Ibid., s. 45(7).
80. Ibid., s. 46(2)(*b*). *See* Chapter Seven for discussion of "fictitious persons".
81. Bills of Exchange Act 1882, s. 45(8).
82. Ibid., s. 52(4).

to the true owner provided that he (the banker) acted in good faith and without negligence.[83] But a banker who collected a bill in similar circumstances would be liable to the true owner even if he acted in good faith and without negligence.

Although a banker is not protected by s. 4 when collecting bills, he is protected by s. 4 when collecting the following instruments:

(a) cheques;

(b) any document issued by a customer of a banker which, though not a bill of exchange, is intended to enable a person to obtain payment from that banker of the sum mentioned in the document;

(c) any document issued by a public officer which is not a bill of exchange, but is intended to enable a person to obtain payment from the Paymaster General or the Queen's and Lord Treasurer's Remembrancer of the sum mentioned in the document;

(d) any draft payable on demand drawn by a banker upon himself, whether payable at the head office or some other office of his bank.[84]

Delay in presentment is excused when caused by circumstances beyond the control of the holder and not imputable to his default, misconduct or negligence. When the cause of delay ceases to operate, presentment must be made with reasonable diligence.[85]

Presentment is dispensed with in the following cases:

(a) where, after the exercise of reasonable diligence, it cannot be effected;

(b) where the drawee is fictitious;

(c) as regards the drawer when the drawee or acceptor is not bound, as between himself and the drawer, to accept or pay the bill, and the drawer has no reason to believe that the bill would be paid if presented;

(d) as regards an indorser, where the bill was accepted or made for his accommodation, and he has no reason to expect that the bill would be paid if presented;

(e) where presentment is waived.

The fact that the holder has reason to believe that the bill will, on presentment, be dishonoured does not dispense with the necessity of presentment,[86] and presentment must still be made on the day the bill falls due.

In *Yeoman Credit* v. *Gregory*,[87] a bill was accepted payable at National Provincial Bank, Piccadilly, London W.1 on 9th December

83. *See* Chapter Eight.
84. Cheques Act 1957, s. 4(2).
85. Bills of Exchange Act 1882, s. 46(1).
86. Ibid., s. 46(2).
87. [1963] 1 All E.R. 245; [1963] 1 W.L.R. 343.

1959. The acceptor informed the holder by telephone shortly before the bill was due that he had had trouble at that bank, and that he had made arrangements with Midland Bank, Golden Square, where there were funds, and that the bill should be presented accordingly. Presentment was made at Midland Bank, Golden Square, on 9th December, the day the bill fell due. Midland Bank dishonoured it, and it was presented next day at National Provincial Bank. It was held that this was not proper presentment, since presentment must be made on the day it falls due and at the place specified in the bill. The presentment on 9th December was not at the right place, and the presentment at National Provincial Bank was not on the right day.

Although there might have been an estoppel against the acceptor, the action was brought against an indorser, and he was entitled to have the bill presented on 9th December to the named bank, National Provincial Bank. What the holder ought to have done, as the judge said, was to have gone to the defendant and all indorsers so that they could, with the holder's consent, alter the bill so as to put a different place of payment on it; they should then each have indicated on the bill their consent to the alteration.

BANKER PRESENTING BILL FOR PAYMENT

When a banker presents a bill for payment on behalf of a customer or correspondent, he must bear in mind the rules given in the preceding paragraphs, and all presentments should be made in accordance with those rules. He must, therefore, present the bill to the acceptor for payment on its due date, and at a reasonable hour. Any delay owing to his negligence may render him liable to make good any loss that may ensue.

If, however, a bill is drawn payable elsewhere than at the residence or place of business of the drawee, and the banker, through presenting the bill for acceptance, does not have time to present the bill for payment on its due date, the delay is excused, and the drawers and indorsers are not discharged from their liability owing to the delay in presenting the bill for payment.

A bill drawn payable at one place, but accepted payable at another, must be presented for payment at the place where it is accepted payable; and since a bill must be presented for payment on its due date, presentment on the previous day is not a good presentment.

The fact that an acceptor has accepted a bill without giving value for it, and merely to accommodate the drawer or an indorser, is not sufficient to excuse presentment for payment in due course. If the banker is informed that the bill will be dishonoured when presented for payment, even if the information is given by the acceptor himself, the bill must nevertheless be duly presented on its due date.[88]

When the services of another banker are necessary in order to present a bill, the bill should as a rule be sent to that banker two or three days before maturity, though some bankers do not care to receive bills until the day preceding maturity. When, however, bills are not made payable at a bank, it is better to dispatch them to the collecting banker in time sufficient for him to make inquiries as to any special expenses that may be incurred by him in effecting presentation at a place some distance away.

If a bill is not domiciled at a bank, i.e. if it is not made payable at a bank, and it is not paid by the acceptor on presentation, a note should be left with the acceptor, containing full particulars of the bill, stating that it is at the bank awaiting payment and that the matter requires to be attended to before close of business. The bill itself must not be left at the acceptor's address, as obviously this would mean surrendering to the acceptor the evidence of his liability. Presentment for payment is quite a different matter from presentment for acceptance. In the latter case, the drawee is entitled to possession of the bill, because until he accepts it he is not liable on it.

Strictly speaking, the acceptor should pay his acceptance in legal tender, and the presenting banker should not give up the bill except for cash, unless he has received instructions to the contrary. If a cheque is offered, it must be one the fate of which can be ascertained in time to give due notice of dishonour of the bill if the cheque be unpaid. The bill should not be given up, but should be attached to the cheque, and surrendered with the cheque on its payment.[89] If the banker were to give up the bill in exchange for the cheque before the cheque were paid, all right of recourse against the drawer and indorsers of the bill would be lost, and he would be left with nothing better than the acceptor's dishonoured cheque and his liability as the drawer of the cheque.

If, when the bill is presented for payment, the acceptor tenders in part payment some but not all of the money due, the banker should accept the money tendered as he does not run any risk by so doing. As Lord Ellenborough said "No one can object to [part payment] because it is in aid of all the others who are liable on the bill."[90] In such circumstances, the bill must not be surrendered; it should, generally speaking, be noted for the unpaid balance, and notice of dishonour must be given, the notice clearly showing that the bill was

88. See Yeoman Credit v. Gregory, supra.
89. Q.B.P., No. 122.
90. Gould v. Robson (1807) 8 East. 756; 103 E.R. 463.

dishonoured by non-payment of part of the amount of the bill.[91] It is usual also to write on the back of the bill a receipt for the money paid. The receipt should state that the payment is a part payment, and should also make it clear that the money has been accepted without prejudice to the rights of other parties liable on the bill, e.g. "Received of ... acceptor of the within written bill, the sum of ... in part payment and without prejudice to the rights of all other parties." If the bill is a foreign bill, it must be protested for the unpaid balance. Part payment discharges a bill *pro tanto*, i.e. to the extent of the amount paid.

PAYMENT OF A BILL

A bill is discharged by payment in due course by or on behalf of the drawee or acceptor.[92] As with a cheque, a bill is not discharged when it is paid by an indorser, since an indorser who pays a bill can enforce the bill against the acceptor, the drawer and any prior indorsers.[93] When a bill is paid by the drawer, it will only be discharged if there is no acceptor liable on the bill. If there is an acceptor who is liable the drawer will be able to enforce the bill against him.[94]

When a drawee accepts a bill payable elsewhere than at his business or private address, the bill is said to be "domiciled" at the place of payment. Unless a banker has expressly or impliedly agreed to pay bills domiciled with him, he is under no legal obligation to do so, even though the customer has a balance sufficient to meet the bills. If, however, a bill is presented to a banker bearing an acceptance domiciling the bill with him, he is entitled to pay it irrespective of the state of the account. Such an acceptance is in itself sufficient authority to justify the banker paying the bill, and charging it to the customer's account.[95]

Instead of the normal relationship of debtor and creditor, the relationship between a customer and a banker paying domiciled bills is that of principal and agent. In the provinces bankers usually require an advice to pay bills domiciled with them, but London bankers generally pay without an advice. If, however, a country banker has been in the habit of paying a customer's bills without advice, he cannot alter his method of procedure without giving due notice to his customer. Advice forms offer some advantages, but they

---

91. *Q.B.P.*, No. 232.
92. Bills of Exchange Act 1882, s. 59; *See also* Chapter Eight.
93. Bills of Exchange Act 1882, s. 59(2).
94. Ibid., s. 59(2)(*a*).
95. *Q.B.P.*, No. 243.

cannot be taken to guarantee the genuineness of any indorsements on the bill.

When paying domiciled bills many of the considerations to be borne in mind are similar to those arising when paying a cheque, the acceptor of a bill being in a position analogous to that of the drawer of a cheque.

The following are the points which the paying banker must consider:

(a) that the instrument is in form a bill of exchange;
(b) that the acceptor's signature is genuine;
(c) that the bill is due;
(d) that the bill is in order as regards words and figures;
(e) that there is confirmation of material alterations and the indorsements.

Furthermore, the acceptor must not have countermanded payment, or be dead or bankrupt.

If the bill is overdue it does not appear that the banker is bound to pay it, but he would be justified in doing so. In such circumstances it is always desirable to get the acceptor's written authority before paying the bill.

As in the case of cheques, if a customer pays money in specially to meet a certain bill, the banker must apply the credit as directed without regard to the condition of the customer's account.

A bill to which the drawee's signature has been forged is not his bill, and if a banker pays such a bill he cannot debit it to the drawee's account, unless the drawee by his acts or conduct is precluded from setting up the forgery. Where the banker has paid to a bona fide holder a bill bearing a forged acceptance, the banker may not be able to compel the bona fide holder to return the money.[96] A banker has no statutory protection against forged indorsements on domiciled bills.

Payment must be in legal tender money, unless the holder agrees to accept some other form of payment. The exact sum must be tendered, but a part payment will discharge the bill *pro tanto*. If the holder takes the acceptor's cheque in exchange for the bill, the holder will lose his rights against the drawer and indorsers of the bill, and if the cheque is dishonoured his only remedy is against the acceptor as drawer of the cheque.

Discharge may occur by merger, as where the acceptor becomes the holder of a bill at or after maturity in his own right.[97]

96. *See* Chapter Eight under "Recovery of money paid under a mistake".
97. Bills of Exchange Act 1882, s. 61.

When the holder of a bill at or after its maturity absolutely and unconditionally renounces his rights against the acceptor the bill is discharged. The renunciation must be in writing unless the bill is delivered up to the acceptor.[98] The liabilities of any party to a bill may in like manner be renounced by the holder before, at, or after its maturity, but the rights of a holder in due course without notice of the renunciation are not affected by it.[99]

When the drawee of a bill is a banker, he will in general, unlike a banker who pays a cheque, not have the protection of s. 60 of the Bills of Exchange Act 1882 or s. 1 of the Cheques Act 1957.[100] He must therefore take great care to examine any indorsements when paying a bill; such indorsements must be correct, unless the bill is a bearer bill. Although s. 1 of the Cheques Act 1957 does not protect a banker when he pays a bill, it does protect him when he pays:

(*a*) a document issued by a customer of his which, although not a bill of exchange, is intended to enable a person to obtain payment from him of the sum mentioned in the document; or

(*b*) a draft payable on demand drawn by him upon himself, whether payable at the head office or some other office of his bank.[101]

DISHONOUR BY NON-ACCEPTANCE OR NON-PAYMENT

When a bill is dishonoured by non-payment or by non-acceptance, notice of dishonour must be given to the drawer and to any indorsers or they will be discharged from liability. The rules regarding notice of dishonour of a bill are the same as those which apply to notice of dishonour of a cheque.[102] Damages for dishonour of a bill are assessed on the same principles as apply to cheques except that the holder of a bill may also recover the expenses of noting or (when protest is necessary and the protest has been extended) the expenses of protest.

NOTING AND PROTEST

A bill is noted in order to secure official evidence that it has been dishonoured. When a bill is to be noted, the notary public to whom the dishonoured bill is taken re-presents it for acceptance or payment

98. Bills of Exchange Act 1882, s. 62(1).
99. Ibid., s. 62(2).
100. *See* Chapter Eight. He will be protected only if it is a bill payable to order on demand.
101. Cheques Act 1957, s. 1(2).
102. *See* Chapter Eight.

whichever is required, and if the drawee or acceptor still refuses to accept or pay the bill (as the case may be) the bill is noted.

The noting is a minute made by the notary public on a dishonoured bill or on a slip of paper affixed to the bill. The minute contains the date of presentment, the notary's charges, a reference to the notary's register, and his initials. A slip of paper is also attached to the bill stating the substance of the answer given to the notary's clerk when he presented the bill, e.g. "No effects", "No advice".

This noting is sometimes followed by a formal document bearing the notarial seal, and attesting the fact that the bill has been dishonoured. This document is called a "protest", and is accepted as evidence in the courts of most countries that the bill has been dishonoured. The law requires a protest to contain a copy of the bill, the notary's signature, the name of the person for whom the bill is protested, the place and date of protest, the cause or reason for protesting, the demand made and the answer given (if any), or the fact that the drawee or acceptor could not be found.[103] Where a bill is lost or destroyed or is wrongly detained from the person entitled to hold it, protest may be made on a copy or written particulars thereof.[104]

When a "foreign bill"[105] has been dishonoured by non-acceptance or non-payment, the holder must "protest" the bill (as well as giving notice of dishonour) in order to preserve his recourse against the drawer and indorsers (unless it does not appear on the face of it to be a foreign bill).[106] As a preliminary step, the holder may if he wishes have the bill "noted" before he protests the bill. If a foreign bill has been accepted as to part, it must be protested as to the balance.[107] A bill which has been protested for non-acceptance may be subsequently protested for non-payment.[108] This may be necessary in order to hold a foreign drawer or indorser liable in his own country.

When an "inland bill" has been dishonoured, the holder may, if he thinks fit, note or protest the bill, but it is not necessary for him to do so to preserve his rights of recourse.[109] The holder of a bill, whether inland or foreign, may also protest a bill if the acceptor becomes bankrupt or insolvent or suspends payment before the bill matures.[110] For the purpose of the Bills of Exchange Act 1882 an

103. Bills of Exchange Act 1882, s. 51(7).
104. Ibid., s. 51(8).
105. See next paragraph for definition of this term.
106. Bills of Exchange Act 1882, s. 51(2).
107. Ibid., s. 44(2).
108. Ibid., s. 51(3).
109. Ibid., s. 51(1).
110. Ibid., s. 51(5).

inland bill is a bill which is or on the face of it purports to be (*a*) both drawn and payable within the British Islands, or (*b*) drawn within the British Islands on some person resident therein. Any other bill is a foreign bill.[111]

Where a bill is to be noted or protested, it may be noted on the day of its dishonour and it must be noted (i.e. signed and dated by a notary) not later than the next succeeding day.[112] If a bill is duly noted and is later protested, the protest may take effect as of the date of noting.[112] The protest must contain a copy of the bill and must be signed by the notary making it; it must specify the person at whose request the bill is protested; the place and date of protest; the reason for the protest; the nature of the demand made of the drawee and the nature of his answer or (if appropriate) the fact that the drawee could not be found.[113] Where a bill is lost or destroyed or is wrongly detained from the person entitled to hold it, protest may be made either on a copy of the bill or on written particulars of the bill.[114]

A bill must be protested at the place (i.e. town) where it is dishonoured, subject to the two following exceptions. If a bill is presented through the Post Office and returned by post dishonoured, it may be protested at the place to which it is returned (on the day of its return if it is received during business hours; otherwise, on the next business day). If a bill drawn payable at the place of business or the residence of some person other than the payee is dishonoured by non-acceptance, it must be protested for non-payment at the place where it is expressed to be payable and no further presentment for payment to the drawee is necessary.[115]

Where a bill or note is required to be protested within a specific time, or before some further proceeding is taken, it is sufficient that the bill has been noted for protest before the expiration of the specified time for the taking of the proceeding; the formal protest may be extended at any time thereafter as of the date of the noting.[116]

Where a dishonoured bill has to be protested and the services of a notary cannot be obtained at the place where the bill is dishonoured, any householder or substantial resident of the place may,

111. Bills of Exchange Act 1882, s. 4(1). "The British Islands" means the United Kingdom, the Isle of Man and the Channel Islands.
112. Ibid., s. 51(4), as amended by the Bills of Exchange (Time of Noting) Act 1971, s. 1. As, however, s. 45(1) of the Act of 1882 states that a bill not payable on demand must be presented on the day it falls due, a notary, when noting such a bill, should do so on the day of maturity, in order that he can testify that the bill was duly presented on the day it fell due and was dishonoured.
113. Ibid., s. 51(7).
114. Ibid., s. 51(8).
115. Ibid., s. 51(6).
116. Ibid., s. 93.

in the presence of two witnesses, give a certificate, signed by them, attesting the dishonour of the bill, and the certificates shall in all respects operate as if it were a formal protest of the bill. Schedule 1 to the Act contains a form which may be used with any necessary modifications.[117]

Protest is dispensed with by any circumstances which would dispense with notice of dishonour.[118] A delay in noting or protesting is excused when the delay is caused by circumstances beyond the control of the holder and not imputable to his default, misconduct or negligence, but when the cause of the delay ceases to operate, the bill must be noted or protested with reasonable diligence.[119] When a foreign bill has been partially accepted, it is necessary to protest the bill for non-acceptance of the balance.[120]

When a bill has been noted or protested, it is still necessary to give notice of dishonour where required.[121]

On the bankruptcy of the acceptor during the currency of a bill, the holder may cause it to be protested for better security against the drawer and indorsers.[122] This must not be taken to imply that the holder, on the acceptor's bankruptcy, can demand further security from the drawer and indorsers that the bill will be met at maturity, though under some foreign codes of protest in such circumstances will enable the holder to do this. The only effect so far as the law of this country is concerned is that anyone who desires to accept the bill for honour may do so as if it had been protested for dishonour by non-acceptance.

When a banker presents a bill which he has received for collection and it is dishonoured, he must carry out his customer's instructions as to noting and protesting, and he will be liable if he neglects to do so.

In the absence of instructions to the contrary, a banker would not usually note a dishonoured inland bill, but if the bill is a foreign bill the banker must protest it, unless he has received precise instructions from his customer or correspondent not to do so. If a notary public is not available a householder's protest must be drawn up. The banker, however, may content himself with noting the foreign bill, pending further instruction as to the formal protest. He is justified in doing this because, as already stated, if the bill is duly noted the formal protest may be extended any time thereafter as of the date of noting.

117. Ibid., s. 94.
118. Ibid., s. 51(9); *See also* Chapter Eight.
119. Bills of Exchange Act 1882, s. 51(9).
120. Ibid., s. 44(2).
121. *Q.B.P.*, No. 270.
122. Bills of Exchange Act 1882, s. 51(5).

It is the custom of some country banks to send bills for noting to the notary a short time before the close of business, but in London the practice is to send them after closing time. This gives an opportunity for the bill to be taken up at the presenting bank right up to the close of business. Inland bills are often marked "N/N", which means "Not to be noted", and this direction is frequently acted on by bankers without further instructions. If a dishonoured cheque bears foreign indorsements, it should be duly noted or protested.

Where an indorser adds the words "sans frais" or "no charges" to his indorsement, it means that the indorser declines liability for return commission expenses, or noting or protesting charges. Subsequent indorsers will not be free from liability for such charges unless they themselves have specifically excluded their liability when adding their indorsement.[123]

ACCEPTANCE AND PAYMENT FOR HONOUR SUPRA PROTEST

Where a bill has been protested for non-acceptance (or for better security if the drawee has become insolvent or suspended payment) and the bill is not overdue, any person who is not already liable on the bill may, with the holder's consent, accept the bill for the honour of any party who is liable.[124] The holder may refuse to allow acceptance for honour, as he may wish to exercise his immediate right of recourse which arises on non-acceptance. An acceptance for honour must be written on the bill, must state that it is an acceptance for honour and must be signed by the acceptor for honour.[125] "Accepted supra protest" or "Accepted S.P." followed by the signature of the acceptor for honour is sufficient, though the person for whose honour it is made may be named. If an acceptance for honour does not expressly state for whose honour it is made, it is deemed to be an acceptance for the honour of the drawer.[126]

By accepting a bill an acceptor for honour becomes liable to the holder and to all parties to the bill subsequent to the party for whose honour he accepted the bill.[127] He engages to them that he will, on due presentment, pay the bill according to the tenor of his acceptance provided that he has notice that it has previously been duly presented for payment to the drawee, has not been paid by the drawee and has been protested for non-payment.[128] An acceptor for honour may

123. *Q.B.P.*, No. 268.
124. Bills of Exchange Act 1882, s. 65(1).
125. Ibid., s. 65(3).
126. Ibid., s. 65(4).
127. Ibid., s. 66(2).
128. Ibid., s. 66(1).

limit his liability by accepting part only of the amount of the bill.[129]

An acceptor for honour should be distinguished from "a referee in case of need". A referee in case of need is a person whose name has been inserted on a bill by the drawer or an indorser as a person to whom the holder may resort for payment of a bill in the event of non-acceptance or non-payment.[130] In both cases the bill must be protested for non-payment before it is presented to such a party for payment.[131]

Thus the holder of a bill which is to be accepted for honour must first present it to the drawee and protest it for dishonour by non-acceptance. Having secured the acceptance for honour, he must again present the bill to the drawee on the due date and protest it for non-payment. This second presentment is made because "effects often reach the drawee who has refused acceptance in the first instance, out of which the bill may and would be satisfied if presented to him again when the period of payment had arrived."[132]

Where an acceptor for honour has his address in the place (i.e. town) where the bill is protested for non-payment, the bill must be presented to him for payment not later than the day after its maturity. If the address of the acceptor for honour is in a different place, the bill must be forwarded not later than the day after its maturity for presentment to him.[133] For the purpose of calculating the maturity of the bill, time runs from the date that the bill is noted for non-acceptance, not from the date of the acceptance for honour.[134] Any delay in presenting a bill for payment to an acceptor for honour (or non-presentment) is excused by any circumstances which would normally excuse delayed presentment (or non-presentment).[135] If the acceptor for honour himself dishonours the bill when it is presented for payment, the bill must be protested for non-payment by him.[136]

After a bill has been protested for non-payment, any person may pay the bill supra protest for the honour of any of the parties liable (as opposed to *accepting* the bill for honour).[137] Payments for honour are not frequent in practice, and their intention is chiefly to preserve the credit of the persons for whom they are made. As the procedure is somewhat cumbrous and expensive, the better plan for a party who wishes to intervene is to obtain possession of the

129. Ibid., s. 65(2).
130. Ibid., s. 15.
131. Ibid., s. 67(1).
132. *Hoare* v. *Cazenove* (1812) 16 East. 391.
133. Bills of Exchange Act 1882, s. 67(2).
134. Ibid., s. 65(5).
135. Ibid., s. 67(3); *See also* Chapter Eight.
136. Bills of Exchange Act 1882, s. 67(4).
137. Ibid., s. 68(1).

bill by paying the holder. A payment for honour supra protest must be attested by a "notarial act of honour" which may be appended to the protest or form an extension of it and must be based on a declaration made by or on behalf of the payer for honour, declaring his intention to pay the bill for honour and declaring for whose honour he pays.[138] Without a valid notarial act of honour, the payment will be regarded as a voluntary payment and not as a payment made on behalf of the party for whose honour the payment was made.[139]

Once a bill has been paid for honour, all parties subsequent to the party for whose honour the payment was made are discharged. All prior parties remain liable, though they are now liable to the payer for honour, not the holder.[140] After the payer for honour has paid the bill and any notarial expenses incidental to its dishonour, the holder is under an obligation to deliver the bill and the protest to the payer for honour.[141]

Where two or more persons offer to pay a bill for the honour of different parties, the person whose payment will discharge most parties is preferred.[142] In other words, a payer for honour on behalf of an acceptor is preferred to a payer for honour on behalf of the drawer; the drawer's payer for honour is preferred to an indorser's payer for honour; and a prior indorser's payer for honour is preferred to a subsequent indorser's payer for honour. If a holder of a bill refuses to accept a payment for honour, he loses his right of recourse against any party who would have been discharged by the payment.[143]

BILLS DRAWN IN A SET

When a bill is drawn in several "parts" (i.e. on several pieces of paper) and each part is numbered and contains a reference to the other parts, the bill is said to be drawn in a "set" and all the parts of the set together constitute a single bill.[144] Except in the circumstances mentioned in the next two paragraphs, discharge of one part of a set (by payment, cancellation, etc.) acts as a discharge of the whole bill.[145]

Where a drawee places his acceptance on more than one part of

138. Bills of Exchange Act 1882, s. 68(3) and (4).
139. Ibid., s. 68(3).
140. Ibid., s. 68(5).
141. Ibid., s. 68(6).
142. Ibid., s. 68(2).
143. Ibid., s. 68(7).
144. Ibid., s. 71(1).
145. Ibid., s. 71(6).

a bill, he is liable on every part which he accepts as if it were a separate bill for the same amount as the whole bill.[146] Where a drawee places his acceptance on only one part of a bill, he must make sure that the part bearing his acceptance is delivered up to him when he pays the bill. Otherwise, if he paid the bill to the wrong person and the holder of the bill at maturity was a holder in due course, he will remain liable to that holder.[147]

Where the holder of a set indorses two or more parts to different persons, he is liable on every such part as if the parts which he indorsed were separate bills. Any subsequent indorser of any of the parts so indorsed will also be liable on the part he indorsed as if it were a separate bill.[148] If the parts of a set have been indorsed to different holders in due course, the holder in due course whose title accrues first is, as between such holders, deemed to be the true owner of the bill (i.e. the person entitled to enforce the bill against the acceptor, the drawer and any indorsers prior to the indorser who indorsed the bill in separate parts);[149] but if the acceptor or the drawer or an indorser prior to the separate indorsements paid that part of the bill which was first presented to him, he would not be prejudiced (i.e. he would not have to pay a second time) merely because the holder in due course who presented his part for payment first was not the earliest of the holders in due course of the various parts.[149]

EFFECT OF LIMITATION ACT 1980 ON BILLS

The limitation period begins to run from the time the cause of action first accrued to the then holder, and no action can be maintained unless it is brought within six years from that time. The Limitation Act 1980 does not apply to Scotland, but by the Bills of Exchange (Scotland) Act 1772, a limitation period of six years is applied to bills of exchange. The barring of a holder's right of action bars also his transferee's right of action.

Normally, the time begins to run in the acceptor's favour from the due date of the bill, unless presentment to the acceptor for payment is requisite, in which case it would appear that the time runs from the date of presentment. If the bill is accepted after its due date, it is considered that the time would probably run from the date of acceptance.[150] If the bill is payable on demand, the time begins to run in the acceptor's favour from the date of issue (presum-

146. Ibid., s. 71(4).
147. Ibid., s. 71(5).
148. Ibid., s. 71(2).
149. Ibid., s. 71(3).
150. Chalmers *Bills of Exchange* (13th Edn.), p. 323.

ably the date of the bill) and not from the date of demand or dishonour. So far as regards the drawer and indorsers, the time generally begins to run from the time when notice of dishonour was first received. The usual rules apply concerning acknowledgments, part payments and persons under a disability.[151]

CONFLICT OF LAWS

Where a bill drawn in one country is negotiated, accepted or payable in another country, the rights, duties and liabilities of the parties to the bill are determined according to the following principles.

(*a*) The validity of a bill as regards requirements of form is determined by the law of the place of issue. The validity of subsequent acceptances or indorsements is determined by the law of the place where such acceptances or indorsements are made.[152] Nevertheless, a bill issued out of the United Kingdom is not invalid merely because it has not been stamped in accordance with the laws of the place of issue; such a bill may be treated as valid between all parties who negotiate, hold or become parties to it in the United Kingdom provided that it conforms to the law of the United Kingdom as regards requirements of form.[153]

(*b*) The interpretation of the drawing, indorsement, or acceptance of a bill is determined by the law of the place where the drawing, indorsement or acceptance is made. Where, however, an inland bill is indorsed in a foreign country, the indorsement will (as regards the person who pays the bill) be interpreted according to the law of the United Kingdom.[154]

(*c*) The duties of the holder with respect to presentment for acceptance or presentment for payment and the necessity for (or sufficiency of) a protest or notice of dishonour, or otherwise, are determined by the law of the place where the presentment is made or the bill is dishonoured.[155]

(*d*) Where a bill drawn outside the United Kingdom is payable in the United Kingdom and the amount of the bill is not expressed in sterling, the amount used to be calculated according to the rate of exchange for sight drafts at the place of payment on the day the bill is payable unless there is an express stipulation to the

151. *See* Chapter Four.
152. Bills of Exchange Act 1882, s. 72(1).
153. Ibid., s. 72(1) provisos.
154. Ibid., s. 72(2).
155. Ibid., s. 72(3).

contrary.[156] Current practice depends on the (express or implied) terms governing the bill.

(e) Where a bill is drawn in one country and is payable in another, the due date of the bill is determined according to the law of the place where it is payable.[157]

PROMISSORY NOTES

The main difference between a bill and a promissory note is that a bill is an unconditional order to the drawee,[158] whereas a promissory note is an unconditional promise by its drawer ("maker"). Thus a promissory note is defined as "an unconditional promise in writing made by one person to another, signed by the maker, engaging to pay on demand or at a fixed or determinable future time, a sum certain in money to, or to the order of, a specified person or to bearer".[159] Most of the rules relating to bills of exchange apply to promissory notes,[160] with a few important exceptions, attributable mainly to the fact that a promissory note has no drawee so that the rules relating to drawees and acceptances will obviously not apply. The following points should be noted.

(a) A note payable to its maker's order is not a promissory note until the maker has indorsed it in favour of a payee or has indorsed it in blank to bearer.[161]

(b) A promissory note is not invalid merely because the maker attaches to the note a pledge of collateral security with authority for the holder to sell or dispose of the security if the maker fails to pay the note.[162] Such a note is still a negotiable instrument.

(c) A promissory note is inchoate and incomplete until it has been delivered to the payee or bearer.[163]

(d) A promissory note may be made by more than one maker. The makers may be liable jointly, or jointly and severally, according to the tenor of the note. A note stating "I promise to pay . . ." which is signed by more than one person is deemed to be their joint and several note.[164]

(e) As with a bill, the holder of a note payable on demand must present it for payment within a reasonable time or the indorsers of

156. Ibid., s. 72(4) (repealed in 1977).
157. Ibid., s. 72(5).
158. Ibid., s. 3(1).
159. Ibid., s. 83(1).
160. Ibid., s. 89(1).
161. Ibid., s. 83(2).
162. Ibid., s. 83(3).
163. Ibid., s. 84.
164. Ibid., s. 85.

the note will be discharged.[165] However, the maker of a note payable on demand will not be discharged if the note is not presented for payment within a reasonable time. Moreover, a holder who takes the note after it has been in circulation for more than a reasonable time can nevertheless be a holder in due course.[166]

(f) Presentment for payment is not necessary to render the maker of the note liable except where a place of payment is specified in the body of the note, in which case the note must be presented to the maker for payment at that place.[167] Presentment for payment is necessary in order to render an indorser liable.[168] Where a place of payment is specified in the body of a note (or in a separate memorandum), the indorser will only be liable if the note is presented for payment at that place.[169]

(g) The maker of a promissory note engages that he will pay it according to its tenor, and is precluded from denying to a holder in due course the existence of the payee and his then capacity to indorse.[170]

(h) The rules relating to presentment for acceptance, acceptance and acceptance supra protest do not apply to promissory notes, nor do the rules relating to bills drawn in a set.[171]

(i) Where a foreign note is dishonoured, it is not necessary to protest the note.[172] A foreign note is a note which does not appear on the face of it to be both made and payable within the British Islands.[173]

INDORSEMENT SANS RECOURS

Reference has already been made[174] to the fact that an indorser has the right to insert an express stipulation negativing or limiting his own liability to the holder.[175] Thus, if an indorser wishes to exclude his liability in the event of a cheque, bill of exchange or promissory note being dishonoured, he can do so by writing the words "Sans recours" or "Without recourse to me" after his indorsement. Even this will probably not save him from liability should there have been

---

165. Ibid., s. 86(1).
166. Bills of Exchange Act 1882, s. 86(3).
167. Ibid., s. 87(1).
168. Ibid., s. 87(2).
169. Ibid., s. 87(3).
170. Ibid., s. 88.
171. Ibid., s. 89(3).
172. Ibid., s. 89(4).
173. Ibid., s. 83(4).
174. See Chapter Seven.
175. Bills of Exchange Act 1882, s. 16(1).

a forgery in the instrument prior to his indorsement, unless the instrument was transferred by way of sale.[176] In recent years a trade has grown up in London, and certain other financial centres, of buying and selling bills of exchange and promissory notes on a "without recourse" basis. This is known as "forfaiting". There have as yet been no cases testing the extent to which the indorser succeeds in negativing his liability in such cases.

176. See *Dumont* v. *Williamson* (1867) 17 L.T.(N.S.) 71, a US case, for an analysis of the effect of such an indorsement.

CHAPTER TEN

The Clearing System

The Clearing System is a contrivance "by which all drafts are brought daily to a common receptacle, where they are balanced against each other".[1] All balances due from or owing to each particular bank at the end of the day's clearing are settled by means of a book entry at the Bank of England. As Dr Ellis Powell says in his *Evolution of the Money Market*,[2] the system of clearing is "a species of highly concentrated representative barter". The system is of incalculable benefit as a time, labour and currency saver. Before the Second World War, the Clearing was divided into Town, Metropolitan and Country. The London Clearing House now deals with Town, General, Credit, BACS[3] and Walks Agency Clearing.

BANKERS' CLEARING HOUSE

The exact date of the foundation of the system which is now known as the Bankers' Clearing House is not known. It probably dates back to a year or so before 1773; its origin is said to have been due to the various clerks of the private banks—there were then no joint stock banks except the Bank of England—meeting at an inn in Lombard Street for refreshment, followed by an exchange of cheques. Soon after the date mentioned we find records of a definite room being engaged as a meeting-place for the clerks. The Bankers' Clearing House is now a limited company, whose shares are held by Barclays Bank, Coutts & Co., Lloyds Bank, Midland Bank, National Westminster Bank and Williams & Glyn's Bank. Other banks having a seat in the Clearing House are the Bank of England, Co-operative Bank, and the Central Trustee Savings Bank. Its premises are situated at 10 Lombard Street, London, EC3V 9AP. Coutts & Co. are only involved in the Town Clearing as their parent bank undertakes the clearance of other items.

The members of the Clearing House clear their own cheques and

1. Report of the Bullion Committee, 1810.
2. Page 305 n.
3. BACS is explained below.

the cheques drawn on those banks for which they act as clearing agents. The various cheques, due bills, bankers' payments, etc., are termed "articles", while bundles of articles are termed "charges". The charges a banker receives from other bankers are termed his "in-clearing", while those he gives are his "out-clearing". A banker's out-clearing, therefore, consists of articles drawn on other banks which have been paid in at his various branches and those branches of the banks for whom he acts as clearing agent.

Cheques and other instruments which are drawn on the collecting bank do not figure in the clearing but are sorted and distributed by the clearing department of the bank concerned.

As far as the General Clearing is concerned, the Clearing House provides nothing more than a place of exchange of the various articles as between banks, and a place of settlement of the ultimate balances to and by the clearing banks.

Articles for the clearing are despatched from the branch of the collecting bank concerned, normally after amount encoding, to that bank's clearing department. There they are sorted according to the various banks on which they are drawn and put into specially designed plastic trays. On the outside of each tray is fixed a label giving the name of the clearing bank to which the tray is to be delivered. The docket (i.e. the machined list showing the cheques and their total in each tray) is placed inside its proper tray. The plastic trays are then put on special hand trolleys and loaded into electric vans. These vans are then driven straight into the exchange centre at the Clearing House. There the trays are unloaded and wait to be collected by similar vans from the drawee banks. The General Clearing takes place in the mornings only and deliveries can be made between 9 a.m. and 11.15 or 11.45 a.m., depending on the day of the week (except on peak days when the times may be extended).

On receipt of cheques by the clearing department of the drawee bank, they are sorted and listed by electronic reader/sorters linked to the computers installed by each bank into the branches where they are payable. Reconciliation of the cheque totals takes place as part of this operation. The cheques are then sent to the drawee branches. These articles cannot therefore be debited until the working day after they are exchanged and the balances for the General Clearing are not therefore included in the Daily Settlement until the next working day after exchange. Accordingly, three working days will normally be required to clear articles including the day on which the article is paid in for collection.

Some articles are inevitably mis-sorted. These are known as "W/Ds" (wrongly delivered items). They must be returned to the presenting banks by 8.15 a.m. the next day and are deducted from the General Clearing make-up summary for that day. The total from the make-up summary is entered into the daily settlement sheet, after agreement by representatives of each of the clearing banks at 10.30 a.m. at the Clearing House.

If on arrival at the drawee branch it is found that an article cannot be paid for any reason, e.g. lack of funds and orders not to pay, it is returned direct by first class post to the collecting branch. An unpaid claim form debiting the collecting bank is then passed through the General Clearing on the same day and ultimately sent to the collecting branch where it is married up with the returned article.

Over 1,310 million articles passed through the General Clearing in 1979.

THE GENERAL CLEARING

Articles included in the General Clearing are as follows.

(a) All cheques payable at a clearing bank with the exception of those of £10,000 and over drawn on and paid in to the offices and branches participating in the Town Clearing.

(b) All cheques payable at non-clearing banks which maintain either a debit or a full agency with a clearing bank. These cheques must bear a sorting code number in a clearing bank range.

(c) Cheques and bankers' payments drawn on town branches other than those paid in to town branches which are eligible for presentation in the Town Clearing.

(d) Channel Islands, Scilly Isles, Isle of Man articles.

(e) Agent claim vouchers and claims for unpaid articles.

(f) Bank of England articles including dividend and redemption warrants.

(g) Inter-bank reimbursement claims.

All cheques, etc., presented in the clearing must conform to the standard laid down from time to time.

Articles *not* included in the General Clearing are as follows.

(a) Standing orders (original bankers' orders).

(b) Coupons and warrants subject to deduction of tax.

(c) Cheques and drafts drawn in currency other than sterling even if converted into sterling.

(d) Cheques, etc., with any attachments.

(e) Cheques to which charges or expenses have been added.

(f) Bills of exchange other than cheques.

(g) Bank of England notes and notes on banks in the Channel Islands and Isle of Man.

(*h*) Articles on non-clearing banks other than those sanctioned by the Committee.

(*i*) Cheques drawn on non-clearing banks which maintain either a debit or a full agency but which do *not* bear a sorting code number in a clearing bank range.

(*j*) "Club and shop cheques" (commonly referred to as "manuscript cheques" or "stationers' forms"), i.e. cheques pre-printed without reference to the bank upon which they are drawn.

(*k*) Punched card cheques.

THE TOWN CLEARING

The only articles to pass through this clearing are certain items drawn on and paid into a "town" branch of a clearing bank. There are at present some 100 or so such branches, all within the City of London and all within easy walking distance of the Clearing House.

The Town Clearing is at present limited to the following.

(*a*) Town articles of £10,000 and over paid in the town offices or branches.

(*b*) Clean due bills of any amount.

(*c*) "Club and shop cheques" of any amount (commonly referred to as "manuscript cheques" or "stationers' forms"), i.e. cheques pre-printed without reference to the bank upon which they are drawn.

(*d*) (*i*) Walks payments of any amount, i.e. items in payment of clearing banks' walks collections and special collections between clearing banks;

(*ii*) credit clearing transactions of any amount including payments given by clearing banks to non-clearing banks and Scottish and Irish banks.

(*e*) Claims for Government Office unpaids and clearing vouchers issued by the Bank of England.

(*f*) Payments of any amount in settlement of Scottish and Irish clearing.

(*g*) Special presentations. For example, an article for which fate is required, and of which the amount may be below the Town Clearing limit, may be passed through the Town Clearing, provided that:

(*i*) it is drawn on a Town Clearing office or branch;

(*ii*) it is paid into a Town Clearing office or branch, or to a general clearing branch and sent to a London clearing department for special presentation;

(*iii*) it bears the crossing stamp of the presenting Town Clearing office or branch and also, where applicable, that of the general clearing branch; and (*iv*) a ticket is attached indicating that it is a special presentation.

(*h*) Special collections. For example, an article drawn on a Town Clearing branch and which has been wrongly delivered to a Town Clearing branch of another clearing bank in the General Clearing may be passed through the Town Clearing, provided that:

(*i*) a ticket is attached indicating that it is a special collection of an article wrongly delivered in the General Clearing;

(*ii*) the presenting bank has indorsed the article to the effect that collection is being made on behalf of the crossing bank; and

(*iii*) where such special collection is dishonoured the article must be returned at the Clearing House to the crossing bank

The Town Clearing is actually conducted at the Clearing House. There is a session in the afternoon of each working day and articles are receivable from 2.30 p.m. onwards. Each clearing bank has one or more long tables at which sit clerks with adding machines. The charges against a bank are brought by messenger and put in a basket on that bank's table. They are then listed and totalled, the totals at the end of the session being agreed by representatives of the clearing banks. The charges are then sorted into the various "town" branches, and delivered by messenger to the branches concerned. At 3.50 p.m. the session ends. A buzzer is sounded and articles are not received after this time without special reason. Any W/D items must be returned to the Clearing House by 4.05 p.m. for settlement on the same day. W/D items received after 4.05 p.m. and unpaid items delivered by 4.45 p.m. are settled on the next business day. The Town Clearing provides an extremely speedy and efficient service; items will be paid (or returned) on the same day that they are paid in for collection, if paid in by 3 p.m. All "town" articles must be presented through the clearing and cannot be presented direct to the drawee bank.

THE CREDIT CLEARING

The Credit Clearing was initiated by the clearing banks on 20th April 1960. It then covered the credit slips used for what was then known as the "trader's credit" procedure and for standing order payments. Basically the articles in the Credit Clearing are bank giro credit vouchers. These vouchers are gathered in bundles of not more than 500 vouchers, and are delivered either direct to the receiving bank or to the exchange room in the Clearing House between 9 a.m. and 10.30 a.m. on every working day. A docket is attached to each bundle. The totals are checked by the receiving bank and returned to the presenting bank with the agreed total.

W/D items must be returned, if possible by 3.30 p.m. on the day of delivery, but otherwise by 9.30 a.m. on the next business day. At 9.30 a.m. the totals of the previous day's clearing are agreed at the Clearing House by representatives of each of the clearing banks and the totals, allowing for W/D items, are then entered on that day's daily settlement sheet.

Accordingly, transactions in the Credit Clearing, like those in the General Clearing, are settled the working day after exchange takes place. The recipient will normally be credited on the second working day after the day on which the voucher leaves the originating branch, on the same day as the settlement takes place.

BANKERS' AUTOMATED CLEARING SERVICES LIMITED

In 1971 a limited company was formed to continue the function formerly performed by the Inter-Bank Computer Bureau. The company is Bankers' Automated Clearing Services Limited; the acronym for this is BACS.

It provides an automated money transfer service, its input being magnetic tapes from approved users and the clearing banks. Through its computer it processes information previously contained on vouchers such as standing order payments, salary payments, and direct debiting facilities. The settlement for these transactions is through the Bankers' Clearing House daily settlement.

THE DAILY SETTLEMENT

The daily settlement takes place at 4.20 p.m. on each working day. A sheet is completed for each clearing bank in accordance with the example set out in Fig. 2. This sheet includes the Town Clearing balances for that day and Town Clearing unpaids for the previous day. The balances for the General Clearing, Walks Agency Clearing, Credit Clearing and BACS Clearing are for the previous day's exchanges and the Credit Clearing W/D items are items wrongly delivered in the previous day's exchanges. The "adjustment of difference" covers any small errors that might have arisen in the previous day's balancing. If the total of the right-hand side exceeds the left the bank is due to make a payment; if the left-hand side exceeds the right, the bank will be a net recipient.

A representative of the Bank of England attends the daily settlement and there is a representative of each clearing bank. Settlement is made in accounts maintained by each clearing bank at the Bank of England, the necessary transfers of money being effected by balance tickets, signed by the Clearing House inspector and the representative of the respective clearing bank.

DAILY SETTLEMENT

NAME OF BANK

Charge   Pay

TOWN CLEARING

Bank of England

Barclays

Co-Operative

Coutts

Lloyds

Midland

National
Westminster

T.S.B.

Williams & Glynn's

$\left(\begin{array}{c}\text{Halfway Balance}\\ \pounds\end{array}\right)$

TOWN CLEARING
UNPAIDS

GENERAL CLEARING

WALKS AGENCY
CLEARING

CREDIT CLEARING

W/Ds CREDIT
CLEARING

COMPUTER BUREAU

ADJUSTMENT OF
DIFFERENCE

BALANCE

Fig. 2   *Daily Settlement Sheet.*

WALKS CLEARING

The majority of items formerly dealt with under this heading are now handled by a different process.

Most of the non-clearing banks have appointed one of the clearing banks as their agent for clearing and where new cheque books have been issued bearing a sorting code number within the range of that clearing bank, the cheques are included in the General Clearing.

WALKS AGENCY CLEARING

Older cheques not bearing such a sorting code number are handled manually through the Walks Agency Clearing. Relevant bank branches are debited for these items.

Articles to be included in this Clearing are all cheques, drafts, bills of exchange, etc., drawn on a non-clearing bank having established agency facilities at a clearing bank other than those items which should properly be included in the General Clearing.

The residual "Walks" items comprise of the London offices of the Scottish banks and HM Customs and Excise.

CHAPTER ELEVEN

Other Monetary Instruments

BANKERS DRAFTS

A bankers draft, properly so called, is a draft drawn by a bank upon itself, drawn either by one branch upon the head office (or vice versa) or by one branch upon another branch. Such an instrument is probably not a bill of exchange or a cheque, since both the drawer and the drawee are the same person, but by virtue of s. 5(2) of the Bills of Exchange Act 1882, the holder may treat it, at his option, either as a bill of exchange or as a promissory note.

Sometimes drafts drawn by one bank upon another are called bankers drafts, but strictly speaking these are cheques for the purposes of the Bills of Exchange Act 1882, and this section is concerned mostly with bankers drafts properly so called.

A bankers draft is usually issued at the request of a customer who needs to pay money to a person when the amount or circumstances involved are such that the recipient needs to have the utmost confidence that the transaction will be completed and the funds definitively and irrevocably transferred; it is used, for example, to make payments from one solicitor to another on completion of conveyancing and other transactions. The customer requiring the draft should complete and sign an application form, stating the amount of the draft required, the name of the payee and the place of payment. He must also provide either a cheque in favour of the banker for the amount of the draft or an authority to debit his account with that amount.

The importance of ensuring that the application is properly made and signed in accordance with the bank's mandate is illustrated by the case of *Bank of Montreal* v. *Dominion Gresham Guarantee & Casualty Co.*[1] The customer's accountant used to attend at the bank's office with cheques duly signed by the company in favour of the bank for the amounts of the drafts, but with no signed instructions regarding the drafts. On numerous occasions he obtained drafts payable to himself, and the bank was held liable to the company

1. [1930] A.C. 659.

for the loss, because it had negligently issued the drafts without an authority signed in accordance with the company's mandate.

Bankers drafts can, and should, be crossed, and they will then be subject to the crossed cheques provisions of the Bills of Exchange Act 1882.[2]

Bankers drafts must not be made payable to bearer on demand, since they would then be equivalent to bank notes and by virtue of ss. 10 and 11 of the Bank Charter Act 1844, no banker other than the Bank of England may draw, or accept, make or issue, in England or Wales, any such draft.

When a customer pays a bankers draft into his account, the collecting banker's duties are similar to those in relation to cheques.[3] Where indorsement is no longer required for a cheque, it is not required for a bankers draft;[4] the paying banker should, however, check that it has been signed by duly authorised officers, and that the particulars on the draft correspond with those on the advice which should be sent to him from the branch by which it was drawn.

The paying banker also has the same statutory protection as he has with regard to cheques. In respect of those drafts (where drawer and drawee are different banks) which in fact count as cheques, he is entitled to the protection of s. 60 of the Bills of Exchange Act 1882. If the draft does not count as a cheque, because both drawer and drawee are the same, the banker may be able to rely on s. 19 of the Stamp Act 1853, if the draft purports to be properly indorsed. The Cheques Act 1957 normally affords protection in the case of unindorsed drafts, whether crossed or uncrossed, where by virtue of that Act indorsement is no longer necessary. But if the draft is crossed, the paying banker will be protected under s. 80, since the crossed cheque provisions of the Bills of Exchange Act 1882 will then apply.[5] This of course is an additional reason why bankers drafts should be crossed.

If a bankers draft is lost, the customer should notify his own bank; it will inform the drawee bank, which can then postpone payment of the draft, if it does turn up, until the title of the person presenting it for payment has been investigated. If he has a good title, the draft must be paid, but it should be borne in mind that if there has been a forged indorsement, the person presenting it has no title and cannot claim payment from the paying bank.

The customer who has lost the bankers draft may ask for a dupli- cate draft, and provided he gives the bank an indemnity against

2. Cheques Act 1957, ss. 4(2)(*d*) and 5.
3. Ibid., ss. 4(1) and (2)(*d*).
4. Ibid., s. 1(2)(*b*).
5. Ibid., s. 5.

liability if the original draft is subsequently presented by someone who has a good title, the custom is to issue such a duplicate. The indemnity should cover all costs and expenses incurred by the bank in investigating the title of any third party who presents the draft, in addition to the amount of the draft itself.

BANKERS PAYMENTS

Bankers payments are drafts or orders drawn by one banker in the United Kingdom upon any other banker in the United Kingdom; they are not payable to bearer or order and are used solely for the purpose of settling or clearing any account between such bankers. They are frequently used in the payment of cheques specially presented by one banker to another, and in particular for the payment of instruments drawn on non-clearing bankers, that is to say "walks items".

BANK GIRO

Bank Giro is the name adopted by the clearing banks and Scottish banks to cover their money transfer services, that is to say, credit transfers and direct debiting.

Generally, a debtor who has a bank account will choose to settle his debt by drawing a cheque on his own bank in favour of his creditor. He then has two options.

(*a*) He may send the cheque to the creditor, who will present it, together with a suitably completed credit slip, to his bankers, and they will credit his account, claiming ("collecting") the proceeds from the debtor's bank through the debit clearing system. In turn they debit the debtor's account. The creditor may negotiate the cheque to a third party, who may again negotiate it to another, but the eventual procedure is the same.

(*b*) Alternatively, the debtor may make use of the bank giro credit system by presenting his cheque, together with a suitably completed credit slip, at any branch of any bank, or his own bank. The credit, and if necessary the cheque, are passed through the clearing systems and arrive at their respective destinations in due course, normally on the third working day. The appropriate accounts are credited and debited in settlement of the debt. The same code numbers are used to identify quickly the payer's and beneficiary's banks. An example is shown in Fig. 3.

Many large concerns, particularly public utility boards, post office telephones, rating authorities and major stores, provide partly com-

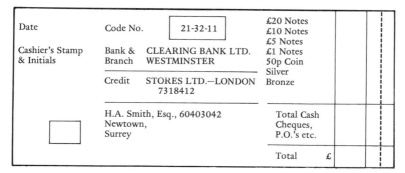

Date	Code No.	21-32-11	£20 Notes £10 Notes £5 Notes		
Cashier's Stamp & Initials	Bank & Branch	CLEARING BANK LTD. WESTMINSTER	£1 Notes 50p Coin Silver		
	Credit	STORES LTD.—LONDON 7318412	Bronze		
	H.A. Smith, Esq., 60403042 Newtown, Surrey		Total Cash Cheques, P.O.'s etc.		
			Total £		

Fig. 3   *Remittance advice/bank Giro credit form.*

pleted bank Giro credit slips with, or as part of, their bills. Code numbers frequently enable computers to effect reconciliation of amounts due and received quickly, and it is possible for the magnetic tapes containing the information to be passed between banker and customer, where systems are compatible, so that a minimum of paper need be generated.

A customer may pay several such bills with one cheque (thus saving charges) provided he makes the cheque payable to his own bank and utilises his own branch for the service. Non-customers may use the system without charge to themselves if they pay in cash. Organisations such as TV rental companies often provide a supply of credit transfer forms in voucher form for use at regular intervals, although for account-holders a banker's order is more convenient.

The credit transfer system was devised as a parallel to the debit clearing system, and offers two other main facilities in addition to those noted above.

(*a*) A standing order is an order from the customer to his bank to make periodic payments on stipulated dates. These are frequently used to pay annual subscriptions, or periodic payments of rent, insurance premiums, or hire purchase or loan instalments. They are now generally made automatically by computer, and quite sophisticated instructions may be pre-programmed.

(*b*) Traders' credits are designed to relieve customers of the trouble and expense of drawing large numbers of cheques to pay creditors. The procedure is for the debtor to draw a single cheque for the total of the bills to be paid, and to take it to his bank with a list of creditors, the names of their bankers, the amounts concerned and a request to the bank to pay over the amounts. Frequently the payer fills in credit slips in duplicate and the paying bank stamps and returns the duplicate slips. This system is often used to pay salaries and wages, too.

DIRECT DEBITING

Direct debiting is a system whereby the creditor originates a debit slip for an amount which is owed to him, and collects the amount due from his debtor's bank through his own bank. Clearly this system cannot be used without a potential debtor's prior authorisation, but once such an authorisation is obtained, it is a useful system for concerns such as insurance companies which can then initiate debits for payments of premiums. The system has an advantage over standing orders, since these must be for amounts certain, whereas the direct debiting system is very suitable when the amounts to be collected are variable. Obviously, with this type of system the interests of debtors must be safeguarded, and a bank customer is only allowed to use the direct debiting service if he first gives an indemnity to all the clearing banks and the Scottish banks, which is lodged with the Committee of London Clearing Bankers. This indemnifies the banks concerned against any actions, claims, etc., arising directly or indirectly from such debiting and authorises each bank to settle a debtor's claim without reference to the creditor. Direct debiting is operated jointly by the English and Scottish banks through Bankers' Automated Clearing Services (formerly the Inter-Bank Computer Bureau). The company using this service, which must involve the collection of at least 1,000 items per month, has the benefit of the immediate use of funds due to it; also, since it generates its own entries (with the aid of its bankers if necessary), it need only be concerned subsequently with the treatment of those debits returned unpaid.

NATIONAL GIROBANK

The National Giro was established in 1968 when the Postmaster-General was empowered to operate "a service of the kind commonly known as a giro system".[6] The system is now operated by the Post Office under powers conferred by s. 7(1)(b) of the Post Office Act 1969, as amended by s. 1(1) of the Post Office (Banking Services) Act 1976, and is known as National Girobank. By s. 40 of that Act, in operating Girobank, the Post Office is deemed to be a bank and a banker and to be carrying on the business of banking and a banking undertaking, but is not required to furnish to the Commissioners of Inland Revenue any returns under s. 21 of the Bank Charter Act 1844, or s. 13 of the Bank Notes (Scotland) Act 1845. The Post Office is subject to supervision by HM Treasury and is therefore exempted

6. Post Office (Borrowing Powers) Act 1967, s. 2.

from the prohibition against carrying on a deposit-taking business under the Banking Act 1979.[7]

The majority of accounts of Girobank customers are kept at a single centre at Bootle in Merseyside, which still processes all transactions. However, two Regional offices have recently been opened, in Birmingham for customers in the Midlands and Wales, and in Liverpool for customers in the North West and Northern Ireland. Accordingly, instead of using cheques, payments between account holders can be made by sending transfer instructions to the centre, which is then in a position to inform both transferor and transferee of the transfer and can advise the transferee of the purpose of the payment. Account holders can make deposits to their own accounts by using a transfer/deposit form. The form with accompanying cash can then be paid in at almost any post office. Cheques to be paid in must be posted to the centre. The same type of form is used to transfer money from one account holder to another. There is provision for standing orders between Girobank accounts where regular transfers of fixed amounts have to be made. The standing order must reach the centre at least four working days before the first payment is due to be made. At least four working days' notice must be given of any change or cancellation. Standing orders may be made to many non-Girobank outlets. A direct debits facility is also to be introduced shortly.

Cash may be withdrawn by means of a payment order called a Girocheque. The Girocheque is completed and signed by the account holder who has nominated, on the form of application to open the account, one or perhaps two post offices at which he wishes to draw the cash. He then takes the Girocheque, his withdrawal record form and his Girobank standard card (which identifies him) to one of the nominated post offices. Up to £50 may be withdrawn every other working day at either of the post offices named on the card. Holders of a Girobank guarantee card may cash a cheque for up to £50 every other working day at any post office transacting Girobank business, and up to £100 at the post office printed on the guarantee card. If over £50 is required by a customer with a standard card, or over £100 by a customer with a guarantee card, or when a customer with a standard card requires cash from a post office other that one of those named on the card, the Girocheque must first be sent to the centre where the account holder's account is debited. The Girocheque is then returned to the account holder who may cash it at any post office (except the very small ones) or, if the amount is £150 or more, at the post office nominated on the Girocheque.

Girocheques are cheques and can be crossed and sent direct to payees for payment into a bank account. Payments to persons

7. Banking Act 1979, s. 2 and Sched. 1. *See* Chapter Three.

who do not have Giro accounts can also be made using Girocheques. These are completed by the account holder, passed by him to the payee, and they can be cashed at a post office, if uncrossed, or can be paid in to the recipient's bank account for collection.

The normal minimum value of any Giro transactions is 25p. A statement of account is sent to the account holder every time money is received for his account, after ten debits or every three months.

At present no charges are made to Girobank account holders provided that their accounts remain in credit. Girobank does not provide overdrafts, and a transaction charge of 30p is made for each payment from an account on any day on which it is overdrawn at the start of business. Other Girobank services available to current account holders include Deposit and Budget accounts, Personal loans and Bridging Loans, Postcheques (for drawing cash in Europe and the USA), Travellers' Cheques, Foreign Currency and Bankers' Drafts. In addition, the Transcash service allows people who do not have Girobank accounts to pay cash into a Girobank account at any post office transacting Girobank business by using a Transcash slip obtainable at the post office.

DEPOSIT RECEIPTS

When a customer places money on deposit with a banker, a receipt is often given to him. Figure 4 is an example.

This receipt is merely a written acknowledgment by the banker that he holds a certain sum to the use of his customer. The document is usually marked "Not transferable", and it is also not negotiable. The customer, therefore, by writing his name on the receipt and transferring it to another person for value, confers no legal right on the person to whom he gives it.[8] Though a deposit receipt does not appear to be transferable by simple indorsement—the judgments on the point are not conclusive—the debt of which it is a memo-randum may be duly assigned in the same way as any other debt provided that due notice of the assignment is given to the banker. Nevertheless, the banker, before paying over the money to the assignee, is entitled to take into consideration any debt due to him by the depositor at the time he received notice of the assignment.[9]

Interest on the deposit may be paid at certain periods at an agreed rate, or the rate may vary from time to time according to either the cost of funds in the London Inter-Bank market or the bank's base rate for the time being. Most banks publish their base rates in the financial press.

8. *Moore* v. *Ulster Banking Co.* (1877) I.R. 11 C.L. 512.
9. *See* under "Set-off" in Chapter Four.

Date_____	.... BANK LIMITED
Deposit Receipt No.	**Deposit Receipt** _____ Branch
Received from (full names)	No. Date _____
_____	Received from _____
_____	the sum of _____
_____	to be placed on Deposit Account
£	FOR ...... BANK LIMITED £
Cheques Prepared by [ ] Initial of Officer signing [ ]	_____ Manager
	This Deposit Receipt is not transferable. It must be returned and discharged at the time of withdrawal

(b)

Received payment of the within named sum of
£ _____ together with the sum of
£ _____ the interest to date.

Signature(s) _____

_____

Date _____

Fig. 4   *Deposit receipt form:* (a) *face;* (b) *reverse.*

Without the express written authorisation of the depositor, the banker should not pay to a third party the sum represented by the deposit receipt. Even when he obtains the necessary written authority, the banker should ask for proof of identity before paying the money. If he pays the money to the wrong person he cannot debit the depositor, but it would appear that if the depositor by his negligence leads the banker to believe that he is paying the right person, the banker might in such circumstances be entitled to debit the depositor. The banker issuing a deposit receipt should require the depositor's written authority before paying over the money to another banker, as he would in the case of any other third party. Presentation of the deposit receipt with the depositor's mere signature is not sufficient; the signature does "not purport to be an authority to the issuing banker to pay over the money".[10] It is nothing more than a receipt for the money, and the banker collecting a deposit receipt would be liable for conversion in case of fraud, as he has no statutory protection whatever.

A deposit receipt has been held to be a good subject of a *donatio mortis causa*, i.e. a gift made in contemplation of death and to take effect only in the event of death. "It is a singular sort of gift ... neither entirely *inter vivos* [i.e. between living persons] nor testa-

10. Collins J in *Evans* v. *National Provincial Bank of England* (1897) 13 T.L.R. 429.

mentary".[11] The banker should refer any claimant to the deceased's personal representatives for their authorisation.

If the deposit receipt merely acknowledges the deposit of the money, the banker cannot demand its production before paying the money. If the form of the receipt is such, however, that the signing of the receipt is a condition precedent to the withdrawal of the money, then the deposit receipt must be returned when the money is handed over, but the banker is not entitled to withhold payment of the money should the receipt be lost or destroyed. All that he can do is to ask the depositor for an indemnity. Whether he is legally entitled to demand such an indemnity, the receipt not being a negotiable instrument, is another question. An overdraft on current account can be safely allowed by the banker on the security of the deposit account before the receipt is actually returned to him, the banker being entitled to set off any overdraft on current account against money placed on deposit. If a deposit receipt is offered to the banker who issued it as a security for the account of a third party or in support of the depositor's guarantee, the banker should obtain a memorandum of charge or a letter showing the object for which the receipt is lodged, and the receipt itself should be duly discharged by the depositor. If it is charged by a company, it must be registered under s. 95 of the Companies Act 1948. Where the receipt offered has been issued by another banker, the same procedure should be adopted and in addition notice must be served on the issuing banker in the manner applicable to the assignment of an ordinary debt.

The form of cheque sometimes printed on the back of the deposit receipt has been held not to change the nature of the account, but to be merely a convenient method adopted by bankers to preserve evidence of the withdrawal of the money. If the deposit stands in the name of a husband and wife the discharge of both is necessary, but if in the name of a firm one signature in the firm's name would be all that is required. When receipts are issued in joint names it is desirable to have instructions as to withdrawals and rights of survivors indorsed on the receipts.

There is another form of deposit receipt issued, generally by foreign and colonial banks, for "fixed" deposits. The money in these cases is deposited for definite periods, such as six or twelve months. The deposit is repayable or renewable on the expiration of the agreed period. The interest may be payable half-yearly, yearly or when the principal is due to be repaid.

Under the Limitation Act 1980 time begins to operate immediately the money is due to be repaid, i.e. after the expiration of the specified notice of withdrawal. If the deposit is for a fixed period,

11. Buckley LJ in *Re Beaumont, Beaumont* v. *Ewbank* [1902] 1 Ch. 889; [1900–3] All E.R. Rep. 273.

the statute begins to run immediately upon expiration of the agreed period. If the repayment of the money is conditional upon the return of the receipt, then the date of its return is the date upon which the statute begins to run.

A garnishee order attaches the balance payable under a deposit receipt notwithstanding any conditions as to the return of the receipt or the absence of notice.[12] Frequently, instead of issuing a deposit receipt, bankers issue deposit pass books. These contain a note of deposits and withdrawals and they usually also contain the main conditions to which the account is subject. For instance, the books usually state that they must be produced at the branch of the bank concerned when making deposits and withdrawals, and also at specified times so that accrued interest may be written in. The books usually further state that moneys deposited bear interest and are subject to a specified number of days' notice of withdrawal. It is quite usual to specify that personal application must be made when any part of the balance is withdrawn and that no payment will be made except on production of the book.[12]

CERTIFICATES OF DEPOSIT

In May 1966 there first appeared in the London market a new form of monetary instrument, namely the certificate of deposit. These are bearer documents which evidence that a sum of money has been deposited with the issuing bank, and include an undertaking to repay the sum deposited on a specified date to the then holder of the certificate, together with interest at a specified rate. Certificates are issued covering deposits for varying periods, are freely transferable and have in all probability now achieved the status of being negotiable instruments. They do not require stamping, being treated for stamp duty purposes as promissory notes.

The first certificates to appear were expressed in US dollars and were issued in respect of Eurodollar deposits (i.e. US dollar balances held by non-US residents). At that time there were legal difficulties in the way of the issue of sterling certificates of deposit, but those difficulties were later removed.

The market in sterling certificates of deposit opened on 28th October 1968. The requirements of the London Discount Market Association are that the minimum denomination should be £50,000, with multiples of £10,000 thereafter up to a maximum denomination of £500,000. The certificates have a minimum duration of three months and a maximum duration of five years. The standard size is ideally 8 in. by 5 in., but this is not compulsory. Interest on issues of one year and less is paid at maturity; on longer issues it is paid

12. *See also* Chapter Four.

annually. Forgery is believed to be one of the major risks and all certificates of deposit must be presented on maximum security paper and must be specially printed on maximum security paper. Certificates of deposit are dealt in without indorsement.

Certificates of deposit were exempt from the provisions of s. 2 of the Protection of Depositors Act 1963, and it was therefore open to a financial house not generally recognised as a bank to advertise for deposits against the issue of certificates of deposit.[13] Since the Banking Act 1979 came into force, only recognised banks may now issue them,[14] together with licensed deposit-taking institutions which have the Bank of England's permission.

```
┌──────────────────────────────────────────────────────────┐
│     NEGOTIABLE STERLING CERTIFICATE OF DEPOSIT            │
│                                                            │
│              BLANK BANK LIMITED                            │
│                                                            │
│                    Address                                 │
│                    £.............................          │
│   Serial No.............   Maturity Date.................  │
│                            London.................19...    │
│                                                            │
│   BLANK BANK LIMITED Certifies that the sum of.........    │
│   pounds sterling has been deposited upon terms that it is pay- │
│   able to bearer on surrender of this certificate, through an  │
│   authorised bank at (address as above) on the............fixed, │
│   with interest at the rate of..............per cent, per annum, │
│   calculated on a 365 day year basis, from the date hereof to  │
│   the date of maturity only, payable at maturity if one year or │
│   less from the date hereof and otherwise annually on the  │
│   anniversary of the date hereof and at maturity.          │
│       For and on behalf of      For and on behalf of       │
│       Blank Bank Limited        Blank Bank Limited         │
│       .....................     .....................      │
│       Authorised Signature      Authorised Signature       │
└──────────────────────────────────────────────────────────┘
```

Fig. 5   *Certificate of deposit.*

DIVIDEND WARRANTS AND INTEREST WARRANTS

A dividend warrant is an unconditional order in writing, addressed by or on behalf of a company to its bankers, ordering them to pay on demand a sum of money to a member of the company or his agent, in respect of a dividend due to the member arising out of his holding of shares or stock in the company. In *Slingsby* v. *Westminster Bank*[15] it was held that a warrant addressed to the Bank of England for payment of interest on 5 per cent War Stock was a dividend warrant.

13. For a specimen certificate of deposit, *see* Fig. 5.
14. Banking Act 1979, s. 1.
15. [1931] 1 K.B. 173.

An interest warrant is in many ways like a dividend warrant, being an order addressed by a borrower to its bankers, and being a payment in respect of interest due to the lender. The borrower is usually a company, municipality, public authority, or government, but warrants for the payment of interest on certain British government stocks must be regarded as dividend warrants.

Most dividend warrants are drawn in the form of cheques, and accordingly are to be treated as cheques. Sometimes, however, the warrant also bears an indication that it will not be honoured after a certain period, usually three months, from the date of issue, unless it is returned to the company for confirmation; it has been held that such a provision does not make the warrant unconditional, and that it is nevertheless a cheque.[16]

Dividend warrants in the form of cheques, payable to order or bearer, would probably be regarded as negotiable on the ground of mercantile custom, provided, of course, that there was nothing on the face of the document precluding negotiability. In practice, however, dividend warrants are frequently marked "Not negotiable". As the question of negotiability has not been settled by the courts, a collecting banker should not, for his own protection, collect such documents for persons other than the payees unless he has good reason. The banker will then not be concerned with the absence of, or irregularity in, indorsements or discharges.

Dividend warrants may be crossed, and if so the crossed cheque provisions of the Bills of Exchange Act 1882 will apply.[17] This section is of little practical importance, however, since nearly all dividend warrants fall within the definition of either a cheque or a bankers draft, and may therefore be crossed apart from this section. For those which do fall within one or other definition, the position of the paying and collecting bankers will be the same as for those classes of instrument.

Dividend warrants usually have counterfoils attached which show the gross amount of the dividend payment, the amount of the tax credit, and the net amount actually paid. The person entitled to the dividend should keep the counterfoil, as he will require it for income tax purposes.

Persons entitled to receive dividends or interest often address dividend or interest mandates to the company or authority making the payment; such mandates request and authorise the company or authority to make the payment either to the bankers of the person entitled to receive them, or to some third party's bankers. Where

16. *Thairlwall* v. *Great Northern Railway Co.* [1910] 2 K.B. 509.
17. Bills of Exchange Act 1882, s. 95.

such warrants are in favour of a third party, it saves the person entitled the necessity of banking the warrant and, if need be, making a cheque out to the third party. Such mandates are a help to the company or authority concerned, to the banks and to the recipients. The company or authority is able to issue one single cheque for all payments mandated to bank accounts; the paying bank then passes the relevant vouchers through the credit clearing and less clerical work is involved for banks. For the recipients, there is much less risk of loss.

When such mandated payments are made, the counterfoils are sent to the paying bank, each counterfoil showing the name of the person entitled to the payment, and the branch of the bank where the account is kept. The bank to which the payment is made forwards the counterfoils to the customers concerned.

It is common practice now for the amounts payable by such warrants to be shown only in figures and not in words and figures, and for the warrants to be signed by printed or lithographed facsimile signatures. It is usual for the company's or authority's bankers to require an indemnity from the company or authority in such cases.

Where dividends or interest are mandated to a bank account, the mandate is probably determined by the death of the holder or borrower who signed it, but where dividends are mandated to his own account, banks usually collect the payments and credit them either to the deceased's account or to a new account which may be operated by the executors or administrators after production of the grant of probate or letters of administration. Where the payments are mandated to the account of a third party and the third party dies, the bank should either return the payments or else seek the instructions of the mandatory.

In the case of dividend warrants there is usually provision in the company's articles of association permitting the company to make the payment by cheque or warrant sent through the post, directed to the registered address of the holder or, in the case of joint holders, to the registered address of the first named, and that any such cheque or warrant shall be made payable to the order of the person to whom it is sent.[18] Local and governmental authority stock is usually issued with similar provisions regarding payment of interest. In other cases, the person entitled to the interest or dividend may impliedly agree that the interest may be paid by cheque or warrant sent through the post.

Where such a cheque or warrant is lost, the person who was the

18. *See*, for example, Table A, No. 121, Companies Act 1948, Sched. 1.

holder of it may apply to the drawer for another bill of the same tenor; he may be required to give security to the drawer, and to indemnify him against all persons whatever in case the bill alleged to have been lost is found again.[19]

WARRANTS ISSUED BY THE DIRECTOR OF SAVINGS

Part V of the Post Office Act 1969 provided for the appointment of a Director of Savings (in place of the Postmaster General) under whose auspices those national savings facilities previously known as the Post Office Savings Bank, the Post Office Register of Stock, National Savings Certificates, Savings Bank Annuities and Insurances, and Premium Savings Bonds would be continued. The Act also provided that the two first-named should be described as the National Savings Bank and the National Savings Stock Register respectively. Savings Contracts are also now issued through the Director of Savings.

Various statutory regulations provide for payment and repayments respecting all media in two forms:

(a) in cash to the depositor/holder or his duly authorised agent or representative at a named post office (a receipt is required for this type of warrant);

(b) by means of a crossed warrant through a bank.

Certain provisions of the Bills of Exchange Act 1882 and the Cheques Act 1957 are applied by the regulations to these crossed instruments which do not, however, share all the characteristics of normal crossed cheques. It is specified that nothing in the regulations may make any such warrant negotiable.

POSTAL ORDERS AND MONEY ORDERS

Postal orders and money orders are instruments embodying instructions for money deposited at one post office to be payable at the same, or a different, post office. Postal orders are of various fixed denominations, up to £10, and their value may be increased by affixing up to two current British postage stamps. The sender of the postal order must enter the payee's name on the order in ink, and he is recommended to fill in the name of the post office of payment in the space provided. If that space is filled in, payment will be made

19. Bills of Exchange Act 1882, ss. 69 and 70. See under "Lost cheques" in Chapter Eight.

only at that office, unless the order is presented through a bank. The order also has a space for the signature of the payee on receipt of the money. Money orders may be obtained for any sum up to £50 (not including fractions of a penny). When a money order is purchased, it is handed to the purchaser to send to the payee. As a protection against theft the money order does not show the name of the person to whom it is payable, but an advice note is sent by the issuing post office to the paying post office, and this advice note shows the name of the payee. The order itself states "Pay to the person named in my advice the sum of ...". Before the money order can be paid at a post office, it must be signed by the payee as named by the payer, and the payee must give the payer's name correctly.

Neither postal orders nor money orders are negotiable instruments. They are both marked "Not negotiable", and a bona fide transferee can never obtain a better title than his transferor. A bank should, therefore, never cash them for a stranger. In each case they must be presented for payment within six months of the date of issue, and payment of a money or postal order completely discharges the post office.[20]

Both postal orders and money orders may be crossed, either generally or specially, and while this means that such orders will be paid only through a bank (in the case of special crossing, through the banker named in the crossing),[21] they are not within the crossed cheque sections of the Bills of Exchange Act 1882; as they are drawn by one post office on another they are not cheques or bills of exchange and are not one of the instruments referred to in the Cheques Act 1957.

A banker collecting postal orders (but not money orders) for customers is absolutely protected against the true owner by s. 21(3) of the Post Office Act 1953, which states that:

... any person acting as a banker ... who, in collecting in that capacity for any principal, has received payment ... in respect of any postal order or of any document purporting to be a postal order, shall not incur liability to anyone except that principal by reason of having received the payment or having held or presented the order or document for payment.

The protection of this section applies whether or not he has been negligent or has acted in the ordinary course of business, and whether or not the postal order is crossed. Since, however, bankers usually do not merely collect such instruments for their customers, but credit them as cash, they lose the protection of this section, and if the order

20. Post Office Act 1969, s. 70.
21. Post Office Scheme P5/1971; Money Order Regulations 1967, S.I. 1967 No. 801, Reg. 6(1). Money orders are to be discontinued in 1982.

proves to have been stolen, the banker would be liable in an action for conversion, and, if his right or recourse against a customer is worthless, he would lose his money.[22] When a postal order is presented for payment by a banker, the payee of the order need not have filled in his name in the space provided or have signed the receipt at the foot of the order, provided that the name of the presenting bank is stamped on the face of the order. The presenting banker, however, usually insists upon the payee writing or stamping his name on the face of the order. The bank usually presents a postal order to the nearest post office for payment, but money orders are remitted to London for presentation to the appropriate department of the Post Office.

There is, however, a danger for bankers in collecting such instruments. Although the Post Office will pay over the proceeds with little formality, if it is afterwards discovered that a money order should not have been paid, the sum paid may be deducted from any money which may subsequently become due from the Post Office to that banker.[23] Thus encashment of these orders for a banker is provisional only. Although the regulations concerning postal orders[24] are not so explicit, it seems that in practice the result is the same. The banker is, in such cases, entitled to debit his customer,[25] but by that time the customer may have closed his account, or died, or become bankrupt.

CHEQUE CARDS AND CREDIT CARDS

Cheque cards and credit cards are cards made of plastic material, carrying a specimen of the holder's signature and with certain information embossed on them so that they can be put into a press and the information on them recorded on an invoice or other document. Cheque cards are issued by all the major British and Irish banks (except for Barclays Bank which uses the Barclaycard credit card); the conditions on the back of such cheque cards state that:

The issuing bank guarantees the payment of one cheque only not exceeding £50 in any single transaction if it:

(a) is signed in the presence of the payee, the signature corresponding with that on this card;

(b) is drawn on one of its cheque forms bearing the code number shown on this card and dated before the expiry date of this card;

(c) has the card number written on the back by the payee.

22. Halsbury, *Laws of England*, (4th Edn.), Vol. 3, para. 121.
23. Post Office Act 1969, s. 71; Money Order Regulations 1967, Reg. 8(3).
24. Post Office Scheme P5/1971.
25. *London and Provincial Bank* v. *Golding* (1918) 3 L.D.B. 161.

These cheque cards make cheques effectively as good as cash so that a cheque card holder can be sure that his cheque will be accepted in payment for goods or services in any amount up to £50 in many cases where his cheque would otherwise not be accepted; he can also obtain cash during banking hours of up to £50 at any one time from any branch of any of the major British and Irish banks. When a cheque card is presented at a bank counter to enable the card holder to obtain cash, the cheque book is stamped. If the card holder wishes to make more than one withdrawal in any day, the bank at which each cheque after the first is presented telephones the card holder's bank before cashing the cheque, in order to minimise the risk of fraudulent use. Card holders may also obtain cash by this means in banks in most European countries.

The customer, when applying for a cheque card, must sign an application form which draws his attention to the fact that as the bank must pay, on first presentation, his cheques up to an amount of £50, he has no right to countermand payment of any cheque which has been accepted with the use of the cheque card.

Credit cards are designed to obviate the use of either cash or cheques, and also, in some cases, to give some measure of credit to the card holder. Like cheque cards, they bear a specimen of the holder's signature, and are embossed with the holder's name and number. They are available for use only in those establishments which have agreed to accept them. In such establishments the credit card may be tendered instead of making payment for goods or services supplied. The supplier puts the card in the imprinter machine supplied by the card organiser, which records his name and number on the sales voucher. The card holder signs the voucher and the supplier checks the signature with the specimen on the card. The credit card organiser then makes payment to the supplier (less a discount agreed with the trader, depending on the average size of the transaction, the volume of trade and, sometimes, the mark-up on particular goods) and once a month sends an invoice to the credit card holder for all his purchases in the previous month. The card holder does not pay any interest, provided he pays the sum due within a specified time; alternatively he may pay some lesser amount (being not less than the then current prescribed minimum amount) and pay interest on the balance. Barclays Bank operates its own credit card service known as Barclaycard and in addition to being credit cards, these cards permit holders to draw cash during banking hours from any branch of Barclays Bank in an amount of up to £50 at any one time.

CASH CARDS AND SERVICETILL

Cash card

With Saturday closing and the desirability of reducing the necessity for carrying large amounts of cash, the major banks have instituted a 24-hour cash card service. Electronically operated cash dispensers have been installed in many branches, particularly at focal points, e.g. branches adjacent to main line railway stations and important shopping centres. Under one system a customer inserts a specially prepared cash card and identifies himself by keying into the machine his personal code number (which cannot be deciphered from the card itself) and then obtains a packet containing £10 (in £1 notes). The cash card is retained in the dispenser, and, following its removal by the branch, the customer is debited £10. The card is then returned to him through his account-holding branch for future use. There is no limit to the number of cash cards held by any one customer, but quite obviously his credit-worthiness will determine whether or not the bank will allow him the facility of holding several cards.

Under another system the card may be used up to twenty times before it is retained; a third system involves the use of vouchers, supplied in books of twenty. With the spread of Servicetill, mentioned below, cash cards have now been largely replaced.

Servicetill

A more sophisticated electronic machine, known as the Servicetill, has recently been introduced, and has found considerable favour with customers through its versatility. Operated by a plastic card similar to a cheque card but containing information coded into a magnetic stripe, and keyed by a personal number known only to the card holder, the machine can dispense cash in any amount up to a daily or weekly limit previously advised to the customer. As it is directly linked to the bank's computer, it can also accept a request for a new cheque book or statement of account and arrange for these to be transmitted to the account holder. During the hours when the computer system is open (generally 8 a.m. to 6 p.m. on Monday to Friday) a customer can also obtain the balance of his current account as at the close of business on the previous working day. After use, the card is returned direct to the customer by the machine, and is immediately available for further use (within the overall cash drawing limit of course).

The application form for a Servicetill card incorporates certain conditions of use designed to protect both bank and customer, prime among which is the authority from the customer to debit his account whenever cash is drawn.

TRAVELLERS' CHEQUES

Travellers' cheques (often called travel cheques) are issued mainly for the convenience of persons travelling abroad and are today the usual method whereby travellers take currency abroad to provide for their expenses. Travellers' cheques issued in the United Kingdom are usually expressed in sterling amounts (though travellers' cheques in other currencies, e.g. US dollars, are available), and are issued in fixed denominations such as £5, £10, £20, £50 and £100. Figure 6 gives an example. Travellers' cheques normally take two forms: either they are expressed to be drawn by the traveller and countersigned by the issuing bank, or else they are drawn by the issuing bank on itself and countersigned by the traveller. The essential thing is, however, that they are signed by the traveller in the presence of the issuing bank and when cashed are signed again by the traveller in the presence of the cashing banker or other person. Some banks issue travel cheques which may be made payable to third parties; if no such name is inserted when the cheque is cashed, it is treated as above; if a third party's name does appear, however, the cheque should be endorsed by him before encashment.

Fig. 6   *Specimen traveller's cheque.*
(*Courtesy of the Financial Times.*)

Travellers' cheques are normally cashed at the current buying rate for demand drafts on London. Normally no commission is charged and the cashing banker makes his profit on the transaction in the rate of exchange. The issuing banker charges a commission (typically 1 per cent), and also has the use of the travellers' funds pending payment.

The value of travellers' cheques not used by the traveller will be credited to him on his surrendering them to the issuing banker. If travellers' cheques are lost, the loss may technically be the traveller's, but most major banks now undertake to replace lost or stolen cheques provided the local police have been informed. Generally an immediate refund can be made up to say £150, with the balance on application and further consideration.

Travellers' cheques are probably negotiable instruments by the law of the United Kingdom. They are certainly so by the law of the United States. Travellers' cheques, however, do not come within the scope of the Cheques Act 1957.

Travellers' cheques should be valid indefinitely and authorised for negotiation in all countries of the world, unless they bear a restrictive indorsement prohibiting negotiation in certain specified countries. With the abolition of exchange control in the UK there is nothing to prevent a traveller using his domestic cheque book to cash a cheque (with cheque card) in any currency he pleases, or in sterling, in any country which will accept them. Such cheques are treated as demand drafts and negotiated at the current buying rate on London.

Travellers' cheques are a security document and incorporate a number of special identification marks which a forger would be unlikely to be able to duplicate.

LEGAL MONEY

The tokens known as money, which constitute a legal medium of exchange, consist in England either of coins made and issued by the Crown under the exclusive powers it enjoys at common law which are now for the most part regulated by statute,[26] or of bank-notes made and issued by the Bank of England under statutory powers.

A bank-note is a promissory note made and issued by a banker and payable to bearer on demand. Bank-notes, said Lord Mansfield, "are treated as money, as cash, in the ordinary course and transaction of business, by the general consent of mankind, which gives them the credit and currency of money to all intents and purposes."[27]

The right to issue bank-notes in England and Wales has become

26. Coinage Act 1971.
27. *Miller* v. *Race* (1758) 97 E.R. 398.

a monopoly of the Bank of England. The Bank of England may only issue bank-notes of such denominations as the Treasury may approve.[28] Any bank-notes so issued may be put into circulation in Scotland and Northern Ireland as well as in England and Wales. Bank of England notes are issued in denominations of £1, £5, £10, £20 and £50.

All Bank of England notes (save those which have been called in) are legal tender in England and Wales for any amount. So long as there remains in force s. 1(1) of the Gold Standard Act 1925, which provides that the Bank of England shall not be bound to pay any of its notes in legal coin, bank-notes are legal tender by the Bank itself. In Scotland and Northern Ireland all Bank of England notes are in circulation, but only notes of £1 are legal tender. Bank-notes issued by Scottish and Northern Irish banks circulate in Scotland and Northern Ireland respectively but are not legal tender.

Although Bank of England notes of over £1 circulate in Scotland and Northern Ireland, they are not legal tender in those parts of the British Isles if, at the time of tender, the person offered payment refuses to accept them.

The finder of a lost note has a good title against everyone except the loser, and if the finder transfers it to a person who takes it honestly and for value, the transferee has a good title against all the world, even the loser. But the loser may always sue the finder for conversion. Notes found on premises not open to the public may belong either to the occupier of the property or to the finder, but it has been held that a bundle of bank-notes found on the floor of a shop belonged to the finder, subject to the true owner's title.[29]

The payment of lost, destroyed or damaged notes is not governed by statute and the method of dealing with such claims is modified from time to time to keep abreast of changing conditions.

The procedure for dealing with mutilated notes depends on whether they are slightly or badly damaged. Slightly mutilated notes can be exchanged at banks and post offices. A mutilated note which satisfies the following requirements is payable at sight.

(a) It must be greater in area than half a whole note, and, if not in one piece, consist of not more than four fragments.

(b) It must contain the whole of the sentence "I promise to pay the Bearer on Demand the sum of ... pound(s)".

(c) It must contain at least one third of the signature.

28. Currency and Bank Notes Act 1954, s. 1.
29. *Bridges* v. *Hawkesworth* (1851) 21 L.J.Q.B. 75.

(*d*) For £5 notes and higher denominations only, the note must bear one complete series index and serial number, not necessarily in one corner, and at least two whole letters or figures in either corner in addition to this requirement.

Mutilated notes which do not satisfy these requirements (and all called-in mutilated notes) must be submitted to the Bank of England accompanied by a form completed by the applicant, giving details of the notes involved in the claim, the circumstances in which they were damaged, and the names and addresses of any witnesses to an accident and a person who can vouch for the applicant's good faith. Applications may be submitted either through a bank, which will provide the necessary form, or direct to the Bank of England by registered post, in which case the appropriate form is obtainable from post offices. Successful claims are paid either by credit to the applicant's bank or through a post office. No payment can be made when there are no identifiable remains available, but a heap of charred or pulped fragments would be worth preserving, since Bank of England experts can often discover how many notes can be traced.

The thief has no title to a stolen bank-note, but a bona fide transferee for value gets a good title even against the true owner.

It is not now the practice of the Bank of England to register stops on the payment of bank-notes of any denomination.

Printing, or stamping, or impressing on any bank-notes by any like means any words, letters or figures, is an offence.[30] This is to prevent any notes being disfigured by advertisements and in particular to enable the Bank to re-issue the notes if so desired. The Bank of England nevertheless permits banks to indorse a name and address and a branch stamp on the back of notes of £5 and upwards of old issues (i.e. those dated prior to 21st September 1956), and they are also permitted to mark current issue notes lightly on the back in lead pencil to assist in checking and identification.

Since bank-notes are promissory notes, many of the provisions of the Bills of Exchange Act 1882 apply to such notes.[31] Thus although a holder with no title or a defective title cannot compel a payment of a note by the Bank of England,[32] if a person takes such a note honestly and for value and without notice of any defect, he can acquire a better title than his transferor, and so acquires a good title and can enforce payment.[33]

30. Currency and Bank Notes Act 1928, s. 12.
31. *See* under "Promisory notes" in Chapter Nine.
32. *Raphael* v. *Bank of England* (1855) 17 C.B. 161.
33. *De la Chaumette* v. *Bank of England* (1829) 9 B. & C. 208.

A person who takes forged or altered notes may recover their value from his transferor. The claim for recovery must, however, be made within a reasonable time. A transferor by delivery who negotiates a bill thereby warrants to his immediate transferee being a holder for value that the bill is what it purports to be.[34] A bill includes a bank-note. In *Suffell* v. *Bank of England*[35] Jessel MR held that the number on a Bank of England note was a material part of the note, and that any alteration of the number vitiated the note, and that even a bona fide holder for value could not recover on it. In this particular case the alteration was effected to prevent its recognition as a stolen note. This judgment shows that the proviso to s. 64(1) of the Bills of Exchange Act 1882[36] does not apply to Bank of England notes.[37]

The Limitation Act 1980 has no application to Bank of England notes. No matter how long such a note remains in circulation, the issuing bank is not discharged from liability. In s. 6 of the Bank Act 1892, there is a special provision with regard to Bank of England notes (other than £1 and 10s.) issued more than forty years ago and not presented for payment. The Bank is permitted to write off the amount of such non-presented notes, but must nevertheless pay them when presented.[38] For £1 and 10s. notes the period is twenty years.[39]

Banks treat foreign bank-notes as foreign bills and send them to London to be sold. Banks should not put their name stamps on foreign notes for identification purposes, as it may possibly affect the value of the notes when negotiated.

The manufacture of coins is carried out by the Royal Mint, and the following are legal tender:

(*a*) gold coins for payment of any amount, though in practice gold coins are unlikely to be tendered since they are now intrinsically worth many times their face value;

(*b*) cupro-nickel or silver coins of denominations of more than 10p, for payment of any amount not exceeding £10;

(*c*) cupro-nickel coins of denominations of not more than 10p, for payment of any amount not exceeding £5.

(*d*) bronze coins for payment of any amount not exceeding 20p.[40]

---

34. Bills of Exchange Act 1882, s. 58(3).
35. (1882) 9 Q.B.D. 555: [1881–5] All E.R. Rep. Ext. 1633.
36. *See* Chapter Eight.
37. Though clearly s. 58 does apply.
38. Bank Act 1892, s. 6. All 10s. notes have been called in.
39. Currency and Bank Notes Act 1928, s. 7.
40. Coinage Act 1971, s. 2.

No piece of gold, silver, copper or bronze, or of any metal or mixed metal, of any value whatsoever, may be made or issued except by or with the authority of the Treasury, as a coin or a token for money, or as purporting that its holder is entitled to demand any value denoted on it.[41]

41. Ibid., s. 9; Goverment Trading Funds Act 1973, s. 7.

PART IV

LENDING AND SECURITY

CHAPTER TWELVE

Bank Lending

LENDING POLICY

One of the main functions of a banker is to accept deposits from certain of his customers and use these funds in his capacity of "expert lender" to satisfy the borrowing requirements of other customers. As a lender of other people's money, he should ideally be assured that those to whom he lends will be able to use the money to such advantage that they are able to repay it at the time and on the terms agreed at the outset, together with the appropriate charges for the use of the money. Thus he can guarantee to the depositors the security of the funds, he can satisfy the liquidity requirements of his borrowers, and he can generate from the process sufficient profit both to maintain and expand his bank's position within the community, and to provide his shareholders with an adequate return on their capital.

Clearly, no banker will lend money on a proposition which manifestly does not satisfy the above criterion or on which he entertains the most serious doubts. It has never been regarded as the duty of a branch banker to provide venture or risk capital. The majority of propositions, however, have one or more features which are to some extent not ideal, and the art of the banker is to minimise the potential risk which those factors may cause. It would be quite unrealistic to expect never to lose money in the course of a career of lending, for even the most far-sighted banker cannot predict the effect on his customer's business of events beyond the control of either, but his experience and training ought to be such that he will in practice lose only a very tiny proportion of what he lends. To this end, a number of criteria have been identified which can assist him in reaching his decision on any particular proposition. Most of these are not rules, but touch-stones, for a good banker will also have learned to be flexible, and it may be that in any particular case there are overriding reasons why one or more of the common principles should not be applied. The following sections detail the main techniques of appraisal.

Integrity, status and competence

This is the cardinal consideration. The banker handling other people's money is being entrusted with its disposition. If he is not entirely satisfied about the creditworthiness of a potential borrower he should not agree to lend. In many cases, of course, the banker will have from his personal experience and files enough information to assess this aspect adequately; more care must be taken with a new customer to establish his background and ability, perhaps by obtaining status reports, by examining balance sheets, if available, to establish previous performance, and by carefully analysing the specific proposition under consideration. Certain detailed techniques may assist here.

The size of the business involved is no criterion. There have been some spectacular collapses of companies whose projected image was such that few foresaw the possibility of failure, although with hindsight the danger signs had been clear enough. A good guide to competence may lie in how well information and the request for assistance is presented. A careless or inadequate approach may well imply poor performance later; one can also assess how quickly and thoroughly queries are answered and additional detail provided.

It is not necessarily a bad sign that another bank has declined to assist on a particular proposition. It may have seemed unattractive for reasons unconnected with the project itself; an initially doubtful or even impossible proposition can often be restructured into an acceptable risk by a helpful and competent banker, and it is part of his duty to his customer to assist in this way if he can.

Special considerations must be borne in mind if a loan to a sovereign country is contemplated, in view of the concept of sovereign immunity. Although this does not seem to have been tested in any courts as a matter of principle, it is certainly true that several countries have effectively refused to meet their obligations (generally those undertaken by previous governments, as, for example, Imperial China). Other countries have defaulted on debt, and had their obligations restructured (e.g. Turkey and Zaire), but in such cases the need for continued assistance generally outweighs the advantage of claiming sovereign immunity. In many international loan agreements, right to claim such immunity is specifically abrogated, and by the State Immunity Act 1978 governments and state organisations may not, under English law, claim sovereign immunity on certain contractual obligations.

No bank will wish to be over-committed in any specific area of lending, or to any particular country, so that its loan portfolio becomes unbalanced. As part of the process of risk assessment, therefore, it is common to assign overall limits to individual countries, and to the less common types of risk undertaken, so that imbalance is avoided—these limits are usually indicative rather than binding as it would obviously be foolish to turn aside an otherwise excellent proposition on purely arbitrary grounds.

There may be special considerations relating to the borrowing powers of a limited company, or a group of trustees or other category of customer, and the appropriate status and possible restrictions must be established at the outset. This is even more important where foreign-controlled companies are involved, as it may be quite difficult to establish what (if any) controls apply.

Other indications of status may be given by the length of time that a company or firm has been established, and, if it is part of a group, what its parentage is or with what (more important) companies it is associated. In the final analysis, much will depend on the banker's own assessment of the man sitting opposite him, and a vital part of a banker's armoury will be a reliable ability to weigh up those intangible factors which, with a good knowledge of human nature, will enable him to come to a sound decision.

Purpose

A banker will want to know exactly what the money he lends is to be used for. There are two main reasons for this: he must assure himself first that the purpose is legal (e.g. no improper company funding of purchases of its own shares),[1] and secondly that the intended use is reasonably likely to produce the sort of profitable result which both parties desire. Bankers are, in general, reluctant to provide "standby" facilities to any except the most reliable and important customers, in view of the lack of control which such provision involves.

Propositions which are purely speculative should be avoided (there are other sources of capital available which are more appropriate), but it is not unreasonable to expect a banker to undertake "a fair trade risk" as long as it is remembered that the parameters defining a fair risk are necessarily narrower for a banker than for an entrepreneur. That one must speculate to accumulate is a truism, but this does not mean that the good banker will have any truck with a purely speculative proposition. It should be noted that borrowing for the acquisition of a particular item differs from that for refinance,

1. *See* Chapter Six.

expansion, construction, or that blanket term covering so many categories, "infrastructure". All the latter are dependent on other factors for their success, whilst the possession of the newly-purchased item, be it a car or a factory, does offer at least some immediate tangible benefit.

One particular area which is usually deemed prudent for the branch banker to avoid is "accommodation banking". This can take various forms, but at its simplest it is borrowing against a future undertaking to pay; if against a bill of exchange, the particular type of bill is defined in s. 28 of the Bills of Exchange Act 1882. The accommodation party[2] puts his name to a bill without receiving consideration, and does not expect to have to pay the bill when due. However, his name on the bill may enable the drawer to discount it for immediate funds, with a view to meeting the bill himself at maturity. A banker may agree to discount such a bill (in which case he becomes a holder for value), but of course he will make the usual charge for providing that service.

Source of repayment

The lending banker will wish to know the source of repayment, so as to ensure that repayment proposals are clear and well thought-out. If the lending is not self-liquidating, that is, if the item acquired or project financed does not of its own accord generate sufficient funds to repay the borrowing within a reasonable period of time, then the lending banker must be satisfied that there are alternative sources of repayment, either from salary or from profits. It is not good to rely on repayment from a third party, even if the relationship is close, and even backing the reliance with a guarantee may not always provide sufficient support. In the case of limited companies, the concept of commercial justification renders directors liable to account to shareholders for any commitments to which they bind their companies. In an extreme case it is quite possible that such planned repayment could be avoided.

Where a term loan is involved for project finance, it may be that the borrower is unable to consider commencing repayments at once, although the project will be self-liquidating once it comes on-stream. In these cases it is common for a grace period to be incorporated in the loan terms. During this period, the borrower will only have to cover interest payments, leaving the capital debt untouched for an agreed term. Occasionally it is agreed that interest payments may be made by further drawings of the loan, effectively capitalising the interest until completion.

2. *See* Chapter Seven.

The mere fact that both the banker and the borrower consider it likely that the borrower will repay the loan out of a particular fund does not amount to a contractual term that repayment is to be made out of this fund and this fund alone, nor does it give rise to an obligation on the part of the bank to ensure that it does nothing to delay or impede repayment out of that fund.

Duration of risk

There are two aspects to be considered with regard to the duration of the risk. First, the banker must not forget that the money which he is lending is, generally speaking, on short-term deposit, or in current account. It is not, therefore, sensible to commit it in long-term loans which cannot be repaid quickly if the need should arise. That said as a basic principle, it is of course normal for the banker to rely on the statistical improbability that at any given time enough depositing customers will demand repayment of their funds actually to cause him any embarrassment. (In fact, if all depositing customers demanded repayment, there is nowhere near enough ready cash in the country to satisfy demand.) So enormous are the deposits held by the clearing banks in particular that it is most unlikely that any serious problems would arise from what is technically known as "mismatching" of deposits and advances, although it is naturally an aspect which is very carefully monitored and controlled by the treasurers' departments and ultimately by the boards of directors.[3] Where it is clear that mismatching could cause problems, as may happen with overseas branches where local currency is in short supply, it is wise, and normal, to ensure that all advances are funded by matching deposits.

Secondly, in the case of long-term lending the banker must be aware of the possible effect of changing economic and political circumstances. This is particularly true of lending on the international market, where a revolution or a coup or a natural disaster may radically alter the chances of repayment of a loan. Most international banks employ sophisticated methods of "risk assessment", assigning particular values to various factors pertaining to the country involved (e.g. import cover, debt service ratio, political vulnerability and so on); in conjunction with other assessments of a more personal nature these quasi-scientific judgments can help to quantify long-term risk and assist the banker's decision.

Profitability

Naturally the banker wants to make a profit on his lending, both

3. Also, to a certain extent, by the Bank of England. *See* Chapter Two.

to enable the business to grow, and to provide the bank's owners with an adequate return on their capital. His calculations must be based on the cost of funds to him (i.e. basically the rate he pays to his depositors), and the overheads of his business. The specific costs of documenting and arranging a particular loan may well be covered by an arrangement fee, but the banker relies on the interest differential to provide the major part of his profit. The actual interest "mark-up" (i.e. over the cost of funds) is determined by many factors, not the least of which is policy. Different types of borrowing attract different formulae of interest representing such considerations as risk of loss, risk of mismatching and so on; generally speaking the appropriate rates are determined by a bank's head office, although individual branch managers may be given some amount of discretion to vary them.

The interest mark-up on Eurocurrency borrowing is usually expressed as a percentage above either the inter-bank offer rate (that is, the interest payable on inter-bank deposits, usually expressed as LIBOR in London, SIBOR in Singapore, BIBOR in Bahrain, etc.), or the lender's offer rate (abbreviated to LOR), which is the rate at which funds are offered to prime names in the inter-bank market.

The interest mark-up in the UK is often expressed as a percentage over the bank's own base rate, a concept which replaced bank rate as a result of Competition and Credit Control[4] in 1971. In practice, competition is so intense that it is very rare for any of the major banks to move out of line with the others for more than a few days. It is also often expressed as a percentage over LIBOR. The advantage of linking the cost of borrowing to the cost of funding is obvious, as their movement in tandem removes the chance of a squeeze on profit margins.

Fixed-rate borrowing is also possible, although a suitable margin is incorporated to cover the possibility that base rates or lender's offer rates rise during the contractual period, when the lender's profit margin would be squeezed by the cost of funding.

Another consideration concerned with profit is "spin-off", the benefit gained from business attracted by, but not directly related to, a particular loan or overdraft, e.g. appointment of bank as executor or trustee, life insurance, or some other related banking service.

Security

The greater part of lending in the UK is unsecured, that is to say, on the strength of the private borrower's personal integrity or the

---

4. *See* Chapter Two.

corporate customer's balance sheet. Techniques for assessing the balance sheet are manifold, and, in the hands of a skilled assessor, fairly reliable. A few of them are mentioned below.

Detailed comments on security will be found elsewhere in this book, but the obvious points to consider are type, value, chargor and realisability.

Obvious differences exist between different types of charge, such as legal and equitable charges, and informal deposit, and also between tangible security (e.g. land, shares) and intangible (e.g. guarantees, indemnities, and letters of comfort or awareness).

It is essential to be realistic in assigning a value to security. Generally speaking the banker likes to consider the "forced sale value" in case, by the time it is necessary to sell the item concerned to recover money, the market is not favourable to the vendor, and he cannot obtain the maximum benefit.

If a borrower has no assets to charge, a third party may act as guarantor. If he provides a guarantee, he undertakes to pay if the borrower fails; he may then, and only then, be subrogated to the right of the lender to receive money or realise assets. In effect this means that the guarantor who has paid up has the right to take over, and realise, any other security given to the lender up to the value of his guarantee. If the guarantor provides an indemnity, he undertakes to pay if called upon under the appropriate circumstances, and his liability remains even if the underlying contract is for any reason invalid (e.g. if the borrower is a minor not borrowing for "necessaries").[5]

The easier it is to realise security, the better. Perhaps the easiest security to take is the guarantee, but it is often the hardest to realise unless the guarantor co-operates. If he does not, co-operation must be enforced by the courts, and even then success is not always achieved. The best security is a legal charge over cash ("cash cover"), followed by legal charges over property and other tangible assets.

Appraising balance sheets

Books have been written on this topic, and the reader is referred to one of them for detailed discussion of the various techniques.[6] Briefly however, the lender may concentrate on certain relationships apparent in annual accounts, and these may assist him in reaching his decision.

Proprietors' stake or *surplus resources* is that amount by which

5. *See* Chapter Fourteen; *see* under "Minors" in Chapter Five for "necessaries".
6. One of the best is *Management Accounting for the Lending Banker* by M.A. Pitcher.

total assets exceed current, medium- and long-term liabilities. In other words, if assets (generally ignoring "intangible assets" like goodwill and short-term leases which may be valueless in the event of winding up) are utilised to pay off all external creditors, whatever remains is the owner's, and represents the worth of the business. If this is negative, the business is insolvent, and the owner would have to inject further cash to pay off all external creditors.

Liquid surplus is the difference between current assets and current liabilities, and represents the margin available to meet the latter. If it is negative, the implication is that fixed assets are being relied on as cover for current liabilities, with obvious problems for the business if those liabilities suddenly fall due. If stock is excluded from current assets, the ratio is known as the *quick assets ratio*, and its common name of "acid test" indicates its importance—it will indicate just how vulnerable the business is to immediate presentation of all its bills, and may be particularly important in time of recession.

The ratio of gross profit to turnover and net profit to turnover can be used to assess the significance of a business's overheads, but of course it is necessary to be aware of the average ratios for the particular business involved.

Other ratios which are useful give the "time allowed to debtors" and "time taken from creditors", the "gearing", the "rate of stock turnover" and so on. Not all will be relevant to every set of accounts, and mechanical calculation of ratios should be avoided as they will only be helpful if used intelligently. They are an aid to assessment, not an assessment in themselves, and there is no substitute for the careful balancing by an experienced banker of all the factors involved in a proposition.

The manager's discretion

A major bank with many branches will have a large number of managers who are authorised to commit the bank to a lending proposition. Not all branches are of equal size, nor is their business of equal complexity; it follows, therefore, that different managers will be granted different discretionary powers, appropriate to their responsibility and seniority. Propositions in excess of an individual manager's discretion will normally have to be referred for approval to his head office, either local or central, and a very large proposition may be referred upwards even until it reaches board level. The method of reference will be individual to each bank, but clearly the submitting manager will need to cover all the various aspects as outlined above, and also add his recommendation on whether the application should be approved or declined.

OVERDRAFT AND LOAN ACCOUNT

The traditional method for banks to provide lending facilities to customers was, and still remains, the overdraft, an agreed line of credit operating directly through the current account, but the last decade has seen the banks willing to provide medium-term finance on a contractual basis by way of loan account. As a general rule, the overdraft is ideal to cover short-term requirements, e.g. for working capital, where considerable fluctuation due to factors such as production cycles or seasonal changes may be expected, whilst the loan account is more appropriate for providing funds for investment projects where repayment can be amortised at predetermined intervals or made in full at the end of an agreed period.

Interest on overdraft is charged only on the outstanding amount borrowed, calculated on a daily basis, so that regular fluctuations can render this type of borrowing considerably cheaper than the amount of the agreed limit might imply. Sometimes, however, a bank may charge a commitment fee on a large overdraft, to cover the cost of ensuring that the necessary funds are available for drawdown whenever required; inevitably some accounts operate in permanent overdraft, although the actual balance may still fluctuate from day to day. The minimum debit balance is known as the "hard-core" and may attract an additional interest weighting. Overdrafts are repayable on demand, but it is not normally the practice to call them in as long as the account is properly conducted; in general, they provide a simple and easily arranged method of covering borrowing requirements.

An overdraft is, unless there is some express or implied term to the contrary, repayable on demand. As an alternative, the bank may offer a term loan. If there is no formal loan agreement, the bank normally reserves the right to claim repayment on demand, but in practice repayments can be spread over several years. If a period is mentioned, and the bank wishes to have the right to call in the loan on demand, it will not be enough simply to describe the money lent as being an overdraft. Unless the right to repayment on demand is expressly reserved, the banker will not be entitled to call for repayment within that period.

The maximum period is generally seven years, although longer terms are possible. The borrower then knows that unless the right to repayment on demand is reserved, he can rely on its availability, and can plan its repayment in advance, with obvious benefits to his cash flow. Even if the banker does reserve the right to call in the loan on demand, the borrower can in practice rely on its availability for the full period unless he misuses the facility or becomes insolvent. The arrangement of such loans is generally very straight-forward, and the absence of complicated legal documentation is of particular advantage to the private customer and the small business. It is not uncommon for a "hard-core" overdraft to be funded on to loan account, and the discipline of providing regular repayments may well enable a customer to reduce his requirement for such "hard-core" borrowing.

Contractual medium-term lending is backed by a legally binding agreement between lender and borrower.[7] It is common for repayments to be deferred for several years when the loan is for major project finance, to allow the project to come "on-stream" before any repayments are required; these can then be achieved from generated profits. This is known as a self-liquidating advance.

In general, banks prefer not to lend for periods longer than ten years because of the possible funding difficulties; however, the clearing banks hold 85 per cent of the shares of Finance for Industry (FFI) which is the holding company of the Industrial and Commercial Finance Corporation (ICFC) and Finance Corporation for Industry (FCI). The former provides long-term capital for companies which are too small to go to the stock market, whilst the latter provides long-term finance for large industrial projects; both fund their loans from debenture and loan stock issues, from moneys provided by the banks, and from public deposits.

Other services provided by banks which enable corporate customers to finance their requirements include factoring, leasing, discounting of bills, and hire-purchase.[8] Frequently, in view of the technicalities peculiar to these types of credit, the services are provided by a subsidiary company specialising in such business.

Both business and personal customers may take advantage of fixed-interest loans (the rate sometimes being finer if security is provided). Monthly repayments cover both interest and principal, and the term is normally up to five years. This type of loan is particularly convenient for financing home improvements and car purchase, and is often covered by an insurance policy which repays the loan outright in the event of the borrower's death. Private customers may also borrow on budget account to finance their regular expenses. An annual estimate of the total is made, and one-twelfth of this sum paid monthly into a special account which is used to meet expenses as they fall due. Interest may not be charged on the borrowing which arises, depending on the particular scheme operated by the bank. If not, the bank takes its profit from an initial commission charge based on the size of the annual commitment.

7. *See* below in this chapter.
8. *See* separate chapters on these topics.

Ideally such an account should show wide fluctuations between credit and debit. Revolving credit loans are also available from some banks, and these are somewhat similar to budget accounts except that no schedule of commitments is required, and interest is usually paid to the customer on any credit balance maintained.

The banks also operate credit card schemes in the form of Access and Barclaycard, and these provide another method of offering lending facilities. The customer has the benefit of free credit on his purchases until the bank's credit card company sends him his monthly bill. He may then choose to settle the bill in full or, subject to an appropriate minimum, pay an amount convenient to himself, spreading the cost of his purchases over a number of months. Each customer has a credit limit agreed with the bank, and may use his card freely and repeatedly within that limit. Interest is charged on a daily basis if the customer makes use of this extended credit facility, and it is also possible to use the card to draw cash direct from the bank; in this case no free credit period is allowed. Barclay card still give a credit free period for this type of withdrawal but charge a fee of one percent for the withdrawal. The schemes are very flexible, and have proved very popular. Diners Club and American Express also offer a credit-free period on their cards pending presentation of the monthly bill, but cash withdrawals are not permitted, and extended payment facilities are not normally available.

LOAN AGREEMENT

Where advances are made for a fixed period, and in some cases where they are repayable on demand, it is the usual practice for the bank to require a formal loan agreement or facility agreement. This will obviously deal with matters such as the amount of the facility, how drawings may be made and when, and how advances are to be used, when repayment is required to be made and how interest is to be calculated. It is becoming increasingly common these days for the interest rate to be geared to LIBOR.[9] In such cases, there will usually be provisions governing how the length of the successive interest periods is to be selected. It is usual in such cases for the lending bank to match the borrowings by taking deposits in the inter-bank market for the same period, and if pre-payments are to be allowed otherwise than at the end of such an interest period, there is usually provision for the borrower to compensate the bank for any loss of interest if the bank is not able to redeploy funds so repaid for the balance of the interest period except at a lower rate of interest.

9. *See* above in this chapter.

Other clauses will require the borrower to pay the interest without any deductions, and, if any deductions are required by law, to pay to the bank such additional amount as will ensure that the bank will, after any such deduction, receive the same net amount as it would have received if no such deductions had been required to be made. The borrower will also be required to compensate the bank if reserve assets or other requirements of any relevant authority increase the cost to the bank of maintaining the advances.

Another clause will govern the various conditions which must be fulfilled before any advance will be made. These will include such formal matters as delivery of the memorandum and articles of association of any relevant company, certified copies of board resolutions, the execution of any necessary guarantees and security documentation, and in addition any commercial conditions which may apply. There may be other requirements imposed on the borrower, such as the need to maintain particular capital or liquidity ratios. Another clause will deal with warranties and representations made by the borrower and any guarantor, dealing with matters such as their corporate status, their powers to enter into the arrangements and carry them into effect, and the fact that no provisions of their constitution or any contractual terms binding upon them will be violated by the arrangements, and that any proper authorisations which may be required have been obtained. There will then be a "default events" clause, permitting the bank to cancel the facility and declare any advances already made to be due and payable if any of the enumerated events should occur.

Finally there will be clauses dealing with matters such as costs, service of notices, and provisions to the effect that the various remedies are cumulative and not exclusive of any remedies provided by law, and that no delay in enforcing any right is to be regarded as a waiver of any breach.

THE CONSUMER CREDIT ACT 1974

This Act is designed to control the working of the credit industry in relation to individuals and unincorporated bodies, and primarily covers credit transactions in that sector up to £5,000. It runs hand in hand with the Fair Trading Act 1973, and both Acts are administered by the Director General of Fair Trading. The Consumer Credit Act 1974 covers all forms of credit and includes conditional-sale agreements and rental agreements as well as the more obvious forms of lending. Many parliamentary orders, regulations and other legislative controls supplement the main Act, and it replaces the protection given to borrowers under all earlier Pawnbrokers, Money-lenders and Hire-Purchase Acts.

Credit business regulation

All institutions which are concerned with consumer credit services, such as banks, finance houses, shops, credit reference agencies and debt-collecting agencies require a licence issued by the Director General to cover one or more of the following categories:

(a) consumer credit[10],
(b) consumer hire[10],
(c) credit brokerage[11],
(d) debt-adjusting and debt-counselling[11],
(e) debt-collecting[11],
(f) operating a credit reference agency[11],
(g) canvassing off trade premises (in relation to (a) and (b) only).[12]

Categories (c) to (f) come under a group heading of ancillary credit services.[13] The licence is valid for ten years in the first case, but may be renewed on application; it authorises only the named licence-holder to carry on the specific business named. It is not transferable, and lapses on the death, bankruptcy or mental incapacity of the holder. In a partnership, however, a change of partners only does not terminate a licence, nor does the appointment of a receiver or liquidator to a limited company. A licence may be suspended or revoked by the Director General, but before doing so he must inform the licensee of his intention and give him an opportunity of making representations.[14]

It is an offence to carry on a business concerned with the credit activities noted above either without a valid licence or under a name not specified in the licence.[15] The maximum penalties are (a) a fine of £1,000 on a summary conviction, (b) two years' imprisonment on indictment and/or an unlimited fine.[16] As agreements entered into by an unlicensed trader may be unenforceable,[17] a bank could be at risk if an unlicensed or improperly licensed customer continues to trade and has a liability to the bank; equally, a bank which lent to a customer under an agreement which falls within the scope of

10. Consumer Credit Act 1974, s. 21.
11. Ibid., s. 147.
12. Ibid., s. 23(3).
13. Ibid., s. 145.
14. Ibid., s. 32.
15. Ibid., s. 39.
16. Ibid., s. 167.
17. Ibid., s. 40.

the Act might be at risk if that customer had been introduced by an unlicensed credit broker.[18]

Certain classes of advisers, notably solicitors, accountants, Citizens' Advice Bureaux and certain Old Peoples' Welfare Organisations have been issued with special group licences which permit them to carry out debt-adjusting and debt-counselling; solicitors and accountants may also carry out the business of consumer credit and credit brokerage under their group licences, and solicitors may engage in debt-collecting, provided these activities arise in the normal course of business.

The categories

(a) *Consumer credit.* Where a person in the course of business provides credit of £5,000 or under to individuals, partnerships, firms or unincorporated bodies, such facilities are provided under regulated consumer credit agreements[19] and that person is required to be licensed[20] unless the credit provided is:[21]

(i) always by way of mortgage over land and the person is a building society, local authority or any other "specified" body including most life assurance/insurance companies, certain friendly societies and charitable trusts and a variety of public corporations and boards; or

(ii) trade credit by way of debtor-creditor-supplier agreements which is always repayable in not more than four instalments; or

(iii) always "low cost credit" by way of debtor-creditor agreements, i.e. the rate of total charge is not more than 13 per cent or minimum lending rate (MLR) plus 1 per cent (MLR being the rate in operation 28 days before the agreement is made), whichever is the higher; or

(iv) always to finance the import or export of goods or services between this country and another, or between overseas countries.

In such cases the consumer credit agreement is exempt.

Besides banks, finance houses, pawnbrokers, moneylenders, retailers offering credit, mail order firms, credit companies, firms offering loans to their employees and trade suppliers offering credit are all examples of persons who are or may be providing credit under regulated agreements.

18. Consumer Credit Act 1974, s. 149(1).
19. Ibid., s. 8.
20. Ibid., s. 39.
21. Ibid., s. 16 and regulations made under it. For the replacement of MLR *see* Chapter Two.

(*b*) *Consumer hire.* Where a person in the course of business hires out, leases, bails or rents goods to an individual, partnership, firm or unincorporated body and the total amount of the payments and charges is £5,000 or less under an agreement which is expected to remain in force for more than three months, such facilities are provided under a regulated consumer hire agreement[22] and that person is required to be licensed.[23] It should be noted that a hire-purchase agreement is consumer credit, not consumer hire.

Leases or hirings of television sets, cars, caravans, office furniture or factory equipment, plant and vending machines are all capable of being consumer hire agreements.

(*c*) *Credit brokerage.* Where a person in the course of business introduces an individual, a partnership, a firm or an unincorporated body to a source of credit or hire or to another credit broker, where the credit being sought

(*i*) is £5,000 or under; or

(*ii*) if over £5,000 is to finance the acquisition or provision of a dwelling to be occupied by the borrower or his relative secured on land; or

(*iii*) if a hire facility is being sought, the total amount of the payments under the agreement is under £5,000;

such introduction constitutes credit brokerage[24] and that person is required to be licensed.[25]

Mortgage and insurance brokers, retailers who introduce customers to finance houses, business transfer agents, motor dealers, estate agents, accountants, solicitors, and building societies are all persons who could be treated as carrying on a credit brokerage business.

Incidentally, that welcome source of introductions to banks, the personal recommendation, is not controlled at all. The Act does not cover introductions which are not in the normal course of business.

(*d*) *Debt-adjusting and debt-counselling.* Where a person in the course of business negotiates terms or is otherwise engaged in the discharge of debts of clients who are individuals, partnerships, firms or unincorporated bodies, where the debts arose under consumer credit or consumer hire agreements (i.e. for credit of £5,000 or under or hire payments totalling £5,000 or under) that person is carrying

22. Consumer Credit Act 1974, s. 15.
23. Ibid., s. 39.
24. Ibid., s. 145(2).
25. Ibid., s. 147.

out debt-adjusting activities[26] and is required to be licensed.[27]

Where a person in the course of business gives advice to an individual, a partnership, a firm or an unincorporated body on the repayment of debts due by that party to another party and the debts have arisen under consumer credit or consumer hire agreements (i.e. for credit of £5,000 or under), such advice is debt-counselling[28] and that person is required to be licensed.[27] A licence is not needed for a business to arrange settlement of its own debts, i.e. debts incurred by the business.

Finance brokers/advisers, e.g. accountants, mortgage brokers, insurance brokers, loan brokers, banks, finance houses, moneylenders, loan and finance companies and financial consultants, all come within this category.

Financial, social and consumer agencies which give financial advice to individuals, e.g. advice and information centres, welfare associations, voluntary service councils, consumer groups, aid societies, legal advice centres, welfare rights groups, consumer councils, trade associations, community relations councils, certain resident associations, and charitable trusts and student unions, also come within the same category.

(e) *Debt-collecting.* Where a person in the course of business takes action to procure payment of debts from an individual, partnership, firm or unincorporated body, those debts being due to a third party arising under consumer credit or consumer hire agreements (i.e. for credit of £5,000 or under or hire payments totalling £5,000 or under), such action constitutes debt-collecting[29] and that person is required to be licensed.[27]

It is not debt-collecting within the meaning of the Act if the debts are due to the person or if they were assigned to the person following a "business transfer", unless that business was a debt-collecting business, i.e. a business does not need a licence to collect its own debts.

Trade protection societies, debt collectors, businesses which take assignments of debts (e.g. factoring companies, finance houses and banks) and traders who collect outstanding hire-purchase, credit or rental instalments on behalf of finance companies could all be carrying on debt-collecting.

(f) *Credit reference agencies.* Where a person in the course of

26. Consumer Credit Act 1974, s. 145(5).
27. Ibid., s. 147.
28. Ibid., s. 145(6).
29. Ibid., s. 145(7).

business furnishes information relevant to the financial standing of individuals, partnerships, firms or unincorporated bodies, having collected the information for that purpose, that person is operating a credit reference agency and is required to be licensed.[30]

Trade protection societies, credit reference agencies, detective and inquiry agencies, even one of a group of companies supplying information to other members of the group, could all come within this category.

A business that keeps records of its own customers for its own use is not a credit reference agency within the meaning of the Act.

Form and execution of credit agreements

Regulated agreements are unenforceable unless they comply with the regulations regarding the form and content of documents, and unless the procedures regarding the execution of such agreements are complied with[31] these provisions would catch overdrafts, where the customer was an individual or an unincorporated body and the amount does not exceed £5,000, even if the overdraft arose without any express agreement such as where a cheque is honoured when the customer's credit balance is insufficient to meet it. Where the bank is a recognised bank for the purposes of the Banking Act 1979, overdrafts are excluded from these requirements.[32]

Control of advertisements

Credit and hire advertisements are now regulated by the Consumer Credit (Advertisements) Regulations 1980,[33] which apply to advertisements containing information about almost all types of credit and represent the first stage in bringing about one of the major objectives of the Consumer Credit Act—that of "truth in lending".

The Regulations, which control both the form and the content of advertisements, apply to most credit and hire advertisements directed at consumers. In relation to consumer credit business, they apply to businesses which lend money, offer credit in any form or give people time to pay for goods or services, such as finance houses or retail stores offering their own credit. In relation to consumer hire business, they apply to businesses which hire, lease or rent out goods, such as television rentals. In relation to credit brokerage business, they apply to businesses which arrange finance for customers, such as retail stores offering finance house credit. They also apply to businesses which provide individuals with credit of any amount secured on land. "Advertise-

30. Ibid., s. 145(8).
31. Ibid., ss. 61, 74. These provisions are not yet in force as the Regulations have not yet been made.
32. Banking Act 1979, s. 38 and Sched. 6, para. 1.
33. S.I. 1980 No. 54 (as amended).

ment" includes information given in visible or audible forms, or both.

The Regulations do not apply if the advertisement indicates clearly that the credit must exceed £5,000 and is either unsecured or is not secured on land, or that the credit is available only to limited companies or for business purposes.[34] Nor will they apply to advertisements for agreements tied to a particular purchase where the credit must be repaid in four instalments or fewer, or where the credit arises because the trader allows customers to charge purchases to a running account and requires them to settle in full at the end of each fixed period, such as at the end of the month.[35]

Traders must give customers who ask for it written information about the credit terms being offered, and many advertisements, and all quotations, are required to show the total credit cost expressed as an annual percentage rate of charge.[36]

Where the Regulations apply, there are three categories of advertisement: simple, intermediate and full. The information which must, may or may not be included in each class is set out in the Regulations and is too detailed to include here.

The word "overdraft", or any similar term, may be used only if it refers to a genuine overdraft such as one given by a bank.[37] An advertisement may not suggest that the terms or conditions are cheaper or easier than that of some other party (unless the advertisement includes with the same degree of emphasis names of the competitors concerned and details of their comparable terms).[37]

As regards form, where an annual percentage rate is stated, it must be given greater prominence than any other rate, and must be given no less prominence than any statement about any period (such as "two year loan") or the amount, number or frequency of any payments.[38] Prominence refers not only to the size of the letters and figures, but also to any other method used to give prominence, such as the colour or kind of type used, the position of the information or the number of times it is repeated. The information must be shown clearly, and together as a whole.[39]

The Regulations apply to advertisements by banks, except where one of the exceptions mentioned earlier applies. They would cover advertisements in newspapers, radio, television, or any other form, including booklets on display in the bank's own premises.

34. Consumer Credit (Advertisements) Regulations 1980, Reg. 2(2), and Consumer Credit Act 1974, s. 43(3).
35. Consumer Credit (Exempt Agreements) Order 1980, s. 1. 1980 No. 52, para. 3(1).
36. The method of calculating the annual percentage rate is set out in the Consumer Credit (Total Charge for Credit) Regulations 1980, S.I. 1980 No. 51.
37. Consumer Credit (Advertisements) Regulations 1980, Reg. 11.
38. Ibid., Reg. 20.
39. Ibid., Reg. 17.

Miscellaneous

(a) *Credit reference agencies.* Where a regulated agreement is involved, an individual has the right to be supplied, upon written request to an actual or prospective lender or hirer, with the name and address of any credit reference agency which has been used to obtain information about his financial standing.[40] An individual has the right to apply in writing to a credit reference agency and, upon payment of a fee of 25p, to receive a copy of the file kept by the agency on him.[41] He also has the right, subject to certain safeguards, to require the agency to correct information which he considers to be wrong.[42]

The need to exercise such rights might normally be expected to arise when a prospective borrower or hirer is refused credit facilities. It is at this point that the individual might wish to ensure that the reason for the refusal is not based on an adverse status report. For instance, a retailer who has declined credit facilities would be required to admit if he has approached an agency and to supply its name and address. He would not be required to reveal the content of the agency's report as it would be open to the applicant to find out by direct approach to the agency. However, the right to approach a credit reference agency may be exercised whenever an individual wishes and it is not confined to occasions when he knows a status report has recently been given.

Fortunately for the clearing banks, their service of answering status inquiries and giving bankers' opinions is deemed to be outside the operation of a credit reference agency. Consequently apart from credit reference agencies, those who seek status inquiries on individuals from the banks have no obligation to reveal that they have made an inquiry, nor to disclose the content of the opinion. If, however, the bank itself has made an inquiry of a credit reference agency in connection with the provision of credit under a regulated agreement, and receives a written request within 28 days of the facility's being granted or declined, then the bank must disclose the name and address of the agency used; there is no obligation to disclose the actual details of the opinion received.

(b) *Approaches to minors.* It is an offence for anyone to send to a minor, with a view to financial gain, any document which invites him to:

40. Consumer Credit Act 1974, s. 157.
41. Ibid., ss. 157, 158.
42. Ibid., s. 159.

(*i*) borrow money;
(*ii*) obtain goods on credit or hire;
(*iii*) obtain services on credit; or
(*iv*) apply for information or advice on borrowing money, obtaining credit or hiring goods.[43]

The penalty is a fine of £1,000 on summary conviction; on indictment, the penalty is an unlimited fine or one year's imprisonment or both.[44] A banker should therefore take care not to send such publicity material to anyone, even customers, under the age of 18. There is nothing to prevent a bank from giving such information personally, however, nor is an offence committed if a minor takes a leaflet from a display stand; the emphasis is on *send*, whether by hand or by post. The specific indication by the bank that borrowing facilities as quoted in publicity material are not available to minors, or even the implication of this by virtue of the type of facility offered (e.g. a business development loan) should be enough to prevent the bank coming within the section; there is nothing to prevent the bank from actually providing credit to a minor if it so wishes.[45]

(*c*) *Powers of enforcement officers.* Powers relating to entry of bank premises and inspection and seizure of documents are set out in ss. 161 to 173 of the Act. The enforcement officers under the Director General of Fair Trading are the local trading standards officers.

With the necessary authority, an enforcement officer may enter a bank's premises "at all reasonable hours" and "on production of his credentials" ascertain if a breach of the Act has been committed.

If an enforcement officer has reasonable cause to suspect that there has been a breach of the Act, he may require any person to produce any books or documents relating to his business. This could include information concerning the customer's affairs, such as memoranda of interviews, copy quotations or agreements, duplicate notices or statutory statements issued under the Act or the customer's statement of account. If any such information is not stored in legible form he may be required to provide a legible reproduction of such information. The officer may also take copies of such relevant information from the books and documents. He may also seize and detain any of a bank's books or documents which may be required as evidence, and if necessary he may require the person to "break

43. Consumer Credit Act 1974, s. 50.
44. Ibid., s. 167(1) and Sched. 1.
45. But *see* Chapter Five.

open" any container, e.g. a safe or a filing cabinet, or, in the face
of refusal, "break it open himself".[46]

Barristers and solicitors may not be required to produce documents covered by privilege, but any of these powers could in theory
apply to banks. In practice the Office of Fair Trading expects the
exercise of these extensive powers to be moderated so that, in the
case of a bank, the Director General will normally instruct enforcement officers to obtain evidence by adopting the procedures laid
down by the Banker's Books Evidence Act 1879.

(d) *Connected lender liability.* A debtor-creditor-supplier agreement is defined by the Act as a regulated agreement to finance a
transaction between a debtor and a supplier made by the creditor
under pre-existing arrangements with the supplier.[47] Within this
definition come credit cards such as Access, which provides credit
to the debtor by "pre-existing arrangements".

Where a customer under a debtor-creditor-supplier arrangement
has any claim against a supplier of goods or services for misrepresentation or breach of contract, he has "a like claim against
the creditor" who is jointly and severally liable with the supplier.[48]
This section applies where the agreement was made on or after 1st
July 1977 and the value of the transaction is more than £30 and
not more than £10,000. Thus all such transactions financed by an
Access or Barclaycard account opened by an agreement entered into
since 1st July 1977 could be covered. Transactions involving credit
agreements entered into before 1st July 1977 are not covered, although both Access and Barclaycard have voluntarily agreed to give
similar protection to cardholders, up to the amount of the transactions actually debited to the cardholder's account. It should be
noted that a potential claimant should always pursue his claim
against the supplier in the first instance. It is only when he decides
to take legal action that he has the option of making such a claim
against the creditor.

(e) *Extortionate credit bargains.* Sections 137–140 of the Act give
powers to the court to examine the terms of a personal credit agreement for any amount. In this context the agreement is referred to
as a "credit bargain". Where it considers the terms to be "extortionate", the court may reopen an agreement and vary the terms.
The onus of showing that a credit bargain is not extortionate is put
on the creditor in all cases.

46. Consumer Credit Act 1974, s. 162.
47. Ibid., s. 12.
48. Ibid., s. 75(1).

It should be noted that the court's powers are not confined to regulated agreements but extend to all credit agreements (including exempt agreements) where the debtor is an individual, partnership or unincorporated body. They also extend to such agreements whenever made. In addition any term of an agreement may be considered by a court, not merely those relating to charges.

Banks should be considered unlikely to experience any difficulty with regard to these regulations, although it must be remembered that the "modified" terms of an agreement which was originally "acceptable" may well have become "extortionate", particularly if the modification has been brought about by the debtor's failing to repay as agreed.

However, if the bank takes, as security from a financial institution, a charge which that institution has taken from one of its own debtors (i.e. a sub-charge), there is a possibility that such security and the credit agreement thus secured could come within the ambit of the Act and be investigated.

The mere fact that the rate of interest is high (even 48 per cent per annum) will not of itself make a bargain extortionate, if factors such as the lack of time to assess the standing of the borrower, and the degree of risk accepted by the creditor, justify a high rate and the borrower is not frail in age or health, or financially very inexperienced or under acute financial pressure.[49]

(*f*) *Canvassing off trade premises.* An individual canvasses a regulated agreement or an agreement for an ancillary credit service if he visits that place without a prior invitation for the purpose of soliciting the entry of another individual into the agreement, or of urging his own ability to provide the service.[50] Canvassing does not include communications by telephone, or in writing, or any kind of non-lending business, or cases where the potential lending is in excess of £5,000. A bank manager suggesting to a client at a golf club that the client should enter into a regulated agreement will not be canvassing unless he went to the club for that purpose; so also if the visit is to the client's home. But if he visits a customer's home for that purpose, he will be canvassing unless the visit is made in response to a previous written request of the customer.

It is a criminal offence to "canvass"[51] and individuals doing so render themselves liable to (*i*) a fine of £1,000 on summary conviction, (*ii*) one year's imprisonment on indictment, and/or an

49. *Ketley* v. *Scott* [1981] I.C.R. 241.
50. Consumer Credit Act 1974, s. 48.
51. Ibid., s. 49.

unlimited fine.[52] Corporate bodies such as banks cannot commit the offence, although a licensee could have the licence revoked for failing to control its employees. An offence is only committed, however, if a visit to a place "off trade premises", that is to say not in the bank itself or the premises in which the business is carried on, is made without a prior invitation, which, in the case of regulated agreements, must have been in writing, signed by a person authorised to do so. Overdrafts and budget accounts for existing customers are specifically exempted[53] as are agreements relating to the finance of foreign trade.

These regulations are very detailed, and considerably reduce the flexibility which was for so many years a feature of British banks' relationships with their customers and potential customers. Different banks will have different internal regulations to ensure that their staff do not run the risk of breaching the complex rules and requirements, and all staff who have any responsibility for the marketing of lending facilities should be thoroughly aware of the need to protect themselves against ever inadvertently committing an offence.

It must be emphasised that these remarks are only a summary of the manifold provisions of the Consumer Credit Act 1974, and that a detailed analysis would be beyond the scope of this book.

52. Ibid., s. 167(1) and Sched. 1.
53. Ibid., s. 49(3).

CHAPTER THIRTEEN

Securities Generally and Banker's Lien

CLASSES OF SECURITIES

A banker in the course of his business has many different kinds of security submitted to him as cover for advances to his customers. Some borrowers tender stocks and shares, others guarantees, land, life policies, bills of exchange, promissory notes or documents of title to goods. Customers less fortunate may have nothing better to offer than second or even third mortgages, bills of sale, mortgages on wasting properties, reversions, partly paid shares (which are rare), or floating charges.[1]

Bankers usually look askance at these latter kinds of securities, since they all lack one or other of the requisites necessary to make them attractive as cover for an advance. After these undesirable forms have been eliminated, there is still a sufficient diversity of types available to enable the banker to avoid advancing too large a proportion of his funds against any one type of security and so incurring an additional risk, namely, the risk of general depreciation in any particular class of security which might affect him seriously if he did not have such a wide spread. It is also a great advantage for a banker to have numerous branches spread all over the country, as he thereby gets a much more varied assortment of security offered him, varying from the title deeds of the country market town to the shipping documents of the seaport.

Whatever class of security a banker agrees to accept, he should only very rarely advance up to the full market price, but should allow a margin, depending upon the class of security, to cover himself against over-valuation and market fluctuations, and the loss which may arise owing to a forced sale.

LIEN, PLEDGE OR MORTGAGE

There are three ways in which a banker may take security for an advance:

1. *See* Chapter Seventeen.

(a) by lien;
(b) by pledge;
(c) by mortgage.

In each case the banker does not become absolute owner of the property, but has rights over the property until the debt due to him is repaid.

In the case of an ordinary lien, the borrower is still the owner of the property, but the creditor is in actual or constructive possession of the property, without as a rule having a right to sell it. The securities subject to the banker's lien are those which come into a banker's hands in the ordinary course of his business, for example bills, cheques and other negotiable instruments deposited with him in order that he may collect the proceeds.[2]

Under a pledge the pledgee is entitled to the exclusive possession of the property until the debt is discharged, and the pledgee, in certain circumstances, has the power of sale, but the ownership remains in the pledgor, subject to the pledgee's rights. In other words, a lien is a mere right to retain a thing, whereas a pledge gives a special property in the thing pledged. Unlike property subject to lien, it is not essential that the thing pledged should be actually owned by the pledgor; it is sufficient if he pledges it with the owner's consent. If the pledgee sells the property he must account to the pledgor for any surplus remaining after liquidating the debt, and he may sell without recourse to the court. Securities subject to pledge are goods and chattels and fully negotiable securities. The legal delivery of the goods to the pledgee is an essential part of a contract of pledge, but it is not essential that there should be an actual physical delivery. Constructive delivery is sufficient, such as delivery of the key of the warehouse in which goods are stored, or delivery of transferable warehouse warrants to the goods.[3]

Under a legal mortgage the mortgagee has a special interest in the property, and also a power of sale, but the possession of the property usually remains with the mortgagor unless and until there is a default and the mortgagee enters into possession, which is rare, or exercises any of his other remedies.[4] Securities subject to mortgage are title deeds, life policies, and stocks and shares and other choses in action.

REALISATION OF SECURITIES

In all cases, even when the document of charge gives him a power

---

2. *See* below in this chapter.
3. *See* under "Goods" in Chapter Eighteen.
4. *See* especially Chapter Fifteen for details of these.

to realise without reference to the borrower or the person who has deposited the security, the banker before selling the security must demand repayment of the advances, and give reasonable notice that he is going to sell, unless the advances are due to be repaid on a fixed date and the banker has power to sell without notice. Bankers' documents of charge usually contain express powers of realisation, and advances are also usually expressed to be repayable on demand. As to the method to be adopted in each case, further particulars are given under the relative headings.

Where the security has been deposited by a third party and is sold, the banker should put the proceeds into a suspense account, so as to leave the full debit balance on the debtor's account for the purpose of proving in his estate.[5]

DISPOSAL OF SURPLUS

If a banker realises a security he must account to the borrower for any surplus remaining after the debt has been discharged, but if the borrower owes him other debts besides the loan for which the realised security was deposited as cover, he is entitled to retain sufficient of the surplus as a set-off against these other debts, provided always that he has received no notice of a second charge upon the security. While any security given to secure a specific advance is in the banker's hands, the borrower has the right of demanding it back upon tendering the amount of the loan which it was deposited to cover, and the banker has no right, apart from express agreement, to retain the security as cover for other liabilities of the borrower, unless the right of consolidation has been preserved.[6] However, as already stated, if the banker realises the security, he has the right of retaining either the whole or a part of the money received from the sale as a set-off against those other liabilities of the borrower to which the right of set-off can apply.[7]

At first sight this distinction may seem difficult to explain, but the reason for it is that as soon as the security is sold the proceeds are a debt due by the banker to the customer, and as such are subject to the banker's right of set-off.[8]

If a third party has given security for a customer's account and pays off the debt, he is entitled to the benefit of any securities the customer himself may have deposited with the banker as cover for the account. But before delivering up these securities or their pro-

5. For the procedure in the event of the borrower's bankruptcy, see Chapter Thirty.
6. See Chapter Fifteen.
7. See Chapter Four.
8. See Paget (8th Edn.), pp. 501–3.

ceeds to the third party, it is desirable for the banker to notify the customer and any other interested party, such as his trustee in bankruptcy, of his intention to give up the securities and obtain consent to their surrender.

COLLATERAL SECURITIES

A collateral security is a security belonging to and deposited by a third party to secure a customer's account. This type of security must be differentiated from a security deposited by and belonging to the customer himself.

The distinction is clearly seen by what happens when a customer becomes bankrupt. All security charged by the bankrupt customer must then be either sold or valued, and the amount realised by sale or determined by valuation is available to reduce the total indebtedness of the bankrupt. The banker can then claim on the estate for the balance remaining. In the case of third party securities, however, the banker is entitled for the time being to ignore the collateral security, and can claim on the estate for the full amount of the customer's debt. If the dividend or dividends he receives from the estate are not sufficient to wipe out the debt, the banker can look to the collateral security for the balance of debt remaining. This double right of remedy makes a collateral security very attractive to a banker, but there are disadvantages which are fully treated in Chapter Fourteen.

Briefly, where a banker has taken a third party security, he must watch that some event does not occur which will change the status of the parties and bring in the rule in *Clayton*'s case.[9] This will arise when any event happens which was not contemplated by the parties at the time the security was deposited and the account is nevertheless continued unbroken. In the normal way, all ordinary events are covered in the form of guarantee or document of charge signed by the third party, but to avoid any risk or trouble, the banker as a general rule should stop the account and open a new account for subsequent transactions whenever changes occur, e.g. in the constitution of a firm by the admission, bankruptcy, retirement or death of a partner; in the case of a limited company by its amalgamation with or absorption by another company; and in the case of an individual by his death, bankruptcy or mental incapacity. These observations with respect to firms and companies apply both when the security is given for them and when it is given by them.

9. (1816) 1 Mer. 529. *See* Chapter Four.

In the case of collateral security a memorandum of deposit showing the purpose of the deposit is essential.

MEMORANDUM OF DEPOSIT

Bankers' mortgage deeds and memoranda of deposit are prepared by their solicitors, and are carefully drawn up so as to provide for most contingencies. They give power to the banker to act in any way that may best preserve his own interests, without prejudicing his right of action against the security. Specimen forms will be found in Appendix I, and should be read in conjunction with this part of the book.

The procedures for and advantages of legal mortgages are explained in the chapters relating to the various types of property concerned. Where property is deposited without a legal charge, it is not essential to take a memorandum of deposit in order to create a charge over the property, but it is always advisable to do so, if only to avoid disputes as to the purpose of the deposit. For example, without some written evidence to the contrary, a borrower might afterwards contend that he deposited the security to cover an overdraft existing at the time of deposit, but not as security for future advances. As already stated, where the security is collateral, a memorandum is essential.

Where the borrower is a firm, the memorandum should provide for any change brought about by the retirement, death or bankruptcy of a partner, or the admission of a new partner; where the borrower is a limited company, provision should be made to cover amalgamation or absorption. It is advisable to include in a third party memorandum the right on the part of the banker to stop the account on any occasion he thinks fit, and the right to open a new account for new transactions.

REGISTER OF SECURITIES

A banker should keep a careful and complete record of all securities deposited with him as cover. In this register should be entered under the name of the account concerned such particulars of each security deposited as will enable the banker to see at a glance the precise nature of the security, its approximate market value, the form of the banker's charge, and whether the security belongs to the customer or to a third party. Any fact which may tend to alter the market value, or any special circumstances connected with the security, should be duly recorded. Some of the entries require periodical revision; for example, the market price of stocks and shares, surrender value of life policies, notes as to the financial position of guarantors.

Security registers are generally ruled so that much of the information necessary, such as the date of deposit, date of the bank's charge and the estimated value, etc., is given in separate columns. A security register should so describe the security that all its salient features can be quickly grasped. Matters affecting the security adversely, such as notice of a second mortgage, should be duly recorded, preferably in red ink. An example of a typical securities register is shown in Appendix I.

BANKER'S LIEN

A lien is the right to retain property belonging to a debtor until he has discharged a debt due to the retainer of the property. A lien may be either (a) particular, or (b) general. A particular lien arises from the particular transaction connected with the property subject to the lien; a general lien arises not only out of the particular transaction but also out of the general dealing between the two parties in respect of other transactions of a similar character.

Bankers have a general lien which derives from the law merchant. This was recognised in the case of *Brandao* v. *Barnett*,[10] where it was stated that "Bankers most undoubtedly have a general lien on all securities deposited with them as bankers by a customer, unless there be an express contract, or circumstances that show an implied contract, inconsistent with the lien."

The securities must have come into the banker's hands in his capacity as banker in the course of banking business; they must not have been deposited for some special purpose inconsistent with the existence of the lien,[11] and they must be securities which a banker ordinarily deals with for his customer when indebtedness on the part of the customer is not in contemplation.

Whether a particular security is in the banker's possession for the purpose of being dealt with by him in his capacity as banker is a question of fact, depending partly on the general usage of bankers, and partly on agreement or the course of dealing between the banker and the particular customer who owns the security.

There is no lien over property deposited by a customer but which the banker knows to belong to a third party, unless the third party is also a customer, in which case there may be a lien against the third party.

10. (1846) 12 Cl. & Fin. 787.
11. *Davis* v. *Bowsher* (1794) 5 Term. Rep. 488.

PROPERTY SUBJECT TO LIEN

In *Brandao* v. *Barnett*, the judgment refers to "all securities". In the earlier case of *Davis* v. *Bowsher*[12] the judgment refers to a banker having a lien on "all the paper securities which come into his hands". The lien is not confined to fully negotiable securities but includes share certificates,[13] an order to pay money to a particular person[14] and certain deposit receipts.[15] The lien does not, however, extend to all documents, since, for example, title deeds of property would not be subject to a lien.[16] This is because they would not normally come into his hands in the ordinary course of banking business but only either when deposited for safe custody or when handed over expressly as security.

PURPOSES INCONSISTENT WITH LIEN

Where securities are deposited for safe custody or for sale through a stockbroker, these are purposes inconsistent with the lien.[17] Difficulties may arise if there is an agreement or understanding that securities are to be returned on the fulfilment of defined conditions. The test is whether there is anything in the circumstances of the transaction, either in the original memorandum of charge if there is one, or some other agreement or arrangement, to exclude the general lien.

In one case the title deed of two properties was deposited with the intention of creating an equitable charge over property A; it was held that no security was intended to be given over property B and there was accordingly no right to retain the deed once the debt for which property A was security had been repaid.[18] In another case a life policy was deposited as security for a loan of £4,000, and it was held that on the construction of the memorandum of deposit the policy was intended to be security for the £4,000 only and that on repayment of this sum, there was no right to retain the policy for other liabilities, since the general lien had been excluded.[19] However, where securities were deposited by brokers for various advances, and were left with the bank when the liabilities outstanding

12. (1794) 5 Term. Rep. 488.
13. *Re United Service Co., Johnston's Claim* (1876) Ch. App. 212.
14. *Misa* v. *Currie* (1876) 1 App. Cas. 554.
15. *Jeffreys* v. *Agra and Masterman's Bank* (1866) L.R. 2 Eq. 674.
16. *Wylde* v. *Radford* (1863) 33 L.J. Ch. 51.
17. *Brandao* v. *Barnett* (1846) 12 Cl. & Fin. 787.
18. *Wylde* v. *Radford* (1863) 33 L.J. Ch. 51.
19. *Re Bowes, Earl of Strathmore* v. *Vane* (1886) 33 Ch. D. 586.

at the time of the deposit were repaid, it was held that there was nothing to exclude the lien.[20]

If securities or moneys are deposited for a purpose which fails, there is a resulting trust which affects the whole of the money or securities and prevents the lien or a right of set-off arising.[21] If, for example, a customer brings documents to his banker to raise a loan on them, and the banker declines to make the loan, but the customer leaves the bank and forgets to pick up the documents, the banker has no lien on the documents for any debt due by the customer on general account.

However, where moneys or securities are lodged to cover a specific advance and the advance is made, the purpose is to provide cover, and since the loan is made the purpose is fulfilled. If the banker has a power of sale and the securities are sold, there is no resulting trust. The moneys representing the surplus after discharge of the liabilities will then be moneys held by the bank either for the debtor's account, or as money had and received to his use, i.e. there is a mere debt to the depositor, and the surplus proceeds are therefore subject to lien or set-off.

The lien, being a right to retain, depends upon possession, and is lost if possession is given up. Thus if a customer instructs his banker to pay out a certain sum in exchange for shares in a company, the banker will have a lien on the share certificate. If, however, the customer takes the certificate away and then brings it back, saying "Take charge of this for me," it is probable that the right of lien would be lost, since the purpose of the deposit would then be safe custody.

COLLECTION

It is perhaps too sweeping to suggest that the sole distinction is between collection and safe custody, but collection is certainly one of the main functions of a banker with regard to securities which can be subject to the lien, and his lien over documents in his hands for this purpose has been repeatedly recognised.

In the case of collections, the lien would cover anything essential to the collection. For example, if bankers are instructed to collect interest on a bond and the bond has to be produced whenever interest is paid, the bond would be subject to the lien. Where coupons are to be cut off for collection of interest, the lien would probably attach to the bonds if the arrangement was for the banker to cut

20. *Re London and Globe Finance Corporation* [1902] 2 Ch. 416.
21. *Stumore* v. *Campbell & Co.* [1892] 1 Q.B. 314; compare *Barclays Bank* v. *Quistclose Investments* [1970] A.C. 567.

off and collect the coupons, but not if the customer himself cut off the coupons, and indeed the lien would not even attach to the coupons unless the coupons were handed to the banker for collection, since the banker would not have the coupons in the course of banking business. If bonds, redeemable at a fixed time or by drawings, are deposited with a banker to be presented for payment at the due date, or in the event of their being drawn, the lien would attach.

Points of this nature will, however, be rare today, since they all relate to bearer bonds which are infrequently encountered; in the case of registered stock, the conditions normally provide for payment to be made through the post to the registered holder. Where certificates in respect of registered debentures or stock are deposited with a bank which is to receive interest or dividends for the customer, it seems doubtful whether the lien would attach to the certificates, since possession of the certificates is not essential for the collection of the interest or dividends and the purpose of the deposit would normally be safe custody.[22] As indicated above interest and dividends are normally paid either through the post to the registered holder or else in accordance with a mandate signed by the registered holder. Of course, when the interest is received by the bank, it becomes the property of the bank, which thereupon owes the customer a corresponding amount, and if the interest is paid into a customer's account which is in credit, it may become subject to the right of set-off.[23]

BILLS OF EXCHANGE, ETC.

With regard to bills, promissory notes, and cheques, where the holder of a bill has a lien on it, arising either from contract or by implication of law, he is deemed to be a holder for value to the extent of the sum for which he has a lien.[24] Normally, a lien does not give any property in the thing subject to lien, but merely a right to retain it[25], but in the case of bills, promissory notes and cheques this rule makes the distinction between lien and pledge immaterial. Thus the banker who has a lien on a bill can, provided he took the instrument in good faith, sue the acceptor and other parties to the bill as holder for value, notwithstanding that his customer had a defective title to the bill,[26] though if he claims under a forged indorsement he has

22. Certificates held by a bank in such circumstances have been held to be subject to the lien; see *Re United Service Co., Johnston's Claim* (1876) Ch. App. 212, but this view is now subject to criticism.
23. *See* Chapter Four.
24. Bills of Exchange Act 1882, s. 27(3).
25. *See* above in this chapter.
26. Bills of Exchange Act 1882, ss. 29 and 38.

no right to retain the instrument or to enforce payment against any party to the bill.[27]

As holder, the banker can sue on the whole bill, but if he has only a part interest he must hand over the surplus to the customer, or to the true owner if the customer's title is defective. In the absence of a contrary agreement, the banker has a lien on all bills, cheques and notes sent to him by a customer for collection. Where the holder of a cheque payable to order delivers it to a banker for collection without indorsing it, the banker, if he gives value for it or has a lien on it, has the same rights as he would have had if, on delivery, the customer had indorsed it in blank.[28]

POWERS UNDER LIEN

A banker's lien has been defined as an "implied pledge".[29] An ordinary lien does not imply a power of sale, but a pledge does. With regard to bills, notes and cheques the distinction is immaterial, since as mentioned above, a person who has a lien on these instruments has full rights of a holder for value, and can sue in his own name.[30] With regard to other securities, since the definition quoted above is generally regarded as accurate, it seems reasonable to assume that the banker has a power of sale over securities over which he has a lien, especially if the securities are fully negotiable. This power enables him to sell on default, if a fixed time has been appointed for repayment, or after a request for payment and reasonable notice of intention to sell if no time has been fixed.[31]

The fact that a banker holds bills, notes or cheques under a lien does not affect his duty as holder to present them for acceptance, where necessary, and for payment in due course, and to give notice of dishonour.

MONEY

It should be mentioned that a banker does not have, nor can he have, a lien over a customer's credit balance. A banker's right over a customer's credit balance is a right of set-off.[32] It is doubtful whether money paid into the bank or received by the bank can be

27. Ibid., s. 24.
28. Cheques Act 1957, s. 2.
29. *Brandao* v. *Barnett* (1846) 12 Cl. & Fin. 787.
30. Bills of Exchange Act 1882, s. 27(3), as extended by Cheques Act 1957, s. 2.
31. *Re Morritt, ex parte Official Receiver* (1886) 18 Q.B.D. 222; *Deverges* v. *Sandeman, Clark & Co.* [1902] 1 Ch. 579.
32. *Halesowen Presswork & Assemblies* v. *Westminster Bank* [1971] 1 Q.B. 25; [1970] 3 All E.R. 473.

the subject of a lien, since first, it would not be possible to identify it, and secondly, when it is received, it constitutes a debt of equivalent amount from the banker to the customer, and a debt is not a suitable subject for a lien.

LIMITATION ACT 1980

Since the effect of the Limitation Act 1939 is to bar the personal remedy, not to discharge the debt, it does not affect property over which the banker has a lien,[33] but as with securities relating to land, the personal remedy is barred after twelve years. The banker can continue to hold securities which become subject to his lien against debts which have become statute-barred, since the debts remain legal; indeed once the right to recover the debt by action has become barred, his remedy will be to retain the securities.

---

33. *London and Midland Bank* v. *Mitchell* [1899] 2 Ch. 161.

CHAPTER FOURTEEN

Guarantees as Security

A guarantee is the simplest form of security a banker may take and is for that reason the commonest. Except where it is desirable for the banker to invite the "guarantor" (referred to in the older cases as the "surety") to take independent advice,[1] no formalities are required apart from obtaining the guarantor's signature on the banker's standard form of guarantee. A guarantee is not a particularly safe form of security, depending as it does on the guarantor's willingness and ability to pay when called upon to do so. Unless a charge is taken over some form of property, a loan secured by a guarantee should be regarded by the banker as an unsecured loan.

When a banker proposes to accept a guarantee as security for a loan, he must first of all, by careful inquiries, satisfy himself as far as is possible that the guarantor will be able conveniently and without embarrassment to carry out his promise to pay if the borrower fails to do so. For instance, the banker should not generally speaking regard persons with fixed incomes terminable at death, who have no other means, as fit persons to guarantee a loan.

At the time of entering into a guarantee the guarantor may be quite able and willing to perform all that he agrees to do, but his financial position, through no fault of his own, may change for the worse. While the guarantee remains operative, the banker should therefore renew periodically his original inquiries. He should make it clear to the source of his information that the inquiry is a renewal, since otherwise the latter might think that the guarantor was undertaking an additional liability which he would not be in a position to meet. In particular, the banker should look out for any evidence that the guarantor has settled (or is about to settle) any substantial part of his property in trust for his dependants or that he is otherwise placing his property beyond the reach of his creditors.

The law has always been jealous of the rights and interests of guarantors, and quick to relieve them of their obligations. As will be seen in the course of this chapter, there are many circumstances

---

1. *See* below under "Undue influence".

in which a guarantor will be released from his guarantee unless an express agreement to the contrary has been reached with the banker. For this reason a banker normally insists that the guarantor should sign the banker's standard form of guarantee which is usually a fairly lengthy document, designed to ensure that the banker will have the greatest possible freedom of manoeuvre in his dealings with the borrower without running the risk that the guarantor will be released from his guarantee. A specimen form of guarantee, incorporating clauses found in many modern forms of bank guarantee, is set out in Appendix I.

NATURE OF A GUARANTEE

A guarantee is an "accessory" contract by which the guarantor undertakes to "answer for the debt, default or miscarriage" of another person[2] known as the "principal debtor"; being an accessory contract, it necessarily involves some other person being primarily liable. A person may be a guarantor either by undertaking liability for the principal debtor's debt or by giving security on behalf of the principal debtor.[3]

Nevertheless a person who promises to pay another person's debt is not necessarily a guarantor and the contract which he makes with the banker is not necessarily a guarantee. Suppose, for example, that Smith promises Brown that if Brown will release Smith's friend Robinson from a debt, he (Smith) will pay the debt instead. This is not a contract of guarantee but a "novation" of the debt or, in other words, a substitution of a new debtor for the original debtor. Alternatively, Smith may agree with Brown that if Brown will let Robinson have certain goods, he (Smith) will see that Brown is paid for them.[4] Such a promise is a contract of "indemnity", not to guarantee, because Smith has undertaken "primary liability" to Brown, and not merely "secondary liability" in the event that Robinson fails to pay for the goods.

FORMAL ELEMENTS OF A GUARANTEE

Consideration
As in the case of any other contract, a guarantee must, unless it is under seal, be supported by "sufficient consideration". In other

2. Statute of Frauds 1677, s. 4.
3. *Re Conley, ex parte Trustee* v. *Barclays Bank* [1938] 2 All E.R. 127.
4. Compare *Davys* v. *Buswell* [1913] 2 K.B. 47 at p. 54: "If a man says to another 'if you will, at my request, put your name to a bill of exchange, I will save you harmless', that is not within the Statute [of Frauds]. It is not a responsibility for a debt of another." It is a contract of indemnity.

words, if the contract is not under seal, the banker will only be able to enforce the contract if sufficient consideration is given by the banker in return for the guarantor's promise to guarantee the debt of the principal debtor. The mere fact that the principal debtor owes money to the banker is not sufficient consideration for the guarantor's promise to the banker. There must be fresh consideration; if there is not sufficient consideration, or if there is a total failure of consideration, the guarantor has no liability under the guarantee.

In accordance with the usual rule that "consideration must move from the promisee" and need not be given to the promisor, the consideration for the guarantee must come from the banker, but need not be given to the guarantor, and indeed may consist wholly of some advantage conferred on the principal debtor by the banker at the guarantor's request. The banker gives sufficient consideration, and may therefore be able to enforce the guarantee, if, at the express or implied request of the guarantor, he agrees to forbear to exercise some legal right. The mere fact of forbearance is insufficient for this purpose. There must be either an undertaking to forbear, or an actual forbearance at the express or implied request of the guarantor.[5] An agreement to forbear for a reasonable period will be sufficient,[6] as will an agreement to forbear for an indefinite period, at least where reasonable time may be inferred.

It is not necessary for the consideration to be commensurate with the promise, since mere inadequacy will not render the guarantee void,[7] although an illegal consideration will not support a guarantee nor will a mere moral, or past, consideration.[8] Thus the existence of an antecedent debt is not in itself valuable consideration.[9]

Provided that there is consideration, the consideration does not need to appear in writing,[10] but may be proved by oral evidence.

Requirement for writing

Under s. 4 of the Statute of Frauds 1677, no action may be brought on a guarantee unless the guarantee itself is in writing or there is a sufficient written "note or memorandum" of the guarantee signed in either case by the guarantor or his agent. If the original written evidence of the guarantee is lost, oral evidence that it once existed is admissible. An oral guarantee is not void on account of the Statute

5. *Crears* v. *Hunter* (1887) 19 Q.B.D. 341. *See also Re Clough, Bradford Commercial Banking Co.* v. *Cure* (1885) 31 Ch. D. 324.
6. *Payne* v. *Wilson* (1827) 7 B. & C. 423.
7. *Johnston* v. *Nicholls* (1845) 1 C.B. 251.
8. *Eastwood* v. *Kenyon* (1840) 11 Ad. & El. 438.
9. *Wigan* v. *English and Scottish Law Life Assurance Association* [1909] 1 Ch. 291.
10. Mercantile Law Amendment Act 1856, s. 3.

of Frauds, but merely unenforceable by action; the contract may nevertheless be valid, and anything actually paid by the guarantor under an oral guarantee cannot be recovered. A personal representative ought not, however, to pay any money under an oral guarantee, since this would amount to wasting the estate's assets.

To satisfy the Statute of Frauds, the written "note or memorandum" need not be made at the same time as the contract of guarantee; it may be made at any time before an action is brought to enforce the guarantee. No special form of words is required, and in particular it is not necessary to use the word "guarantee". What is necessary is that the writing must name the parties as being parties and must contain all the essential terms of the contract. For reasons which will be evident throughout this chapter, however, it is highly desirable for a banker to use a comprehensive written form of guarantee.

"Original", as opposed to accessory, promises are outside the Statute of Frauds, since they bind the promisor to do something independently of, and without regard to, another's liability.[11] Thus a promise to pay a certain sum to a person if he will withdraw a disputed claim against a third party,[12] a promise that another person will not leave the kingdom without paying his debt,[13] and a promise to procure the signature of a third party to a guarantee[14] have all been held to be original promises; such promises are indemnities, not guarantees, and do not need to be evidenced in writing.

The discussion should be largely academic, since no prudent banker would deliberately lend money on the security of a mere oral promise by a third party, but there have been cases where, no doubt owing to an oversight, money was advanced before the guarantee was evidenced in writing.

A guarantee does not have to be under seal unless no consideration is given for the guarantee. Guarantees under seal attract a fixed duty of 50p.[15] Guarantees under hand ("simple contracts" of guarantee) are not now liable to stamp duty.[16]

---

11. "Thus if two come to a shop, and one buys, and the other to gain him credit promises the seller that, if the buyer does not pay him, the promisor will do so, this is a collateral undertaking, and not actionable without writing—but on the other hand, if the buyer's friend says to the seller, 'Let him have the goods, and I will see you paid', this is an original undertaking for the promisor himself and outside the statute." *Birkmyr* v. *Darnell* (1704) 1 Salk. 27; 1 Smith LC (13th Edn.) 331.
12. *Read* v. *Nash* (1751) 1 Wils. 305.
13. *Elkins* v. *Heart* (1731) Fitz-G. 202.
14. *Bushell* v. *Beavan* (1834) 1 Bing. N.C. 103.
15. Stamp Act 1891, Sched. 1.
16. Finance Act 1970, s. 32 and Sched. 7.

CAPACITY TO GIVE A GUARANTEE

Any person other than a minor or a mentally disordered person or an undischarged bankrupt may give a guarantee. A minor or a bankrupt may give a guarantee when acting as an agent for someone else. Any partner has power to give a guarantee which is binding on the other partners if he is authorised to do so by the other partners or if the guarantee is in the ordinary course of the business of the partnership.[17] In general, however, it is safer for the banker to obtain the signatures of all the partners either on the guarantee itself (if there is sufficient space on it for all the partners to sign) or on an authority expressly referring to the guarantee. If the guarantee is under seal and is not signed by all the partners, it is essential that those partners who do sign the guarantee should have been authorised to do so under seal, since authority to execute a contract under seal can only be conferred under seal.[18]

A company may give a guarantee only if it is expressly permitted to do so by its memorandum. If a company is proposed as a guarantor, the banker should examine the memorandum to make sure that the company has power to give the guarantee. If it is proposed that the company should charge some of its property in support of the guarantee, the banker should ensure that the company has capacity to charge property in support of a guarantee and not merely as security for its own borrowings. A trading company has an implied power to do certain things necessary for the conduct of its business even if it is not expressly permitted to do so by its memorandum, but a trading company would probably never be considered to have an implied power to give a guarantee.

If, after examining the memorandum, the banker discovers that the company which is proposed as guarantor does have capacity to give the guarantee, he should see that a board resolution is passed, conferring authority on one or more of the directors to give the guarantee, and should obtain a certified copy of the resolution. Sometimes, however, a banker will accept a guarantee signed by one or more of the directors on behalf of the company without obtaining a certified copy of the board resolution. This is because under the rule in *Royal British Bank* v. *Turquand*,[19] a banker is entitled to assume that anything which relates purely to the internal management of the company has been duly carried out. He would be able to enforce a guarantee given by one or more of the directors, even

17. Partnership Act 1890, s. 5.
18. *Berkeley* v. *Hardy* (1826) 5 B. & C. 355.
19. (1856) 6 E. & B. 327; [1843–60] All E. R. Rep. 435; 25 L.J.Q.B. 317. *See* Chapter Six.

if those directors did not have express authority to give the guarantee, unless the banker knew or ought to have suspected that those directors did not have authority. In general, it is the articles which give the directors power to manage the business of the company; since everyone has notice of what is in the articles, he would be deemed to know of the absence of such a power, or the fact that there were limitations on it.

In any event, directors are bound to exercise their powers in the interests of the company, and if a person dealing with the company knows that a transaction is not in the interests of the company he will be unable to enforce it. One of the reasons why the banker should see that a board resolution is passed, and that it states both that and why the directors considered the transaction to be in the interests of the company, is so that he can rebut any allegation that he knew it was not in the interests of the company. It is particularly difficult to decide whether a guarantee is given in the interests of the company when one company in a group guarantees the debts of another company in the same group. Following the discussion of this problem in *Charterbridge Corporation* v. *Lloyds Bank*,[20] it would seem that the directors of the guarantor company are allowed to take into account not only the interests of their own company, but also the interests of the group as a whole.

Section 9(1) of the European Communities Act 1972 provides in favour of a person dealing with a company in good faith that any transaction decided upon by the directors is deemed to be one which it is within the capacity of the company to enter into, and the power of the directors to bind the company will be deemed free of any limitation under the memorandum or articles of association; a party to a transaction so decided on is not bound to inquire into the capacity of the company or as to any limitation on the powers of the directors, and is presumed to have acted in good faith unless the contrary is proved.

At first sight, it would seem that as a result of s. 9(1) bankers need no longer examine the memorandum and articles of a company. This would, however, be a dangerous conclusion to draw for two reasons. First, it only applies to "any transaction decided upon by the directors", and so it is desirable for the banker to see that a board resolution is passed, so that he can establish that the transaction was "decided upon by the directors". Secondly, since it is established English banking practice to examine the memorandum and articles, it is thought that the banker would probably not be considered to have acted in good faith if he had failed to make a

20. [1970] Ch. 62; [1969] 2 All E.R. 1185.

proper examination of the memorandum or articles[21] or if he was aware that the guarantee was not given in the interests of the company. Thus s. 9 is probably of assistance only to persons who are not in the ordinary course of business accustomed to inspecting such documents as the memorandum and articles of a company. When the directors of a company give a guarantee, they should take great care to ensure that the guarantee is worded in a way that makes it clear that they are acting solely as the agents of the company and not on their own behalf at all. Otherwise, they may be personally liable to the banker under the guarantee.

LIABILITY OF THE GUARANTOR

Unless the guarantee provides otherwise,[22] the liability of the guarantor arises when the principal debt becomes due. The guarantor will be liable from that date even if the banker does not inform him that the principal debt has become due and does not demand payment under the guarantee. Unfortunately, it is not entirely clear when the principal debt does become due if the contract between the banker and the principal debtor fails to deal with the point expressly. In *Parr's Banking Co.* v. *Yates*[23] it was held that, in the case of an overdraft, each advance becomes due as and when it is made by the banker, but in *Joachimson* v. *Swiss Bank Corporation*[24] it was suggested that an advance made on overdraft does not become due until the banker has actually demanded repayment. The second view is now generally preferred, and in any event the point can be put beyond doubt as regards the guarantor by specifying in the guarantee that the liability of the guarantor arises only when demand has been made on the guarantor.[25]

Except where there is an agreement to the contrary,[26] the banker does not have to request the principal debtor to pay[27] or to sue the principal debtor before suing the guarantor.[28] However, the banker can in no event sue the guarantor before the principal debt has become due, so that if the principal debt only becomes due after

21. *See Q.B.P.*, No. 72.
22. E.g. if the guarantee is to pay "on demand"; *see* below.
23. [1898] 2 Q.B. 460.
24. [1921] 3 K.B. 110, [1921] All E.R. Rep 92, a case concerning a current account in credit. *See* Chapter Four.
25. *See* for example, *Bradford Old Bank* v. *Sutcliffe* [1918] 2 K.B. 833, where such a provision was effective. *See* Clause 1 in the form in Appendix I.
26. *Holl* v. *Hadley* (1835) 2 Ad. & El. 758.
27. *Belfast Banking Co.* v. *Stanley* (1867) 15 W.R. 989; *Re Brown, Brown* v. *Brown* [1893] 2 Ch. 300.
28. *Wright* v. *Simpson* (1802) 6 Ves. 714 at p. 734, where Lord Eldon LC stated that it is the surety's business to see whether the principal debtor pays, not the creditor's; but *see Ewart* v. *Latta* (1865) 4 Macq. 983.

a demand by the banker for repayment, the banker must demand repayment of the principal debt before he can sue the guarantor. The limitation period for contracts of guarantee is the same as for any other type of contract.[29]

If the banker wishes to take a guarantee from a guarantor who has already given the banker a guarantee or some other security in respect of the principal debt, it may not be clear whether the guarantee is in addition to the earlier guarantee or security or in substitution for it. Most standard bank forms of guarantee provide expressly that the guarantee is intended to be in addition to any earlier guarantee or security.[30]

When the banker demands payment from the guarantor under a guarantee, questions might be raised about the actual amount of the principal debt. For this reason most standard bank forms of guarantee provide expressly that a certificate from any of the bank's officers should be regarded by the guarantor as conclusive evidence of the amount of the principal debt.[31]

It is not advisable that the moneys covered by the guarantee should be described as a "debt due or owing from" the principal debtor, because it is possible, though the matter is open to doubt, that if the principal debtor becomes bankrupt, the guarantor may evade liability by contending that the bankruptcy annulled the debt, and substituted in its place the right to prove against the principal debtor's estate,[32] and since there was nothing "owing" by the principal debtor, the guarantor's promise to be collaterally answerable has come to an end. To avoid all risk of such a repudiation, the guarantor's liability should be expressed in terms that cover all moneys advanced to, paid for, or incurred by the bank on behalf of the principal debtor, together with interest and all other charges that may be payable thereon.[33]

LIMITED, SPECIFIC AND CONTINUING GUARANTEES

A person who gives a bank guarantee today usually guarantees all the liabilities of the principal debtor to the banker, including any liabilities in respect of any joint account or partnership account. If the guarantor wishes to confine his guarantee to any particular

29. *See* Chapter Four.
30. *See* Clause 4 in the form in Appendix I.
31. *See* Clause 12 in the form in Appendix I.
32. *See Re Moss, ex parte Hallet* [1905] 2 K.B. 307; but the point was not taken in *Re Rees, ex parte National Provincial Bank of England* (1881) 17 Ch. D. 98 and *Re Sass, ex parte National Provincial Bank of England* [1896] 2 Q.B. 12.
33. *See* Clause 1 in specimen form in Appendix I.

account of the principal debtor, he should ensure that the guarantee is worded accordingly. The banker should, however, be cautious about agreeing to any such suggestion and care should be taken over any necessary amendment to the standard wording. If any such amendment is agreed, the banker should ensure that the principal debtor's account is conducted in the manner contemplated by the guarantee, or he may find that the guarantor is discharged from his guarantee.

A form of words such as "in consideration of your agreeing to advance a sum of £500 to A, I hereby guarantee you due payment of that amount" ought to be avoided, since the guarantee may be totally invalidated if the banker advances more, or even less, than £500.[34]

In one case, the guarantor wished to be liable for a year only, and added at the end of the guarantee the words "This guarantee will expire upon 30th June 1925." In October 1925 the banker called upon the guarantor to pay the money which was owed by the principal debtor on 30th June 1925. The guarantor argued that she was not liable as the claim was made after 30th June 1925.[35] Although in that case the bank won in the Court of Appeal, the case should stand as a warning against hasty or ill-considered amendments to carefully drawn standard forms. The bank should have insisted on some wording such as "This guarantee shall not extend to indebtedness incurred after 30th June 1925."

If it has been agreed that the liability of the guarantor should be limited to a specified sum, the guarantee should state that the guarantee is of all the principal debtor's debts with the proviso that the guarantor should not have to pay more than the specified sum.[36] The reason is that as soon as a guarantor makes any payment under the guarantee he has an immediate right not only to claim repayment from the principal debtor and, in the insolvency of the principal debtor, to prove against his estate in competition with the bank, but also to share *pro rata* in all securities held by the banker on account of the principal debtor.

If the guarantor is not liable for the whole of the debtor's liability, the banker will clearly wish both to retain any securities, whether furnished by the principal debtor or other guarantors, and to prove against the principal debtor for the whole debt. For this purpose the bank should ensure that the guarantee is expressed to be a guarantee of the whole debt, even if the guarantor's liability is

34. *See,* for example, *Burton* v. *Gray* (1873) 8 Ch. App. 932, a case concerning third party security.
35. *Westminster Bank* v. *Sassoon* [1926], *The Times*, 27th November.
36. *See* Clause 1 in the form in Appendix I.

limited, and that it excludes any right of the guarantor to prove against the principal debtor until the whole amount due to the bank from the principal debtor has been repaid.[37] If the guarantor then pays the amount for which he is liable, the banker need not apply it in reduction of the debt, nor refuse the money, but may place it to a suspense account or securities-realised account and prove against the debtor for the whole debt.

A guarantee may refer to a specified transaction only. Such a guarantee is called a "specific guarantee", and is discharged on repayment of the particular advance it was given to secure. Alternatively, a guarantee may be worded so as to cover the amount of the fluctuating overdraft on an account during the continuance of the guarantee. This is called a "continuing guarantee"; most bank guarantees are continuing guarantees.

If a specific guarantee is taken by the banker, the money lent to the principal debtor should be lent on a separate loan account. If the money is not lent on a separate loan account, but by way of an overdraft on the borrower's current account, the rule in *Clayton's* case[38] will apply in the absence of express appropriations and payments into the account will be used to reduce the amount of the debt which is covered by the guarantee.

For as long as it remains in force a continuing guarantee is not affected by any payments into the principal debtor's account, for it does not secure any particular advance to the principal debtor but the final combined debit balance on all the principal debtor's accounts. The liability of the guarantor to be answerable for the final balance must be clearly stated in the guarantee and the words "ultimate balance" are often used in continuing bank guarantees.[39] This phrase points both to the continuing nature of the guarantee and to the fact that the sum secured by the guarantee is the sum finally owing after combining all the accounts of the principal debtor. In *Re Sherry, London and County Banking Co.* v. *Terry*[40] Cotton LJ said of a continuing guarantee, "The balance which the surety guarantees is the general balance of the customer's account and, to ascertain that, all accounts existing at the time the guarantee came to an end must be taken into consideration."

Where a guarantee is given in connection with the grant of a specific facility, the view is gaining ground among lawyers that it should be regarded as being restricted to that facility, even if

---

37. *See* Clause 8 in the form in Appendix I. *See also Re Rees, ex parte National Provincial Bank of England* (1881) 17 Ch. D. 98; *Re Sass, ex parte National Provincial Bank of England* [1896] 2 Q.B. 12.
38. (1816) 1 Mer. 572. *See* Chapter Four.
39. *See* Clauses 3 and 10 in the form in Appendix I.
40. (1884) 25 Ch. D. 692.

expressed to be unlimited. This view is not supported by any decided cases and rests upon a feel for what a court would hold if the point were to be raised, but it is now being advocated by some fairly senior barristers and a banker would be wise to take note of the possibility. The way to deal with it in practice, where a further facility is made available and is intended to be covered by an existing guarantee, is to arrange for any guarantor to confirm that the guarantee will apply to the new facility before any advances are made under it.

CASES WHERE THE PRINCIPAL DEBTOR IS NOT LIABLE

A guarantee is, as mentioned above, an accessory contract, and therefore presupposes that some other person is primarily liable. If for any reason the principal debtor is not liable or if in fact there is no principal debtor, the guarantor will not be liable under the guarantee. This point can be illustrated by the case of *Coutts & Co.* v. *Browne-Lecky and others*[41] where two persons had guaranteed the overdraft of a minor. It was held that since the loan to the minor was absolutely void under s. 1 of the Infants Relief Act 1874, neither the minor nor the guarantors were liable.[42]

To prevent this happening it is usual to provide in the guarantee that the guarantee should operate as an indemnity if the contract with the principal debtor cannot be enforced.[43] In *Yeoman Credit* v. *Latter*,[44] where a minor had entered into a hire purchase agreement, the father of the minor signed a document which was construed by the court as an indemnity, not as a guarantee; being an indemnity, it was held to be enforceable even though the contract made by the minor was void by reason of the Infants Relief Act 1874.

The clause usually adopted in guarantees to meet this point would also cover lending to unincorporated associations, unauthorised borrowings by limited companies, or borrowings in excess of the powers of either the company or its directors. The effectiveness of such a clause was upheld in *Garrard* v. *James*,[45] a case which concerned an agreement by a company to repurchase certain preference shares. The company was unable to perform this obligation because it is not lawful for a company to purchase its own shares. In that case Lawrence J said as follows:[46]

41. [1947] K.B. 104.
42. *See* Chapter Five.
43. *See* Clause 6 in the form in Appendix I.
44. [1961] 2 All E.R. 294.
45. [1925] Ch. 616.
46. At pp. 622–3.

It seems to me immaterial whether the failure or omission by the company to perform its obligations is attributable to its financial inability or to statutory disability, as the liability of the defendants arises, whatever may be the cause of failure. The gist of the bargain entered into by the defendants, in my opinion, was: "If you, the plaintiff, will advance this £1,500 we, the defendants, will pay you, if the company does not pay".

The essence of such a clause is that the document, besides being a guarantee, constitutes also an indemnity. A person agreeing to give an indemnity undertakes a separate and independent obligation which does not presuppose that some other person is primarily liable. Nevertheless, it must be doubtful whether even such a clause would be effective in the case of a regulated consumer credit agreement which was unenforceable by virtue of the Consumer Credit Act 1974.[47]

JOINT AND SEVERAL GUARANTEES

Where two or more persons join in the giving of a guarantee their liability may be joint, or several, or joint and several.

In a joint guarantee each co-guarantor is liable for the whole of the sum which is guaranteed; all should be sued together; if proceedings are taken against only some of them, the co-guarantors not included in the action are no longer discharged from liability if the banker fails to obtain satisfaction from those he has elected to sue.[48] On the death or bankruptcy of a joint co-guarantor his estate is freed from all liability under the guarantee and the banker must look to the remaining co-guarantors for the whole amount. Such, at least, is the old law of survivorship. It has been argued[49] that the law has in this respect been changed by the Law Reform (Miscellaneous Provisions) Act 1934. The point has not been decided by the courts and it is safer for the bank to act on the assumption that the old law remains and that when a joint guarantor dies his liability ceases altogether.

In a several guarantee each of the co-guarantors may be sued separately for the whole of the sum which is guaranteed. An unsatisfied judgment against one does not prevent the banker taking proceedings against each of the others. In fact the parties may be sued in any way the banker wishes, and the only limit is that he cannot recover in total more than the amount which the guarantee is drawn to cover. The death or bankruptcy of any one of the several co-guarantors does not of itself release his estate from liability for

47. *See* especially s. 113.
48. *See* the Civil Liability (Contribution) Act 1978, s. 3
49. *See* Glanville L. Williams, *Joint Obligations* (1949), p. 63.

advances made before the banker receives notice of these events.[50]
From the point of view of the banker, it does not matter much whether the guarantee is several or joint and several. It is usually made joint and several and this may afford advantages for the guarantors. The guarantee should expressly state whether the liability is several or joint and several. It should also include a provision entitling the bank to release or discharge or make any arrangements with any one or more of the guarantors without discharging the rest, thereby excluding the rule that the release of one or more co-guarantors releases the others.[51]

The guarantee should also make it clear that it is a continuing guarantee and cannot be determined by notice unless the notice is signed by all the guarantors or their personal representatives.[52]

Whenever there are co-guarantors, the banker should take care that all the proposed co-guarantors execute the contract and no advance should be made to the principal debtor until all the co-guarantors have signed. For if one or more of the co-guarantors fails or refuses to sign, and those that have already signed can prove that they agreed to enter into the contract on the faith of its being signed by one or more of those who have not signed, they will be discharged from all liability.[53] Accordingly, if any of the proposed co-guarantors wishes to withdraw or refuses to sign, the best course for the banker is to get the willing co-guarantors to sign a new guarantee. A similar point arises if any of the co-guarantors is to be liable for a limited amount. No alteration must be permitted to the amount of the limit unless all are aware of the alteration; if one seeks to limit his liability or to reduce the agreed limit of his liability, the safest course is to get them all to sign a new guarantee.[54]

RIGHTS OF THE GUARANTOR

Rights against banker

From the very moment when the guarantee is entered into, the guarantor has certain implied rights against the banker.

(a) The guarantor has the right, at any time after the principal

---

50. See below.
51. See Mercantile Bank of Sydney v. Taylor [1893] A.C. 317; Barclays Bank v. Trevanion, The Banker, Vol. XXVII (1933) p. 98. See Clause 2 in the form in Appendix I.
52. See Egbert v. National Crown Bank [1918] A.C. 903, where it was held that a reference to notice being given "by the undersigned" meant all of the persons who signed by guarantee. See Clause 10 in the form in Appendix I.
53. National Provincial Bank of England v. Brackenbury (1906) 22 T.L.R. 797.
54. Ellesmere Brewery Co. v. Cooper [1896] 1 Q.B. 75.

debt is due, to apply to the banker and pay him off. Then, on giving a proper indemnity to the banker for costs, he may sue the principal debtor in the banker's name.[55] In practice this right is rarely exercised.

(b) The guarantor has the right to require the banker to call upon the principal debtor to pay the debt at any time after it has become due.[56]

(c) While the guarantee is in force the guarantor has the right to ask the banker at any time for particulars of the extent of his liability and the banker is bound to give the necessary information. The banker should not disclose to the guarantor the details of his dealings with the principal debtor for these are covered by his duty of secrecy to his customer[57] but he may tell the guarantor how much he would have to pay if the guarantee were to be called immediately.

(d) A guarantor has the right to raise against the banker any defence or right of set-off or counterclaim which is open to the principal debtor.[58]

(e) As soon as the guarantor has paid off the debt, he has the right to be subrogated to all the rights of the banker against the principal debtor unless he has already waived the right. In other words, he may sue the principal debtor in the place of the banker. The guarantor has exactly the same rights against the principal debtor as the banker had previously. Thus, if the banker was a "preferential creditor",[59] the guarantor will also be a preferential creditor, and so on.

(f) After paying the principal debt the guarantor also has a right to any security given to the banker by the principal debtor (or by a co-guarantor).[60] It does not matter whether the security was given before or after the guarantor entered into the guarantee or whether the guarantor knew or did not know that the security had been given.[61] If the guarantee is for a limited sum only, the guarantor, on payment of that limited sum, has all the rights of the creditor in respect of that sum. He is entitled to share *pro rata* in any security

55. *Swire* v. *Redman* (1876) 1 Q.B.D. 536 at p. 541.
56. *Rouse* v. *Bradford Banking Company* [1894] 2 Ch. 32. The existence of this right has been questioned: *Ewart* v. *Latta* (1865) 4 Macq. 983 at p. 989, per Lord Westbury LC. The way to reconcile these authorities may be that unless and until the creditor applies to the guarantor for payment, the guarantor has the right to insist that the creditor calls upon the debtor to pay, but that once the creditor has called upon the guarantor, the guarantor then becomes bound to pay.
57. *See* Chapter Four.
58. *Bechervaise* v. *Lewis* (1872) L.R. 7 C.P. 372; *Bowyear* v. *Pawson* (1881) 6 Q.B.D. 540.
59. *See* Chapter Twenty-Nine.
60. Mercantile Law Amendment Act 1856, s. 5. *See also Duncan, Fox & Co* v. *North and South Wales Bank* (1880) 6 App. Cas. 1.
61. *Forbes* v. *Jackson* (1882) 19 Ch. D. 615.

held by the creditor for the whole debt.[62] It is usual for bank guarantees to exclude this right until the whole debt has been recovered by the bank.[63]

(g) Although the banker may, provided the guarantee is appropriately worded, claim the whole amount both from the principal debtor and from each guarantor (subject to any limit in the guarantee), he may not retain more than one hundred pence in the pound, and as soon as he reaches such sum he must, in addition to handing any remaining securities over to the guarantor, refund any surplus to the guarantor. For the purpose of calculating what is "surplus", he is entitled to look to the guarantor for any interest for which he may have been unable to prove in the principal debtor's estate,[64] provided, of course, the guarantor is not insolvent.

If there are two or more guarantors, each is entitled *pro rata* to the liabilities he has discharged. In any such case it is safer for the banker to withhold payment of the refund until the guarantors reach agreement as to their respective entitlements, unless he pays the money into court.

Rights against principal debtor

A guarantor has an implied right to an indemnity from the principal debtor if he gives the guarantee at the request of the principal debtor. The principal debtor may give the guarantor an express right of indemnity, in which case the guarantor's rights will be governed by the terms of the express indemnity. If, however, the guarantee is given without any request from the principal debtor the guarantor may not have any implied right to be reimbursed.[65]

Under the implied right of indemnity, the guarantor has, unless the guarantee provides otherwise, an immediate right against the principal debtor,[66] as soon and as often as he pays anything to the banker in pursuance of the guarantee, though he is not entitled to accelerate this right by paying the guaranteed debt before it falls due.[67] If goods of the guarantor are taken in execution of a judgment of the court,[68] or if the guarantor pays a sum to prevent an execution,[69] that constitutes payment by the guarantor.

Until the guarantor has paid the banker, the guarantor's right of

62. *Goodwin* v. *Gray* (1874) 22 W.R. 312.
63. *See* above in this chapter, and Clause 8 in the form in Appendix I.
64. *See* Bankruptcy Act 1914, s. 66, Companies Act 1948, s. 317 and Chapters Twenty-Nine and Thirty.
65. *Owen* v. *Tate* [1975] 2 All E.R. 129.
66. *Davies* v. *Humphreys* (1840) 6 M. & W. 153.
67. *See Coppin* v. *Gray* (1842) 1 Y. & C. Ch. Cas. 205 at R. 210.
68. *Rodgers* v. *Maw* (1846) 15 M. & W. 444.
69. *Edmunds* v. *Wallingford* (1885) 14 Q.B.D. 811.

indemnity against the principal debtor does not constitute a debt owed by the principal debtor to the guarantor. Thus although the guarantor may petition as a prospective or contingent creditor to wind a company up he may not prove in the winding up so long as he has not paid the guaranteed debt.

The guarantor's right of indemnity entitles him to recover from the principal debtor the full amount he has paid together with interest and he is also entitled to recover damages for any other loss.[70] Where the principal debtor is a company in liquidation or a bankrupt, the guarantor is entitled to interest only up to the commencement of the winding up or the date of the receiving order, irrespective of when he made his payment under the guarantee; even then the usual restriction on the maximum rate of interest on which dividends will be paid will apply.[71]

Where the principal debt has become due, the guarantor need not wait until the banker demands payment from him;[72] he is entitled to call upon the principal debtor to pay the guaranteed debt, so as to relieve the guarantor from his obligation.[73] This relief is not generally available until the debt is due, so that the guarantor cannot require the principal debtor to make provision for payment to the banker before the debt is due.

Rights of a co-guarantor against other co-guarantors

A co-guarantor has a "right of contribution" against the other co-guarantors. In other words, any co-guarantor who has paid more than his fair share of the common liability is entitled to compel the others to contribute. The right of contribution applies whether co-guarantors are bound severally,[74] or jointly and severally,[75] and whether by the same or different contracts.[76] It does not apply in the case of a joint but not several liability or in any case where the guarantors are not liable to a common demand.[77]

There is no right of contribution if the co-guarantors are liable under separate contracts for equal portions of the same principal debt as in this case each guarantor has entered into a separate transaction with the bank;[78] nor does the right arise against any person

70. *Badeley* v. *Consolidated Bank* (1886) 34 Ch. D. 536.
71. Bankruptcy Act 1914, s. 66. *See* Chapters Twenty-nine and Thirty.
72. *Ascherson* v. *Tredegar Dry Dock and Wharf Co.* [1909] 2 Ch. 401; *Watt* v. *Mortlock* [1964] Ch. 84, [1963] 1 All E.R. 388; *Thomas* v. *Nottingham Incorporated F.C.* [1972] Ch. 596; [1971] 1 All E.R. 1176.
73. *Earl of Ranelaugh* v. *Hayes* (1683) 1 Vern. 189 at p. 190; *Antrobus* v. *Davidson* (1817) 3 Mer. 569 at p. 579; *Berchervaise* v. *Lewis* (1872) L.R.7 C.P. 372 at p. 377.
74. *See Ward* v. *National Bank of New Zealand* (1883) 8 App. Cas. 755 at p. 765.
75. *Underhill* v. *Horwood* (1804) 10 Ves. 209 at p. 226.
76. *Ellesmere Brewery Co.* v. *Cooper* [1896] 1 Q.B. 75.
77. *Hunter* v. *Hunt* (1845) 1 C.B. 300.
78. *Coope* v. *Twynham* (1823) Turn. & R. 426.

who became a co-guarantor with another at the request of that
other[79] or on the promise of an indemnity from that other,[80] where
the circumstances show that the intention was that, of the two, only
one of them should in fact be liable. If the right of contribution does
arise, it applies whether or not the guarantor who has paid more
than his fair share of the common liability knew of the existence
of any other co-guarantors at the time when he became a
guarantor.[81]

The right of contribution may arise before or after the guarantor
who seeks the contribution has paid the banker.[81] Before making
payment to the banker any co-guarantor can compel the other co-
guarantors to contribute to the common liability and can apply to
the court for a declaration of his right to contribution.[82] If a co-
guarantor is sued by the banker for payment under the guarantee,
he can assert his right of contribution by joining the other co-
guarantors as defendants in the action, or by obtaining an order
directing that, when he has paid his own share of the common
liability, the co-guarantor should indemnify him from further
liability.

A guarantor who has paid has no right of contribution unless and
until he has paid more than his true share of the debt which is
guaranteed,[83] though possibly if the debt is payable by instalments,
there is a right of contribution in respect of each instalment.[84] If
a co-guarantor pays a sum which is not more than his true share
but which the banker accepts in full and final satisfaction of his claim
against all the co-guarantors, the co-guarantor who made the payment can claim contribution from the other co-guarantors based
upon the sum which he paid.[85]

The extent of the right of contribution depends upon the number
of solvent co-guarantors[86] and on the amount for which each
guarantor is liable. If co-guarantors are each liable for the whole
of the principal debt or for equal amounts of the principal debt,
each solvent co-guarantor is liable to contribute equally. Thus, if
there are five co-guarantors, one of whom is bankrupt, and one of
whom has paid the whole liability, the true liability of the co-
guarantor who has paid the whole debt is one-quarter, so he may
claim a contribution of one-quarter from each of the other three

79. *Turner* v. *Davies* (1796) 2 Esp. 478.
80. *Rae* v. *Rae* (1857) 6 1 Ch. R. 490.
81. *Craythorne* v. *Swinburne* (1807) 14 Ves. 160 at R. 165.
82. *Wolmershausen* v. *Gullick* [1893] 2 Ch. 514.
83. *Ex parte Gifford* (1802) 6 Ves. 805; *Davies* v. *Humphreys* (1840) 6 M. & W. 153.
84. *Re Macdonald, ex parte Grant* [1888] W.N. 130.
85. *Re Snowdon, ex parte Snowdon* (1881) 17 Ch. D. 44.
86. *Ramskill* v. *Edwards* (1885) 31 Ch. D. 100.

solvent co-guarantors. If the co-guarantors are not liable for equal amounts, the right of contribution is calculated proportionately to the amount for which each is liable.[82]

Any co-guarantor who pays the banker more than his true share of the liability under the guarantee is entitled to an assignment of the banker's rights against the principal debtor and the other co-guarantors in respect of the guaranteed debt, including the banker's right to any security given by the principal debtor or the other co-guarantors.[87] If the co-guarantor who paid the banker had himself been given any security by the principal debtor or the other co-guarantors, that security must be taken into account when calculating the amount of the contribution owed by each of the other co-guarantors.[88]

DISCHARGE OF THE GUARANTOR

Discharge by payment

A guarantor is "revocably" discharged from his obligations under the guarantee if the principal debtor pays the principal debt. The reason that the guarantor is only revocably discharged is that the payment made by the principal debtor may turn out to have been a "fraudulent preference" any may therefore have to be refunded to the liquidator or trustee in bankruptcy of the principal debtor.[89] Because the guarantor is only revocably discharged, the banker should not return the guarantee to the guarantor, nor should he write the word "cancelled" across the guarantee.

Where the debt which is guaranteed is the overdraft on the principal debtor's bank account, any payments made by the principal debtor to his banker may be appropriated in the normal way, either to paying off the overdraft or to some other purpose. The liability of the guarantor of an overdraft could be materially affected by the way in which payments made to the principal debtor's banker were appropriated. If, however, as is the case with most modern bank guarantees, the guarantee is not in fact a guarantee of the overdraft on a particular account, but a guarantee of the "ultimate balance" on all the principal debtor's accounts with his banker, this will not apply.[90]

A guarantor is also discharged from liability under the guarantee

87. *Duncan, Fox & Co.* v. *North and South Wales Bank* (1880) 6 App. Cas. 1.
88. *Steele* v. *Dixon* (1881) 17 Ch. D. 825.
89. *See* Chapter Twenty-Nine.
90. *See* this chapter under "Limited, specific and continuing guarantees".

if he himself pays the principal debt, but as in the case of payment by the principal debtor, the discharge will be revocable until it is clear that the payment will not be upset as a fraudulent preference.

Discharge by release of the principal debtor

An express release of the principal debtor from all further liability will discharge the guarantor since such release extinguishes the guaranteed debt.[91] This is so whatever express reservations there may be,[92] except where the principal debtor obtained the release by fraudulent means.[93] However, a mere covenant not to sue the principal debtor, with a reservation of the banker's rights against a guarantor, does not discharge the guarantor.[94] If it can be shown that, even though a document was called a "release", the real intention was merely to covenant not to sue the principal debtor, the document is construed as a covenant not to sue.

The reason for this distinction was explained in *Kearsley* v. *Cole*[95] where the principal debtor compounded with his creditors, who covenanted not to sue the principal debtor, but the composition was expressed to be without prejudice to any security (which included guarantees) or to any guarantor's rights against the principal debtor. One of the creditors then sued the guarantor successfully, and the guarantor in turn sued the principal debtor. It was held that where the principal debtor's creditors expressly reserve their rights against the guarantor, the guarantor automatically retains his implied right to an indemnity from the principal debtor. Even though the guarantor was not a party to the composition, the principal debtor's consent for the creditor to have recourse to the guarantor constituted an implied consent for the guarantor to have recourse to the principal debtor, and consequently the principal debtor could not complain when the guarantor sought to enforce his rights against the principal debtor. It seems, therefore, that it would be sufficient if the creditor expressly reserves his rights against the guarantor, but it is clearly safer for the express reservation to include the guarantor's rights against the principal debtor.

There can be no effective reservation of rights against the guarantor where the transaction between the creditor and the principal

---

91. *Burke*'s Case (circa 1780) cited in 2 Bos. & P. 62; *Perry* v. *National Provincial Bank of England* [1910] 1 Ch. 464; *Rees* v. *Berrington* (1795) 2 Ves. 540; *Clarke* v. *Henty* (1838) 3 Y. & C. Ex. 187.
92. *Commercial Bank of Tasmania* v. *Jones* [1893] A.C. 313.
93. *Scholefield* v. *Templer* (1859) 4 De G. & J. 429.
94. *Price* v. *Barker* (1855) 4 E. & B. 760.
95. (1846) 16 M. & W. 128.

debtor amounts to a novation,[96] or a satisfaction of the guaranteed debt.[97]

There is some conflict of authority as to whether the reservation of the banker's rights against the guarantor must appear on the face of the covenant not to sue; in one case it was said that it must,[98] though in another case it was held that the reservation can be proved by oral evidence.[99] It seems that oral evidence may be given to prove a general understanding that the guarantor was not to be discharged,[100] but only if this evidence does not vary the terms of the covenant not to sue.

Where an agreement made between the principal debtor and the banker is construed as a release rather than as a covenant not to sue, the guarantor will be released even if the release of the principal debtor is not express but results from the legal consequences of some transaction. He will, for example, be released if the banker accepts a second security in discharge of the original one,[101] or if a security is substituted for the personal liability of the principal debtor.[102] Although the taking of a second security in discharge of the original one, or in replacement of the principal debtor's personal liability, will discharge the guarantor, the mere acceptance of additional security from the principal debtor will not have this effect[103] unless the intention of the parties is manifestly that the original security is not to remain in force.[104]

A guarantor is not automatically discharged from liability if the principal debtor is discharged under the Bankruptcy Acts, nor if the creditor accepts a scheme or composition after adjudication under the Bankruptcy Acts. If, however, the creditor assents to a composition deed outside the Bankruptcy Acts, which releases the principal debtor, the guarantor will be released unless the creditor either obtains the guarantor's consent or expressly reserves his rights against the guarantor. In practice, bankers' forms of guarantee usually give them power to accept compositions or make other arrangements with the principal debtor without prejudicing their rights against the guarantor.[105]

96. *Commercial Bank of Tasmania* v. *Jones* [1893] A.C. 313.
97. *Webb* v. *Hewitt* (1857) 3 K. & J. 438.
98. *Re Renton, ex parte Glendinning* (1819) Buck. 517.
99. *Re Blakely, ex parte Harvey, ex parte Springfield* (1854) 4 De G.M. & G. 881 at p. 899.
100. *Wyke* v. *Rogers* (1852) 1 De G.M. & G. 408.
101. *Clarke* v. *Henty* (1838) 3 Y. & C. Ex. 187.
102. *Lowes* v. *Maughan and Fearon* (1884) Cab. & El. 840.
103. *Twopenny* v. *Young* (1824) 3 B. & C. 208.
104. *Overend, Gurney & Co. (Liquidators)* v. *Oriental Finance Corpn. (Liquidators)* (1871) L.R. 7 H.L. 348; *Twopenny* v. *Young supra*; *Munster & Leinster Bank* v. *France* (1889) 24 L.R. Ir. 82.
105. *See* Clause 2 in the form in Appendix I.

If, by separate contract with the guarantor, made on good consideration and without the concurrence of the principal debtor, the creditor gives the guarantor further time for payment of a bill of exchange accepted by the guarantor, and the principal debtor is subsequently released from the debt by the creditor, the guarantor is not discharged from liability, since his liability derives now from the new contract, rather than the original guarantee.[106]

Discharge by agreement to give time

A binding agreement[107] between the banker and the principal debtor[108] to give more time to the principal debtor to repay his debt will discharge the guarantor from liability[109] if made without his consent, whether or not he is in fact prejudiced by the agreement.[110] The reason appears to be that in theory such an agreement necessarily prejudices the guarantor by preventing him from exercising his right to require the banker to call upon the principal debtor to pay off the debt or his right to pay off the debt himself, and then sue the principal debtor. This point was explained by Smith LJ as follows.[111]

A surety is entitled at any time to require the creditor to call upon the principal debtor to pay off the debt, or himself to pay off the debt, and when he has paid it off, he is at once entitled in the creditor's name to sue the principal debtor; and if the creditor has bound himself to give time to the principal debtor, the surety cannot do either the one or the other of these things until the time so given has elapsed, and it is said that by reason of this the surety's position is altered to his detriment without his assent.

It would appear, however, that the guarantor will not be discharged if, when making the agreement to give time to the principal debtor, the banker expressly reserved his rights against the guarantor, even if the guarantor did not consent or even know that this was so.[112] The guarantor will not be discharged by an agreement to give time to the principal debtor if the agreement was made after the banker had obtained judgment against the principal debtor and the guarantor,[113] or against the guarantor alone,[114] or if the guarantor

106. *Defries* v. *Smith* (1862) 10 W.R. 189.
107. *Clarke* v. *Birley* (1889) 41 Ch. D. 422.
108. The agreement giving time will not discharge the guarantor if it is made with a stranger (*Lyon* v. *Holt* (1839) 5 M. & W. 250) or with one of several guarantors (*Clarke* v. *Birley* (1899) 41 Ch. D. 422).
109. *Burke*'s Case (circa 1780) cited in 2 Bos. & P. 62; *Bolton* v. *Buckenham* [1891] 1 Q.B. 278.
110. *Ex parte Gifford* (1802) 6 Ves. 805.
111. *Rouse* v. *Bradford Banking Company* [1894] 2 Ch. 32 at p. 75; affd. [1904] A.C. 586.
112. *Kearsley* v. *Cole* (1846) 16 M. & W. 128.
113. *Re a debtor* (*No. 14 of 1913*) [1913] 3 K.B. 11.
114. *Jenkins* v. *Robertson* (1854) 2 Drew. 351.

agrees either in the guarantee or after the agreement giving time[115] that time may with impunity be given to the principal debtor.[116]

The guarantor is not discharged from liability if the banker does not make an agreement to give time to the principal debtor but merely refrains from taking any steps to recover the principal debt, or refuses to take proceedings which are bound to be abortive.[117] The guarantor is discharged only if there is an agreement which is binding and capable of enforcement,[118] for valuable consideration,[119] made with the principal debtor,[120] and which actually gives more time to the principal debtor to pay the principal debt.[121] If the banker agrees to give time to the principal debtor because that is the custom of a particular trade, the existence of this custom will not prevent the guarantor from being discharged. An agreement whereby the banker agrees not to demand due repayment in return for a promise by the principal debtor to pay a higher rate of interest is not an agreement to give time if the creditor retains the right to demand repayment at any time.[122] The agreement to give time need not, however, be an express agreement and may be written or oral. An omission to do something which the creditor is bound to do for the protection of the guarantor will release the guarantor,[123] for example, if the creditor has a bill of exchange and fails to take steps to obtain payment of it from the drawer or acceptor which might reasonably have been taken before their insolvency.[124]

If the guarantee is a continuing guarantee, an agreement to give time may only partially discharge a guarantor from liability. For example, if goods are supplied by instalments to the principal debtor and a longer period of credit is allowed in respect of one instalment than the guarantor had anticipated when he gave the guarantee, he will be relieved from liability in respect of that instalment, but not in respect of earlier or later instalments.[125] The same rule will apply to any other principal debt which is "severable".[126] Liability for

115. *Mayhew* v. *Crickett* (1818) 2 Swan. 185.
116. *Yates* v. *Evans* (1892) 6 L.J.Q.B. 446; and *see Midland Counties Motor Finance Co.* v. *Slade* [1950] 2 All E.R. 821 C.A. *See also* Clause 2 in the form in Appendix I.
117. *Musket* v. *Rogers* (1839) 5 Bing. N.C. 728.
118. *Clarke* v. *Birley* (1889) 41 Ch. D. 422; *Rouse* v. *Bradford Banking Co.* [1894] A.C. 586.
119. *English* v. *Darley* (1800) 2 Bos. & P. 61.
120. The agreement giving time will not discharge the guarantor if it is made with a stranger (*Lyon* v. *Holt* (1839) 5 M. & W. 250) or with one of several guarantors (*Clarke* v. *Birley* (1889) 41 Ch. D. 422.
121. *Prendergast* v. *Devey* (1821) 6 Madd. 124; *Bolton* v. *Buckenham* [1891] 1 Q.B. 278; *Rouse* v. *Bradford Banking Co.* [1894] A.C. 586.
122. *York City & County Banking Co.* v. *Bainbridge* (1818) 43 L.T. 732.
123. *Mansfield Union Guardians* v. *Wright* (1882) 9 Q.B.D. 683.
124. *Philips* v. *Astling* (1809) 2 Taunt. 206.
125. *Bingham* v. *Corbitt* (1864) 34 L.J.Q.B. 37.
126. *Croydon Gas Co.* v. *Dickinson* (1876) 2 C.P.D. 46.

payments under a hire purchase agreement has been held not to be severable, so that the creditor's agreement to give time for payment of some instalments does discharge the guarantor from all liability under the guarantee.[127]

Discharge by material variation of principal contract

As we have seen a guarantor will be discharged from liability if the principal debtor is given more time to pay without the guarantor's consent, unless the banker expressly reserves his rights against the guarantor. On the same principle, a guarantor will be discharged if the banker makes any other material variation of the principal contract without obtaining the guarantor's consent and without reserving his rights against the guarantor.[128] The reason for this is that the contract between the banker and the principal debtor will no longer be the contract which the guarantor agreed to guarantee.

If a guarantor has guaranteed that the principal debtor will perform several obligations which are separate and distinct and if the principal contract is then varied in respect of one of the obligations, the guarantor will be discharged from liability in respect of that obligation, but will not be discharged from liability in respect of the other obligations.[129]

Acceptance by the banker of a breach of contract by the principal debtor does not amount to a material alteration of the principal contract, so the guarantor will not be discharged. A breach of contract by the principal debtor should be regarded equally as a breach of contract by the guarantor because the guarantor has a duty to see that the principal debtor performs his obligations. The guarantor is therefore liable to the banker in damages to the same extent as the principal debtor.[130]

If the principal debtor enters into a composition with his creditors, and one creditor obtains from the principal debtor an agreement binding the principal debtor to pay his debt in full, this agreement would be a fraud on the other creditors and would thus invalidate the composition. A guarantor for the payment of the composition will thus be discharged from the liability to that creditor as this amounts to a dealing with the principal debtor in a manner at variance with the contract guaranteed, and a guarantee of the original debt will in any event already have been discharged by virtue of the composition.[131]

Any banker will wish to retain the utmost freedom of action in

127. *Midland Motor Showrooms* v. *Newman* [1929] 2 K.B. 256.
128. *Ward* v. *National Bank of New Zealand* (1883) 8 App. Cas. 755 at p. 763.
129. *Skillett* v. *Fletcher* (1867) L.R. 2 C.P. 469.
130. *Moschi* v. *Lep Air Services* [1972] 2 All E.R. 393.
131. *Mayhew* v. *Boyes* (1910) 103 L.T. 1.

his dealings with his customer, the principal debtor. The banker will therefore insert in his contract with the principal debtor a "time and indulgence clause" which will enable the banker to vary the terms of his lending to the principal debtor, grant further time to pay when the advances become repayable, take additional security or release existing security, either from the principal debtor or a co-guarantor, or even agree compositions with the principal debtor. Any of these will discharge the guarantor, unless the guarantor agrees otherwise, either in the guarantee or at the time of the action in question or even subsequently.[132] To be sure of preserving his rights against the guarantor in such a case, it is essential for the banker to have a clause permitting any such steps without releasing the guarantor.[133]

Such a clause was upheld in *Perry* v. *National Provincial Bank of England*,[134] where a firm became insolvent and a new limited company was incorporated to take over the firm's business. The creditors, including the bank, agreed to accept debentures from the new company at the rate of twenty-five shillings for each pound of the firm's indebtedness, in full and final satisfaction of all claims against the firm, except to the extent that particular creditors had security. The bank had security from a third party, which was valued at a certain figure, and accepted the debentures in respect of the balance of the claim. The firm, the principal debtor, was totally released, and the third party claimed back the security, but it was held that because the "time and indulgence" clause covered such matters, the balance of the old indebtedness was still effectively charged against the security.

Despite the protective provisions of some such clause the banker should be careful not to prejudice the guarantor's position without giving him notice and getting his consent, even if the action contemplated is covered by the terms of the guarantee.

Discharge by a material variation of contract of guarantee

The guarantor will also be discharged if the banker materially varies or departs from the terms of the guarantee. This is so whether the departure injures the guarantor or not,[135] unless the departure is obviously quite insubstantial,[136] since in either case the departure will constitute an alteration in the guarantor's obligations. Thus, for example, if a guarantee stipulates that a certain period of credit is

---

132. *Yates* v. *Evans* (1892) 61 L.J.Q.B. 446; *Cowper* v. *Smith* (1834) 4 M. & W. 519.
133. *See* Clause 2 in the form in Appendix I.
134. [1910] 1 Ch. 464.
135. *General Steam-Navigation Co.* v. *Rolt* (1858) 6 C.B.N.S. 550.
136. *Holme* v. *Brunskill* (1878) 3 Q.B.D. 495 quoted in *Egbert* v. *National Crown Bank* [1918] A.C. 903 at p. 908.

to be given to the principal debtor, this stipulation must be strictly adhered to.[137] A guarantor who has agreed to pay whatever another party is made to pay under an insurance policy is not liable for sums paid by that other party under a scheme of arrangement substituted for the policy.[138] In one case a guarantor gave an undertaking in the belief, to which he was led by the form of the undertaking, that others named in it would also execute the document. When the others did not sign, it was held that he was not bound.[139] In a case concerning a bank guarantee where the document was to be signed by four parties but only three signed, the three who did sign were held not to be bound.[140]

Where there are co-guarantors, all the co-guarantors will be discharged if the banker gives one of the co-guarantors more time to pay or if he materially varies the terms of the guarantee in any other way in favour of one of the co-guarantors without obtaining the consent of the other co-guarantors and without reserving his rights against the other co-guarantors. Thus all the co-guarantors will be discharged if one of the co-guarantors is released by the banker,[141] and any security given by the others will also be discharged;[142] but if the banker merely covenants not to sue one of the co-guarantors, the other co-guarantors will not be discharged if the banker reserves his rights against them.[143]

Where the guarantors are severally (not jointly, or jointly and severally) liable for the same debt, release of one does not involve release of the others, unless they can prove that there was a right of contribution between the released guarantor and the other guarantors and it has been prejudiced by his discharge. Accordingly, a banker's guarantee should expressly provide that the liability of the remaining co-guarantors shall not be affected by the release of or the giving of time or other indulgence to one or more of the co-guarantors.[144] If there is no such provision in the guarantee, the banker must not prejudice his rights against all by varying the contract in favour of any particular guarantor without the consent of all.

If the banker makes a binding agreement with the principal debtor to give time to the guarantor, this discharges the guarantor, on the gounds that the guarantor's position has been varied, since the

137. *Bacon* v. *Chesney* (1816) 1 Stark. 192.
138. *Mortgage Insurance Corporation* v. *Pound* (1894) 64 L.J.Q.B. 394; affd. (1895) 65 L.J.Q.B. 129.
139. *Hansard* v. *Lethbridge* (1892) 8 T.L.R. 346.
140. *National Provincial Bank of England* v. *Brackenbury* (1906) 22 T.L.R. 797.
141. *Mercantile Bank of Sydney* v. *Taylor* [1893] A.C. 317.
142. *Hodgson* v. *Hodgson* (1837) 2 Keen. 704.
143. *Price* v. *Barker* (1855) 4 E. & B. 760; *Mercantile Bank of Sydney* v. *Taylor*, *supra*.
144. *See* Clause 2 in the form in Appendix I.

banker cannot receive payment from the guarantor and thus enable the guarantor to sue the principal debtor.[145]

Where several parties enter into a guarantee, but are liable for different amounts, the dangers in allowing one of them to alter the amount for which he is liable without the consent of the others are illustrated by *Ellesmere Brewery Co. v. Cooper.*[146] In that case, there were four guarantors for a debt of £150; two of them were to be liable for £50 and two for £25. One of the parties who was expressed to be liable for £50 signed after the other three, and added words after his signature limiting his liability to £25. This was done in the presence of the manager of the plaintiffs, and not in any way surreptitiously, but because of the alteration the rights of contribution were affected. The other three guarantors had entered into a contract under which they would have certain rights of contribution against the fourth, and since the alteration of his maximum reduced the amount for which the other three were entitled to compel contribution from the fourth, they were discharged. Since the other three were discharged, he was also discharged, for just as the other three had entered into a contract under which they were to have full rights of contribution against the fourth, he correspondingly had entered into a contract under which he was to have rights of contribution against the other three. As neither of these conditions was fulfilled the result was that none of the four guarantors were liable.

If, therefore, there is any deviation from previously agreed figures as expressed in the document which any of the guarantors signs, it is essential for the banker to have a fresh form signed by all the guarantors before making any advances, or to have the existing documents re-executed or initialled by the others.

A guarantor is entitled, on paying the principal debt, to have any security held by the banker for the principal debt handed over to him by the banker, whether the security was given by the principal debtor before the guarantor entered into the contract of guarantee or whether it was given subsequently.[147] Any act of the banker interfering with that right will, at least to the extent of any loss suffered, discharge the guarantor from liability, and if the effect is to alter the guarantee materially, the guarantor may be discharged altogether.[148]

Thus if a guarantor executes the guarantee on the basis that the creditor will take certain securities from the principal debtor, or that there will be other guarantors, the guarantor will be completely

145. *Overend, Gurney & Co. (Liquidators)* v. *Oriental Finance Corpn. (Liquidators)* (1871) L.R. 7 H.L. 348.
146. [1896] 1 Q.B. 75.
147. Mercantile Law Amendment Act 1856, s. 5. *See* above in this chapter.
148. *See* Taylor v. *Bank of New South Wales* (1886) 11 App. Cas. 596 at p. 603.

released if the securities are not duly taken and retained,[149] or if the other guarantors do not execute the guarantee,[150] or they limit their liability under it.[151]

The banker will be regarded as interfering with the right of the guarantor to receive any security given by the principal debtor if, for example, he loses the security, or realises the security in satisfaction of another debt,[152] or fails to make the security effective by giving any necessary notice[153] or making any necessary registration.[154]

A co-guarantor also has a right to any security given to the banker by any of the other co-guarantors in the event that he pays to the banker more than his true share of the common liability. A co-guarantor will therefore be discharged from liability under the guarantee if the banker interferes with his right.

Except where there is an express provision to the contrary, a guarantor will be discharged from liability if the banker exchanges or surrenders any security given by the principal debtor or a co-guarantor. Most bank guarantees contain an express provision covering this point.[155]

Discharge by a change in legal position of the parties

If a guarantee is given to a partnership, the guarantor will be discharged if there is "any change in the constitution" of the partnership.[156] In other words, the guarantor will be discharged if any existing partner leaves the partnership or dies or becomes bankrupt or if any new partner enters the partnership. Similarly, if a guarantee is given of the debts of a partnership, the guarantor will be discharged if there is any change in the constitution of the partnership.[156] If a principal debtor who is an individual enters into partnership with another person, the guarantor will be discharged. The guarantor will also be discharged if he gives a guarantee to a partnership or any other unincorporated body which subsequently becomes incorporated. Bankers' guarantees usually provide for any such contingency, but if this is not so, the account must be stopped and a new account opened, otherwise the rule in *Clayton*'s case[157] will operate. Apart from any provisions in the guarantee, it is prefer-

---

149. *Polak* v. *Everett* (1876) 1 Q.B.D. 669; *Smith* v. *Wood* [1929] 1 Ch. 14.
150. *Evans* v. *Bremridge* (1856) 8 De G.M. & G. 100.
151. *Ellesmere Brewery Co.* v. *Cooper* [1896] 1 Q.B. 75.
152. *Pearl* v. *Deacon* (1857) 1 De G. & J. 461.
153. *Strange* v. *Fooks* (1863) 4 Giff. 408.
154. *Wulff* v. *Jay* (1872) L.R. 7 Q.B. 765.
155. *See* Clause 2 in the form in Appendix I.
156. Partnership Act 1890, s. 18.
157. (1816) 1 Mer. 572. *See* Chapter Four.

able for the account to be broken, so as to bind the estate of the deceased, bankrupt, or retiring partner.

If a guarantee is given to a company, the guarantor will be discharged if the company is absorbed by another company or if the company merges or amalgamates with another company[158] except where the merger is effected by Act of Parliament as was the case with the merger of the old National Provincial and Westminster Banks to form National Westminster Bank. A guarantor will not, however, be discharged if the company to which the guarantee was given merely changes its name.

In any of these circumstances the guarantor will only be discharged with regard to future transactions of the principal debtor, but will remain liable with regard to past transactions of the principal debtor. Any of these rules may be excluded or modified by agreement with the guarantor. In the case of guarantees given to a bank, these rules usually are excluded.

DETERMINATION OF A GUARANTEE

Determination by notice

Guarantees frequently provide expressly that the guarantor may totally or partially revoke, or determine, the guarantee by notice to the creditor. In the absence of any express provision, a continuing guarantee under hand may definitely be revoked by notice at any time. The same probably applies to a guarantee for a limited period or a guarantee under seal.[159] If a guarantee is revoked by notice, the guarantor is discharged in respect of future transactions of the principal debtor, but remains liable in respect of past transactions of the principal debtor. If the guarantee was given by more than one person the guarantee cannot be revoked by notice unless the notice is signed by all the co-guarantors, except where the guarantee contained express provisions to the contrary.[160]

If a continuing guarantee is revoked by notice, and there are no express provisions in the guarantee regarding such matters as unpresented cheques, the banker will not know whether he should honour cheques drawn before receipt of notice of revocation but not presented until afterwards. For this reason it is highly desirable for a bank guarantee to include detailed provisions regarding the revocation of the guarantee by notice. In particular the guarantee should provide for a period of notice long enough to allow time for

158. *Bradford Old Bank* v. *Sutcliffe* [1918] 2 K.B. 833.
159. *See* Paget, (8th Edn.), pp. 610–11.
160. *Egbert* v. *National Crown Bank* [1918] A.C. 903.

all outstanding cheques to be presented, and for the principal debtor and the banker to make alternative arrangements for the future if the principal debtor's account is to be continued.[161]

When notice is given, the guarantor will be liable for all matters outstanding at the date of receipt by the bank of such notice, and for subsequent items accruing by reason of engagements made before the receipt of notice, such as bills accepted by the bank before the notice was received.

It is, however, inadvisable for the banker to make purely voluntary advances between receipt of notice and the date when it expires since these might not be recoverable against the guarantor. The banker should confine himself to obligations incurred to the principal debtor before receipt of the notice. This would be in line with the general duty for the guaranteed party to behave equitably towards the guarantor.[162] There would be little point in the guarantor being able to give notice if the banker could still increase the amount of the liability up to the limit.[163]

The banker should give notice to the principal debtor immediately he receives notice of revocation from the guarantor; as with all such notices, the banker should be in a position to prove delivery of the notice to the principal debtor if necessary. The notice to the principal debtor should therefore be in writing and sent by registered or recorded delivery post. The banker should then stop the guaranteed account so as to prevent the operation of the rule in *Clayton*'s case,[164] for although he is not permitted to rule off the account and place future payments into a separate account so as to deprive the guarantor of the benefit of them while the guarantee continues in force, the banker is justified in doing so once the guarantee has been determined.

Determination by death

In the absence of any express provision in the guarantee, it is not clear whether a guarantor is discharged by his death. If the guarantee provides specifically that the personal representatives of the guarantor may revoke the guarantee by giving notice, then the guarantee will certainly not be revoked by the death of the guarantor since it expressly contemplates that it may continue beyond the guarantor's death.[166] In any event a guarantee will not be revoked

161. *See* Clause 10 in the form in Appendix I.
162. *See Holland* v. *Tead* (1848) 7 Hare. 50.
163. *See* Paget (8th Edn.), pp. 611–12.
164. *See Bradford Old Bank* v. *Sutcliffe* [1918] 2 K.B. 833.
165. *Re Sherry, London & County Banking Co.* v. *Terry* (1884) 25 Ch. D. 692.
166. *See Egbert* v. *National Crown Bank* [1918] A.C. 903.

until the banker receives notice that the guarantor has died.[167]

A guarantee will be revoked by notice of the guarantor's death if the consideration for the guarantee is supplied from time to time, as in the case of a continuing guarantee of a current account, so that the guarantee is by its very nature revocable at any time by the guarantor, and there is no stipulation for determination by notice, or if notice can only be given in accordance with the contract by the guarantor in his lifetime.[168] When it is so revoked, it is only revoked as to the future transactions of the principal debtor and the personal representatives will remain liable in respect of past transactions of the principal debtor.

Where co-guarantors are jointly liable, the estate of a deceased guarantor is discharged altogether by the death. If, however, the co-guarantors are jointly and severally liable, the estate of a deceased co-guarantor will remain liable under the guarantee, especially if the guarantee provides that notice to determine may be given by the personal representatives of a deceased guarantor. It is not entirely clear whether the surviving co-guarantors remain liable under the guarantee if one co-guarantor dies.[169] For this reason the guarantee should expressly provide that whatever happens to any one co-guarantor, the other co-guarantors will remain liable both for past and future advances to the principal debtor.[170] In all cases of death of (or determination by) one of two or more co-guarantors, it is advisable that the account of the principal debtor should be stopped by the banker; a new account should be opened, and should be kept in credit until the surviving guarantors can enter into another guarantee or write a letter continuing their responsibility.

Where a guarantee is revoked, either by notice of the guarantor's death or by express notice from the personal representatives, the banker should immediately rule off the account and pass all future transactions through a new account. The necessity for doing this is illustrated by the case of *Bradford Old Bank* v. *Sutcliffe*,[171] where a company had a loan and a current account with the bank, guaranteed by several of the directors. In 1898 one of the guarantors became mentally incapacitated, and the bank had notice of this in 1899. Demand was made on the guarantors, including the estate of the incapacitated guarantor, in 1915. It was held that the guarantee of the incapacitated guarantor ceased as a continuing guarantee in 1899, when the bank had notice of the incapacity, and thereupon his liability crystallised in respect of the amount then outstanding. The

167. *Ashby* v. *Day* (1885) 33 W.R. 631; affd. on appeal (1886) 54 L.T. 408.
168. *Coulthart* v. *Clementson* (1879) 5 Q.B.D. 42.
169. Except in the case of the death of a guarantor who was joint only.
170. *See* Clause 11 in the form in Appendix I.
171. *Bradford Old Bank* v. *Sutcliffe* [1918] 2 K.B. 833.

current account continued to be operated actively. Under the rule in *Clayton*'s case[172] payments in were deemed to have paid off the earliest advances, so that with the turnover on the account the whole of the amount outstanding when demand was made against the guarantors was held to represent advances made after the bank received notice of insanity, and so the estate of that guarantor was not liable in respect of the current account. There was, however, no set-off of credit balances on the current account against the balance on the loan account, so that the estate of the incapacitated guarantor remained liable on the loan account.

Determination by mental incapacity or bankruptcy

A guarantor who has been been declared incapable is discharged as regards future transactions of the principal debtor as soon as the banker has received notice of the incapacity, but the guarantor remains liable as regards past transactions of the principal debtor.[173] Similarly, a guarantor who has been declared bankrupt is discharged as regards future transactions of the principal debtor.

The bank should, therefore, as soon as it receives notice of the mental incapacity of a guarantor, close the account and pass all future transactions through a new account. This was not done in the *Sutcliffe* case, and the effect was that under the rule in *Clayton*'s case[172] the liability of the insane guarantor was satisfied by subsequent payments into the account.

Even the standard "Cond" clause[173] would not have helped the bank in this case, since that applies only to determination by notice. To guard against this, one should add to the standard wording a reference to determination ". . . or by any other cause or reason whatsoever" to cover the possibility of insanity.

Where the guarantor is declared bankrupt, the banker has the right to prove against the guarantor's estate in respect of the contingent liability even if the principal debt has not yet become due.[174] When proving against the guarantor's estate, the banker must take into account any security or any part payment he has received from the principal debtor. Once a bankrupt guarantor is discharged from bankruptcy, he has no remaining liability under the guarantee.[175]

If one of a number of joint and several guarantors is adjudicated bankrupt, the bank will be faced with a choice. Does it call in the guarantee, claiming against the others and proving in the estate of the bankrupt guarantor, or does it rely on the remaining guarantors?

---

172. (1816) 1 Mer. 572. *See* Chapter Four.
173. *See Westminster Bank* v. *Cond* (1940) 46 Com. Cas. 60, referred to below.
174. Bankruptcy Act 1914, s. 30(3).
175. Ibid., s. 28(2).

In the latter case, since the bankrupt guarantor will have been released by bankruptcy, there is a risk that the remaining guarantors may also be released, since the standard "time and indulgence" clauses refer only to releases by the bank, and such a release would be by operation of law.

Unless, therefore, the guarantee provides that the liability of the remaining guarantors is not revoked or impaired by the bankruptcy of one or more guarantors, it is safer for the banker to arrange for a new guarantee from the remaining guarantors; pending such new arrangement the banker should stop the account. Where there is only one guarantor, the banker should, as soon as he learns of his failure, stop the account, demand payment from the principal debtor, and if he defaults, prove against the guarantor's estate.

Where there are co-guarantors and one co-guarantor is declared incapable or bankrupt, the declaration operates as a release of that co-guarantor and, as we have seen, the release of one co-guarantor can have the effect of discharging the other co-guarantors as well. Most standard bank guarantees expressly provide that if one co-guarantor is released, the other co-guarantors will not be discharged,[176] but these provisions normally apply only to an express release by the banker and not to a release by "operation of law", as in the case of mental incapacity or bankruptcy. For this reason, the banker should in most cases assume that the mental incapacity or bankruptcy of one co-guarantor discharges the other co-guarantors. He should therefore obtain a new guarantee from any of the co-guarantors who wish to continue to guarantee the debt of the principal debtor.

CONDUCT OF THE PRINCIPAL DEBTOR'S BANK ACCOUNT ON DISCHARGE OF A GUARANTOR

When a guarantee is determined, either wholly or as regards any one guarantor, the banker should stop the principal debtor's account and open a new account for subsequent payments in. If the banker allows the old account to continue, any payment in will, in the absence of an express appropriation, be appropriated according to the rule in *Clayton*'s case.[177] This will mean that payments in will be used to pay off the guaranteed debit balance on the account, leaving any subsequent debit balance unguaranteed.

It is usual for bank guarantees to have a clause expressly permitting the bank to close the account concerned and to pass all future trans-

176. *See* Clause 11 in the form in Appendix I.
177. (1816) 1 Mer. 572. *See Bradford Old Bank* v. *Sutcliffe* [1918] 2 K.B. 833.

actions through a separate account so that the guarantor remains liable for the indebtedness outstanding at the day the account is closed,[178] though the case of *Re Sherry, London & County Banking Co.* v. *Terry*[179] suggests that such a clause is, strictly speaking, unnecessary. In that case it was held that there was nothing express or implied in the contract to prevent the bank from carrying such payments by the customer to the new account.

Sometimes, either through an oversight or because the bank has some reason for not wishing to close the account, the account is not closed but is continued. Subsequent payments made by the customer will, under the rule in *Clayton*'s case,[177] go to reduce the oldest indebtedness first; thus all new payments in will reduce the amount for which the guarantor is liable and may extinguish it altogether.[180] In order to counteract this a clause was devised stating that the liability of the guarantor was to continue for the amount due from the principal debtor at the date when the guarantee was determined notwithstanding any subsequent payment into or out of the account by or on behalf of the principal debtor; such a clause was upheld in *Westminster Bank* v. *Cond*.[181]

It is, however, the normal practice of bankers to stop the old account and to open a new account for subsequent payments in, whether or not there is a "Cond clause" in the guarantee.

AVOIDANCE OF A GUARANTEE

Avoidance by reason of misrepresentation

Guarantees, unlike contracts of insurance, are not contracts *uberrimae fidei*, or contracts "of the utmost good faith", under which one or both parties is under an obligation to disclose to the other all material facts known to him which might influence the decision of the other. Non-disclosure by the banker of facts which led the banker to suspect that the principal debtor was defrauding the guarantor would not necessarily invalidate the guarantee.[182]

The test, laid down in *Hamilton* v. *Watson*,[183] is whether there is any contract between the banker and the principal debtor which would mean that the position of the guarantor was not what he might reasonably expect. If there is, the guarantor is entitled to have this disclosed to him; he must make his own specific inquiries if he is concerned about other points.

178. *See* Clause 8 in the form in Appendix I.
179. (1884) 25 Ch. D. 692.
180. *Bradford Old Bank* v. *Sutcliffe* [1918] 2 K.B. 833.
181. (1940) 46 Com. Cas. 60.
182. *National Provincial Bank of England* v. *Glanusk* [1913] 3 K.B. 335.
183. (1845) 12 Cl. & Fin. 109.

The principle established in *Hamilton*'s case was applied strictly in *Cooper* v. *National Provincial Bank*.[184] In that case the banker did not disclose to the guarantor that the husband of the principal debtor, who was an undischarged bankrupt, had authority to operate the principal debtor's account and that the account had been operated in an improper and irregular way because certain cheques had been stopped. The guarantee was nevertheless held to be enforceable, since there was nothing concerning the principal debtor's account which a guarantor might not reasonably have expected. Similarly, in *Lloyds Bank* v. *Harrison*[185] it was held that the banker had no duty to disclose that the principal debtor was in difficulties and that the banker had insisted for six months that the principal debtor should accept only such business as would reduce his stock.

If, however, the guarantor does make inquiries of the banker with reference to matters which the banker does not have a duty to disclose, the banker must then give a straightforward reply and not one capable of being misconstrued, and must give the information honestly and to the best of his ability. While the banker is not bound to disclose all that he knows about the principal debtor's dealings, he must not conceal from the guarantor any fact materially affecting the transaction between the banker and the guarantor. As Fry J put it in *Davies* v. *London & Provincial Marine Insurance Company*,[186] "the avoidance of a contract of guarantee by the non-disclosure of a material fact depends in each case upon whether, having regard to the nature of the transaction, and the relations of the parties, *the fact not disclosed is impliedly represented not to exist*", and "very little said which ought not to have been said and very little omitted which ought to have been said will suffice to avoid the contract".

Avoidance by reason of undue influence

A guarantor may be discharged if he can show that he was induced to enter into the guarantee by reason of undue influence. There is a presumption of undue influence where the guarantor was persuaded to enter into the guarantee by someone in whom he placed his "trust and confidence" and where the banker knew that this was so. In *Lloyds Bank* v. *Bundy*,[187] for example, the guarantor was an old man in poor health. He had already given two guarantees to the bank in respect of an overdraft to his son, and had mortgaged a farm, which had been in the family for generations and was his only asset, in support of the guarantees. He had been advised by

184. [1945] 2 All E.R. 641.
185. (1925) 4 *Legal Decisions Affecting Bankers* 12.
186. (1878) 8 Ch. D. 469.
187. [1975] Q.B. 326.

his solicitor not to commit his assets beyond the figure of £6,500, the amount for which he was liable after signing the second guarantee. The assistant bank manager now visited the father at his home, saying he would only continue the facilities to the son if the father gave a third guarantee and increased the mortgage on the farm.

The father had relied for financial advice on his bank manager for a long time. Although the assistant bank manager realised that the father relied on him implicitly to advise him about the transaction "as a bank manager", he did not appreciate that there was a conflict of interest and never suggested that the old man should take independent advice. Even though the father had previously been warned by his solicitor, the third guarantee was set aside by the court by reason of undue influence.

The law has always recognised that there are some cases of "inequality of bargaining power" where the intervention of the courts is required. These include cases of "undue influence" where the stronger party gains from the relationship with the weaker some gift or advantage for himself.[188] In some cases there is a presumption of undue influence from the relationship of the parties, such as parent over child, solicitor over client; in other cases a relation of confidence must be proved to exist. In *Bundy*'s case the relation of confidence was found to exist because of the age of Mr Bundy and the long relationship between his family and the bank.

The bank conceded that relations of confidentiality could arise between a banker and a customer, and the father conceded that in the normal course of transactions by which a customer guaranteed third party obligations the relationship did not arise. However, it was held that this was a case which "cried out for independent advice", and in such cases the stronger party must not be allowed to retain any benefit from the transaction unless the other person can be shown to have formed an independent and informed judgment.

Sachs LJ pointed out that nothing in his judgment affected the duties of the bank in the normal case where it was obtaining a guarantee and in accordance with standard practice the banker explained the legal effect and the sums involved. When the bank, as in this case, went further and advised on the wisdom of the transaction, it might be crossing the line into the area of confidentiality; the court might then have to examine all the facts to see if the line had been crossed.

It will be evident from the above remarks that it will not be necessary in every case for the banker to ensure that a guarantor

188. See *Allcard* v. *Skinner* (1887) 36 Ch. D. 145.

takes independent advice and it would be tiresome and superfluous for banks to suggest this on every occasion. Clearly in the case of substantial men of business it would be unnecessary.

Where guarantees are taken from persons who are not men of business, the banker should never seek to advise them himself. He should always suggest that independent advice be obtained by any guarantor who may seem unlikely to be able to form an independent and informed judgment without it. This is particularly important where the proposed guarantor has in the past looked to the bank for advice, and where the guarantor is giving a guarantee for a relation, or a company owned by a relation.

Bearing in mind that the undue influence might be exerted not only by the bank but also by the person whose account is guaranteed, there may be other circumstances, especially in the case of spouses.

Husband and wife

There is no presumption of undue influence in the case of husband and wife,[189] and the burden of proving undue influence lies on those who allege it.[190]

In *Bank of Montreal* v. *Stuart*[191] the same solicitor acted on behalf of the bank, the husband and the wife. The husband had already given the bank a guarantee in respect of the company which was the principal debtor. The solicitor was also a director, secretary and shareholder of the debtor company. The wife was a confirmed invalid, who acted throughout in passive obedience to her husband's directions, and had no means of forming an independent judgment. In a series of transactions spread over eight years she charged all her extensive real and personal estate to the bank as security for the liabilities of the company for which the husband had already exhausted his own assets.

The court found that these transactions could not stand, as the wife was under the husband's influence and the solicitor was in a position in which he could not advise fairly. The lawyer "ought to have endeavoured to advise the wife and to place her position and the consequences of what she was doing fully and plainly before her. Probably, if not certainly, she would have rejected his intervention. And then he ought to have gone to the husband and insisted on the wife being separately advised, and if that was an impossibility owing to the implicit confidence which Mrs Stuart reposed in her husband, he ought to have retired from the business altogether and told the bank why he did so."

189. *Mackenzie* v. *Royal Bank of Canada* [1934] A.C. 468.
190. *Nedby* v. *Nedby* (1852) 5 De G. & Sm. 377.
191. [1911] A.C. 120.

The above remarks apply equally to either spouse; a husband might require separate advice where he is to guarantee a loan to his wife's business.

In all cases where independent advice is sought at the request of the bank, it would be wise to have the signature on the guarantee witnessed by a solicitor. In such cases the solicitor should, either on the guarantee which he witnesses or in a separate letter, acknowledge that he explained the nature and effect of the document and the transaction to the guarantor, who fully appreciated what he or she was signing, and what obligations he or she was undertaking, before he or she signed the guarantee. Even if this does not preclude the allegation of undue influence it will give the bank a method of establishing that the guarantor was separately advised and fully understood the transaction.

Avoidance by reason of mistake

A guarantor cannot claim to be relieved from his guarantee by reason of mistake on the ground that he did not understand some particular provision of the guarantee or even, since modern guarantees contain much in addition to the basic guarantee clause, the general drift of the guarantee.

Where, however, a person signs a guarantee under a fundamental mistake as to the nature of the document he is signing, the guarantee may in some cases be void by reason of mistake. The essence of the defence here is the old plea of *non est factum* (literally "it was not my act"). This defence is clearly available when the guarantee was not in fact signed not by the guarantor or his agent, but by some other person. The law has also recognised the need to offer some protection in favour of persons who, because they are illiterate or blind, cannot read, and have to trust other persons to tell them what they are signing, and the plea of *non est factum* has also been extended to persons who are permanently or temporarily unable, through no fault of their own, to understand without explanation the purport of the document, whether the inability is through defective education, illness, or incapacity.

In *Foster* v. *Mackinnon*,[192] Byles J said "if a blind man or one who cannot read, or one who for some reason (not implying negligence) forbears to read, has a written contract falsely read over to him, the reader misreading to such a degree that the written contract is of a nature altogether different from the contract pretended to be read from the paper which the blind or illiterate man afterwards signs, then, at least if there be no negligence, the signature so obtained

192. (1869) L.R. 4 C.P. 704.

is of no force. And it is invalid not merely on the ground of fraud, where fraud exists, but on the ground that the mind of the signer did not accompany the signature; in other words, that he never intended to sign, and therefore in contemplation of law never did sign, the contract to which his name is appended."

In *Saunders* v. *Anglia Building Society*,[193] the House of Lords decided that where a person signed a document, the plea of *non est factum* can only succeed if he can show that the document which he signed was not the document he intended to sign and that when he signed the document he was not acting carelessly. It follows from this that the plea of *non est factum* will rarely succeed if the document was signed by an adult and literate person.

Clearly in the case of fraud, the question is still one of lack of consent, however the lack of consent was brought about, but where innocent third parties are concerned, if a person of ordinary education and competence chooses to sign without informing himself of the purport and the effect of the document, he cannot escape its consequences.

Problems arise where the person concerned is careless (meaning ordinary carelessness, not negligence in the sense in which that word is used in the law of torts). The general conclusion must be that the plea will inevitably be rare in the case of adult and literate persons; in the case of illiterates, blind persons or those lacking in understanding, the dilemma is to reconcile the need to relieve them and the need to protect both parties.

If a person signs a deed without knowing or inquiring about its contents but signs simply because his solicitor or other adviser tells him to do so, then his intention is to sign the deed placed before him, whatever it is; the plea of *non est factum* is not available in such cases. Again a busy managing director may sign, without reading, a pile of papers placed before him by his secretary. He knows there is a possibility of the fraudulent insertion of a document in the pile, but disregards this risk as improbable. Nevertheless, a person who signs in such circumstances should be held by the consequences, since he takes on himself the responsiblity for the documents and assumes the risk of fraudulent substitution.

The old distinction between differences in the character and the contents of the documents must now be rejected as unsatisfactory. In so far as it is possible to derive a short principle from the judgment of the House of Lords in this case, it is one of ascertaining whether the person who signs must in all the circumstances be treated as having intended to sign the document he did sign. In ascertaining

193. [1970] 3 All E.R. 961 (affirming *Gallie* v. *Lee* [1969] 1 All E.R. 1062); *see also Credit Lyonnais* v. *P. T. Bernard & Associates* [1976] 1 Lloyd's Rep. 557.

this objective intention from the surrounding circumstances one must have regard to the extent to which he did or, for whatever reason, did not read the document; if he did not read the document, the nature and the extent of the inquiries he actually made as to its contents are crucial. The busy managing director is bound by his signature because he does intend to sign the documents placed before him, whatever they may be.

CHAPTER FIFTEEN

Land as Security

DISADVANTAGES OF LAND AS A SECURITY

Land is probably the most common form of security taken by bankers, and in many ways it is the most convenient. Even so, there was at one time a strong prejudice among bankers against lending on land as security. By the 1960s this prejudice had been overcome, and bankers had begun to look upon property as a security which would tend, with time, to increase in value. Then, in 1973–74, the property market collapsed, there was a general crisis in liquidity, and many bankers who had made substantial loans on the security of land suffered heavy losses.

That crisis has drawn attention once again to some of the drawbacks of land as security. In the first place, recent experience has shown that the traditional view that land could be relied upon, in the face of market forces, to increase in value, as against other forms of security, no longer holds good. Secondly, such security cannot easily be realised, and when, as in 1974, too much property becomes available on a depressed market, its value will almost certainly fall. Thirdly, there is the difficulty of valuing property, and of deciding whether to value it on the basis of its use to the present owner or on the basis of a forced sale. Usually the latter is preferred by bankers.

Other disadvantages for the banker are, first, the risk that the bank might not get a good title to the property under its mortgage. Second, if the customer obtains an improvement grant in respect of a house which is mortgaged to a bank, the bank would, in the event of default, be unable to sell the house with vacant possession because of the conditions which apply automatically to such loans.[1] Third, where a bank takes a mortgage on a customer's home, the bank may find itself unable to sell the property with vacant possession because of the spouse's rights of occupation,[2] or because of the rights of another person living in the house.[3] Even if there is no

1. Local authorities may make improvement grants under the Housing Act 1974, ss. 56–84.
2. Matrimonial Homes Act 1967, s. 1.
3. *Williams & Glyn's Bank* v. *Boland,* and *Williams & Glyn's Bank* v. *Brown* [1981] A.C. 487. *See also* the Matrimonial Homes and Property Act 1981, ss. 1–6 (not in force at the time of writing).

such difficulty a banker will often be reluctant to enforce his security by obtaining a court order to sell a customer's home. Finally, and from the customer's point of view, there is the expense of obtaining a mortgage. The customer may have to pay for a professional valuation of the property, for the fees of the bank's solicitors for reporting upon the title, and for land registry fees if the title is registered.

Nevertheless, provided the banker is satisfied that a conservative valuation has been obtained, that the customer has a sound title to the land, and that he, the banker, will, if the customer defaults, be able to realise his security, he will usually be willing to lend money on land.

LEGAL DEFINITION OF LAND

For almost a millennium the law relating to ownership of land in England was based on the proposition that the ultimate ownership of all land remained vested in the Crown. Occupiers of land held it in return for an obligation owed to the Crown, or to an intermediate occupier who himself held from the Crown. In early times the obligations were often of a practical and personal nature, for example, to provide personal, military or agricultural services.

As commerce and industry advanced, and the personal power of the monarch declined, such arrangements became impractical and the attempt to reconcile historical principles to modern necessities produced a legal system concerning the ownership of and dealing with land of considerable complexity and obscurity.

Reform of the law was consequently felt to be desirable and manifested itself in what has come to be referred to as "the 1925 legislation". The various statutes comprising this legislation must be considered an outstanding example of legal craftsmanship. Some anomalies and obscurities have revealed themselves since 1925, but in general the sweeping reforms in the law which the 1925 legislation brought about have proved eminently practical and just.

The principal statutes making up the 1925 legislation are:

(a) Law of Property Act 1925 (LPA 1925);
(b) Land Registration Act 1925 (LRA 1925);
(c) Land Charges Act 1925 (LCA 1925) (now replaced);
(d) Settled Land Act 1925 (SLA 1925);
(e) Trustee Act 1925 (TA 1925); and
(f) Administration of Estates Act 1925 (AEA 1925).

Later statutes have amended certain of these Acts, in particular the Land Registration Act 1966 (LRA 1966), the Law of Property Act 1969 (LPA 1969) and the Land Charges Act 1972 (LCA 1972), but the structure of law established by the 1925 legislation remains essentially unchanged.

The first thing a banker should know about land as a security is that in legal terminology "land" possesses a much wider meaning than in everyday speech. The legal definition of land embraces not only the land itself but also the air above the land to an infinite height and the earth beneath the land to an infinite depth, including any mines and mineral wealth. The legal definition of land also embraces any building which is on the land and any "fixtures" which are attached to the land. A fixture is any item which is attached to land in such a way as to suggest that it was intended to form a permanent part of the land.[4] So a light bulb is probably not a fixture whereas a light fitting probably is a fixture. When a banker is offered "land" as a security, he may therefore be offered the ground itself or a building or a mine or fixtures or all of these things together.

The second thing a banker should know about land as a security is that, strictly speaking, land cannot be offered as a security. The reason for this is that in theory all land has been owned by the Crown for many centuries and anybody else can own only an "interest" in land or, in other words, a right to possession of land for a certain period, either immediately or at some future date. Thus, strictly speaking, this chapter should not be entitled "Land as Security", but "Interests in Land as Security". Before he is in a position to accept an interest in land as a security, a banker must be able to understand what interest it is that he is being offered and how much it is worth. To understand these things the banker must acquire at least a basic understanding of land law, which is perhaps the most complex area of the law.

The interests in land which a banker is most likely to be offered as security for a loan are "legal estates" and "equitable interests". Since the property legislation of 1925, these can be sub-divided as follows.

Legal estates

The only two legal estates capable of subsisting in land are a fee simple absolute in possession (a freehold) and a term of years absolute (a lease).[5]

Fee simple absolute in possession (freehold)

A fee simple is an interest in land which is not for a limited period, such as a set term of years or the life of a particular person. In

---

4. LPA 1925, s. 205(*ix*).
5. Ibid., s. 1(1).

theory a fee simple is an interest which "endures" until the owner (or "tenant") for the time being "dies without heirs". What this formula means in practice is that the owner of a fee simple has an interest in land which endures for ever.

An interest is "in possession" if it entitles the holder to immediate possession of the land. An absolute interest which is not in possession, or an interest in possession which is not absolute, is not a legal estate in land, but an equitable interest in land. For this purpose, "possession" includes the right to enjoy the income from the land, not merely the right to occupy it.

Term of years absolute (lease)

A term of years is an interest in land which entitles its owner to exclusive possession of a clearly defined piece of land for a "term of years". Where a person does not have the right to exclusive possession of land or where the piece of land is not clearly defined, the person has a "licence", not a term of years. A licence is not an interest in land, nor is it any other form of property. Therefore, it cannot be sold or given away or given as security for a loan.

A term of years is "absolute" if (a) it is for a fixed period and it is possible to say with certainty when the period begins and what the maximum duration of the period will be; or (b) if it is for a series of fixed periods and it is possible to say with certainty when the first period begins and what the maximum duration of each of the periods will be.

A term of years may be absolute even if it is contingent, conditional or determinable. So a term of years may be absolute even if it may be determined prematurely, for example, by the giving of notice. It follows that the word "absolute" does not mean the same in the phrase "term of years absolute" as it means in the phrase "fee simple absolute in possession".

A term of years absolute may be a legal estate even if it is not in possession. This means that a term of years absolute may be a legal estate even if its owner does not have an immediate right to possession of any land. In most cases, however, a term of years absolute will be void if it does not "take effect" in possession within twenty-one years of its creation. A term of years absolute may be of any duration, from a few minutes to thousands of years.

A term of years which is created for a single period is known, in everyday speech, as a "lease". This term is also used to refer to the document by which the term of years is created. A term of years which is created for a single period with the possibility of renewal for subsequent periods is usually referred to as a lease, but it is sometimes referred to as a "periodic tenancy".

The person who grants a lease is the owner of the fee simple absolute in possession.[6] He is known as the "landlord" (or "lessor") and the person to whom the lease is granted is known as the "tenant" (or "lessee"). In the lease, the landlord and the tenant make certain "covenants" with one another. The tenant, for example, may covenant to pay rent or to use the land only for a specified purpose. The landlord may covenant to carry out certain repairs on the land. In the absence of any express covenants to the contrary, certain covenants may be implied. There is usually provision in the lease for the lease to be "forfeited" if the tenant is in breach of one of his more important covenants, particularly his covenant to pay rent to the landlord.

After the landlord has granted a lease, his fee simple absolute in possession is referred to as the "reversion" to the lease. This is an interest in land which entitles its owner (the "reversioner") to possession of the land at the end of the term of years which he has granted. Until the term of years is over, the reversioner is not entitled to possession of the land and is only entitled to the rent from the land.

The reversioner or the tenant may sell (or "assign") their interests to third persons who are known as "assignees". By the doctrine of "privity of estate" the assignee of the landlord enjoys the benefit of any covenant in favour of the landlord and the assignee of the tenant enjoys the benefit of any covenant in favour of the tenant. The doctrine of privity of estate only applies, however, to any covenant which "touches and concerns" the land. The benefit and burden of a purely personal contract between the landlord and the tenant do not pass to their assignees.

Instead of assigning his lease, a tenant may create a "sublease". The difference between an assignment and a sublease is as follows. An assignment of a lease is an assignment of the whole of the tenant's interest in the land or, in other words, an assignment of the whole of what remains of the term of years granted to the tenant by the landlord. A tenant who has assigned his lease has no further interest in the land. A sublease, on the other hand, is a grant by the tenant of less than what remains of the term of years granted to him by the landlord. Thus, if the original term of years was 99 years and 50 years of the term still remain, the tenant will be granting a sublease, not an assignment, if he grants a term of 49 years and 364 days.

The relationship of the tenant and the sublessee is the relationship of landlord and tenant. This means that the tenant and sublessee enter into covenants with one another and the tenant, as sublessor, retains an interest in land, namely the reversion on the sublease. The

6. Sub-leases are discussed below.

sublessee may himself assign or sublet and the same applies to any sub-sublessees. Assignment or subletting may, however, be restricted or excluded by a covenant in the lease or the sublease. As between a landlord and a sublessee (or a sublessor and a sub-sublessee), the doctrine of privity of estate does not apply. This means that a landlord or his assignee cannot normally enforce a covenant against a sublessee (or vice versa). However, under a special rule a landlord or his assignee can enforce a covenant against a sublessee if the covenant is a restrictive covenant. Restrictive covenants are discussed later in this chapter.

To be a legal estate a term of years absolute, whether a lease or a sublease, must normally be created by deed, or in other words by a document executed under seal.[7] However, a term of years absolute may still be a legal estate if it is created orally provided that the term is for a maximum of three years, to take effect in possession, at the best rent obtainable, without payment of a "fine".[8] The normal practice when a lease is granted is first to enter into a contract and then to "complete" the transaction by the execution of a lease by deed. As soon as the contract is created, the tenant acquires an equitable interest in land.

Equitable interests
The only equitable interests which are at all commonly offered as security are interests of a minor in land, an interest in an estate or interest which is co-owned, and a contract to grant a legal estate.

Any interest in land owned by a minor is an equitable interest. The reason for this is that a minor is prevented by statute from holding a legal estate.[9] A banker should never accept such an interest as security.[10]

Where any legal estate or equitable interest is co-owned, each of the co-owners has an equitable interest in that interest. The interest of a co-owner can be either a joint tenancy or a tenancy-in-common.

A person who has entered into a contract to purchase a legal estate has an equitable interest in that legal estate.

BANKER'S INQUIRIES ABOUT LAND OFFERED AS SECURITY

It follows from what has been said that a large number of legal estates and equitable interests may exist in the same land at the

7. LPA 1925, s. 52.
8. Ibid., s. 54(2).
9. Ibid., s. 19.
10. See "Minors" in Chapter Five.

same time. Any of these interests may be offered as security for a loan and from the point of view of a banker some of these interests will be more valuable than others. For example, the relative values of the freehold, a lease and any subleases will depend upon the length of the terms created by, and the rents payable under, the lease and the sublease.

When a legal estate or equitable interest is offered to a banker as security for a loan, the banker should make inquiries in order to discover whether the estate or interest is subject to any mortgage or to any contract such as a right of pre-emption or an option.[11] In the case of a legal estate, the banker should also make inquiries in order to discover whether the estate is subject to any lease or to any "easement", "profit", "restrictive covenant" or "rentcharge" or to any other "charges" such as an Inland Revenue charge, a compulsory purchase order, a listed building charge or a spouse's charge on the matrimonial home. Where a lease or a reversion to a lease is being offered as security, the banker should make inquiries regarding the covenants in the lease. The more arduous the covenants, the smaller the value of the security.

Mortgages, easements, profits, restrictive covenants and rentcharges are themselves all interests in land and may themselves be given as security for a loan, though in practice only a mortgage is particularly likely to be offered. These interests may be "legal interests" or "equitable interests", depending on the manner of their creation and the length of time for which they will endure.[12] Mortgages are discussed in considerable detail later in this chapter and need not be dealt with here. Basic definitions of the other four "interests in the land of another person" are given below.

(a) *Easements.* An easement is an interest which entitles the owner of one legal estate to do certain things on land the legal estate of which is owned by another. A common example of an easement is a right of way.

(b) *Profits.* A profit is an interest which entitles one person to take certain things, such as sand or gravel, away from the land of another.

(c) *Restrictive covenants.* A restrictive covenant is an interest which entitles the owner of one legal estate to restrict the rights of the owner of the legal estate in neighbouring land. For example, a legal estate might be subject to a restrictive covenant which prevents its owner from erecting any buildings on the land.

11. These terms are discussed below.
12. LPA 1925, s. 1(2) and (3).

(*d*) *Rentcharges.* A rentcharge is an interest which entitles its owner to receive recurring payments out of the income of another person's legal estate in return for some payment or other consideration from the owner of the rentcharge. The Rentcharges Act 1977 has (in effect) prevented the creation of any new such charges.

At the same time as he inquires whether the estate or interest which he is being offered as security is subject to any of the interests just described, the banker should also inquire whether the would-be borrower has "good title" to the estate or interest which he is offering.

When a banker is offered as security a legal estate in unregistered land he should apply on Land Registry Form No. 96 for an official search of the index map of registered titles.[13] This will show whether the land has in fact been registered even though the usual Land Registry stamp has not been impressed on the last document of title.

PROOF OF BORROWER'S TITLE

In any examination of title the object is to establish that the purported owner is, in fact, the true owner of the interest offered as security. In the case of a legal estate, the method adopted is to consider the recent history of the transmission of the legal estate from successive owners and this is done by examining the documents which effect and evidence such transmission.

The document by which title to unregistered freehold land is transmitted is known as a conveyance, which must be a deed.[14]

The statutory minimum period for which title is to be shown is fifteen years.[15] This is the minimum period to which a person is entitled under an "open contract", that is to say, a contract for the sale of land which does not specify any particular conditions of sale, but it may be reduced by agreement between the parties. Often it is much longer, if the earliest appropriate document is appreciably more than fifteen years old. The document from which the title is to commence is known as the "root of title". A "good root" is a deed of conveyance (or mortgage) dealing with the entire legal estate in the whole of the land in circumstances which render it highly likely that the title to the land prior to the date of the document in question was examined at the date of that document. A conveyance or mortgage for value is thus usually accepted as a good root of

13. The rules which apply where the title to land is registered are discussed at the end of this chapter.
14. LPA 1925, s. 52(1). There are certain technical exceptions set out in ss. 52(2) and 55.
15. It was reduced from thirty years to fifteen years by the LPA 1969, s. 23.

title, but a devise by will or a voluntary conveyance by way of gift is not.

The root of title of a leasehold property must always be the lease itself, whatever its age. The remainder of the title may consist of assignments of the lease for a period not less than the statutory fifteen years (unless modified by contract) even though this may leave a considerable gap in time between the date of the lease and the assignment with which the title continues.

The subsequent documents must be scrutinised in date order to ensure that they evidence an unbroken transmission of the legal estate to the assumed present owner. It is rare for a title to consist exclusively of a series of conveyances of the whole of the property originally included in the root of title. An owner may die, in which event the grant of probate of his will (but not the contents of it, which remain "behind the curtain"), or the grant of administration if he should die intestate, will form part of the title, followed by either a sale by the executors or administrators or the vesting by them of the title in a beneficiary under the will or intestacy by means of an assent (which may be considered as a special form of conveyance). A previous owner may have borrowed money on the security of the property, in which event a mortgage or charge of the property will appear on the title followed by either a discharge of the mortgage (evidenced by a receipt indorsed upon it) and a conveyance by the borrower or a sale by the mortgagee.

The intending mortgagor should be able to produce the original documents of title for examination. If this cannot be done, an explanation of the absence of the documents should be insisted upon. There are wholly legitimate explanations for the inability to produce original documents. The potential borrower may require an advance upon the security of property to enable him to complete his purchase of it, or he may seek an advance for the purpose of paying off an existing loan. In the former case, he will be entitled to particulars of his vendor's title before completion. In the latter case, the lender will usually be prepared to hand over title documents in his possession to a solicitor in exchange for a solicitor's undertaking to hold the documents to the lender's order and to return them on demand, or alternatively to pay the amount due to the lender. A borrower is entitled to access to his documents of title in the hands of a lender and to make abstracts or copies of them, upon payment of expenses.[16]

Particulars of title are produced in the form of either an "abstract" or, more usually today, an "epitome". An abstract is a summary

16. LPA 1925, s. 96.

of the documents constituting the title. An epitome is a list of the relevant documents, accompanied by photocopies of them all.

Copies will, of course, show directly impressed stamps and details of execution. An abstract should show particulars of the execution of documents, and of any stamps impressed on the originals for stamp duty or pursuant to the Finance Act 1931. Where the investigation has been on the basis of an abstract or an epitome, the original documents should be checked before completion, and this should include a check of execution and stamping.

LOCAL LAND CHARGES REGISTER

Examination of an abstract or epitome of title to land by no means reveals all of the rights and obligations which may affect it. Some external matters are the subject of registration in official registers maintained by the State pursuant to statute.

The registers of local land charges, kept under the provisions of the Local Land Charges Act 1975, are of universal application, since they affect all land, whether title to it is unregistered, or registered under the LRA 1925.

The register is kept by the local authority for the area in which the land in question is situated.[17] It is divided into twelve parts in which there can be recorded a great number of matters, themselves usually arising as a result of the operation of other statutory provisions which may affect either a particular property alone or a designated area including a large number of properties. Some of the more important parts of the register deal with the following matters:

(*a*) general and specific financial charges,
(*b*) planning charges,
(*c*) some compulsory purchase orders,
(*d*) lists of buildings of special architectural or historical interest,
(*e*) light obstruction notices.

These subject headings indicate the nature of the entries to be found in the relevant parts of the registers. They range in scope from purely financial entries, such as legal charges, to restrictions based upon aesthetic considerations designed to preserve buildings noteworthy in some special respect.

Although it is possible in some cases to obtain information from the register by personal attendance at the offices of the local authority, the usual search procedure is to lodge a formal requisition for an official certificate of search in the register with the local

17. LLCA 1975, ss. 1–5.

land charges section of the local authority within whose jurisdiction the property under examination is situated. If a charge in existence at the time of a search is not registered on the register when a personal search is made, or is not shown on an official search certificate, a purchaser is still bound by the charge, but he is entitled to compensation.[18]

It is the invariable practice to lodge with the requisition a standard set of inquiries, in a form agreed by the Law Society with various bodies representing local authorities, requesting information upon a very wide range of matters important to a potential purchaser or lender but not within the ambit of the formal register. These inquiries deal, for instance, with intended road works, matters relating to drainage, town and country planning, the Rent Acts, compulsory purchase, smoke control, general rates and many other matters. The form also provides for additional inquiries specific to the property. The property must be identified by description or plan since the search and replies will only deal with matters affecting that particular property.

When particulars of the entries in the various parts of the register and the replies to inquiries are returned by the local authority they should be carefully perused, and particular regard be paid to matters affecting title and value. Some entries may affect both.

Title to property is affected in two ways only. First by the existence of a specific or general financial charge which may affect the priorities of bankers or others taking a charge on the same property, and secondly by the existence or intimation of a compulsory purchase order which will result in the removal of title from the current owner.

Value may be affected by a number of the entries and replies, not always prejudicially. The listing of a building as one of special architectural or historical interest, although restricting what may be done to the structure and appearance of the building, may well enhance its value. The conditions attached to a planning permission, which itself may be limited in time or personal to the occupier, or an intimation of enforcement proceedings in respect of breaches of planning control, may reduce value. Similarly, the carrying out of major road works close to the property, or the possibility of payment of additional rates (if the property is an empty commercial building)[19] reduces value.

Careful perusal of any entries in the register and replies to the standard inquiries will usually reveal any item upon which further information is desirable. It should be noted that, while proper care

18. LLCA 1975, s. 10.
19. General Rate Act 1967, Sched. 1.

is taken by local authorities, they do not give any warranty as to the accuracy of replies given to inquiries accompanying an official requistion for a search certificate.

LAND CHARGES REGISTER

The next series of registers to which consideration must be given are those maintained by the Chief Land Registrar. Although the Chief Land Registrar is often thought to be concerned exclusively with land the title to which is registered or registrable under the LRA 1925, he is also responsible for the operation of the registers of land charges which deal exclusively with matters affecting land the title to which is unregistered.

The registers were set up under the LCA 1925; this Act and subsequent amendments are now consolidated by the LCA 1972. There are five registers, of

(a) land charges,
(b) pending actions,
(c) writs and orders affecting land,
(d) deeds of arrangement affecting land, and
(e) annuities.

Entries in the registers of pending actions, writs and orders and deeds of arrangement are not very common and almost always arise out of matrimonial disputes or insolvencies. For example, a claim to have the matrimonial home transferred to one spouse,[20] or a bankruptcy petition may be registered as a pending action; an order appointing a receiver, or a receiving order in bankruptcy, may be registered in the register of writs and orders affecting land.[21] Entries in these registers cease to be effective after expiry of five years from the date of registration unless renewed.[22]

The register of annuities was closed in 1972 to new entries and will cease to exist when the existing entries are vacated.[23]

The register of land charges is the most important. There are six classes of land charges: A, B, C, D, E and F.[24]

Class A

This deals with rents, annuities and money payable by instalments which are charged upon land, not by an instrument of charge but

---

20. *Whittingham* v. *Whittingham;* (*National Westminster Bank (Intervener)*) [1979] Fam. 19.
21. LCA 1972, ss. 5–7.
22. Ibid., s. 8.
23. Ibid., s. 1 and Sched. 1.
24. Ibid., s. 2.

pursuant to the application of some person under the authority of an Act of Parliament.[25]

Class B

This deals with charges of the same kind as Class A, but created otherwise than pursuant to the application of some person.[26] Entries of Classes A and B are rare.

Class C

These are subdivided in the Act as follows:

(*i*) a "puisne mortgage", or legal mortgage not protected by deposit of the title deeds;

(*ii*) a limited owner's charge, such as a charge acquired by a tenant for life who has paid death duties, capital transfer tax or other liabilities out of his own pocket;

(*iii*) a general equitable charge—this is a sweeping-up category, which includes equitable charges which (*a*) are not secured by deposit of title deeds, (*b*) do not arise or affect an interest arising under a trust for sale or settlement, and (*c*) are not included in any other class of land charge;

(*iv*) an estate contract, or contract by an estate owner, or person entitled to have a legal estate conveyed to him, to convey or create a legal estate. It includes contracts to purchase, options to purchase, pre-emptions and the like.[27]

A Class C(*i*) land charge, a puisne mortgage, is important in itself and particularly so in the context of this work. A puisne mortgage is a legal mortgage not protected by a deposit of documents relating to the legal estate affected. As will be seen, a first legal mortgagee normally has the right to custody of the documents of title. A second or subsequent legal mortgagee's principal protection against competing mortgagees is, therefore, registration of his mortgage as a Class C(*i*) land charge. (A second equitable charge would be registered as a Class C(*iii*) land charge.)

Class D

These are subdivided in the Act into three groups, namely:

(*i*) Inland Revenue charges to secure payment of death duties or, after 1974, capital transfer tax;

(*ii*) restrictive covenants, i.e. covenants or agreements restricting

25. LCA, s. 2(2)
26. Ibid., s. 2(3).
27. Ibid., s. 2(4).

the user of land (otherwise than between landlord and tenant);[28]
(*iii*) equitable easements—for example, rights of way—except those created by deed, which are legal interests.[29]

Entries of Class D(*ii*) and D(*iii*) are relatively common. The Revenue rarely exercise their right to register charges of Class D(*i*).

Class E
These are extremely rare and relate only to annuities created before 1st January 1926 not registered in the register of annuities.[30]

Class F
These are charges affecting land by virtue of the Matrimonial Homes Act 1967;[31] the head note to this Act, which reads "Protection against eviction, etc., from matrimonial home of spouse not entitled by virtue of estate, etc., to occupy it", sufficiently illustrates its purpose. A Class F charge registered in respect of a property will normally protect the right of occupation of a spouse having no title to the property itself and in the usual case will normally prevent any dealing with the property prejudicial to the interest of such spouse.[32]

Effect of registration
The importance of the LCA 1972 consists in the fact that rights and claims which are capable of being registered under it must be so registered if they are to bind purchasers who acquire the land affected by the entry after the date upon which the right or claim arose.

The Act distinguishes between purchasers simpliciter, and purchasers for money or money's worth, but a purchaser is defined, for the purposes of the Act, as any person (including a mortgagee or lessee) who, for valuable consideration, takes any interest in land or in a charge on land.[33]

Land charges of Classes A, B, C (other than Class C(*iv*)), E and F are void against a purchaser of the land charged with them or of any interest in such land unless the charge is registered before completion of the purchase.[34] Class C(*iv*) charges and Class D charges are void against a purchaser for money or money's worth of a legal estate in the land affected unless registered before completion of the purchase.[35]

28. *See* below for discussion of these.
29. LCA 1972, s. 2(5).
30. Ibid., s. 2(6)
31. Ibid., s. 2(7).
32. For further discussion of Class F charges *see* below.
33. LCA 1972, s. 17(1); compare LPA 1925, s. 205(*xxi*).
34. LCA 1972, s. 4(5).
35. Ibid., s. 4(6).

If the title to the land is registered, any charges will become apparent at an early stage. If the title is unregistered, only the charges of which the purchaser is actually knew will bind him: the state of the register is not relevant.[36]

It is, nevertheless, an essential element in unregistered conveyancing that before completion of the purchase of such land the appropriate searches are made in the land charges registers.

Entries are made against the names of the estate owners of the land affected by the entry, and searches must be made against all persons named in the abstract of title. The normal method of search is by means of a written requisition sent to the Registry by post with the appropriate fee.[37] Searches by telephone and telex are permitted if the person searching maintains a credit account at the Registry.

A certificate of search is issued by the Registry. If entries exist against the names searched, the certificate will only reveal the class of the entry, its date, and the Registry's identifying number; an office copy of the application leading to the entry can be supplied by the Registry, on payment of the appropriate fee.

In the normal course, any entries revealed will be explained by the abstract or by inquiry of the vendor or prospective borrower, but this is not invariably so. A Class F charge may have been registered by one spouse without the knowledge of the other, or a party claiming a charge, other than a first legal mortgage, may have registered a Class C(i) charge. It is essential, therefore, that a full explanation be obtained of all entries revealed by a search certificate and, if appropriate, arrangements made for their removal from the register in the prescribed manner before completion of any purchase or mortgage.

An official search certificate is conclusive in favour of a purchaser, unless the application leads the Registry into error[38] or the search was made against a wrong version of a registered name.[39] Though registration is deemed to constitute actual notice of the instrument registered, there is legal protection for a purchaser who acts in reliance on the basis of a search certificate which erroneously omits to disclose a registered charge, or where no charge comes to light and he therefore suffers loss: there is a statutory scheme for the payment of

---

36. LPA 1925, s. 198(1) as restricted by LPA 1969, s. 24..
37. LCA 1972, s. 10.
38. *Du Sautoy* v. *Symes* [1967] 1 All E.R. 25, where the purchaser was buying two plots of land and should have submitted two applications but submitted only one.
39. *Oak Co-operative Building Society* v. *Blackburn* [1968] 2 All E.R. 117; [1968] Ch. 730, where a vendor called Francis B traded under the name Frank B, and the purchaser searched against Frank B.

compensation to the purchaser in such cases.[40] He is still affected by any properly registered charges.

RIGHTS OF PRE-EMPTION AND OPTIONS

Sometimes an investigation of title will disclose rights of pre-emption or options. These are more frequently encountered in leasehold than in freehold titles, and, to be effective, must be very precisely defined.

A right of pre-emption, colloquially called a right of first refusal, inhibits the free disposal of the property in the market because the owner is first obliged to offer it upon defined terms to the named person. The law is uncertain as to whether such a right constitutes an interest in land capable of registration as an estate contract under the LCA 1972, but the Land Charges Registry will normally not object to the registration of such a right. Rights of pre-emption are not common, but they are frequently imposed by local authorities selling houses to sitting tenants at concessionary prices (and are bound to do this in sales under the Housing Act 1980, Part I).

Options confer upon the person entitled to the benefit thereof the right to acquire property upon compliance with defined conditions. For example, a lessee may have an option to acquire the freehold reversion from his landlord. There can be both put and call options in respect of land; a put option enables the owner of land to require a third party to buy from him and a call option enables an individual to require a land owner to sell the land to him.

As an option is a contract "for the sale or other disposition of land or any interest therein", the contract must, if it is to be enforceable by action, be in, or be evidenced by, writing containing all the essential terms, signed by the party to be charged or his duly appointed agent.[41] An option is without doubt an interest in land and is thus registrable (and indeed should be registered) as an estate contract under the LCA 1972.

RIGHTS OF OCCUPIERS

Searching inquiries should always be made as to whether there is any person in occupation of a particular property, other than the owner of the legal estate, by virtue of either a formal lease or tenancy agreement, or other less formal rights.

The rights of the person in occupation by virtue of a lease or agreement will be defined by the appropriate document and the position will be ascertained by the normal investigation of title. A person otherwise in occupation may have rights prejudicial to the

40. LPA 1925, s. 198 and LPA 1969, s. 25.
41. LPA 1925, s. 40.

interest of the owner of the legal estate and thus to the lender of money on the security of such estate. These rights can subsist without the formality of any written document.

They arise in two main ways, either by reason of what is, in the case of registered land, called an overriding interest,[42] or by virtue of registration of a Class F land charge, first introduced by the Matrimonial Homes Act 1967.[43]

RESTRICTIONS ON OWNER'S RIGHT TO OFFER LAND AS SECURITY

In general, the estate owner of freehold property is not restricted in any way from creating a mortgage of his property to secure an advance of money. With leasehold property, there may be a prohibition against charging, or the landlord's consent may be required.[44] There are, however, two sorts of case where special problems arise, namely trusts and the matrimonial home.

Trusts

A person who holds the entire legal estate in land or who has statutory or other power to dispose of the legal estate may, nevertheless, only hold it or be able to dispose of it subject to the rights of others. This is the position, for instance, of trustees holding land upon trust for others within the scope of the TA 1925, or of a tenant for life of a settlement under the SLA 1925. Both of these Acts confer power upon a trustee or tenant for life to create a valid mortgage of land within the trust or settlement, but only for defined purposes.[45]

The general principles of law, which apply to such trusts as well as to any other equitable interests, are firstly that a bona fide purchaser of the legal estate without notice of any prior equitable interest takes priority over such equitable interests. This is because of the general superiority of a legal title over equitable rights, at least where the person taking the legal title does so bona fide, for value and without notice of the equitable rights. Secondly, where a purchaser (even if bona fide and for value) acquires an equitable interest only, then under the general rule that where the equities are equal the first in time prevails, he will take subject to any equitable interests subsisting at the time of his purchase, whether or not he has notice of them. This risk attaches to any equitable charge.

42. LRA 1925, s. 70(*i*)(*g*). *See* below.
43. *See* below.
44. *See* below.
45. TA 1925, s. 16; SLA 1925, s. 71.

One of the principal objects of the 1925 legislation was to convert the majority of beneficial interests in land into equitable interests, and to remove them from the legal title, so that a person dealing with the legal title was no longer concerned with them. They are, in the conveyancer's hallowed phrase, "behind the curtain" and the person investigating the legal title will never know of them. The beneficiaries' rights are exercisable against the trustees only.

Nevertheless, a banker may have notice of the existence of equitable interests. For example, persons applying for a loan may describe themselves as being trustees of the John Smith Trust, or may use other words implying that they are trustees. Indeed a prudent banker should always ask the potential borrower whether the land offered by him as security is held by him for his own absolute use and benefit, and if the reply indicates that any other person has an interest in the property, the banker is at least on notice that there may be trust interests. In any case such as the above, where the banker is deemed to have notice of a trust, he risks being subordinated to the equitable interests of the beneficiaries.

At common law, trustees had no implied powers to borrow, still less power to mortgage the trust property, and accordingly unless the trust instrument gave the trustees power to borrow and mortgage, any mortgage by trustees in favour of a banker who has notice of the trust would not be binding on the beneficiaries, who could take free of the mortgage.

The position is now alleviated to some extent by certain provisions in the TA 1925. Where trustees are authorised, either by the trust instrument or by general law, to pay or apply capital moneys subject to the trust for any purpose or in any manner, they have power to raise the money required by sale, conversion, calling in, or mortgage of all or any part of the trust property.[46] No purchaser or mortgagee, paying or advancing money on a sale or a mortgage purporting to be made under any trust or powers vested in trustees, is concerned to see that such money is, in fact, wanted or as to its application.[47] These provisions should cover most cases, so that where a banker acquires a legal mortgage, he will prevail over the beneficiaries' rights; if he is taking an equitable mortgage, or if he has notice of the existence of a trust, he should examine the trust instrument to ensure that the trustees have power to borrow and to mortgage the trust property. If they have no such power, he should insist upon the trust instrument being properly varied. If all the beneficiaries are *sui juris*, they can either consent to the mortgage (and join in

46. TA 1925, s. 16.
47. Ibid., s. 17.

the mortgage in order to mortgage their equitable interests) or else consent to a deed of variation varying the trustees' powers. If, however, any of the beneficiaries is not *sui juris*, it would be necessary to apply to the court for such variation.

The matrimonial home

The other case where an ostensible legal owner may be incapable of creating an effective charge on his own concerns the matrimonial home. The Matrimonial Homes Act 1967 gave a spouse living in the matrimonial home, but who nevertheless has no formal title to the property, the right not to be evicted. This right constitutes a charge over the land, and can be protected, in the case of unregistered land, by registration, under the LCA 1972, of a Class F charge, and in the case of registered land by registration of a caution.[48] The 1967 Act followed a line of cases in which Lord Denning MR had evolved a "deserted wife's equity" to remain in the matrimonial home, a principle overturned by the House of Lords as having no basis in conveyancing law.[49] Registration of such a charge or caution effectively protects the interest of such a spouse, and in practical terms prevents any dealing with the property affected by such charge unless and until the spouse by whom it is registered has been satisfactorily provided for.

If the wife has commenced proceedings for the transfer to her of the matrimonial home, the matrimonial proceedings are a pending action, registrable in the register of pending actions,[50] and if the husband subsequently creates a charge and the wife's pending action is not registered before the completion of the charge, the chargee will take free of the wife's rights.[51]

In *Williams & Glyn's Bank* v. *Boland*[52] the title was in the name of the husband and he had created a mortgage in favour of the bank for advances made at his request without the consent of the wife. It concerned registered land, but the wife had not registered a caution; the wife's right not to be evicted was not an overriding interest.[53] Her rights in respect of the property derived from the fact

---

48. Matrimonial Homes Act 1967, ss. 1 and 2(6) and (7), and LCA 1972, s. 2(7). For the position in relation to registered land, *see* below in this chapter. *See also* footnote 3.
49. *National Provincial Bank* v. *Ainsworth* [1965] 1 All E.R. 472, reversing the Court of Appeal decision reported *sub nom. National Provincial Bank* v. *Hastings Car Mart* [1964] 1 All E.R. 688; [1964] 3 All E.R. 93.
50. LCA 1972, ss. 5(1) and 17(1).
51. *Whittingham* v. *Whittingham* (*National Westminster Bank* (*Intervener*)) [1979] Fam. 19.
52. *Williams & Glyn's Bank* v. *Boland*; and *Williams and Glyn's Bank* v. *Brown* [1981] A.C. 487.
53. Matrimonial Homes Act 1967, s. 2(7).

that, besides being in actual occupation, she had an interest in the property through having contributed to the purchase price for the house. Actual occupation of itself would not have been sufficient. In these matters it is not so much a case of "I am in occupation therefore I have a right", but "I have a right and I am in actual occupation". Her rights in respect of the property were held to be not merely an interest in the proceeds of sale, as had previously been thought, but an interest in the land itself. Lord Wilberforce described it as being "just a little unreal" to refer to the interests of the spouses in the matrimonial home being an interest in the proceeds of sale.

Although the case concerned registered land, the principle will apply to unregistered land as well. The point was that there was a spouse with rights over the property who was in actual occupation. In the case of registered land, the rights of a person in actual occupation are an overriding interest unless inquiry is made of such a person and such rights are not disclosed.[54] In the case of unregistered land, almost certainly the rights of any person in actual occupation will be rights of which a purchaser has constructive notice. The decision, therefore, is not restricted to matrimonial homes but has a much wider application; any person (not only spouses but also girlfriends, tenants and others in actual occupation) who has rights in respect of any property and is in actual occupation will prevail over those of a mortgagee or a purchaser. Moreover, a person would not have to be physically present on any particular day in order to be in actual occupation; a person who lives there but is away on holiday would clearly be in actual occupation.

The moral for banks is that before taking mortgages on property they must inspect to see who is in actual occupation. The inspection must include steps such as opening wardrobes in residential property, seeing what nameplates are visible in commercial premises and the like. If any person is found to be in actual occupation, he should be asked what rights he claims to have and such inquiry must be directed to and answered by the person in occupation. An answer from the intending mortgagor or purchaser is insufficient. A banker should ensure that before advancing money on the property, he takes a document from any person found to be in actual occupation, in which such person consents to the mortgage and postpones his rights.

MORTGAGES

The fundamental difference between a mortgage and a charge is that a mortgage is a conveyance of property, legal or equitable,

54. LRA 1925, s. 70(1)(g).

subject to a right of redemption, whereas a charge conveys nothing, it only gives the chargee certain rights over the property charged. In land law, because of the concept of the "charge by way of legal mortgage", and because equitable mortgages and equitable charges are identical, the difference is now more theoretical than actual and the two terms are practically interchangeable.

Mortgages (or charges) are of two kinds: legal and equitable. A legal mortgage vests in the mortgagee the legal estate to the property charged, whereas an equitable mortgage does not. It follows that if the mortgagor has no legal estate but only an equitable interest, he can effect only an equitable mortgage.

LEGAL MORTGAGES

Before the 1925 legislation, a legal mortgage of freehold property was created by the actual conveyance of the fee simple estate to the mortgagee, who took it subject to the right of the mortgagor to have it reconveyed upon repayment in full of the amount advanced and interest and costs. A legal mortgage of leaseholds was created either by assignment of the lease to the mortgagee or, less usually, by the grant of a sub-lease for a term at least one day shorter than the lease. The mortgagor had the right to have the lease re-assigned to him, or for the sub-lease to cease, on repayment.

A legal mortgage of a freehold estate may now be created only by (*a*) a demise of the property to the mortgagee for a term of years absolute subject to a proviso for cesser on redemption, or (*b*) a charge by deed expressed to be by way of legal mortgage.[55] In the case of a demise, the usual length of the term is 3,000 years, so that, quite apart from the special legal effect of a mortgage, virtually the whole of the value of the property is represented by the leasehold term. In fact no lease, as a separate document, is ever brought into existence apart from the mortgage deed itself. Upon repayment of the mortgage debt, the leasehold term ceases to exist ("cesser on redemption") and the mortgagor regains the fee simple estate free of the leasehold term.

Leaseholds may now be mortgaged by either (*a*) a sub-demise for a term of years absolute at least one day shorter than the term vested in the mortgagor, and subject to a proviso for cesser on redemption; or (*b*) a charge by deed expressed to be by way of legal mortgage.[56]

The charge by way of legal mortgage is a creation of the LPA 1925. It gives the mortgagee the same protection, powers and

55. LPA 1925, s. 85(1).
56. Ibid., s. 86(1).

remedies as if he had, in the case of freehold land, a mortgage term for 3,000 years, and, in the case of leaseholds, a sub-term less by one day than the term vested in the mortgagor.[57] This form has certain advantages over the demise, or sub-demise. It can conveniently be used for mortgages of freeholds or leaseholds, or both together, and regardless of whether the land is registered or unregistered,[58] and there is no danger that, by creating a sub-lease, a mortgagor may be in breach of a covenant against sub-letting. It is now more usual for the standard forms of mortgage used by bankers to create a charge by way of legal mortgage rather than a demise or sub-demise.

One of the most valuable means of protecting the rights of a first legal mortgagee is his entitlement to possession of the documents of title to the property mortgaged as if the fee simple estate or the lease were vested in him.[59] It is very difficult (in the absence of fraud) for a mortgagor to effect any dealing adverse to the interests of a first mortgagee if the documents of title cannot be produced.[60] Only the first mortgagee can normally have custody of the title deeds.[61] Nevertheless, second (and subsequent) mortgages can be created over the same property and they should be protected by registration under the LCA 1972 as land charges.[62]

Sometimes a customer who has mortgaged a property to the bank may ask the bank to release the deeds to him for a short period, for example to make them available to prospective purchasers of the property.

A banker should usually part with the deeds only if he is satisfied that the reason for the request is valid, and he obtains an undertaking from a solicitor to hold the documents to the order of the bank, and to return them to the bank on demand in the same condition as they are given to the solicitor, without permitting any other dealing, or to account to the bank for the proceeds of sale.

If a banker is considering parting with the deeds in any other circumstances, he should first register his mortgage as a land charge. This will obviate the risk that the customer might fraudulently create

57. Ibid., s. 87(1).
58. Ibid., ss. 85(3) and 86(3); the only point to note in the case of registered land is that the title number should be quoted as part of the description of the property charged: LRA 1925, s. 25.
59. LPA 1925, ss. 85(1) and 86(1).
60. *See* above.
61. Milnes Holden points out (Vol. 2, p. 66) that a first mortgage without custody of title deeds could be created if A's title to Blackacre and Greenacre is in one set of title deeds, and A mortgages Blackacre to X, depositing with X the deeds which will include Greenacre, and then mortgages Greenacre to Y. Y will have a first mortgage over Greenacre without custody of the deeds, and must register his mortgage as a puisne mortgage to preserve priority over subsequent mortgages.
62. Class C(*i*) for legal mortgages, Class C(*iii*) for equitable mortgages; *see* above.

a second mortgage, and that the second mortgagee might, by registration, obtain priority over the banker who failed to retain the deeds.

EQUITABLE MORTGAGES

A mortgage which is not under seal and in the form of a demise (or sub-demise) or a charge by way of legal mortgage cannot be a legal mortgage. Accordingly, any document or act of the parties which creates a charge over property, or is intended to do so, in some other way is an equitable mortgage.

In normal commercial practice, equitable mortgages may be created, without much formality, in one of three ways.

(*a*) By deposit of the documents of title with the lender, without any accompanying document, provided that the deposit is made by way of security for money lent or to be lent. A mere deposit of deeds with a bank for safe custody, for example, creates no sort of charge.

(*b*) By deposit of the documents of title, as before, together with a written memorandum setting out the terms and conditions upon which the deposit is made.

(*c*) By the execution of a memorandum, without any deposit of deeds, but showing an intention that a charge over the property be created.

Since the banker should always be in a position to prove, if necessary, that the deeds were deposited as security, and since a memorandum of deposit says, *inter alia*, precisely that,[63] the second method is by far the best.

The prudent banker would adopt the third method only if the title deeds were not available, presumably because they were mortgaged elsewhere. He should always protect such a charge by registration as a land charge of Class C(*iii*) under the LCA 1972.[64] Where the charge (legal or equitable) is protected by deposit of the title deeds, registration is not possible by definition.[65]

In all these cases, the charge, however created, must be a present charge of specific or specified property. If there is a memorandum, it is possible by including suitable terms to catch property which comes into the possession of the mortgagor at a future date and the charge will take effect over such after-acquired property when it is acquired.

63. *See* the specimen form in Appendix I; *see also* Chapter Sixteen.
64. LCA 1972, s. 2(4)(*iii*).
65. *See* the definition of puisne mortgage and general equitable charge in LCA 1972, s. 2(4)(*i*) and (*iii*).

Equitable charges have, over the years, been popular with customers, and therefore with their bankers, for several reasons, of which the first two are, or were, the most important. First, in the days when mortgages attracted stamp duty, they attracted a lower rate of duty provided that they were under hand and not under seal; secondly, they do not, in the case of unregistered land, form part of the title.[66]

There is also some merit in presenting the borrower with a short form of document for execution rather than a long form.

It is sometimes thought that the borrower is spared the expense of having to pay the costs of a full investigation of title by the bank's solicitors. This is not true, since a banker might equally well decide to dispense with investigation of title on taking a full legal charge as on taking an equitable charge, and conversely might on occasion insist upon a full investigation of title even if taking only an equitable charge.

In order to obtain a satisfactory equitable mortgage, a banker should take certain precautions. He should obtain the documents of title and not part with them during the currency of the mortgage; he should obtain a signed memorandum from the borrower, setting out the terms upon which the deeds are deposited and the advance made; and he should make the appropriate searches against estate owners revealed by the title deeds and investigate any entries revealed thereby, as well as any suspicious or unusual matters revealed by an examination of the title generally.

If, after having obtained possession of the title deeds, he allows them out of his possession without adequate safeguards (such as only sending them to a solicitor in exchange for a solicitor's under-taking)[67] and thus enables the mortgagor (albeit fraudulently) to effect another mortgage in favour of a mortgagee acting in good faith, without notice of the prior equitable mortgage, he may be postponed to that mortgage although it is later in time.

The big disadvantage, from the bank's point of view, in the traditional form of equitable charge, was that there was no power of sale. There is an implied power of sale in any mortgage under seal, but to qualify for the lower rate of stamp duty, the mortgage had to be executed under hand. Stamp duty is no longer applicable, but as an equitable mortgagee has no legal estate in the property charged, even an equitable mortgage under seal does not give the mortgagee a power of sale unless certain additional steps are taken.

It is quite common for legal mortgages to contain a clause giving

66. For registered land, see below.
67. See above.

the mortgagee a power of attorney to act in the name of and as agent of the mortgagor. Such a power of attorney must be under seal, and as there is now no disadvantage in having an equitable charge or memorandum of deposit under seal, such a document should now always be under seal and should contain a power of attorney clause.

A memorandum of deposit should also always contain an undertaking by the depositor to execute a full legal charge on request. The combination of these two clauses may now be used to give the bank the choice of either selling in the name of and on behalf of the mortgagor, as beneficial owner, or of executing, in the name of and as agent of the mortgagor, a full legal charge and then selling as mortgagee.

PRIORITY OF MORTGAGES

If advances upon the same property have been made at different times by different mortgagees and these advances are secured in some cases by legal mortgages and in others by equitable mortgages, it is necessary to be able to determine in what order of priority the various mortgages rank.

The basic rules for determining the order of priority have already been stated.[68] They are now subject to many qualifications, mostly as a result of the system of registration introduced by the 1925 legislation. A banker (or his solicitors) should take particular care to observe all the practical and statutory requirements to ensure that a particular mortgage ranks where it is intended to rank.

Certain protective procedures are available before completion of any mortgage and the making of the advance thereunder. The first step to be taken is to make an ordinary search in the registers of land charges. The certificate of search will show both the date upon which it was issued and the date upon which the protection given by it expires. The "protection" conferred is that an entry made in the register after the date of the certificate and before completion of the purchase shall not affect the purchaser, provided the purchase is completed within the period of validity of the certificate,[69] i.e. fifteen working days (days upon which the Registry is open to the public).[70] "Purchaser" is defined for this purpose as meaning any person (including a legal or an equitable mortgagee) who, for valuable consideration, takes any interest in land or charge on land.[71]

68. See above.
69. Law of Property (Amendment) Act 1926, s. 4(2) and LCA 1972, s. 11(5). The one exception is in the case of priority notices (see below).
70. LCA 1972, s. 11(6).
71. Ibid., s. 17(1).

This is, in practice, usually the only step taken, since bankers, and mortgagees in general, seem strangely reluctant to use the priority notice procedure explained below.

Priority notices

The only entry which can be made in the register during the period of protection and still bind a purchaser is one made pursuant to a priority notice.[72] A priority notice may be given to the Land Charges Registry in a prescribed form in respect of any *contemplated* charge or other event registrable under the LCA 1972. It must be given at least fifteen days before the creation of the charge and operates as a kind of temporary reservation of priority for the contemplated dealing.[73] It is entered in the register appropriate to the document or event which it foreshadows[74] and if the application to register the substantive transaction is made within thirty days after the date of registration of the priority notice, the registration takes effect as if it had been made on the date of the document or the date of completion of the transaction.[75]

Priority notices are probably not used as frequently as they ought to be, but a banker proposing to complete a mortgage who knows or suspects that a subsequent mortgage is to be entered into by his borrower should always insist upon registration of a priority notice before completing his advance.

The importance of the search will be readily appreciated when it is remembered that a mortgagee will not have priority over earlier mortgages if an earlier mortgage was registered before he acquired his mortgage and a clear search is the way of establishing that no such mortgage is registered. Indeed the absence of such registration makes the relevant charge void against a purchaser.[76] The banker's protection depends on the issue by the Land Charges Registry of a clear search certificate.

Section 97 of the LPA 1925 provides that legal and equitable mortgages not protected by deposit of the title deeds shall rank in the order of their registration as land charges and not in order of their date of execution. Section 4(5) of the LCA 1972 provides that registrable charges are void against a purchaser unless registered before completion of the purchase. So, just as it is essential to search in the Land Charges Registry before completing a mortgage, it is a matter of considerable importance for such a mortgage to be

72. Ibid., s. 11(1).
73. Ibid., s. 11(1).
74. Ibid., s. 11(2).
75. Ibid., s. 11(3).
76. Ibid., ss. 4(5) and 17(1); and LPA 1925, ss. 198 and 199.

registered against the name of the mortgagor as a Class C(*i*) or C(*iii*) charge at the earliest opportunity after execution.

If each mortgagee after the first (who keeps the deeds) registers his mortgage at the time of execution, and each is registered before the next is completed, there will be little difficulty in determining the priority of mortgages. If, however, all fail to register, or if, for example, the third mortgagee registers before the second, the position is more complex.

If the third mortgage is executed before the second is registered, the second mortgage is void against the third mortgagee, even if the third mortgagee had actual notice of the second mortgage at the time when he, the third mortgagee, acquired his interest.

If, however, the third mortgage is created before the second mortgagee registers his mortgage, and then they register in order of creation, the two sections produce an unresolved conflict. According to s. 97 of the LPA 1925, the second mortgage should prevail, having been registered before the third was registered, but under s. 4 of the LCA 1972, the second mortgage is void against the third mortgagee. Furthermore, if the second and third mortgagees both complete after obtaining clear search certificates, and the third registers before the second, the LCA 1972 itself produces a conflict, since the second's mortgage is void against the third, but the third's mortgage is void against the second.

The conflict has been pointed out by textbooks for many years, but when the LPA 1969 and the LCA 1972, amending and consolidating Acts, were passed, the opportunity to resolve the problem was not taken. It is uncertain which way the courts would decide the point if such a case came before them.

If neither of the mortgagees registers, the second mortgage is void against the third mortgagee for want of registration, and so the third mortgage will prevail. If a fourth person takes a mortgage and registers before either of the others register, he will take priority over both second and third mortgagees.

The moral for the prudent banker is to use the priority notice procedure, as well as searching beforehand and, if appropriate, registering without delay. If this procedure was always followed, such problems would disappear.

UNPAID VENDOR'S LIEN

A banker should not omit to take into account what is known as the "unpaid vendor's lien". If a vendor of property executes a conveyance of it, so as to pass the legal estate to a purchaser and, for whatever reason, the vendor is not paid the full price for the property, he retains a lien over the property which is not overridden by the execution by the purchaser of a subsequent legal mortgage. An unpaid vendor's lien is necessarily an equitable charge, but as it arises by operation of law and not by the act of the parties to the transaction, it is not susceptible to the rules of registration under the LCA 1972, which would otherwise require to be observed if the priority of the equitable charge were to be maintained against a subsequent legal mortgagee. The right to an unpaid vendor's lien can pass, by way of subrogation, to a third party, such as a banker, who actually makes payment to the vendor on behalf of the purchaser, or who lends the purchaser the money with which to pay the vendor.[77]

It is, however, unwise to rely on this, and the banker will not be able to fall back upon this lien if he has agreed to advance upon some other form of security. It is an implied equitable remedy, and will be excluded if the circumstances show that the vendor, or the lender, agreed to take some other form of security, and such security is effected. Even if the other security subsequently becomes void, e.g. for want of registration under s. 95 of the Companies Act 1948, the lien is still excluded.[78]

MORTGAGOR'S RIGHT TO REDEEM THE MORTGAGE

In the days when mortgages were created by transferring the whole of the mortgagor's interest, there used to be a proviso giving the mortgagor a legal right to redeem on the appointed day; in addition, equity intervened to enable the mortgagor to redeem after the contractual date of repayment.

Although mortgages no longer take that form, the mortgagor now has both a legal or contractual right to redeem on the appointed day, and an equitable right to redeem thereafter. Where principal and interest are repayable by instalments, the mortgage is often made redeemable six months from its date, and the date for redemption should be the same date as any date fixed by the covenant for payment. Where a time is fixed for redemption, a mortage is not redeemable until that time has arrived (subject to the exceptions mentioned below). A mortgagee may object to an attempt to redeem at an earlier date, even if the mortgagor tenders interest for the whole of the intervening period,[79] unless the mortgagee has taken steps to recover payment in the meantime, in which case he cannot

---

77. *Congresbury Motors* v. *Anglo-Belge Finance Co.* [1970] 3 All E.R. 385.
78. *Capital Finance Co.* v. *Stokes* [1968] 3 All E.R. 625, and *Burston Finance* v. *Speirway* [1974] 3 All E.R. 735.
79. *Brown* v. *Cole* (1854) 14 Sim. 427.

object.[80] Where no date for redemption is specified and the debt is repayable on demand by the mortgagee, it seems that the mortgagor may redeem at any time, even if the mortgagee has covenanted not to call in the mortgage until a specified date.

The right of redemption may be postponed by a covenant that during a certain period the mortgage shall remain irredeemable. The mere length of time of any such postponement is not itself an objection to the enforceability of such a covenant,[81] but it may be an important consideration in this respect. The court will not interfere so long as the essential requirements of a mortgage are observed, and oppressive and unconscionable terms are not imposed. The right of redemption must not be rendered illusory; if, for example, the interest mortgaged is a short term of years, a postponement until six weeks from the end of the term would render the equity of redemption illusory, and is unenforceable.[82] In determining whether terms are oppressive or unconscionable, relevant considerations would be matters such as the absence of a corresponding restraint on the mortgagee, the size of the loan,[83] the character and bargaining power of the parties and whether they are companies or individuals,[84] the circumstances surrounding the loan[85] and the duration of any covenants in restraint of trade.[86]

In the case of a security for a regulated agreement, the Consumer Credit Act 1974 provides that the borrower may complete the payments ahead of the time stipulated, and there can be no contracting out.[87]

Although a mortgagee cannot, as part of the mortgage transaction, expressly stipulate that the equity of redemption will be extinguished if the debt is not paid by a certain time, it is nevertheless possible for the equity of redemption to be released under a separate transaction. There is no reason why the mortgagee should not purchase the equity of redemption from the mortgagor, provided he does not bring this about by fraud or oppression.

The security may contain a stipulation that the mortgagor will do something in addition to repaying the loan with interest. Such

80. *Bovill* v. *Endle* [1896] 1 Ch. 648.
81. *Knightsbridge Estates Trust* v. *Byrne* [1938] Ch. 741; [1938] 2 All E.R. 444; reversed [1939] Ch. 441; [1938] 4 All E.R. 618; affirmed on other grounds [1940] A.C. 613; [1940] 2 All E.R. 401.
82. *Fairclough* v. *Swan Brewery Co.* [1912] A.C. 565.
83. *Knightsbridge Estates Trust* v. *Byrne, supra.*
84. *Samuel* v. *Jarrah Timber and Paving Corpn.* [1904] A.C. 323.
85. *Knightsbridge Estates Trust* v. *Byrne, supra.*
86. *Esso Petroleum Co.* v. *Harpers Garage (Stourport)* [1968] A.C. 269; [1967] 1 All E.R. 699 (21 years unreasonable; 5 years reasonable).
87. Consumer Credit Act 1974, ss. 94, 113 and 173. For further discussion of the effect of this Act, *see* Chapter Twelve.

a collateral advantage will, if reasonable, be valid until redemption, but will in general become invalid upon redemption, though if it is contained in a separate agreement the stipulation may be independent of the mortgage, in which case its validity will be determined on general principles. If it can be construed as a term of the mortgage, even though in a separate instrument, it will not be enforceable if it is either unfair or unconscionable, or is in the nature of a penalty clogging the equity of redemption, or is inconsistent with or repugnant to the contractual and equitable right to redeem.[88] In appropriate cases, such a collateral advantage may survive repayment of the mortgage debt.[89]

A provision in the mortage for a bonus or premium payable on redemption will be in the same category as any other collateral advantage. If the bonus or premium is reasonable, i.e. if it is in lieu of interest and is at a reasonable rate, or the security is of a hazardous nature, it will be upheld. If the provision is unreasonable, the bonus or premium will not be payable,[90] but the court would award interest on the principal sum at a rate to be fixed by the court.

RIGHTS OF THE MORTGAGEE

Right to tack

A banker, having obtained his security and then made an initial advance, sometimes makes a further advance, especially where the mortgage is effected to secure a current overdraft account at a bank, and the amount of the indebtedness fluctuates up to a limit agreed between banker and customer.

Before the 1925 legislation, a first mortgagee (who was then the only possible legal mortgagee) who had no notice of a second mortgage could make further advances which could be "tacked on" to the initial advance and thus take priority over the second mortgagee. The general right to tack has now been abolished,[91] and the right

---

88. *Kreglinger* v. *New Patagonia Meat & Cold Storage Co.* [1914] A.C. 25.

89. Contrast *Noakes & Co.* v. *Rice* [1902] A.C. 24 (covenant in a mortgage of a public house to buy all liquor from the mortgagee during the mortgage term, whether or not any money still owing on the security, held unenforceable after repayment) and *Bradley* v. *Carritt* [1903] A.C. 253 (covenant in mortgage of shares in tea company to secure that company continued forever to sell tea through the lender, a tea broker, or pay commission on sales through third parties, not binding after repayment) with *Kreglinger* v. *New Patagonia Meat & Cold Storage Co.* [1914] A.C. 25 (agreement not to sell skins for five years except through lenders, provided lenders were willing to pay the best price offered elsewhere, was upheld when the loan was paid off after three years).

90. *Cityland and Property (Holdings)* v. *Dabrah* [1968] Ch. 166; [1967] 2 All E.R. 639.

91. LPA 1925, s. 94(3).

remains in three cases only. A prior mortgagee has the right to make further advances ranking in priority to subsequent mortgages:

(a) if an arrangement has been made to that effect with the subsequent mortgagees; or

(b) if he had no notice of such subsequent mortgages at the time when the further advance was made; or

(c) whether or not he had such notice, where the mortgage imposes an obligation on him to make such further advances.[92]

This applies whether or not the prior mortgage was made expressly for securing further advances.[92]

The first of these cases requires no explanation, but should be discounted by the prudent banker. It may well be possible to make such an arrangement with subsequent mortgagees, and such arrangements are in practice sometimes made, but the banker cannot rely on being able to do so.

The second case is not as helpful as may at first sight appear, in view of the rule that registration under the LCA 1972 constitutes actual notice of the instrument or matter registered.[93] There is, however, some limited protection for bankers; where the prior mortgage was made expressly for securing a current account or other further advances, a mortgagee is not deemed to have notice of a mortgage merely because it was registered as a land charge, if it was not so registered at the date of the original advance, or when the last search (if any) by or on behalf of the mortgagee was made, whichever is later.[94] This effectively means that a banker whose mortgage expressly secures a running account need not search every time a further advance is made (which in practice means every time a cheque is debited to an overdrawn account), and would not be deemed to have notice of a registered charge unless either it was registered when he made his last search, or, of course, he has express notice from the second mortgagee. It should, however, be borne in mind that any prudent second mortgagee will in practice give notice to the banker, and if the banker does in fact make a search which discloses a subsequent mortgage, he will then be unable to make further advances in priority to that mortgage under this rule.

Where a banker does in fact receive notice of a second mortgage he should immediately rule off any running account secured by his mortgage. Because of the rule in *Clayton*'s case,[95] if the account is continued each subsequent payment in will go to reduce the indebted-

92. LPA 1925, s. 94(1).
93. Ibid., s. 198(1). *See also* footnote 36.
94. LPA 1925, s. 94(2).
95. *Devaynes* v. *Noble* (1816) 1 Mer. 572. *See* Chapter Four.

ness subsisting at the date on which notice of the second mortgage was received and each subsequent debit will be treated as a new advance, which will rank after the second mortgage.[96]

To counteract this, the account is ruled off so that all subsequent payments in may be credited to a new account, against which will be debited all advances subsequent to the date of receipt of notice; the indebtedness subsisting at the date of receipt of notice will then continue to rank in priority to the subsequent mortgage, and will not be reduced. The balance of the indebtedness, representing net advances on the new account, will be kept to a minimum, which is desirable since, though secured, it ranks after the subsequent mortgage.

If the second mortgage is expressly subject to the charge in favour of the bank securing an amount up to a specified sum, the bank may lend up to that amount by way of fixed advance and still preserve priority. If, however, the bank's mortgage is to secure a running account, the rule in *Clayton's* case[95] will still apply, so that the amount which ranks in priority will represent not the net amount due to the bank at any time, but advances up to the specified sum less the aggregate of all repayments (credits to the account) after notice of the second mortgage. If the bank is intended to have priority up to a specified amount in respect of a running account, the second mortgagee should expressly agree that the bank shall have power to make advances from time to time by way of fluctuating overdraft, up to an amount not exceeding at any one time the specified sum.

Thus the only case in which a banker may be sure of being able to tack further advances on to his original mortgage, whether or not he has notice of a subsequent mortgage, is if the mortgage imposes an obligation on him to make further advances. The obligation must be in the mortgage itself and not in some other document, e.g. a facility letter. However, it seems that the banker may qualify the obligation, for example, so that it ceases to apply if the mortgagor is in breach of his obligations to the banker, without losing the protection of the rule.

There is a price to be paid for preserving the right to tack further advances, namely an obligation, even if qualified, to make the advances, and bankers are reluctant to take advantage of it. This course should, however, always be considered where a banker is making advances to finance the construction of a building, where the work is to be paid for in stages, such as against architects' certificates under the building contract. Without such a right, the

96. *Deeley* v. *Lloyds Bank* [1912] A.C. 756.

banker may find that he receives notice of a second mortgage at a time when the building is incomplete and is then unable to make further advances in priority to the second mortgage. It will at this stage be irrelevant that the second mortgage may have been created in breach of the borrower's obligations to the banker; even if the banker has personal remedies against the mortgagor, this will not enable him to make the further advances in priority. Yet until the building is complete, he will almost certainly not have a saleable security.

Right to sue

The mortgage usually contains, in addition to a charge over the property, a personal covenant by the mortgagor to repay the mortgage debt, and the right to sue on this covenant exists independently of the mortgagee's rights against the property. Indeed, since any mortgage must secure some liability, even if the liability is that of a third party, there would be a right to sue the mortgagor or other person so liable even without the covenant.

The right of action will, however, only rarely be of interest to the banker unless bankruptcy proceedings (or the threat of them) are contemplated. A petition to wind up a limited company may be presented without first obtaining a judgment, but with personal debtors a judgment is a necessary preliminary to bankruptcy proceedings. Even so, the banker will be reluctant to sue on the debt unless he believes that the debtor will, under threat of bankruptcy proceedings, be able to borrow the necessary funds from a relative or friend, or he intends to use the judgment as a means of levying execution on other assets of the mortgagor[97] or to use the bankruptcy procedure itself as a means of flushing out other assets. As a general rule, one of the purposes of taking security is to avoid having to incur the trouble and expense of suing on the debt.

If the banker does decide to sue on the debt, he must be careful to make proper demand. Clearing banks' standard forms of mortgage usually make the debt payable on demand, so that a demand would be a necessary preliminary. Unless the terms on which the money was advanced include a fixed date for repayment, such a provision has the additional advantage that time does not begin to run, for the purposes of the Limitation Act,[98] until demand has been made.

Great care should be taken to ensure that the correct sum is

97. *See* Chapter Twenty.
98. *See* Chapter Four.

demanded, and that the demand is sent to the correct address by registered or recorded post.

Right to possession

A legal mortgagee has the right to possession of the mortgaged property, or to the rents and profits, immediately upon completion of the mortgage deed, whether or not there has been any default by the mortgagor in observing the terms of the mortgage deed, unless the mortgage provides for the mortgagor to retain possession.[99]

An equitable mortgagee has no right to possession without obtaining a court order,[100] though if his mortgage is by deed he has the right to appoint a receiver.

If the property is occupied by the mortgagor, or a tenant whose tenancy is not binding on the mortgagee,[101] he can take possession by entering on the land, if he may do so peaceably, or by bringing an action for possession. If the property is let to a tenant whose tenancy is binding on the mortgagee, he can exercise his right by giving notice to the tenant to pay the rent to him.

The taking of possession, while it enables a mortgagee, for instance, to cultivate a farm if it is untenanted or to take the rents and the profits of property if it is let, puts the mortgagee in a position of responsibility towards the mortgagor which is generally considered onerous. He must, after paying himself out of the income he receives for principal, interest and expenses, account to the mortgagor for any balance of rents and profits which he has or might or ought to have received out of the property while he continues in possession.[102] If any part of the property is unlet, he must use due diligence to let it,[103] and if it remains unlet through his default, he is charged with the rents which ought to have been obtained. If he goes into actual occupation himself[104] he must pay a fair occupation rent.

He must keep the property in a reasonable state of repair at least to the extent of surplus rents in his hands after satisfying the interest due on the mortgage.[105] This liability derives from the fact that by

99. *Fourmaids* v. *Dudley Marshall* (*Properties*) [1957] Ch. 317; *Pope* v. *Biggs* (1829) 9 B. & C. 245; *Doe d. Roylance* v. *Lightfoot* (1831) 8 M. & W. 553; *Rogers* v. *Grazebrook* (1846) 8 Q.B. 895.
100. *Barclays Bank* v. *Bird* [1954] Ch. 274; [1954] 1 All E.R. 449.
101. See below under "Right to grant leases of mortgaged land".
102. *Hughes* v. *Williams* (1806) 12 Ves. 493; *Quarrell* v. *Beckford* (1816) 1 Madd. 269; *Rowe* v. *Wood* (1822) 2 Jac. & W. 553; *Gaskell* v. *Gosling* [1896] 1 Q.B. 669; *Chaplin* v. *Young* (*No. 1*) (1864) 33 Beav. 330.
103. *Blacklock* v. *Barnes* (1725) Cas. Temp. King 53.
104. *Metcalf* v. *Campion* (1828) 1 Mol. 238.
105. *Richards* v. *Morgan* (1753) 4 Y. & C. Ex. 570.

taking possession he has excluded the mortgagor from control of the property and that the rents are the proper fund out of which to provide for repairs. He may make reasonable improvements without notice to the mortgagor,[106] but must not make a large outlay on permanent improvements unless the mortgagor either consents or acquiesces after notice.[107] He cannot make any charge for his own personal inconvenience and may not embark upon any speculative ventures with the property. So, although superficially the taking of possession might appear to be advantageous to a mortgagee, in practice the ability to do so is hedged about with so many restrictions and disadvantages that it is rarely resorted to, except where necessary in order to sell with vacant possession.

Right to sell the mortgaged land

A power of sale is implied by statute[108] in all cases where the mortgage is by deed (as a legal mortgage must be) unless a contrary intention is shown. It may also be given by an express power in the mortgage deed. The statutory power arises on the legal date for redemption but cannot be exercised until:

(*a*) notice requiring repayment has been given to the mortgagor and there has been a failure to repay for three months after service of such notice; or

(*b*) there has been default in paying interest for at least two months after it became due; or

(*c*) there has been a breach of any provisions contained in the mortgage deed or implied by statute.[109]

The statutory power may, however, like the other powers of a mortgagee, be varied or extended by the mortgage deed,[110] and most mortgages, and bankers' mortgages in particular, provide that the power of sale (and other statutory powers of the mortgagee) arise and are exercisable after a demand for repayment has been made and has not been complied with, or after a much shorter period than is prescribed by the section.

Although a mortgagee has only a limited legal interest in the property charged to him, a conveyance by him, in exercise of his power of sale, operates to pass to the purchaser the whole estate and interest in the property which was vested in the mortgagor

106. *Shepard* v. *Jones* (1882) 21 Ch. D. 469.
107. *Sandon* v. *Hooper* (1843) 6 Beav. 246.
108. LPA 1925, s. 101(1)(*i*).
109. Ibid., s. 103.
110. Ibid., s. 101(3).

immediately before the creation of the mortgage deed, freed and discharged from both the mortgage pursuant to which the power of sale was exercised, and any subsequent mortgages.[111]

A purchaser buying from a mortgagee selling in exercise of the statutory power of sale need not inquire into the state of affairs existing between the mortgagor and the mortgagee, and the sale to him cannot be impeached on the ground that the power of sale had not become exercisable, or no notice was given, or the power was not properly exercised.[112] The remedy of an aggrieved mortgagor lies in damages against the mortgagee and not against the property or the purchaser.[112]

Just as sale is by far the most frequently used of a mortgagee's remedies, so it is also the one most likely to give rise to difficulties between the mortgagee and the mortgagor. Every mortgagor considers his property to be worth far more than it fetches when sold by a mortgagee, and mortgagors frequently complain that the mortgagee would have done much better to sell at some later time. The banker should, therefore, know something of the principles governing the exercise by a mortgagee of the power of sale.

A mortgagee can sell when and to whom he wishes, and by auction or by private treaty. A mortgagee is not a trustee of the power of sale, i.e. he does not have to act as the mortgagor wishes or to act in the best interests of the mortgagor, and is entitled to sell when it suits him to do so. However, the mortgagee owes a duty to take reasonable precautions to obtain whatever was the true market value of the mortgaged property at the moment he chooses to sell it. The banker must realise therefore that it is not sufficient for him to act honestly and without a reckless disregard of the interests of the mortgagor. The leading case is *Cuckmere Brick Co.* v. *Mutual Finance*[113] where the mortgagee sold a property without mentioning that the property had planning permission for 100 flats and where it was held by the Court of Appeal that the mortgagor was entitled to damages from the mortgagee, representing the difference between the price obtained and what should have been obtained. Building societies are obliged to take reasonable care to ensure that the best price is obtained.[114]

It would obviously be a wise precaution for a banker to obtain an independent valuation before selling. The property crisis in 1973–74 was an example of times when there was no market in certain types of property, but one of the guidance notes issued by the Royal

111. Ibid., ss. 88, 89 and 104(1).
112. Ibid., s. 104(2).
113. *Cuckmere Brick Co.* v. *Mutual Finance* [1971] 2 All E.R. 633.
114. Building Societies Act 1962, s. 36.

Institution of Chartered Surveyors states that even when the property market is in an uncertain and volatile condition,

... the Institution holds the view that members have the capability of providing proper valuations reflecting the prevailing circumstances at any particular date. The Institution does not subscribe to the view that it has been impossible to make appropriate valuations in recent times.[115]

A mortgagee cannot sell to himself, either alone or with others, nor to a trustee for himself.[116] Where a sale is being conducted by the court, the mortgagee may obtain leave to bid, if the mortgagor does not object, but otherwise he will not be allowed to become the purchaser, unless no purchaser at an adequate price can be found.[117]

Unless there are different persons in the position of vendor and purchaser, the transaction is not a sale at all, and is not an exercise of the power. The fact that a trustee is interposed does not affect the substance of the matter,[118] nor can a sale be made to an agent or solicitor acting for the mortgagee in the matter of the sale.[119]

Many banks have associated companies. It is settled law that a company and its shareholders are different persons;[120] a fortiori two companies of which the same persons are shareholders are different persons. Therefore a sale by a mortgagee to an associated company in exercise of the power of sale cannot be set aside on the grounds that it is a sale to the mortgagee himself. In such a case, however, the propriety of the exercise of the power of sale may be more open to objection on the grounds of lack of bona fides or the price. A sale must be "one which the [purchaser] company must prove to have been bona fide and at a price at which the mortgagees could properly sell, yet, if such proves to be the fact, there is no rule of law which compels the court to set aside the sale."[121]

It may be, of course, that the mortgagor would be willing to sell the property himself to the bank's associated company at an agreed figure. Provided the bank had not acted unconscionably by exerting undue pressure on the mortgagor, this would be quite proper. In

---

115. Guidance Note No. A. 3 issued in October 1975, from *Guidance Notes on the Valuation of Assets* prepared by the Assets Valuation Standards Committee of the Royal Institution of Chartered Surveyors.
116. *Downes* v. *Grazebrook* (1817) 3 Mer. 200; *Robertson* v. *Norris* (1857) 1 Giff. 421.
117. *Tennant* v. *Tenchard* (1869) 4 Ch. App. 537.
118. *Farrar* v. *Farrars* (1888) 40 Ch. D. 395. *See also William* v. *Wellingborough Borough Council* [1975] 1 W.L.R. 1375.
119. *Whitcomb* v. *Minchin* (1820) 5 Madd. 91; *Martinson* v. *Clowes* (1882) 21 Ch. D. 857.
120. *Salomon* v. *Salomon & Co.* [1897] A.C. 22; *Kodak* v. *Clark* [1903] 1 K.B. 505.
121. *Farrar* v. *Farrars* (1888) 40 Ch. D. 395.

any such case, the requirements regarding market value are just as important.

A mortgagee's duty of care does not extend to guarantors of the mortgage debt. A receiver owes a similar duty to guarantors in the disposal of the property, as a guarantor is only liable to the same extent as the mortgagor.[122]

If the proceeds of sale, after deduction of the expenses of selling, exceed the mortgage debt, the mortgagee is obliged to account to the mortgagor or other the person entitled thereto for the surplus.[123] In these circumstances, before making payment, a mortgagee should always make a land charges search to discover what other charges (if any) are registered against the name of the mortgagor, since registration is notice in this respect[124] and the mortgagee is under an obligation to account to a subsequent mortgagee of whose entitlement he has notice. In case of doubt as to the person entitled to a surplus, the funds may be paid into court.

If, after sale, the net proceeds are insufficient to discharge the mortgage debt in full, the mortgagee has a right of action against the mortgagor on the personal covenant to pay if, as is usual, one is contained in the mortgage, and if not, he still has a right of action on the debt against the debtor, whether he be the mortgagor or a third party.

If the power of sale (whether express or statutory) is made exercisable by reason only of the commission of an act of bankruptcy by the mortgagor or his adjudication as a bankrupt, the power of sale can only be properly exercised with the leave of the court.[125]

Right to appoint a receiver

The right to appoint a receiver arises as soon as a mortgagee becomes entitled to exercise his power of sale.[126] Although a receiver is appointed (and may be removed and replaced) by the mortgagee, in each case by instrument in writing under the hand of the mortgagee, the receiver is deemed to be the agent of the mortgagor who becomes solely responsible for his acts and defaults.[127] Such agency comes to an end on bankruptcy or liquidation, in that the receiver can no longer bind the mortgagor personally, but continues to the extent that it is used to give effect to the power of sale.[128]

Since a receiver can, in practice, act nearly as effectively as a

122. *Standard Chartered Bank* v. *Walker* [1982] The Times, June 21.
123. LPA 1925, s. 105.
124. Ibid., s. 198(1). *See also* footnote 36.
125. LPA 1925, s. 110.
126. Ibid., ss. 101(1)(*iii*) and 109(1).
127. Ibid., s. 109(2).
128. *See* Chapters Seventeen and Thirty.

mortgagee in possession without imposing upon the mortgagee the liabilities arising out of taking possession, the appointment of a receiver is very much the preferred choice of a mortgagee. The statutory powers of a receiver and the order in which he is to apply money coming into his hands are set out in s. 109(8) of the LPA 1925. As in other cases, however, these statutory powers may be varied by express provision in the mortgage deed,[129] and these powers are commonly varied to such an extent that he becomes capable of doing virtually everything that the mortgagor or the mortgagee might do personally.

Right to foreclose

This remedy is rarely used, because of the somewhat cumbersome procedure for obtaining it and because the court will, even after an order for foreclosure has become absolute, be prepared in a proper case to reopen the matter and enable a mortgagor to repay the mortgage debt and recover the title to his property.

The mortgagee may apply to the court at any time after the legal date for redemption for a foreclosure decree nisi. An account is taken of the amount owing under the mortgage and the mortgagor is directed to pay it within a specified period, usually six months. If the mortgagor defaults, i.e. fails to pay by that date, a foreclosure decree absolute is made vesting the mortgagor's property in the mortgagee subject to prior mortgages but free from subsequent ones and free from the mortgagor's equity of redemption.

Foreclosure is sometimes sought by an equitable mortgagee whose charge is created by a mere deposit of deeds without any memorandum giving him a power of sale; the court has power in such cases to make an order vesting the title to the mortgaged property in a purchaser or to appoint a person to make the conveyance or to vest in the mortgagee a legal term of years absolute as if his charge had been created by a legal mortgage to enable him to exercise a power of sale.[130]

Ad valorem stamp duty is payable on a foreclosure order which for the purposes of s. 54 of the Stamp Act 1891 is included in the definition of "conveyance on sale".[131] The *ad valorem* stamp duty upon any such decree or order will not exceed the duty on a sum equal to the value of the property to which the decree or order relates, and where the decree or order states that value that statement is conclusive for the purpose of determining the amount of the duty. Where *ad valorem* stamp duty is paid upon such decree or order,

129. LPA 1925, s. 101(3).
130. Ibid., s. 90.
131. Finance Act 1898, s. 6.

any conveyance following upon such decree or order is exempt from the *ad valorem* stamp duty.[132] The effect of this is that the duty is paid by the mortgagee instead of the ultimate purchaser.

Right to grant leases of mortgaged land

Subject to contrary agreement in writing, a mortgagee, if he is in possession, or has appointed a receiver, may grant leases of the mortgaged land (*a*) for 50 years for agriculture or occupation, and (*b*) for 999 years for building.[133] Such leases must take effect in possession within twelve months of the grant,[134] be at the best rent without taking a fine (i.e. full market rent without a premium)[135] and contain a covenant to pay the rent with a proviso for re-entry if the rent is in arrear for a specified period not exceeding thirty days.[136] A counterpart of the lease must be executed by the lessee and delivered to the lessor.[137]

It is important to note that neither a mortgagee, nor his receiver, may grant long leases at a premium, such as where a building is divided into flats and the flats are sold on long leases, without express powers in the mortgage.

A mortgagor in possession has the same statutory powers of leasing as the mortgagee.[138] However, if the mortgagor grants the lease he must, within one month after making it, deliver to the mortgagee the counterpart duly executed by the lessee.[139] If this is not done, the lease is valid but the mortgagee's power of sale or appointment of a receiver becomes exercisable.[140]

The statutory power to lease may be modified or excluded by agreement between the parties in writing,[141] but it cannot be excluded in a mortgage of agricultural land made after 1st March 1948,[142] nor will an exclusion prevent the grant of a new lease to a business tenant ordered by the court under Part II of the Landlord and Tenant Act 1954.[143]

If the mortgagor grants a lease where the mortgage excludes his power to do so, the lease is binding on the mortgagor by estoppel,[144]

132. Ibid., s. 6.
133. LPA 1925, s. 99(2) and (3).
134. Ibid., s. 99(5).
135. Ibid., s. 99(6).
136. Ibid., s. 99(7).
137. Ibid., s. 98(8).
138. Ibid., s. 99(1).
139. Ibid., s. 99(11).
140. *Public Trustee* v. *Lawrence* [1912] 1 Ch. 789.
141. LRA 1925, s. 99(14).
142. Agricultural Holdings Act 1948, s. 95 and Sched. 7, para. 2.
143. Landlord and Tenant Act 1954, s. 36(4).
144. *Alchorne* v. *Gomme* (1824) 2 Bing. 54.

but it is not binding on the mortgagee,[145] although the tenant, as a person interested in the equity of redemption, could redeem or take a transfer of the mortgage.[146]

It will thus be apparent that where the mortgage is silent, a mortgagor has the power to grant certain leases in accordance with the terms of s. 99 of the LPA 1925. Such leases will be binding upon both the mortgagor and the mortgagee. In a case where the mortgage excludes the mortgagor's right to grant leases, the mortgagor has no power to grant leases which will bind the mortgagee, unless the covenant in the mortgage is that the mortgagor will not without the mortgagee's consent grant a lease of the mortgaged property, and the mortgagee's consent is in fact obtained. A mortgagor who grants a lease which is not binding on the mortgagee cannot restrict the mortgagee's right to take possession so that any lessee would have no protection at all as against the mortgagee.

Where a banker lends money on the security of property which is already subject to a lease which is disclosed to the banker, the lease will of course be binding on the mortgagee banker. Where a purchaser purports to grant a legal lease and lets the tenant into occupation before completion of his purchase and after completion enters into a mortgage, the mortgagee will be bound by the tenancy.[147]

Right to consolidate

Consolidation was an advantage previously available to a mortgagee without restriction. Generally speaking, it arises if a single borrower has mortgaged more than one property by separate mortgages to a single lender. If then the borrower seeks to repay the advance made under one mortgage, the lender may "consolidate" his mortgages and refuse repayment under one mortgage unless the debts due on each mortgage are simultaneously paid. The right of consolidation is now abolished by s. 93(1) of the LPA 1925, but this sub-section does not apply if a contrary intention is shown in any one of the mortgage documents in respect of which consolidation might apply. The practical effect of the legislation has been largely nullified by the almost universal exclusion in mortgage deeds of the operation of s. 93.

A banker who has several mortgages of separate properties from a single customer should always consider whether consolidation is available, if a request is made for the redemption of any single

---

145. *Keech* v. *Hall* (1778) 1 Doug. K.B. 21; *Rust* v. *Goodale* [1957] Ch. 33 at p. 44; [1956] 3 All E.R. 373 at p. 380.
146. *Tarn* v. *Turner* (1888) 39 Ch. D. 456.
147. *Church of England Building Society* v. *Piskor* [1954] Ch. 553.

mortgage. The values of properties, as security, differ, and no banker should release the most valuable securities or those with the greatest margin of cover and be left with those of lesser value or with lower cover if he has a choice in the matter.

Right to insure mortgaged land

A mortgagee has a statutory right of insurance against loss or damage by fire[148] but the restrictions on the statutory right are such that the mortgage should always contain express provisions as to insurance.

Under the statutory power, the amount of the cover must not exceed the amount specified in the mortgage, or, if no amount is so specified, two-thirds of the re-instatement value.[149] Moreover, there is no such right if, *inter alia*, an insurance is kept up by or on behalf of the mortgagor in accordance with the mortgage deed, or, if the mortgage deed contains no stipulation as to insurance, if an insurance is in fact kept up by the mortgagor with the consent of the mortgagee up to the amount to which the mortgagee may insure under the provisions of the Act.[150]

It will be seen that the above provisions are highly unsatisfactory. A well-drafted mortgage ought to contain an obligation on the mortgagor to insure, either in the name of the mortgagee or in joint names, for an amount equal to the full re-instatement value, and to produce evidence that such insurance cover has been effected and is maintained in force. If the mortgage then provides that if the mortgagor defaults in this obligation, the mortgagee may himself insure and recover the premiums paid as part of the moneys secured by the mortgage, and the mortgagee will be fully protected.

The mortgagee may, of course, insure up to the full value without any such provision in the mortgage, but in such case he may neither recover the premiums from the mortgagor (certainly not that part of the premium which represents the excess over two-thirds and possibly not any part) nor recoup them out of the security.

The banker should, as a matter of routine administration, check that all such insurances are renewed as and when they fall due, and the appropriate column of the securities register[151] should be used for this purpose.

There is in addition a risk that the policy might be avoided by virtue of some act or omission of the mortgagor affecting the risks insured. There is little a banker can do about this, unless he can persuade the insurance company to agree in the policy not to avoid

148. LPA 1925, s. 101(1)(*ii*).
149. Ibid., s. 108(1).
150. Ibid., s. 108(2).
151. *See* Chapter Twelve.

the policy as against the bank for any reason, so long as the bank is still interested in the policy. The banker should, of course, take a covenant in the mortgage not to allow the policy to be so avoided, but this will not prevent it from happening. It could only give the bank rights against the mortgagor.

There is an agreement in force between the Committee of London Clearing Bankers and the British Insurance Association covering policies where the interest of a member bank has been notified on a policy issued by members of the British Insurance Association.[152] As regards property, it does not cover residential property where the sum insured is £70,000 or less, but where the agreement applies member companies will, instead of indorsing the policy with a note of the bank's interest—

(*a*) advise the bank if the policy is not renewed as soon as practicable after such non-renewal has come to its notice;

(*b*) advise the bank if the cover in which the bank is interested is reduced or if any risk hitherto covered is restricted or cancelled; and

(*c*) pending receipt of instructions from the bank keep its interest in the policy in force up to the full sum insured and for the same risks as were covered when the bank's interest was notified (subject to the insurance not having been replaced elsewhere with the consent of the bank).

SECOND MORTGAGES

A second or later mortgage is normally not protected by deposit of title deeds since these will be with the first mortgagee. A second mortgagee risks tacking, sale, foreclosure or consolidation by a prior mortgagee. He should therefore carry out the following steps.

(*a*) He should check the amount of the prior loan to ensure that there is adequate equity to spare in the property. The banker should remember that a first mortgagee on a sale has the right to keep not only the principal sum but also arrears of interest. It will therefore not be satisfactory, for example, to lend £3,000 on a second mortgage on a property worth £8,000 on which the first mortgagee has lent £5,000.

(*b*) He should see if the prior mortgagee has a right to tack.

(*c*) He should register his second mortgage at the Land Charges Registry as a Class C(*i*) land charge in the case of a legal mortgage, or as a Class C(*iii*) land charge in the case of an equitable mortgage.

(*d*) After completion of the mortgage he should give notice to the prior mortgagee to ensure that the deeds are passed on to the second

152. There are similar agreements covering some other banks.

mortgagee when the prior mortgage is redeemed, and to prevent tacking.

(e) If possible he should indorse a note of his mortgage on the prior mortgage.

Section 96(2) of the LPA 1925 (as amended) provides that a mortgagee who has been repaid shall not be liable if he then delivers the title deeds to the person "not having the best right thereto" unless he has notice of the right or claim of a person having a better right. Notice in this respect does *not* include notice implied by reason of registration under LCA 1925 (now LCA 1972). Accordingly, in the absence of express notice and notwithstanding registration of a subsequent mortgage as a Class C(*iii*) land charge, a prior mortgagee could, without risk to himself, deliver the title deeds to the mortgagor upon repayment of his advance, and not to the subsequent mortgagee, whose position might be prejudiced without the custody of the title deeds to which he would then become entitled.

The remedies of a second mortgagee are largely the same as the remedies of a first mortgagee. Thus, a second mortgagee may sue the mortgagor on the covenant to pay; he may take possession of the property provided that his mortgage is by deed; he has a statutory power to appoint a receiver if his mortgage is by deed and does not exclude the power; or he may apply to the court for a foreclosure order.

DISCHARGE OF MORTGAGES

Under s. 115 of the LPA 1925, a statutory receipt will be sufficient to discharge the mortgage, i.e. a receipt indorsed on the mortgage deed, signed by the mortgagee and naming the person paying the money. If the receipt shows that the money was paid by a person not entitled to the immediate equity of redemption it operates as a transfer of the mortgage to him (unless there is a provision to the contrary).[154] The effect of this may be shown as follows: where a first mortgagee is paid off by the second mortgagee, the second mortgagee is not the person entitled to the equity of redemption (since the mortgagor is so entitled), so generally the second mortgagee obtains a transfer of the mortgage.

A receipt sealed by a building society does not need to name the payer but will be a sufficient discharge.[155]

If there are two or more mortgagees in one mortgage, the mort-

153. LPA 1925, s. 96(2), as amended by the Schedule to LP(A)A 1926.
154. *Cumberland Court* (*Brighton*) v. *Taylor* [1964] Ch. 29.
155. Building Societies Act 1962, s. 37.

gagor may treat them as joint tenants (even though they are not) and may get a good receipt from the survivor or survivors of them.

SUB-MORTGAGES

A mortgage, whether it be legal or equitable, is an asset which is itself capable of being mortgaged or disposed of outright by the mortgagee.

A sub-mortgage is appropriate where the value of the mortgage in the hands of the original mortgagee is used as the security for an advance to that mortgagee (who thus becomes a sub-mortgagor) by another (the sub-mortgagee).

A legal sub-mortgage should be effected by deed and its form is governed by the form of the original mortgage. That mortgage will either create a term of years absolute by way of demise or sub-demise, or a charge by way of legal mortgage.

In the former case, the deed may create, as the security for the sub-mortgagee, a sub-term of years absolute, normally equal to the term vested in the sub-mortgagor less one day.[156] The essentials of a sub-mortgage of this type are therefore:

(*a*) the sub-demise of the term of years;

(*b*) a covenant by the sub-mortgagor to repay the amount advanced to the sub-mortgagee, together with interest;

(*c*) a transfer of the debt secured by the original mortgage and the benefit of the security for it, including the powers and rights vested in the sub-mortgagor.

The sub-demise is not only subject to the right of redemption created by the original mortgage, but the sub-term is also subject to a proviso for cesser, when the amount advanced on the security of the sub-charge is repaid.

As an alternative to the creation of a sub-term where the original mortgage is by demise, the sub-mortgage may take effect by means of the creation of a charge by way of legal mortgage over the property comprised in the original mortgage, with a proviso for the discharge of the charge upon repayment.[157]

If the original mortgage is a charge by way of legal mortgage, the mortgagee has no estate for a term of years and it would appear that the proper method of effecting a sub-mortgage of such an original mortgage is to transfer the benefit of the original mortgage under s. 114 of the LPA 1925.

---

156. LPA 1925, s. 86(1).
157. Ibid., s. 86(1).

The form of the sub-charge is again different if the original charge is of registered land and is registered in the charges register of the title. In these circumstances, the sub-charge is expressed to be a charge over the original charge, the moneys secured by it and the benefit of all securities for their repayment. It is provided by Rule 163 of the Land Registration Rules 1925 (which, with Rules 164–6, sets out the Land Registry practice) that the registered proprietor of a sub-charge has the same powers of disposition over the land affected as the proprietor of the principal charge.

A sub-charge of registered land must be registered and the charge certificate of the principal charge included in the application. Before completing an advance, a lender on the security of a sub-mortgage should require a statement of the mortgage debt (confirmed by the original mortgagor), and should, immediately after completion, give notice to the mortgagor. Before such notice, the mortgagor is entitled to continue payments to the original mortgagee and to obtain a good discharge from him for them. After notice, the mortgagor must make the payments required of him under the mortgage to the sub-mortgagee.

The sub-mortgagee should also ensure that he receives not only the principal mortgage which is to be sub-charged to him, but also all the documents evidencing the title of the property charged by the principal mortgage, so that, in case of need, he is in a position to exercise his ultimate remedy of a sale of the property.

In addition to the creation of a legal sub-mortgage by one of the foregoing means, a sub-mortgage may be created as an equitable charge or a legal mortgage by means of a deposit of the documents by which the initial legal mortgage is created, preferably accompanied by a memorandum or other evidence of the terms of the sub-mortgage. The state of the original mortgage debt should be investigated and notice given to the original mortgagor. In the same way, an equitable sub-mortgage of an equitable charge may be created by a new deposit of the documents creating the charge.

TRANSFERS OF MORTGAGE

A sub-mortgage is by its nature intended as a temporary document, the effect of which is spent, as with any other mortgage, when the debt it secures is repaid. A mortgage can, however, be disposed of absolutely by way of sale or gift, and such a disposal is normally described as a transfer of mortgage. The form of the document used is not greatly dissimilar from a form of sub-mortgage, but it does, of course, state that the mortgage debt and the securities for it are transferred absolutely to the transferee without any question of a right of redemption other than that appropriate to the mortgage transferred.

The rights which pass to the transferee of a mortgage are set out in s. 114 of the LPA 1925 and, in brief, consist of the right to sue for and recover the mortgage debt and interest, the benefit of all securities for the debt and all the estate in the mortgaged property vested in the mortgagee.

Again, as with a sub-mortgage, it is necessary to inquire into the state of affairs as between mortgagor and mortgagee. The transferee should therefore obtain an admission of the amount of the mortgage debt from the mortgagor and require the mortgagor to be a party to the deed of transfer to confirm the state of the mortgage debt and interest. In the latter case, it is desirable to request a direct covenant from the mortgagor in favour of the transferee to pay the mortgage debt and interest.

Formal notice of the transfer should always be given to the mortgagor and to any prior mortgagee[158] and the documents of title to the property mortgaged must be obtained by the mortgagee. If the mortgaged property is registered land, the transfer of a mortgage registered in the charges register must be perfected by registration of the transfer itself.

A transfer of an equitable mortgage may be accomplished by a delivery of the documents constituting the equitable mortgage to the transferee, but is more satisfactorily evidenced by a deed of transfer, in which both the equitable mortgage and the underlying security are expressed to be transferred to the transferee.

RATES AND TAXES RELATING TO MORTGAGED LAND

Rates

In areas where a resolution of the rating authority has brought the necessary provisions into effect, liability to be rated in respect of unoccupied property attaches to owners of relevant hereditaments. "Owner" means the person entitled to possession of the hereditament.[159] It has been held that a receiver for debenture-holders who was the agent of the company and who had gone into possession of the premises which he subsequently vacated, was an "owner" as defined.[160] A relevant hereditament is one which consists of, or of part of, a house, shop, office, factory, mill or other building what-

158. LPA 1925, ss. 96 and 136.
159. General Rate Act 1967, Sched. 1, para. 15.
160. *Bannister* v. *Islington Borough Council* (1973) 17 R.R.C. 191.

soever. The hereditament must have been unoccupied for a continuous period exceeding three months or, in the case of a newly erected dwelling-house, six months.

The amount of rates payable by an owner in respect of an unoccupied hereditament is a proportion of the rates which would be payable if he were in occupation of the hereditament, such proportion (which may be the whole or any less amount) being specified by resolution of the rating authority.

The principle of the rating of unoccupied property has been greatly extended by the provisions of the Local Government Act 1974 which seek to prevent commercial property from remaining empty or unused for its intended purpose by means of a progressively increasing surcharge imposed by way of rates. In certain circumstances a banker or a receiver may incur liability for void rates or the rating surcharge, or at the very least will find that such liability is charged on the property and that such charge can only be discharged, so as to enable the property to be sold free of such charge, if these are paid either before sale, or else out of the proceeds of sale. The owner (i.e. the person entitled to possession) of a commercial building which for a continuous period exceeding six months is not used for the purpose for which it was constructed or has been adapted must pay a surcharge in respect of that period (the period of non-use) in addition to the rates otherwise payable. The surcharge is levied in the form of rates by doubling the normal rates for the first twelve months of the period of non-use, trebling the normal rates for the second twelve months, quadrupling the normal rates for the third twelve months and so on progressively while the period of non-use lasts.[161]

The surcharge is not payable if, *inter alia*, the owner has tried his best to let the building[162] or to "sell his interest" in the building.[163] Apart from the difficulty of proving that one has tried one's best to sell or let, there is the additional problem, in the case of attempts to sell, that a mortgagee when selling sells more than "his interest". He does not merely transfer the mortgage; he sells the property, free of the mortgage. A banker would be well advised to consult the local rating officer at an early stage.

These provisions relate solely to a situation where the mortgagor is solvent. The situation is very much more complicated where the mortgagor is insolvent and it is too technical to be dealt with in this work.

161. General Rate Act 1967, ss. 17A and 17B, inserted by Local Government Act 1974, s. 16. Since April 1981 these provisions have been suspended (*see* S.I. 1980 No. 2015) without fully being repealed.
162. General Rate Act 1967, s. 17A(2).
163. Rating Surcharge (Exemption of Unused Commercial Buildings) Regulations 1977 (S.I. 1977 No. 1515).

Taxes

In relation to income tax and capital gains tax where an individual is concerned, and corporation tax where a company is concerned, the general rule is that when a mortgagee sells the mortgaged property the mortgagee is entitled to keep the amount of the loan and all arrears of interest before giving the balance to the mortgagor. The mortgagor is liable to pay the tax and it is no concern of the mortgagee if the net proceeds handed to the mortgagor are less than the mortgagor's liability to tax.[164]

In relation to development land tax, s. 32 of the Development Land Tax Act 1976 contains similar provisions. Accordingly, on a sale by a mortgagee, the mortgagee is entitled to keep the amount secured and the mortgagor is liable for any DLT payable.[165]

A person who acquires an interest in development land (broadly land with the benefit of planning permission for material development which has not been commenced) from a person whose usual place of abode is outside the UK is required either (*a*) to deduct at source when handing over the consideration the DLT which the DLT office has told him to deduct, or (*b*) if he has not been instructed to make a specific deduction to withhold one half of the consideration on account of the non-resident's DLT liability and forthwith to remit the amount withheld to the Inland Revenue.[166] Solicitors acting for mortgagees where the mortgagor is non-resident should always bear in mind this trap. If they have overlooked it, they could turn up on completion to find the net proceeds of sale are unexpectedly insufficient to discharge the mortgage. Further, anyone proposing to lend money to a non-resident on the security of land in the UK should bear in mind that the loan should not exceed the mortgagor's best base value for DLT purposes, otherwise this deduction at source procedure may mean that part of the loan is unsecured.

Where land is sold to a local authority, the local authority, when paying the completion moneys, will make payment net of DLT. This will occur whether the sale is compulsory or voluntary.[167]

164. *See* in particular Capital Gains Tax Act 1979, s. 23(2).
165. Detailed reference should be made to Development Land Tax Act 1976, Sched. 7, para. 5 (as amended) and 7, para 8.
166. Development Land Tax Act 1976, s. 40 as supplemented by the Development Land Tax (Disposals by Non-Residents) Regulations 1976 (S.I. 1976 No. 1190).
167. Development Land Tax Act 1976, s. 39.

JOINT OWNERS

Where land is jointly owned, a mortgage of the legal estate can only be effected by both (or all) the joint owners; any purported mortgage by only one of them would not operate to effect a mortgage. It sometimes happens that a mortgage is taken from one person and it subsequently transpires that the legal estate in the property mortgaged is held by that person and another. A typical example is where a husband grants a mortgage to a bank when the property is held jointly by the husband and his wife.

If only one of the spouses executes a document expressed to be a charge on land, it used to be considered that such a mortgage was not effective to charge that spouse's beneficial interest in the proceeds of sale.[168] This view has been stated in the House of Lords to be incorrect, and the case in question wrongly decided, on the grounds that it is "just a little unreal" to describe the spouse's interest in the matrimonial home as being an interest in the proceeds of sale rather than an interest in land.[169] In spite of this, it would appear to be safer to use a special document, appropriately drafted, where it is intended that one of the spouses (usually the husband) should charge his interest in the property, rather than use a normal form of charge over land. Such a charge is worth having if it is all the husband has to offer, since it can be effective as against the husband's trustee in bankruptcy, but it is in many ways unsatisfactory. As it affects only the husband's interest in the proceeds of sale the banker has no power to bring about a sale and can only wait until the property is in fact sold. Even then, as his charge does not form part of the title to the property, he cannot be sure of bringing his interest to the notice of prospective purchasers, and must rely on the integrity of the husband in informing him of the sale and paying over his share of the net proceeds.

COMPULSORY ACQUISITION

If a loan is made on the security of a property which is later compulsorily acquired by the local authority, there is a risk that the local authority will pay the money to the borrower and the mortgagee will lose his security. There is the additional risk that the price paid by the local authority will not be enough to cover the loan.

In the case of a first legal mortgage, the mortgagee will hold the title deeds. Accordingly, no compulsory sale will be effected without

168. *Cedar Holdings* v. *Green* [1981] Ch. 129.
169. *Williams & Glyn's Bank* v. *Boland*, and *Williams & Glyn's Bank* v. *Brown* [1981] A.C. 487.

the mortgagee being aware of the situation and joining in negotiations with a view to handing over the title deeds to the local authority. In this situation the local authority will pay the money to the mortgagee and the mortgagee will account to the mortgagor for the balance, if any, in the usual way.

In most mortgages, there is a covenant by the borrower to inform the mortgagee of any notice of compulsory acquisition. In practice of course the borrower cannot be relied upon to inform the mortgagee of the notice of compulsory acquisition.

If the local authority buys the property for less than the loan, the mortgagee will receive the amount of money which the local authority pays and will thereafter have to look to the borrower for the balance on the personal covenant to repay the loan and interest.

LENDING MONEY ON LEASEHOLDS

When considering making an advance against a leasehold property, there are various additional matters to be considered which might affect the value.

There will invariably be some rent to pay, whether a mere ground rent, a full market rent or rack rent. In addition, it has become increasingly common in present times for landlords to require a service charge or maintenance charge to cover the cost of performing common services such as lighting, cleaning, possibly heating, and in some cases, lifts. There will also be provisions for forfeiture if the rent or service charges are not paid, and the banker must always consider the ability of the borrower to be able to pay the rent and the service charges. Even if the rent is low, the service charges may, with current levels of inflation, mount up in future years. There may, in addition, be provision for a sinking fund to cover matters such as renewals of lifts or boilers.

Commercial and industrial premises are usually let at a rack rent except where the lease was granted in consideration of the tenant (or a builder through whom the tenant derives his title) having erected the building. In such cases, the banker must again consider not merely the current rent and service charges. With inflation at its present levels, the practice of frequent rent reviews has become almost universal, and not only will the value of the lease reflect the amount by which the rent at any time is less than current market rent, but also the maintenance of the security will depend upon the rent and the service charges being paid as and when these accrue.

Although leases invariably contain provisions enabling the landlord to forfeit the lease if the rent or service charges are not paid, or if there is any breach of other covenants in the lease, some relief is available to the tenant. Under s. 146 of the LPA 1925 a landlord is not entitled to enforce a right of re-entry or forfeiture on the grounds of a breach of covenant other than non-payment of rent unless and until he serves a notice on the lessee specifying the breach complained of and requiring the lessee to remedy the breach, if the breach is capable of remedy, and if thought fit, requiring the lessee to pay money compensation for the breach. The lessee then has a reasonable time within which to remedy the breach or make reasonable money compensation.

In an action for forfeiture, the lessee has the right to apply to the court for relief.[170] This right is not limited to the tenant whose breach of covenant has caused the action to be brought but extends to all sub-tenants of the property (and, indeed, to mortgagees of any leasehold interest in the property) even in those cases where the tenant cannot apply for relief. The right also extends to a person entitled to call for a legal mortgage of the lease to be executed in his favour.[171] If the breach is remedied, the court almost invariably grants relief.

Where a lessor is proceeding to enforce a right of forfeiture or re-entry by action, any underlessee may apply to the court for relief, and the court has power to make an order vesting the property comprised in the lease in such underlessee for the whole of the remainder of the term, subject to the underlessee undertaking liability for payment of the rent, costs, damages and compensation and, if appropriate, giving security.[172]

It will be recalled that the two ways of taking a mortgage over leasehold property are by sub-demise and by charge by way of legal mortgage. In the case of a sub-demise, the mortgagee is an underlessee, and since a charge by way of legal mortgage puts the mortgagee in the same position as if he had a sub-demise, a mortgagee with a charge by way of legal mortgage is also regarded as an underlessee. A mortgagee therefore has power to apply for relief against forfeiture of a lease, upon terms involving the mortgagee taking over liability under the covenants contained in the lease.

Where there is a condition for forfeiture on the insolvency of the lessee, s. 146 applies if the lessee's interest is sold within one year of the insolvency, and for this reason landlords rarely seek forfeiture of a lease if the mortgagee effectively takes over liability for payment of the rent.[173] Indeed, although there is no statutory reason for this, landlords sometimes refrain from enforcing forfeiture pro-

---

170. LPA 1925, s. 146(2).
171. *Re Good's Lease, Good* v. *Trustee of the Property of W.* [1954] 1 W.L.R. 309.
172. LPA 1925, s. 146(4).
173. Ibid., s. 146(10).

visions even after the end of the year if the mortgagee is paying the rent.

Section 146 does not apply to leases of agricultural land, mines or minerals, public houses, furnished houses or a lease of any property where the personal qualifications of the tenant are of importance.[174]

Section 146 does not apply to forfeiture for non-payment of rent.[175] Technically a landlord is entitled to forfeit without going to court, but a prudent landlord would always apply to the court for forfeiture even for non-payment of rent. The tenant may apply for relief within six months after the date of re-entry if re-entry is effected without a court order, or within six months after an order for forfeiture has been made, and in either case the court will grant relief if the tenant puts the landlord in the same position as if the rent had been paid.[176] Thus even if a court order is obtained, the landlord is effectively unable to deal with the property for six months, while he waits to see if the tenant pays the rent and applies for relief. The rules as to who may apply for relief are the same as those mentioned above.

Where the rent is in arrears the landlord has the right to distrain for all arrears of rent upon all goods found on the premises. The right originally extended to all goods on the premises, whether or not belonging to the tenant, but has now been hedged in with restrictions so that many goods of third parties, and certain articles used in the tenant's trade, are protected. For a banker the significance is that some goods which he may have considered covered by a floating charge in his favour risk being seized by the landlord. Distress is completed by seizure, which may be actual or constructive, such as preventing the removal of goods from the premises, or walking round the premises after intimating the intention to distrain followed by written notice that one has distrained.

The banker must also consider the terms of the lease, with a view to satisfying himself that if he needs to enforce the security, he will effectively be able to do so either by assigning the lease or by granting an underlease. Many leases contain prohibitions against assignment or underletting. In the case of an absolute prohibition, a mortgagee would be unable to sell the lease without the landlord's consent which could be arbitrarily withheld. If the covenant is not to assign or underlet without the landlord's consent, there is an implied condition that such consent is not to be unreasonably withheld.[177] Where

174. LPA 1925, s. 146(9).
175. Ibid., s. 146(11).
176. Common Law Procedure Act 1852; Judicature Act 1875.
177. Landlord and Tenant Act 1927, s. 19.

a lease contains a tenant's covenant not to charge the lease without the landlord's consent, the banker will need to ensure that such consent is obtained prior to making the loan to the lessee. There may also be other covenants which affect the marketability of the lease. There may, for example, be restrictions on the user of the property. A restrictive user clause will render the lease less marketable than a lease with a user clause drafted in such wide terms as for example "to use the premises only for offices".[178] These contractual limitations contained in leases are wholly different from those arising under the general legislation relating to town and country planning. It can fairly easily happen that a use permitted by the lease is, or may become, prohibited by the planning legislation.

Any lease offered as security which contains rent review provisions should be scrutinised with particular care to ensure that the provisions are in such terms that they are clear, unequivocal and provide an effective mechanism for the establishment of a new rent. This is important where a freehold property, with the benefit of the rent receivable from a lease of it, is under consideration, as the value of the property is directly related to the rental income.

It may also be necessary to consider the terms of a lease where freehold property is offered as security subject to existing leases. The mortgagee will wish to be satisfied that the terms of the lease are sufficiently stringent to afford adequate protection to the mortgagee if he wishes to take over the security, or to a prospective purchaser if the need arises to sell the security. Paradoxically where the terms of the lease are such as to make it an attractive security for a banker lending against the lease, the same property may not be attractive security for a person lending on the security of the freehold, and vice versa. Incidentally, one advantage of the charge by way of legal mortgage of leaseholds is that although this form of charge gives the same protection as a mortgage by sub-demise, it is not in fact a sub-demise, so that the granting of a charge by way of legal mortgage of such a lease would not be a breach of a prohibition against underletting. Most modern forms of covenant, however, also contain a prohibition against charging without consent.

AGREEMENTS FOR LEASE

Another form of interest in land which is now often offered as

---

178. The other side of the coin is that the more restrictive the user clause the lower the rent will be on the next review. Thus, the user clause is an important point for the banker to bear in mind when considering either the landlord's freehold or the tenant's lease as security.

security is an agreement for lease. Frequently a developer enters into an agreement, often with a local authority, under which he is required to construct a building on land vested in the authority or other land owner. Provided the building is completed to the satisfaction of the putative landlord and otherwise in compliance with the terms of the agreement, the developer becomes entitled to the grant of a long lease on completion of the building. In the meantime, he needs to raise money to finance the construction of the building, and offers the agreement for lease to the bank or other lender as security for advances to cover the cost of the building work up to an agreed maximum.

This is obviously technically less satisfactory as a security than a leasehold interest, since the maintenance of the security depends upon the observance of the developer's obligations in the agreement, and such agreements commonly contain provision for termination without compensation in the event of the developer's default. The developer has no right to the lease until the building has been completed in accordance with the landlord's requirements and the terms of the agreement. It is equally common, however, for such agreements to contain provisions designed to protect a banker or other mortgagee. These normally prevent any termination of the agreement unless notice of the intention to do so is given to the mortgagee, who may then elect to assume and complete the developer's outstanding obligations and thereafter to take up the lease.

The banker's advance is normally made in instalments as the work proceeds, in amounts certified by the developer's architect. The certificates are invariably for amounts less than the value of the work done at the date of issue of the certificate so that there should, at all times, be a margin of security in the work for the benefit of the banker. However, the banker must appreciate that if the developer defaults before the building is completed, he will be virtually obliged to elect to complete the development himself if he is to preserve his security.

Agreements of this nature are becoming an increasingly common form of security in the present property climate. Repayment of any advances normally depends upon there being a buyer willing to purchase the lease, or an institution willing to advance long-term funds on the security of the lease, when the building is completed. Indeed, many bankers will refuse to consider an advance upon this form of security unless the developer has, at the time the advance is agreed, already negotiated a forward sale of the leasehold interest with the completed building at a price sufficient to repay the advance and interest. Coupled with the ability to complete the building itself upon the developer's default, a forward sale of this kind significantly improves the bank's position.

Certain additional precautions should be taken to safeguard the banker's interest during the construction if he is to have an effective form of security. He should arrange for a surveyor instructed by him to monitor the progress of the construction and (if possible) the contracts of engagement of the architect, quantity surveyor and other professionals concerned with the development. He should also be in a position to take over the benefit of any building contract as well as the agreement for lease in the event of the insolvency of the borrower during the course of the construction. It is increasingly common for landlords, particularly local authorities, to require a licence fee or some other form of premium before the developer is permitted to enter upon the land. The banker should try to arrange for this (or some part of it) to be refunded if the landlord repossesses the land because of some default by the developer. Finally, as in any other case where a lender is providing funds to finance the construction of the building, he should consider accepting an obligation in the mortgage to make further advances, so as to be sure of retaining priority if he receives notice of a subsequent mortgage.[179]

BANKER'S INQUIRIES WHERE REGISTERED LAND IS OFFERED AS SECURITY

Registered land is governed by the Land Registration Act 1925 (as amended) and the rules made thereunder.[180]

The register of title contains all the material facts about the title and so investigation of title is easier where registered land is concerned. No trusts may be entered on the register. If the register is wrong a purchaser can obtain compensation.[181] The validity of the title, once registered, is generally speaking guaranteed by the State.

The remainder of this chapter deals with aspects of the registered land system that are of interest to mortgagees, in particular in relation to the practice of bankers.[182]

---

179. *See* above in this chapter under "Mortgagee's right to tack".

180. The LRA 1925 has been amended by the LRA 1936 and LRA 1966 and by the Land Registration and Land Charges Act 1971. Reference should also be made to the Land Registration Rules 1925 and 1967 and to the registered land practice notes and practice leaflets.

181. Rectification of the register and compensation are discussed further below.

182. For a detailed discussion of the subject *see* especially Ruoff & Roper, *Registered Conveyancing*, (4th Edn.).

THE REGISTERS

Five registers are kept at each District Land Registry. They are:

(*a*) the register of titles to freehold and leasehold land;
(*b*) the index map which shows the position and extent of each registered title;
(*c*) the alphabetical index of proprietors' names;
(*d*) a list of pending applications;
(*e*) the minor interests index. This deals with equitable interests and governs the priority of them *inter se*.[183]

Of these, the most important is the register of titles. The register is a vast card index system. Each title is on a separate card and has a distinguishing title number.

Each register is in three parts.

(*a*) The property register contains a description of the land comprised in the title by reference to a plan. Exceptions and reservations should be noted and also benefits enjoyed with the land can be noted. In the case of leasehold land, short particulars of the lease are included.

(*b*) The proprietorship register states the nature of the title, the name and address and description of the proprietor and any entries affecting his right of disposal, i.e. restrictions, inhibitions and cautions, e.g. a caution registered to protect, *inter alia*, an estate contract, or a bankruptcy inhibition.

(*c*) The charges register contains details of charges and encumbrances affecting the land such as restrictive covenants. Notices appear here such as of a right under the Matrimonial Homes Act 1967. Details of mortgages appear here together with the name and address of the proprietor of the charge. On discharge of the mortgage, the entry is deleted. The charges register cannot be treated as conclusive evidence of the existence or otherwise of a subsisting lease; it is possible for there to be an entirely valid and subsisting lease particulars of which do not appear in the charges register. The banker should, therefore, always investigate, independently of the evidence offered by the land or charge certificate, whether or not there are any subsisting unregistered leases of the property intended to be charged.

The register of an individual title is private and may only be

183. Priority between assignees of certain equitable interests in registered land (life interests, remainders, reversions, and executory interests) depends on the order of lodging priority cautions or inhibitions in this index which does not concern a purchaser of the legal estate (LRA 1925, s. 102). *See* below.

inspected by the registered proprietor and those authorised by him.

As evidence of his title, a land certificate is issued to the registered proprietor. This is a complete copy of the entries in the register of his title as at the date when it was last examined with the register. The land certificate must be produced at the Registry when any disposition by the registered proprietor is made,[184] or when a notice or restriction is entered against it,[185] or on rectification of the register.[186] The object is to keep the land certificate up to date with the register. If the land is subject to a registered charge, the land certificate is kept at the Registry until the charge is cancelled, and a charge certificate is prepared and issued to the chargee.

The registers of title themselves are kept under the authority of the Chief Land Registrar at the District Land Registries throughout England and Wales. These deal with registration of and dealings with titles in defined districts.

TITLES CAPABLE OF REGISTRATION

Only the following titles may be registered:

(*a*) a fee simple absolute in possession ("title absolute");

(*b*) a term of years absolute, except (*i*) a lease with less than 21 years to run, (*ii*) a mortgage term with a subsisting right of redemption,[187] (*iii*) a lease containing an absolute prohibition against *inter vivos* dealings.

Overriding interests

Some incumbrances, interests rights and powers are not capable of being entered on the register, but all registered dispositions nevertheless take effect subject to them. These are known as overriding interests.

Overriding interests are listed in s. 70(1) of the LRA 1925 and include various public rights, legal easements, rights acquired, or in the course of being acquired, under the Limitation Act, rights of every person in actual occupation of the land, local land charges, and legal leases not exceeding 21 years granted at a rent without a fine.

Where a husband is sole registered proprietor and his wife has contributed to the purchase price of the house her interest is a

---

184. LRA 1925, s. 64(1).
185. Ibid, s. 58, Land Registration Rules 1925, s. 235.
186. LRA 1925, s. 82(6).
187. This can be registered as a charge, but not as a lease in its own right.

tenancy-in-common, which ranks as a minor interest (*see* below). But where she is in actual occupation (in other words living there) it amounts to an overriding interest so as to bind a mortgagee of the house, whether he knew of it or not.[188] A mortgagee of any residence must, therefore, take particular care to find out who is living there, as the rights of any person who is living there will be overriding interests. As neither banks nor their solicitors usually inspect personally, they must ensure that their surveyors take note of all persons living there. Indeed this is a precaution which should not be confined to matrimonial homes or other residential property; it applies to all property, though the consequences of finding someone in occupation, particularly authorised occupation, and especially a wife (with or without the husband), of a home are probably relatively more drastic than in the case of other property.

Minor interests
All interests in registered land except legal estates capable of substantive registration and overriding interests take effect in equity as minor interests.[189]

Minor interests include (*a*) interests of beneficiaries under a trust for sale or settlement, (*b*) registrable interests not yet registered, (*c*) non-registrable interests which depend for enforceability on some entry on the register.

Third party interests
Interests in land not capable of registration with separate title are either:

(*a*) overriding interests which bind every purchaser and donee of registered land, even though not entered on the register; or

(*b*) minor interests which bind every donee but which generally only bind a purchaser if protected by an entry on the register.

COMPULSORY AND VOLUNTARY REGISTRATION

Compulsory registration
The system of land registration is not yet operative throughout the whole of England and Wales. The LRA 1925 specified certain areas in which registration of title was to be compulsory and made provision for further compulsory areas to be designated in the future. The areas of compulsory registration have expanded and continue

---

188. *Williams & Glyn's Bank* v. *Boland,* and *Williams & Glyn's Bank* v. *Brown* [1981] A.C. 487.
189. LRA 1925, s. 2(1).

to expand, principally in urban areas where dealings are frequent. In an area where compulsory registration is in force, the following must be registered within two months of the disposition:

(a) every conveyance on sale of freehold land;
(b) every grant of a lease for 40 years or more;
(c) every assignment on sale of a lease with 40 or more years still to run.

Failure to apply for registration within the time limit renders void the legal estate granted or transferred unless an extension of time has been granted by the Registrar.[190] Where compulsory registration is in force, registrable estates can be registered even if there has been no dealing with them, if the estate owner so desires. It is important to note that after a title has been registered (whether or not compulsorily and whether or not in an area of compulsory registration) all registrable dealings with the registered estate must be registered.

Where a lease is granted for more than 21 years out of a registered superior title and the lease does not contain an absolute prohibition against assignment and is not a mortgage term with a subsisting right of redemption, it must be registered with its own title.[191] On the assignment of an unregistered lease with between 21 years and 40 years still to run, registration is optional.

The two-month time limit does not apply to dealings, but on a dealing no legal estate passes to the purchaser until registration has been completed.

Voluntary registration

In an area of compulsory registration, a title which is not compulsorily registrable within s. 123 of the LRA 1925 may be registered voluntarily. Outside compulsory areas, voluntary registration has been suspended[192] except for:

(a) properties in respect of which the deeds were destroyed by enemy action during World War II, or lost or destroyed whilst in a solicitor's proper custody;

(b) applications by local authorities or development corporations which intend to sell or lease residential property;

(c) applications in connection with the development of a building estate of 20 or more houses or plots.

190. Ibid., s. 123.
191. Ibid., s. 19(2).
192. LRA 1966 s. 1(2).

BORROWER'S TITLE WHERE REGISTERED LAND OFFERED AS SECURITY

The effect of first registration depends upon the class of title registered, i.e. absolute, possessory, qualified or good leasehold. Registration with absolute title vests in the registered proprietor the freehold or leasehold estate in the land, together with all rights and privileges pertinent thereto but subject to:

(a) incumbrances and other entries, if any, appearing on the register;

(b) overriding interests, if any;

(c) any minor interests of which the proprietor has notice where he is not entitled for his own benefit. In effect this means that if the first registered proprietor is a trustee, he holds subject to the equitable interest of the beneficiaries; and

(d) in the case of leaseholds, the express and implied liabilities both under the lease and affecting the superior titles.

Save for the above, registration with absolute title vests the estate in the proprietor free from all other estates and interests whatsoever (but subject to rectification).[193]

Registration with possessory title has the same effect as registration with absolute title except that it is subject to all adverse interests existing at the time of first registration. These adverse interests take effect as overriding interests. Title is guaranteed in respect only of dealings after registration and the prior title must be investigated as if the land was not registered.[194]

Registration with qualified title (which is rare) has the same effect as registration with absolute title save that it is subject to rights or interests arising under a specified instrument or before a specified date.[195] Registration with good leasehold title has the same effect as registration with absolute title save that it is subject to defects in the lessor's title.[196]

An absolute title to a leasehold cannot be registered unless and until the title both to the leasehold and to the freehold and to any intermediate leasehold that may exist is approved by the Registrar, as it amounts to a guarantee not only that the registered proprietor is the owner of the lease but also that it was validly granted. Hence, good leasehold title is common.

In certain circumstances it is possible for title to be upgraded.

193. LRA 1925, ss. 5 and 9. *See also Bridges* v. *Mees* [1957] Ch. 475.
194. LRA 1925, ss. 6 and 11.
195. Ibid., ss. 7 and 12.
196. Ibid., ss. 8 and 10.

Where a possessory title is registered and the proprietor is in possession, the Registrar is bound on application to convert:

(a) to absolute a freehold possessory title so registered for at least
15 years;
(b) to good leasehold a leasehold possessory title so registered for
at least 10 years.

In addition, the Registrar may at his discretion:

(a) on any dealing for value upgrade to absolute or good leasehold
a qualified, possessory or good leasehold title;
(b) at the request of the proprietor, upgrade to absolute a good
leasehold title so registered for at least 10 years, provided he is satisfied that successive lessees have been in occupation during that
period.[197]

How to protect minor interests

(a) *By notice.* This is entered on the charges register of the title
affected. Any interest protected by notice automatically binds the
transferee of the land. It may protect, for example, a lease of
registered land which is not an overriding interest (e.g. an agreement
to grant a lease or a lease for any period granted at a premium)
or interests which would be registrable as land charges under the
LCA 1972 (except puisne mortgages). A notice can be entered only
if the land certificate is lodged at the Land Registry, but a registrable
lease granted out of a registered title will automatically be noted
on the superior title even though the superior land certificate has
not been lodged at the Land Registry.[198]

(b) *By caution.* This is entered on the proprietorship register and
entitles the person lodging it to notice of any proposed dealing with
the land. Broadly speaking, a caution is designed to protect an
interest, such as an estate contact, where the registered proprietor
will not consent and lodge his land certificate in the Land Registry
for a notice to be entered. There are two types of caution:

(i) *a caution against dealing:* any person interested under an unregistered instrument or as a judgment creditor or otherwise in any
land registered in the name of any other person may lodge a
caution against dealings with such land by the registered
proprietor;
(ii) *a caution against registration of unregistered land:* any person

197. Ibid., s. 77.
198. Ibid., s. 64.

having or claiming an interest in the land which entitles him to object to any disposition of it being made without his consent may lodge a caution. Production of the land certificate is not required for entry of a caution.

(c) *By restriction.* This is entered on the proprietorship register and curtails the proprietor's powers of disposition without prior conformity to some specified requirement. The entry is made by or with the consent of the registered proprietor. An example would be a joint proprietors' restriction, which is entered unless the applicant states on the registration application form that the survivor of the joint proprietors can give a valid receipt for capital money. Production of the land certificate is required for the entry of a restriction.

(d) *By inhibition.* This is entered on the proprietorship register and prevents any dealing with the land during a specified period. It can only be entered by order of the registrar or the court. An inhibition may be entered for example where a receiving order in bankruptcy has been made against the registered proprietor.

CONVEYING REGISTERED LAND

Dealings with unregistered land leading to first registration of title
There are three types of dealing leading to first registration:

(a) the sale of a freehold or assignment of a lease with 40 years or more still to run, or the grant of a lease for 40 years or more of land in a compulsory registration area under s. 123 of the LRA 1925;

(b) voluntary registration of land in a non-compulsory area where this is permitted by the LRA 1966;

(c) voluntary registration of dealings apart from s. 123 dealings, e.g. assignment of lease with between 21 years and 40 years still to run affecting land in a compulsory registration area.

The pre-completion procedure is the same as for unregistered land. After completion application is made to the appropriate District Land Registry accompanied, *inter alia*, by the conveyance to the applicant and any mortgage. The application is then put in the pending list. The Registrar investigates the title and decides what title to grant. If there is a mortgage, he issues a charge certificate to the mortgagee and keeps the land certificate in the Registry. The Registrar normally returns to the registered proprietor (or, if there is a registered charge, to the proprietor of the charge) the deeds relating to the unregistered title with the Land Registry stamp placed on the last conveyance or, in the case of a leasehold, on the lease and on the last assignment. As a matter of course, the title deeds of any land within an area of compulsory registration presented by way of security or otherwise, without an accompanying land or charge certificate, should be examined to ensure that they do not bear the Registry stamp. Equally, if there has been a recent dealing for value with the title, it should be ascertained whether the property is within an area of compulsory registration and if so, whether registration should have been effected. Any District Land Registry will supply, upon request, a list of areas of compulsory registration showing the date upon which registration became compulsory in each area and indicating future areas of compulsory registration.

While land with registered title can only satisfactorily be dealt with by the methods of disposition and charge laid down in the LRA 1925, land which becomes subject to the obligation of compulsory registration by means of a dealing with the title in its unregistered state can nevertheless continue to be dealt with as an unregistered title. It is the ultimate transferee of the land dealt with in this way upon whom the responsibility for first registration will rest.

Searches on transfer of registered land

Even when land is registered a search must be made in the local land charges register since the matters registered there are overriding interests. When dealing with land registered with absolute title, there is no need to search in the Land Charges Registry. It is provided that a purchaser of registered land is not affected with notice of any matter registrable there under the LCA 1972 merely by reason of registration under that Act if the interest can be protected on the registered title by a restriction, inhibition, caution or notice. It is common for bankruptcy searches under the LCA 1972 to be made on behalf of a mortgagee before completion of the mortgage in order to discover whether the mortgagor is on the road to bankruptcy. In buying registered land from a registered company, there appears to be no need so far as registration of a charge is concerned to search in the Companies Registry, but a search should always be made there before completion of a mortgage.

Before completion, the purchaser should make an official search of the register to ascertain whether any entries have been made since either (a) the date of the office copy entries supplied, or (b) the date on which the land or charge certificate was last officially compared with the register.

An official certificate of search gives the purchaser priority over subsequent entries on the register for fifteen working days after delivery of the search application provided the purchaser applies for registration within that period. The applicant may, before the priority period expires, obtain one extension for a further fourteen days.[199]

The official search certificate is not conclusive in the purchaser's favour. If an error occurs and the purchaser suffers loss thereby, he can claim compensation from the Registry.[200]

MORTGAGES OF REGISTERED LAND

In general, the registered proprietor of registered land has the same powers of creating a mortgage of his land as the owner of unregistered land. Such a mortgage may be legal or equitable. The banker's remedies in relation to either of such mortgages are largely the same as his remedies in relation to unregistered land.

A registered proprietor may mortgage or charge his land by any of the following methods.

Registered charge by deed

This may be in any form applicable to unregistered land provided that it adequately identifies the land. The charge is completed by registration of the mortgagee as proprietor thereof on the charges register of the title affected. The land certificate is retained at the Registry for as long as the registered charge subsists and the mortgagee is issued with a charge certificate which is his document of title.

A charge created by a limited company must be registered at the Companies Registry[201] before being lodged for registration at the Land Registry. The charge must be accompanied by a copy of the memorandum and articles of association of the company certified by the secretary or solicitor of the company and by a certificate by the secretary or solicitor that the charge does not contravene the memorandum and articles of association of the company. Floating charges cannot be registered but may be protected by notice or caution.

Subject to any entry to the contrary on the register, the chargor impliedly covenants: (a) to pay the principal and interest on the appointed date, and (b) in the case of leaseholds, to pay the rent, perform and observe the covenants in the lease and indemnify the chargee against breach.

199. For the procedure, *see* the Land Registration (Official Searches) Rules 1969.
200. See the case of *Parkash* v. *Irani Finance* [1970] Ch. 101 where the official certificate of search failed to reveal a caution. It was held that the purchaser took subject to the caution which, having been lodged, was effective. The purchaser could, however, claim compensation from the Land Registry.
201. Under s. 95 of the Companies Act 1948. *See* Chapter Seventeen.

Unregistered mortgage

A registered proprietor may mortgage land by deed in any form applicable to unregistered land. Such mortgages take effect only in equity and will be capable of being overriden as a minor interest unless protected by entry on the register of a notice or caution. Before 29th August 1977, an unregistered mortgage by deed could be protected by entry of a special form of caution known as a "mortgage caution".[202] This device was rarely used and has now been abolished; being replaced by the ordinary caution against dealings;[203] the effect of such a caution is that no dealing with the land may be registered unless notice is given to the cautioner.[204]

Lien by deposit of land certificate

A registered proprietor may create a lien on the land by deposit of his land certificate.[205] The mortgagee/depositee should give written notice of the deposit to the Registrar who enters a notice of deposit on the charges register. This operates as a caution.

Where a loan is made in connection with the purchase of land, the land certificate must first be sent to the Registry for registration of the purchaser as proprietor following completion of the purchase before it can be deposited. In this case, a notice of intended deposit should be given to the Registrar on Form 85C.

The deposit is generally accompanied by a memorandum under seal and in such a case, the memorandum, not the deposit, creates the mortgage. Such a mortgage should be protected by notice or caution in the usual way. However, in the case of *Re White Rose Cottage*[206] it was held that notice of deposit of the land certificate was sufficient protection for the mortgagee, though notice or caution of the memorandum would be the proper course for protection of the mortgagee. In *Barclays Bank* v. *Taylor*[207] an unregistered mortgage by deed was held to be protected by an earlier notice of deposit.

Discharge of mortgages

A registered charge is discharged by cancellation of the entry on the register pursuant to receipt by the Registry of the Charge Certificate and Form 53.

202. LRA 1925, s. 106 (now replaced; *see* note 203).
203. Administration of Justice Act 1977, s. 26, inserting a new s. 106 into the LRA 1925.
204. LRA 1925, s. 54.
205. Ibid., s. 66.
206. [1965] Ch. 940.
207. [1974] Ch. 137.

Where an equitable mortgage has been created by the deposit of the land certificate, or by an unregistered legal mortgage, such a mortgage is protected by entry on the register of a notice or caution. A notice of deposit may be withdrawn from the register on the written request of the person entitled to the lien created by the deposit. The land certificate must accompany this request. Application to remove a caution should be made to the Registry in cases where the equitable mortgage has been protected by entry on the register of a caution.

RIGHTS AND REMEDIES

The proprietor of a registered charge has all the powers of a legal mortgagee of unregistered land. He can exercise the statutory power of sale, and if he enters into possession and acquires a title under the Limitation Act 1980, he can procure himself to be registered as proprietor of the land (subject to the rights of persons entered in the register as prior incumbrancers) and he will be in the same position as a purchaser on sale made in exercise of the mortgagee's statutory power of sale.[208]

An equitable mortgagee enjoys the same remedies as an equitable mortgagee of unregistered land. A mortgagee is unable to effect a sale unless his mortgage is registered. If, therefore, the banker has taken a legal mortgage which he has protected merely by a caution, he must have his mortgage registered before he will be in a position to sell. Similarly, if the banker has taken merely an equitable mortgage by deposit of the land certificate, but has nevertheless obtained his borrower's signature to a legal mortgage, this must be registered before the banker can effect a sale. If the banker's security consists simply of the deposit of the land certificate, application will have to be made to the court to order a sale.

Registered charges on the same land rank for priority according to their order of entry on the register and not the order of creation.[209] Tacking is only possible if the chargee is under an obligation to make further advances and the right to do so is noted on the register.[210]

When a registered charge is made for securing further advances, the Registrar must, before making any entry on the register which would prejudicially affect the priority of any further advance thereunder, give to the proprietor of the charge at his registered address notice by registered post of the intended entry, and the proprietor of the charge is not, in respect of any further advance, affected by

208. LRA 1925, s. 34.
209. Ibid., s. 29.
210. Ibid., s. 30.

such entry unless the advance is made after the date when notice ought to have been received in course of post.[211] If the proprietor of the charge suffers loss in relation to a further advance as a result of any failure on the part of the Registrar or the Post Office, he is entitled to be reimbursed by the Registrar out of moneys provided by Parliament. This does not apply if the loss occurred because the proprietor of the charge changed his address without notifying the Registrar.[212] Accordingly, when an overdraft secured by a registered charge is transferred from one branch to another, the Registrar should be informed.

The minor interests index has been referred to above. Priority as between assignees of certain equitable interests in registered land (for example, life interests, remainders, reversions and executory interests) depends on the order of lodging priority cautions or inhibitions in this index. This does not concern a purchaser of the legal estate.[213] The banker advancing against an equitable interest should search this index in order to discover whether the customer has already mortgaged it. The banker should also register a priority caution in respect of his mortgage. Once the caution is entered in the index, notice thereof is given to the registered proprietor of the land. A mortgagee of an equitable interest is not entitled to notice of any intended disposition of the land, even though he has registered a priority caution. Such a person has a charge not upon the land itself but upon the proceeds of sale in the hands of the previous registered proprietor. Since a life interest is a minor interest under the LRA 1925, it cannot be made subject to a registered charge.

SECOND MORTGAGES AND SUB-MORTGAGES OF REGISTERED LAND

The general rules relating to second mortgages of unregistered land apply also to registered land. The banker should ensure that notice is always given to the first mortgagee and acknowledged. If the first mortgage contains an obligation to make further advances, this obligation will have been recorded on the register. The Land Registration Acts prescribe no compulsory form which a second mortgage must take. The mortgage should be completed and registered in the usual way. When the charge is sent to the Registry it should be accompanied by a copy thereof and by the search certificate. The Registry will issue to the second mortgagee a charge certificate which will contain a reference to the prior charge.

211. Ibid., s. 30(1).
212. Ibid., s. 30(2) and Land Registration and Land Charges Act 1971, s. 1.
213. LRA 1925, s. 102.

A person who has a mortgage of registered land may create either a legal sub-mortgage or an equitable sub-mortgage.[214] However, if the mortgage is equitable, any sub-mortgage which he creates will necessarily be equitable.

The banker should carry out the same procedure as upon a sub-mortgage of unregistered land, except that there are certain requirements arising from the fact that the land is registered. The banker should discover how much is still owing by the mortgagor under the head mortgage; a valuation of the property should be carried out; notice of the sub-mortgage must be given to the mortgagor under the head-mortgage and an acknowledgment should be obtained. If the sub-mortgagor is a company, the sub-mortgage must be registered with the Registrar of Companies.[215]

Legal sub-mortgage

The proprietor of a charge or incumbrance may at any time charge the mortgage debt with the payment of money in the same manner as the proprietor of land can charge the land; such charges are referred to in the Land Registration Rules 1925 as "sub-charges".[216] The proprietor of a sub-charge has, subject to any entry to the contrary on the register, the same powers of disposition in relation to the land as if he had been registered as proprietor of the principal charge.[217] In order to have the sub-charge registered, the charge certificate must be produced at the Registry and a note of the sub-charges entered therein. The sub-mortgagee is then issued with a certificate of the sub-charge.

Equitable sub-mortgage

The proprietor of a registered charge may create a lien on the charge by deposit of the charge certificate.[218] Such lien is equivalent to a lien created in the case of unregistered land by the deposit of the mortgage deed. A banker who takes an equitable sub-mortgage in this way should give notice in duplicate on the appropriate form to the Registrar, who will enter notice of it in the charges register and return the duplicate notice to the bank by way of acknowledgment.

The banker will recall that it is advisable, when taking a deposit of a land certificate, to ask the borrower to execute a form of legal mortgage without proceeding to register it. Similarly when a

214. *See* above for a discussion of these.
215. Companies Act 1948, s. 95(2)(*d*).
216. Land Registration Rules 1925, Rule 163(1).
217. Land Registration Rules 1925, Rule 163(2).
218. LRA 1925, s. 66.

customer mortgagee creates a sub-mortgage by deposit of the charge certificate, it is often advisable to ask him to execute a form of legal sub-mortgage. At any time in the future this instrument can be registered as a sub-charge.

RECTIFICATION OF REGISTER AND COMPENSATION

The register may be rectified by order of the Registrar or the court in certain cases, e.g. (a) where all interested parties consent, (b) where an entry has been obtained by fraud, (c) where the legal estate is registered in a person who would not have been the estate owner had the land been unregistered, and (d) where by reason of error or omission in the register or by reason of an entry made under a mistake, it may be deemed just to rectify the register.[219]

The register will not be rectified so as to affect a proprietor in possession, unless:

(a) the proprietor has caused or substantially contributed to the error or omission by fraud or lack of proper care; or

(b) for any other reason it would be unjust not to rectify; or

(c) to give effect to an overriding interest or order of the court.[220]

Compensation for errors of the Land Registry
Under s. 83 of the LRA 1925, a person may claim compensation if he suffers loss by reason of:

(a) rectification of the register; or

(b) any omission or error in the register where it is not rectified; or

(c) loss of a document lodged at the Registry; or

(d) an error in the official search certificate.

The claimant must suffer loss, and he only suffers loss if his position is worse after rectification than it was before. Thus, no compensation can be paid to a proprietor where the register is rectified to give effect to an overriding interest.[221]

A proprietor who claims in good faith under a forged disposition is deemed to have suffered loss where the register is rectified against him. No compensation is payable if the applicant or someone through whom he claims as a volunteer has caused or has substantially contributed to the loss by fraud or lack of proper care.[222]

---

219. Ibid., s. 82(1).
220. Ibid., s. 82(3) as amended by Administration of Justice Act 1977, s. 24.
221. See Bridges v. Mees [1957] Ch. 475.
222. Land Registration and Land Charges Act 1971, s. 3.

Where the register is rectified, any indemnity will not exceed the value of the estate immediately prior to rectification. Where the register is not rectified, any indemnity will not exceed the value of the estate when the error was made. The amount of indemnity is determined by the court and paid by the State.

CHAPTER SIXTEEN

Stocks and Shares as Security

REGISTERED STOCKS AND SHARES AS SECURITY

The two types of stocks and shares most likely to be offered to a banker as security for a loan are "registered" stocks and shares and "fully negotiable" stocks and shares. Where stocks and shares are registered, the names of the owners are recorded on a register, and there can be no change of legal ownership until the name of the old owner has been removed from the register and the name of the new owner has been registered instead, though in some circumstances the legal owner may hold the title on trust for others. Where stocks and shares are fully negotiable, they are "bearer documents", which means that they are owned by whoever is their bearer at a particular time, subject to certain qualifications which are discussed later in the chapter.

The main types of registered stocks and shares are public body bonds and stocks, and stocks and shares of companies. These will now be discussed in turn.

Public body stock

Public body stock is issued by governments, local authorities, nationalised industries and other public bodies as security for loans made to the public body. The holder of a public body stock is normally entitled to receive a fixed rate of interest and repayment of capital at a fixed date. Some public body stocks are "listed" (or "quoted") on the Stock Exchange and these are better security for a loan made by a banker than stocks which are not listed. This is because listed stocks are readily marketable and it is possible to ascertain their precise value at any given time. When a banker accepts listed stock as security for a loan, he should be careful to lend a sum which is smaller than the value of the stock. In this way, he will be protected if the value of the stock in the market moves downwards. A banker should take great care when lending money on the security of foreign public body stocks. The reason for this is that the banker will only be able to enforce his security according to the law of the foreign country concerned. The registers of ownership for British Government stocks are kept in the Bank of England, though several British Government stocks are also registered on the National Savings Register or the registers of the Trustee Savings Banks. Ownership of Government Stock (Marketable Securities), British Savings Bonds and National Savings Income Bonds is recorded on the National Savings Stock Register. Public body stock may in general be given as security either by a legal mortgage or by an equitable mortgage.[1] National Savings Certificates, Premium Bonds and British Savings Bonds can only be given as security by an equitable mortgage, because, as will be seen later in the chapter, a legal mortgage of registered stocks and shares cannot be created until the name of the mortgagee has been recorded on the register, and the Director of Savings will not give his consent to a change in the National Savings Register in favour of a mortgagee.

Stocks and shares of companies

For most practical purposes, there is no difference between company shares and company stock. Fully paid shares may be converted into stock, and stock converted back into fully paid shares. Thus by definition stock must always be fully paid.[2]

Some types of company stocks and shares are safer security for a loan than others. The safest security for a loan is "debenture stock";[3] the holder of debenture stock has a right to receive interest from the company, usually at a fixed rate, and is a secured creditor of the company. What the security is will depend upon what assets are charged by the debenture trust deed. The next safest security is "unsecured loan stock". The holder of unsecured loan stock is also a creditor of the company and has a right to receive interest from the company. The next safest security for a loan is a "preference share"; the holder of a preference share is not a creditor and does not have a right to any interest or to a dividend on his share, but he does have a right to a dividend on his share before any dividend can be paid to the holders of "ordinary shares". In an insolvency, the holder of a preference share is usually next in line of priority after all the creditors have been paid.

The least safe security (now that "deferred shares" are rarely

---

1. *See* below in this chapter.
2. This form of conversion, effected by resolution of the company and applying to all shares or stock of the class in question, should not be confused with convertible debenture or loan stock, or indeed preference shares issued on terms on which each holder has the right to convert his own stock into shares, or into shares of a different class, at the price specified in the terms of issue of the stock or shares concerned.
3. The term debenture stock is generally used for secured stocks; stocks issued without security are generally known as unsecured loan stocks.

issued) is an ordinary share. Ordinary shares represent the company's venture capital and they carry the greatest risk, but also, if the company prospers, the greatest reward. The holder of an ordinary share does not have a right to a dividend on his share and ranks last in priority in a winding up.

The shares of a private company are poor security for a loan. Under the old classification of public and private companies, the right to transfer the shares of a private company had to be restricted by the articles of association.[4] Although the classification under the Companies Act 1980 is on a different basis,[5] it is likely that the articles of many companies which were previously private companies will not have been altered in this respect. Thus if a banker does agree to accept the shares of a private company as security for a loan, he should always examine the articles of association to see whether, and if so in what way, the right to transfer its shares is restricted. A banker cannot obtain a legal mortgage of the shares of a private company unless the transfer of the shares is registered in accordance with the articles of association; if the banker subsequently wishes to enforce his security, he will not be able to transfer the shares to anyone else except as permitted by the articles. This makes it more difficult for the banker to find a purchaser.

The shares of a public company are better security for a loan if the articles do not restrict the right to transfer the shares, but if the company is not listed on the Stock Exchange the shares may still not be readily marketable. The shares of a public company which is listed are the best sort of shares for the purposes of security.

The registers of both public and private companies are kept either by the company itself or by an outside "registrar", usually a bank or a chartered accountant. The register shows the names and addresses of the stockholders or shareholders and the quantity of the stock or shares held. Holders are given a stock or share certificate and may transfer the stock or shares by executing a stock transfer form and delivering it, with the certificate, to the transferee.[6]

---

4. Companies Act 1948, s. 28(1)(*a*) (now repealed). *See* below in this chapter.
5. *See* "Companies" in Chapter Five.
6. If part only of a registered holding is being transferred, and the registered holder does not wish to hand over his certificate to the transferee because he is retaining some of the shares represented by the certificate, he can, at least in the case of listed shares, send his share certificate to the company's registrar together with an executed transfer in respect of the shares he is transferring and arrange for the registrar to certify the transfer against the register and to return it to him together with a certificate for the balance of his holding. He can then deliver the certified transfer to the transferee.

CREATION OF A LEGAL MORTGAGE OF REGISTERED STOCKS AND SHARES

A banker takes a legal mortgage of registered stocks and shares by obtaining from the registered holder a properly executed form of transfer, together with the stock or share certificate, and then having himself registered as the new registered holder of the registered stocks and shares.[6] Where the registered holder is not the mortgagor himself, but the mortgagor's nominee, the form of transfer must be executed by the mortgagor's nominee, not by the mortgagor.[7] The form of transfer cannot be registered unless the certificate on the back of the form is signed by the transferor or by a solicitor or stockbroker and the transfer is then stamped with a 50p deed stamp.

It is usual for banks to register mortgaged shares in the names of one of the bank's own nominees. To make it easier to identify particular shareholdings some banks, particularly the clearing banks, have a separate nominee company for each area of the country and even, in some instances, for individual branches. A legal mortgage is not created unless and until the registered stocks and shares have been registered in the name of the bank or its nominee.

When taking a legal mortgage of registered stocks and shares, the banker should give the mortgagor a "facility letter" or formal "loan agreement", describing the loan, the terms of repayment and the nature of the security. The banker should also take from the mortgagor a memorandum of deposit, containing details regarding the banker's powers in relation to the stocks and shares.[8] The memorandum of deposit should either list the mortgaged stocks and shares or be expressed to cover all stocks and shares from time to time deposited with the banker. Where the mortgagor, or the banker on his behalf, has the right to sell the mortgaged stocks and shares and invest the proceeds in other forms of property which will themselves be deposited as security, the memorandum of deposit should reflect this.

The memorandum of deposit should state which debts owed to the banker are secured by the mortgage. If the mortgage is given to secure a fluctuating debt, such as an overdraft, the memorandum should state that the mortgage is given as continuing security for the balance on the debtor's accounts with the banker so that the rule in *Clayton*'s case[9] will not have the effect of reducing the debt which is

7. In such cases any memorandum of deposit or other mortgage document should be signed by the beneficial owner.
8. A specimen form of memorandum of deposit is set out in Appendix I.
9. *Devaynes* v. *Noble* (1816) 1 Mer. 572; *see* Chapters Four and Fourteen.

secured.[10] The memorandum should preferably also state that the mortgage is being taken in addition to any other securities given to secure the same debt, not in substitution for them.

The memorandum normally includes provision for the banker to sell the mortgaged stocks and shares if the mortgagor defaults. However, even if there is no express provision in the memorandum, the banker will have an implied right of sale if the mortgagor fails to make repayment by the agreed date or, where no date was agreed, if the mortgagor fails to make repayment after the banker has given him a reasonable period of notice.[11] The notice should state that the banker will enforce his security if the mortgagor fails to make repayment by the end of the period. Where stocks and shares are mortgaged, a month's notice (or perhaps even a fortnight's notice) has been held to be reasonable.[12] Where no date has been fixed for repayment, the mortgagor must be given a reasonable opportunity of repaying. Banker's advances are frequently repayable on demand. In today's volatile market conditions a banker would normally wish to be able to sell immediately after demand has been made for repayment; the specimen memorandum contained in Appendix I provides for this.[13]

As will be seen later in the chapter, a legal mortgagee is liable for any "calls" on partly-paid stocks and shares, so where a legal mortgage of partly-paid stocks and shares is taken by a banker, the memorandum should normally provide for the mortgagor to indemnify the banker in respect of any such calls. For the protection of the banker the memorandum should also perhaps provide that in the event of the mortgagor redeeming his security, the banker will not have to return exactly the same stocks and shares as were originally deposited, but may give the mortgagor shares "of the same class or denomination". In this way the banker would be protected if an English judge followed the decision in a Scottish case[14] where it was held that a mortgagor had a right to the specific stocks and shares which he had deposited with the banker except where the mortgagor had agreed otherwise.[15]

---

10. *See* Clauses 2 and 6 in the form in Appendix I.
11. *Re Morritt, ex parte Official Receiver* (1886) 18 Q.B.D. 222; *Deverges* v. *Sandeman Clark & Co.* [1902] 1 Ch. 579.
12. *Deverges* v. *Sandeman Clark & Co.* [1902] 1 Ch. 579.
13. *See* clause 3.
14. *Crerar* v. *Bank of Scotland* [1922] S.C. 137; (1922) 3 Legal Decisions Affecting Bankers, 248; *Journal of the Institute of Bankers*, Vol. 43, p. 50.
15. It is perhaps difficult to see what would be the basis of a customer's claim in such a case. Although on a pledge of chattels the pledgor is entitled to have the very object he pledged returned to him, it is doubtful whether this principle ought to extend to shares, since one block of shares is just as good as any other of the same class and denomination, and specific return, instead of damages, is not normally ordered unless

A memorandum of deposit may be given under hand or under seal. In either case the memorandum, being a mortgage document, would be exempt from stamp duty.[16]

CREATION OF AN EQUITABLE MORTGAGE OF REGISTERED STOCKS AND SHARES

An equitable mortgage of registered stocks and shares is created when the mortgagor enters into a binding agreement to execute a proper form of transfer in favour of the banker or his nominee, or when a proper form of transfer is executed in favour of the banker or his nominee and the banker or his nominee has not yet been registered as the new registered holder of the mortgaged stocks and shares. In most cases, however, an equitable mortgage is created by the mortgagor depositing his stock or share certificate with the banker by way of security, which, as Cozens-Hardy J pointed out, "seems ... to amount to an equitable mortgage or, in other words, to an agreement to execute a transfer of the shares by way of mortgage."[17]

Deposit of the stock or share certificate will not amount to an equitable mortgage unless it can be shown that the deposit was by way of security. It may be difficult for the banker to show that the deposit of the certificate was by way of security unless the mortgagor also gives the banker a memorandum of deposit or a blank form of transfer (i.e. a transfer signed by the transferor, but with a blank for the name of the transferee), the intention being that the purchaser or mortgagee shall be at liberty later on to fill up the blank and perfect his security by getting himself registered. In most cases the banker will insist that he be given both. A person who has an equitable mortgage by taking a blank transfer and the certificate can sell after reasonable notice.[18] Alternatively he has the mortgagee's usual right to foreclose.[19].

The memorandum of deposit should contain essentially the same terms as the memorandum of deposit which, as we have seen, a banker should obtain when a legal mortgage is created. However, in addition, the memorandum should describe the circumstances in

---

the article is of unique or very special value. Whatever the precise claim, the measure of damages could hardly be other than the value of equivalent shares at the market price on the day of judgment, and these would already have been transferred or tendered to the mortgagor.

16. Finance Act 1970, s. 32 and Sched. 7.
17. *Harrold* v. *Plenty* [1901] 2 Ch. 314 at p. 316.
18. *Stubbs* v. *Slater* [1910] 1 Ch. 632.
19. *Harrold* v. *Plenty* [1901] 2 Ch. 314 at p. 316.

which the banker would be permitted to complete the blank form of transfer in favour of himself or some third party. If the transfer may be under hand, authority to fill up the blank may be oral, and may be implied from the nature of the transaction.[20] Where shares can only be transferred by deed the banker cannot have authority to execute a blank transfer unless the mortgagor has given him a power of attorney which enables him to do so. Whether a transfer may be under hand or must be under seal is governed partly by the articles of association of the company, but by s. 1 of the Stock Transfer Act 1963, shares which are fully paid may be transferred under hand and the transfer need not be executed by the transferee, whatever the articles of association might provide. Shares which are partly paid, however, must still be transferred by deed if the articles so provide. In addition any transfer of shares by a company must be by deed.

A blank transfer, however, is not a deed. A deed must be signed, sealed and delivered.[21] If a person seals and delivers a writing which is left blank in any material part, it is void for uncertainty and is not his deed, and it cannot be made his deed merely by filling up the blanks after execution.[22] It can, of course, be filled in and executed by a duly authorised agent, but such authority can only be conferred by deed.

Where the transfer must be by deed, the banker should insist that, in addition to the blank form of transfer, he is given either a power of attorney or a memorandum of deposit containing a power of attorney. In either case it should be under seal. The banker's power of attorney to complete a blank form of transfer, or to execute a form of transfer, secures an obligation owed to the banker, and so if it is expressed to be irrevocable, it cannot be revoked except with the consent of the banker.[23]

If the mortgagee sells to a purchaser who fills in his own name on a blank transfer, the purchaser can only hold the shares as security for the amount due under the mortgage to the mortgagee.[24] The purchaser cannot get a better title than the vendor mortgagee because the fact that the transfer is in blank puts him on notice of third party rights.

20. *Powell* v. *London and Provincial Bank* [1893] 2 Ch. 555; *France* v. *Clark* (1884) 26 Ch. D. 257.
21. *Powell* v. *London and Provincial Bank* [1893] 2 Ch. 555.
22. *Markham* v. *Gonaston* (1598) Cro. Eliz. 626. *See also Powell* v. *London and Provincial Bank* [1893] 2 Ch. 555 at p. 560: "We all know that both at common law and under these statutes, if you execute a transfer in blank, that instrument with the blanks is not a deed."
23. Powers of Attorney Act 1971, s. 4. *See* Chapter Four. For new provisions *see* the Stock Transfer Act 1982 (not in force at the time of writing).
24. *France* v. *Clark* (1884) 26 Ch. D. 257.

As well as obtaining a memorandum of deposit and a blank form of transfer from the mortgagor, a banker who has an equitable mortgage over British Government stock or company stock or shares can further protect his position by means of a "stop notice".

The Rules of the Supreme Court provide that such a notice may be served by any person claiming to be beneficially entitled to an interest in any government stock, any stock of any company registered under any general Act of Parliament, or any dividend of or interest payable on such stock, who wishes to be notified of any proposed transfer or payment of those securities.[25] He must file in Chancery Chambers or in a district registry an affidavit and a notice addressed to the Bank of England or the company concerned in the prescribed form, and must serve an office copy of the affidavit, and a copy of the notice, sealed with the seal of the Chancery Chambers or district registry, on the Bank or the company.[26]

The effect of the stop notice (which replaces the old writ of distringas, and which is sometimes referred to in the earlier cases as a notice in lieu of distringas) is to prevent any dealing in the securities or the payment of a dividend without the person who issued the stop notice having an opportunity of asserting his claim, since the stop notice requires the Bank of England or the company to give the person who served the stop notice fourteen days' written notice before registering a transfer of any stock or making payment of any dividend or interest on such stock.

Upon receiving such notice, the banker can then proceed to obtain a restraining order or an injunction against the customer, but the banker must act quickly, as he has only fourteen days in which to take action to prevent the distribution or the dealing.

Where the stocks and shares which are mortgaged are company stocks and shares, the banker can also protect his position to a limited extent by sending a letter to the company, informing the company that the stock or share certificate has been deposited with the banker and asking the company whether the company has any lien over the mortgaged stocks and shares or knows of any prior equitable interest in the mortgaged stocks and shares. Although the company secretary is under no obligation to reply to these inquiries, it is still a good idea for the banker to give the company notice of deposit. This is because a company is bound by a notice of deposit even though, under s. 117 of the Companies Act 1948, a company is not bound by notice of a trust because no notice of any trust can be entered on its register.

25. Rules of the Supreme Court, Order 50, Rules 11 and 12.
26. The prescribed form of affidavit and notice is Form No. 80 in Appendix A of the Rules of the Supreme Court.

The principle that a company is bound by a notice of deposit was established by the House of Lords in *Bradford Banking Co. v. Henry Briggs Son & Co.*[27] where the company had by its articles of association a lien upon "every share for all debts due from the holder thereof". One of the shareholders owed money to the company and then gave the bank an equitable mortgage over his shares. The bank then gave notice of deposit to the company. After the notice of deposit was given, the shareholder incurred a further debt to the company. It was held that the notice of deposit was not notice of a trust for this purpose and was binding on the company so that with regard to the debt incurred by the shareholder to the company after the notice of deposit was given, the bank's equitable mortgage over the shares had priority over the company's lien.

Whether a company does or does not have a lien over the shares of the company in any particular circumstance will depend upon the articles of association of the company. Most companies have a lien over partly paid shares, and private companies normally have a lien over all shares, whether fully paid or partly paid.

In the case of listed securities, however, the rules of the Stock Exchange effectively prevent the company claiming any lien on fully paid shares, since an official listing will not be granted for any fully paid shares on which the company may claim a lien.[28] In such cases the only purpose to be gained by serving notice of deposit would be to prevent the customer obtaining a duplicate share certificate by stating that he had lost the original one, and then selling the shares using the duplicate. Such frauds are, however, rare, and it must be doubtful whether it is worth going to the expense of serving such a notice in every case merely to guard against this possibility.

ADVANTAGES OF A LEGAL MORTGAGE OR REGISTERED STOCKS AND SHARES

The main advantages of obtaining a legal mortgage of registered stocks and shares are as follows.

(*a*) A banker who obtains a legal mortgage over registered stocks and shares is not affected by any prior equitable interest in the same stocks and shares, including any prior equitable mortgage, unless he had notice of that interest by the date when he or his nominee was registered as the new registered holder. A banker who obtains an equitable mortgage is affected by any prior equitable interest, whether he had notice of it or not, by virtue of the rule that "where

27. (1886) L.R. 12 A.C. 29.
28. Rule 159(2) and Appendix 34, Schedule VII, Part A.

the equities are equal, the earlier in time prevails". The importance of obtaining a legal rather than an equitable mortgage may be illustrated by the cases of *Powell* v. *London and Provincial Bank*,[29] and *Coleman* v. *London County and Westminster Bank*.[30]

In *Powell*'s case, the bank took a deposit of the stock certificate, together with a blank form of transfer, so that an equitable mortgage was created in favour of the bank. The bank did not also obtain from the mortgagor a power of attorney which, as we have seen, would have enabled the bank to convert its equitable mortgage into a legal mortgage, but it subsequently filled in its own name and had itself registered. Later it emerged that the morgagor was in fact a trustee and was not entitled under the terms of his trust to mortgage the stock. It was held that the equitable interests of the beneficiaries of the trust had priority over the equitable interest of the bank because the interests of the beneficiaries were created before the equitable mortgage was created. The beneficiaries were therefore entitled to the stock which had been mortgaged by the trustee, and the bank lost the benefit of its mortgage. If, on the other hand, the bank had been authorised by power of attorney to execute the transfer on behalf of the morgagor, it would have obtained a legal mortgage of the stock, and so would have prevailed over the interests of the beneficiaries because at the time the legal mortgage would have been created, the bank would not have had notice of the existence of the trust or of the prior equitable interests of the beneficiaries.

In *Coleman*'s case, Annie Coleman executed a transfer of certain debenture stock to Edward Coleman. The transfer was never registered, so Annie Coleman remained the registered holder of the stock which she held on constructive trust for Edward Coleman, who therefore had an equitable interest in the stock. Some time later Annie Coleman regained possession of the stock certificate which she deposited with the bank as security for a loan. This meant that the bank also had an equitable interest in the stock, as it had an equitable mortgage. Some years later the bank learned of the original transfer to Edward Coleman and in order to defeat Edward Coleman's prior equitable interest, it obtained a legal mortgage of the stock. After Edward Coleman died, his personal representatives sued the bank to recover the stock. It was held that the bank's legal mortgage did not have priority over Edward Coleman's prior equitable interest because at the time that the legal mortgage was created, the bank had notice of Edward Coleman's interest. If, on the other hand, the bank had obtained a legal mortgage of the

29. [1893] 2 Ch. 555.
30. [1916] 2 Ch. 353.

stock from the outset, the legal mortgage would have had priority over Edward Coleman's interest because at that time the bank did not have notice that the prior interest existed. The bank would therefore have been entitled to retain the mortgaged stock.

The longer the banker refrains from taking a legal mortgage, the longer the possibility remains open that he will come to have notice of earlier equitable interests which will rank ahead of him but which would have been postponed to him if he had obtained a legal mortgage, without notice of them, right at the outset.

(b) If the banker does not obtain a legal mortgage of registered stocks and shares, the mortgagor remains the registered holder and can therefore dispose of the mortgaged stocks and shares or exercise any other right of a registered shareholder, to the prejudice of the banker. If the mortgagor sells or mortgages the mortgaged stocks and shares, the transaction will inevitably be fraudulent. The mortgagor would have either to give the purchaser or mortgagee a false explanation of his inability to produce the share certificate or to obtain a new certificate by falsely representing that he had lost his original certificate.[31]

It would, however, be possible for a mortgagor to engage in certain other transactions to the prejudice of the banker without behaving fraudulently. For example, one instance is known where a mortgagor gave an equitable mortgage to a banker over shares representing 100 per cent of the share capital of a small private company. Due to a misunderstanding with the banker the mortgagor then increased the share capital from £100 to £1,000. As a result the banker was left with a mortgage over shares which now represented only 10 per cent of the share capital instead of the original 100 per cent.

(c) If the banker obtains a legal mortgage of registered stocks and shares, any documents relating to such matters as rights issues, bonus issues and shareholders' meetings will be sent to the banker as registered holder of the mortgaged stocks and shares. Access to these documents represents a positive advantage to the banker, in particular because the mortgagor will not be able to deal in any rights issue or bonus issue without the banker's knowledge. Any rights issue or bonus issue will reduce the value of shares already issued, so that if the mortgagor was able to take up the issue without the banker's knowledge or, in the case of a rights issue, was able to sell the rights, he could reduce the value of the security which he gave to the banker without the banker's knowledge and consent. The banker normally insists, whether his mortgage is legal or

---

31. In the case of Savings Bonds, National Savings Certificates or Premium Bonds the mortgagee can obtain duplicate bonds or certificates and encash them without the bank's knowledge.

equitable, that there should be a clause in the memorandum of deposit stipulating that any shares issued to the mortgagor by virtue of a rights issue or bonus issue should be subject to the mortgage. If the shares are registered in the name of the mortgagor, he cannot prevent the mortgagor from taking up the rights in his own name, or selling them, or keeping any bonus shares, and can only take steps to recover the shares or the rights or their proceeds afterwards. In any event he will need to be particularly vigilant to check when such issues are made, and will then have to make sure he secures the benefit of them. If the shares are registered in his own name, the documents will automatically come to him.

(d) If the banker obtains a legal mortgage of registered stocks and shares, he will be able to transfer the shares as soon as he has power to do so under the terms laid down in the memorandum of deposit. If, on the other hand, the banker only obtains an equitable mortgage, he will not be able to transfer the shares without an order of the court unless he has been given a blank form of transfer by the mortgagor and, where necessary, a power of attorney.

(e) If the banker obtains a legal mortgage of registered stocks and shares, he will have priority over any lien which the company has over the same stocks and shares. If, on the other hand, the banker only obtains an equitable mortgage, he will, as we have seen, have priority over the company's lien only in respect of debts incurred by the shareholder after the banker gave notice of deposit to the company.

DISADVANTAGES OF A LEGAL MORTGAGE OF REGISTERED STOCKS AND SHARES

Although the advantages of a legal mortgage far outweigh the disadvantages, the banker should know what the disadvantages are.

(a) Where registered shares are partly-paid, the registered holder is liable for any "calls" by the company for further payments on the shares. He remains liable if the company is wound up within twelve months after the date on which he ceases to be the registered holder.[32] A banker who takes a legal mortgage should therefore insist on a clause in the memorandum of deposit stipulating that the mortgagor will indemnify him the event that he has to pay any future calls. These points do not apply to registered stock because, by definition, all stock is fully paid.

(b) A banker who takes a legal mortgage by a transfer which is forged is liable to indemnify the company or public body for any

32. Companies Act 1948, s. 212(1).

resulting loss even if he acted in good faith. This principle was established in *Sheffield Corporation* v. *Barclay*[33] where Sheffield Corporation stock was mortgaged to a bank by a transfer from trustees on which the signature of one of the trustees was forged. The bank later sold the stock to a third party who was registered as the holder, and at this stage the forgery was discovered. The innocent trustee successfully brought an action against Sheffield Corporation, which was compelled to buy an equivalent amount of stock and register it in his name. The corporation claimed an indemnity from the bank and succeeded on the grounds that the bank, by sending in the forged transfer for registration, had impliedly warranted that it was genuine.

The only sure way of guarding against this risk would seem to be to have transfers executed in the banker's own presence, and if any of several transferors were unable to be present, the transfer should be sent to him for signature by the banker himself, and not left to be dealt with by the other transferor. This is perhaps a counsel of perfection, and might be dispensed with in suitable cases.

(*c*) A banker who takes a legal mortgage is entitled, as the holder of the shares or stock, to receive any interest or any dividends paid by the company or public body. However, as against the mortgagor he is not entitled to keep any interest payments or dividends unless and until the mortgagor defaults. Until that time he must pay them over to the mortgagor. This will involve the banker in a certain amount of administrative expense unless he takes the simple precaution of giving the company a mandate to make the payments directly to the mortgagor.

(*d*) The articles of association of a company frequently provide that a director of the company must at all times be the registered holder of a specified minimum number of shares in the company if he is to remain qualified to be a director. The shares which make up this specified minimum shareholding are known as "director's qualification shares". If a director of a company offers a banker directors' qualification shares as security for a loan and if it is important to the banker that the director should remain a director, the banker cannot obtain a legal mortgage of the shares. This is because the director would no longer be qualified to remain a director if the bank were to be registered as the holder of the director's shares. One possible solution to the problem is for the director to procure a change in the articles of association with regard to director's qualification shares. If this cannot be achieved, the banker might be well advised to ask the director to provide alternative security.

33. [1905] A.C. 392.

STOCKS AND SHARES OF THE LENDING BANK AS SECURITY

A bank which is a company (as nearly all banks are) is sometimes offered stocks and shares in itself as security for a loan. A bank may accept stocks and shares in itself as security provided that it is permitted to do so by its articles of association and the circumstances are not such as to involve a breach of s. 42 of the Companies Act 1981,[34] and, if it is a public company, provided it is permitted under s. 38 of the Companies Act 1980.[35]

SHARES IN PRIVATE COMPANIES

Although this chapter has been concerned mostly with securities listed on the Stock Exchange, the principles governing the methods of taking security and the advantages and disadvantages of legal and equitable charges apply also to shares in private companies. There are, however, certain inherent defects in any form of security over shares in a private company.

As mentioned above the articles of association of a private company usually restrict the right to transfer its shares in some way.[36] There is no prescribed method and frequently the articles provide that the directors may in their discretion refuse to register a transfer. Sometimes the articles contain detailed pre-emption provisions under which shares may not be transferred, except to another member, unless they are first offered to all the members. This precludes registration of a bank mortgagee, or its nominee, as holder of any such shares unless either the pre-emption procedure is followed or all the registered shareholders agree. If the directors agree to register a bank as the holder of shares in a case where the pre-emption procedure has not been followed, any shareholder may apply to the Court for the register to be rectified by restoring the name of the transferor/mortgagor.[37]

Clearly where the articles contain pre-emption provisions, the bank cannot acquire a good legal mortgage and must rest content with an equitable mortgage, unless the procedure is followed.

---

34. *See* Chapter Six. Section 42 of the Companies Act 1981 prohibits a company from giving any assistance in connection with the purchase of its shares; the exceptions include cases where money is lent in the ordinary course of business, and employee share schemes.
35. One of the permitted cases is where the transaction is in the ordinary course of business of a money-lending company.
36. Companies Act 1948, s. 28, for companies which were private under the 1948 classification. *See* earlier in this chapter.
37. *Hunter* v. *Hunter* [1936] A.C. 222.

Even if there are no pre-emption provisions, there is a risk that the directors may decline to register a bank mortgagee as holder of the shares. The only effective method of taking security in such cases may be to serve a stop notice.[38]

In either case, there may be difficulties if and when the bank wishes to realise its security. If there are pre-emption provisions, these will have to be followed when the bank comes to sell. These sometimes provide for the price to be the value as certified by the company's auditors. Auditors tend to be very conservative in their estimate of the value and their figure tends to be significantly lower than a vendor or mortgagee would expect. Even if there are no such provisions, a purchaser cannot be certain the directors will agree to register him, and this will restrict the marketability of the shares.

In practice, in the case of any private company, a bank mortgagee may have to reckon with the fact that for all practical purposes the only likely purchasers for the shares will be the other members, and knowledge of this will clearly affect the price which such other members are likely to be willing to offer for the shares.

For all these reasons, shares in a private company are an unattractive form of security, and not to be recommended unless there is no alternative.

UNITS OF A UNIT TRUST AS SECURITY

Many investors today purchase "units" in a unit trust as an alternative to investing directly in stocks and shares, property, commodities and so on. The unit trust is managed by the "managers" of the trust whose function is to invest the assets of the trust in accordance with the terms of the trust deed for the benefit of the "unitholders" who are the beneficiaries of the trust. The trust deed normally provides for unitholders to be given certificates in the form specified in the deed and for the trustees of the unit trust to maintain a register of unitholders; it normally stipulates that the trustees are not bound to have regard to the interest of any person other than the registered unitholder in any unit of the trust. Many trust deeds permit unitholders to transfer their units by gift, sale or mortgage.

Since the unitholders have only an equitable interest under the trust, it is impossible to take a legal mortgage and any mortgage will of necessity be equitable.[39] The best protection is for the banker to

38. *See* earlier in this chapter.
39. In *Re Pain, Gustavson* v. *Haviland* [1919] 1Ch. 38 it was held that it was possible to have a legal assignment by way of mortgage of an equitable interest in a trust fund, but this decision has been criticised.

take a transfer of the units and have himself, or his nominee company, registered as holder of the units. Then, under the terms of the trust deed, he will be recognised as holder of the units by the trustee. This does not, however, prevent any person with a prior equitable title claiming through the transferor, since the banker will not have the protection conferred on a bona fide purchaser of the legal estate without notice. To minimise the risk of this, the banker should, before making his advance, inquire of the trustees whether the trustees have received notice of any other equitable interests, and should not advance until he receives a reply confirming that the trustees have not. He should then give the trustees notice immediately after his advance and have the notice receipted by the trustees.

The reason for this is that the priority of competing assignments (and a mortgage of such an interest is effected by an assignment) of equitable interests is, under the rule in *Dearle* v. *Hall*,[40] governed by the order in which notice of the assignments is received by the trustee. The banker should therefore protect himself by obtaining confirmation before taking his mortgage over a unit in a unit trust that the trustee has not received notice of any other dealings in the unit, and by giving notice of his dealing immediately after taking the mortgage. Even this, however, would not help him if the mortgage was being given by a company which had created a floating charge which covered the unit and the charge was registered at the Companies Registry under s. 95 of the Companies Act 1948.[41] Such registration would constitute constructive notice of the charge to all persons and if he makes the loan with knowledge of a prior assignment he cannot gain priority by being the first to give notice to the trustees.[42] If, however, he advances money without knowledge of a prior assignment of the unit and subsequently acquires knowledge of such an assignment, such knowledge will not prevent him from claiming priority if he is first to give notice to the trustees.[43]

The alternative to registration is for the holder to deposit his unit certificates, with or without a blank transfer, with the banker, together with a memorandum of deposit. The disadvantage of this is that the unit-holder is left in a position to obtain a new certificate and transfer and dispose of his units to a third party. The banker may prevent this by making the same inquiries of, and giving the same notice to, the trustee as set out above.

40. (1828) 3 Russ. 1. *See* under "Assignment of interests under a trust" in Chapter Eighteen.
41. *See* Chapter Six.
42. *Re Holmes* (1885) 29 Ch. D. 786; *Spencer* v. *Clarke* (1878) 9 Ch. D. 137.
43. *Mutual Life Assurance Society* v. *Langley* (1886) 32 Ch. D. 460.

FULLY NEGOTIABLE STOCKS AND SHARES AS SECURITY

Fully negotiable securities taken in good faith and for value may be retained by the purchaser (including a mortgagee) against the true owner even though the latter may be a beneficiary under a trust and the trustee has fraudulently transferred them to the purchaser, or the securities are stolen. They are in this respect the best security a banker can get. If he takes them bona fide and for value and without notice of any defect in title, he can still hold them against the true owner, as in the case of a bank note, or a bill of exchange or cheque drawn payable to bearer, without any risk of his title being upset by proof of an earlier theft or forged indorsement or that they were obtained from the issuer by fraud. Fully negotiable securities can also be realised very easily upon the customer's default.

Fully negotiable securities are charged by way of pledge rather than mortgage.[44] Although the mere deposit of a fully negotiable security gives the banker a complete title, it is always desirable to take a memorandum of deposit showing the purpose of the deposit.[45] The memorandum will contain essentially the same terms as one for registered stocks and shares, including a statement that the securities are deposited as a continuing security and that the rule in *Clayton's* case[46] is excluded.

Requirements for negotiability

In order to be fully negotiable a security must satisfy the following requirements.

(*a*) It must be in a form which renders it capable of being sued on by the holder *pro tempore* in his own name without reference to any other document.

(*b*) It must show on the face of it that it is, in its existing condition, transferable by delivery and must be recognised, either by statute or by the law merchant, as being so transferable and as conferring, upon a person who takes it bona fide and for value, absolute title to it and a right of action on it. It must, like cash, be transferable by delivery.

Failure to comply with either of these requirements prevents the instrument being a negotiable instrument at all.[47]

---

44. *See* Chapter Thirteen.
45. *See* the form contained in Appendix I.
46. *Devaynes* v. *Noble* (1816) 1 Mer. 572; *see* Chapters Four and Fourteen.
47. *Crouch* v. *Credit Foncier of England* (1873) L.R. 8 Q.B. at p. 381.

Bearer bonds and Treasury bills are examples of negotiable securities. Because of exchange control legislation bearer bonds have been virtually eliminated in the case of British Government securities and securities of English corporations, except for letters of allotment and certificates for newly issued shares which are commonly renounceable for a limited period and are sometimes renounced in blank and so become bearer documents for such period. With the abolition of exchange control in the United Kingdom in October 1979, bearer bonds may now come back into use, though they will still have stamp duty disadvantages.[48] They are in any event relatively common outside the United Kingdom.

Bearer bonds are always issued with interest coupons attached. As and when they mature, these coupons are presented to the issuer or his paying agent who retains them and pays the interest to the person presenting them. Bearer bonds must have the coupons attached to them, for deposit of the bonds without the coupons is not a good delivery of the stock, nor should the coupons be deposited without the related bonds.

The fact that a mercantile custom which treats a particular class of instrument as negotiable is of recent origin is no bar to negotiability. What is important is the prevailing mercantile custom at the time, and commercial needs and developments in mercantile custom have over the years brought an increase in the number of different negotiable instruments recognised by the English courts.

Foreign government bonds and foreign corporation bonds may be negotiable[49] provided they are negotiable according to the law of the country of issue and are negotiable by custom in this country. The fact that a foreign instrument is negotiable in its country of issue is not of itself sufficient for it to be negotiable here.[50]

Pledges of bearer securities by agents and others not entitled to pledge them

If a banker taking fully negotiable instruments as security from a customer who is not entitled to pledge them is to acquire a good title to them he must take them in good faith and for value, and without notice of any defect in the pledgor's title.

Whether a banker takes securities in good faith is a question of fact depending on the circumstances of the individual case. Mere negligence in taking the negotiable security will not deprive the banker of his rights, but negligence or carelessness, when considered

---

48. Stamp Act 1891, Sched. 1: the duty payable on the issue of a bearer instrument is three times the transfer duty.
49. *London Joint Stock Bank* v. *Simmons* [1892] A.C. 201.
50. *Picker* v. *London and County Banking Co.* (1887) 18 Q.B.D. 515.

in connection with the surrounding circumstances, may be evidence of bad faith.

A banker takes a security for value if he expressly or impliedly agrees to do or not to do something which will be sufficient to induce the customer to deposit the security. For example, a banker takes a security for value if he forbears to sue for a debt already incurred.[51]

It was once thought that if a banker took negotiable instruments by way of pledge from an agent, such as a stockbroker, he might be affected by constructive notice of a defect in the pledgor's title or of a lack of authority to pledge them. The House of Lords in *Sheffield* v. *London Joint Stock Bank*[52] held that if negotiable securities were tendered as cover by a person who, from the nature of his business, was likely to have securities of other persons in his hands, it was the duty of the bank to inquire into the nature and extent of his authority to deal with the securities, and that if no such inquiry was made, the banker might be held to have notice of the defect or the lack of authority.

That case was, however, decided purely on its particular facts, and was distinguished by the House of Lords in *London Joint Stock Bank* v. *Simmons*[53] on the ground that in *Sheffield* the bank had notice or knowledge of the limited title of the pledgor, or rather knew or had notice that the pledgor was himself a pledgee for a limited amount and knew or had reason to believe he was exceeding his authority. In the *Simmons* case it was expressly stated that there was nothing in the position of broker and customer to make reasonable the inference that the broker was exceeding his authority, or even to raise a doubt about the subject. It is perhaps worth noting that in those days brokers were, in the words of Lord Watson, "in the ordinary course of business, employed to sell, to buy, and to raise money upon as well as to keep in custody the securities of their customers" and that a banker was then "entitled to assume, in the absence of aught to indicate to the contrary, that whether the bonds belonged to [the broker], or to a customer, he had full authority to deal with them." The mere fact that the pledgor was assumed to be an agent for the owner does not of itself put the bank on inquiry as to his title to the property.

On the question of notice, Lord Herschell stated that although there is no doctrine of constructive notice in the law of negotiable instruments, the facts of which a person has actual notice are relevant in considering whether he takes in good faith. The law does not

51. *Glegg* v. *Bromley* [1912] 3 K.B. 474.
52. (1888) 13 App. Cas. 333.
53. [1892] A.C. 201.

lay any obligation on him of inquiring into the title of the person whom he finds in possession of them, provided there is nothing to arouse suspicion. If, however, there is any cause for suspicion in a particular case, "the person taking the instrument is not acting in good faith if he shuts his eyes to the facts presented to him and puts the suspicions aside without further inquiry."

Negotiability by estoppel

Instruments which by their nature are not strictly negotiable may become so in particular cases because the issuer or holder is estopped from denying their negotiability after they have been transferred without his authority. Title acquired by estoppel is sometimes called "negotiability by estoppel", but this term is misleading. An instrument not recognised by law as negotiable cannot acquire the characteristics of negotiability; it is rather a case of a person in a particular transaction becoming estopped by his conduct from denying that a third party has acquired title as if the instrument were negotiable.

The principle of these cases is that an instrument which is not recognised by law as having the attributes of a negotiable instrument nevertheless indicates on the face of it that it is a bearer document. If a person allows such a document out of his possession so that it comes into the hands of an innocent third party who takes it bona fide and for value (usually through a broker or agent acting fraudulenty and in breach of his principal's instructions) the first person is precluded from denying that the innocent third party acquires as good a title as he would have acquired if the instrument had been a negotiable instrument, and so in effect becomes bound to treat the instrument as a negotiable instrument in that transaction.

There are two conditions which must be satisfied for such representation to be effective or to justify a person in acting on it so as to acquire title by estoppel. First, the instrument must be complete, so that no further formalities are required on the face of it to entitle the taker to full right and title. In *Colonial Bank* v. *Cady & Williams*,[54] executors of a deceased registered holder signed the form of transfer indorsed on the share certificate and sent it to their stockbroker for him to arrange for them to be registered, but he procured a loan for himself on the security of the shares. In this case the document was not "in order" and complete on the face of it; the document with the signature of the registered holder's executors was not accepted in commercial circles as being a sufficient voucher of title unless accompanied by an extract of

54. (1890) 15 App. Cas. 267.

probate and an attestation of the genuineness of the executors' signature.

Secondly, the possession of the agent must, in conjunction with the nature and condition of the instrument, be consistent only with the intention on the part of the principal that the agent shall have power to transfer it by way of sale or pledge. It is not sufficient if the agent's possession is compatible with either authority to transfer or some other purpose. In *Cady*'s case, even though delivery of the instrument signed by the registered holder himself would have passed a good title to the bank, signature by his executors was consistent with either an intention to dispose of the shares or to hold them as part of the estate, and so there was no representation that the broker had authority to sell or pledge.

CHAPTER SEVENTEEN

Company Debentures as Security

DEBENTURES

The precise meaning of the term "debenture" is uncertain. It has been defined as meaning any document issued by a company which creates or acknowledges a debt owed by the company.[1] Some have found the definition too wide. It is certainly not necessary for a debenture to constitute a charge over any assets of the company.[2] In practice, however, the term is normally only used to describe a document which does constitute a charge over some or all of the assets of the company.

Where a single debenture is to be issued, as when a banker lends money to a company on the security of a debenture, the charge is normally created by the company in favour of the debentureholder himself. Where, on the other hand, a number of debentures are to be issued, as when the public lends money to a company on the security of an issue of debenture stock, the charge is normally created by the company in favour of trustees who have a duty to hold and possibly enforce the security for the benefit of the debentureholders in accordance with the terms of the trust deed.

A banker may be offered company debentures as security for a loan in two different circumstances. He may be offered a newly issued debenture if he lends money to a company, or the company may already have raised money by the issue of debenture stock and he may be offered debenture stock as security for a loan to a debenture-holder. This chapter is concerned with the position as between the company and its debentureholder, whether he be the banker or the investing public. The subject of debenture stocks as security for loans to investors is dealt with in Chapter Sixteen.

Before lending money to the company the banker should examine the memorandum and the articles of association of the company in order to make sure that the company and its directors have power to

---

1. Per Chitty J in *Levy* v. *Abercorrie Slate and Slab Co.* (1887) 37 Ch. D. 260 at 264.
2. Companies Act 1948, s. 455(1).

borrow the money which is to be secured by the debenture and to charge the assets which are to be charged by the debenture. He should also check whether the charge which is being offered is a "fixed charge" or a "floating charge", and whether the assets to be charged by the debenture are subject to any prior charge.

These points are discussed in the next three sections of this chapter.

FIXED AND FLOATING CHARGES

A fixed (or "specific") charge is a charge given by a company over specified assets. Once a fixed charge has been given, the company cannot dispose of the specified assets covered by the charge except subject to the charge. The rights and duties of the company and the chargee are the normal rights and duties of mortgagor and morgagee.[3] Like most other mortgages a fixed charge may be either legal or equitable, depending on the nature of the asset which is charged and the manner in which the charge is created.

The best general description of a floating charge is contained in certain observations of Lord MacNaghten in *Illingworth* v. *Houldsworth*.[4]

I should have thought there was not much difficulty in defining what a floating charge is in contrast to what is called a specific charge. A specific charge, I think, is one that without more fastens on ascertained and definite property or property capable of being ascertained and defined; a floating charge, on the other hand, is ambulatory and shifting in its nature, hovering over and so to speak floating with the property which it is intended to affect until some event occurs or some act is done which causes it to settle and fasten on the subject of the charge within its reach and grasp.

If, for example, a floating charge is given over the stock-in-trade of the company, the company can continue to dispose of its stock-in-trade as if the charge did not exist, but as soon as the charge crystallises, the charge will fix upon whichever specific assets comprise the company's stock-in-trade at the moment of crystallisation. A floating charge will crystallise not on mere default alone, whether such default be a failure to pay some moneys due under the debenture or some other default, but when the debentureholder appoints a receiver or applies to the court to do so,[5] or when the company ceases business or winding up commences.[6]

A number of attempts have been made by the courts to describe

---

3. *See* Chapters Twelve and Fifteen.
4. [1904] A.C. 355.
5. *Re Griffin Hotel Co.* [1941] Ch. 129.
6. *Edward Nelson, Co.* v. *Faber & Co.* [1903] 2 K.B. 367 at p. 376.

a floating charge. The best description is probably that given by Romer LJ in *Re Yorkshire Woolcombers Association.*[7]

I certainly do not intend to give an exact definition of the term "floating charge" nor am I prepared to say that there will not be a floating charge within the meaning of the Act which does not contain all of the three characteristics that I am about to mention, but I certainly think that if a charge has the three characteristics that I am about to mention, it is a floating charge: one, if it is a charge on a class of assets of the company both present and future; two, if that class is one which, in the ordinary course of the business of the company, would be changing from time to time; and three, if you find that by the charge it is contemplated that, until some future step is taken by or on behalf of those interested in the charge, the company may carry on its business in the ordinary way as far as concerns the particular class of assets I am dealing with.

It was established in *Re Panama, New Zealand, etc. Co*[8], the first case in which the validity of a floating charge was recognised, that a floating charge may be created over any or all of the assets of a company, whether fixed or current. In that case, the charge which was held to be a floating charge over all the assets of the company was a charge on the "undertaking" of the company. However, a floating charge may also be created over all the assets of a company by expressions such as "all the property of the company, both present and future" or "all the property now belonging to or hereafter acquired by the company".

From the point of view of the company the advantage of a floating charge is that the company can continue to deal freely with assets subject to it. It formerly had the disadvantage that it tended to suggest in some cases that the company was in financial difficulties, but this is less so today as bankers are increasingly taking some sort of security as a matter of course and frequently a floating charge is the only form available. Even so, other prospective lenders do not always view favourably the fact that a company has given a floating charge.

From the point of view of the chargee, however, since, as will be seen below, floating charges suffer from certain disadvantages which do not apply to fixed charges, it is the practice of many banks, even when taking floating charges, to take fixed charges over as many assets of the company as possible so as to minimise the effect of those disadvantages. For example, land, whether owned at the date of the charge or acquired thereafter, stocks and shares, book debts, goodwill and uncalled capital are frequently expressed to be charged

7. [1903] 2 Ch. 284.
8. (1870) L.R. 5 Ch. 318.

by way of fixed charge. Inevitably the charge over some of these assets will take effect as an equitable charge only, and a fixed charge on book debts, as will be seen below, is itself subject to certain reservations, but the attempt may overcome some of the inherent disadvantages of floating charges.

DISADVANTAGES OF A FLOATING CHARGE

From the point of view of the chargee the main disadvantages of a floating charge are as follows.

Floating charge void owing to liquidation within twelve months

Unless a floating chargee is able to show that the company was solvent immediately after the creation of the floating charge, he runs the risk that his security will prove to be void unless twelve months have elapsed since the creation of the floating charge. The reason for this is that by virtue of s. 322 of the Companies Act 1948, if the company were to go into liquidation within twelve months after the creation of the floating charge and was not solvent immediately after the charge was created, the charge would be void except to the extent that any money had been advanced by the chargee to the company for the benefit of the company and in consideration of the charge. Any such advances would be secured by the charge, together with interest on the advances at the highly disadvantageous rate of 5 per cent per annum, or such other rate as may be prescribed from time to time by the Treasury.[9]

As far as banks are concerned, if the floating charge is given to secure a running account, the disadvantage of this rule may be wholly negated by the rule in *Clayton*'s case.[10] This provides that where there is a running account, each debit to an overdrawn account (which includes each cheque which is paid) is a fresh advance and each payment into the account will go to repay the earlier advances before the latter advances,[11] so that there may come a time when the whole of the debit balance then outstanding is represented by advances made after the creation of the charge.

An advance would not normally be considered to be for the benefit of the company if it was made to enable the company to pay off one of its creditors in preference to the general run of creditors.[12] Similarly, an advance would not normally be considered to be for

9. As yet no such other rate has been prescribed.
10. *Devaynes* v. *Noble* (1816) 1 Mer. 572; *see also* Chapters Four and Fourteen.
11. *Re Yeovil Glove Co.* [1965] Ch. 148.
12. *Re Destone Fabrics* [1941] Ch. 319.

the benefit of the company if it was made to enable the company to pay off an unsecured debt which it already owed the lender, which the lender had previously been content to allow to remain unsecured.

Under the statutory wording, the advance must have been made "at the time of or subsequently to the creation of, and in consideration for, the charge". However, an advance might be allowed to come within the exception if the advance was made as part of the consideration for the security and in anticipation of its creation and in reliance on a promise to create it, provided that the charge was executed within a few days after the advance was made and the chargee was in no way responsible for any delay in executing the charge.[13]

Where a charge is taken to secure a guarantee, or other liabilities which do not arise directly from new loans to the company, such as liabilities in respect of performance guarantees or under acceptance credit facilities, where the banker accepts bills of exchange drawn on it by a customer, discounts them in the market and remits the proceeds to the customer, cash will not have been paid to the company by the chargee, and so the exception for "cash paid to the company" can never apply; in such cases the chargee will have to wait twelve months until he can be sure that the charge will not be avoided under this section.

If any question arises as to whether a company was solvent at the time of the charge the onus of proof is on the person to whom the charge was given.

Value of floating charge reduced

A second important disadvantage of a floating charge is that when the charge becomes fixed, the chargee may discover that the value of the charge is substantially lower than he had anticipated. This may happen for a number of reasons. Suppose, for example, that the company paid a number of debts out of its bank account or the proceeds of sale of the assets secured by a floating charge while the charge was still floating. The value of the assets left in the charge would obviously be reduced by the amount of those payments (or, if payment was made out of an overdrawn account, the debt secured on the same assets would have increased). Again, suppose that the company owns assets which are situated in a country where the law does not recognise the concept of a floating charge. Unless the chargee has taken a charge over the foreign assets which the law of the foreign country does recognise, he will, as against the

---

13. *Re Stanton (F. & E.)* [1929] 1 Ch. 180.

creditors of the company in that country, have no security with regard to those assets and the value of the floating charge to the chargee will be reduced accordingly.

The value of a floating charge will also be reduced if the company owes any "preferential debts" at the time that a receiver is appointed or the debentureholder takes possession of the assets. Preferential debts are debts which must be paid before a floating chargee can benefit from his security. They include any one year's assessment of corporation tax; any wages or salary owing to any clerk, servant, workman or labourer of the company in respect of the four months preceding the relevant date up to a maximum sum; any rates or value added tax owing in respect of the twelve months preceding the relevant date.[14]

The value of a floating charge will also be reduced if, before the charge crystallises, any of the assets which were subject to the floating charge have been seized and sold by the sheriff in execution of a judgment of the court and the proceeds paid by the sheriff to the judgment creditor,[15] or have been seized by the company's landlord as "distress" for unpaid rent.[16] Where, however, a garnishee order[17] has not yet become absolute before the charge crystallises, the chargee is entitled to the assets in priority to the judgment creditor.[18]

The value of a floating charge will also be reduced if it turns out that some of the assets which the chargee might have thought were subject to the charge were not in fact subject to the charge because the company never owned them. This might happen, for example, if any of the company's assets was held under a hire purchase agreement. In such cases the assets are owned by the hire purchase owner, and the company's interest in the assets is subject to his rights. Thus when the floating charge crystallises, the chargee would have no better rights than the company in respect of these assets, unless he paid off the owner.[19]

Furthermore, it might happen that there was a "Romalpa" clause in the company's purchase contracts, i.e. a clause similar to the one considered by the court in the recent case of *Aluminium Industrie Vaassen N.V.* v. *Romalpa Aluminium*.[20]

In the *Romalpa* case, there was a clause in a supplier's contract

14. Companies Act 1948, s. 94. The relevant date is the date of the appointment of the receiver or the taking of possession: s. 94(2). For details of what debts are preferential, *see* s. 319, and Chapter Twenty-Nine.
15. *Taunton* v. *Sheriff of Warwickshire* [1895] 2 Ch. 319.
16. *Re Roundwood Colliery Co., Lee* v. *Roundwood Colliery Co.* [1897] 1 Ch. 373.
17. *See* Chapter Four.
18. *Evans* v. *Rival Granite Quarries* [1910] 2 K.B. 979.
19. *Re Morrison, Jones & Taylor* [1914] 1 Ch. 50.
20. [1976] 2 All E.R. 552.

with the company which provided that all goods supplied to the company by the supplier were to remain the property of the supplier and would be held by the company as trustee for the supplier, and were to be stored and marked separately for so long as the company was in any way indebted to the supplier. The clause went on to provide that, although the company could sell such goods, the benefit of the contract of sale and the proceeds of sale were to be held on trust for the supplier, and if the goods had been mixed with other goods or made up by the company into manufactured goods, the title to the mixed or manufactured goods was to remain with the supplier. Where, as in the *Romalpa* case, such a clause is upheld, the value of a floating charge may be materially reduced since assets which do not belong to a company, but are merely held by the company as a trustee, clearly cannot be comprised in the floating charge.

Such clauses will not, however, always be upheld. Much will depend upon the wording of the clause and the circumstances of the case. It was decided, for example, in the later case of *Re Bond Worth*[21] that a clause which spoke of "equitable and beneficial ownership remaining with [the supplier] until full payment has been received" did not constitute the company a trustee for its supplier, but merely created a floating charge in favour of the supplier which was in the event void because it had not been registered under s. 95 of the Companies Act 1948.[22] Moreover, if the goods supplied lose their identity completely when they are mixed with other goods in the manufacturing process the supplier cannot claim title to the made up goods.[23]

It will be evident that if any company whose assets consist in the main of stock, work in progress and debtors is purchasing a substantial quantity of raw materials from suppliers supplying on conditions such as those of the Dutch supplier in the *Romalpa* case, the banker's security may be substantially eroded. There is in practice very little a banker can do to prevent this happening. Clearly a banker would be wise to inquire of any such customer before taking the floating charge, or before making advances in reliance on it, whether it is purchasing goods from suppliers selling under similar conditions of sale, and to make repeated inquiries as to whether this remains the case. If, however, a company does start purchasing on such conditions without informing the banker, the banker is unlikely to discover the fact until too late. Of course, if the amount outstanding

---

21. [1980] Ch. 228.
22. *See* Chapter Six.
23. *Borden (UK)* v. *Scottish Timber Products* [1971] Ch. 25 (resin used in the manufacturing process).

to suppliers forms only a small proportion of the aggregate realisable value of the stock, work in progress and debtors, this risk is correspondingly smaller, but this is a factor which requires frequent monitoring by the banker.

Such is the position in theory, but unless the company is taking all its supplies, or all its supplies of a particular material, from one supplier, the predicament of the banker with a floating charge may be less formidable than the *Romalpa* case might suggest, since the first reply the receiver appointed by the bank will make to the supplier who claims title under such conditions will be to require the supplier to show which of the goods in stock were his. With a mixed stock of goods this may, unless they are still in the supplier's packaging or are otherwise distinguishable from the goods of other suppliers, be impossible for the supplier to comply with, but unless the supplier can identify his goods his claim must inevitably fail.

Finally, the value of a floating charge may be reduced if any of the assets subject to the floating charge were acquired by the company from an individual or partners other than in good faith. If the transfer of the assets to the company was held to be "fraudulent" under s. 1 of the Bankruptcy Act 1914 and the transferor was declared bankrupt, the trustee in bankruptcy of the transferor would be entitled to reclaim the assets from the company if the bankruptcy petition had been presented within three months of the transfer.[24] This would obviously reduce the value of the floating charge. The assets could also be reclaimed by the trustee in bankruptcy if they were subject to a fixed charge, but before a banker lent money on the security of a fixed charge, he would normally make sure that the title of the company to the assets was not liable to be overturned.

A banker should be aware that the value of a floating charge may be reduced in any of the ways just described. A banker should not lend money on the security of a floating charge without making proper inquiries and taking whatever other measures are appropriate to protect the value of his charge.

Priority of a subsequent fixed charge

A third important disadvantage of a floating charge is that if a fixed charge is given over assets which are already subject to a floating charge, the fixed charge may have priority over the floating charge even if the fixed chargee had notice of the floating charge at the time that the fixed charge was created. The reason for this is that a

24. *Re Simms* [1930] 2 Ch. 22. *See* Chapter Thirty.

floating charge leaves the company in possession of its assets, with implied authority to deal with them, including creating charges. This rule does not, however, apply if the floating charge contains a prohibition against the creation of subsequent charges ranking in priority or *pari passu* and the fixed chargee had notice of the prohibition at the time that the fixed charge was acquired.

The fixed chargee will in most instances have notice of the floating charge because most charges created by a company must be registered at the Companies Registry[25] and registration of a charge constitutes constructive notice of the charge to all subsequent chargees. Notice of the charge, however, does not amount to notice of the prohibition in the charge.[26] It is not clear whether a floating chargee can ensure that a subsequent fixed chargee will be deemed to have constructive notice of a prohibition in the floating charge. The normal practice of a floating chargee is to record a prohibition on the Form 47 which a chargee must complete when he wishes to register his charge,[25] but the Registrar of Companies does not always enter a note of the prohibition on the charges register. It is not certain that the mere entry of the prohibition on the Form 47 constitutes constructive notice to a subsequent fixed chargee if the Registrar does not include a note of the prohibition on the charges register; this has not yet been tested in the courts.

The textbook writer, Milnes Holden, has suggested that a special resolution of the company authorising the creation of the floating charge and including details of the prohibition might amount to constructive notice of the prohibition because special resolutions have to be filed at the Companies Registry. This has also not yet been tested in the courts.[27] Another possibility, also not confirmed, is that the floating chargee should take possession of the title deeds or other documents of title to the assets charged on the grounds that the absence of these documents at the time that the fixed charge is acquired might amount to implied notice of the prohibition. Where the assets subject to a floating charge include registered land, the problem need not arise, at least as regards those assets; this is because the prohibition can be registered as a "restriction" at the Land Registry and this would constitute notice of the prohibition, as least as regards that land.[28]

Furthermore, a mortgage to secure an advance of the purchase price of after-acquired property may take priority over a floating charge even if the mortgagee has actual notice of the restriction,

25. *See* Chapter Six.
26. *Wilson* v. *Kelland* [1910] 2 Ch. 306; *Re Castell and Brown* [1898] 1 Ch. 315.
27. Milnes Holden, *The Law and Practice of Banking* (5th Edn), Vol. 2, p. 359.
28. *See* Chapter Fifteen.

since in reality the company may have acquired merely the equity of redemption subject to the mortgage.[29]

CHARGE OVER BOOK DEBTS

Where a floating charge is created by an assignment of the "book debts" of a company (or, in other words, where a floating chargee takes as his security an assignment of the company's right to receive debts owing to the company), a subsequent fixed charge created by a further assignment of the same book debts will not have priority over the earlier floating charge merely because the fixed chargee did not have notice of a prohibition in the floating charge. For the fixed charge to have priority over the earlier floating charge it is also necessary that the assignment which created the fixed charge should be a "legal assignment" under s. 136 of the Law of Property Act 1925.

The subject of assignments of book debts is discussed in greater detail elsewhere.[30] The essentials of a "legal assignment" are that it must be in writing and be absolute and not purporting to be by way of charge[31] and notice of the assignment must be given to the debtor, otherwise the assignment will be an "equitable assignment". A fixed chargee who takes a written assignment of any book debt of a company should give notice to the relevant debtor immediately because the fixed charge cannot have priority over the earlier floating charge until the assignment has become legal, and the assignment cannot become legal until notice has been given to the debtor in question. This would be an example of the usual rule that a subsequent legal mortgage may in some circumstances take priority over an earlier floating charge.

In the case of book debts, a fixed charge created by a legal assignment may have priority not only over an earlier floating charge, but also over an earlier fixed charge if the earlier chargee had not given notice of assignment to the debtor; if the later fixed chargee did not have notice of the earlier fixed charge at the time that the later fixed charge was acquired, he can acquire priority over it by being first to give notice to the debtor. For this reason too, a fixed chargee should give notice to the debtor immediately so that his assignment can become a legal assignment. The giving of notice will also prevent the debtor from acquiring new rights of set-off or other equities against the assignee.

29. *Re Connolly Brothers* (*No. 2*) [1912] 2 Ch. 25.
30. *See* under "Assignment of debts" in Chapter Eighteen.
31. But *see* the special definition of these expressions under "Life policies and assignments of debts" in Chapter Eighteen.

Where a large number of book debts are assigned by fixed charge, it may not be administratively possible for the fixed chargee to give notice to all the debtors in order to convert the assignment of each debt into a legal assignment. In most circumstances it will not matter if the earlier assignment remains equitable, for the assignment will have to be registered under s. 95 of the Companies Act 1948,[32] and registration amounts to constructive notice of the charge to a later legal assignee. The equitable assignee will therefore retain his priority as against the later legal assignee because the later legal assignee will have notice of the earlier equitable assignment.

However, in one increasingly important circumstance an assignment of book debts is by way of sale, not by way of charge. This occurs when a company sells its book debts to a "factor".[33] Since such an outright sale does not constitute a charge, it does not need to be registered at the Companies Registry, which means that a later assignee will not be deemed to have constructive notice of the assignment and may in fact know nothing about it. Factors usually arrange for notice of assignment to be given to the debtors as soon as the company sends them the invoices. Indeed the invoices are often printed with a form of notice of assignment included. The risk for the banker taking a charge over such debts is that he has no foolproof way of knowing whether the debts have already been factored or not. Unless he inquires of the company or the debtors, and receives a truthful answer, he may not know until too late.

For reasons already mentioned in this chapter, banks usually prefer to take fixed charges over whatever assets they can, and book debts come into the category of assets over which they can take fixed charges. A fixed charge over future book debts[34] is inevitably equitable, and if the bank leaves the company free to deal with the book debts it is likely that the charge would be held to be a floating charge even if described in the instrument of charge as a fixed charge. If, however, the company is required to pay all moneys received in respect of the book debts which have been charged into its account with the chargee, and is prevented from disposing of them to third parties or dealing with them in any way, the charge will be effective as a fixed charge.

Indeed, if a subsequent assignee has notice of the restriction he can be prevented from acquiring any rights which conflict with the rights of the first chargee.[35] Restriction in this context means a restriction

---

32. *See* Chapter Six.
33. *See* Chapter Twenty-Six.
34. A future book debt is a debt which has not yet arisen, as opposed to a debt which is simply due to be paid at some future date.
35. *See Siebe Gorman & Co.* v. *Barclays Bank* [1978] *The Times* 15th May.

against dealing with the book debts which are the subject of the fixed charge, and again it is not settled whether a note of the restriction on the Form 47 would be adequate notice to a subsequent assignee. It follows from what has been said that unless it is administratively impossible, a banker who takes an assignment of a book debt as security for a loan should obtain a legal assignment by giving notice to the debtor, first, because he will retain his priority as against a later legal assignee whether or not the later assignee had notice of the assignment to the banker; secondly, because he himself will take priority over an earlier equitable assignment by way of fixed charge unless he had notice of the earlier assignment at the time when he took his assignment; thirdly, because he will also take priority over an earlier assignment by way of floating charge (which will necessarily be an equitable assignment) unless he had notice of a prohibition in the floating charge.

There are two other reasons for a banker who takes an assignment of a book debt from a company to give notice to the debtor in order to become a legal assignee. First, a legal assignee can sue the debtor in his own name without having to join the company as a party to the action. Secondly, the debtor cannot plead against a legal assignee any "equity" (or, in other words, any defence, set-off or counterclaim which he could have pleaded against the company) unless the equity either arose before he received notice of the assignment or is directly connected with the book debt which is assigned.[36]

REGISTRATION OF CHARGES

Most charges created after 1st July 1908 by companies registered in England must be registered with the Registrar of Companies.[37] It makes no difference whether the charge is fixed or floating, legal or equitable, and whether the company is private or public, limited or unlimited. The charges which must be registered are:[38]

(a) a charge created to secure any issue of debentures;

(b) a charge on the uncalled share capital of the company;

(c) a charge created (or evidenced) by a document which would have had to be registered as a bill of sale if it had been executed by an individual;[39]

(d) a charge on land wherever situate, or any interest in land, but not including any charge to secure rent or other periodical sums issuing out of land;

36. *See* under "Assignment of debts" in Chapter Eighteen.
37. Companies Act 1948, s. 95(1).
38. Ibid. s. 95(2).
39. *See* under "Bills of sale" in Chapter Eighteen.

(e) a charge on book debts of the company;

(f) a floating charge on the undertaking or property of the company;

(g) a charge on calls made but not paid;

(h) a charge on a ship or on an interest in a ship;

(i) a charge on the goodwill or a trademark of a company or on a patent or copyright (or on a licence under a patent or copyright).

The charges created by a registered company which do not have to be registered are:

(a) charges created over the shares or debentures of another company;

(b) charges on a life policy;

(c) pledges of goods;

(d) charges on a negotiable instrument, such as a bill of exchange, given to the company by a debtor of the company to secure an advance to the company;[40]

(e) charges created by an assignment of the company's interest in an export credit guarantee policy.[41]

It is not always clear whether a debt which is assigned by the company is or is not a book debt. It is therefore not always clear whether the charge created by the assignment of the debt has to be registered. The test would seem to be that a debt is a book debt if it is a debt which would be entered in the books of a well-run company. A "contingent debt" or, in other words, a debt which will not arise unless a particular contingency occurs, will not normally be entered in the books of a well-run company and will therefore not normally be regarded as a book debt. A charge created by an assignment of a contingent debt will therefore not have to be registered. This is why, for example, a charge created by an assignment of the company's interest in an export credit guarantee policy does not have to be registered.[41]

Where a charge created by a company does have to be registered, the prescribed particulars of the charge, together with the instrument (if any) which created the charge, must be delivered to the Registrar of Companies within 21 days after the creation of the charge.[42] If these formalities are not observed, the charge will become void against the liquidator or a creditor[43] unless a court order is obtained authorising an extension of the 21 day period.[44] When a charge is

40. Companies Act 1948, s. 95(6).
41. *Paul & Frank* v. *Discount Bank* (*Overseas*) [1967] Ch. 348.
42. Companies Act 1948, s. 95(1). The prescribed particulars are set out in the form known as Form 47.
43. Companies Act 1948, s. 95(1).
44. Ibid., s. 101.

void, the debt which the charge was intended to secure becomes an unsecured debt and becomes immediately repayable.[42] It is not possible to evade the 21 day period by postdating the instrument which creates the charge or by leaving the instrument undated.[45]

When a company acquires property subject to a charge which would have been registrable if it had been created by a company, the particulars of the charge must be delivered to the Registrar within 21 days after the company acquires the property.[46]

The company has a duty to register a registrable charge and it and its officers are subject to statutory penalties if it fails to do so.[47] A charge may also be registered by any person who has an interest in the charge.[48] For his own protection a banker who lends money on the security of a registrable charge over the assets of a company should make certain that the charge is properly registered; indeed charges are in practice usually registered by the chargees. If a charge is properly registered, a "certificate of registration" will be issued by the Registrar. The certificate is conclusive evidence that the requirements of the Act as to registration have been complied with[49] even if some of the property charged is omitted from the particulars[50] or other details are incorrectly stated.[51] A copy of the certificate of registration must be indorsed on every debenture or on every certificate of debenture stock issued by the company.[52] After payment of a debt which is secured by a registered charge the company should file the appropriate form at the Companies Registry. The Registrar will then enter a "memorandum of satisfaction" on the register.[53]

As we have seen, most charges created by a registered company must be registered on the companies register. Charges on registered land belonging to the company must also be registered at the Land Registry,[54] and some charges on unregistered land must be registered at the Land Charges Registry.[54] In addition, every charge created by a limited company (as opposed to an unlimited company) must be entered on a register which the company itself is required to

---

45. *Esberger* v. *Capital and Counties Bank* [1913] 2 Ch. 366. But since the facts in this case are substantially similar to those in *Re C.L. Nye* [1971] Ch. 442; [1970] 3 All E.R. 1061 referred to below, there is some doubt as to whether this case would be decided the same way today, but it would not be safe to rely on this.
46. Companies Act 1948, s. 97.
47. Ibid., s. 96(1) and (3).
48. Ibid., s. 96(2).
49. Ibid., s. 98.
50. *National Provincial and Union Bank of England* v. *Charnley* [1924] 1 K.B. 431.
51. *Re C.L. Nye* [1971] Ch. 442; [1970] 3 All E.R. 1061.
52. Companies Act 1948, s. 99.
53. Ibid., s. 100.
54. *See* Chapter Fifteen.

keep.[55] This register must be kept at the company's registered office and may be inspected by any person.[56]

Before a banker lends money on the security of a debenture, he should inspect the relevant registers in order to find out whether the assets charged by the debenture are subject to any prior charge. Even if he does not inspect the registers, he will not be able to claim priority over an earlier charge which is entered on the register because, as we have seen, an entry on the register constitutes constructive notice to subsequent chargees. A banker should be particularly careful if he discovers that the assets which will be charged by the company in his favour have previously been charged by an issue of debentures which has already been redeemed. In that circumstance he should inspect the debenture or trust deed and the articles of association of the company before lending any money because unless they provide otherwise the company may re-issue the same debentures or issue others in their place with the same priority as the original debentures had when they were first issued.[57]

APPOINTMENT OF A RECEIVER

When a banker lends money on the security of a debenture, the debenture will almost invariably provide for the appointment of a "receiver" in the event of a default by the company. Subject to any express provision in the debenture, the task of the receiver will be to run the business, to collect and realise the assets with a view to paying the debentureholders in full (subject to any preferential creditors), and when the debentureholders have been paid in full, to hand the remaining property of the company back to the company, or, if the company has gone into liquidation, to the liquidator.

A well-drawn debenture will provide that the receiver is the agent of the company and not of the debentureholders and that the company is liable for his actions and his remuneration. This agency ceases when the company goes into liquidation, though even then it remains in force for the purpose of giving effect to the power of sale.

Although receivers are normally appointed under express provisions in the debenture, a receiver may sometimes be appointed by an order of the court. As a general rule, a receiver will be appointed by the court whenever the security is in jeopardy. This would include cases where the company has become insolvent and closed its

55. Companies Act 1948, s. 104.
56. Ibid., s. 105.
57. Ibid., s. 90.

works,[58] where a winding up takes place or is imminent,[59] where the company is disposing of its undertaking in breach of the terms of the debenture,[60] or where there are judgments against the company.[61] A body corporate, such as a company, cannot be appointed a receiver either by the debentureholders or by the court.[62] A bankrupt can be appointed a receiver, but only with leave from the court.[63] In most cases the person appointed as receiver is a qualified accountant.

When a banker who holds a debenture wishes to appoint a receiver, he must observe any formalities laid down in the debenture. He may, for example, have to make a demand for payment before making the appointment; if he is required to and does not do so, the appointment will be void. He should also be careful to make demand for the correct amount. If the demand is made for more than the banker is entitled to demand the appointment may be ineffective.

The timing of the appointment may be important. The banker should ensure that all interest and other charges are debited to the account before the appointment is made; for example, if interest is to be allowable against tax, it must actually be borne, and so must be debited to the account before the appointment; if it is only debited after the appointment, the company may have ceased trading, or it may not be allowable on other grounds. Yet since the tax may be a preferential debt, it could be important for the tax assessment to be reduced by the interest charges. If, on the other hand, the banker does not appoint a receiver until after a liquidator has been appointed, the costs incurred on the winding up, including any corporation tax payable in respect of any capital gain arising on the sale of company assets, will have priority over the debt owed to the debentureholder.[64] Another reason for not delaying is that any execution which is completed, or distress for rent which is levied, before a receiver is appointed will have priority over the debentureholder.[65]

Once a receiver is appointed, the company and its directors have no power to deal with the assets which the receiver was appointed to administer until the receivership has ended unless the receiver abandons any particular assets.[66] When a receiver is appointed by the

58. *McMahon* v. *North Kent Ironworks* [1891] 2 Ch. 148.
59. *Re Victoria Steamboat Co.* [1897] 1 Ch. 158; *Hodson Tea Co* (1850) 14 Ch. D. 859; *Wallace* v. *Universal etc. Co* [1894] 2 Ch. 547.
60. *Hubbuck* v. *Helms* (1887) 56 L.J. Ch. 536.
61. *Edwards* v. *Standard Rolling Stock Syndicate* [1893] 1 Ch. 574.
62. Companies Act 1948, s. 366.
63. Ibid., s. 367.
64. *Re Barleycorn Enterprises* [1970] 2 All E.R. 155.
65. *See* above in this chapter.
66. *See* below in this chapter.

court, all servants of the company, including the directors, are automatically dismissed.[67] They do not, on his appointment, become his employees, though they may be re-engaged by the receiver.[68] When a receiver is appointed "out of court", the servants of the company are not automatically dismissed unless the appointment of the receiver is inconsistent with the terms of their contracts of service with the company.[69]

A banker or any other person who appoints a receiver must give notice of the appointment to the Registrar of Companies within seven days after the appointment is made.[70] On payment of the prescribed fee, the Registrar must register the appointment on the register of charges.[71] After the appointment has been made, every letter and other company document sent out by the company must contain a statement referring to the appointment.[72] Notice must also be given to the Registrar when a receiver ceases to act.[73] Registration of the appointment of a receiver amounts to constructive notice to any other person of the appointment.[74]

As soon as a receiver is appointed, he has a duty to give notice of his appointment to the company.[75] Then, within fourteen days, the company must send the receiver a "statement of affairs", giving details of the assets and liabilities of the company and of any securities given by the company to its creditors.[76] The statement of affairs should be verified by the secretary of the company and at least one director.[77] The receiver may also require verification of the statement of affairs from the promoters of the company and from any officer or employee of the company, past or present.[77] On receiving the statement of affairs the receiver should give notice of his appointment to the debtors of the company. After a debtor has received notice of the appointment, he must act according to the directions of the receiver and not according to the directions of the company.

67. *Reed* v. *Explosive Co.* (1887) 19 Q.B.D. 264.
68. *Re Marriage, Neave & Co., North of England Trustee, Debenture & Assets Corpn.* v. *Marriage Neave & Co.* [1896] 2 Ch. 663.
69. *Re Mack Trucks (Britain)* [1967] 1 All E.R. 977; *Griffiths* v. *Secretary of State for Social Services* [1973] 3 All E.R. 1184, where employment of managing director under service contract subject to control of board not determined by appointment of receiver.
70. Companies Act 1948, s. 102(1).
71. Ibid., s. 102(1). At present no fee has been prescribed.
72. Ibid., s. 370.
73. Ibid., s. 102(2).
74. Under the doctrine of constructive notice; *see*, for example, *Mahony* v. *East Holyford Mining Co.* (1875) L.R. 7 H.L. 869.
75. Ibid., s. 372(1)(a).
76. Ibid., s. 372(1)(b) and 373(1).
77. Ibid., s. 373(2).

Within two months after receiving the statement of affairs, the receiver has a duty to give copies of the statement, together with his comments on the statement, to the company, to the debenture-holders, to the trustees for the debentureholders and to the Registrar of Companies.[78] Within two months after the end of each twelve months following his appointment, and within two months after ceasing to act, the receiver has a duty to give the same persons an abstract of his receipts and payments.[79]

If the receiver is appointed by another person, the banker is probably protected as to his transactions with the company up to the moment he receives notice of the appointment, even though made after the date of such appointment. Notice to the Registrar and record of the fact in the official register of charges would not, it is considered, be deemed sufficient notice to the banker.[80] If the appointment is under a debenture containing a floating charge, no further payments out of the company's credit balances may be made without the consent of the receiver, who is entitled to collect the balances, less any set-off due to the banker.[81] Section 31 of the Bankruptcy Act 1914, requiring set-off of mutual credits and dealings,[82] does not apply on the appointment of a receiver. The banker, therefore, in such circumstances, has no right of set-off against the credit balance of a company for its contingent liability on bills discounted.[83]

The appointment of a receiver takes effect when the document appointing him is handed to the receiver and he accepts the appointment. Nobody can be forced to act as a receiver against his will and the date from which the receiver is entitled to act is therefore the date of acceptance, not the date of any document offering or acknowledging the appointment.

RIGHTS, POWERS AND DUTIES OF A RECEIVER

Basically the duty of a receiver is to preserve the goodwill of the buisness where he is authorised to carry on the business, but he owes no duty to the unsecured creditors or contributories[84] to do so and it would seem that, so long as the preferential debts are provided for, he would be justified in paying an unsecured debt due before his appointment where payment is necessary to ensure the continuation

---

78. Ibid., s. 372(1)(c).
79. Ibid., s. 372(2).
80. Q.B.P., No. 79. For the extent of the right of set-off, see Chapter Four.
82. See Chapters Twenty-Nine and Thirty.
83. Q.B.P., No. 80. The case is different when a company is wound up (see Chapter Twenty-Nine).
84. See the definition of this term in Chapter Twenty-Nine.

of a supply of goods essential to the company's business; he must not, however, pay statute-barred debts.

The receiver's power to make contracts and to effect other transactions will be governed by the terms of the debenture, though as agent of the company he cannot exceed the company's own powers. It is, therefore, desirable for the powers in the debenture to be as wide as possible. It is virtually impossible to think of every conceivable eventuality and provide for it in the debenture; for example, one receiver needed power to purchase an easement over adjoining land in order to realise the company's own land most favourably. In the absence of the necessary powers, the receiver could apply to the court. A fairly comprehensive list of the most likely powers is contained in the specimen form of debenture in Appendix I.

A receiver does not have implied power to run or "manage" the company's business. Since it is generally necessary to continue the business in order to realise the assets most beneficially, he is usually given express power to run or manage the business, in which case he is technically known as a "receiver and manager", though he is usually referred to simply as a receiver. In fact the appointment of a receiver only, without powers of management, would inevitably cause the loss of any goodwill owned by a company, which could only be preserved for the benefit of the chargees if a manager is appointed. Even if there is no goodwill of any saleable value, it is often necessary to carry on the business for a time so that the assets may be sold as a going concern. Consequently, where the appointment is made by the court (if for example the charge does not contain the power of appointing a receiver) it is usual to appoint a receiver and manager, though the manager is appointed for a fixed period, usually between one and six months; if a sale is not completed before the end of the period, application must be made to the court, before the period expires, for the appointment to be continued.

Where a receiver is appointed by the court, his remuneration is fixed by the court. If he is appointed by the debentureholder, his remuneration is normally fixed by agreement with the debentureholder under express powers in the charge. If there are no express powers, s. 109(6) of the Law of Property Act 1925 will enable it to be fixed at a rate not exceeding 5 per cent of what he receives. Where the company is in liquidation the court may, on an application by the liquidator, fix the amount to be paid to the receiver even if he has been appointed out of court, and the receiver can be required to account for any excess over the amount specified in the order.[85]

85. Companies Act 1948, s. 371.

A receiver appointed by the court is an officer of the court; he is therefore not an agent for any person but a principal, and as such is personally liable on all contracts made by him, unless his personal liability is expressly excluded in the contract. He does, however, have a right of indemnity against all the assets under his control for all liabilities properly incurred.[86] The liability of a receiver appointed by the debentureholders is the same as that of a receiver appointed by the court.[87] A receiver appointed by the court cannot sue without leave of the court.

If the receiver ratifies a contract made on behalf of the company by a person acting without the receiver's authority, such ratification does not result in a novation of the contract and does not entail his becoming personally liable thereon, since he was never a party to the contract. Ratification will have the normal result of relating back to the date of the contract.

A receiver who is also a manager does not have a duty to perform a contract which was made before his appointment unless the company is likely to continue business after the receivership has ended and refusal to perform the contract would be damaging to the goodwill of the company.[88]

If the receiver is an agent for the company, neither the trustees for the debentureholders who appointed him, nor the debentureholders themselves, are under any personal liability for debts incurred in carrying on the business. If the receiver continues to carry on the business after his agency has been determined,[89] he does not do so as agent for the debentureholders but becomes a principal, but he may be entitled to an indemnity from the debentureholders.

So long as the company is not in liquidation, receivers may contract in the name of the company rather than in their own name, and may include clauses expressly excluding any personal liability.[90] Suppliers are, however, reluctant to permit this. In such cases the practical remedy is for the receiver to buy for cash only; he would be financed by the debentureholder, who would normally agree not to look to the receiver personally for payment.

If and when the company goes into liquidation, the receiver ceases as from the commencement of the liquidation to have power to bind the company personally as its agent, though he may enter into contracts in his own name (for which he would be entitled to an

86. *Burt, Boulton and Hayward* v. *Bull* [1895] 1 Q.B. 276; *Re Glasdir Copper Mines* [1906] 1 Ch. 365.
87. Companies Act 1948, s. 369(2).
88. *Re Newdigate Colliers* [1912] 1 Ch. 468; *Re Thames Ironworks Shipbuilding and Engineering Co.* (1912) 106 L.T. 674.
89. For example, by liquidation. *See* below in this chapter.
90. *Re British Power Traction Co.* [1910] 2 Ch. 470.

indemnity out of the assets of the company and would in any event look to the debentureholders to indemnify him); further he is still able, notwithstanding the commencement of the liquidation, to exercise in his own name all the powers contained in the debenture or his appointment for the purpose of giving effect to the power of sale contained in the debenture.

It was formerly thought that after the commencement of liquidation, the receiver could no longer execute conveyances or transfers as the agent of the company, and that any conveyances or transfers of the property of the company would have to be executed by the liquidator. Since the interests of the liquidator and the receiver were frequently at variance, this gave rise to difficulty for receivers.

This view has now been shown to be incorrect by two cases concerning "secondary banks" which went into liquidation after receivers had been appointed during the secondary banking crisis of 1974/5.[91] Notwithstanding liquidation, (a) the debentureholder may himself sell as mortgagee under the power of sale, and (b) if the debenture contains a power for a receiver to get in and dispose of the company's property in the name of the company, the receiver may continue to sell and dispose of the company's property in the name of the company, even though the receiver's power to bind the company, or to pledge the company's credit, ceases on liquidation. The debentureholder may sign contracts of sale or seal conveyances as attorney of the company, at least for the purpose of giving effect to the power of sale, if the power of attorney clause permits this, but this may be inconvenient and defeats at least part of the object of appointing a receiver. If the power of attorney clause is also expressed to operate in favour of any receiver appointed by the debentureholder, then the receiver may also act as attorney for and in the name of the company, for in this respect also the authority to act in the name of the company to sell its property will survive liquidation.

In each case the receiver of the bank entered into a contract to sell the property mortgaged to the bank in exercise of the power of sale contained in the mortgage to the bank. In the *David Samuel Trust* case, a conveyance was made by the bank as mortgagee acting by its attorneys, the debentureholders, at the request of the receiver and in exercise of the power of sale conferred on the bank by the mortgage and by statute; in the *G. T. Whyte & Co* case, the conveyance was executed by the receiver of the bank.

A receiver who makes any contract outside the limits of his

91. *Sowman* v. *David Samuel Trust* [1978] 1 W.L.R. 22; *Barrows* v. *Chief Land Registrar* (1977), *The Times*, 20th October (the *G.T. Whyte & Co.* case).

authority or after his authority has been revoked will, according to the normal laws of agency, be personally liable on the contract.[92] The contract will be binding on the receiver alone, and will not be binding on the company or the debentureholders. A receiver is in the position of a trustee *vis-à-vis* the company and the debenture-holders. Thus, if he makes a secret profit out of his office or he causes loss by his own wilful default, he can be sued in breach of trust.

If a receiver is appointed in respect of only some of the assets of the company, the directors will continue to control the remaining assets and can sue the receiver for any loss which he causes to those assets by his acts or omissions. Furthermore, if a receiver fails to pursue a right of action, the directors are not only entitled to pursue the right of action themselves, but also bound to do so since the directors must continue to safeguard the interests of the other creditors. This point arose in a recent case where the directors were permitted to sue a debentureholder for breach of contract after the receiver who had been appointed by the debentureholder had failed to do so.[93]

The assets realised by the receiver must first be applied to paying off the costs and expenses of realisation and the remuneration of the receiver before any money can be paid to the debentureholders. Preferential debts must be paid next,[94] followed by any remuneration to which the trustees for the debentureholders are entitled and only then will the debentureholders be entitled to receive anything.[94] Once the receiver has paid over the assets he has realised, he can apply for a discharge. The discharge will be given by the court if the receiver was appointed by the court;[95] it will be given by the debentureholders (or the trustees for the debentureholders) if the receiver was appointed under the terms of the debenture.

As a general rule a receiver has a right to take control of any asset which is subject to the charge he is appointed to enforce. There is, however, one important exception to this rule. If the company entered into a contract with a third party before the receiver was appointed and if, by reason of that contract, the third party had a lien over assets of the company which came into his hands, the receiver would not be entitled to take control of any assets which actually came into the hands of the third party and which the third party held by reason of his lien.[96] Once a receiver is appointed, he should

92. Companies Act 1948, s. 369(2).
93. *Newhart Developments* v. *Co-operative Commercial Bank* [1978], Q.B. 814.
94. Companies Act 1948, s. 94; *see* above.
95. *Thomas* v. *Brigstocke* (1827) 4 Russ. 64.
96. *George Barker* v. *Eynon* [1974] 1 All E.R. 900.

check whether any such contract has been made by the company. If so, he has a duty to prevent any of the assets which are subject to the charge from falling into the hands of the third party.

When a banker or any other debentureholder takes steps to appoint a receiver, he normally does so because this remedy is more convenient than other remedies available to him, such as sale of the assets which are charged or entering into possession.[97] Strictly speaking the banker has no standing in the matter of the conduct of the receivership, but many bankers like to keep a close eye on it and discuss the matters with the receiver before he makes decisions or takes actions, and in practice many receivers pay close attention to what bankers say in this regard as they wish to preserve good relationships with the bankers who appoint them. The banker should, however, be careful not to appear to be too closely involved with the activities of the receiver or he may be deemed to have entered into possession of the assets. He will then be subject to precisely the inconveniences which the appointment of the receiver was intended to avoid.

When a banker appoints a receiver to enforce a company debenture which the banker has been given as security for a loan, he may find that the receiver realises substantially less money than the banker had anticipated. We have already seen how the value of a floating charge may be substantially reduced. In addition, there are a number of other reasons why any charge, whether fixed or floating, may prove less valuable than expected.

First, a number of debts owed to the company may be "bad debts" and therefore irrecoverable. Secondly, some of the other debts owed to the company may be reduced because the debtors are able to plead defences or set-offs against the company. Thirdly, the company was probably short of cash before the receiver was called in, so it had probably deferred expenditure on repairs to the assets charged by the debenture. Fourthly, trading conditions may well have turned against the company before the receiver was called in, so the stock and work-in-progress are likely to realise less than their book value; in any event the best and most readily saleable assets will probably have been sold already. Fifthly, the cost of realising the assets, and the cost of the receiver's remuneration, may be substantial.

Experience shows that in a receivership the assets tend to realise only 20 to 30 per cent of their book value, and if a banker is working on the basis of the last audited balance sheet, which will probably be the only figures available, he should not expect to receive more than about 10 to 20 per cent of the amounts shown there. Thus

97. *See* Chapter Fifteen.

as a rough guide it is unlikely to be worth appointing a receiver for a debt of under £2,000.

For all these reasons, a banker who lends money on the security of a floating charge should lend less than the apparent value of the assets charged by the debenture.

CHAPTER EIGHTEEN

Miscellaneous Securities

1. LIFE POLICIES

The assignment, legal or equitable, of a life assurance policy is a very general form of security for an advance up to the surrender value of the policy, and is moreover a security that increases in value the longer it is held, provided that any premiums due are paid. It is also useful as a supplementary security, because in the event of the borrower's death, part or the whole of the debt is liquidated as soon as the policy moneys are paid over by the insurance company. If the borrower has a fixed income terminable at death, or has merely a contingent interest in property, the taking of a policy on the life of the borrower is a necessary precaution that no prudent banker should neglect.

TYPES OF POLICY

There are various types of life insurance policy, the following being the most common.

A *pure endowment policy* provides for the sum assured to be payable not on the death of the life assured, but on the arrival of a specified date, the insured being still alive. What are normally known as endowment policies are a mixture of pure endowment and strict life assurance, and these provide for the sum assured to be payable on a specified date or on the death of the life assured, whichever occurs earlier.

The sum assured may be payable "with profits" or "without profits". In the case of a "with profits" policy, the policy holder is entitled to have added to the value of the policy a proportion of the profits made by the insurance company on its life fund. These profits are ascertained by periodical valuations (usually triennial or quinquennial).

Whole life policies provide for the sum assured to be payable on the death of the life assured, whenever it occurs. Again, the sum assured may be payable "with profits" or "without profits".

There are various types of *family protection policy*. Some provide for payment of the sum assured on a reducing scale, such as, for example, £10,000 if the life assured dies during the first few years of the policy, reducing by stages to a lower figure, or nothing at all, by a specified later date.

Some policies are written under s. 11 of the Married Women's Property Act 1882, which provides that—

... a policy effected by any man on his own life and expressed to be for the benefit of his wife or of his children or of his wife and children or any of them, or by any woman on her own life and expressed to be for the benefit of her husband or of her children or of her husband and children or any of them, shall create a trust in favour of the objects therein named, and the moneys payable under any such policy shall not, so long as any object of the trust remains unperformed, form part of the estate of the insured or be subject to his or her debts.

The most usual form of policy issued under this Act is one effected by the husband for the benefit of his wife only, and vice versa, and without appointment of a trustee. This is the only policy under the Act that is a fit subject of mortgage, the husband and wife being jointly capable of dealing with it in any way they please. Even then the policy is suitable for charging only if it names the wife, for in such cases the named wife takes an absolute vested interest in the policy and its proceeds immediately upon issue.[1] If the policy is expressed to be "for the benefit of his wife", this means the person who at his death shall become his widow, whether it be his wife living at the date of his policy or some future wife who shall survive him,[2] and such a policy is incapable of being charged.

If the policy is effected by a husband for the benefit of his wife (or vice versa) and for the benefit of named children, the policy may be charged if all the children are of full age, the two spouses and all the children beneficiaries joining in.

Here again, if the policy is to be capable of being assigned, it must be effected for the benefit of his named wife and named children, since a policy written "for the benefit of his wife and children" means the person who at his death shall become his widow, and those of his children by any marriage and whenever born who shall survive him.[3]

ADVANTAGES AND DISADVANTAGES

There are three main advantages in this type of security.

(a) The value of the security may be easily ascertained. As a general rule, there is no surrender value on a policy until two (and some-

1. *Cousins* v. *Sun Life Assurance Co.* [1933] Ch. 126.
2. *Re Collier* [1930] 2 Ch. 37.
3. *Re Browne's Policy* [1903] 1 Ch. 188.

times more) full premiums have been paid on it. The surrender value depends on the age of the assured and the duration of the policy, and is greater on policies of long duration and on lives where the age is considerably advanced than on those of short duration and on young lives. The surrender value has no direct connection with the number of premiums paid, though it increases—and at a more rapid rate—with the payment of each successive premium. The actual surrender value can always be ascertained from the company.

(b) A life policy can easily be realised. The banker does not in this case have to sell the mortgaged property, since, at least if he has a legal mortgage, he may surrender the policy and obtain payment of the surrender value. A customer may be anxious that the banker should not take this drastic course, and it may instead be possible for the banker to arrange for the insurance company to make a loan against the policy. Needless to say, when the life assured dies, the policy moneys become payable.

(c) The value of the security does not fluctuate. Provided any premiums due are paid regularly, the surrender value will increase over the years.

There are, however, a number of disadvantages.

(a) Except in the case of paid-up policies, the premiums must be paid regularly, but the customer may be unable to pay future premiums. The banker should have power to pay the premiums himself, if the customer does not do so, but this may be of little comfort to the banker if the customer has already reached the limit of his facility and the increase in the surrender value is less than the increase in the advance (and interest).

(b) There is a possibility that the policy may be avoided either for non-disclosure or for breach of condition. Avoidance for non-disclosure is rare in practice, but there is nothing the banker can do to guard against this. The risk of avoidance for breach of condition is again small, because stringent conditions are rare, but there may be restrictions against engaging in certain activities, such as private flying or mining.

(c) There is a rather remote possibility that the life assured may die in circumstances in which the sum assured will not be payable, such as execution after conviction for a capital offence,[4] or some cases of suicide.

(d) The insured might not have had an insurable interest in the life assured. This risk is slight, since a reputable insurance company

---

4. *Amicable Society* v. *Bolland* (1830) 4 Bligh (N.S.) 194. The death penalty for murder does not at present apply.

would not knowingly issue such a policy, and even if it did, it is likely that it would waive the illegality in favour of the banker.

VALIDITY OF THE POLICY

Uberrimae fidei

A contract of life assurance is a contract *uberrimae fidei*, that is to say, the "utmost good faith" is required on the part of the assured, who must when applying for the policy disclose all material facts within his knowledge affecting the life. Non-disclosure of a material fact may avoid the policy. "Probably a material fact means for this purpose a fact such that its concealment makes the statement actually furnished, though literally true, so misleading as it stands as to be in effect untrue." [5] If the insurers are to avoid the policy on the grounds of non-disclosure, they must prove the fact to be a material one, that is to say a fact which would tend to increase the risk or influence their decision on whether to accept the proposal and if so on what terms. Now, however, most proposal forms for such policies contain an exhaustive list of questions, and the answers to these are made into warranties by the forms. In such cases the assured cannot deny that the answers are material.

Suicide

Suicide was formerly a crime in English law and it invariably avoided the policy, on the grounds of public policy and the general legal principle that no person may be allowed to benefit from his own criminal act.

The leading case is *Beresford* v. *Royal Insurance Co.*[6] In this case the deceased had insured his life for £50,000 and the policy provided for the sum to be payable to his executors or assigns on his death, even if he should die by his own hand, whether sane or insane, provided one year had elapsed from the commencement of the insurance. The deceased committed suicide some nine years later, a few minutes before the insurance was due to expire, and it was clear that he took his life so that the policy moneys would be made available for payment of his debts. The House of Lords held that the contract was unenforceable, since it was contrary to public policy that a person, or his personal representatives, should be permitted to benefit from his crime.

Suicide is no longer a crime under English law,[7] but it might still

5. Pollock, *Principles of Contract* (8th Edn.), p. 566 n.
6. [1938] 2 All E.R. 602; [1938] A.C. 586.
7. Suicide Act 1971, s. 1.

be argued that it was contrary to public policy for personal representatives to be allowed to recover policy moneys in circumstances such as those in *Beresford's* case, since there is a presumption in every insurance contract that the assured cannot by his own intentional act bring about the event upon which the insurance money is payable and then recover under the policy.[8]

Beresford's case left open the question of whether a banker, or any other bona fide assignee, would be allowed to recover in such circumstances. The presumption may be displaced if the policy provides, either expressly or by clear implication, that the policy money is payable to the assured's representatives in the event of a sane suicide, or is payable to an assignee taking before the suicide, especially where the policy contains an express term to this effect in favour of assignees only.[9]

An insane suicide will not generally affect the right of the assured's personal representatives to recover under the policy, unless there is an express term of the policy to the contrary. It is not unusual these days for insurance policies to contain a clause to the effect that the insurance shall be forfeited and become void if the assured shall within one year after such assurance shall have been effected die by suicide. Even so, there is often a proviso specifically protecting assignees. The Forfeiture Act 1982, s. 2, also may give rise to exceptions.

Insurable interest
Section 1 of the Life Assurance Act 1774 (also known as the Gambling Act 1774) provides that no life insurance policy shall be made unless the person on whose behalf the policy was made has an insurable interest in the life assured, and that a life policy taken out in contravention of this principle shall be null and void. The preamble to the Act states that "the making insurances on lives or other events where the assured shall have no interest had introduced a mischievous kind of gaming."

There is no statutory definition of what constitutes an insurable interest, but it is established that any person has an unlimited[10] insurable interest in his own life[11] and that of his spouse,[12] but unless there is some pecuniary interest, a parent does not have an insurable interest in the life of his child,[13] nor a child in the lives of his parents; there may in some circumstances be a pecuniary interest,

8. *Bell* v. *Carstairs* (1811) 14 East. 374.
9. *Moore* v. *Woolsey* (1854) 4 E. & B. 243.
10. *M'Farlane* v. *The Royal London F.S.* (1886) 2 T.L.R. 755.
11. *Wainwright* v. *Bland* (1835) 1 Moo. & R. 481.
12. *Griffiths* v. *Fleming* [1909] 1 K.B. 805; *Reed* v. *Royal Exchange Assurance Co.* (1795) Peake Add. Cas. 70.
13. *Halford* v. *Kymer* (1830) 10 B. & C. 724.

such as if the life assured renders domestic or other services to the assured so that his death would cause the assured to incur expense. A creditor has an insurable interest in the life of his debtor,[14] though the extent of the insurable interest is not certain. It is clear that a creditor has an interest at least to the amount of the debt and interest due thereon at the time he effects the insurance,[15] but an insurance limited to that amount would not fully protect him because future interest and the cost of maintaining the insurance up to the date of the debtor's death are not provided for.[16]

PROCEDURE

Examination of the policy

Before taking, or at least making advances against, the security of a life policy, the banker should examine the policy closely.

He should note the name of the insurance company which issued the policy. He should consider whether he is satisfied with the financial strength of the company, as will be the case with most British companies, or whether he needs to make inquiries. In addition, policies issued by overseas companies which do not have offices in this country may give rise to difficulties in recovering the policy moneys when they become payable.

The banker should also note whether there are any special conditions attaching to the policy, such as a special suicide clause, a clause limiting the amount recoverable in the event of the death of the life assured within a specified period, or even restrictions against certain activities.

The banker should check by inquiry of the insurance company concerned, before making the advance, whether the policy is still in full force and effect, whether the last premium has been paid and whether it has received notice of any other assignments.

Some insurance companies do not insist upon the age of the assured being admitted before the policy is issued, but they will insist upon proof of age when the sum assured is claimed under the policy. The banker should, therefore, insist upon the assured proving his age and, if necessary, obtaining an indorsement to that effect from the insurance company. Since the customer will usually be more compliant before any advance has been made than after, the banker should insist upon this before allowing the customer to make any borrowings.

14. *Godsall* v. *Boldero* (1807) 9 East. 72.
15. *Law* v. *London Indisputable Life Insurance Policy Co.* (1855) 1 K. & J. 223; *Hebdon* v. *West* (1863) 3 B. & S. 579.
16. *Amick* v. *Butler*, 12 N. E. 518 (Ind., 1887).

Age is usually proved either by sending the birth certificate to the company, or if the assured has lost the birth certificate, by obtaining a "short" birth certificate from the Registrar-General, General Register Office, St Catherine's House, 10 Kingsway, London WC2B 6JP.

If the life assured is a woman who has married since the policy was issued, a certificate of her marriage should be obtained and registered with the insurance company.

Equitable mortgage

This is a very simple and inexpensive way of taking a life policy as security for an advance. All that is necessary is a deposit of the policy, together with a written undertaking on the part of the borrower to assign the policy, if and when called upon to do so. Whether this memorandum should be under hand or under seal will depend on the circumstances. If under hand, the banker has to face the risk of the borrower refusing to carry out his undertaking to assign, in which case considerable trouble and expense might be incurred in realising the security. If under seal the banker would have a power of sale by s. 101 of the Law of Property Act 1925, but, as mentioned above, sale is not usually the most satisfactory remedy for the banker.

An equitable mortgage of a life policy has this advantage over a legal mortgage, that when the advance is repaid no formal re-assignment of the policy is necessary. All that is required to re-establish the title of the assured is a letter from the bank to the insurance company stating that the bank has no further claim on the policy. This, however, is more an advantage for the customer than one for the banker, and there are some disadvantages to this method of taking a charge over a life policy.

The method of enforcing the banker's rights is cumbersome, if the mortgagor does not co-operate. When the policy matures, the banker cannot sue the company in his own name, since the banker in this case would not be entitled to the benefit of the Policies of Insurance Act 1867[17] nor, if the policy moneys have not matured, could the banker surrender the policy without the co-operation of the mortgagor, and if the banker preferred to sell the policy, he would have to apply to the court for an order for sale or foreclosure.

In any event, if the banker is content with an equitable mortgage, he should certainly give notice to the insurance company, since s. 3 of that Act provides that the priority of claims under any assignment is regulated by the date on which notice is received by the company,

17. *See* earlier in this chapter.

and the banker must be careful to retain possession of the policy at all times.

Legal mortgage

From the banker's point of view, the more fitting way of taking a life policy as security is by a deed assigning it to the banker, with a proviso for redemption.

Until the passing of the Policies of Assurance Act 1867, life policies were not assignable at law and were assignable in equity only. Under that Act, in order for the right to sue at law without joining in the assignor, and hence in order for the ability to give a legal discharge to the insurance company, to pass to the assignee, three conditions must be satisfied.

(a) At the time when the action is brought, the assignee must be entitled in equity to receive the policy.[18]

(b) The assignee must have a properly stamped assignment in writing in words to the effect set out in the Schedule to the Act.[19]

(c) Written notice must have been given to the company at its principal place of business.[20]

The form prescribed in the Schedule to the Act reads as follows.

I, A B of ... in consideration of ... do hereby assign unto C D of ... his Executors Administrators and Assigns, the [within] policy of assurance granted ... [here describe the policy].

In witness, ...

This form must either be indorsed on the actual policy or be contained in a separate instrument. It is not necessary to use the exact words, so long as the parties and the policy are sufficiently identified and the document shows a clear intention to effect an immediate unqualified assignment of the policy.

The first condition, however, causes difficulty. Entitlement in equity at the time when the action is brought is a condition precedent to the validity in law of the assignment, and so the insurance company, before being able to pay out to the claimaint, must consider all equities of which they have notice, whether formal or informal, in order to determine whether or not the claimant has the equitable right to receive the insurance money. If, under the equitable rules governing the priority of assignments, the person who gave the first formal notice is not in fact entitled to the policy, the company will not obtain a valid discharge from him or any assignee from

18. Policies of Assurance Act 1867, s. 1.
19. Ibid., s. 5.
20. Ibid., s. 3.

him. Since, therefore, equitable entitlement is a condition precedent to the legal validity of an assignment under the 1867 Act, most assignments of life insurance policies are now made not under the 1867 Act but under s. 136 of the Law of Property Act 1925. The requirements of s. 136 are that:

(a) the assignment must be by writing under the hand of the assignor;

(b) it must be absolute and not purporting to be by way of charge only;

(c) express notice in writing must have been given to the debtor, trustee or other person liable to pay.

If these conditions are satisfied, the assignment transfers from the date of such notice the legal right to the policy, all legal or other remedies for the same and the power to give a good discharge without the concurrence of the assignor, though the assignment takes effect subject to all equities subsisting as between the assignor and the debtor at the date on which such notice is given.

Form

Although s. 136 requires only writing under hand, it is usual for such assignments to be by deed.

The deed will normally begin with a covenant to pay, covering all moneys due, and an assignment clause itself. Although s. 136 states that the assignment must be absolute and not purport to be by way of charge, a mortgage in the form of an assignment of the whole debt with a proviso for redemption is an absolute assignment for the purposes of the section.[21]

The deed should also contain a covenant by the mortgagor to pay the premiums punctually and make provision that if premiums are not paid, the bank may pay them and debit the debtor's account and that they will be charged on the policy. It should also give the bank power to sell the policy, or convert it to a paid up policy, or surrender it. There is usually a clause reserving the right of consolidation.[22]

All parties having an interest in the policy must sign the deed of assignment. If the policy taken out by the assured is expressed on the face of it to be for the benefit of his named wife, then the wife must concur in the charge when it is executed, and if any children are included, then all those expressed to benefit must also sign. If any of the children interested are under age the policy is not assignable, as a minor has no power to assign.[23] A policy expressed to be "for the

21. *Tancred* v. *Delagoa Bay Railway Co.* (1889) 23 Q.B.D. 239.
22. *See* a specimen form of mortgage in Appendix I.
23. *See* later in this chapter.

benefit of his wife" or "for the benefit of his wife and children" is non-assignable.[24]

No stamp duty is payable in respect of the assignment.

Notice of assignment to company

Whether the assignment is under the Policies of Insurance Act 1867 or s. 136 of the Law of Property Act 1925 the banker should, immediately the deed is executed, give written notice to the insurance company at its principal office. The notice should be sent in duplicate with the statutory fee of not exceeding 25p. Some companies make no charge while with others the fee is less than 25p. The company must stamp the acknowledgment of the receipt of notice on the duplicate form and return it to the banker.[25]

The giving of notice is most important. Until notice of the banker's interest is received by the company, the policy holder may surrender or deal with the policy, and the banker cannot sue in his own name. The date on which a notice of assignment is received by the insurance company regulates the priority of all claims under any assignment.[26]

This provision, however, applies only as between an insurance office and the persons interested in the policy, and does not affect the right of those persons *inter se*.[27] An equitable assignee for value can never gain priority over any equity of which he had notice, actual or constructive, at the time that he took his assignment by giving formal notice to the company. It is the time when this assignment was made which is important, the knowledge of the assignee at the time of his giving notice being immaterial.[28]

The banker should, when asking the company to acknowledge receipt of the notice on the duplicate, ask the company whether they have received notice of any other assignments or whether they have any charge on the policy themselves. The banker should keep with the policy the receipted notice of assignment, together with any previous assignments, reassignments and receipted notices of assignment. When a claim is made under the policy, the insurance company will require not only the policy but all such assignments and reassignments.

Although the Life Assurance Act 1774 prohibits persons from effecting insurances on lives in which they have no insurable interest, this prohibition does not affect the purchase of policies by third parties. If the policy was valid when taken out, it does not become invalid through being assigned to a person who purchases as an

24. *See* later in this chapter.
25. Policies of Assurance Act 1867, s. 6.
26. Policies of Assurance Act 1867, s. 3.
27. *Newman* v. *Newman* (1885) 28 Ch. D. 674.
28. *Mutual Life* v. *Langley* (1886) 32 Ch. D. 460.

investment. As an assignee, such person is in no different a position from the banker who takes an assignment of such a policy as security.

There is an exception with regard to this rule of priorities, for it has been held that a trustee in bankruptcy, who serves a company with notice of his claim, cannot get priority over an assignee for value, even though the assignee for value has failed to give notice to the company. This is so because a trustee in bankruptcy is regarded as a statutory assignee, and not as an assignee for value, and as such he takes over the debtor's property subject to all equities in existence at the time.

REMEDIES

Equitable mortgage

If the policy moneys have become payable, the banker, if he has only an equitable mortgage, cannot claim payment from the insurance company without joining the personal representatives of the deceased (if the deceased owned the policy at his death) or without the concurrence of the beneficiary if it was a settlement policy. In practice, if the policy was owned by the deceased at his death and the estate is solvent, it is likely that his personal representatives will co-operate (when a grant of representation has been obtained), since delay will increase the interest running on the account.

If the policy moneys have not yet become payable, the banker can do nothing without either the co-operation of the customer or an order of the court. In the first instance, the banker should request the customer either to execute a legal mortgage or to consent to the surrender or sale of the policy. If he does not do so, the banker may apply to the court for an order for foreclosure or sale.

Legal mortgage

If the banker has a legal mortgage, and the policy moneys have become payable, he is in a position to give a good discharge, and the banker may claim from the insurance company under the policy, subject to proof of death if the life assured has died.

If the policy moneys have not yet become payable and the customer is not willing to co-operate, the obvious remedies are either surrender or sale. Since both of these will inevitably involve the customer in loss, the banker is usually, out of consideration for the customer, willing to allow him a certain latitude before exercising such drastic remedies, and may, if the customer so requests, consider either an approach to the insurance company for a loan against the policy or alternatively conversion of the policy into a paid up policy for a reduced amount.

If the policy is to be sold, there are certain companies which specialise in the purchase of policies and reversionary interests, and they advertise regularly in the financial press. The purchase price will, in such case, often be higher than the surrender value.

MINORS' POLICIES

A minor may propose for and take out a policy of insurance, but he cannot, whilst still a minor, assign the policy as security for a loan. Any such assignment would be void under the Infants Relief Act 1874, and the lender would have no rights either against the minor or under the policy.

Parents sometimes take out endowment policies on the lives of minors. Provided these are owned by the parents and do not create any trust in favour of the minors, they are suitable for charging, but such policies are relatively rare and are difficult to distinguish from policies effected by parents on the lives of their children taken out in trust for the children. These latter policies are incapable of being charged as security for the parents' account.

INDUSTRIAL POLICIES

These are of no value as a banker's security, for, apart from the fact that many of them are not capable of being assigned, mortgaged or sold without becoming void, they are effected with numerous conditions which make them quite unsuitable for the purpose of covering an advance.

2. ASSIGNMENT OF DEBTS, CREDIT BALANCES, INTERESTS UNDER TRUSTS

ASSIGNMENT OF DEBTS

Debts due or accruing due to a person may be assigned by him to another person, either absolutely or by way of security. Debts are by no means ideal security, since the value of the security depends upon both the ability of the debtor to pay and the ease or otherwise of enforcing payment if for any reason the debtor does not pay promptly.

Legal assignment

By virtue of s. 136 of the Law of Property Act 1925, debts or other legal things in action may be assigned at law. The requirements are:

(*a*) the assignment must be by writing under the hand of the assignor;

(*b*) the assignment must be absolute and not by way of charge only;

(*c*) express notice in writing must be given to the debtor, trustee or other person liable to pay.

If these requirements are satisfied then, subject to any equities subsisting at the date upon which notice is received by the debtor, the legal right to such debt or chose in action passes to the assignee, together with all legal and other remedies for the same and the power to give a good discharge for the same without the concurrence of the assignor.

Section 136 requires only that the assignment should be in writing, though such assignments are frequently effected by deed. Although the section specifies that the assignment must be absolute and not by way of charge only, an assignment of the whole debt by way of mortgage with a proviso for redemption is an absolute assignment for the purposes of the section.[29]

If all three requirements are satisfied, then the legal right to the debt passes to the assignee, and the assignee will take priority over any prior assignees who have not given notice of assignment to the debtor, provided the assignee did not have notice, actual or constructive, of any prior assignment at the date he took his assignment. For this purpose it is the time that the assignment was made which is important, the knowledge of the assignee at the time of his giving notice being immaterial.[30]

Express notice in writing must be given to the debtor and it is wise for the banker to send the notice in duplicate asking the debtor to sign the duplicate by way of acknowledgment and return it to the banker. Ideally, the form of acknowledgment should provide for the debtor to confirm the amount of the debt, whether or not he has any right of set-off or counterclaim against the assignor and whether he has received notice of any prior assignments.

Since an assignment which satisfies those three requirements passes the right to give a good discharge for the debt, the assignee can, if the debtor notwithstanding such notice pays the assignor, still recover the debt from the debtor.[31]

Conversely, if the bank does not give notice, not only would the assignment not be effective at law (though it may be effective in equity), but the banker also runs the risk that further equities or

---

29. *Tancred* v. *Delagoa Bay Railway Company* (1889) 23 Q.B.D. 239.
30. *Mutual Life* v. *Langley* (1886) 32 Ch. D. 460.
31. *Brice* v. *Bannister* (1878) 3 Q.B.D. 569.

rights of set-off might thereafter arise as between the debtor and the assignor, and these would rank ahead of the banker, whereas after notice is given, any subsequent equities arising between the debtor and the assignor will not affect the banker's right. Furthermore, the banker runs the risk that a subsequent assignee of the same debt, who takes by assignment without notice of the banker's rights, may acquire a legal title in priority to that of the banker by giving notice to the debtor.

In the case of an assignment of a trade debt, if notice is not given to the debtor and the assignor is adjudicated bankrupt, the debt will be regarded as within the "order or disposition" of the assignor under s. 38 of the Bankruptcy Act 1914 and title to the debt will pass to his trustee in bankruptcy.[32]

If the assignment is executed by a registered company, it must be registered at the Companies Registry under s. 95 of the Companies Act 1948.[33]

An assignment of part of a debt or of a future debt can take effect in equity only.

There is no stamp duty payable on an assignment by way of mortgage.[34]

Prohibition against assignment

Sometimes the contract under which the moneys are payable contains a prohibition against assignment. If there is a such a prohibition, and the debt is assigned notwithstanding, the assignee will have no right to recover the debt from the debtor, and it seems that the assignment may be completely invalid.[35]

Equitable assignment

If the assignment is of part of a debt or is by way of charge, this can take effect in equity only and the assignee cannot recover from the debtor without the concurrence of the assignor. The reason is that in both such cases, the absolute right to the debt has not passed to the assignee and it is therefore material for the debtor to know the state of the accounts between the assignor and the assignee. Consequently, in any action on the debt, the assignee must join the assignor, either as co-plaintiff if he consents, or as co-defendant if he does not, but since most of the considerations mentioned above in relation to notice will apply to equitable assignments, written notice should always be given to the debtor.

32. *See* Chapter Thirty.
33. *See* Chapter Six.
34. Finance Act 1971, s. 74.
35. *Helstan Securities* v. *Hertfordshire County Council* [1978] 3 All E.R. 262.

An assignment of an equitable interest (whether under an express trust or otherwise) must, on general principles, take effect in equity only.[36]

Future debts

Bankers are sometimes offered as security debts which have not yet accrued due, such as debts which will fall due under contracts to supply goods or services when the assignor has performed his part of the contract, or when the time for payment arises under the contract. Such debts are clearly a less satisfactory form of security for the banker, since the assignor may not perform his part of the contract or the other party may have some counter-claim under the contract, and in any event an assignment of future debt takes effect in equity only.

If the banker agrees to accept such debts as security, notice must be given to the other party to the contract, since otherwise the other party will be free to pay the assignor. Such an assignment is, however, effective as security between the assignor and the assignee, and would prevail over a liquidator or trustee in bankruptcy of the assignor (subject to the requirements referred to above as to notice and registration under s. 95 of the Companies Act 1948), so that unless and until the debtor pays the assignor, the banker may recover the debt from the debtor (subject to joining the assignor in any proceedings). If, however, the debtor has already paid the assignor before receiving notice, the banker would lose the benefit of his security over the amount so paid and would be an unsecured creditor of the assignor.

If an advance is made to a registered company against such a contract and the company agrees to instruct the other party to remit all moneys payable under the contract direct to the company's account with the banker, and states that the instructions are irrevocable unless the banker consents in writing, such form of instruction will be regarded as an assignment of a book debt for the purposes of s. 95 of the Companies Act 1948, and would be void unless registered at the Companies Registry under that section even if there is no express document of assignment.[37]

Where a banker's customer has a sole or major customer, such as a statutory corporation or a big public company, and has a long-term supply contract with him the customer may ask the banker for short-term advances against an assignment of moneys which will

---

36. *See* under "Unit trusts" in Chapter Sixteen. In *Re Pain, Gustavson* v. *Haviland* [1919] 1 Ch. 38 it was held that it was possible to have a legal assignment by way of mortgage of an equitable interest in a trust fund, but this decision has been criticised.
37. *Re Kent & Sussex Sawmills* [1947] Ch. 177.

become payable to him under his contract with such a customer. Section 43 of the Bankruptcy Act 1914, which does not apply to companies, provides that:

(1) Where a person engaged in any trade or business makes an assignment to any other person of his existing or future book debts or any class thereof, and is subsequently adjudicated bankrupt, the assignment shall be void against the trustee as regards any book debts which have not been paid at the commencement of the bankruptcy, unless the assignment has been registered as if the assignment were a bill of sale given otherwise than by way of security for the payment of a sum of money, and the provisions of the Bills of Sale Act 1878 with respect to the registration of bills of sale shall apply accordingly, subject to such necessary modifications as may be made by rules under that Act:

Provided that nothing in this section shall have effect so as to render void any assignment of book debts due at the date of assignment from specified debtors, or of debts growing due under specified contracts, or any assignment of book debts included in a transfer of a business made bona fide and for value, or in any assignment of assets for the benefit of creditors generally.

(2) For the purposes of this section, "assignment" includes assignment by way of security and other charges on book debts.

Thus an assignment of all sums due or to become due to the customer under the existing contract with his customer will be valid, even against his trustee in bankruptcy. An assignment of all sums which may become due under any future contract with such customer would be void in the event of his bankruptcy, except as regards moneys paid before the commencement of the bankruptcy. It is, however, effective unless and until he becomes bankrupt, and so notice may be given to the third party, and should be given to stop the assignor attempting to raise moneys from another source on the same security. Notice to the other party is essential for the protection of the banker, since this would constitute an assignment of an equitable interest, and under the rule in *Dearle* v. *Hall*[38] the priority of successive assignments of equitable interests is governed by the order in which notice is received by the trustee or other person liable to pay.

An assignment by a customer of all book debts, present or future, as security would, in the case of any individual or partnership of individuals, be void against the trustee in bankruptcy under s. 43.

CREDIT BALANCES

Somewhat similar considerations apply where it is desired that credit balances with a banker be used as security for advances to a third

38. *See* "Interests under trusts" below.

party or, sometimes, to the customer himself. In this section the person with the credit balance is called "the depositor" and the person to whom the advances are made is called "the borrower"; in practice they may, of course, be the same person.

In such a case there should be a written document signed by the depositor stating that the credit balance for the time being is held as security for all moneys due from the depositor and giving the bank power either to debit the account with the depositor's liability, or to transfer from the credit balance such moneys as may be necessary to discharge the depositor's liability at any time without notice to the depositor.

If the charge is created by a registered company, it will require registration at the Companies Registry under s. 95 of the Companies Act 1948,[39] as being a charge on a book debt.

If the borrower is a third party, then either the document of charge should expressly state that the credit balance is held as security for the liability of the borrower, rather than the depositor's own liability, and the document should also include certain of the usual "guarantor" clauses,[40] or there should in addition be a separate form of guarantee signed by the depositor.

If there is an objection from the depositor to executing a document which requires registration at the Companies Registry, bankers sometimes agree to dispense with an express charge over the credit balance. In such cases, there should be some document containing a clause giving the bank a lien over "all securities belonging to me now or hereafter held by the bank and all moneys now or hereafter standing to my credit with the bank on any account or other account", or preferably, since it has been stated that the right of the banker to resort to a credit balance is not truly a lien, but in reality a right of set-off,[41] the banker should have, either in the guarantee if there is one, or in a separate agreement or letter if the credit balance is that of the borrower, a clause conferring on the banker an express right of set-off.[42]

In either case, it would be a sensible precaution for the credit balance to be deposited either for a fixed period, expiring a day or two after the liability of the borrower will mature, or withdrawable on a specified period of notice, so that in the period before maturity, or during the period of notice, the banker and the borrower will

39. See Chapter Six.
40. See especially Clauses 2, 6, 8 and 11 in the specimen form of guarantee in Appendix I.
41. Halesowen Presswork and Assemblies v. National Westminster Bank [1971] 1 Q.B. 25; [1970] 3 All E.R. 473.
42. See Clause 13 in the specimen form of guarantee in Appendix I.

have time to make other arrangements and, if necessary, the banker will resort to the credit balance to satisfy the liability.

INTERESTS UNDER TRUSTS

It occasionally happens that a banker is offered as security an interest under a trust. The interest offered may be a life interest under a will, or possibly the remainder expectant upon the determination of a life interest, but the principles referred to in this chapter would apply to any equitable interest in property.

As a general rule, any equitable interest may be assigned, provided the assignor is of full age and capacity. The exceptions are that some trusts contain provisions under which, if the beneficiary attempts to change or alienate his interest under the trust, the interest passes to someone else; such restrictions are expressly permitted by s. 33 of the Trustee Act 1925. In addition, there may be some restriction in the contract or other instrument creating the trust preventing the party entitled to the interest from charging or alienating it, and if there is such a restriction and it is valid and effective, alienation or charge might have the consequence of either terminating or giving the other party the right to terminate the arrangement.

Where there is no effective prohibition against assignment, any disposition of an equitable interest or trust must be in writing signed by the person disposing of the same (or by an agent duly authorised in writing or by will).[43] In practice, the mortgage would be by deed, and the deed would be substantially in the same form as a mortgage of a debt or other chose in action.

Defects of the security

This form of security has, however, inherent weaknesses. In the case of a legal mortgage of land, the banker can, if the mortgagor defaults, effectively exercise all the powers of the mortgagor in relation to the land and either sell it or appoint a receiver to manage the property. However, since the beneficiary's powers in relation to the trust property are very limited, and no mortgagee can be in a better position than the mortgagor himself, the mortgagee's powers are similarly limited where the mortage is of an interest under a trust. The beneficiary may require the conduct of the trustees to be supervised by the court, if they are not managing the trust property correctly, and is entitled to see annual accounts. Apart from that his basic right will be limited to receiving either the income if he is a life tenant, or the fixed sum if he is entitled to a fixed annuity,

43. Law of Property Act 1925, s. 53(1)(c).

or to waiting for the appropriate amount of capital to be paid to
him when he becomes entitled to capital, and the banker mortgagee
can be in a better position than this. In particular, if the beneficiary
is a life tenant, the banker cannot give directions to the trustees
as to how the trust property is to be managed, or how the capital
should be invested.

Notice to the trustees

As in the case of assignments under s. 136 of the Law of Property
Act 1925, notice should be given to the trustees, but under the rule
in *Dearle* v. *Hall*,[44] as amended by s. 137 of the Law of Property
Act 1925, the priority of successive assignments of equitable interests
is governed by the order in which written notice of the assignments
is received by the owner of the legal estate. There is a further difficulty
here in that one cannot tell simply by examining the trust instrument
who is the owner of the legal estate, as there may have been changes
in trustees since the will or other trust instrument or the governing
document was executed.

It is, therefore, a wise precaution for the banker to write to the
persons who were the original trustees, or who are suspected by the
banker as being the current trustees, to inquire of them whether
they are indeed still the trustees. Moreover, since a trust corporation
may be nominated either by the original trust instrument or by the
trustees at any time as being the person to whom notices of dealings
affecting the property may be given,[45] the banker should also inquire
whether any such trust corporation has been so nominated. The
inquiry should also ask whether any other notices of assignment
have been received. Notice of assignment should be given to the
current trustees, or the trust corporation as appropriate, immediately
after the assignment. Such notice should be given in duplicate and
the trustees or trust corporation should be asked to acknowledge
receipt, and to confirm both that they are the current trustees (or
the trust corporation nominated for receipt of notices of dealings)
and that no notice of any previous assignment has been
received. For safety's sake such steps should all be taken, and such
acknowledgement and confirmation should be received, before any
advances are made.

Enforcement

The method of enforcing such a charge is not particularly attractive.
As with any other mortgage, so long as the mortgagor is not in

44. [1828] 3 Russ. 1.
45. Law of Property Act 1925, s. 138(1).

default, the income will belong to the mortgagor, unless specific arrangements to the contrary are made between the banker and the mortgagor. So, even if the income is paid to the banker in the first instance, the banker will, unless any such other arrangement has been made, have to account to the mortgagor for it, until the mortgagor defaults. After he does default, the banker may still be able to do no more than continue to receive the trust income so long as the life interest lasts or, as the case may be, wait for the right to the capital to mature. In the last resort, the banker may be able to sell the interest. In this case, what the banker can sell will, of course, be restricted to the interest of the beneficiary, and except in the case of a reversionary interest for which there is a limited market in the City of London, there may be difficulties in finding a buyer, especially of a life interest, unless the life tenant's life is insured for an appropriate sum and the life policy is also assigned to the buyer.

3. GOODS

Goods may be taken as security for advances. This is most frequently done where merchants, usually importers of raw materials, are buying goods for the purpose of resale. More rarely this method of raising finance is used by manufacturers who will be processing the goods or mixing them with other goods and making them up into a finished product. For various reasons, this is less satisfactory.

The advantages to a bank in lending against this form of security are twofold. There is usually a fairly rapid turnover, and, provided that the banker is acting in good faith and is dealing with honourable merchants, the banker will get a good title. The disadvantages are that it may be difficult to put a true value on the security, especially if the market in the goods concerned is volatile; much detailed clerical work may be required by the banker; there may be heavy insurance and storage charges; and there is ample scope for fraudulent customers to defeat the banker's rights.[46]

DOCUMENTS OF TITLE TO GOODS

Since the security is almost invariably effected by taking actual delivery of the documents of title to the goods, it is necessary to consider the various forms of documents of title, and to distinguish between (a) those documents that give a title to the goods named in them, and (b) those documents which are merely receipts acknow-

46. *See* below in this chapter.

ledging that the goods have been lodged in the warehouse. Bills of lading, dock and warehouse-keeper's transferable warrants are documents of the first category; warehouse-keeper's certificates and delivery orders are documents of the second category.

The bona fide possession of bills of lading and warrants gives a complete title to possession of the goods, whereas possession of the certificates and delivery orders is merely a means to an end, namely delivery of the goods, or the issue of a document of the former class, which will give a complete title to the goods.

The distinction is important in the event of bankruptcy, since the bona fide possession of a bill of lading or a dock warrant by a banker is sufficient to take the goods out of the "order and disposition" of the bankrupt.[47] Possession, however, of a non-transferable warehouse-keeper's warrant or a warehouse-keeper's certificate or a delivery order is of no avail against the claim of the trustee in bankruptcy to the goods unless the goods have been registered in the banker's name.[48]

The chief Acts regulating these documents are the Factors Act 1889 and the Sale of Goods Act 1979. Section 1(4) of the Factors Act 1889 defines documents of title as including "any bill of lading, dock warrant, warehouse-keeper's certificate, and warrant or order for the delivery of goods, and any other document used in the ordinary course of business as proof of the possession or control of goods, or authorising, or purporting to authorise, either by in-dorsement or by delivery, the possessor of the document to transfer or receive goods thereby represented." Section 4 of the Bills of Sale Act 1878 expressly excludes all such documents of title from the definition of a bill of sale, so that they do not require registration as bills of sale.

DEFINITIONS

Bill of lading

A bill of lading is a document issued and signed by the master of a ship or by his agent, and is given to the person shipping goods on board the vessel.[49] The document performs a threefold function:

(a) it acknowledges that the goods have been received on board;
(b) it is evidence of the contract of affreightment; and
(c) it is an undertaking to deliver the goods, in the order and condition in which they were received, to the consignee or to his

47. Bankruptcy Act 1914, s. 38.
48. *See* under "Reputed ownership" in Chapter Thirty.
49. A specimen is set out in Appendix I.

order, provided that the freight and any other charges specified in the bill have been duly paid.

By virtue of the third function, it is a document of title.

Bills of lading are exempt from stamp duty.[50]

A dock warrant

A dock warrant, or warehouse-keeper's warrant, is a document issued by a warehouse-keeper in exchange for goods deposited. It describes the goods, acknowledges receipt of them and contains an undertaking to deliver them to the order of the depositor or his assigns.[51]

Some warehouse-keepers have statutory authority to issue warrants which are transferable, but where a warrant is issued by a warehouse-keeper who does not have such statutory authority, the warrant is not transferable, and indorsement and delivery is insufficient to pass the property in the goods. A banker who accepts a pledge of goods in a warehouse must bear the distinction in mind; moreover, even those warrants which are transferable are not negotiable instruments, and so a transferee cannot obtain a better title than the transferor.

Warehouse-keeper's warrants are exempt from stamp duty.[52]

Warehouse-keeper's certificate

A warehouse-keeper's certificate, or warehouse-keeper's receipt, is a document given by a warehouse-keeper certifying that he holds certain goods described in the certificate, and awaits instructions for their disposal from the person to whom the certificate is addressed. This is simply a receipt for the goods and indicates on the face of it that it is not transferable.[53]

It is not a document of title. If the owner wants to get the goods out of the warehouse, he must send delivery instructions to the warehouse-keeper, or obtain a warrant from the warehouse-keeper, by which the goods are deliverable either to the owner or to his assigns by indorsement. Conversely, if the owner wishes to sell them, he must execute in favour of the buyer either a transfer order directing the warehouse-keeper to hold the goods in the name of the purchaser, or a delivery order directing the warehouse-keeper to deliver the goods to the purchaser.

Warehouse-keeper's certificates are exempt from stamp duty.[54]

50. Finance Act 1949, s. 35 and Sched. 8.
51. A specimen is set out in Appendix I.
52. Finance Act 1949, s. 35 and Sched. 8.
53. A specimen is set out in Appendix I.
54. Finance Act 1949, s. 35 and Sched. 8.

Delivery order

A delivery order is a document containing the owner's instructions regarding delivery, addressed to the proprietors of the warehouse where the goods are lodged.[55] The owner fills in the name of the person—either himself or his assigns—who is authorised to receive the goods. The document does not require stamping.[56]

FORMS OF SECURITY

Goods may be made security either by pledge or by mortgage.

Mortgage

A mortgage is the conveyance or transfer of a legal or equitable interest in the property as security. There is no delivery of the goods, but the general property passes to the mortgagee by the mortgage document.

Mortgages of goods in writing are rare, for they are subject to the Bills of Sale Acts. These involve registration, and so are disliked by the business community. A further drawback is that a bill of sale given by way of security is void unless in the prescribed form,[57] and the prescribed form is frequently inappropriate for the type of transaction contemplated.

A parol mortgage of goods is possible, if completed by actual delivery, and the terms of the mortgage may be proved by oral evidence.[58] Indeed a parol mortgage is good at common law even without delivery, but since the chattels then remain in the order and disposition of the customer, the mortgagee would have no priority over the general creditors if the customer was an individual and became bankrupt.[59]

Even where the banker is not dealing with an individual or partnership, a parol form of security is not to be recommended, and in the case of a registered company, a floating charge would be preferable.

Pledge

A pledge arises when goods (or documents of title to goods) or bearer securities are delivered by the pledgor to the pledgee, on the understanding that the property will be restored to the pledgor when the

55. A specimen is set out in Appendix I.
56. Finance Act 1949, s. 35 and Sched. 8.
57. Bills of Sale Act 1882, s. 9.
58. Compare *Woodgate* v. *Godfrey* (1879) 5 Ex. D. 24; *North Central Wagon Co.* v. *Manchester, Sheffield and Lincolnshire Rail Co.* (1887) 35 Ch. D. 191.
59. *See* under "Reputed ownership" in Chapter Thirty.

debt or obligation has been discharged. Unlike a mortgage, a pledge is incomplete without delivery.[60] A pledge transfers only a special property which enables the pledgee to deal with the goods, if necessary, in order to enforce his rights; the general property remains as a legal interest in the pledgor.

The method of enforcing a pledge is by sale. If there is a fixed time for payment, the pledgee has an implied power to sell on default; if no time has been fixed for payment, the pledgee must demand payment and may only exercise the power of sale after giving notice to the pledgor of his intention to sell if payment is not made.[61]

Although delivery is essential, delivery need not be physical delivery of the goods. Constructive delivery, in the sense of delivery of the documents of title to the goods, is sufficient.

Lien
Both mortgages and pledges differ from liens, since a lien is only a personal right to hold the goods of another until a debt is paid; a lien cannot be assigned and continues only so long as the possessor of the right holds the goods.

Letter of hypothecation
Security over goods is frequently created by the execution of a letter of hypothecation. "Hypothecation" is in fact a misnomer, since strictly speaking a hypothecation is a transaction whereby goods may be made available as security for a debt without a transfer of either the property or the possession to the lender. What is usually known as a "letter of hypothecation" is in fact a form of pledge.[62] It is not subject to the Bills of Sale Acts, since the definition of a bill of sale excludes any documents used in the ordinary course of business as a proof of possession or control of goods, or authorising, or purporting to authorise, the possessor of the document to transfer or receive goods thereby represented.[63]

When documents of title are lodged as security, a letter of hypothecation should always be taken. The banker for his protection should see that the goods are adequately insured. Where the banker holds the documents but is not registered as owner of the goods, he may sometimes find it necessary, in order to prevent dealings in the goods without his consent, to lodge a "stop order" with the warehouse-keeper or dock company.

60. *Martin* v. *Reid* (1862) 11 C.B.N.S. 730.
61. *Burdick* v. *Sewell* (1883) 10 Q.B.D. 363 at pp. 366, 367; *Re Morritt, ex parte Official Receiver* (1886) 18 Q.B.D. 222.
62. A specimen of a general letter of hypothecation is set out in Appendix I.
63. *See* under "Bills of sale" in this chapter.

Trust receipt

A trust receipt is a document used where goods over which a banker already has security, generally in the form of a letter of hypothecation, and possession of the documents of title is prepared to release the documents of title to the customer in order for the customer to sell them. In exchange for the documents of title, the banker receives from the customer a trust receipt by which the customer undertakes to hold the goods in question on trust for the banker, to warehouse the goods in the name of the banker, to pay the proceeds of sale to the banker without deduction, to keep the transaction and the relative documents separate from all other transactions and documents, and to deliver the documents of title to the banker upon request at any time.[64].

GENERAL CONSIDERATIONS

It is generally more convenient to make advances against goods by way of loan, each parcel or consignment being the subject of a separate loan. In this way each advance can be more readily followed. Advances against goods and produce are essentially of a short-term character.

When a banker takes a document of title as security for an advance, he does not obtain a security of the premier class. Documents of title do not guarantee the value, or even, in extreme cases, the existence, of the goods described in them. Moreover, unlike the case of title deeds to land, possession of the documents of title to goods does not prevent the customer from dealing physically with the goods without the knowledge of the banker. Any such dealing would, of course, be fraudulent, and may be impossible without the connivance of the warehouse-keeper, but the banker must be aware of the risk that such dealings may take place.

Since documents of title are not negotiable instruments, a title to the goods cannot under any circumstances be acquired through a thief who has stolen the documents of title. They are, however, transferable. There are three classes of persons from whom they may be taken as security:

(a) the owner of the goods;
(b) his transferee;
(c) a mercantile agent in possession of the documents as agent.

---

64. A specimen is set out in Appendix I.

A seller who has sold goods and has not been paid for them[65] has a lien on the goods if they are still in his possession[66] and the right, so long as the goods are in transit to the buyer, to stop delivery of them if the buyer has become insolvent.[67] This latter right is called the right of stoppage *in transitu*, and is lost if the goods have passed into the possession of the buyer.[68] It is not necessary, in order to defeat the right, that the goods should have reached the destination intended. If the buyer gets possession of them on the way to the destination, the right is lost.[69] So also, if by arrangement between the carrier and the buyer, the goods are held by the carrier in his warehouse as bailee for the buyer.[70] If, however, the carrier has only delivered part of the goods, he is as a rule bound to stop delivery of the remainder as soon as he receives notice.[71]

This right of the seller to stop *in transitu* is not affected if the buyer re-sells the goods without his consent,[72] but if the buyer lawfully obtains possession of the bill of lading or other document of title to the goods, and transfers the document to a person who takes it bona fide and for value so that he becomes a buyer of the goods, then the seller's right of stoppage *in transitu* is gone.[73] The banker is not usually affected by the unpaid seller's right of stoppage *in transitu*, since if a transfer is made by way of pledge or other disposition for value, the unpaid seller's right of lien or retention or stoppage *in transitu* can only be exercised subject to the rights of the transferee.[73] However, in order that the unpaid seller's rights may be defeated, it is essential that the original buyer shall have obtained the document of title from the unpaid seller with his consent.

The second buyer, to get a good title, must also be "without notice of any lien or other right of the original seller in respect of the goods".[74]

When the seller sends the documents of title to the buyer, it is quite usual to send with them a bill of exchange for the price of the goods. If this is done the buyer must accept or pay the bill, according to the terms of the contract, or he is bound to return

---

65. *See* Sale of Goods Act 1979, s. 38 for definition of unpaid seller. The rights of an unpaid seller under that Act may be negatived or varied by express agreement or by the course of dealing between the parties, or by usage (ibid., s. 55).
66. Ibid., s. 41.
67. Ibid., s. 44.
68. Ibid., s. 45(1).
69. Ibid., s. 45(2).
70. Ibid., s. 45(3).
71. Ibid., s. 45(7).
72. Ibid., s. 47(1).
73. Ibid., s. 47(2).
74. Ibid., s. 25(1).

the documents. If he refuses the bill but retains the documents, the property in the goods does not pass to him.[75] At the time the contract was made, the buyer may not have had any intention of paying for the goods, but since he is considered to be in possession of the documents with the consent of the owner, he can give a good title to a transferee who takes them in good faith and for value, in spite of the fact that the transferor fails to fulfil his bargain with the original seller, namely to pay or, as the case may be, accept a bill of exchange for the price of the goods.[76]

Where a mercantile agent is with the consent of the owner in possession of the documents of title to goods, any pledge or other disposition of the goods made by him when acting in the ordinary course of business of a mercantile agent has the same effect as if he were expressly authorised by the owner to make the same, provided that the person taking the goods acts in good faith and at the time of the disposition is not aware of the absence of authority.[77]

As a general rule, any form of valuable consideration is sufficient consideration for the validity of a sale, pledge or other disposition of goods in pursuance of the Factors Act.[78] The qualifications are as follows.

(a) If goods are pledged by a mercantile agent in consideration of the delivery or transfer of other goods, or of a document of title to goods, or of a negotiable security, the pledgee acquires no right or interest in the goods so pledged in excess of the value of the goods, documents or security when so delivered in exchange.[78]

(b) Where a mercantile agent pledges goods as security for a debt or liability due from the pledgor to the pledgee before the time of the pledge, the pledgee acquires no further right to the goods than could have been enforced by the pledgor at the time of the pledge.[79] This would amount to nothing more than what the agent could have claimed for commission and expenses.

A mercantile agent is defined as a person "having in the customary course of his business as such agent authority either to sell goods, or to consign goods for the purpose of sale, or to buy goods, or to raise money on the security of goods."[80]

Bills of lading
Bills of lading are, as we have seen, (a) contracts between the ship-

75. Sale of Goods Act 1979, s. 19(3).
76. *Cahn* v. *Pockett's Bristol Channel Steam Packet Co.* [1899] 1 Q.B. 643.
77. Factors Act 1889, s. 2.
78. Ibid., s. 5.
79. Ibid., s. 4.
80. Ibid., s. 1(1).

owners and the shippers of goods, (*b*) documents of title to the goods. They are symbols of the goods while at sea and until the goods are delivered to the person entitled to receive them. From the banker's point of view, a disadvantage is his dependence upon the word of the shipper that the bill of lading represents the kind and quantity of goods it purports to represent. The banker must be sure that the merchandise is in good demand and readily marketable, and that there is an adequate margin of value over the amount of the relative advance. He must remember that the margin has to take care of accruing charges for storage and insurance.

As a general rule bills of lading are issued in triplicate, one copy being retained by the shipper and the other two being sent by different mails to the consignee. As soon as the consignee gets possession of the bill of lading, he is entitled to sell or otherwise deal with the goods, even while they are at sea. This he does by indorsing the bill of lading and transferring it for value to the buyer of the goods.

When the goods arrive at the port of destination the person rightfully entitled to the goods, whether as consignee, indorsee, or holder of the bill of lading, should be ready to receive the goods. He proves his right to the goods by presenting the bill of lading to the captain. If two parts of a bill of lading are transferred to two different parties, the first transferee for value has the legal title to the goods.[81] To avoid any difficulty for the ship's captain, should the first presenter of one part of the bill of lading happen not to be the legal owner of the goods, bills of lading drawn in a set always contain the clause, "one of which being accomplished, the others to stand void." This clause enables the ship's master to hand over the goods to the first presenter, provided always that in so doing he acts in good faith and without notice of an alleged prior claim.[82] If he does receive notice of a prior claim before he has delivered the goods, he may interplead, i.e. claim the protection of the court and force the opposing parties to prove to the satisfaction of the court who has the right to the goods.

The possibility of such a twofold claim to the goods makes it necessary that the banker should get all the parts of the bill of lading into his own hands. If this is not possible he should give notice to the shipowner as soon as possible. If the goods have been warehoused, notice of his claim should be sent to the warehouse-keeper.

A "Through bill of lading" is one given when the goods in transit have to pass through the hands of more than one carrying company, whether shipowners or railway companies. The contract is made with

81. *Barber* v. *Meyerstein* (1870) L.R. 4 H.L. 317; *Caldwell* v. *Ball* (1786) 1 Term. Rep. 205.
82. *Glyn Mills & Co.* v. *East and West India Dock Co.* (1882) 7 App. Cas. 591.

the first carrying company, which charges an inclusive rate for the whole journey. Through bills of lading usually incorporate by reference the usual form of bill of lading used by the shipowner, and other clauses and terms limiting the liability of each company to loss or damage incurred while the goods are actually under the control of the company.

Another type of shipping document is the "Received for shipment bill of lading". Having regard to the definition of a proper bill of lading, the "Received for shipment" variety is a contradiction in terms. It enables the shipowner to ship the relative goods as and when he can, but from the banker's point of view there is a risk that the goods may have to wait for some time at the quay, either deteriorating or arriving too late for the market. Hence, if the banker is operating under a credit which calls for "On board" or "Shipped" bills of lading (the proper and normal kind) or shipment by a specified time, it is essential that the document be indorsed "Received on board" and dated with the actual date of receipt and the name of the carrying steamer if not the same as that on the bill of lading.

A bill of lading is a peculiar document in that it has (when drawn "to order or assigns") some of the qualities of a negotiable instrument and yet is not really negotiable. The person transferring it can as a general rule give no better title to the goods than he has himself. If he has stolen the bill of lading, he cannot confer any title to the goods, even to an innocent transferee for value. In some cases, however, he can give a better title, if, for example, he fails to accept the accompanying bill of exchange yet transfers the bill of lading to a bona fide transferee for value.[83] However, the bill of lading is similar to a negotiable instrument, in that possession of it by a bona fide transferee for value defeats the lien of the unpaid vendor and his right of stoppage *in transitu*, but this may be said to be due to the peculiar nature of the unpaid seller's right, rather than to any truly negotiable quality of the bill of lading, and it may be stated definitely that a bill of lading is not a negotiable instrument.

Another drawback to a bill of lading as a security is to be found in the provision safeguarding the interest of the shipowner and limiting his liability. In addition to the ordinary clauses, another clause frequently introduced, namely "and all other conditions as per charter party", may involve the payment of possibly heavy charges for dead freight and charter party demurrage—charges incurred through no fault on the part of the banker or the shipper. The banker, therefore, before lending on this kind of security should ascertain what the "other conditions" are. Another point to be considered

83. Sale of Goods Act 1979, ss. 19(3) and 25(2).

is that though the goods as described on the bill of lading are signed for by the ship's captain, it does not follow that these are the actual goods shipped. A bill of lading in the hands of a consignee or indorsee for valuable consideration representing goods to have been shipped on board a vessel is conclusive evidence of such shipment as against the master or other person signing the same, but the master or other person so signing the same may exonerate himself in respect of such misrepresentation by showing that it was caused without any default on his part and wholly by the fraud of the shipper, or of the holder, or some person under whom the holder claims.[84] The onus rests upon him.

If the bill of lading states that the goods are shipped "in good order and condition", without any qualifying indorsement, it is termed "clean". This does not constitute a warranty, but does amount to a representation of fact that the goods were shipped in apparent good order and condition,[85] and if an indorsee changes his position on the faith of this representation and sues the shipowner for delivering the goods in bad condition, the shipowner may be estopped from denying that the goods were shipped in apparent good order and condition.[86] He will not, however, be estopped from proving that the internal condition of the goods was bad.[87] In view of this, the bill of lading usually has a note to the effect that "weight and contents are unknown", and all that the shipowner contracts to do is to deliver them in the same condition as when they were received.

As already stated, the actual value of the goods depends upon the honesty of the person shipping the goods. The value stated in the invoice and the amount for which the goods are insured are as a general rule a very fair guide as to the value of the shipment. After all, as Lord Bowen once said: "Credit, not distrust, is the basis of commercial dealings; mercantile genius consists principally in knowing whom to trust and with whom to deal, and commercial intercourse and communication are no more based on the supposition of fraud than on the supposition of forgery."[88] If this were not so the relationship of banker and customer would be an impossible one.

Where a bill of lading is delivered to the consignee, or transferred by indorsement to an indorsee, with the intention of passing the property in the goods, the rights and liabilities contained in the bill of lading are transferred to the consignee or indorsee as if the bill

84. Bills of Lading Act 1855, s. 3.
85. *Compania Naviera Vasconzada* v. *Churchill & Sim* [1906] 1 K.B. 237.
86. *Silver* v. *Ocean Steamship Co.* [1930] 1 K.B. 416; *The Skarp* [1935] p. 134.
87. *Compania Naviera Vasconzada* v. *Churchill & Sim* [1906] 1 K.B. 237.
88. *Sanders Bros.* v. *Maclean & Co.* (1883) 11 Q.B.D. 327.

of lading had been made with himself.[89] However, although the indorsement and pledge of a bill of lading by way of security gives the pledgee the right to claim delivery of the goods,[90] it was held in *Sewell* v. *Burdick*[91] that the pledgee is not liable to the shipowner under the contract contained in the bill of lading for freight and other charges unless and until he exercises this right and claims delivery.

This decision is an important one for bankers. The lender had advanced £300 on a bill of lading indorsed in blank. The goods were landed in Russia, and by Russian law the lender had no power to sell the goods to pay the shipper's charges—the cause of action—which amounted to nearly £180. As it turned out, when the goods were actually sold by the Russian authorities, they only realised sufficient to pay customs duties and other charges. It was decided that the shipper retained "the real and substantial property in the goods, subject to the security". If the lender had lost the action, he would have had to pay the freight and charges, plus the costs of the action, besides being a (by then) unsecured creditor for the £300 he had lent the shipper. However, if the lender, whether he has actually indorsed the bill of lading or not, wishes to obtain delivery of the goods in order to sell them, then he must pay all outstanding freight and charges.

To avoid all possible risk of liability, the better course is for the bill of lading to be indorsed in blank, and for the banker's name not to appear in them at all. The banker's claim in such circumstances would have to be supported by a memorandum or letter of hypothecation, and when the goods were to be warehoused, the banker would have to give notice to the warehouse-keeper to protect his position.

The insurance policy or certificate of insurance should always accompany a bill of lading. In the case of a c.i.f. (cost, insurance and freight) contract, it has been held that the buyers are entitled to demand that a policy of insurance be produced and that a broker's note or certificate of insurance is not sufficient.[92]

It should be carefully noted whether the description of the goods in the bill of lading tallies with that in the policy. If the policy is a "floating policy", it should be ascertained that the particular shipment has been "declared", and indorsed and initialled by the underwriter to show that it has been noted and approved. This kind of policy is often called an "open policy". The name is not strictly

89. Bills of Lading Act 1855, s. 1.
90. *Bristol and West of England Bank* v. *Midland Railway Co.* [1891] 2 Q.B. 653.
91. (1884) 10 App. Cas. 74.
92. *Wilson, Holgate & Co.* v. *Belgian Grain & Produce Co.* (1920) 2 K.B. 1 cited with approval in *Scott* v. *Barclays Bank* [1923] 2 K.B. 1.

accurate, since an open policy is really a policy in which the value of the subject matter of the insurance is not stated, but left to be ascertained and proved.

Trust receipt

The essence of arrangements for advances secured on goods is that the customer sells the goods and repays the advance out of the proceeds of sale, but the customer cannot effect a sale without having the bills of lading and any other documents of title. It is, therefore, necessary for the banker to release the documents of title to the customer, but without releasing his security over the goods. It is usual for the documents to be released to customers against signature of a "trust receipt".

By the trust receipt, the customer in effect agrees to hold the proceeds of sale of the goods as the banker's security in place of the goods themselves, and a trust receipt should only be used in a case where the goods were previously in the actual or constructive possession of the banker and were duly pledged to the banker.[93]

The purpose of the trust receipt is to maintain the original charge, and if the customer becomes bankrupt, the trustee or liquidator cannot claim the goods for the benefit of the unsecured creditors. The effectiveness of trust receipts has been upheld. They are appropriate only where the security has already been created, so that the banker, being entitled to realise the goods himself, is merely entrusting the realisation of the goods to an expert in this field, the pledgor customer, on his behalf. It was held as long ago as 1905[94] that trust receipts are documents used in the ordinary course of business as proof of possession or control of goods. They are therefore not bills of sale, and so do not require registration under the Bills of Sale Acts, and so long as the pledge existed before, they are not used to create security and so do not require registration under the Companies Acts either.[95]

Although trust receipts have been described as "a very convenient business method", there are risks in permitting the customer to deal with the goods in this way, since if the customer deals dishonestly with the goods, a bona fide transferee may prevail over the banker's security.

Just as land law has always favoured the bona fide purchaser for value of the legal estate without notice of prior equitable interests, so the law merchant has always favoured his equivalent in other fields. In the case of bills of exchange, he is a holder in due course.

93. A specimen is set out in Appendix I.
94. *Re Hamilton Young & Co.* [1905] 2 K.B. 772.
95. *Re David Allester* [1922] 2 Ch. 211.

In sales of goods, where a buyer obtains possession of goods or documents of title to goods with the consent of the seller, and delivers or transfers the goods or documents of title under a sale, pledge, or other disposition to any person receiving the same in good faith and without notice of any lien or other right of the original seller, the delivery or transfer has the same effect as if he were expressly authorised to make the same by the owner, so long as the person taking the goods acts in good faith and was not aware of the absence of authority.[96] This in effect means that if the customer dishonestly pledges the goods to another banker, the second banker will, provided he acts in good faith and without notice, take priority over the first banker, who will accordingly lose the benefit of his security.[97]

Another disadvantage is that the goods supposedly represented by the documents of title may simply not be there. If the bills of lading are released by the banker in order that the goods may be warehoused, the banker should expect to receive a warehouse-keeper's warrant from the customer within a reasonable time. Indeed, the bank may wish to warehouse the goods in its own name without releasing the documents of title to the customer and may therefore send the documents of title to the warehouse-keeper so that the warehouse-keeper may arrange for their collection from on board the ship. The banker must then ensure that he receives the warehouse-keeper's warrant from the warehouse-keeper without delay, and if, as most warehouse-keepers attempt to do today, the warehouse-keeper insists upon importing into his contract with the banker some standard conditions of contract which seek to exclude all liability on the part of the warehouse-keeper for loss or damage to the goods, except in cases of fraud, wilful default or gross negligence, and limit the liability of the warehouse-keeper, the banker should seek to have such conditions excluded. Such conditions may be more difficult to enforce now, since the coming into effect of the Unfair Contract Terms Act 1977, but it is clearly safer to secure the removal of such clauses in advance.

When the customer wishes to take up the goods from the warehouse, or sell them to a purchaser, he will require a release note from the banker, who should first obtain a trust receipt from the customer. Even here there is some possibility of fraud, if the customer persuades the warehouse-keeper to allow the customer to take up the goods before the warehouse-keeper receives a release note from

96. This is the combined effect of the Sale of Goods Act 1979, s. 25(1), and the Factors Act 1889, ss. 2 and 9.
97. *Lloyds Bank* v. *Bank of America National Trust and Savings Association* [1938] 2 K.B. 137; [1938] 2 All E.R. 63.

the banker, either by persuading the warehouse-keeper to join in some deception on the banker or by convincing the warehouse-keeper that he will not be under any risk in releasing the goods without a release note, since the release note will assuredly follow shortly from the banker. Indeed, if such conduct is repeated and the warehouse-keeper regularly receives the release note after releasing the goods to the customer, there may come a time when the warehouse-keeper may be entitled to rely on the customer's assurances about the release note, so that he will not be responsible to the banker for release of the goods without a release note. This risk may be minimised if the banker receives from the warehouse-keeper regular certificates as to the goods currently held by the warehouse-keeper on behalf of the banker.

It is, however, beyond the scope of this book to go in detail into all the various possibilities of fraud and how to avoid them. Business of this nature, as has been noted above, is conducted on the basis of trust, rather than on the supposition of fraud, but the banker ought to be aware of the possibility of fraud.

4. SHIP MORTGAGES

By s. 2(1) of the Merchant Shipping Act 1894, every British ship must be registered, except certain ships up to 15 tons.[98] The property in a ship is divided into sixty-four shares. A registered ship or any share therein must be transferred by "bill of sale", but the purchaser does not get a complete title until the bill of sale has been registered at the ship's port of registry. A registered ship or a share therein may be made a security for a loan. The Act prescribes the form of the mortgage, which must be duly registered by the Registrar at the ship's port of registry.[99] The prompt registration of the mortgage deed is essential for the security of the mortgage, because the mortgage takes its priority from the date of production for registration, and not from the date of the instrument. Every registered mortgagee has power to dispose of the ship or share in respect of which he is registered, but except under the order of the court a subsequent mortgagee cannot sell without the concurrence of the prior mortgagee.[100] A charge given by a company on a ship or any share in a ship must also be registered with the Registrar of Companies.[101]

98. Merchant Shipping Act 1894, s. 5(1).
99. Ibid., s. 31(1).
100. Ibid., s. 35.
101. Companies Act 1948, s. 95.

Before taking a charge the banker should search the register to ascertain whether any prior charges exist. When the mortgage is discharged, the Registrar on production of the mortgage deed, with a receipt for the mortgage money indorsed thereon, must enter the fact of discharge in the register book.[102] The certificate of registry, which can only be used for the lawful navigation of the ship,[103] is of no value to the mortgagee. Instruments used in connection with the registry, ownership or mortgage of a British ship are exempt from stamp duty.

Though no notice of any trust can be entered in the register book, equitable interests are recognised, but a registered legal mortgagee has priority over every equitable charge, even though the equitable charge was prior in order of date.[104] Priority is determined by order of date in the register, and equitable charges cannot be registered,[105] but if a second mortgagee gives notice of his charge to the banker he can claim priority over any advance made by the banker under the legal mortgage after receipt of the notice.

The value of a ship's mortgage as a security can be seriously diminished by the priority over the mortgage of certain maritime liens, such as seamen's wages, master's wages, salvage and collision damage to another vessel.

When a ship is owned by several persons, one of them is usually entrusted with the control and management of the ship. This person is called the "managing owner". Where the controller of the ship is not one of the owners he is called the "ship's husband". The powers of a managing owner or a ship's husband include the borrowing of money for purposes necessary for the ship, but the borrowing must not be on the credit of the shipowners except in circumstances of necessity.[106] The managing owner (or ship's husband) is entrusted with the management of the ship, but he cannot bind his co-owners unless he is in fact their agent.[107] The name of the managing owner or other person to whom the management of the ship is entrusted must be entered on the register at the ship's port of registry.[108] Unless expressly or impliedly authorised, the co-owners will not be liable for any overdraft created by the managing owner or ship's husband since the latter are acting as agents, and to avoid all risk the co-owners should join in a mandate respecting the opening of the account and the borrowing powers of the signatories.

102. Merchant Shipping Act 1894, s. 32.
103. Ibid., s. 15.
104. Ibid., s. 56.
105. Ibid., s. 33.
106. *Pringle* v. *Dixon* (1896) 2 Comm. Cas. 38.
107. *Frazer* v. *Cuthbertson* (1880) 6 Q.B.D. 93.
108. Merchant Shipping Act 1894, s. 59.

The banker who advances money on this kind of security should obtain possession of the marine insurance policy (or policies), the assignment being indorsed on the policy, or, preferably, the banker should transfer the money into his own name or into the names of his nominees. The fact that ships heavily depreciate in value year by year should be carefully borne in mind by the banker when, as frequently happens, he is periodically asked to lend money on the same ship.

The subject of ship mortgages is a vast topic, and what has been said is no more than the barest sketch.

5. BILLS OF SALE

A bill of sale is a document under seal which, for consideration, transfers the title to personal chattels from one person to another. The full definition is to be found in s. 4 of the Bills of Sale Act 1878; the essence of a bill of sale is the transfer of ownership without possession, and certain documents, including documents used in the ordinary course of business as proof of the possession or control of goods, are excluded. Bills of sale are of two kinds: (a) absolute, or (b) conditional. Absolute bills of sale pass the property absolutely to the transferee; conditional bills of sale pass it by way of security for the payment of money. Conditional bills of sale, the only kind with which we are concerned, are in the nature of a mortgage of personal chattels, i.e. goods, animal stock, household furniture and "other articles capable of complete transfer by delivery". Trade machinery is also deemed to be personal chattels.[109]

A banker taking this kind of security must see that the bill is registered at the Central Office of the Supreme Court within seven days of its execution and, if the loan is continued, must re-register it every five years.[110] A bill "given by way of security for the payment of money" must be in accordance with the form prescribed in the schedule to the 1882 Act, and the consideration must be not less than £30.[111] Every conditional bill must truly set forth the consideration. It was held that where the consideration was stated to be "£90 now due and owing", whereas £50 was advanced at the time of execution, the consideration was not truly stated.[112] It is not necessary that the bill of sale should be drawn up in the statutory form, but if it is not drawn up substantially in accordance with the

109. Bills of Sale Act 1878, s. 5.
110. Ibid., ss. 8 and 11.
111. Bills of Sale Act (1878) Amendment Act 1882, ss. 9 and 12.
112. *Davies* v. *Jenkins* [1900] 1 Q.B. 133.

statutory form, it is void. However, though such a bill is void, if the right to possession of the goods can be proved without reference to the bill of sale, then the fact that the bill of sale is not expressed in the statutory form, or in substantially the same form, will not vitiate the right to possession. If two or more bills of sale are given comprising in whole or in part any of the same chattels, they will have priority in the order of the date of their registration.[113] Provided a bill of sale is duly registered, any subsequent assignment or transfer does not require registration.

The grant of a bill of sale does not affect the right of the rate or tax collector (or the landlord) to levy distress on the goods included in the bill of sale, for rates or taxes (or rent).[114] Subject to these prior claims, the grantee may seize the goods assigned to him provided that the grantor (a) makes default in payment of the sum secured, or (b) becomes bankrupt, or (c) fraudulently removes the goods, or (d) fails to produce (without reasonable excuse) his last receipts for rent, rates and taxes, or (e) has had execution levied against the goods under any judgment at law.[115] A bill of sale is not valid if it is executed (a) by a bankrupt, (b) by a person who has to the knowledge of the grantee committed an act of bankruptcy within three months from its date, (c) in fraudulent preference over other creditors.

Because of the statutory requirements as to registration and form bills of sale are not as a rule acceptable to bankers as security, and when a bill of sale is registered against one of his customers, the banker should regard it as a warning that the customer is probably at the end of his tether, at any rate so far as personal efforts at extrication from his financial difficulties are concerned.

An agricultural charge given under the Agricultural Credits Act 1928 is not a bill of sale within the meaning of the Bills of Sale Acts.[116]

---

113. Bills of Sale Act 1878, s. 10.
114. Bills of Sale Act (1878) Amendment Act 1882, s. 14.
115. Ibid., s. 7.
116. Agricultural Credits Act 1928, s. 8(1).

CHAPTER NINETEEN

Agricultural Credit

INTRODUCTION

This chapter is concerned with the Agricultural Credits Act 1928 which, according to the long title, is

... an Act to secure, by means of the formation of a company and the assistance thereof out of public funds, the making of loans for agricultural purposes on favourable terms, and to facilitate the borrowing of money on the security of farming stock and other agricultural assets, and for purposes connected therewith.

The two purposes outlined in the long title are, briefly (*a*) long-term credits by means of loans on mortgage of agricultural land, and (*b*) short-term or seasonal credits secured by a charge on farming stock and other agricultural assets.

The Act is of particular importance and interest to bankers, since the shareholders of the company formed in pursuance of Part I of the Act are all banks, while Part II creates a security available only to banks.

It will be observed that the Act separates very distinctly long-term credit and short-term credit, the former in general being made by the Agricultural Mortgage Corporation Limited, and the latter by the banks. Thus, the Act has made easier the application of the sound principle that permanent loans should be raised against permanent assets.

LONG-TERM MORTGAGES

The mortgage company formed under Part I of the Act is called the Agricultural Mortgage Corporation Limited; it commenced business on 14th January 1929 and is now located at Bucklersbury House, 3 Queen Victoria Street, London EC4N 8DU. The shareholding banks are the Bank of England, Barclays Bank, Lloyds Bank, Midland Bank, National Westminster Bank and Williams & Glyn's Bank.

The essential motives for establishing AMC were the provision of facilities by which farmers could obtain long-term loans at favourable rates secured by first mortgages on their farms and repayable over an agreed number of years, not normally more than 40, and the provision of the necessary finances to make these loans. Accordingly, AMC has power to issue debentures secured by a first floating charge on the whole of its undertaking, property and assets.

To increase the security behind the debentures, the Minister of Agriculture, Fisheries and Food, with the approval of the Treasury, is authorised to advance up to an amount not exceeding £30 million for the purpose of establishing a guarantee fund. These advances are free of interest for a period of 60 years.[1] Under the provisions of the Agricultural Credits Act 1928, Part I, the Minister was empowered to contribute £10,000 per annum for ten years towards the cost of the administration of AMC. This provision was in due course superseded by various Acts, but all grants taken up have now been repaid, and there is now no provision for AMC to receive any grant from the Minister.

AMC debenture stock is a trustee security, and it will be seen that adequate measures have been taken to ensure its safety and make it an attractive security. It has therefore become a useful channel by means of which the capital of the private investor may become available for agriculture.

At the time of writing AMC has £366 million of debenture stock and bonds outstanding, some at fixed rates ranging from $4\frac{1}{2}$ per cent to $16\frac{1}{4}$ per cent depending on monetary conditions at the time of issue, and some at variable rates. The loan contributed by the State at present amounts to £14.6 million and the paid up capital is £1.5 million. This Government loan has to be invested in British Government stocks. AMC's memorandum of association provides that issues of debentures and the like securities shall be restricted so that the total of the Government loan, paid-up capital and reserves shall never be less than 10 per cent of the aggregate amount of such issues up to a total of £50 million and $7\frac{1}{2}$ per cent of the aggregate amount of such issues in excess of £50 million.

Operating under the provisions of the Agricultural Credits Acts 1928 and 1932, AMC offers loans on agricultural properties in England and Wales secured by first mortgages of the freehold or on suitable long leaseholds. The proceeds of a loan from AMC may be used for many purposes and include the following:

(a) farm or land purchase,

(b) repayment of loans borrowed from other sources,

1. The sum was fixed at £2.5 million by the Agricultural (Miscellaneous Provisions) Act 1944, s. 2(1), and has been increased by various Acts; the present limit derives from the Agriculture (Miscellaneous Provisions) Act 1976, s. 2.

(*c*) capital improvements (e.g. reconstruction or provision of new cottages or farm buildings, electricity or water supplies, drainage, farm roads),

(*d*) provision of working capital, or

(*e*) for any other reasonable agricultural purpose.

AMC offers the following two basic loans:

(*a*) long-term loans which are offered for periods of 10–40 years and include provision for repayment of capital during the life of the loan;

(*b*) 5–10 year straight loans at interest only with capital to be repaid at the end of the agreed period.

Borrowers can elect to repay all loans on a fixed or variable interest rate basis or by a combination of both.

Main methods of repaying a long-term loan
Borrowers taking out a long-term loan may repay the loan by any of the following methods:

(*a*) *annuity*: half-yearly comprising interest plus an instalment of capital;

(*b*) *endowment assurance*: half-yearly payment comprising interest only, plus endowment assurance policy premiums which are paid by a borrower direct to a company of his choice;

(*c*) *equal instalments of capital*: half-yearly payments comprising equal instalments of capital plus interest at the mortgage rate on the reducing balance;

(*d*) *straight loan option*: AMC also offers borrowers of long-term loans the option of taking half their loan on a straight basis at interest only with capital to be repaid at the end of the period, the remaining half to be repaid by the annuity, endowment assurance or equal capital instalment methods outlined.

AMC is always willing to consider other repayment methods or combination of methods which may best suit an individual borrower's requirements.

Applications are considered on the understanding that:

(*a*) AMC's lending terms (other than the rate of interest) will be those which are current on the date when the loan is offered;

(*b*) the rate of interest will be that which is ruling on the date when the loan is actually completed.

The property should normally be an agricultural unit with an income potential sufficient to enable the borrower to meet his loan commitments and provide a reasonable livelihood. In suitable cases, loans are granted on bare land or specialised units.

In the case of 10–40 year long-term loans, the maximum advance must not exceed two-thirds of the value of the property as certified by AMC's valuer for the area. With 5–10 year straight loans, the maximum advance is restricted to one half of the AMC valuation. In the case of specialist units, the term of repayment is restricted to 10 years, and again the maximum advance is restricted to one half of the AMC valuation.

Where, following a valuation, AMC is unable to offer a loan, no charge will be made. If a loan offer is made but not accepted, a fee amounting to one-quarter of one per cent of the amount of the loan offer will be payable by the applicant towards AMC's expenses.

Acceptance of the offer commits the applicant to payment of a loan fee, amounting to $1\frac{1}{2}$ per cent of the amount of the loan. In normal cases the fee is deducted from the loan completion moneys, but it will be payable in cash by applicants who withdraw after accepting the offer. Valuation permitting, AMC is willing to add the fee to the loan at the mortgage rate of interest. This fee covers the valuation cost, all AMC's office and legal expenses, including the cost of searches in the appropriate registries, and any necessary fees for registration of the legal charge.

Applications for loans should be made on Forms AMC 1 and 27 and should be accompanied by the following documents:

(*a*) copies of the applicant's farming accounts for the last three years for the confidential information of AMC and its valuer;

(*b*) forward budgets for the next two years' farming operations;

(*c*) a schedule of the Ordnance Survey numbers and areas together with an exact plan of the property offered as security;

(*d*) sale particulars, where appropriate.

The farmer has the certainty that his loan will not be called in, as in the case of a private mortage, by the death of the mortgagee, or because the money is wanted for other purposes. Furthermore, in the event of a borrower's death, a loan is not subject to recall but can continue undisturbed in favour of his representatives unless it is covered by endowment assurance.

Where the representatives vest the property in the beneficiary of the borrower's estate, AMC is always willing to consider transferring the loan undisturbed, the account to be in the name of the beneficiary provided he is regarded as being capable of observing the mortgage deed covenants. Where the loan is on the endowment assurance basis of repayment, the proceeds of any assigned insurance policies are normally required for reduction or repayment of the loan.

By virtue of the Agricultural Credits Act 1932, borrowers have no legal right to repay otherwise than by the means set out in the mortgage deed, but AMC is always prepared to consider earlier repayment arising out of a sale or otherwise on terms to be arranged at the time it is desired to make partial or full repayment. AMC is always willing to consider the release for building or other purposes of parts of the land mortgaged, on terms to be arranged at the time.

The interest due is notified annually by AMC to the local inspector of taxes. Relief appropriate to the tax situation of the borrower and/or his farming business is normally obtainable but it is recommended that a borrower should consult his accountant who is best placed to advise on the individual taxation questions involved.

SHORT-TERM PAYMENTS

Part II of the Agricultural Credits Act 1928 is entitled "Agricultural short-term credits", and is of direct interest to bankers as it authorises the creation of a charge, called an "agricultural charge", on farming stock and assets, available only to banks.[2]

Prior to this Act it was only possible to give a charge on such assets as crops and live-stock, by means of a bill of sale, a form of security generally associated with the last efforts of an impecunious debtor, and hence fatal to the borrower's credit. In many other countries, however, as, for example, Canada, Australia and parts of the West Indies, special legislation has existed for many years under which the farmer has been able to pledge his crop, live-stock, etc., to secure the money required to sow, cultivate and harvest his crop, or maintain his live-stock. By means of these facilities the farmer can borrow part of the floating capital required for investment in his floating assets on the appropriate security of those assets, thus leaving his other resources free to provide for his more permanent assets, or to enable him to operate on a larger or more economical scale. These agricultural statutes have undoubtedly been of benefit to the farming community and materially assisted in the agricultural development of these countries.

In the absence of any appropriate form of giving a legal security, many farmers can be restricted in fully utilising the resources locked up, either permanently in implements and plant, or for the season in crops. Probably in the majority of cases this represents by far the greater part of their capital. They have therefore to rely on getting unsecured credit from their bankers or suppliers. It is of course

2. Agricultural Credits Act 1928, s. 5.

appreciated that farmers, whether owners or tenants, have been supported by the banks, but the Agricultural Credits Act gives opportunities for credit facilties and creates a form of borrowing which it was hoped would become recognised in time as being in the usual course of business, as it is for industrial enterprises to borrow. It is better, cheaper and more economically sound for the farmer to get all his credit from his bank, where the cost can be definitely ascertained.

A well-known authority who had many years' experience with this class of legislation in other parts of the Commonwealth felt that the Act should have proved a distinctly beneficial measure. Nevertheless, it must be admitted that the agricultural charge has not been the success it was hoped. The effect of registering a charge has resulted in some cases in the farmer's other creditors calling for payment of their debts, and, as some of these were somewhat over-generous or of a semi-long-term nature, it soon became evident that the banker's seasonal advances were insufficient to enable the farmer to settle his other creditors and finance his crops. Hence both banker and farmer have been reluctant to use the agricultural charge. Obviously some of the difficulty is due to the fact that many farmers are under-capitalised, a highly dangerous feature in any kind of industry. The mechanisation of farming has led to the necessity of using expensive implements, though much of this can be financed under hire purchase or leasing and lease purchase. It is evident that some further scheme is necessary to enable the tenant farmer to get the requisite finance on the cheapest terms possible, so as to encourage the fullest use of the land. Point of sale finance schemes through agricultural merchants are now available.

It has been stated elsewhere that the personal character of the borrower is one of the banker's first considerations when examining an application for an advance. In no case is this more important than with agricultural advances. Another essential point is that of the farmer's capability, since so much depends on his knowledge and energy. With well-selected borrowers, agricultural advances possess certain features attractive to bankers. The advances gradually increase up to the harvest, when they are at the highest, while at the same time the security is also at its maximum. Another favourable feature is that the advances are seasonal, and should run off each year on sale of the produce. To watch this, it is the practice in some countries to make each crop year's advances on a separate account. This system, however, is more suited to one large crop, such as wheat or sugar, than to mixed farming.

For the purposes of Part II of the Act, a "farmer" means any person (not being an incorporated company or society) who, as tenant or owner of an agricultural holding, cultivates the holding for profit, and "agriculture" and "cultivation" include horticulture and the use of land for any purpose of husbandry, inclusive of the keeping or breeding of live-stock, poultry or bees, and the growth of fruit, vegetables and the like.[3] "Farming stock" means crops or horticultural produce, whether growing or severed from the land, and after severance whether subjected to any treatment or process of manufacture or not; live-stock, including poultry and bees, and the produce and progeny thereof; any other agricultural or horticultural produce whether subjected to any treatment or process of manufacture or not; seeds and manures; agricultural vehicles, machinery and other plant; agricultural tenant's fixtures and other agricultural fixtures which a tenant is by law authorised to remove.[3] "Other agricultural assets" means a tenant's right to compensation under the Agricultural Holdings Act 1948 for improvements, damage by game, disturbance or otherwise, and any other tenant right.[4]

A farmer may create by an instrument in writing in favour of a bank an agricultural charge on all or any of his farming stock and other agricultural assets as security for sums advanced or to be advanced to him or paid or to be paid on his behalf under any guarantee by the bank, together with interest, commission and charges.[5] An agricultural charge may be either fixed, or floating, or fixed and floating.[6] In the case of a fixed charge, the property affected shall be such part of his farming stock and other agricultural assets belonging to the farmer at the date of the charge as may be specified in the charge. It may include, in the case of live-stock, any progeny born after the date of the charge, and, in the case of agricultural plant, any plant substituted for that specified in the charge.[7] The property affected by a floating charge shall be the farming stock and other agricultural assets from time to time belonging to the farmer, or such part thereof as is mentioned in the charge.[8]

The principal sum secured may be either a specified amount, or a fluctuating amount advanced on current account not exceeding at any one time such amount (if any) as may be specified in the charge. In the latter case the charge is not deemed to be redeemed by reason only of the current account having ceased to be in debit.[9]

3. Agricultural Credits Act 1928, s. 5.
4. Agricultural Credits Act 1928, s. 5, as amended by Agricultural Holdings Act 1948, ss. 98–100 and Sched. 8.
5. Agricultural Credits Act 1928, s. 5(1).
6. Ibid., s. 5(2).
7. Ibid., s. 5(3).
8. Ibid., s. 5(4).
9. Ibid., s. 5(5).

No specific form of charge is required. Sureties may be made parties to the charge.[10]

When considering the assets behind a floating charge, it is necessary to keep in mind current legislation relating to farming. In view of the pressing urgency of the need to increase the productivity of our farms there has been a considerable quantity of legislation, grants, subsidies and schemes of one sort or another, designed to encourage or assist the farmer to greater output. It is essential therefore to keep up to date in order to know the present position, and what may or may not be regarded as an asset behind a floating charge, or whether or not a separate charge is possible. Even if the banker is not relying on a floating charge, it is very desirable to keep in close touch with the current position.

On the other hand, amounts due to a farmer under the Milk Marketing Scheme would be included in an agricultural charge. In cases where the latter is not taken, milk payments can be charged separately. The milk contract should be lodged with the banker and should show that it has been registered with the Board. It should bear the address of the branch bank concerned, to which payments will be made direct. If it is desired to complete the security, notice should be given to the Milk Marketing Board, but such notice is of no avail in bankruptcy. If a charge is taken from a registered company, it must be registered with the registrar of companies.[11]

FORM AND EFFECT OF CHARGE

No statutory form of charge is laid down in the Act, and bankers will, as is usual, use their own standard forms prepared by their solicitors.

In regard to the fixed charge, the Act states that it will confer on the bank the right, upon the happening of any event specified in the charge as being one authorising the seizure of the property, to take possession thereof, and, where possession has been so taken, the right after an interval of five clear days (or such less time as the charge provides) to sell the property by auction (or by private treaty if the charge allows), either for a lump-sum payment or payment by instalments.[12] The farmer is under an obligation, whenever he sells any of the property or other agricultural assets subject to the charge, forthwith to pay the bank the proceeds, except to the extent allowed by the charge or the bank. The farmer is under a similar obligation in regard to moneys received from any insurance policy

10. Agricultural Credits Act 1928, s. 5(6).
11. *See* Chapter Seventeen.
12. Agricultural Credits Act 1928, s. 6(1).

or by way of compensation under statutory provisions for the destruction of animals or crops, so far as the sums so received relate to property covered by the charge.[13]

It should be noted that a fixed charge does not prevent a farmer selling any of the property, and third parties are not concerned with the fact that there is a charge on the property.[14] In the event of the proceeds being paid to some other person, the bank cannot recover the money from such person unless it proves that the person knew the proceeds were being paid to him in breach of the obligation to pay such proceeds to the bank.[15] For this purpose, notice of the charge is not sufficient evidence of knowledge of any contemplated breach.[15] Hence in special cases it may be desirable to serve express notice in writing of the charge and to demand payment of the proceeds to the bank, for example, on an auctioneer who is selling property the proceeds of which the bank wishes to ensure receiving.

The Act states that the effect of a floating charge is similar to one created by a duly registered debenture issued by a company,[16] a description not entirely apposite, but sufficient to convey the general idea. A floating charge becomes a fixed charge on the property comprised in the charge as existing at the date of the charge becoming fixed:

(a) upon a receiving order in bankruptcy being made against the farmer;

(b) upon the death of the farmer;

(c) upon the dissolution of partnership in the case where the property charged is partnership property;

(d) upon notice in writing to that effect being given by the bank on the happening of any event which by virtue of the charge confers on the bank the right to give such a notice.[17]

The farmer is under the same obligation in respect of proceeds of sale as in the case of a fixed charge, except that instead of paying the proceeds to the bank, he can expend the money in the purchase of other farming stock, which on purchase becomes subject to the charge.[18]

The previous paragraphs have detailed the provisions of the Act in regard to fixed and floating charges. The bank's form should make the moneys payable on demand, and cover all liabilities now due

13. Ibid., s. 6(2).
14. Ibid., s. 6(3).
15. Ibid., s. 6(4).
16. Ibid., s. 7(1).
17. Ibid., s. 7(1)(a).
18. Ibid., s. 7(1)(b).

or to become due in the usual exhaustive style of bank forms. There is no need to specify any amount in the charge. The form should create a fixed charge on the farming stock and other agricultural assets specified in the charge, and also a floating charge on the farming stock and other agricultural assets from time to time belonging to the farmer. The following conditions and covenants should be incorporated.

(*a*) It should include, in the case of the fixed charge, the progeny of any live-stock born after the date of the fixed charge, and any agricultural plant substitued for the charged plant.

(*b*) It should give the bank power to seize the property subject to the fixed charge without any further notice on the happening of the following events:

(*i*) any demand for repayment;

(*ii*) the death of the farmer or the making of a receiving order in bankruptcy against the farmer;

(*iii*) any failure or refusal of the farmer to perform or observe the conditions and obligations imposed by the Act or the charge;

(*iv*) if a distress or execution be levied or attempted on any of the farmer's property;

(*v*) the dissolution of any partnership;

(*vi*) the expiration or determination, or threatened determination, of the farmer's lease or tenancy;

(*vii*) if the farmer shall cease or threaten to cease to farm the land subject to the charge or in the bank's opinion cease or neglect to farm the land in a husbandlike manner.

(*c*) The happening of any of the above events should confer on the bank the right to give the requisite notice fixing the floating charge.

Among the usual clauses of a well-drawn bank form there should be included a covenant to keep in effect all proper insurances, the receipts for which the bank should be entitled to have produced. The bank should be permitted to sell by private treaty either for a lump-sum payment or payment by instalments. The usual clause regarding the appointment of a receiver should also be included.

Another important clause is one in which the farmer should covenant to cultivate his land in a good and husbandlike manner, to look after, keep up and replace all live farming stock and maintain in good condition and replace all dead farming stock, and generally to maintain the same in the condition as when charged. Since the Act is silent on the subject of the mortgagee's right to inspect the property charged, it would not be unreasonable to include a clause allowing inspection and valuation at any time and at the borrower's expense.

The Act makes reference to the farmer's obligation forthwith to pay to the bank the proceeds of any sale or other receipts relating to the property charged. It is obvious that unless some limit, below which the farmer need not account to the bank, is named, the farmer's position would be very irksome, since he would render himself liable to penalties if he sold, for example, a fowl and omitted to pay the proceeds to the bank.

If the farmer is operating more than one farm, his farming stock and other agricultural assets on all the farms he occupies should be included in the charge, as otherwise there is a danger of controversy or evasion arising.

If a farmer is adjudged bankrupt on a bankruptcy petition presented within three months of giving an agricultural charge, unless it is proved that the farmer was solvent immediately after the execution of the charge, the charge is only available for advances made after the execution thereof. This is to prevent a bank taking a charge to secure present indebtedness to the detriment of the other creditors. The bank can in such circumstances claim for any balance as an unsecured creditor.[19]

The banker will need to bear in mind that his floating charge is subject to certain preferential claims, such as those for rent, rates and taxes.

If, with intent to defraud, a farmer who has given an agricultural charge fails to make payment over to the bank of any sums received by him by way of proceeds of sale, or in respect of other agricultural assets, or under a policy of insurance or by way of compensation, he commits an offence and is liable on conviction to imprisonment for a term not exceeding three years.[20] The penalty is the same if with intent to defraud he removes or suffers to be removed from his land any property subject to the charge. Such a clause is not unusual in legislation of this kind.

REGISTRATION OF CHARGE

An agricultural charge must be registered within seven clear days after its execution; if not so registered, it is void as against any person other than the farmer.[21] Registration must be effected against the name of the farmer giving the charge with the land

19. Agricultural Credits Act 1928, s. 8(5).
20. Ibid., s. 11. If tried summarily, the maximum penalty is £1,000 and/or six months' imprisonment: ibid.
21. Ibid., s. 9(1).

registrar of the Land Registry.[22] A fee is due for the registration or cancellation of an entry, both of which have to be made on the official forms. The fees must be prepaid by the prescribed methods. The register is open to inspection and a certified copy of any entry can be obtained.[23] Registration of a charge is deemed to constitute actual notice of the charge, but where it has been created expressly to secure a current account or other further advances, the bank is not deemed to have notice of another agricultural charge registered later, so long as the register was clear when its charge was created or the last search (if any) was made on its behalf.[24] This follows a similar provision of the Law of Property Act 1925.[25] Since registration of charges is necessary, it follows that a search should be made before taking a charge.

In relation to one another, agricultural charges have priority in accordance with the times at which they are respectively registered.[26]

An instrument creating an agricultural charge is exempt from stamp duty.[27]

In connection with registration, it should be noted that the Act prohibits the publication of any list of agricultural charges or of the names of the farmers concerned. This restriction, however, does not preclude the confidential notification by trade protection societies to their members carrying on business in the district in which the property charged is situated.[28]

While in other cases the Act applies only to farmers trading either as individuals or in partnership, a provision is made in favour of agricultural societies. A debenture issued by a society registered under the Industrial and Provident Societies Acts 1893 to 1965, creating in favour of a bank a floating charge on "farming stock", may be registered as an agricultural charge and under the same regulations. The secretary of the society must also send notice of any registration of a charge to the Central Office established under the Friendly Societies Act 1974 for registration there.[29]

---

22. Agricultural Credits Act 1928, s. 9(3).
23. Ibid., s. 9(4).
24. Ibid., s. 9(8).
25. Law of Property Act 1925, s. 94(2). *See* Chapter Fifteen.
26. Agricultural Credits Act 1928, s. 8(2).
27. Ibid., s. 8(8).
28. Ibid., s. 10.
29. Ibid., s. 14.

CHAPTER TWENTY

Enforcement of Debts and Security by Action

1. DEBTS AND GUARANTEES

CHOICE OF COURT

Proceedings in respect of simple contract debts may be commenced in a County Court or in the High Court of Justice.

There are some 300 County Courts in England and Wales, each having a specified district. In general, proceedings must be commenced in the court for the district in which the defendant resides or carries on business, or in the court for the district in which the cause of action wholly or partly arose.

The scope of the County Court jurisdiction is restricted to claims not exceeding £5,000.[1]

The High Court of Justice consists of the Central Office in London and many District Registries.[2] Proceedings can be commenced in the Central Office or any of the District Registries. If they are commenced in a District Registry and the defendant does not have a place of residence or place of business within its district the defendant may no longer have an absolute right to acknowledge service[3] at the Central Office,[4] but if he does, the proceedings continue there.[5]

It will be seen from the above that the jurisdictions of the High Court and the County Court overlap. Unless, however, there is reasonable ground to suppose that more than £5,000 is recoverable, a plaintiff bringing proceedings in the High Court and recovering less than £3,000 is penalised to the extent that any costs recoverable will only be allowed on the lower, County Court, scale, and in the High Court if less than £120 is recovered or reasonably recoverable, no costs will normally be recoverable.[6]

1. County Courts Act 1959, s. 39, as amended by the County Courts Jurisdiction Order 1981, S.I. 1981 No. 1123.
2. Rules of the Supreme Court, Order 32, rule 23.
3. *See* below.
4. R.S.C. Order 12, rule 2, revised by R.S.C. (writ and Appearance) 1979 (S.I. 1979 No. 1716).
5. Ibid., Order 4, rule 5.
6. County Courts Act 1959, s. 47, as amended by the County Courts Jurisdiction Order 1981, S. I. 1981, No. 1123.

In the County Court, where less than £500 is recovered court fees only are recoverable, and no solicitor's charges except in certain specified cases.[7]

THE HIGH COURT

Procedure in the High Court

This is governed by the Rules of the Supreme Court which lay down a detailed practice and to which reference must be made in bringing proceedings. What follows is, of course, only a very general summary.

The High Court is divided into three Divisions, the Family Division, Chancery Division, and Queen's Bench Division. Certain types of matter are assigned to each division although there is a certain overlap. Proceedings for recovery of simple contract debts are usually brought in the Queen's Bench Division.

Proceedings are commenced by issuing a writ of summons. This is a document containing (*inter alia*) the division of the High Court in which the plaintiff is proceeding, the names and addresses of the parties to the action and either a concise statement of the nature of the claim and of the relief sought, or a full statement of claim. The writ gives the defendant notice of the claim and requires him either to satisfy the claim or to return to the court the accompanying acknowledgment of service, stating whether he intends to contest the proceedings, in either case within 14 days of service of the writ.

The writ is issued in the Central Office or District Registry and a copy is then served personally on the defendant together with a form for acknowledgment of service also issued in the court office in accordance with the Rules of the Supreme Court. Leave is required for a writ to be served outside the jurisdiction,[8] and will only be granted in certain specified cases.[9]

If a defendant, either himself or through his solicitor, confirms that a solicitor is authorised to accept service, any pleading may be served on that solicitor, who will normally accept service through the post.

Personal service is usually effected through firms of specialist process servers. If several attempts to effect service prove unsuccessful, the plaintiff may use the new, alternative, procedure set out below or may apply to the court for substituted service, such as by advertisement.

7. County Court Rules 1981, Order 9r. 6.
8. Scotland counts as outside the jurisdiction.
9. Examples are if the action relates to land in England, or a contract made in England or governed by English law, or a tort committed in England; R.S.C., Order 11, rule 1.

A document may be served on a company registered under the Companies Acts by leaving it or sending it by post to its registered office.[10]

An attempt was made in 1979 to alleviate the position of banks and other creditors where debtors consistently evade service by a set of amendments to the Rules of the Supreme Court.[11]

These rules provide that a writ for service on a defendant within the jurisdiction may, instead of being served personally on him, be served by sending a copy of the writ by ordinary first class post to him at his usual or last known address, or, if there is a letter-box for that address, by inserting through the letter-box a copy of the writ enclosed in a sealed envelope addressed to the defendant. In both cases the copy of the writ must, as in the case of personal service, be accompanied by a form for acknowledgment of service.

Where the writ is served in accordance with this procedure, the date of service is, unless the contrary is shown, deemed to be the seventh day after the date on which the copy was sent to, or inserted through the letter-box for, the address in question, with the exception of postal service on a company in which case the writ is deemed served one day after posting. An affidavit proving service of the writ must contain a statement to the effect that in the opinion of the deponent (or in some circumstances the plaintiff) the copy of the writ, if sent to, or inserted through the letter-box for, the address in question, will have come to the knowledge of the defendant within seven days thereafter and, in the case of service by post, that the copy of the writ has not been returned to the plaintiff through the post undelivered to the addressee.

This enables the plaintiff to proceed as if the defendant had been served personally, but the rules further provide that if, after judgment has been entered, the copy of the writ sent to the defendant is returned to the plaintiff through the post undelivered to the addressee, the plaintiff must, before taking any further steps in the action or for the enforcement of the judgment, apply to the court either for the judgment to be set aside on the ground that the writ has not been duly served, or for directions. The significance of this is that a party applying for a judgment to be set aside normally has to pay the costs of the application. Since with the vagaries of the post, it may take anything up to eight weeks or more for a letter to be returned undelivered, a plaintiff proceeding in this manner risks losing costs.

10. Companies Act 1948, s. 437.
11. Rules of the Supreme Court (Amendment No. 2) Order 1979, S.I. 1979 No. 402, and Rules of the Supreme Court (Writ and Appearance) Order 1979 S.I. 1979 No. 1716.

There would appear to be less risk as to costs if the plaintiff's solicitors arrange for a copy of the writ to be inserted through the letter-box; it is perhaps unlikely that in such cases the writ will be returned through the post undelivered, and if application were made to set judgment aside, it would have to be made by the defendant, with the consequent risk as to costs being on the defendant.

Yet the letter so delivered could be returned to the sender by an occupier of the property indicating that the defendant had "gone away" or was "not known at this address" thus putting a plaintiff who had proceeded to a default judgment in the same position as having to apply to the court for directions. This course is thus free of risk only if the defendant is known to be still resident at the address in question and the letter is put through the letter box at that address.

The new procedure is cheaper and simpler in straightforward cases, and avoids the need to instruct process servers, but it is not entirely free of risk on the question of costs. If, however, the old, cumbersome, procedure of obtaining an order from the court for substituted service, either by post or advertisement, is adopted, any judgment is unlikely to be set aside and in any event the plaintiff himself is under no obligation to take steps to set it aside. Any defendant who was able to persuade a court to set a judgment aside would almost certainly be ordered to pay the costs thrown away. More importantly, if given leave to defend the action at all, it would be likely that he would be ordered to pay the amount of claim, or a substantial sum, into court to abide the event as a condition of being granted leave to defend.

Within fourteen days after service the defendant should acknowledge service of the writ. This is done by filing at the Court Office where the writ was issued the completed form of acknowledgment of service which was served on the defendant with the writ. In order to complete this form the defendant must give his full name and state whether or not he intends to contest the proceedings. He must also give his address for service, i.e. the address at which documents can be served on him. The form tells the defendant that he may be entitled to legal aid and also gives full directions as to how to obtain any necessary legal advice. The completed form is then sent to the appropriate Court Office by hand or by post. The proper officer at the Office then sends a copy of the completed form of acknowledgment of service to the plaintiff or to his solicitor.

A company may only acknowledge service of the writ by solicitors or by a person duly authorised to act on the company's behalf.[12]

---

12. R.S.C., Order 12, rule 1.

If the defendant fails to acknowledge service of the writ within fourteen days after service, the plaintiff may, provided the writ is indorsed with a statement of claim, enter judgment in default of acknowledgment of service upon production of proof of service as defined by the Court rules.[13] In addition, if the defendant in his acknowledgment of service states that it is not his intention to defend the plaintiff's claim the plaintiff may enter judgment against the defendant at any time after the acknowledgment of service has been received by the appropriate court office.

If the defendant acknowledges service and gives notice of intention to defend, documents known as pleadings are exchanged. Strict rules govern the contents of pleadings. Briefly, pleadings contain in summary form the material facts upon which each party relies for his claim or defence. The main pleadings are the statement of claim by the plaintiff, and a defence by the defendant, although often futher pleadings are served. For example, the defendant will sometimes ask for further and better particulars of the statement of claim.

The statement of claim, if not indorsed on the writ, must be served within fourteen days after acknowledgment of service and the defence within fourteen days after service of the statement of claim or, if this is indorsed on the writ, within 28 days after service of the writ. These time limits (and indeed all time limits that are laid down) can be, and usually are, varied by agreement or by order of the court.

If the defendant fails to serve a defence on time, the plaintiff may enter judgment in default.[14]

After all pleadings have been served, at a stage known as "close of pleadings", discovery of documents takes place.[15] The parties are required to exchange lists of all documents which are or have been in their possession, custody or power relating to the matters in question in the action within fourteen days after close of pleadings. The lists must contain a notice stating a time and place where the specified documents can be inspected within seven days after service.

Within one month after close of pleadings, the plaintiff takes out a summons for directions, whereby the parties attend before a High Court official called a master in order to obtain directions for trial.[16] Such directions will depend on the case in question but include provision for the amendment to or provision of further and better particulars of pleadings where required, obtaining experts' reports, discovery (where this has not yet taken place) and setting down

13. Ibid., Order 13, rules 1 and 7.
14. Ibid., Order 19, rule 2.
15. Ibid., Order 24.
16. Ibid., Order 25.

of the action for trial, giving the place and mode of trial and estimated length of hearing.

The action is then set down for trial in accordance with the direction and, unless application is made to fix a date for trial, the action takes its place in the general list and in theory can come on for trial at any time, subject to disposal of actions above it on the list and to the hearing of other actions in respect of which a fixed date of trial has been allocated.

The time taken for an action to come to trial after setting down is obviously dependent on the state of the lists and the estimated length of trial, but it will usually be a matter of months before the trial is heard.

At the trial the judge, after hearing evidence and submissions by counsel, will give judgment. Appeal can be made on certain grounds to the Court of Appeal and from there, with leave, to the House of Lords, if a point of law of general public importance is involved.

Summary judgment

Where the plaintiff believes that the defendant has no defence it is open to the plaintiff to apply for summary judgment at any time after notice of intention to defend has been given and after service of the statement of claim.[17] Application is made in chambers to a master, who hears the matter on the basis of affidavit evidence only.

The plaintiff has by now set out his case in the statement of claim, and when applying for summary judgment he has sworn in his affidavit that he believes that there is no defence. The onus is therefore on the defendant to show that he has a defence which at least raises a triable issue. Unless the master decides that the defendant has raised a triable issue, the master will give judgment for the plaintiff. If he comes to the conclusion that there is an issue to be tried, he will give leave to defend, which may be unconditional or subject to conditions (usually paying the money in question into court or giving security).

There is a right of appeal to a judge in chambers, with a further right of appeal in certain circumstances to the Court of Appeal and House of Lords. The plaintiff cannot appeal from the judge in chambers on an order giving unconditional leave to defend.

The time taken by the procedure for summary judgment obviously varies according to the complexity of the case and the state of the lists, and according to whether any appeals are made, but in simple cases where no appeal is made it should be possible to obtain judgment in a matter of weeks.

17. R.S.C., Order 14.

Costs

Unless otherwise provided by some statute or Rule of the Supreme Court, costs are in the discretion of the judge,[18] but in general will be ordered to "follow the event". The costs awarded will not generally amount to a full indemnity but will be on a "party and party" basis only, comprising only those costs necessary or proper for the attainment of justice or for enforcing or defending the rights of the party in question. As mentioned above costs will be limited if proceedings are brought in the wrong court.

At any time after the defendant has been served with the writ he may, before or without acknowledging service, pay into court a sum of money in satisfaction of the cause of action in respect of which the plaintiff claims.[19] The defendant must serve on the plaintiff notice of payment in. If the plaintiff accepts the payment in, the proceedings are at an end, and, unless the trial has begun (when it is for the judge to award costs), the plaintiff is entitled to party and party costs up to the time of receipt of notice of payment in.

Where a payment into court is made but not accepted by the plaintiff, and the matter proceeds to trial, the judge is not informed of the payment in. If the judgment, including any interest awarded by the court, is for a sum equal to or less than the amount of the payment in, then, subject to the discretion of the judge, the plaintiff will only be awarded costs up to the date of receipt of notice of payment in, and will be required to pay the defendant's costs as from that date.

Enforcement of judgment

A judgment for payment of money may be enforced by bankruptcy (in the case of an individual) or winding-up proceedings (in the case of a company) where the judgment debt is not less than £200.[20] There are six other methods of enforcement of judgment.[21]

(a) Writ of *fieri facias* (or "fi fa") directs the sheriff of the county in which the goods of the debtor are situated to seize and sell such of the goods of the debtor within that county as may be sufficient to satisfy the amount of the judgment debt and interest until payment together with costs of execution.[22] Exempted from execution are freeholds and equitable interests of the debtor,

---

18. Ibid., Order 62.
19. Ibid., Orders 22 and 62.
20. Bankruptcy Act 1914, s. 4(1)(a); Companies Act 1948, s. 223(a); Insolvency Act 1976, Sched. 1.
21. R.S.C., Order 45.
22. Ibid., Order 47.

and also the debtor's wearing apparel, bedding and tools of trade to the total value of £150.[23]

(b) By means of garnishee proceedings debts due to the judgment debtor from third parties (garnishees) may be attached by the judgment creditor.[24] The procedure is commonly used against bank credit balances. A garnishee order nisi is made on *ex parte* application supported by affidavit, and served on the garnishee and the judgment debtor. The order nisi specifies a time and place for further consideration of the matter and in the meantime attaches sufficient of the debt to answer the judgment. At the return date of the order nisi, unless cause is shown by the garnishee, the order may be made absolute by the court against the garnishee and enforced as against the garnishee in the same way as any other money judgment.

(c) A charging order may be obtained by the judgment creditor on land or an interest in land or on stocks and shares of the judgment debtor, on money standing in court to the credit of the judgment debtor,[25] or on a partnership interest of the judgment debtor.[26] For charging orders other than on partnership interests, the procedure is for a charging order nisi to be made *ex parte* on application supported by affidavit. This order has the effect of imposing a charge until the return date of the order nisi. At the hearing, unless cause is shown, the order may be made absolute.

(d) A receiver may be appointed by way of equitable execution where prima facie other means of enforcement are not available. It operates to collect moneys receivable by the judgment debtor such as rents, profits, proceeds of sale from property belonging to the judgment debtor, etc.[27] Application is made *ex parte* on affidavit in the first instance for leave to issue a summons, and at the hearing of the summons the court may make an order appointing the receiver. If necessary, application can be made for an injunction restraining disposal of the property in question until the hearing of the summons.

(e) Attachment of earnings is a County Court procedure. High Court judgments are enforceable in the County Court for the appropriate district.[28]

(f) Where it is not clear how to proceed in enforcing judgment due to lack of information as to the assets and financial standing of the judgment debtor, it is possible to obtain an order for attendance of

23. Administration of Justice Act 1956, s. 37(2); Protection from Execution (Prescribed Value) Order 1980, S.I. 1980 No. 26.
24. R.S.C., Order 49. *See* Chapter Four.
25. R.S.C., Order 50. *See* generally the Charging Orders Act 1979.
26. R.S.C., Order 81, rule 10.
27. Ibid., Order 51.
28. County Courts Act 1958, s. 139.

the judgment debtor before a master to be orally examined as to the debts owing to him, and whether he has any, and if so what, property or other means of satisfying the judgment.[29] The court may also order the production of relevant books or documents in the possession of the judgment debtor.

THE COUNTY COURT

Procedure in the County Court

This is governed by the County Court Rules 1981 as amended, and where these do not expressly provide for a case, the general principles of practice in the High Court may be adopted and applied to proceedings in the County Court.[30]. There are two classes of action, the "default" action which must be used for every monetary claim whether the damages are liquidated or unliquidated and the "fixed date summons" which is used e.g. for claims for injunctions, specific performance, possession of land, return of goods.[31]

In the case of fixed date summons, the old procedure by ordinary action still applies. A summary of procedure is given as follows. The plaintiff files in the court office a request for issue of a fixed date summons together with particulars of the claim. A summons is then issued by the court and served on the defendant, generally by the court. Within fourteen days the defendant must either pay into court the amount claimed and costs indorsed on the summons, or file a form of admission, defence and/or counterclaim (and, if he makes admission, he must make an offer of payment).[32] The return day stated in the final date summons will be for a pre-trial review unless the court otherwise directs.[33]

At the pre-trial review the registrar gives directions similar to those given in a High Court summons for directions, and the action follows the same steps (exchange of pleadings, discovery, etc.) to trial as in the High Court.

If the defendant does not make a payment into court or file the form described above under fixed date summons, within fourteen days of service, inclusive of the day of service, the plaintiff may enter final judgment in the case of a debt and, in a claim for damages, interlocutory judgment or damages to be assessed and costs.[34]

If the defendant does respond as described above within the fourteen-day time limit or before judgment has been entered, then a

29. R.S.C., Order 48.
30. County Courts Act 1959, ss. 102 and 103.
31. C.C.R., Order 3 rule 2.
32. Ibid., Order 9.
33. Ibid., Order 3 r. 3 (3)(4).
34. Ibid., Order 9 r. 6 (1)(2).

date will be fixed for a pre-trial review and the action will proceed to trial as in the case of a fixed date action.

Similar rules to those described above for the High Court apply to costs in the County Court.[35]

Enforcement of judgment

All the methods described above as available in the High Court can also be used to enforce a County Court judgment for payment of money, proceedings being brought in the relevant County Court.[36]

There is one extra method of enforcing judgment which can be used in the County Court only, namely attachment of earnings.[37] By this procedure application for an attachment of earnings order is made to the court for the district in which the debtor resides. Notice of the application which sets out the return date and a form of reply for completion by the defendant, in which he is to set out details of his employment, pay and income, liabilities, and proposals for payment, are served on the defendant. The defendant must file the completed reply in the court office within eight days of service of the notice of application.

At the application, the attachment of earnings order may then be made. This is an order directed to a person who appears to the court to have the debtor in his employment. It operates as an instruction to that person to make periodical deductions from the debtor's earnings and pay these to the court. The order will specify protected earnings below which no deduction will be made and the normal deduction rate, and attachment is made of that amount of income (net of income tax and certain other statutory payments) left after payment of the protected earnings, at the normal deduction rate. Any arrears must be deducted from income remaining after these deductions.

The attachment of earnings order is served on the employer. If the debtor has left his employment, the employer is under a duty to inform the court within seven days. Similarly the employee is under a duty to inform the court within seven days of cessation of his employment.

While the attachment of earnings order is in force the debtor is also under a duty to notify the court of changes in his employment within seven days.

Failure to comply with the various requirements can in certain circumstances render the debtor or the employer liable to criminal proceedings.

35. C.C.R. 1981, Order 38.
36. Ibid., Order s. 25 to 32.
37. Attachment of Earnings Act 1971; C.C.R., Order 27.

Since an attachment order relates only to the employment current at the date of the order, the procedure has proved to be of limited value where debtors have not been in stable or regular employment, or wish to evade payment by changing employment without notifying the Court.

2. MORTGAGES

CHOICE OF COURT

Proceedings to enforce a mortgage of land can be commenced in the High Court or in the County Court, and procedure relating to second mortgages is broadly the same as for first mortgages. The choice of court is governed by the value of the property, where it is situated, and also by the type of action that the mortgagee wishes to take to enforce his security. He can apply in most cases for payment of the money secured, sale of the mortgaged property, foreclosure (in which the mortgagor's legal rights to the property are extinguished and transferred to the mortgagee), delivery of possession, or a combination of them.[38] It also depends to some extent on the powers given to the mortgagee in the mortgage deed. In practice an application by a mortagagee usually includes several of these remedies, as in the case where a mortgagee applies for possession of the mortgaged property and payment of the mortgage debt.

The County Court has exclusive jurisdiction in cases where the property is in Greater London, or the annual value for rating purposes is over £1,000, or the property is not a dwelling-house.[39] Otherwise the claim must be brought in the Chancery Division of the High Court.[40] The County Court does not, however, have exclusive jurisdiction in an action for foreclosure where a claim for possession of the mortgaged premises is also included.

The Chancery Division of the High Court has jurisidiction where there is a claim for payment of money secured by a mortgage of land.[40] The mortgagee may also bring proceedings in the County Court which has an overlapping jurisdiction in proceedings for foreclosure where the amount owing under the mortgage does not exceed £30,000.[41] The High Court may transfer to the County Court an action begun in the High Court.[42]

---

38. *See* Chapter Fifteen.
39. Administration of Justice Act 1970, s. 37, as amended by the Courts Act 1971.
40. R.S.C., Order 88, rule 2.
41. County Courts Act 1959, s. 52; County Courts Jurisdiction Order 1981, S.I. 1981 No. 1123.
42. County Courts Act 1959, s. 75A.

The Chancery Division of the High Court has jurisdiction in actions where the claim is for the sale of the mortgaged property.[43] The County Court has overlapping jurisdiction where the amount owing under the mortgage does not exceed £30,000,[44] as in the case of actions for foreclosure as above.

Where the security is personal property, as where a bank has a mortgage of shares or other securities, proceedings are usually brought in the Queen's Bench Division of the High Court.

PROCEDURE IN THE HIGH COURT

Where an action is brought in the High Court on a mortgage of land, either for payment of the money secured, sale of the property, foreclosure, possession, or a combination of them, the procedures are governed by the Rules of the Supreme Court[45] as for the enforcement of debts discussed earlier.

The action is usually commenced by the issue of an originating summons, which is similar to the writ described earlier, although there are some technical differences. Strictly speaking a writ can also be used but the usual practice is to begin proceedings by originating summons except where an issue of fraud is involved.

The mortgagee issues the writ out of chancery chambers or certain District Registries. Other district registries may be used only when the mortgaged property is in the district of that registry.[46] The originating summons or writ is indorsed with a statement showing where the property is situated and, where the mortgagee claims possession of the mortgaged property and the property is outside Greater London, whether it is a dwelling-house and, if so, whether its rateable value exceeds £1,000.[47] If the property does fall into any of these categories the mortgagee will be required to bring proceedings in the County Court.

The originating or writ summons should state full details of the mortgaged property and of the grounds upon which the mortgagee claims to be entitled to enforce his security. The originating summons is served on the mortgagor and notice of the proceedings is given to all occupiers of the mortgaged property, who are told they may be added later as defendants. Where a mortgage is taken out in the husband's sole name a wife need not be joined as a defendant initially although the court may order her to be

43. R.S.C., Order 88, rule 2.
44. County Courts Act 1959, s. 52; County Courts Jurisdiction Order 1981, S.I. 1981 No. 1123.
45. R.S.C., Order 88.
46. Ibid., rule 3(2).
47. Ibid., rule 3(3).

added as a defendant later, and it seems that it may now be advisable to join the spouse in every action.[48] Where the mortgagee is seeking foreclosure any prior mortgagee must also be made a defendant in the proceedings.[49]

The originating summons is supported by an affidavit which must show the circumstances under which the right to possession arises and the state of account between the mortgagor and mortgagee, showing particulars[50] of:

(a) the amount of the advance;

(b) the amount of periodic payments required to be made under the mortgage;

(c) the amount of any interest or instalments in arrear at the date of issue of the originating summons and at the date of the affidavit;

(d) the amount remaining due under the mortgage;

(e) where the mortgagee claims possession, particulars of every person who to the best of the mortgagee's knowledge is in possession of the mortgaged property.

The affidavit must exhibit a true copy of the mortgage and the original mortgage or legal charge must be produced at the hearing. After issuing the proceedings and serving the parties named in the proceedings, the mortgagee then applies for an appointment for his summons to be heard by a master, who is a junior judge, producing the originating summons and acknowledgment of service if one has been filed within fourteen days after service of the originating summons. Where the defendant has failed to acknowledge service of the originating summons the defendant must be served not less than four days before the date of the hearing with a copy of the notice of appointment for the hearing together with a copy of the affidavit in support of the originating summons.[51]

If the mortgagee claims possession of the premises the affidavit served on the defendant must be indorsed with a notice informing the mortgagor, the defendant, that the mortgagee intends to apply at the hearing for an order that the defendant give possession of the mortgaged property to the mortgagee.[51] The mortgagee may be required to certify the manner in which the notice and affidavit was served on the defendant.

In cases where proceedings in the High Court are begun by writ,

48. *Williams & Glyn's Bank* v. *Boland* [1981] A.C. 487, and *see* Chapter Fifteen for cases involving husband and wife.
49. *Westminster Bank* v. *Residential Properties Improvement* [1938] W.N. 160.
50. R.S.C., Order 88, rule 5.
51. Ibid., rule 4.

it is not possible to enter judgment in default of giving notice of intention to defend.

The hearing in the Chancery Division is before a master. He will consider the evidence given by the mortgagee in his affidavit and any affidavit evidence submitted by the defendant. Depending on whether or not he is satisfied with the evidence as to the morgagee's claim he may give judgment for payment of the moneys owing to the mortgagee or make an order for delivery of possession. The master may stay or suspend execution of the judgment, or postpone the date for delivery of possession, for such period or periods as he thinks reasonable.[52] This is usual, in order to give the mortgagor a final period to repay the amount owing before the order takes effect. If the money is paid during that period the order will not be executed. These suspended orders are used frequently, but the master must be satisfied that the mortgagor is likely within a reasonable period to pay off the amount owing.

If the master is not satisfied with the evidence given by the mortgagee, or the mortgagor requests further time to file evidence, or for any other reason, he may adjourn the hearing to a later date.

If either the mortgagor or the mortgagee is dissatisfied by the master's order or course of action, he has an absolute right to have the summons adjourned to a judge;[53] the judge decides whether the hearing will be in chambers or in open court.

Where the mortgagee seeks foreclosure, the procedure is similar to that described above, but the mortgagee produces an affidavit setting out the amount due under the mortgage and any special circumstances which affect the state of account between the parties. If the master is satisfied of the mortgagee's claim, he makes an order *nisi* which gives the mortgagor six months in which to redeem his mortgage and appoints a time and place for the redemption to take place, the place for redemption being chosen in relation to the location of the mortgaged property and address of the mortgagor. If the mortgagor fails to redeem by the date fixed by the master, the mortgagee is entitled to apply by summons for the order for foreclosure to be made absolute and for the order for possession to be given. Stamp duty is payable on the order for foreclosure as for a conveyance on the sale;[54] this is one of the reasons why banks rarely seek foreclosure as a remedy.

If the mortgagor is in possession of the mortgaged property, it is usual for the originating summons to claim possession as well.

---

52. Administration of Justice Act 1970, s. 36(2). *See also* the Administration of Justice Act 1973, s. 8 (which extends the 1970 provisions).
53. *Birmingham Citizens Permanent Building Society* v. *Caunt* [1962] Ch. 883.
54. Finance Act 1898, s. 6.

Where the mortgagee claims an order for sale of the mortgaged property, the procedure by way of originating application and supporting affidavit is the same as for foreclosure. In the case of an equitable mortgage the court on an order for sale may vest the legal title in the mortgagee to enable him to sell the property.[55]

PROCEDURE IN THE COUNTY COURT

On account of the exclusive jurisdiction of the County Court in certain possession cases mentioned earlier, the majority of actions for possession and for payment under mortgages are brought in the County Court. Proceedings are brought in the County Court for the district in which the property is situate,[56] and the procedure is governed by the County Court Rules.[57] The mortgagee applies by summons and the particulars of claim which are served on the mortgagor contain the same information as set out in the originating summons and supporting affidavit as in the Chancery Division procedure described above. The matter is heard before a judge and the type of order made is similar to that made by a master in the Chancery Division in the High Court.

TIME TAKEN

In the Chancery Division in a simple case a mortgagee could expect to obtain a judgment within five or six months from commencing proceedings. If, however, the case were adjourned under the registrar's jurisdiction, as when the mortgagor is given time to sell his mortgaged property and pay off the mortgage debt, the case could take much longer. In the County Court, in a simple case, judgment could be obtained within about four months, subject to the same caveat in cases where there is an adjournment.

MORTGAGES OF CHATTELS

Where security consists of property other than land, such as stocks and shares or money in a bank account, the action can be brought in either the County Court or the High Court depending on the amount involved. The County Court has jurisdiction to hear any claim to enforce any charge or lien where the amount owing does not exceed £30,000.[58] Proceedings may also be brought in the Queen's

---

55. Law of Property Act 1925, s. 90.
56. C.C.R. 1981, Order 4.
57. Ibid., Order 6 rule 5.
58. County Courts Act, s. 52, as amended by the County Courts Jurisdiction Order 1981, S.I. 1981 No. 1123.

Bench Division of the High Court for any sum, and where the amount owed is under £30,000 the mortgagee can choose which court to use; as in the case of simple contract debts, he will be penalised as to the costs he can recover in the High Court unless the amount recovered exceeds £3,000 or there where reasonable grounds to suppose that the amount recovered would exceed £5,000.[59] In the High Court proceedings are commenced in the Queen's Bench Division by a writ and the procedure is basically the same as for a normal action for a contract debt described earlier.

59. County Courts Act 1959, s. 47, as amended by the County Courts Jurisdiction Order 1981, S.I. 1981 No. 1123.

PART V

INTERNATIONAL BANKING

CHAPTER TWENTY-ONE

Dealing in Foreign Exchange

INTRODUCTION

In order that countries may trade with one another it is necessary for there to be mechanism whereby payments may be made across national boundaries, and for the currency of one country to be valued in terms of that of another. Between 1879 and 1914 the currencies of the major trading nations were valued in terms of gold. Trading deficits and surpluses were matched by inflows or outflows of gold, and exchange rates were adjusted accordingly. Because of the discovery of gold in South Africa in 1887, a substantial increase in the level of world trade was able to take place, and adherence to the gold standard did not cause economic performance to drag. During the Great War the belligerents were forced to create vast new supplies of printed money which by 1919 was in excess of the supply of gold. The period between the wars was characterised by a mixture of fixed and floating exchange rates. The United Kingdom returned to the gold standard in 1925 after a period of floating exchange rates, but was forced to abandon it and return to floating rates which lasted until the outbreak of war in 1939.

In 1944 the major western trading nations attended a conference at Bretton Woods, New Hampshire, at which a system was devised which sought to achieve exchange rate stability, linked to gold but without restricting any country's domestic monetary policy. As a result of the conference, the International Monetary Fund (IMF) was set up, which was designed to provide a pool of gold and foreign currency from which member countries could borrow to iron out temporary deficits in their balance of payments. On joining the IMF each country established a value for its currency against the United States dollar and the extent to which each currency could deviate from its base rate was limited. Subsequently in 1969 the IMF created a new instrument, the Special Drawing Right (SDR), against which each currency was valued. These units of value were designed to create extra liquidity in the international monetary system and to reduce the reliance on gold and US dollars. The SDR is now valued daily against a "basket" of sixteen currencies each of which is given a weighting based on its importance in international trade.

Since 1972 the major currencies of the world have been allowed to float, with varying degrees of government intervention to influence their levels. Attempts have, however, been made within the European Economic Community (EEC) to establish a fixed rate structure for the member countries. The latest such attempt is the European Monetary System (EMS) (to which the United Kingdom has not yet agreed to subscribe) in which each currency is allocated a central rate against the European Currency Unit (ECU), which is another unit of value based on a trade-weighted basket of currencies. Each EMS currency is permitted to move only a certain amount against each other EMS currency and is only permitted to deviate by a certain percentage against its ECU general rate. There is a presumption that central bank action will be taken to keep each currency within its EMS limits.

THE LONDON FOREIGN EXCHANGE MARKET

The London Foreign Exchange Market does not have a floor like the Stock Exchange or the Baltic Exchange where buyers and sellers meet, but operates by telephone through sixteen firms of foreign exchange brokers. Until January 1980 there was an agreement between the banks operating in the market in London that foreign exchange deals between London banks would only be transacted through the broking system. Since that date direct dealing in foreign exchange between banks in London has been permitted. Transactions with overseas banks have always been carried out direct without going through a broker. Deposits and loans in Euro-currencies may also be carried out direct between banks in London, though in practice the brokers are extensively used for this purpose. The existence of the brokers greatly facilitates the operation of the market, since without them each bank dealing in the market would have to telephone a large number of banks in order to identify the best rate for a transaction available in the market. As it is, each bank need only have direct telephone lines to each of the brokers in order to cover the whole market.

EXCHANGE CONTROL

Between the outbreak of war in 1939 and October 1979, the United

Kingdom was subject to exchange control which restricted the ability of residents to make payments to and receive payments from non-residents, or to deal in foreign exchange or hold foreign currency, except in certain cases and under certain conditions laid down by the Bank of England by virtue of its authority derived from the Exchange Control Act 1947. In October 1979 all the restrictions were withdrawn except those relating to Zimbabwe, and in December 1979, following the lifting of sanctions, the Zimbabwe restrictions were also lifted. The Exchange Control Act 1947 has not, however, been repealed, with the result that the mechanism for reintroducing exchange control exists.

EXCHANGE RATES

Foreign exchange rates are determined by supply and demand, just as in the case of any other commodity which is bought and sold. In theory the basic factor affecting the exchange rate of a currency is the balance of payments position of the country concerned. If there is a balance of payments surplus, where exports exceed imports, then demand for the currency will exceed supply and the rate will rise against currencies of countries which have a balance of payments deficit. In practice many other factors affect exchange rates, and many transactions in the foreign exchange markets do not relate to trading transactions. For instance, movements of capital also affect exchange rates. A demand for foreign currency is created by a British company investing overseas in the same way as an import of goods. If domestic interest rates in a particular country are high, then that financial centre may attract deposits from overseas. The demand for the country's currency will cause the exchange rate to rise. The level of foreign exchange and gold reserves of a country and its inflation rate compared with other countries can also affect the market's view of the relative strength of the currency concerned. Economic and political events in the country concerned can influence the market's confidence in its currency. Finally government intervention can cause exchange rates to move. The country's central bank can enter the market to buy or sell its own currency or domestic interest rates can be adjusted to attract or dispel foreign currency. Exchange controls are also used by governments to regulate the exchange rate.

TYPES OF TRANSACTION

Foreign exchange transactions fall into three types. First there are sales or purchases for immediate delivery. These are known as spot transactions and the normal rate quoted for one currency against another is the spot rate. Spot rates are quoted for two days' delivery which means that a deal concluded on one day takes effect in terms of payment two business days later. In this way time is given for the necessary payment instructions to be carried out.

Secondly there are transactions where the currency is to be delivered more than two days after the deal is concluded. These are known as forward deals. If a United Kingdom importer is buying from an overseas supplier and the invoice is in a foreign currency, the importer may wish to fix in advance the sterling price to his customer. In such an event the importer can buy the foreign currency from his bank for delivery on the day on which the invoice becomes payable. This may be several months in advance if credit is being given by the overseas supplier. Similarly a United Kingdom exporter can sell currency forward if he is giving credit and invoicing in a foreign currency. The rate quoted for forward deals normally differs from the spot rate, since the supply and demand for a currency in the future may vary from the immediate supply and demand, and will depend partly on the difference between interest rates in the two currencies for the forward period and partly on the market's views of the future weakness or strength of the currencies concerned. Thus, if, for example, it is thought that sterling will be weaker than the US dollar in the future, there will be more buyers of US dollars in the forward market than sellers, and the forward rate will reflect the greater demand. If the three-month interest rate for sterling is higher by, say, 2 per cent per annum than the equivalent US dollar rate, then the pound will be at a discount of 2 per cent per annum (or $\frac{1}{2}$ per cent flat in the case of a three-month forward) to the US dollar. It is normally the case that interest rate differentials have more effect on forward foreign exchange rates than vice versa.

Thirdly, if an importer does not know when an amount in foreign currency has to be paid out but knows the extent of his liability, he may take out what is known as an option contract. For example, if he knows in January that he will have to make a payment before June, he can fix the rate in January and the currency will be delivered any time between January and June. Alternatively, he may know in January that the payment will fall due at any time between March and June and he will be able to fix the rate for delivery at any time during that period. In such cases, given that the bank does not know at the time the deal is done on what day it will be called upon to deliver the currency, it will assume, when quoting the exchange rate, that the currency will be delivered at the time which is least favourable to the customer.

METHODS OF PAYMENT

Reference is made in Chapter Twenty-Three to the use of documentary credits and collections and foreign bills to effect payments in foreign currency. Where an exporter is prepared to deal with an importer on open account, which is to say without keeping control of the shipping documents prior to payment or acceptance of a draft, or where the payment is not related to a trading transaction, there are three methods by which payment can be made.

For all large amounts payment is made by means of a telegraphic transfer (TT). If an importer in the United Kingdom is required to make a large payment to a supplier in the Unted States, he will normally issue instructions to his bank to make the payment by telegraphic transfer. The bank will send a tested telex to its correspondent in New York requesting the payment to be made to the exporter, and will buy the necessary dollars in the market. It will simultaneously enter into a contract with the importer to sell the dollars against sterling, which it will receive by debiting the importer's account with the sterling equivalent. In practice banks may group together several payment requests from a number of customers before buying the necessary currency in the market, or a bank may have a customer who is selling the same currency in which case it will not need to go into the market.

The cost of sending the telex is either covered by the customer on whose behalf the payment is being made or deducted from the payment to the beneficiary, depending on the arrangement between the parties. For smaller amounts where there is no particular urgency, payment is normally made by air mail transfer or by draft. The procedure for air mail transfers is the same as for telegraphic transfers except that the instructions are sent by air mail and it is unlikely that the bank will match the amount in the market. If a draft is used, the bank will, on instructions from its customer, draw a cheque on its correspondent bank. The draft will be sent to the beneficiary who will present it to his own bank for collection on the correspondent bank on which it is drawn. Each bank keeps accounts in its own books which reflect the accounts in its name in the books of its correspondents. These accounts are known as *nostro* accounts. Thus when an amount is paid out by a correspondent, a credit entry is made in the *nostro* account in the books of the bank requesting the payment, and if an amount is received by the correspondent, the *nostro* account is debited. When a correspondent bank sends in its statement of the bank's account in its books, a reconciliation between the statement and the *nostro* account is carried out.

EUROCURRENCIES

A Eurodollar is a dollar deposited with a bank outside the United States. Similarly any unit of currency deposited with a bank outside its country of origin is Eurocurrency, e.g. Eurosterling, Euroyen. Where the local exchange controls of a country restrict the payment of the local currency overseas, then no market in deposits in that currency will exist. Thus there is no such thing as a Eurorand, since the authorities in South Africa have successfully prevented non-residents from holding their currency overseas. Where a Euro-currency is deposited with a bank in London, the underlying payment for the transaction still normally takes place in the financial centre in the country of origin of the currency. For instance if a German resident deposits Eurodollars with a London bank the payment will be made by a New York bank to the New York correspondent of the London bank for account of the London bank. Similarly a Euro-sterling deposit in Luxembourg will be cleared through London. Clearing for US dollars can, however, be effected in London.

In a perfect market the rates of interest paid to a depositor or charged by a lender would be the same whether the deposit or loan was with a bank inside or outside the country of origin of the currency concerned. In such circumstances the rate of interest required by a depositor would be a function of his willingness to hold the currency concerned in preference to another currency. Thus weaker currencies would attract higher rates of interest to compensate the depositor against the possibility of their falling in value against other currencies. In practice, however, a variety of factors distort the market. First the authorities may wish to influence the domestic level of interest rates for purely internal reasons but so that the external level of rates is also affected. Secondly the imposition of exchange controls can cause differences to appear between internal and external rates, particularly if the ability of residents of the country of origin of the currency concerned to borrow or lend abroad is restricted. Thirdly, credit controls can affect the scarcity of funds domestically whilst Eurocurrencies are not in general subject to such controls. Fourthly, the deduction of withholding taxes from interest payments between countries can affect the attractiveness to a depositor of making deposits in the country making the deduction.

PRESS REPORTS

A report on foreign currency is produced every day in the *Financial Times*. An examination of the constituent parts of the report as given in the various parts of Fig. 7 on the following pages will give an indication of the way in which foreign exchange rates are quoted in the market. It should be remembered that no newspaper is a member of the market. The rates quoted are an indication given to the newspaper at a particular point in time and should only be used as such. It must also be made clear that the rates quoted are for large amounts between banks. Dealings for smaller amounts or with customers may be at different rates from those shown in the newspapers. The report contains a text (*see* Fig. 7(a)) which attempts to highlight the main events during the previous day's trading in the principal financial centres. High and low points are mentioned and influences, such as central bank interventions or domestic interest rate changes, are identified.

CURRENCIES, MONEY and GOLD

$ & £ soft

The dollar was slightly weaker in dull foreign exchange trading yesterday. Sterling had a generally softish undertone but finished unchanged at 73.7 on a trade-weighted basis, according to the Bank of England, after opening at 74.0 but declining to 73.7 at noon. There was no sustained selling of the pound, but the market lacked buying interest. Sterling fell quite sharply at one time in the morning, touching a low of $2.3330-2.3340, after a peak of $2.3460-2.3470. The pound quickly recovered however and closed at $2.3390-2.3400, a rise of 50 points on the day.

Further cuts in the U.S. banks prime lending rates depressed the dollar. The U.S. currency's trade-weighted index, as calculated by the Bank of England, fell to 83.3 from 83.4.

The dollar fell to DM 1.7625 from DM 1.7645 against the D-mark; to Swiss franc 1.6250 from SwFr 1.6285 against the Swiss franc; and to Y216.75 from Y217.50 in terms of the Japanese yen.

D-MARK—Showing renewed strength against the dollar and steady within the European Monetary System, following firmer rates in Frankfurt, and lower U.S. interest rates—The D-mark lost ground against most major currencies at the Frankfurt fixing, although the Swiss franc eased to DM 1.0830 from DM 1.0862. The dollar rose to DM 1.7646 from DM 1.7635 without any intervention by the Bundesbank at the fixing or on the open market. Sterling improved to DM 4.1240 from DM 4.1190, but eased slightly from the early morning level of DM 4.1330. Within the EMS the French franc rose to DM 42.9250 per 100 francs from DM 42.90; the Dutch guilder to DM 91.18 per 100 guilder from DM 91.13; the Belgian franc to DM 6.2470 per 100 francs from DM 6.2300; and the Italian lira to DM 2.1180 per 1,000 lira from DM 2.1170.

ITALIAN LIRA — Weakest member of EMS, after rising to the top of the system in February, and remaining firm for most of last year—The lira was firmer against other members of the EMS at the Milan fixing, but declined against the dollar and sterling. The D-mark was fixed at L472.23 compared with L472.47; the

French franc at L202.73 compared with L202.74; the Danish krone at L151.72 against L152.05; and the Dutch guilder at L430.44 against £430.48. Outside the EMS the dollar rose to L833.05 from L832.80 and sterling to L1,947.30 from L1,946.80, but the Swiss franc fell to L510.80 from L513.02.

BELGIAN FRANC—Remaining firm within EMS despite easing of interest rates by Belgian authorities—The Belgian franc improved against the dollar, sterling, Swiss franc and members of the EMS at the Brussels fixing. The dollar fell to BFr 28.2550 from BFr 28.30; sterling to BFr 66.1125 from BFr 66.1350; and the Swiss franc to BFr 17.3450 from BFr 17.4290. The D-mark fell to BFr 16.01525 from BFr 16.0525 and the French franc to BFr 6.8750 from BFr 6.88175.

JAPANESE YEN—Energy and balance of payments problems reflected in sharp decline last year. More recently lower U.S. interest rates have helped the yen recover—Fears of political instability following the death of the Japanese Prime Minister depressed the yen in heavy foreign exchange trading. The dollar rose to Y218.175 from Y217.675, after opening at Y218.50.

Fig. 7 (a)   *Foreign currency report—text.*

(*Courtesy of the Financial Times.*)

The other sections contain detailed information about foreign exchange rates during the previous day. The first section (*see* Fig. 7(*b*)), "The Pound Spot and Forward", gives the rates at which the pound was traded against the major currencies in terms of the number of units of foreign currency per one pound sterling. The first column shows the day's spread, the first rate quoted being the lowest rate at which banks sold currency against sterling and the second rate being the highest rate at which banks bought currency against sterling.

THE POUND SPOT AND FORWARD

June 12	Day's spread	Close	One month	% p.a.	Three months	% p.a.
U.S.	2.3330-2.3470	2.3390-2.3400	1.72-1.62c pm	8.57	4.45-4.35 pm	7.52
Canada	2.6850-2.6950	2.6860-2.6870	1.13-1.03c pm	4.82	3.32-3.22 pm	4.87
NethInd.	4.51-4.55	4.52¼ -4.53¼	3-2c pm	6.63	7¼ -6¼ pm	5.96
Belgium	65.95-66.40	66.05-66.15	15-5c pm	1.82	42-32 pm	2.24
Denmark	12.81-12.87	12.83½ -12.84½	1¼ -3 ore dis	−1.99	6¼ -8¼ dis	2.34
Ireland	1.1050-1.1110	1.1055-1.1065	0.03pdis-0.02 pm	−0.11	0.20-0.15 pm	0.63
W. Ger.	4.11½ -4.15½	4.12-4.13	3¼ -2¼ pf pm	8.00	8⅛ -7⅛ pm	7.39
Portugal	114.00-115.00	114.15-114.35	10c pm-20c dis	1.05	55pm-45 dis	0.35
Spain	163.50-164.25	163.90-164.00	5c pm-50c dis	1.65	10pm-100 dis	−1.10
Italy	1946-1956	1948-1949	¼ lire pm-1¾ dis	0.62	7¼ -9¼ dis	−1.69
Norway	11.32-11.39	11.33¾ -11.34¾	8½ -6⅞ ore pm	8.13	19⅞ -18½ pm	6.77
France	9.60-9.65	9.61¼ -9.62¼	4¾ -3¾ c pm	5.30	10¾ -9¾ pm	4.26
Sweden	9.71½ -9.77½	9.72-9.73	3½ -2¼ ore pm	3.55	5¾ -5 pm	2.21
Japan	505-515	506½ -507½	2.15-1.80y pm	4.67	6.95-6.50 pm	5.31
Austria	29.32-29.55	29.35-29.40	20-16gro pm	7.35	52-45 pm	6.60
Switz.	3.79½ -3.83½	3.79¾ -3.80¾	3⅜ -2⅜ c pm	9.07	10⅛ -9⅝ pm	10.39

Belgian rate is for convertible francs. Financial franc 66.85-66.95.
Six-month forward dollar 6.90-6.80c pm, 12 month 10.20-10.10c pm.

Fig. 7 (*b*)   *Foreign currency report—the pound spot and forward.*
(*Courtesy of the Financial Times.*)

From the second column it will be seen that the closing rates for the day are quoted in pairs. The first rate is the bank's selling rate and the second rate is the bank's buying rate, the difference between the two being the bank's turn. Thus if immediately before the close of business on 12th June a bank had one customer wishing to buy US $250,000 and another customer wishing to sell US $250,000 both against sterling, then it would have quoted a rate of US $2.3390 to the first customer, from whom it would receive £106,883.28 and US $2.3400 to the second customer, to whom it would pay out £106,837.60. The bank's profit on the two transactions would therefore be £45.68.

The next four columns deal with forward rates, and show the premium (pm) or discount (dis) at which each currency stands to the pound for one and three months' forward delivery. Premiums are deducted from the spot rate to arrive at the forward rate. Thus the rate at which a bank would have sold US dollars against sterling for

delivery on 14th July 1980 (one month forward) would have been
US $2.3218 (US $2.3390 minus 1·72 cents), and the rate at which
it would have bought Danish Kroner for delivery on 12th
September 1980 would have been DKr 12.87½ (DKr 12.84½ plus
3 ore). The columns marked "% p.a." show the premium or discount
expressed as a percentage per annum. The figures are arrived at by
taking the middle spot rate, and multiplying by twelve in the case of
the one-month rate or four in the case of the three-month rate.
The section entitled "The Dollar Spot and Forward" (see Fig.
7(c)) gives the same information for the US dollar as for the pound
except that all rates other than the pound sterling and the Irish Punt
are quoted on the basis of units of currency per one dollar. Where a
forward rate is shown as being at par, it is the same as the spot
rate. Thus the rate at which the bank sells Deutsche Marks against
US dollars three months forward is 1.7620.

THE DOLLAR SPOT AND FORWARD

June 12	Day's spread	Close	One month	% p.a.	Three months	% p.a.
UK†	2.3330-2.3470	2.3390-2.3400	1.72-1.62c pm	8.57	4.45-4.35 pm	7.52
Ireland†	2.1085-2.1100	2.1090-2.1100	1.55-1.45c pm	+8.54	4.45-4.35 pm	+8.34
Canada	1.1473-1.1483	1.1478-1.1481	0.47-0.52c dis	−5.17	0.81-0.86 dis	−2.90
NethInd.	1.9340-1.9380	1.9350-1.9365	0.28-0.38c dis	−2.04	0.73-0.83 dis	−1.61
Belgium	28.24-28.27	28.25-28.27	13-15c dis	−5.94	33-38 dis	−5.02
Denmark	5.4820-5.4865	5.4820-5.4835	4.30-4.80oredis	−9.96	13¾-14¼	−10.12
W. Ger.	1.7610-1.7670	1.7620-1.7630	0.05-0.15pfdis	−0.68	par-0.10 dis	−1.13
Portugal	48.80-48.95	48.83-48.93	32-42c dis	−9.08	70-110 dis	−7.36
Spain	70.12-70.20	70.15-70.19	45-60c dis	−8.98	135-155 dis	−8.26
Italy	832.50-833.40	832.50-833.00	1.3-1.4liredis	−10.45	19.0-20.0 dis	−9.36
Norway	4.8475-4.8525	4.8505-4.8525	0.1orepm-0.4dis	−1.83	0.75-1.25 dis	−0.82
France	4.1065-4.1135	4.1120-4.1135	1.12-1.22c dis	−3.41	3.25-3.40 dis	−3.23
Sweden	4.1605-4.1627	4.1617-4.1627	1.85-1.95oredis	−5.47	5.20-5.35 dis	−5.06
Japan	216.40-218.50	216.70-216.80	0.65-0.85y dia	−4.15	0.95-1.15 is	−2.07
Austria	12.54-12.58	12.55-12.56	0.85-1.45grodis	−1.10	1.75-3.55 dis	−0.84
Switz.	1.6225-1.6320	1.6245-1.6255	0.44-0.37c pm	2.99	1.54-1.47 pm	3.70

†UK and Ireland are quoted in U.S. currency. Forward premiums and
discounts apply to the U.S. dollar and not to the individual currency.

Fig. 7 (c)   *Foreign currency report—the dollor spot and forward.*

(*Courtesy of the Financial Times.*)

The table entitled "Currency Rates" (see Fig. 7(d)) shows the bank
rate in the countries with major currencies, and the rate against
SDRs and ECUs. Each day the Bank of England and Morgan
Guaranty Trust Company of New York, the American Bank,
publish a figure for each major currency which shows the amount
by which each currency has depreciated or appreciated against other
currencies on a trade-weighted basis since December 1971. These
figures are shown in the table headed "Currency Movements". It will
be seen from the table that according to the Bank of England's
reckoning the pound has depreciated to 73.7 per cent of its December

V. INTERNATIONAL BANKING

CURRENCY MOVEMENTS   CURRENCY RATES

June 12	Bank of England Index	Morgan Guaranty Changes %	June 11	Bank rate %	Special Drawing Rights	European Currency Unit
Sterling.........	73.7	−32.2	Sterling....	17	0.565950	0.610177
U.S. dollar.......	83.3	−10.4	US. $.....	12	1.32189	1.42446
Canadian dollar...	81.7	−15.9	Canadian $.	11.83	1.51594	1.63627
Austrian schilling.	156.3	+24.1	Austria Sch.	6¾	16.6135	17.8912
Belgian franc.....	115.9	+14.2	Belgian F. ..	14	37.4095	40.2623
Danish kroner....	107.2	−4.2	Danish K ..	13	7.25387	7.80175
Deutsche mark...	155.7	+44.5	D'Mark....	7½	2.33115	2.51246
Swiss franc......	198.4	+80.1	Guilder....	10	2.55786	2.75661
Guilder.........	125.7	+19.8	French Fr..	9½	5.43330	5.85737
French franc.....	101.3	−5.9	Lira.......	15	1100.80	1186.22
Lira	53.4	−51.0	Yen.......	9	286.850	308.751
Yen...........	130.8	+28.9	Norwgn. Kr	9	6.41117	6.89651
Based on trade weighted changes from			Spanish Pts.	8	92.5548	99.7405
Washington agreement December,			Swedish Kr.	10	5.49919	5.92930
1971 (Bank of England Index = 100).			Swiss Fr...	3	2.14569	2.31460

Fig. 7 (*d*)   *Foreign currency report—currency rates and movements*
(*Courtesy of the Financial Times.*)

1971 value or by 26.3 per cent. The Morgan Guaranty figure shows a depreciation of 32.2 per cent for the pound.

The section entitled "Other Currencies" (*see* Fig. 7(*e*)) gives the spot rates against the pound and the US dollar for currencies which are dealt in on the market but which are not regarded as major currencies, and also the rates for buying and selling notes against sterling. It will be noticed that the rates for notes are in line with the spot rates, but that the spread between the selling and the buying rate is much wider.

OTHER CURRENCIES

June 12	£	$		£ Note Rates
Argentina Peso	4276-4296	1831-1838	Austria	29.15-29.45
Australia Dollar	2.0210-2.0230	0.8652-0.8656	Belgium	66.35-66.95
Brazil Cruzeiro	118.21-119.21	50.61-50.81	Denmark	12.76-12.86
Finland Markka	8.5095-8.5179	3.6410-3.6430	France	9.55-9.61
Greek Drachma	99.909-102.232	42.80-43.00	Germany	4.11-4.14
Hong Kong Dollar	11.46-11.48	4.9070-4.9090	Italy	1910-1975
Iran Rial	n/a	n/a	Japan	509-514
Kuwait Dinar (KD)	0.624-0.630	0.2670-0.2700	Netherlands	4.51-4.54
Luxembourg Frc	66.05-66.15	28.25-28.27	Norway	11.29-11.38
Malaysia Dollar	4.990-5.003	2.1365-2.1385	Portugal	110-115.5
New Zealand Dlr	2.3590-2.3610	0.9895-0.9905	Spain	158.75-165.25
Saudi Arab. Riyal.	7.77-7.83	3.3280-3.3310	Sweden	9.69-9.77
Singapore Dollar	4.9525-4.9645	2.1210-2.1230	Switzerland	3.79-3.82
Sth. African Rand	1.8139-1.8145	0.7752-0.7758	United States	2.3300-2.3390
U.A.E. Dirham	8.65-8.71	3.7000-3.7030	Yugoslavia	61.00-66.50

Rate given for Argentina is free rate.

Fig. 7 (*e*)   *Foreign currency report—other currencies.*
(*Courtesy of the Financial Times.*)

The section called "EMS European Currency Unit Rates" (*see* Fig. 7(*f*)) gives details of the currencies whose countries have joined the EMS. The table shows the actual rate against the ECU and the amount by which each country has diverged and is permitted to diverge from the central rate.

EMS EUROPEAN CURRENCY UNIT RATES

	ECU central rates	Currency amounts against ECU June 12	% change from central rate	% change adjusted for divergence	Divergence limit %
Belgian Franc . . .	39.4582	40.2451	+1.14	+0.55	±1.53
Danish Krone . . .	7.08592	7.81698	+1.21	+0.62	±1.635
German D-Mark. .	2.51064	2.51379	+1.28	+0.69	±1.1325
French Franc. . . .	5.79831	5.85668	+0.17	−0.42	±1.35
Dutch Guilder . . .	2.72077	2.75794	+0.52	−0.07	±1.5075
Irish Punt	0.662638	0.675235	+1.05	+0.46	±1.665
Italian Lira	1148.15	1185.86	+2.42	+2.34	±4.0725

Changes are for ECU, therefore positive change denotes a
weak currency. Adjustment calculated by Financial Times.

Fig. 7 (*f*) *Foreign currency report—EMS European currency unit rates.*
(*Courtesy of the Financial Times.*)

The "Exchange Cross Rates" table (*see* Fig. 7(*g*)) shows the value of each major currency against each other major currency. Thus it show that £1 = US \$2.340 and that US \$1 = £0.427. It will be seen that the rate for one currency against another is the reciprocal of the rate quoted the other way around. The table shows that DM 1 = Swiss Fr 0.922, which is the reciprocal, to the nearest three decimal places, of 1.085 which is shown as the number of Swiss Fr per Deutsche Mark.

Finally the table entitled "Euro-Currency Interest Rates" (*see* Fig. 7(*h*)) gives the day's spread of the middle rates for Eurocurrencies and for US dollars deposited in Singapore (in the Asian dollar column). Like currency rates, Eurocurrency interest rates are quoted as double rates, with the offered rate (the rate at which banks lend) quoted first and the bid rate (the rate at which banks will borrow) quoted second. The offered rate is normally about 1/8 per cent per annum above the bid rate, the difference representing the bank's turn. As in the case of currency rates, the rates shown here are for large amounts between banks.

THE LONDON GOLD MARKET

The London Gold Market has five members: Mocatta and Goldsmid (a subsidiary of Standard Chartered Bank); Sharps Pixley (a subsidiary of Kleinwort Benson); N. M. Rothschild & Sons; Johnson Matthey Bankers; and Samuel Montagu & Co. Unlike the foreign exchange market, with its large number of members, the gold market is small enough in terms of the number of members for meetings to take place twice a day at which the price of gold is fixed. Each fixing is attended by a representative from each member of the market, who is in contact with his firm's dealing room by telephone.

EXCHANGE CROSS RATES

June 12	Pound Sterling	U.S. Dollar	Deutschem'k	Japan'se Yen	French Franc	Swiss Franc	Dutch Guild'	Italian Lira	Canada Dollar	Belgian Franc
Pound Sterling	1.	2.340	4.125	507.0	9.618	3.803	4.528	1949	2.687	66.10
U.S. Dollar	0.427	1.	1.763	216.7	4.111	1.625	1.935	832.9	1.148	28.25
Deutchesmark	0.242	0.567	1.	122.9	2.332	0.922	1.098	472.4	0.651	16.02
Japanese Yen 1,000	1.972	4.614	8.136	1000.	18.97	7.500	8.930	3843.	5.299	130.4
French Franc 10	1.040	2.433	4.269	527.2	10.	3.954	4.708	2026.	2.793	48.73
Swiss Franc	0.263	0.615	1.085	133.3	2.528	1.	1.191	512.4	0.707	17.38
Dutch Guilder	0.221	0.517	0.911	112.0	2.124	0.840	1.	430.4	0.593	14.60
Italian Lira, 1,000	0.513	1.201	2.117	260.2	4.936	1.952	2.324	1000.	1.379	33.92
Canadian Dollar	0.372	0.871	1.535	100.7	3.580	1.415	1.685	752.3	1.	24.62
Belgian Franc 100	1.513	3.539	6.241	767.0	14.55	5.753	6.849	2948.	4.064	100.

Fig. 7 (*g*) *Foreign currency report—exchange cross rates.*

(*Courtesy of the Financial Times.*)

EURO-CURRENCY INTEREST RATES (Market Closing Rates)

June 12	Sterling	U.S. Dollar	Canadian Dollar	Dutch Guilder	Swiss Franc	West German Mark	French Franc	Italian Lira	Asian $	Japanese Yen
†Short term.....	$17\frac{1}{4}-17\frac{1}{2}$	$8\frac{3}{8}-8\frac{5}{8}$	13-15	$11-11\frac{1}{4}$	$2\frac{1}{4}-2\frac{1}{2}$	$9\frac{1}{2}-9\frac{5}{8}$	$12\frac{1}{4}-12\frac{1}{2}$	14-17	$8\frac{1}{8}-8\frac{3}{8}$	14-15
7 days notice.	$19-19\frac{1}{4}$	$8\frac{1}{2}-8\frac{3}{4}$	13-15	$11-11\frac{1}{4}$	$2\frac{5}{8}-3\frac{1}{8}$	$9\frac{1}{2}-9\frac{5}{8}$	$12\frac{3}{8}-12\frac{1}{2}$	$17-18\frac{1}{2}$	$8\frac{1}{2}-8\frac{3}{4}$	$13\frac{1}{2}$
Month.........	$17\frac{5}{8}-17\frac{7}{8}$	$8\frac{7}{8}-9\frac{1}{8}$	$12-12\frac{3}{8}$	$10\frac{7}{8}-11\frac{1}{8}$	$5\frac{5}{8}-5\frac{3}{4}$	$9\frac{1}{2}-9\frac{5}{8}$	$12\frac{3}{8}-12\frac{1}{2}$	$16\frac{1}{2}-18$	$9\frac{1}{16}-9\frac{3}{16}$	$12\frac{3}{8}$
Three months...	$16\frac{5}{8}-16\frac{7}{8}$	$9-9\frac{1}{4}$	$11\frac{1}{8}-11\frac{1}{2}$	$10\frac{3}{4}-11$	$5\frac{9}{16}-5\frac{11}{16}$	$9\frac{1}{4}-9\frac{3}{8}$	$12\frac{3}{8}-12\frac{1}{2}$	$17\frac{1}{2}-18$	$9\frac{1}{4}-9\frac{3}{8}$	$11\frac{3}{8}$
Six months.....	$15\frac{3}{8}-15\frac{5}{8}$	$9\frac{1}{8}-9\frac{3}{8}$	$10\frac{1}{2}-11\frac{7}{8}$	$10\frac{3}{8}-10\frac{5}{8}$	$5\frac{1}{2}-5\frac{5}{8}$	$8\frac{7}{8}-9$	$12\frac{3}{8}-12\frac{1}{2}$	$17\frac{1}{2}-18$	$9\frac{1}{4}-9\frac{3}{8}$	$10\frac{1}{4}$ 3/16
One year.......	$14\frac{1}{8}-14\frac{3}{8}$	$9\frac{3}{16}-9\frac{5}{16}$	$10\frac{1}{4}-10\frac{5}{8}$	$10\frac{1}{8}-10\frac{3}{8}$	$5\frac{1}{8}-5\frac{5}{8}$	$9\frac{5}{16}-9\frac{7}{8}$	$12-12\frac{1}{2}$	18-19	$9\frac{5}{16}-9\frac{7}{16}$	$8\frac{7}{8}-9\frac{1}{8}$

The following nominal rates were quoted for London dollar certificates of deposit: one-month 8.60-8.70 per cent: three-months 8.65-8.75 per cent: six-months 8.65-8.75 per cent: one year 8.75-8.85 per cent.

Long-term Eurodollar two years $10\frac{1}{8}-10\frac{3}{8}$ per cent: three years $10\frac{1}{2}-10\frac{3}{4}$ per cent: four years $10\frac{5}{8}-10\frac{7}{8}$ per cent: five years $10\frac{3}{4}-11$ per cent: nominal closing rate. Short-term rates are call for sterling, U.S. dollars, Canadian dollars and Japanese yen: others two-days notice. Asian rates are closing rates in Singapore.

Fig. 7 (*h*) *Foreign currency report—Euro-currency interest rates.*

(*Courtesy of the Financial Times.*)

Each price quoted at the meeting is relayed back to customers of the members until a price is reached at which the market is in equilibrium, where the size of buying and selling balances. At this point, the chairman of the meeting, traditionally the representative of N. M. Rothschild & Sons, declares the price to be "fixed". The fixed price is then published and communicated around the world and is used internationally by industrialists and producers to establish prices for their products.

The advantage of operating a fixing system is that at one point in time a wide range of buyers and sellers is brought together and customers are offered the opportunity of buying and selling at a single quoted price. In volatile market conditions it can be a useful reference point. At other times of the day members quote buying and selling prices for spot and forward deliveries. The prices are subject to fluctuation depending on supply and demand and they are normally

GOLD
Further fall

Gold fell $11 to close at $589-593 after an active day in the London bullion market. The metal also opened at $589-593, and was fixed at $588.75 in the morning, and $590.00 in the afternoon. Trading was generally cautious following the recent fall in the price, and gold touched a low of $581-583 and a peak of $595-597.

In Paris the 12½-kilo bar was fixed at FFr 78,000 per kilo ($590.13 per ounce) in the afternoon, compared with FFr 78,990 ($597.77) in the morning, and FFr 79,100 ($598.56) Wednesday afternoon.

In Frankfurt the 12½-kilo bar was fixed at DM 33.250 per kilo ($590.05 per ounce), compared with DM 33.850 ($597.04) previously, and finished at $586-590, compared with $598-602.

In Zurich gold closed at $585-590, against $601-606 previously.

	June 12		June 11	
Gold Bullion (fine ounce)				
Close..........	$589-593	(£252-254)	$600-604	(£257-259)
Opening	$589-593	(£251-253)	$587-591	(£251¾ -253¾)
Morning fixing . . .	$588.75	(£251.253)	$595.00	(£254.687)
Afternoon fixing..	$590.00	(£251.814)	$596.00	(£255.465)
Gold Coins				
Krugerrand	$608-611	(£260-263)	$620½-624	(£265-267½)
Mapleleaf	$603-608	(£258-261)	$615-620	(£262½ -265½)
New Sovereigns...	$150-151	(£64-65)	$152-153½	(£65-66)
King Sovs	$180-183	(£77-79)	$180-183	(£77-79)
Victoria Sovs	$180-183	(£77.79)	$180-183	(£77-79)
French 20s	$153½ -156½		$155-158	
50 pesos Mexico ..	$732-737		$744-749	
100 Cor. Austria..	$575-580		$586-592	
$20 Eagles.......	$682-686		$683-687	
$10 Eagles.......	—		—	
$5 Eagles........	—		—	

Fig. 8   *Gold market report.*

expressed in US dollars per fine ounce troy. The standard unit of trading is a bar weighing approximately 400 ounces troy (12.5 kgs) with a minimum fine gold content of 995 parts per 1000. However, bars of various weights are available to meet the individual requirements of a customer.

For the smaller investor wishing to buy gold, a variety of coins is available such as the sovereign or the krugerrand. Because of the manufacturing costs involved with coins, they normally trade at a premium over their gold content. Since the removal of exchange controls in October 1979, residents of the United Kingdom have been completely free to deal in gold bullion and coins.

Figure 8 shows a report on the gold market from the *Financial Times*, giving an indication of the sort of movements which can take place during a day's trading and listing the coins for which a price is quoted in London.

CHAPTER TWENTY-TWO

Handling Trade Documents

GENERAL CONSIDERATIONS

Documentary credits are used to facilitate commercial relations, say, between an importer or exporter in the UK and a merchant abroad, or in financing the shipment of merchandise from one country to another. The importer gets his banker to issue a documentary credit which incorporates an undertaking to accept or pay bills of exchange up to a certain amount by the merchant abroad, provided that they are accompanied by specified documents.

Since 1st July 1963, UK banks have operated under the *Uniform Customs and Practice for Documentary Credits* of which the current edition is the 1974 Revision,[1] which should be read in conjunction with this chapter.

The functions of a documentary credit can best be described and the parties identified by giving a simple example. Suppose that a buyer in London wishes to buy a consignment of raw jute from a seller in Bangladesh at a cost of £45,000. The contract for the sale of the jute, which is on c.i.f. (cost, insurance and freight) terms, provides that payment shall be by confirmed irrevocable letter of credit against delivery of the shipping documents covering the jute, i.e. bill of lading, invoice and policy or certificate of insurance. The contract further provides that the letter of credit must be opened by the buyer at least one month before the intended shipment date. The buyer therefore goes to his bank and asks the latter to open the required letter of credit by the required date. The bank will require the buyer to complete and sign a request form. The request form sets out details of the required letter of credit, specifies that the letter of credit is to be subject to the *Uniform Customs and Practice* and specifically gives the bank a charge over the shipping documents and the goods represented thereby together with, if necessary, a power of sale. The bank may also require other security since, by opening the credit, the bank will be making itself primarily liable to make payment under it.

1. Available from the International Chamber of Commerce.

The bank, which is called the issuing bank, then opens the letter of credit and sends it to its correspondent bank in Bangladesh by letter, or in urgent cases communicates the terms of the letter of credit by telex or cable, in either case asking the bank in Bangladesh to add its confirmation to the letter of credit and notify the seller (i.e. the beneficiary under the letter of credit). By adding its confirmation, the confirming bank itself accepts liability to make payment under the letter of credit[2] and in that way, the seller has a bank resident in his own country to look to for payment.

When the goods are shipped, the beneficiary draws a draft as instructed in the letter of credit, i.e. on the confirming bank or on the issuing bank or on the buyer, and hands this draft to the confirming bank, or to his own bank in Bangladesh (i.e. a negotiating bank), together with the letter of credit and the shipping documents specified therein. If he presents these to the confirming bank, that bank honours the draft if drawn on itself or negotiates (i.e. buys) the draft if drawn on another party, always provided that the accompanying documents are in order. If he presents them to his own bank, that bank negotiates the drafts in reliance on the undertaking of the confirming bank supported by that of the issuing bank. In this way, the seller is paid immediately but the buyer does not have to pay for the goods until the draft and the shipping documents are presented to the issuing bank for payment.

Depending upon the payment terms in the underlying contract for the sale of the goods, a letter of credit may stipulate a sight draft or a usance draft, i.e. a draft providing for payment so many days after date or sight. In the latter case, the drawee bank will accept the draft (if in order) when presented for acceptance and will pay it when presented for payment at maturity. By means of a usance draft, the buyer can be granted credit, while the seller can get his money immediately by negotiating the draft on the strength of the undertakings given by the issuing and confirming banks in the letter of credit. Specimens of documentary credits using standard forms recommended by the International Chamber of Commerce Brochure No. 268 are given in Figs. 9, 10 and 11.

TYPES OF CREDIT

Credits may be revocable or irrevocable, confirmed or unconfirmed. A revocable credit is one which gives no undertaking by the issuing or advising bank that drafts issued thereunder will be honoured and the issuing bank can cancel it at any time by merely advising the

2. *See Uniform Customs*, Article 3.

Banque X/Bank X   Original

Except so far as otherwise expressly stated, this documentary credit is subject to the "Uniform Customs and Practice for Documentary Credits" (1974 Revision) International Chamber of Commerce (Brochure No 290).

Sauf stipulations particulières expressément définies, ce crédit documentaire est soumis aux "Règles et Usances uniformes relatives aux Crédits Documentaires" (Revision 1974) Chambre de Commerce Internationale (Brochure No. 290).

| Address télégraphique / Cable address | No. de télex / Telex number | Lieu d'émission et date / Place and date of issue |

CREDIT DOCUMENTAIRE - DOCUMENTARY CREDIT IRREVOCABLE
Banque notificatrice / Advising bank

Numéro du crédit / Credit number
de la banque émettrice /of issuing bank de la banque notificatrice /of advising bank
Donneur d'ordre / Applicant

Bénéficiaire / Beneficiary

Montant / Amount

Date / Date
à / in

Validité / Expiry
pour négociation / for negotiation

M   / Dear Sir(s),

Nous émettons en votre faveur ce crédit documentaire / We hereby issue in your favour this documentary credit

qui est utilisable par négociation de votre traite à
which is available by negotiation of your draft at

tirée sur
drawn on

et portant la mention: "Tirée en vertu du crédit documentaire No.   de (nom de la banque émettrice)"
bearing the clause: "Drawn under documentary credit No.   of (name of issuing bank)"

accompagnée des documents suivants:
accompanied by the following documents:

(SHIPPING DOCUMENTS REQUIRED).

concernant
covering   (GOODS AND PRICE BASIS).

Expédition/Embarquement de / Despatch / Shipment from
à / to

Expéditions partielles /Partial shipments   Transbordements /Transhipments

ALLOWED/NOT ALLOWED   ALLOWED/NOT ALLOWED

Conditions spéciales:
Special conditions:

Nous garantissons aux tireurs et / ou porteurs de bonne foi que les traites émises et negociées en conformité avec les termes de ce crédit seront dûment honorées à présentation et que les traites acceptées conformément aux terms de ce crédit seront dûment honorées à leur échéance.

Le montant de chaque traite doit être inscrit au verso de ce crédit par la banque négociatrice.

We hereby engage with drawers and or bona fide holders that drafts drawn and negotiated in conformity with the terms of this credit will be duly honoured on presentation and that drafts accepted within the terms of this credit will be duly honoured at maturity.

The amount of each draft must be endorsed on the reverse of this credit by the negotiating bank.

indications de la banque notificatrice / Advising bank's notification

Including whether credit is to be confirmed.

Vos dévoués / Yours faithfully,

Nom et signature de la banque émettrice. / Name and signature of the issuing bank.

Lieu, date, nom et signature de la banque notificatrice. / Place, date, name and signature of the advising bank.

Fig. 9   Negotiation credit.

Banque X/Bank X   Original

Address télégraphique Cable address	No. de télex Telex number	Lieu d'émission et date Place and date of issue

CRÉDIT DOCUMENTAIRE · DOCUMENTARY CREDIT
IRRÉVOCABLE

── Banque notificatrice / Advising bank ──

── Numéro du crédit / Credit number ──
de la banque émettrice /of issuing bank de la banque notificatrice /of advising bank

── Donneur d'ordre / Applicant ──

── Bénéficiaire / Beneficiary ──

── Montant / Amount ──

── Validité / Expiry ──

Date /Date
aux guichets de:
at the counters of:

M   / Dear Sir(s),
Nous émettons en votre faveur ce crédit documentaire qui / We hereby issue in your favour this documentary credit which est utilisable   is available
par paiement contre remise des documents suivants:
by payment against presentation of the following documents:

(SHIPPING DOCUMENTS REQUIRED).

concernant
covering

(GOODS AND PRICE BASIS)

Chaque présentation de documents doit indiquer le numéro du crédit de la banque émettrice et le numéro du credit de la banque notificatrice.
Each presentation of documents must indicate the credit number of the issuing bank and the credit number of the advising bank.

Expédition/Embarquement de Despatch / Shipment from à to	Expéditions partielles /Partial shipments	Transbordements /Transhipments
	ALLOWED/NOT ALLOWED	ALLOWED /NOT ALLOWED

Conditions spéciales:
Special conditions:

Vous garantissons que le paiement sera dûment effectué contre les documents présenté en conformité avec les termes de ce crédit. We hereby engage that payment will be duly made against documents presented in conformity with the terms of this credit.	indications de la banque notificatrice / Advising bank's notification Including whether credit is to be confirmed.

Vos dévoués / Yours faithfully,

Nom et signature de la banque émettrice. Name and signature of the issuing bank.	Lieu, date, nom et signature de la banque notificatrice. Place, date, name and signature of the advising bank.

Fig. 10   *Irrevocable credit available for payment.*

Banque X/Bank X

Original

| *Address télégraphique*
Cable address | *No. de télex*
Telex number | *Lieu d'émission et date*
Place and date of issue |

CREDIT DOCUMENTAIRE - DOCUMENTARY CREDIT
IRREVOCABLE
Banque notificatrice / Advising bank

Numéro du crédit / Credit number
de la banque émettrice /of issuing bank *de la banque notificatrice* /of advising bank
Donneur d'ordre / Applicant

Bénéficiaire / Beneficiary

Montant / Amount

Validité / Expiry

Date /Date
aux guichets de:
at the counters of:

M   / Dear Sir(s),
Nous émettons en votre faveur ce crédit documentaire qui / We hereby issue in your favour this documentary credit which
est utilisable   is available
par acceptation de votre traite à   *tirée sur*
by acceptance of your draft at   drawn on

accompagnée des documents suivants:
accompanied by the following documents:

(SHIPPING DOCUMENTS REQUIRED).

concernant
covering
(GOODS AND PRICE BASIS)

Chaque traite accompagnant les documents doit indiquer "Tirée en vertu du crédit No. . . . . . . de (banque émettrice) et No. . . . . . . de (banque notificatrice)"
Each draft accompanying documents must state: "Drawn under credit No. . . . . . . of (issuing bank) and No. . . . . . . of (advising bank)"

| *Expédition/Embarquement de*
Despatch / Shipment from
à
to | *Expéditions partielles* /Partial shipments
ALLOWED /NOT ALLOWED | *Transbordements* /Transhipments
ALLOWED/NOT ALLOWED |

Conditions spéciales:
Special conditions:

Nous garantissons que les traites tirées en conformité avec les termes de ce crédit serond dûment acceptées à présentation et dûment honorées à leur échéance.

We hereby engage that drafts drawn in conformity with the terms of this credit will be duly accepted on presentation and duly honoured at maturity.

indications de la banque notificatrice / Advising bank's notification
Including whether credit is to be confirmed.

Vos dévoués / Yours faithfully,

Nom et signature de la banque émettrice.
Name and signature of the issuing bank.

Lieu, date, nom et signature de la banque notificatrice.
Place, date, name and signature of the advising bank.

Fig. 11 *Irrevocable credit available for acceptance.*

beneficiary through the correspondent bank, with one important proviso. Any negotiations, acceptances or payments effected prior to receipt by the correspondent bank of any amendment or cancellation must be honoured by the issuing bank and its customer.[3] This revocable form of credit is not usually acceptable to the seller of the goods unless there is considerable trust between himself and the buyers. It will definitely be unacceptable to a seller who requires certainty.

An irrevocable credit is a definite undertaking on the part of an issuing bank and constitutes the engagement of that bank to the beneficiary or, as the case may be, to the beneficiary and bona fide holders of drafts drawn and/or documents presented thereunder, that the provisions for payment, acceptance or negotiation contained in the credit will be duly fulfilled provided that all the terms and conditions of the credit are complied with.[4] Once established, an irrevocable credit cannot be altered or cancelled without the agreement of all concerned. Partial acceptance of amendments is not effective without the agreement of all parties to the credit.[5]

An irrevocable credit may, in itself, mean little or nothing to the exporter who may not know the issuing bank, but, if the correspondent bank in his own country adds its confirmation, the seller will have a bank in his own country legally committed to paying, irrespective of what happens to the issuing bank. This means complete certainty for the seller and ensures that the importer obtains the documents he requires. "Confirmation constitutes a definite undertaking on the part of the confirming bank either that the provisions for payment or acceptance will be duly fulfilled, or in the case of a credit available by negotiation of drafts, that the confirming bank will negotiate drafts without recourse to the drawer." This undertaking can be neither modified nor cancelled without the agreement of all concerned.[6]

An unconfirmed credit is one on which the issuing bank advises the credit as either revocable or irrevocable but the correspondent bank does not add its confirmation thereto.

Another form of credit, frequently used in connection with the finance of shipments of merchandise and produce from countries overseas to this country and between foreign countries, is one under which bills are drawn on the importer himself, the bank's services in the matter being requisitioned in order that the foreign exporter may be able to negotiate the bills he has drawn on the buyer. The credit

3. *Uniform Customs*, Article 2.
4. Ibid., Article 3.
5. Ibid., Article 3(c).
6. Ibid., Article 3.

is communicated by the bank to the beneficiary who can sell (i.e. negotiate) his draft to his local banker, sometimes "without recourse", and so obtain payment for his produce. This is known as a negotiation credit.

Two other types of credit are frequently encountered. The first is a revolving credit. It may be revolving as to time or amount, which is to say that it can be valid for three months and is then automatically renewable, or it can be made available for a sum of, say, £50,000 and the value of any utilisations that reduce this amount will be reinstated immediately such utilisation has been settled with the issuing bank by the ultimate buyer, so that the amount available under the credit reverts to the original credit amount. Variations on the point at which the credit is to be reinstated occasionally occur but, of course, each revolving credit stipulates the necessary conditions as laid down by the buyer.

The second is a transferable credit.[7] In its simplest form, it allows a middleman, such as a merchant or agent, to enter into a transaction without disclosing the buyer's name to the seller. The transferable credits are operated in the following manner. The importer is requested to arrange with his bank for a letter of credit to be opened in favour of the merchant, and for it to be stated in the credit that it is transferable. The extent of the transferability will depend upon the exchange control restrictions of the buyer's country and may be limited to the same monetary area as that in which the original beneficiary is resident. Subject to that, and unless the credit specifies otherwise, it may be transferred once only to a second beneficiary in any country under advice to the correspondent.[8] The merchant names the supplier as the second beneficiary and the shipping documents are presented to the correspondent bank under the credit. At this point the merchant's invoices, which will include his mark-up or commission, are substituted for the supplier's invoices before the documents are handed over to the opening bank against payment under the credit. The invoices which are substituted must conform in all respects with those specified in the credit. In this way, the correspondent bank is able to pay the merchant his mark-up, and the merchant is not required to establish his creditworthiness for the purpose of establishing a letter-of-credit line from his bank.

When a credit has been transferred and the first beneficiary is to supply his own invoices in exchange for the second beneficiary's invoices but fails to do so on demand, the paying, accepting or

7. For full details, see Uniform Customs, Article 46.
8. Uniform Customs, Article 46(e).

negotiating bank has the right to include the second beneficiary's invoices despite the fact that the names of the original seller and ultimate buyer will then become known to one another.

There are several other variations of documentary credit, such as red clause credits, but these do not fall within the scope of this work.[9]

TERMS OF THE CREDIT

In order to be able to take advantage of a credit opened in his favour, the beneficiary must see that he complies strictly with the terms of the credit in every respect. The bank opening the credit cannot be expected to make all sorts of external inquiries as to whether the description of the merchandise as given in the documents presented to him does in fact conform to the credit, although expressed in a different way. The drawee banker is concerned only with documents which must conform precisely on their face with the terms of the credit, these terms having been settled by the issuing bank's principals. This principle was emphasised in *JH Rayner & Co.* v. *Hambros Bank*[10] and *Bank Melli Iran* v. *Barclays Bank (DC & O).*[11] If the buyer is not satisfied with the goods or they are not up to the sample, his remedy is not against the bank (provided that the documents are exactly as specified) but against the sellers under his contract. "Banks must examine all documents with reasonable care to ascertain that they appear on their face to be in accordance with the terms and conditions of the credit"[12] and "in documentary credit operations all parties concerned deal in documents and not in goods."[13]

Disclaimer clause

When handling documents in connection with documentary letters of credit, it is the practice of banks to disclaim any responsibility on behalf of themselves and their correspondents for the genuineness, correctness or form of any documents or any indorsements thereon, or any misrepresentations as to quantity, quality or value of any goods comprised therein, or for shipper's charges. This principle is expressed in *Uniform Customs*, Article 9. If foreign currency is to be held abroad to meet the payments under the credit, then the customer will be required to accept full responsibility for such currency.

---

9. For more detailed information, *see* H. C. Gutteridge and Maurice Megrah, *The Law of Bankers' Commercial Credits* (6th Edn.).
10. [1943] K.B. 37.
11. [1951] 2 Lloyd's Rep. 367; [1951] 2 T.L.R. 1057.
12. *Uniform Customs*, Article 7.
13. Ibid., Article 8.

Documentary credits may be expressed in sterling or in foreign currency. If they are expressed in foreign currency, then the exchange risk is that of the customer and he may cover this by buying the currency in advance.

Documents

The documents required to accompany a bill under a documentary credit will depend upon many things, e.g. the health requirements for the import into this country of fruit and vegetables, the documents required in respect of tariff preferences, the exchange control regulations of the importing country and the terms of the contract between buyer and seller. These requirements will not be examined in detail here but, for example, if goods are bought on a c.i.f. basis, then the usual documents required will include at least commercial invoices, insurance policy or certificate and bills of lading. The bills of lading, which are documents of title, are of particular importance to the banker as they constitute his security in the event that he is unable to obtain reimbursement for his payment under the credit if, for example, his customer, the applicant, became bankrupt or was wound up or if he refused the documents as not conforming to the credit. The documents of title are hypothecated to the bank by means of a letter of pledge and this is usually contained in the request form signed by the customer for the opening of a documentary credit.[14] However, modes of transport are changing and it is therefore important to read this paragraph in conjunction with the final paragraph of this chapter.

Indemnities

It is in connection with documentary credits and bills that bankers are so often called upon to join with their customers in giving indemnities to cover such things as discrepancies in the documents, or to shipowners for the non-production of the bills of lading due to the arrival of the carrying vessel before the documents or, in the case of a claim, to underwriters to cover the absence of one or more of a set of bills of lading. Wherever possible, a maximum value and an expiry date should be included in the indemnity for the bank's protection.

Liability entries are required in the bank's books when an indemnity is issued and frequent checks should be made to see whether the cause for the indemnity has been satisfied, thus enabling the bank to obtain the return of the indemnity for a cancellation. It should be remembered that indemnities create a real and not a merely

14. Ibid., Articles 14–33.

nominal responsibility. It is usual for the bank to take a counter-indemnity from its customer.

DISCOUNTING AND ADVANCING AGAINST DOCUMENTARY BILLS

If a banker discounts a documentary bill in connection with an import, he can do so on the security of the goods which are pledged to him by a letter of hypothecation or a memorandum of deposit supported by a document of title, e.g. bill of lading. The letter should contain a clause giving the bank power to sell the goods if necessary.

Documentary bills drawn on foreign countries and payable abroad are sometimes sold to (or negotiated by) bankers. In some cases, the bank may make advances against the bills up to an agreed percentage. The bank should secure full sets of the bills and of the relative documents, i.e. bills of lading, invoices, certificates of origin, insurance certificates covering marine and all usual risks, etc. It is usual for the documents of title, i.e. the bills of lading, to be to the shipper's order, and the whole set must be duly indorsed by him in blank if this is the case. In the case of certain countries, the bills of lading are sometimes made out to the order of the local bank so that they may better ensure control of the goods. In that event the bank to whose order the bills of lading are issued should be the branch or correspondent in that country of the bank making the advance. One drawback to this system however is that the bank's name would appear as the consignee in the ship's manifest and, as a result, the bank might be held liable for import duties, landing charges, freight charges, etc., incurred by the local bank, although it could cover itself in this respect by the understanding it has with its customer. If eventually it did have to rely on the goods for its cover, it would then be obliged to pay duties, landing charges, etc.[15]

The original set of documents is despatched to the bank's branch or correspondent at the place drawn on for presentation to the drawee for payment or acceptance, according to the terms of the bill of exchange. The second or duplicate set of documents follows by a later mail. It will be appreciated that if a bank is negotiating or advancing against these bills, it is essential that it has possession of all sets. As a safety measure, the bill of exchange should be indorsed to the collecting bank or correspondent. The bill should be accompanied by full instructions as to noting or protest if dishonoured, whether or not cable notice of dishonour is required, as to

15. *See Sewell* v. *Burdick* (1884) 13 Q.B.D. 159; reversed (1884) 10 App. Cas. 74.

storage and insurance of the relative goods if the drawee does not take up the documents promptly or does not meet the bill of exchange and the powers of any case of need or other agent, etc. The counterpart of these instructions will be contained in those given to the banker by the drawer. In particular, it is essential to get the powers of any case of need or drawer's agent clearly defined. It is also necessary for the bank to be acquainted with the requirements of the country of destination in the way of consular invoices, certificates of origin or any other documents required by the foreign customs authorities. The drawer and his bank should make every endeavour to ensure that the documents arrive in the country of destination before, or at least not later than, the vessel carrying the relative goods. Reference should also be made to Chapter Twenty-Three, where similar procedures regarding documents are followed but without necessarily involving advances.

DOCUMENTS WITHOUT TITLE

In the preceding pages there is frequent reference to bills of lading as documents of title. However, it must be appreciated that in modern practice goods are often despatched by airfreight and no system has yet been satisfactorily devised which would enable a third party (a bank) to keep control of the goods in the same manner as with a shipping company's bill of lading. The air consignment note is not a quasi-negotiable document like a bill of lading and does not convey any title to the goods as it must evidence consignment to a named party at destination and cannot be made out "to order". Therefore, in such cases, the banker would not have effective control of the goods to support the letter of hypothecation or memorandum of deposit as he would have with despatch by sea. Similar difficulties can arise with despatch of goods by road which is becoming more commonplace where only short sea passages or no sea passage is involved (e.g. within Europe). In this case, the usual document produced is a CMR (Contrat Marchandise par Route) which again has no quasi-negotiable properties, and the bank's only protection in such cases is to try to ensure that the goods are despatched to a named agent to be held at the bank's disposal until release is authorised by the bank.

CHAPTER TWENTY-THREE

Commercial Paper and Finance for Foreign Trade

THE COLLECTION OF COMMERCIAL PAPER

One of the functions of a banker is to collect bills of exchange and other instruments for customers. The collection of inland instruments has already been dealt with in earlier chapters and the present chapter is concerned with the collection of instruments payable overseas and vice versa. Such instruments are now generically known as "commercial paper".

The "Uniform Rules"

A revised code for the collection of commercial paper, known as *Uniform Rules for the Collection of Commercial Paper* (Brochure No. 322) was drawn up the International Chamber of Commerce in 1978 and, as from 1st January 1979, members of the British Bankers' Association and the Accepting Houses Committee decided to apply this code. There is, however, the proviso that "certain British banks with branches overseas may wish to opt out regionally in areas where such branches are in competition with other banks which do not subscribe to the code or where long established commercial practice makes full observance impossible." The banks of many other countries have indicated their intention to adopt the code and it is anticipated that it will in time be as universally applied as the *Uniform Customs and Practice for Documentary Credits.*

What follows is a general summary of some of the main points. For further details, the reader is referred to the text of the *Uniform Rules.*[1]

The letter of instructions and the remittance letter

The *Uniform Rules* will, of course, only be binding on a bank's customers and others concerned who have agreed to be bound by them, expressly or impliedly. It is therefore usual, when a bank accepts commercial paper for collection, for the bank to require the customer concerned to complete and sign a letter of instructions.

1. Available from the International Chamber of Commerce.

This will contain the stipulation: "Collections are handled subject to *Uniform Rules for the Collection of Commercial Paper* (1978 revision), International Chamber of Commerce Brochure No. 322."

Similarly, when the commercial paper is sent forward, it must be accompanied by a remittance letter,[2] which in addition to giving complete and precise instructions regarding the collection, would also state that the collection is sent forward on terms that it is subject to the *Uniform Rules*.

The customer's letter of instructions to his bank will also contain his instructions with regard to the collection, e.g. if it is a documentary drafts whether documents are to be delivered against acceptance (D/A) or against payment (D/P); whether acceptance or payment may or may not be deferred until the arrival of the goods; whether the proceeds are to be remitted by air or sea mail; whether collection charges and remittance expenses are to be for account of the drawer or drawee; whether charges may or may not be waived; whether or not the draft is to be protested for non-payment or non-acceptance, and any instructions with regard to the case in the remittance letter. The *Uniform Rules* provide in paragraph (c) of the preamble that banks are only permitted to act upon the instructions contained in the remittance letter and that if a collecting bank cannot for any reason comply with the instructions given in the remittance letter it must advise the remitting bank immediately.

The letter of instructions will contain a clear statement that overseas collections are undertaken only on terms that the remitting bank is not liable to its customer for loss, damage or delay, howsoever caused. Article 3 of the *Uniform Rules* provides that banks utilising the services of another bank for the purpose of giving effect to the instructions of the principal do so for the account of and at the risk of the latter.

Definition of "commercial paper"

In paragraph (b) of the preamble to the *Uniform Rules*, documents are defined as being either financial or commercial. Financial documents are instruments used for obtaining the payment of money, such as bills of exchange, promissory notes, cheques and payment receipts. Commercial documents mean all documents which are not financial documents, such as invoices, shipping documents and documents of title.

The parties to a collection are the customer, who is referred to as "the principal", the remitting bank, which is the bank to which the principal has entrusted the collection, the collecting bank, which is

---

2. *See* paragraph (c) of the preamble to the *Uniform Rules*.

any bank other than the remitting bank which is involved in the collection, the presenting bank, which is the collecting bank when making a presentation to the drawee, and the drawee, who is the person to whom presentation is made.

Presentation

Article 7 of the *Uniform Rules* provides that commercial paper is to be presented to the drawee in the form in which it is received from the customer, except that the remitting and collecting banks are to affix any necessary stamps. Remitting and collecting banks have no obligation to examine the commercial paper or the accompanying documents, if any, and assume no responsibility for the form and/ or regularity thereof.

Payment

In the case of commercial paper expressed to be payable in local currency, the collecting bank must only release the commercial paper against payment in local currency which can be immediately be disposed of.[3] In the case of commercial paper expressed to be payable in a currency other than that of the country of payment (foreign currency) the collecting bank must only release the commercial paper to the drawee against payment in the relative foreign currency which can immediately be remitted.[4]

Acceptance

The collecting bank is responsible for seeing that the form of the acceptance appears to be complete and correct, but is not responsible for the genuineness of any signature or for the authority of any signatory to sign the acceptance.[5] This is a reasonable provision since the formal validity of an acceptance will depend upon the law of the place where the bill is accepted, and the collecting bank should therefore be in a position to know the appropriate law.

Case of need

If the customer nominates a representative to act as case of need in the event of non-acceptance or non-payment, the remittance letter should clearly and fully indicate the powers of such case of need. Whether a case of need is nominated or not in the absence of specific instructions the collecting bank has no obligation to take any action in respect of the goods represented by a documentary remittance.[6]

3. Uniform Rules, Article 11.
4. Ibid., Article 12.
5. Ibid., Article 15.
6. Ibid., Article 19.

Waiver of liability

Banks concerned with the collection of commercial paper assume no liability or responsibility for the consequences arising out of delay and/or loss in transit of any messages, letters or documents, or for delay, mutilation or other errors arising in the transmission of cables, telegrams, or telex, or for errors in translation or interpretation of technical terms.[7]

Inward collections

If banks in this country accept commercial paper for collection from banks abroad on terms that the *Uniform Rules* are applicable, such banks will be collecting banks in terms of the *Uniform Rules* and their rights and duties will be as set out in the Rules.

THE USE OF BILLS IN FINANCING FOREIGN TRADE

Foreign bills

Bills drawn by an exporter on another country are generally denominated either in the currency of the exporter or in US dollars. British exporters to South Africa, Australia and New Zealand often embody in the bill the clause "Exchange as per indorsement". The rate at which the exchange is to be made is indorsed on the bill in London at the time of its first negotiation and before it is sent overseas for acceptance. The effect of this is to transfer to the overseas buyer the risk of fluctuations in the exchange rate after the bill has left the United Kingdom. The phrase can only apply, therefore, where there has been agreement to its inclusion between the drawer and the drawee of the bill. Figure 12 gives an example of a bill containing the phrase "Exchange as per indorsement" and a referee in case of need.

Foreign bills drawn by British exporters can be sent for collection through a bank which charges a collection commission, or they can be sold. The bank which buys the bill quotes a discount rate which takes into account the interest cost to the bank of holding the bill until the proceeds can be collected from the overseas drawee.

If a bank in the United Kingdom buys a bill on a country where it has no agent or correspondent, it can sell the bill to another bank which is represented in the country concerned. When a bank sells a foreign bill it indorses it and thus becomes liable to the buyer if the bill is ultimately dishonoured. The contingent liability is recorded in the bank's books on an account styled "Liability for foreign bills negotiated". Since the bank will have a claim against its

7. Ibid., Article 4.

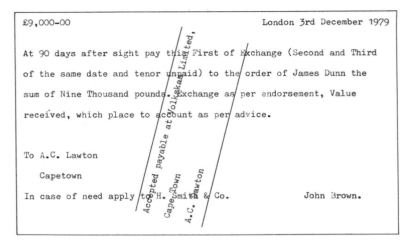

£9,000-00   London 3rd December 1979

At 90 days after sight pay this First of Exchange (Second and Third

of the same date and tenor unpaid) to the order of James Dunn the

sum of Nine Thousand pounds. Exchange as per endorsement, Value

received, which place to account as per advice.

To A.C. Lawton

   Capetown

In case of need apply to H. Smith & Co.   John Brown.

Accepted payable at Volkskas Limited,
Cape Town
A.C. Lawton

Fig. 12   *Bill of exchange.*

customer (the drawer of the bill) in the event of the bill being dishonoured, a contra entry is recorded on an account styled
"Customer's liabilities for foreign bills negotiated". Once sufficient
time has elapsed for the bill to be returned if dishonoured, the
entries are reversed and the record of the contingent liability is extinguished.

Re-exchange
Re-exchange arises when bills are dishonoured in a country different
from that in which they were drawn or indorsed, and covers the loss
to the bank holding the bill arising from such dishonour. For
example, if a bill drawn in London on a buyer in Trinidad which has
been sold to a bank in London is dishonoured, the bank will be
able to claim from the drawer such a sum as will realise in Trinidad
the amount of the bill at the rate of exchange prevailing in Trinidad
at the time of its dishonour, plus the usual expenses of protest,
stamps, etc. The bank is in this way able to pass back to its
customer any exchange risk involved in dishonour by the drawee.

Referee in case of need
The specimen bill of exchange given in Fig. 12 contains the expression
"In the case of need apply to H. Smith & Co." Section 15 of the
Bills of Exchange Act 1882 states that "the drawer of a bill and any
indorser may insert therein the name of a person to whom the holder
may resort in case of need, that is to say, in case the bill is dishonoured

by non-acceptance or non-payment. Such person is called the referee in case of need. It is in the option of the holder to resort to the referee in case of need or not, as he may think fit."

In some foreign countries presentment to a case of need is obligatory but in this country it is optional. On acceptance the case of need becomes an "acceptor for honour".[8] A person does not become a party to a bill by merely being named as a "case of need", and any person who satisfies the conditions may intervene without being mentioned on the bill. The practice is naturally more frequently encounted in bills drawn abroad on the United Kingdom or vice versa, than in inland bills. In the case of foreign bills the drawers, and possibly the indorsers also, are not in a position quickly to take up bills dishonoured by the drawees or acceptors. The practice is of particular value with documentary bills where there is merchandise to be attended to. A bank should not give up the documents to a case of need, except against payment, unless there are written instructions from the drawer. Full instructions should always be obtained as to the powers of the drawer's agent or representative to deal with extensions of bills, the documents or goods, if the relative bill is dishonoured, with particular reference to their storage and insurance.[9]

Bills in a set
A bill in a set is a bill of exchange that is drawn in two or three parts, each part being on a separate piece of paper. Each part must be worded exactly the same as the other parts, except that the parts are called respectively "First of exchange", "Second of exchange" and "Third of exchange", and are so referred to in each of the other parts. Inland bills—that is, bills drawn by one person on another both of whom are resident in this country—are not usually drawn in sets. Bills are drawn in sets by foreign traders on persons in this country, and vice versa, and are so drawn to minimise the risk of loss in transmission from one country to another. Banks usually issue drafts on foreign countries in two parts, one being marked "Original" and the other "Duplicate".

When a bill is drawn in two or three parts, the first part is often sent to a bank or correspondent in the country drawn on, in order that it may present the bill to the drawee for acceptance. After acceptance has been obtained, the correspondent retains the first part until it is claimed by the holder of the other part or parts. In order that such holder shall know to whom to apply for the "First of

---

8. *See* Chapter Nine.
9. *See also* earlier in this chapter.

```
┌─────────────────────────────────────────────────────────────────────┐
│                                  703, Commercial Buildings,           │
│                                  London,                              │
│  £10,000.                        3rd December 1979                    │
│                                                                       │
│  Sixty days after sight pay this First of Exchange (Second and        │
│  Third of the same date and tenor being unpaid) to the order of       │
│  F. Jaasma and Co. the sum of ten thousand pounds, value received.    │
│                                                                       │
│                                  James Norton.                        │
│                                                                       │
│  To Fritz Evers,                                                      │
│     Amsterdam.                                                        │
└─────────────────────────────────────────────────────────────────────┘
```

```
┌─────────────────────────────────────────────────────────────────────┐
│                                  703 Commercial Buildings,            │
│                                  London,                              │
│  £10,000.                        3rd December 1979.                   │
│                                                                       │
│  Sixty days after sight pay this Second of Exchange (First and        │
│  Third of the same date and tenor being unpaid) to the order of       │
│  F. Jaasma and Co. the sum of ten thousand pounds, value received.    │
│                                                                       │
│                                  James Norton.                        │
│                                                                       │
│  To Fritz Evers,                                                      │
│     Amsterdam.                                                        │
└─────────────────────────────────────────────────────────────────────┘
```

```
┌─────────────────────────────────────────────────────────────────────┐
│                                  703, Commercial Buildings,           │
│                                  London,                              │
│  £10,000.                        3rd December 1979.                   │
│                                                                       │
│  Sixty days after sight pay this Third of Exchange (First and         │
│  Second of the same date and tenor being unpaid) to the order of      │
│  F. Jaasma and Co. the sum of ten thousand pounds, value received.    │
│                                                                       │
│                                  James Norton.                        │
│                                                                       │
│  To Fritz Evers,                                                      │
│     Amsterdam.                                                        │
└─────────────────────────────────────────────────────────────────────┘
```

Fig. 13   *Bill in a set having three parts:* (*a*) *first part;* (*b*) *second part;*
(*c*) *third part.*

exchange" a reference, "First with Messrs A.B. & Co", is written on the remaining part or parts. On seeing this statement, the holder knows that A.B. & Co hold the first and accepted part, and all he has to do to secure possession of it is to produce the remaining part or parts. All parts are then together and the whole constitutes one bill.[10] By sending the first part forward in this manner the advantage of earlier acceptance is obtained.

Figure 13 gives an example of a bill in a set having three parts.

Statute law governing bills in a set

Although the whole of the parts constitute one bill, where the holder of a set indorses two or more parts to different persons he is liable on every such part, and every indorser subsequent to him is liable on the part he has himself indorsed as if the said parts were separate bills.[11] Where two or more parts of a set are negotiated to different holders in due course, the holder whose title first accrues is, as between such holders, deemed the true owner of the bill. This, however, does not affect the rights of a person who in due course accepts or pays the part first presented to him.[12] The acceptance may be written on any part but it must be written on one part only. If the drawee accepts more than one part, and such accepted parts get into the hands of different holders in due course, he is liable on every such part as if it were a separate bill.[13] When the acceptor of a bill drawn in a set pays it without requiring the part bearing his acceptance to be delivered up to him, and that part at maturity is outstanding in the hands of a holder in due course, he is liable to the holder thereof.[14] Subject to the preceding rules, where any one part of a bill drawn in a set is discharged by payment or otherwise, the whole bill is discharged.[15]

Conflict of laws

Where a bill drawn in one country is negotiated, accepted or payable in another country, difficulties may arise as to which country's laws govern each transaction. In the general way, the maxim *locus regit actum*, which means "the place governs the act", decides the matter. There are some exceptions, but this is the general rule followed when determining the rights, duties and liabilities of the parties. Thus the validity of a bill as regards its form is determined by the law of the place of issue, and the validity as regards requisites

10. Bills of Exchange Act 1882, s. 71(1).
11. Ibid., s. 71(2).
12. Ibid., s. 71(3).
13. Ibid., s. 71(4).
14. Ibid., s. 71(5).
15. Ibid., s. 71(6).

in form of the supervening contracts, such as acceptance, or indorsement, or acceptance supra protest, is determined by the law of the place where such contract was made.[16] However, a bill issued out of the United Kingdom is not invalid by reason only that it is not stamped in accordance with the law of the place of issue,[17] and if a bill conforms as regards requisites in form to the law of the United Kingdom, it may, for the purposes of enforcing payment, be treated as valid as between all persons who negotiate, hold or become parties to it in the United Kingdom.[18] The interpretation of the drawing, indorsement, acceptance or acceptance supra protest of a bill is determined by the law of the place where such contract is made, but where an inland bill is indorsed in a foreign country the indorsement as regards the payer is interpreted according to the law of England.[19] The duties of the holder with respect to presentment for acceptance or payment, and the necessity for or sufficiency of a protest or notice of dishonour or otherwise, are determined by the law of the place where the act is done or the bill is dishonoured.[20]

ACCEPTANCE CREDITS

Reference has been made in the section on documentary credits to the arrangement whereby the beneficiary under a credit draws usance drafts on the confirming or advising bank. Such an arrangement enables the exporter to be paid immediately upon shipment, provided that the documents are in accordance with the terms of the credit, and the importer to pay for the goods some time after they have been shipped, depending on the tenor of the bill. Because the bill has been accepted by a bank rather than by the importer it can be sold more easily and at a finer rate. In the case of drawings on London banks the bills are normally sold to members of the London Discount Market. The proceeds of discount are then paid away to the exporter, and the importer is obliged to put the bank in funds on the maturity date of the bill so that the bank can make payment to the presenter of the bill. The bank is therefore taking a risk on the importer since by virtue of its acceptance of the bill, it renders itself primarily liable to meet the bill at maturity.

At one time a large proportion of bills accepted by banks in the United Kingdom were drawn under letters of credit. It is now the

16. Bills of Exchange Act 1882, s. 72(1).
17. Ibid., s. 72(1)(a).
18. Ibid., s. 72(1)(b).
19. Ibid., s. 72(2).
20. Ibid., s. 73(3).

case, however, that the majority of bills in the London market arise from clean acceptance credits, where no documents pass through the hands of the bank. Under such an arrangement the bank makes available to its customer a facility for a specified amount and period, under which the customer may draw bills on the bank for usances of up to six months. The bills are then sold in the London Discount Market normally by the banks at a discount rate which is determined by the usual market forces affecting interest rates. The bank, which is once again primarily liable under the bill, receives an accepting commission by way of remuneration for the risk it takes on its customer. In order to meet the requirements of the Discount Market a bill sold must have at least two good names as parties and must bear a clause indicating that it is drawn against exports, imports or some other self-liquidating transaction. Thus the discount house may refuse to buy the bill if the drawer is not considered a good enough name to appear in the market, or if the bill is not drawn against turnover of some sort. A property company would not normally be able to raise money by means of an acceptance credit since its underlying business is not self-liquidating within six months. The Bank of England polices the market by taking sample parcels of bills from the Discount Market. If any bills are found which are not thought to be suitable for the market, the accepting bank may be asked to buy back the bills.

Bills accepted by certain banks are eligible for re-discount with the Bank of England. This means that the holder of a bill can at any time sell it to the Bank of England for cash. Since these bills are more liquid than bills drawn on ineligible names, the Discount market will normally buy eligible bills at a finer rate than ineligible bills. In addition, eligible bills qualify to a limited extent as reserve assets[21] which further increases their attractiveness to the holder. Banks whose bills are eligible for re-discount at the Bank of England are the London Clearing and Scottish banks, the accepting houses, the British overseas banks, the London branches of the Australian, New Zealand and Canadian banks and certain other British banks, and one or two customers of long standing of the Bank of England.

One advantage of acceptance credits to the accepting bank is that it makes funds available to its customers by lending its name rather than cash. It is for this reason that the accepting houses have been pre-eminent in the provision of acceptance credits. In the accounts of the accepting bank two entries appear to record the existence of an acceptance credit. On the asset side of the balance

21. *See* Chapter Two.

sheet is to be found the item "Liabilities of customers on acceptances" and this is matched on the liabilities side by the contra entry "Acceptances on behalf of customers". In Britain the standard accounting practice is for these items to be included in the main body of the balance sheet. In many other countries acceptances are recorded as a note to the accounts.

THE EXPORT CREDITS GUARANTEE DEPARTMENT

The Export Credits Guarantee Department (ECGD) is a government department whose function is to support British exports. It was founded in 1919, and derives its present powers from the Export Guarantees and Overseas Investment Act 1978. The assistance afforded to exporters by the ECGD falls into two principal categories. First it provides insurance against the risk of not being paid, for such reasons as the default of the buyer, restrictions on the transfer of currency or the cancellation of valid import licences. Secondly it furnishes guarantees to banks in respect of loans either to the exporter (supplier credit) or to the overseas buyer (buyer credit). In addition, the ECGD insures new investment overseas against such risks as war, expropriation and restrictions on currency transfers, provides support for the issue of performance bonds in respect of export contracts, gives protection against increases in United Kingdom costs for large contracts with long manufacturing periods and covers members of a United Kingdom consortium against loss caused by the insolvency of another member of the consortium.

The ECGD was formed on the basis that its operations would involve no expense to the taxpayer. Accordingly it operates mainly on a commercial basis and applies normal commercial principles to its underwriting. About 10 per cent of its business is, however, undertaken where no commercial justification exists, but where the writing of the business is considered to be in the national interest.

Insurance

The basic insurance policy available to exporters is the comprehensive short-term guarantee. It applies to consumer and other production-line goods where the business is of a continuous and repetitive nature. The exporter is normally expected to insure all his export turnover for which credit terms of up to 180 days are granted. In this way the ECGD is able to spread its risk between high and low risk countries and keep its premiums low. An exporter can in some circumstances obtain cover for selected markets, at a higher premium, but only if a reasonable spread of countries is offered, which represents a significant proportion of the exporter's total overseas business. The exporter is insured against 90 per cent of losses arising from political events in the country of the buyer. No cover is available where the exporter is in default of his contractual obligations to the buyer.

Where comprehensive cover is inappropriate, as in the case of non-standard, individual contracts for the supply of capital goods or construction projects, the ECGD issues specific insurance policies which are tailor-made to suit the circumstances of the case. The exporter is not obliged to offer all his business and may select only the worst risks. The premiums for such cover are therefore higher than in the case of comprehensive insurance. The cover is broadly the same as that provided by comprehensive policies.

Guarantees

The ECGD does not itself provide finance for exporters, but facilitates export credit by means of guarantees to banks. In addition, an exporter is able to assign his rights under ECGD insurance policies to banks as security for export finance. Where an exporter grants less than two years' credit and the buyer accepts a bill of exchange or issues a promissory note, ECGD may give an unconditional guarantee to the exporter's bank that it will pay 100 per cent of the face value of any bills or notes plus the interest on them up to the date of default three months after the due date. In order to operate the scheme, which is known as the comprehensive bill guarantee scheme, the exporter presents the bills or notes to his bank together with the relevant shipping documents and a warranty that the transaction is covered by an ECGD insurance policy. British banks have agreed to finance 100 per cent of such transactions at an interest rate of $\frac{5}{8}$ per cent per annum over base rate. The ECGD agrees a limit for the amount of finance it will guarantee, which is determined by the amount of the exporter's business insured with the ECGD and the financial standing of the exporter. The ECGD has recourse to the exporter in respect of payments made by the ECGD in excess of or in advance of amounts payable under the standard ECGD policy.

Where goods are sold on open account, unsupported by bills or notes, and under credit terms of up to six months, the ECGD may give a comprehensive open account guarantee to the financing bank on terms similar to the comprehensive bills guarantee. The exporter provides the bank with evidence of shipment and the terms of payment, and in addition gives the bank a promissory note for the amount of the loan. In the event that the exporter fails to make repayment to the bank, the ECGD pays the bank and has recourse to the exporter, the exporter's obligation to repay the bank being independent of the receipt of payment from the buyer on the due date.

Supplier credits

Where the terms of payment are two years or more, the ECGD is normally prepared to issue a specific bank guarantee to the financing bank in respect of all principal and interest remaining unpaid up to the date of default three months after the due date. The buyer must pay not less than 15 per cent on or prior to shipment in cash and the balance by bills of exchange or promissory notes maturing at six-monthly intervals over the period of credit approved by the ECGD, normally up to five years. With this type of guarantee banks which are incorporated in the United Kingdom make finance available to the exporter at minimum subsidised fixed rates of interest ranging from $7\frac{1}{2}$ to 8 per cent per annum for periods over five years. These subsidised fixed rates of interest are no longer available for exports to members of the EEC. The minimum interest rates charged on such facilities are fixed by agreement between the member countries of the Organisation for Economic Co-operation and Development (OECD). Supplier credits are available in sterling for amounts up to £1 million. Amounts in excess of that figure can be financed in US dollars or Deutsche Marks.

Buyer credits

Export contracts worth £1 million or more may be financed by a bank or a syndicate of banks lending direct to the overseas buyer or a borrower acting on his behalf. The loan normally covers 80 or 85 per cent of the United Kingdom value of the contracts, and the obligation to repay the lender rests solely with the overseas buyer. The ECGD has recourse to the exporter only if he is in default under his contract with the buyer and the buyer is also in default under the loan. The terms on which banks lend under buyer credits are the same as those applicable to supplier credits except that the available period of credit may be extended to ten years. Since December 1976 the ECGD have required that most countries borrow under buyer credits in US dollars or Deutsche Marks rather than sterling, except where the loan is for £5 million or less.

Other facilities

Other facilities provided by the ECGD include insurance cover for merchanting transactions, sales by overseas subsidiaries of United Kingdom exporters and stocks held abroad. Insurance can also be obtained in respect of exports of semi-capital goods, where the business is of a repetitive nature but where credit terms of between six months and five years are necesary. Buyer credits can take the form of lines of credit to cover cases where an overseas buyer regularly purchases equipment from the United Kingdom of an individual value which would not normally warrant the setting up of a buyer credit.

OTHER SERVICES IN FINANCING FOREIGN TRADE

Export houses

Various types of export house provide additional services to the United Kingdom exporter. There are three principal types of export house.

(*a*) *Merchants who act as principals.* The exporter, instead of selling to an overseas importer, sells to a merchant who in turn sells to the overseas importer. The responsibility for financing the shipment and collection from the buyer thus falls on the merchant, and the exporter receives cash immediately upon the sale of the goods.

(*b*) *Export agents or export managers.* These companies act on behalf of the exporter and make payment against evidence of shipment. The exporter therefore receives payment immediately but, unlike in the case of dealing with a merchant, remains responsible to the overseas buyer in respect of the performance of the sale contract. The export agent provides credit to the overseas buyer in its own name.

(*c*) *The confirming or indent house.* This acts for the overseas buyer. The confirming of an order from an overseas buyer involves an undertaking to the exporter that payment for the goods will take place on evidence of shipment. The confirming house then gives credit to the buyer. As in the case of export agents, the seller and buyer remain in a contractual relationship as far as performance of the contract is concerned.

Many banks have subsidiaries or associates which fulfil some or all of the export house functions referred to above.

Bonds and guarantees

The exporter of capital goods may be required to provide a bank bond or guarantee in respect of a percentage of the value of the contract. There are three types of bond which commonly arise.

(*a*) *A tender or bid bond* is designed to prove to the buyer that the exporter's tender is serious. The bank guarantees that if the contract is awarded to the tenderer, he will comply with the terms of the tender and enter into the contract. Tender bonds are normally for up to 5 per cent of the tender value.

(*b*) *A performance bond* guarantees that, once the contract has been awarded to the exporter, he will comply with its terms. The amount of the bond is normally for 10 per cent of the value of the contract.

(*c*) *A bank guarantee* may be required by the buyer where a contract provides for payments in advance by the buyer to the exporter, to the effect that if the contract is not completed, any loss arising from the fact that an advance payment has been made will be covered.

Banks will usually take a counter-indemnity from the exporter in respect of bonds issued. Bonds may be conditional, in which case it is the responsibility of the buyer to show that he has suffered loss as a result of default by the exporter, and the amount payable is limited to the extent of that loss. Other bonds are unconditional. These may be called for their full amount whether the exporter is in default or not. The ECGD provides cover in the form of an indemnity to the issuer of the bond in respect of certain types of export contract.

Where a bond is unconditional, the bank is not concerned with any question of the propriety or otherwise of any call made by the buyer. If a call is made, the bank is bound to pay (subject to any maximum liability under the bond), and if the exporter wishes to dispute the buyer's right to make the call, his remedy is against the seller, not the bank. It is not appropriate for the exporter to seek an injunction to restrain the bank from making payment.[22]

Other sources of export finance

Exporters of capital goods can offer medium-term credit to the overseas buyer by means of *à forfait* paper. Under this type of arrangement, a bank buys bills of exchange or promissory notes without recourse to the exporter. The bank then looks to the buyer for payment on the due date of the bills or notes. If the buyer's creditworthiness is considered insufficient to justify the giving of credit without recourse to the exporter, the buyer may be required to obtain the guarantee by means of an indorsement of a bank which is acceptable to the bank providing the finance.

In addition, factoring, leasing and hire purchase[23] may be used for export trade in the same way as for domestic trade.

---

22. *See R. D. Harbottle* (*Mercantile*) v. *National Westminster Bank* [1977] 2 All E.R. 862, and *Edward Owen Engineering* v. *Barclays Bank International* [1978] Q.B. 159.

23. *See* separate chapters on these topics.

CHAPTER TWENTY-FOUR

The Underwriting and Syndication of Loans

INTRODUCTION

Other chapters of this book are intended to provide the legal framework within which UK banking and financial institutions operate. This chapter is more general, since it deals with the subject of current legal and financial practices in the Eurocurrency banking markets which operate from London. It is common practice for borrowers and lenders in these markets to nominate the laws of England as the governing basis of the contract between them, and the English courts as having jurisdiction over any dispute which may arise. It can, however, be appreciated that the choice of any one set of laws, or indeed a favourable judgment by an English court, may not solve the problems of a lending bank with a client who has not paid moneys due and whose assets lie within the jurisdiction of a foreign court which may not be inclined to accept the validity of the choice of English law or to follow an earlier ruling of an English court. It is therefore necessary for banking law and practice in the Eurocurrency market to be viewed in the light of the historic growth pattern of the markets and the protection which lenders have developed in the loan documentation specifically for this type of international banking.

The Eurocurrency market has become an increasingly important source of bank finance for international and UK borrowers over the past few years and during the 1970s the size of the Eurocurrency market grew at a compound rate of over 20 per cent per annum. The larger part of the annual increases in the net size of the market (i.e. of loans to the non-banking sector, exclusive of inter-bank transactions) has consistently comprised advances by Eurocurrency lending banks as opposed to Eurobond issues or other Eurocurrency financings. By the end of 1979 the net liabilities of the Eurocurrency banking sector were estimated to be of the order of US $700 billion, while during the year ended 31st December 1979, the value of new bank loans arranged in this market was in excess of US $90 billion.

To put the Eurocurrency market into perspective the net liabilities outstanding of over US $700 billion compare with the total sterling liabilities of the UK banking sector of US $205 billion, that is the Eurocurrency sector is over three times as large as the entire UK banking sector.

When a borrower approaches the market for a loan at a fixed interest rate (generally a "Eurobond issue") or a floating interest rate (generally a bank credit but sometimes a "floating rate note" issue) the amount of the loan is often too much for one bank to provide from its own funds. In this event the bank originally approached (the "managing bank") provides the borrower with a commitment to lend (in other words it will "underwrite" all or part of the loan) but will require the opportunity to invite other banks or investors to participate in the loan and thereby reduce the final amount of funds to be provided by the managing bank (in market terminology the loan will be "syndicated" to achieve a lending syndicate).

The purpose of this chapter is therefore to provide a general introduction to the development of this fast-growing financial market and to explain in more detail some of the financing techniques and banking practices which accompany loan underwriting and syndication.

EUROCURRENCIES

The Eurocurrency market is centred upon the Eurodollar, although there are other currencies such as Euro-Deutsche Marks, Euro-Swiss francs and Eurosterling. A Eurocurrency deposit is merely a deposit located at a bank in one country but denominated in the currency of another. A Eurodollar is therefore a dollar deposit held at a bank in any financial centre outside the United States, usually London, Paris, or Zurich.

The practice of making dollar deposits with banks outside the US developed in the early 1960s, when the US started to produce large annual balance of payment deficits, which in the first instance led to an accumulation of dollar claims by non-US residents. Governmental restrictions at that time tended to discourage the retention by European exporters of dollar deposits at banks in the US and since the dollar was widely regarded by Europeans as an attractive currency in which to hold assets, it was convenient for them to place the dollar deposits with non-US banks or subsidiaries in Europe of US banks. Commercial banks in Europe found a steady demand from borrowers for dollars held in Europe and, typically, would offer interest rates for dollar deposits which were slightly higher than deposits for dollars left in the US. Once commercial banks in Europe started making dollar-denominated loans, they were able to quote interest rates at which they themselves would bid for dollar deposits and, dependent on the interest rate paid by commercial banks in Europe and the willingness of European exporters to hold dollar assets, European corporations and banks could choose between making "domestic" or "Eurodollar" deposits.

London was originally the principal financial centre through which Eurodollar deposits were made, and once the financial market had become well established in this centre, the ease of communication and the existence of a developed financial infrastructure and experienced personnel tended to attract market operators to the same location.

Development of Eurobanks

For commercial banks in Europe to be willing to accept dollar deposits they must perceive a demand for dollar loans. There are no detailed statistics regarding the identity of early borrowers but extensive data is available concerning borrowings in the Eurocurrency markets during the past five years.

The Eurocurrency market is founded on the large deposits made by European corporations and commercial banks with Eurobanks (i.e. banks making a market in Eurocurrencies). Since their deposit base is therefore heavily dependent on "wholesale" funds there has been a strong incentive for these banks to prefer to make "wholesale" loans to major corporations or governments.

Borrowers of Eurocurrencies

In the formative years of the Eurocurrency markets it was common practice for Eurocurrency loans to be made for comparatively short periods to match the tenor of the deposits taken by the Eurobanks. These loans would normally be regularly rolled-over at the banks' discretion but would not provide the borrower with the medium-term loan which he often required. For this reason, the typical borrowers in the early years of the market were European subsidiaries of US corporations which could use the dollars to pay for services and goods received from their parent companies (and avoid any net foreign exchange exposure for the US group on a consolidated basis), and European exporters who wished to hedge their foreign exchange position by fixing their dollar/domestic currency exchange rate through a spot market sale.

As lending practice developed and commercial banks recognised the increasing stability of the Eurodollar market it became standard practice to grant longer-term loans with the interest rate subject to change at regular intervals to reflect the cost of funds to the banks as they replaced short-term deposits with new deposits. As a precautionary measure the banks limited their obligation to provide dollar funds to the extent that they could in practice obtain dollar deposits. The interest rate became subject to three- or six-month revisions since deposits of these maturities were regarded as being freely available to the banks.

The development of a true medium-term Eurocurrency market attracted further borrowers to the market. Corporations wanted to borrow dollars to pay for imported capital equipment which would be used to produce consumer goods for export and generate the dollars needed to repay the loans over the life of the dollar facilities. Governments were prepared to borrow dollars to finance external payments deficits over a number of years until they believed the external account would return to surplus and liquidate the temporary borrowings taken to bridge the deficit period.

A further innovation of the market which encouraged borrowers was the development of "syndicate" lending to one borrower by a group of banks. In a syndicated bank credit the lending banks agree to act together in lending under one loan agreement. Thus the borrower has only one series of documentation and pricing negotiations to complete at the outset of a loan, and only one series of interest and principal payments to make (to an agent bank acting on behalf of all the banks).

The development of the syndicated bank credit concept can be seen as having been one of the most important stimuli to the growth of the Eurocurrency market. A borrower could now obtain very large amounts of money at one time from one source with the only constraints on the size of a borrowing being the overall liquidity of the Eurocurrency system and the ultimate creditworthiness of the borrower. As the size of the borrowing grew so the unit cost of borrowing was reduced.

Demand for bank credit facilities has been maintained during periods of low interest rates when borrower preference might have been expected to favour long-term fixed rate finance to such an extent that the demand for floating-rate bank credit would decline. The Eurobond market cannot generally provide amounts in excess of US $100 million in a single issue, whereas the average size of individual medium-term loans raised in the Eurocurrency market during 1979 was US $95 million.

The economies of scale offered by the bank credit market are also applicable in periods of low interest rates and, although it is at first sight contradictory, they may be seen by borrowers as being even more attractive at such times since interest margins over the cost of funds will be depressed by competitive pressures within the banking sector.

For some borrowers the attraction of raising finance by way of a syndicated bank credit is enhanced by virtue of the willingness of lending banks to tailor the credit facility to fit the individual requirements of a borrower. It can be appreciated that a small group of banks all of which are familiar with the techniques of Euro-currency lending are more willing and able to discuss amending the terms attached to the loan than a much larger group of bond holders (with perhaps several hundred for one bond issue) can possibly be. The terms of a bank credit facility can be negotiated to provide, for example, extended draw-down periods or unequal repayment instal-ments, and can be modified to enable pure "project financings" for new ventures to be successfully financed.

The average life of loans made by bank syndicates is generally shorter than the average life of a Eurobond. This differential reflects the differing risk profiles assumed by the private individuals or institutions who hold bonds, and by the lending banks which, as a group, have a relatively less stable deposit base and whose willingness to lend for long periods is accordingly less than that of the bond holders.

The limitation of the shorter average life of loans in the bank lending sector, while unattractive for some smaller borrowers, is not generally regarded as being a major deterrent to prime borrowers wanting large loans and being confident of their ability to refinance the loans at maturity. Such borrowers can be expected to include governments and, in recent years, it has been normal for over 80 per cent of the total volume of syndicated bank credits to be for governments or public bodies of one sort or another.

Approaches to the Eurocurrency market have tended to be made most frequently by borrowers from a relatively small number of countries, and the cumulative borrowings of borrowers from the ten major countries (the United Kingdom, France, Italy, Spain, Sweden, Denmark, Brazil, Mexico, Venezuela and Canada) in the bank credit market in the period January 1977 to December 1979 totalled US $95 billion and represented 48 per cent of the total volume of credits arranged during the period.

THE LOAN AGREEMENT

As previous sections of this chapter have explained, bank loans made in the Eurocurrency market have typically been made by syndicates of banks lending currencies, which may not necessarily be their domestic currency, for periods of time which are commonly much longer than is typical in their respective domestic markets. To meet these unique features of the Eurocurrency market the banks have demanded an increasingly complex form of loan agreement which has specified in detail the mechanisms whereby funds are made available to the borrower by banks in the syndicate, by way of an agent bank, and has incorporated extensive protection for the banks in the event of the currency of denomination not being available to them or of additional costs (of any nature whatsoever) being incurred by the banks. As Eurocurrency loans are sometimes made for periods of twelve years or longer, there are also extensive requirements for the borrower to maintain its financial condition within stipulated boundaries and to provide general undertakings to conduct its business in a prudent fashion.

The general philosophy behind floating rate syndicated bank credits is that banks will typically fund their loan portfolio by means of deposits taken in the inter-bank market and bearing interest at the London Inter-bank Offered Rate (LIBOR), and on-lend funds to borrowers on the basis of the LIBOR rate plus an appropriate additional interest margin. Over the past ten years margins have on average been around 1 per cent for prime borrowers with small variations above or below this figure being charged for better or worse quality borrowers to reflect the credit risk attached to each loan. With such narrow profit margins the banks evidently do not contract to absorb any risk other than that directly associated with the creditworthiness of the borrower, and the loan agreement is intended to specify and limit any risk to which the banks might be exposed by requiring the borrower to absorb any extra costs which may be incurred by the bank as a result of the loan. Obvious examples of additional costs relate to withholding taxes (either existing or which may be imposed at some time in the future), requirements to provide reserve assets to the appropriate banking authority in the country in which the bank is domiciled, extra interest costs incurred by the bank as a result of funds not being available at the LIBOR rate, or extra costs incurred by the bank as a result of payment of principal or interest being made in currency other than the currency in which the loan is drawn.

It is thus predictable that a typical Eurocurrency loan agreement is significantly longer than a domestic facility letter relating to, say, an overdraft or acceptance credit. The bulk of the text will normally extend to 30–35 pages and some of the essential topics covered in such an agreement are reviewed below.

DEFINITIONS

The agreement relates to an obligation of banks in various countries
to make funds available on agreed terms and conditions, usually to a
corporate or sovereign borrower in a given jurisdiction. To avoid
any subsequent misunderstandings and to define various essential
mechanisms relating to payment of principal and interest it is the
market custom to define apparently obvious items. Examples are
given below.

London Inter-bank Offered Rate (LIBOR)

In view of the historical importance of London as a principal
financial centre for the Eurocurrency markets, it has become
standard practice in syndicated bank credit facilities for the interest
rate to be based upon a rate at which one or more specified
"reference banks" offer deposits to leading banks in the London
Inter-bank Market at or about 11.000 a.m. (London time) two
business days prior to the commencement of any interest period. The
reason for the two business-day lead in fixing the interest rate is that
payments in the New York dollar market are typically made in so-
called clearing house funds for which delivery lags two days behind
the date on which payment instructions are given. The interest rate
fixed by the reference banks is, therefore, applicable to the corresponding clearing house funds which are delivered two days after the
interest-fixing date.

Business day

In view of the necessity for funds to be made available in New
York (for dollar transactions) it is necessary for all payments
associated with the loan to be made on a date on which banks are
open for business in New York City.
   Since the banks are generally working from a London base and,
therefore, are closed for English holidays, it is normal to define a
business day as being a day on which relevant London financial
markets are open for business.

Majority banks

Whatever contentious points arise in relation to the loan agreement
it is necessary for the lending banks to act together. Experience has
shown that it is not always possible to obtain the unanimous consent
of any lending group, and for this reason many agreements introduce
the concept of "majority banks", whose decision will be binding upon
the whole syndicate. Naturally, it is necessary to define what percentage of the lending banks need to be in favour of the decision in

order for a majority decision to be taken, and the figure of two-thirds in aggregate value of the loan outstanding is often used as this required majority.

DRAWING DOWN THE LOAN

As many Eurocurrency loan agreements contain provision for there to be more than one lending bank it is to be expected that the payment mechanisms of such loans are more complex than the normal one bank/one borrower loan agreements common in domestic lending.

It is mentioned above that payments in the dollar market are customarily made in clearing house funds where an interest rate has to be established two days before the value date for delivery of the funds. Using the interest-fixing date as a reference point and recognising that all banks need to be aware of a borrower's intention to draw funds in order to be in a position to fix an interest rate on a specified day, it has become normal for loan agreements to require a borrower to give five business days' advance warning of any draw-down. Thus the importance of the concept of business day and its need to be defined can be appreciated in the light of the requirement for each participating bank to have adequate notice of any drawing of funds. Clearly notice given over a weekend or over a holiday is of no help to a bank in arranging a payment.

The loan agreement provides for the obligations of the banks to advance funds to the borrower to be "several" obligations, although in practice each bank does not make its loan available directly to the borrower, but rather advances funds through an agent bank. The duties of an agent bank are generally restricted to that of a paying agent, but in some instances, discussed below, the duties can be increased. Once a borrower has requested funds to be made available it is necessary for the agent bank to satisfy itself that the borrower has complied with all conditions which the loan agreement might require to have been satisfied before the drawing (i.e. conditions precedent) and then to advise all participating banks of the date on which funds will be required. The agent will require each bank to make available, on its own account, dollar funds on the draw-down date and will, on that same day, transfer all such amounts thereby made available to it to the account of the borrower. Naturally the volume of payments being made through New York on any day is immense, and it is not generally feasible for an agent bank to have confirmed that it has received all amounts due from the participating banks before disbursing the aggregate total of the drawing to the borrower. For that reason, it is important that the agent is indemnified by the borrower against non-receipt of funds from any participating bank, and the loan agreement should therefore specify that if the agent pays in good faith money which has not in fact been made available to it, then the agent will be entitled to recover such amount and any interest charges thereon from the borrower.

OTHER EVENTS PRIOR TO DRAW-DOWN

In view of the cross-border nature of so many Eurocurrency transactions, and the fact that the borrower may be borrowing a currency for which it needs the express approval of its own central bank, it is essential for lending banks to ensure that all regulatory and other requirements have been complied with by the borrower and that the borrowing is correctly authorised. No funds will be advanced until the lending banks are satisfied that all such requirements have been complied with and authorisations have been received. In addition the borrower will be required to make a variety of relevant representations as to all relevant factors as at the draw-down date. Such conditions and representations may include the following.

(*a*) Copies of all appropriate government and regulatory authority consents must be produced.

(*b*) Copies of all relevant corporate or constitutional documents and consents must be obtained.

(*c*) A legal opinion will often be provided by independent counsel in the country of the borrower to confirm that from a legal point of view the borrower has complied with all relevant matters in its country of domicile, and that the agreement will constitute a legally binding obligation.

(*d*) The borrower will normally confirm that no event of default has occurred before either the date of the loan agreement or the date of drawing or each of them, that it has the power to enter into the agreement, and that the agreement will constitute a legally binding obligation.

(*e*) The borrower will warrant that its latest published financial accounts are correct and that there has been no material change in its financial or business position since the date of the last accounts.

In view of the term-loan nature of many Eurocurrency agreements and the objective of the banks to monitor the financial stability of the borrower, it is customary for the borrower to repeat in each draw-down notice the essential representations and warranties given in the loan agreement, e.g. the representations and warranties relating to its ability to borrow the funds and that there has been no event of default or change in its financial position since the loan agreement date.

OPTIONAL CURRENCY CLAUSES

Some Eurocurrency loan agreements allow a borrower to draw down funds either in US dollars or in other freely convertible currencies. Examples of freely convertible currencies which are often selected include Euro-Deutsche Marks, Euro-Dutch florins, Euro-Swiss francs and Euro-Canadian dollars. If a clause of this type is included in a loan agreement it is helpful for the following protective items to be incorporated.

(*a*) The option to draw funds in a currency other than dollars may only be exercised if the selected currency is freely available to all banks and is convertible into the base currency (usually US dollars) of the loan.

(*b*) A limitation is needed relating to the number of currencies in which the total amount of the loan can be drawn. A facility usually becomes difficult for the banks and the borrower to administer if the loan is drawn in more than three currencies at any one time.

(*c*) If the original agreement to lend was based on a commitment of a specified amount denominated in a base currency, the amount of a drawing in any selected optional currency, while being liable to fluctuation, must, at the start of any interest period, be calculated with reference to the exchange rate prevailing at that time between the base currency and the optional currency selected at the beginning of the interest period during which the loan is to be drawn in the optional currency. At the start of each interest period the banks will agree what amount of optional currency they are prepared to lend for that forthcoming period, and if the loan continues to be denominated in an optional currency in subsequent interest periods, the optional currency equivalent amount of the base commitment will be recalculated at the beginning of each subsequent interest period to ensure that any movement in exchange rates between the start of one interest period and the next will be accompanied by corresponding reduction or increase in the amount of the optional currency which is recorded as outstanding on the borrower's advances account with the agent bank. In other words, the borrower will never, on any interest payment date, draw an amount of a loan which is greater in dollar terms than the original dollar commitment of the banks.

It can be appreciated that an optional currency clause is both complicated in wording and difficult to administer and is not generally included in loan agreements unless specifically requested by the borrower. Many lending banks have a natural deposit base in US dollars and the average cost to them of funds is often substantially below the London Inter-bank Offered Rate for dollar deposits. Their effective margin on dollar drawings is thus greater than the notional margin attached to the loan, and they will naturally resist the inclusion of multi-currency options which, if exercised by the borrower, will result in their having to take from the market non-dollar funds where their cost of funds is exactly equal to the LIBOR rate and where their total return is correspondingly reduced. Nevertheless the multi-currency clause continues to be attractive to many borrowers to whom the possibility of borrowing, say, Euro-Swiss francs at a LIBOR rate of 1 per cent or 2 per cent is appealing. It must, however, always be remembered that the level of domestic interest rates is often an indication of the relative strength or weakness of the currency itself, and that an apparent saving in the interest cost in borrowing Swiss francs can be more than offset by an exchange loss incurred by having to repay a greater amount in US dollar terms. During the early- to mid-1970s many European borrowers discovered this fact and incurred net borrowing costs of up to 20 per cent per annum when the exchange losses were incorporated into their borrowing cost calculations.

PAYMENTS

Many Eurocurrency loan agreements contain a provision for the commitment of the lender to be terminated and the moneys outstanding to be prepaid by the borrower either on an interest payment date or even on other agreed dates. In the light of the historic development of the market it can be appreciated that originally the term loan was in essence only a series of three- or six-month loans continued on a best-efforts basis by the lending banks and subsequently institutionalised through a term-loan agreement whereby the sequence of succeeding loans represented a commitment on the part of the banks qualified only by various sets of pre-defined circumstances.

From the point of view of a lending banker, the freedom for a borrower to prepay is undesirable since it allows the borrower the right to terminate a loan with a high interest margin at a time when interest margins may have narrowed in favour of the borrower, or, alternatively, to use the threat of an unwanted prepayment to force the bank to accept a renegotiation of the terms onto a basis more favourable to the borrower. To a very limited extent the loss of earnings incurred by the bank can be covered by way of a prepayment premium included in the loan agreement, but typical pre-payment premiums have seldom exceeded $\frac{1}{2}$ per cent flat on prepaid amounts whereas reductions in interest rates have often been as much as 1 per cent per annum.

Recent trends in practice associated with prepayments have been to remove any prepayment premiums whatsoever and therefore as interest margins decline there is an incentive for borrowers either to prepay or renegotiate their loans to new lower interest rates. Naturally this trend has a dramatic impact on banks' profits, and since there is no provision in the agreement for banks to increase interest margins on existing loans when market conditions move in favour of the banks and interest margins increase, it is a one-way movement. It is hard to speculate how this trend may be halted, but there is a growing body of opinion amongst international banks that loan agreements written during periods of high margins will include a substantial prepayment premium or, alternatively, will preclude any prepayment unless such prepayment is caused by an identifiable increase in the cost of borrowing, such as can result from increased taxes payable by the borrower or by, for example, the imposition of reserve asset requirements on the banks which increase the cost of borrowing for the borrowers.

As a point of procedure, loan agreements often permit a borrower to prepay a loan between interest payment dates, that is, in the middle of a period for which a three- or six-month deposit has been taken by a lending bank. In these circumstances the bank may have returned to it unwanted funds which may have to be redeployed in the money markets at a lower interest rate than the rate being paid for the deposit (i.e. the prevailing LIBOR rate may have fallen since the previous interest payment date) and in these circumstances the borrower will be required to indemnify the bank for all loss of interest income or of interest margin incurred by it as a result of the pre-payment.

TAXATION

Banks generally require all payments made by borrowers to be made free of any deductions of taxes in the country in which the borrower is domiciled. Whereas many countries impose a withholding tax on remittances of interest paid by domestic borrowers to foreign banks, such withholding taxes are often waived by the taxing authorities in respect of the major public or sovereign borrowers which com-prise the majority of borrowers in the Eurocurrency market. Many major corporations are also able to obtain exemption from with-holding taxes if the foreign moneys are being borrowed to support projects of national importance. Nevertheless, the problem remains that many corporate borrowers are not able to obtain exemptions from withholding taxes and as such there may be deductions made from interest payments associated with the loan. The loan agreement will therefore provide for the borrower to make additional payments such that the moneys received by the foreign lending banks are the same as would have been received had there been no such deduction. This concept of the borrower paying additional moneys is commonly known as "grossing up". In some circumstances the banks which receive the grossed-up amount undertake to reimburse the borrower to the extent of any tax credit received by them.

Other loan agreements do, however, provide for withholding taxes to be paid yet for the borrower not to be obliged to gross up for the full amount of the deduction. Circumstances in which such allowances are made occur when the withholding tax paid on the remittance of funds is recognised by the taxing authority of the bank's own country of domicile, under double taxation treaties, to represent an advance payment of its own income taxes. In these circumstances the bank will receive less than the full amount of interest needed to pay the corresponding interest on the corresponding three- or six-month deposit, but also receives a tax certificate which will be offset against its domestic tax bill. Furthermore, the bank would expect to earn a slightly higher interest income which will be sufficient to cover the additional cost to the bank of having to fund the unpaid interest element until its next scheduled tax payment date when the cash benefit of the tax certificate can be received.

SUBSTITUTE INTEREST RATES

As explained earlier, the base interest rate (LIBOR) is determined as the arithmetic average of the rate quoted to lending banks by three or more reference banks two days prior to the value date for payment of funds. During the history of the Eurocurrency markets it has always been possible for the reference banks to quote a LIBOR rate for dollar deposits, but this period is comparatively brief as syndicated loans have only been a widely used instrument since the late 1960s. For this reason most Eurocurrency loan agreements contain a clause providing for the introduction of a substitute interest rate if, for some improbable reasons, the reference banks are not capable of quoting an offered rate for dollar deposits.

The provisions of the substitute interest rate clause have grown into a highly complex but largely theoretical mechanism which in essence says that if dollar deposits are not available in the ordinary course of business, or if adequate and fair means do not exist for ascertaining the rate of interest, or if as a result of a change in any national, economic, international or political conditions it is impractical for any one bank to fund or continue to fund its participation in the loan, then the undrawn portion of the loan facility will not be allowed to be borrowed and any drawn amount will be continued by the banks only after discussions with the borrower to establish a substitute basis for the interest rate to reflect the lenders' individual costs for obtaining dollar deposits or, failing dollar deposits, of obtaining deposits in any other currency which might be available to them. If the borrower does not accept the increased costs resulting from this exercise, the loan must then immediately be repaid.

It may be questioned how, if major Eurobanks have been unable to obtain dollar deposits freely from the Eurocurrency markets, the corporate or sovereign borrower would be better able to obtain such funds in order to make the required repayment to the banks. This paradox highlights the practical weakness of the substitute interest rate clauses. These have never been adequately tested in real-life circumstances, and for the time being must remain a theoretical, but in practice dubious, protection for Eurobanks.

UNDERTAKINGS OF THE BORROWER

To protect the position of the banks during the life of the loan, the loan agreement will usually contain provisions for the borrower to commit itself to various undertakings relating to its general business activities and to the loan itself. Such undertakings will generally include the following.

(a) The obligation of the borrower to produce regular financial reports to the banks.

(b) The obligation of the borrower to notify the agent bank in writing of any event of default as soon as it occurs.

(c) The inclusion of a "negative pledge" provision to the effect that the borrower will not provide general or specific security to other loans such that those loans will rank senior to the loan being made by the lending bank. In the event that other lenders require security the negative pledge clause will require the borrower to give equal and rateable security to the banks participating in the subject loan.

(d) The loan agreement will, in the case of corporate borrowers, often contain financial covenants relating to debt/equity and other ratios which must be adhered to by the borrower during the life of the loan. These are considered by many lending banks to be of the utmost importance and for this reason a separate section is devoted to these ratios later in this chapter.

DEFAULT BY THE BORROWER

If the financial or business circumstances of a borrower deteriorate substantially from those prevailing at the date of granting the loan, the banks naturally need to have the right to recover their loans prior to the agreed maturity date. The circumstances in which such accelerated repayment will take place are defined by a variety of "events of default". Some of the more important events of default commonly included in Eurocurrency loan agreements are as follows.

(a) Failure to pay the amounts due under the loan agreement on the stipulated dates.

(b) Failure by the borrower to comply with any other provision contained in the loan agreement (e.g. maintenance of financial ratios).

(c) If the representations or warranties made by the borrower in connection with the loan agreement turn out to be incorrect or untrue when made or repeated (e.g. at draw-down) or in the event of failure by the borrower to fulfil any of the covenants or undertakings.

(d) Cross default. If the borrower defaults under any other agreement to which it is a party, this may give other lenders the opportunity to initiate bankruptcy proceedings against the borrower. The lending banks would naturally wish to be in a similar position to press claims in those proceedings and would therefore draft their loan agreement to the effect that any default by the borrower under other loan agreements may be construed as a default under this loan agreement.

(e) Bankruptcy or similar proceedings, which may include a moratorium on the payment of borrowed moneys, appointment of receivers or similar circumstances.

(f) Material adverse changes in the borrower's financial conditions or, in the case of a sovereign borrower, in the general economic, political or social environment which may impair the borrower's ability to repay the loan. It should be noted that the right of banks to insist on an accelerated repayment as a result of some perceived material adverse change is difficult to prove and may be expected to be contested by the borrower. During November 1979 changes in the international relationship between the United States and Iran resulted in the United States Government freezing the assets of the Iranian Government held in the United States. As a result various US banks which were acting as agents for international lending syndicates maintained that there had been such a material adverse change in the ability of Iran to repay its international loans, and consequently called an event of default which was contested by the borrower. The decision of the US banks was not widely supported by European banks and has effectively proved how little credence can be attached to the ability of lending banks to insist on repayment as a result of the material adverse change clause.

The occurrence of an event of default will entitle the banks to terminate their obligations to lend and to call for an immediate repayment of loans already made. An event of default does not, however, automatically result in an accelerated repayment, and a decision to call for an immediate repayment will generally only be taken by the agent bank on instructions from a majority of the lending banks.

THE AGENT BANK

In view of the historic development of the syndicated bank credit market and the underlying concept of a group of banks joining together to lend on the basis of one common loan agreement with all payments being made through one agent bank, it can be appreciated that the responsibilities of the nominated agent bank could be considerable. The loan agreement must therefore contain provisions defining the relationship of the participating banks both between themselves and with the agent bank. The latest trends in Eurocurrency documentation are to include extensive protective clauses relieving the agent bank from responsibility for losses incurred by the banks as a result of their participating. Generally the agent bank is only required to perform in a reasonable manner specific duties delegated to it within the framework of the loan agreement, and the agent is not responsible to the banks for losses incurred unless it fails to perform its designated functions as a result of its gross negligence or wilful misconduct.

Where the Unfair Contract Terms Act 1977 applies to loan agreements (i.e. only where the proper law governing the agreement is that of the United Kingdom other than by a mere choice of the parties) the agent bank can only disclaim liability for negligence if the disclaimer satisfies the requirement that it is reasonable in all the circumstances. The banks are often required to represent to the agent bank that they have made independent investigations of the credit condition of the borrower and have not relied on information supplied to them by the agent. This latter provision is clearly totally at odds with the spirit of the syndicated bank credit market since the agent bank is in many cases instrumental in having formed the lending syndicate, and the information on the financial and economic position of the borrower has almost invariably been supplied to participating banks either by the agent or by another bank having a managing role in the transaction.

JURISDICTION AND SOVEREIGN IMMUNITY

The choice of governing law (i.e. the substantive law of the contract) and the jurisdiction (i.e. the choice of procedural law and the courts which will resolve disputes) are important issues in a loan agreement, particularly when the borrower is a sovereign state and is therefore able to claim immunity from suit in foreign courts.

The issue of sovereign immunity is a problem to lending banks as certain jurisdictions recognise the "absolute" right of a sovereign borrower to immunity from suit in any action, whether sovereign or private. Furthermore, a jurisdiction of this nature will not recognise the possibility that a sovereign borrower can irrevocably waive its right to immunity.

It is for these reasons that lending banks will try to choose a jurisdiction (preferably exclusive) which applies a "restrictive" interpretation of sovereign immunity, and will incorporate into the loan agreement extensive provisions relating to jurisdiction and immunity. The nature of such clauses will depend on the specific circumstances of the case. However, the borrower may irrevocably agree, in so far as this is permitted by the law, to waive its rights to sovereign immunity, to submit to each of the relevant jurisdictions, to appoint an agent who will accept service of process in each of the relevant jurisdictions, and to allow the lending bank or agent to choose the jurisdiction within which it wishes to bring an action.

Countries such as the United States and Great Britain have legislated in favour of the restrictive doctrine of immunity. Naturally therefore the choice of such a jurisdiction would be advantageous from the lender's point of view.

TIMETABLE FOR A SYNDICATED BANK CREDIT

Prime borrowers approaching the Eurocurrency markets in today's conditions of high liquidity can hope to draw funds under a syndicated bank credit facility within a few weeks of giving instructions to a lead managing bank to act on their behalf.

Once such instructions have been given the most important decisions to be made by the borrower in conjunction with the lead manager relate to syndication strategy. In many instances where a borrower is seeking a very large loan it is advantageous to form a small management group of banks which will underwrite the full amount of the loan among themselves and will give the borrower an offer of finance within a matter of days thus removing any risk of the market conditions moving against the borrower. After the offer has been accepted by the borrower, additional banks may be invited to join the lending syndicate. The composition of this group of banks will generally reflect the existing banking relationships of the borrower and will in any event be subject to approval by the borrower.

During the syndication process a loan agreement will be prepared by the lead banks' legal advisors, and, through negotiation, developed into a form which is acceptable to both the borrower and lending banks.

It is customary, although not mandatory, in larger transactions, for a syndication memorandum in which the financial position of the borrower is described to be prepared by the lead manager.

With a near ideal set of market circumstances and a well-known prime borrower for which banks invited to participate will have minimal need to quantify the credit risk, a loan agreement can often be completed and signed by all parties in less than six weeks after the mandate has been issued by a borrower. Notice to draw funds can be given at any time thereafter. Some private corporations reapproaching the market—and many sovereign states perhaps approaching the market for the first time—will often be advised to spend more time in the preparation of the syndication memorandum than would a well-known prime borrower, and to allow longer response times for the banks invited to participate. The total time likely to elapse between the issue of a firm mandate and the availability can therefore sometimes amount to two to three months.

FINANCIAL RATIOS

In order to continue the underlying requirement of a term loan, that is, that the financial condition of a borrower throughout the life of a loan should not materially worsen from the date on which the loan is made, many lending banks require that corporate borrowers give undertakings in the loan agreement that their financial condition will be preserved. The problem of how adequately to measure and monitor financial condition is often solved by defining various financial ratios which, if breached, give the banks the opportunity to call for corrective measures to be undertaken by the borrower, or failing that, to call for an accelerated repayment.

The subject of financial ratios is complex but it may be helpful to remember that the ratios which are commonly used are briefly reviewed below and include:

(*a*) debt/equity ratio, commonly called a leverage ratio;
(*b*) working capital ratio (i.e. current assets divided by current liabilities);
(*c*) minimum net worth requirement;
(*d*) restriction on dividend payments;
(*e*) interest coverage ratio (i.e. net profit before interest and taxes divided by interest charges).

Leverage ratio

There is much written material available on the mechanics of debt/equity ratios but the philosophy is simple. Prudent lending bankers require the stockholders of companies to accept a higher level of the business risk depending on the riskiness of the business operations. The ratio of debt/equity merely defines the amount of risk being assumed by external lenders in relation to that assumed by the equity holders. For this purpose debt is defined as "total liabilities" and equity as "tangible net worth" (i.e. as net worth less intangible assets such as goodwill). It is good lending practice to require the stockholders to finance all intangible assets (which do not actually exist).

Working capital ratio

This ratio is helpful in establishing the solvency of a company during the forthcoming trading period. An excess of current assets, that is assets which are likely to be converted into cash during the coming twelve months, over the current liabilities (i.e. the liabilities which will result in a cash outflow from the company during the coming twelve months) is clearly an encouraging sign for the short-term prospects of the company. This type of ratio is normally applied to manufacturing companies and is a recognition of the difficulty referred to above of making reliable forecasts of the profitability of trading companies. If the ratio is set at a level of 1.5:1 and the company is obliged to produce statements half-yearly then there is clearly a reasonable prospect for a lending bank to detect any unfavourable movement in the company's solvency position.

Minimum net worth requirement

Once again this ratio is particularly helpful when applied to a manufacturing company which may incur losses over a number of years during which period its external debt also declines. In these circumstances the debt/equity ratio may be maintained but the overall size of the company may shrink to a level at which the corporation cannot continue to operate efficiently. A minimum net worth level of, say, 70 per cent of the level on the date on which the loan is granted might be a reasonable point from which to start negotiations with the company. It must, however, be emphasised that this figure must be subject to extensive discussion with the borrower.

Restriction on dividend payments
This restriction may be imposed to prevent the company paying out too high a level of its profits to its shareholders or to avoid the situation where the level of net worth was unexpectedly reduced to unacceptably low levels.

Interest coverage ratio
As interest is intended to be paid from the profits of a company and as interest payments are a tax-deductible item, it is useful to relate the level of profit before interest and taxes to the level of interest charges in any one year. If a manufacturing company is unable to cover its interest charges by a factor of at least 2, then the lending banks would normally have cause for concern. This ratio is often set at a level of around $4\times$, but it is also a ratio which can be breached without banks feeling it necessary to call for an immediate accelerated repayment.

PART VI

CORPORATE FINANCE

CHAPTER TWENTY-FIVE

Raising Money on the Stock Exchange

EXISTING LISTED COMPANIES

In order to raise money on the Stock Exchange it is necessary for the security involved to be listed. Where the company is already listed, the listing for a further security is a matter of the company satisfying certain requirements, many of them formalities, with the department which deals with listings. These requirements are set out in Appendix 34 of The Stock Exchange Rules and Regulations which are obtainable from the Stock Exchange, and anyone wishing to study the requirements in detail should obtain a copy. Since this is the most common and simplest way in which money is raised, this subject is dealt with first, and companies new to the Stock Exchange are treated at the end of the chapter.

Where a company is already listed, the first decision to be made is the form of the security which will be appropriate to raise the money required.

The company has the alternatives of issuing loan capital in various forms, preference shares or equity. The choice must largely depend on the market conditions at the time of the issue and on the state of the company's balance sheet.

DEBENTURES

In the past, many companies favoured raising money by debenture issues—longer term loans at a fixed rate of interest secured on the company's assets—as this involves a fairly direct calculation as to the cost of the new money and where companies have been putting substantial sums into reserves, it increases the shareholders' equity. It introduces an element of gearing which can, in certain circumstances, help a company to grow more quickly. Where the company already has a debenture listed, it may be convenient to issue a further tranche of the same debenture.

Over a period, interest rates may vary considerably and if the price of existing debentures is too far away from par, this may not be practicable. If the price is over par, potential subscribers who are taxpayers will object because the loss of capital is not desirable. On the other hand, if the price is much below par, the company may object because the discount has to be provided out of its net income. Protection for debentureholders is provided by a trust deed, which contains a wide variety of restrictions on the company, and a trustee (usually a specialist department of an insurance company) is appointed to ensure that the provisions of the trust deed are complied with. It is usually possible to issue further debenture stock under the same trust deed, but with a different interest rate and different repayment terms, but this will of course depend on the particular provisions of the deed.

If the company has not previously issued a debenture, then the terms and amount must be such that the asset cover and the interest cover are acceptable to the institutional investor. The standards set for each industry depend upon the degree of risk in that industry and the cover acceptable for a brewery or property debenture will not be sufficient for a mining debenture. For a normal industrial debenture, the investor would expect to see the issue covered at least twice by assets and the interest covered four times by the available income.

The form of trust deed acceptable to the institutions has become fairly standard, and if a company attempts to obtain clauses particularly favourable to it, organisations such as the British Insurance Association Investment Committee quickly draw the attention of their members to what they regard as undesirable clauses, with the result that it becomes impossible to find buyers in any quantity for any debenture not having the standard clauses.

The Stock Exchange has developed a method of issuing debenture stocks for cash (a cash placing) which is both efficient and cheap, and has become a standard way of issuing debentures. The detailed rules of such placings are set out in Paragraph 15 of Chapter 1 of Appendix 34 of the Rules and Regulations. This involves the preparation of a small advertisement giving brief details of the issue, and a statistical card circulated in the Extel Statistical Service which contains the full particulars of the security. The advertisement will state that up to 20 per cent of the issue is available for subscription by the general public through their stockbrokers. This offer stays open for one day only. The main buyers of such debentures are usually a small circle of institutional investors who are used to having to take speedy decisions. These institutions value the new debenture on the basis of existing yields of comparable securities and it is therefore possible to fix a keen price, particularly in view of the short time-scale involved, and on issue only a small premium is seen.

UNSECURED LOAN STOCKS

An alternative to the debenture is the unsecured loan stock, which may be suitable for some companies. Because of the lack of mortgage security, it is important to the institutional investor that special safeguards are written into the trust deed of an unsecured loan. Not only must there be restrictions on the amount of stock issued relative to the company's assets, but in addition there are clauses which prevent the company disposing of any substantial amount of its assets, or substantially altering the nature of its business. There was a famous case some years ago when the courts held that under statute law a jam-making company could convert itself into an artificial silk manufacturer without the consent of its loan stockholders,[1] and so now this type of transaction is precluded by the Trust Deed. The method of issuing unsecured loan stocks is identical to that used for debentures.

CONVERTIBLE LOAN STOCKS

A very popular type of unsecured loan stock has been the convertible loan stock, where holders are given the option at certain stated times of tendering their stock to the company and receiving equity in exchange. The income from such stocks is higher than from an equivalent investment in the company's equity and the price at which conversion takes place will be at a premium on the market price of the equity at the time of issue. The intention is that conversion will take place once the dividend yield on the equity rises above that available on the convertible. This type of issue is particularly suitable for companies such as property companies where there is a considerable delay between the commencement of an investment project and a return being received from that project. This has been particularly true in past years when the yields on what are regarded by the stock market as rapidly growing companies were too low for the investor depending on income. By acquiring a convertible stock, such holders could obtain a reasonable income immediately, while having the chance to share in the capital appreciation of the equity in the longer term if things went well with the company.

1. *R.* v. *Board of Trade* (*ex parte St. Martin Preserving Co.*) [1964] 2 All E.R. 564.

In order to comply with Stock Exchange rules regarding the issue of equity or equity-type securities, where a company wishes to issue a convertible for cash, it has to restrict the issue to its own equity holders, unless the dilution of the equity holders' interests is small (usually below 5 per cent). The issue will be offered to the existing holders *pro rata* to their present shareholdings; if there are existing convertible stocks, holders of these may be offered the right to take up the appropriate amount of the new stock or else the conversion price of the stock will be adjusted by a formula set out in the trust deed for their stock.

PREFERENCE SHARES

The incidence of distributed profits tax has made the issue of preference capital very much less common than in the pre-1939 period, and the market for preference capital has shrunk. There are, however, some companies to whom preference capital is the only possibility as they find it impossible to issue loan capital and do not wish to issue equity, probably because a family controlling a company is unwilling to see its voting rights diluted and is unable to subscribe for further equity.

Because the demand from the ordinary investor for preference shares is very small, issues of preference shares usually take the form of a placing with those institutional investors who find this type of investment acceptable. Twenty per cent of the issue must be made available to the general public in the same way as previously described for debentures. In order to increase the attraction of preference capital companies will sometimes make the issue redeemable at par at some date long in the future (probably 20–25 years) and set up a redemption fund to provide the necessary moneys. It is also possible for preference shares to carry the right to convert into equity on certain stated dates and conditions in the same way as for convertible loan stocks. The voting rights of preference shareholders must be considered with some care. It is unusual in a modern company for a preference share to have an automatic vote (except at meetings of its own class) but it is usual for votes in general meeting to be given when the preference dividend falls into arrears, or when proposals are made which could affect the way in which the company's business is conducted.

ORDINARY SHARES

Assuming the company has decided that its new funds must be provided by way of equity, it has then to decide on the terms of the issue.

The current market price will provide a guide as to the price at which the issue can be made and, at the time of writing, the company will put a discount on the price of somewhere between 15 and 25 per cent. This will depend on the number of shares to be issued, and will be expressed as a ratio of the existing issued capital. For convenience it is usual to express issues as 1 for 10, 2 for 9, etc. Any issue over 1 for 4 is regarded as a heavy issue and will tend to depress the market. Consequently, the discount to be offered has to be increased. The first decision to be made is whether the proposed rights will involve an increase in the company's authorised capital. If so, a shareholders' meeting will need to be called and the timetable must be adjusted to take this into account.

Again, since an equity issue sometimes involves a profit forecast, it is convenient that such issues are made at a time when yearly or half-yearly figures are available. By moving the date of publication of the accounts, it is possible to vary these by a few weeks, but the date to which the company's accounts are made up obviously provides some inelasticity in the dates of a rights issue.

It is possible to make a rights issue which is not underwritten, but this means that if the issue fails to be taken up either wholly or in part the company does not receive its new money and it may find that it has entered into certain commitments which become very onerous. Thus, where an issue has not been underwritten, it is usual for it to be issued on terms well below the market price. The effect of this is that the number of shares to be issued has to be substantially increased and the dilution of the equity is that much greater.

A few companies have in the past issued shares at very low prices compared with their market price and such issues have not been underwritten. The reasoning behind such issues was that as well as raising money the companies wished to give their shareholders an element of a bonus issue, as the effect of such issues is that the rights stand at a very substantial premium. The disadvantage of this type of issue is that the price of the equity will appear to fall substantially, although probably the adjustment in price will only be *pro rata*, and usually dividends per share are reduced. These results, although only optical, can have an effect on the future performance of the company's share price and shareholders who do not take up their rights may have a substantial capital gains tax liability.[2]

The great majority of rights issues are made at the highest price the market can stand, so as to provide the highest proceeds in cash

2. Capital Gains Tax Act 1979, s. 25(2). *See also Floor* v. *Davis* [1979] 2 All E.R. 677.

for the issue of a given number of shares. This therefore involves underwriting the issue. The underwriter (usually an issuing house but occasionally a stockbroker) undertakes to subscribe for any shares not taken up as of right. The underwriter then arranges that a number of others (known as sub-underwriters) will each take up a proportion of whatever shares the underwriter may be required to take up. Each stockbroker who provides a corporate finance service has a list of potential investors who, for a small fee (of the order of $1\frac{1}{4}$ per cent), are willing to act as sub-underwriters. These potential investors are the large insurance companies, pension funds, etc., who normally have a flow of income to invest, and use issues of new shares as a convenient and cheap method of investing such moneys. Such institutions will have funds available to take up shares where owing to market factors a fall in price makes the offer of the new share unattractive to the shareholders to whom they are offered. It follows that in general where these institutions are left with shares, such shares are valued at a price which, if the shares were sold, would show a loss, and so they will not sub-underwrite an issue unless there is a good chance that they will not have any liability. The interest of the sub-underwriter is best served if the issue is made at a low price, whereas the issuing company would wish to issue the shares at as high a price as possible. If the price is fixed too low, the company may find that the moneys raised when reinvested in the new project may not produce enough income to service the new equity capital.

The expertise of the broker or merchant bank enables them to advise the company of the kind of price which would be acceptable to the sub-underwriters, although there is always a caveat that the final price agreed must be dependent on market conditions at the time the issue is launched. Since the timing of the issue is also dependent on the production of the necessary documents it is clear that much preliminary work must be done to prepare for the issue, including the preparation of a circular to shareholders. This will contain an explanation of the reason for the issue, will review current trading prospects, and will often contain profit and dividend forecasts for the current financial year. The Stock Exchange also requires that certain prescribed information is included such as:

(*a*) a statement that the group has sufficient working capital for its present requirements;

(*b*) an up-to-date statement of total group indebtedness;

(*c*) a summary of any material contracts (other than in the ordinary course of business) entered into in the previous two years and sundry other matters set out in Schedule II, Part B of the booklet "Admission of Securities to Listing" issued by the Stock Exchange.

If an increase of share capital is required the circular will also contain the notice to shareholders convening the necessary meeting.

The procedure is that an underwriting agreement is prepared, with warranties by the company that any statements in the draft letter to shareholders regarding future trading and profits are true, and more particularly that there are no other factors which have not been revealed which would affect the company's prospects. A sub-underwriting letter will be prepared on the basis of the underwriting agreement, and is sent out to prospective sub-underwriters with the draft circular to shareholders attached. Of necessity, since sub-underwriters regularly receive such letters from different stock-brokers, the sub-underwriting letter is a fairly standard document in which the timing of the sub-underwriting is clearly set out.

Until 1939 it was common for the document offering the shares to be a letter of rights which was subsequently exchanged for an allotment letter, which was then exchanged for a certificate. It is now standard for the document offering the shares to be a provisional allotment letter, which automatically becomes an allotment letter when the shares are paid up. This procedure eliminates one document in the new issue procedure.

The provisional allotment letter is a standardised document as this is the document of title which passes on the Stock Exchange, but will be adapted to the particular requirements of the organisation which has to process it. This will usually be one of the specialist registration organisations, the largest of which are departments of the clearing banks. This organisation will process all the allotment letters received from accepting shareholders together with their cheques on behalf of the company. They will carefully check the level of acceptance and then inform the issuing house of the number of shares not taken up. If these shares can be sold at a premium over the issue price, this will be done and the net proceeds distributed *pro rata* to the non-accepting shareholders. Otherwise, the shares will be allotted to the sub-underwriters.

The final documentary requirements on the new issue are the Companies Act requirements, such as the return to be made of allotments, etc.

NEW COMPANIES

Where a company does not already have a listing, the first decision to be made is whether the costs and trouble involved in obtaining listing are worthwhile and desirable for the particular company or corporation concerned. Normally the professional advisers to a company, the accountants, the solicitors, or the bankers, will be willing to give some preliminary advice as to whether it would be appropriate for the company to seek listing. If the answer appears to be positive, the next question to be answered is who is to carry out the feasibility study on the arithmetic of listing. If the company enjoys a close relationship with its bankers, it is likely they will be recommended to the merchant banking arm of the commercial bank, which is equipped to carry out the necessary investigation and to make recommendations. On the other hand, if the company is heavily indebted to the bank, it may feel that it is better to seek completely independent advice, and so would go to one of the dozen or so merchant banks which specialise in these investigations. If the company's accountants happen to have a department which has specialised in investigations for listing, or perhaps are associated with a larger practice which has such a department, it may be appropriate to ask the accountants to carry out the preliminary work.

In any case, before obtaining a listing, the company must obtain the services of a sponsoring broker, who will become the broker to the company and will represent the company in its dealings with the Stock Exchange. The relationship between a company and its broker, if it is to work properly, is one of mutual trust and is something which develops. When it looks as though the time may be approaching when the services of a broker will be required, thought should be given to making a contact, and personal recommendation usually works best. Because of the specialised nature of the work, only a minority of brokers on the Stock Exchange have departments which carry out the corporate finance work for companies new to the Stock Exchange. The most usual bar which prevents a company obtaining a listing is the question of size. In former days, when size was not a criterion, some quite tiny companies were listed. For some years the Stock Exchange has imposed limits as to size, and at the moment no company with a prospective market capitalisation of less than £500,000 may obtain listing. This figure is, however, unrealistically low, since the costs of obtaining a listing will probably be in excess of £100,000. Probably a company has to have a prospective market capitalisation of £4–5 million before it should consider coming to the market.

In the early days of the feasibility study most of the work falls on the accountant. A report has to be prepared stating the previous five years' financial record including source and application of funds, statements for each financial period and a balance sheet as at the last date reported on. This may cause difficulties, especially in cases where the company has been run in harness with other family-owned businesses. The accountants have to produce a statement of adjustments which shows how their present report reconciles with the previous annual accounts of the company, and discussions between the Stock Exchange and the accountants on difficult points may take some time.

Once a satisfactory report has been prepared it is necessary to decide the method to be used for obtaining the initial listing. There are three possibilities.

(a) *Offer for sale.* This is the method most commonly used. The prospectus is advertised in full in two leading daily newspapers with a minimum of 25 per cent of the company being offered to the public for subscription.

(b) *Placing.* This method is suitable for smaller companies as the maximum amount with the Stock Exchange will permit to be raised is £1.5m. The broker to the company will place a minimum of 25 per cent of the equity of the company with his clients, with 25 per cent of the shares being placed being offered to the market, which will be retained to supply demand from the general public.

(c) *Introduction.* An introduction does not involve the offering or placing of any shares with the public and can only be used by those companies which already have a wide spread of shareholders.

Whichever method is chosen for obtaining a listing the contents of the prospectus will be the same. The main matters to be dealt with are:

(a) a brief summary of the company's history and the main constituents of its current business;

(b) a commentary on the company's financial record;

(c) a statement of future trading prospects, usually including a profit and dividend forecast for the current fiscal year;

(d) a description of the function of the company's senior executives including directors (giving age, business background, etc.);

(e) a report by the accountants on the company's financial record for the previous five years which will include five years' profit and loss accounts, five years' source and application of funds statements and the latest balance sheet; the accountants will also be expected to set out the main accounting policies of the company and to have adjusted the figures so that they are all shown on a consistent basis;

(f) an up-to-date valuation of the property portfolio by a leading firm of valuers, required if the company is a property company;

(*g*) a general appendix covering *inter alia*:

(*i*) directors' shareholdings;
(*ii*) details of directors' service contracts;
(*iii*) a summary of the main provisions of the articles of association;
(*iv*) details of material contracts;
(*v*) details of recent share issues;
(*vi*) details of any share options outstanding.

Once the documentation has been prepared and the method of issue decided, it only remains for the issue price to be agreed between the sponsor and the company. This is dictated by market conditions at the time and will be related to the market ratings of any similar companies. If an offer for sale is the chosen route and there are no similar companies listed it can be very difficult to gauge the right price; in these circumstances the sponsors may feel an offer for sale by tender is appropriate. This means that instead of the shares being offered at a fixed price, a minimum subscription price is set and subscribers are invited to tender either at or above that price. Depending on the level of applications a striking price is established which it is felt will create a reasonable market at the commencement of dealings; all applications below that price are rejected and appropriate allotments made to the others.

Whether the method of raising money chosen is an offer for sale, an offer for sale by tender or a placing, a receiving banker will be chosen, whose duty it will be to receive all applications with cheques attached. He will check carefully that all the applications have been properly completed, looking particularly, in the case of an offer for sale, for multiple applications, which the issuing house reserves the right to reject. If an offer for sale is oversubscribed the receiving banker will prepare a schedule setting out the number of applications received at each level, and in consultation with the issuing house and the company the basis of allotment will be decided. The basis chosen will depend on whether the company wishes to favour small shareholders or the large institutions. Once the basis of allotment has been chosen it is the receiving banker's duty to issue letters of acceptance to succesful applicants and return cash due to unsuccessful applicants. The final proceeds are then remitted to those entitled.

In November 1980 the Stock Exchange introduced a new second-tier market known as the Unlisted Securities Market. This market is intended for companies which are unable or unwilling to satisfy the full listing requirements. The requirements for obtaining a listing, and so also the costs of raising money, in this market are somewhat less than those for obtaining a full listing. The overall cost will, however, depend on the depth of the investigation carried out by the sponsors and the reporting accountants. Potential investors in the unlisted securities market should therefore be aware that in order to cut costs the same standard of care in preparing the prospectus may not have been applied as is usual for a full listing. This means that the sponsor is even more important than usual; those with a good reputation built up over many years are unlikely to risk their standing in the City of London by putting their name to a prospectus until all their normal inquiries have been made.

This chapter contains a very brief summary of the present methods of raising money on the Stock Exchange. New methods are evolving all the time and the removal of exchange controls, which opens the London capital market to foreign borrowers, will undoubtedly bring changes. The student should try to follow these in the financial press.

CHAPTER TWENTY-SIX

Factoring

THE NATURE OF FACTORING

In essence factoring is an arrangement for the outright purchase by a finance company (the "factor") of all the book debts of a supplier of goods and services to trade customers as such debts arise in the normal course of the supplier's business.[1] It is further normally accepted that factoring as distinguished from its blood relations, invoice discounting and accounts receivable financing, postulates (a) the giving of notice of the transfer of ownership of each debt as it arises to such trade customers, and (b) the purchase of the debts without recourse to the supplier as regards the risk of non-payment by a customer by reason of the customer's insolvency (subject to approval by the factor of the customer's credit standing).

When notice is given to the customer, he is directed to pay the factor direct, and this relieves the supplier from the need to keep a sales ledger and to carry out the related tasks such as the collection of his claims on his customers. The value of each sale made, less the factor's charges, may be debited to one account in his books (that of the factor) as soon as a sale is made and ownership of the resulting debt has been transferred to the factor. Similarly, the factor's acceptance of ownership of debts without recourse to the supplier provides the supplier with protection against bad debts. For the relief from these two burdens of administration and the risk of loss, the factor makes an *ad valorem* charge on the value of each debt sold to him. This charge will vary from a fraction of 1 per cent up to around 2 per cent according to the pattern of trade, the nature of the business and the quality of the trade customers.

The supplier may also be largely relieved from providing the credit requirements of his trade customers, because the factor will make

1. *See* Biscoe, *Law and Practice of Credit Factoring*: "... a continuing legal relationship between a financial institution (the "factor") and a business concern (the "client") selling goods or services to trade customers (the "customers") whereby the factor purchases the client's book debts either with or without recourse to the client and in relation thereto controls the credit extended to the customers and administers the sales ledger."

available a large percentage of the purchase price of each debt (usually in the region of 80 per cent) to the supplier as soon as the transfer of ownership has taken place. The balance of the purchase price is retained, so that the factor may set off against it his rights in respect of recourse for disputes and counterclaims raised by customers in relation to any of the debts sold to the factor. The retention will be released either when the customer pays or on an agreed maturity date calculated by reference to the average period of credit taken by customers of the supplier. Should the supplier take advantage of this availability of early payment, he will normally be charged a discounting charge calculated on the amount of the early payment on a day-to-day basis from the date of such payment, either to the date of payment by the customer or to a fixed maturity date according to the system used.

THE USE OF FACTORING

There are many ways in which a merchant, manufacturer or supplier of services may finance the trade credit granted to his customers. For example, he may use his own capital resources, bank credit or the credit granted to him by his own suppliers. However, the insufficient and recessive supply of risk capital externally and internally generated, coupled with inflation, makes the smaller independent business look increasingly to other means of financing. The amount of bank credit granted to the supplier will be determined to a large extent by criteria other than the value of trade debts outstanding from time to time. Moreover, the credit granted to a merchant or manufacturer with a growing business or seasonal needs will not necessarily match his requirements for the credit to be allowed to his own customers. Thus factoring is most suitable to meet the needs of such businesses, because the factoring company in its arrangements with the merchant or manufacturer, will, to the extent of 80 per cent or so, exactly match with its funds the credit required, for the factor undertakes to buy without recourse every debt which arises from the sale of acceptable goods on acceptable terms to creditworthy customers, without formal limit as to the funds provided.

Factoring is not, however, suitable for all businesses. It is suitable for those who sell raw materials, components or consumer goods. It is not suitable for those who sell capital equipment or whose sales or services are provided under long-term contracts. A buyer of capital equipment, who intends to repay credit out of the profit generated by the use of the equipment, would better look to instalment credit companies to provide the credit by hire purchase, leasing or similar means. Moreover, where the debts purchased arise from any form of long-term contract or where there is a substantial element of after-sales service, the factor can only rely on collection of the purchased debts for the recovery of the funds he has laid out and has no opportunity in most cases to have the business carried on for his benefit. His prospects of recovery may be in jeopardy owing to the probability of heavy counterclaims from customers on the insolvency of the supplier. Thus a factor may safely purchase only debts arising out of contracts of sale under which all or substantially all of the supplier's obligations have been discharged on the delivery of goods or the invoicing of the service when the ownership of the debts is usually transferred to the factor.

METHOD OF OPERATION

Factors normally expect that suppliers of goods and services will enter into agreements which will last at least a year. At the outset the supplier will advise all his customers and prospective customers of the arrangement and in particular that they will henceforth be expected to pay the factor in discharge of their obligations for goods or services supplied.

The factor will examine the creditworthiness of each of the customers and prospective customers and advise the supplier of the extent to which the debts created by sales to each such customer will be accepted by the factor without recourse to the supplier. This may be done in one of two ways, either by the approval of orders as received or by the approval of a limit of credit on each customer account. In the latter case the factor must provide sufficient information regarding each customer's account to enable the supplier to know if any order taken or delivery made will cause the approved limit to be exceeded.

It is usual for a factor in the United Kingdom to purchase the debts in existence at the starting date of the agreement. The procedure used is for the supplier to bring his sales ledger up to date to the day before the starting date, send statements of account to his customers bearing notices of the assignment by which payments are directed to the factor and send copies of the statements (with or without supporting documents such as invoices and credit notes) to the factor. From the details on these copy statements or the supporting documents the factor will make a credit to the account of the supplier of the aggregate value of the debts less his charges and will debit each of the customer accounts in his records.

Although some factors will require that there should be full recourse to the supplier for such existing debts and that the "non-recourse" arrangements should start with deliveries after the starting date, the supplier will in any case be allowed to draw immediately against the credit on his current account subject to an agreed retention. The amount of any such drawing will be debited to the supplier's account.

From then on the supplier will send out his invoices to his customers in the normal way on delivery of the goods or on completion of the services; such invoices will however bear the notice of the assignment. Periodically, normally at least once a week, the supplier will send copies of these invoices to the factor who will credit the supplier with the value thereof (less his charges) and debit the relevant customer accounts. As a corollary, copies of any credit notes issued by the supplier will be sent to the factor who will debit the amounts thereof to the supplier's account and credit the applicable customers' accounts. The supplier may continue to draw against the net credit on his account subject to the agreed retention which is calculated daily on the basis of a percentage of debts remaining outstanding and unpaid.

The collection of the indebtedness of each customer is the factor's responsibility as he owns the debts; he will send out further monthly statements, follow up in suitable ways and where accounts are seriously overdue threaten and, if necessary, arrange for the implementation of legal proceedings for recovery. Where any part of the indebtedness has not been the subject of an approval, and is irrecoverable by reason of the customer's insolvency, it will be charged back to the supplier, and a debit will be made to the supplier's account and a credit to the customer's account to clear that part of the indebtedness from the factor's records. The loss of the approved amount of any indebtedness by reason of the customer's insolvency will be borne by the factor.

Factors cannot accept responsibility for the acceptance by the customer of the goods or services of the supplier, for the compliance by the supplier with the terms of any sale contract or for the accuracy of invoices and credit notes issued. Factors also require undertakings by suppliers that the debts sold to them are free from any rights of set-off or counterclaims from the customers. Accordingly, should any query or dispute be raised by a customer on a demand for payment by the factor, the supplier will be notified immediately and given an opportunity to dispose of the matter. In the absence of agreement between the supplier and the debtor, the disputed or queried indebtedness will be charged back to the supplier and the customer notified of its reassignment.

In addition to the notifications of approvals of orders or credit limits and of disputed or queried invoices, the factor sends a statement of account to each supplier at least once a month. This statement will normally be in the form of a current account showing the credits for debts purchased (i.e. their value less the factor's charges) and the debits for credit notes issued, items charged back, and cash drawn. The balance on the account will represent the undrawn balance owed by the factor to the supplier, which the supplier may draw subject to the agreed retention. Such accounts are normally accompanied by a statement showing the calculation of the factor's charges for the month.

Most United Kingdom factors supply information regularly to the supplier. Relations between supplier and customer are seen as paramount to the supplier's selling and marketing efforts and the state of the account, albeit between the factor and the customer, relating to supplies by the supplier, is seen as an essential part of the relationship. Thus most factors in this country send to each supplier at least once a month a list of their customers showing the outstanding indebtedness of each customer, aged by reference to due dates for payment, and analysed to show how much of the indebtedness of each customer is approved, unapproved or disputed. Other returns such as sales analyses by area, product or salesmen, and totals of monthly VAT outputs, may be made available by the factor to the supplier.

The simplicity of the concept of factoring described above is in direct contrast to the complexity and difficulties relating to the law under which factoring operates in England. The difficulties seem to have arisen by the transfer of the system direct from the United States, where the service is recognised in the Uniform Commercial Code and the factor may normally see precisely the relationship between the parties, to England where there is no such code. There are important gaps in the law and it is surprising, in view of these gaps, that there is little case law involving factors in the twenty or so years since the service was introduced into England.

THE FACTORING AGREEMENT—THE GIVING OF EFFECT TO ASSIGNMENTS

A factor's principal demand of the law is that it should give him an unfettered ownership of the debts which he purchases; this is the principal purpose of the factoring agreement between a supplier and a factor. An assignment of a chose in action is a legal, or statutory, assignment if it is in writing, is absolute and does not purport to be by way of charge, and is of the whole debt and written notice is given to the debtor. Such an assignment confers upon the assignee the legal right to such debt, subject only to equities having priority at the date that the debtor receives notice of assignment.[2] If any one of those essentials is missing, the assignment may nevertheless be effective in equity. The assignee should never omit to give notice to the debtor, because to omit to do so might permit a subsequent assignee to take priority, or might permit equities arising after the date on which he could have given notice of the assignment to the debtor to arise and take priority over him. The main difference between a legal and an equitable assignment is that an equitable assignee cannot sue on the debt in his own name, but must join the assignor either as co-plaintiff, if he consents, or as co-defendant, if he does not. This may not be a major disadvantage as between factor and supplier, where the supplier would be willing to lend his name to an action by the factor.

The precise form such agreements take in practice is governed largely by stamp duty considerations. Where the consideration exceeds £35,000, an assignment attracts *ad valorem* stamp duty at the rate of 2 per cent on the amount of the consideration.[3] Where the amount is less than £20,000, the assignment is exempt from duty and there are reduced rates where the amount is between £20,000 and £35,000. In assessing the amount of the consideration, all linked transactions should be aggregated.

Some factors seek to take advantage of this exemption by making the agreement contain not an assignment but a requirement that the supplier should offer to the factor every trade debt as it arises. Every now and then the supplier sends a batch of copy invoices to the factor, thereby constituting an offer, with a form of assignment of the debts represented by the invoices. The factor then accepts each batch as it is sent to him. The supplier ensures that the aggregate value of each batch of copy invoices is less than £20,000. Notice of assignment is not sent out to the suppliers' customers, the debtors, until after the assignment in question has been completed. It is not entirely clear that the duty would be successfully avoided if this method were challenged, but it does not seem to have been challenged as yet.

Other factors use a form of agreement under which the parties agree that the supplier will sell, and the factor will purchase, each trade debt as and when it arises, and that ownership of the debts is transferred to the factor as soon as they come into existence, without further formalities. Since the agreement is executed before the arrangements have come into force, at a time when no debts are in existence, no debts are assigned by the agreement, and the

2. Section 136 of the Law of Property Act 1925. For further discussion of this topic, *see* "Assignment of book debts" in Chapter Eighteen.
3. Stamp Act 1891, Sched. 1, and Finance Act 1980, s. 95.

agreement will therefore be exempt, if it is under hand, or attract fixed duty of 50p if it is under seal.[4] The factor's title to each debt will be equitable, unless and until any debt is that the subject of a subsequent formal assignment.[5] A formal assignment is usually taken to simplify the proceedings if it becomes necessary to sue the debtor, but not otherwise.

Whichever form of agreement is used it will be a document which will ensure, as far as it is possible, that the debt which the factor purchases shall vest in him free from any encumbrance and that the benefits of such debts may be enjoyed without any difficulties.

At the minimum such document will include:

(a) warranties by the supplier that the debts sold by him are bona fide arising from his sale and delivery of goods (or the provision of services) free from encumbrance, set-off, dispute and counterclaim, and that such debts arise from contracts of sale the terms of which have been approved by the factor either generally in the factoring agreement or specifically;

(b) arrangements whereby the factor may enforce payment of such debts without further reference to the supplier, usually by means of a power of attorney granted to the factor by the supplier enabling the former to perfect his legal title to the debts if this is necessary;

(c) a provision by which any payments received by the supplier from debtors in respect of debts sold are held in trust for the factor;[6]

(d) the factor's charges and method of calculating the finance charge;

(e) the regulations for determining how any debts sold to the factor by the supplier may rank as an approved debt (i.e. there is no recourse to the supplier in the event of non-payment owing to the insolvency of the debtor) or unapproved;

(f) a guarantee by the supplier of due payment to the factor of any unapproved debts which the factor may purchase;

(g) provisions by which, on the assignment of any debt, all other rights of the supplier under the relevant contract for sale are

---

4. Stamp Act 1891, Sched. 1.

5. For the difficulties which this form of agreement may raise for a factor who wishes to provide his services for a sole trader or partnership, *see* below in this chapter.

6. For confirmation that such a provision in the factoring agreement will give the factor a proprietary right to a cheque drawn by a customer in respect of an assigned debt and made payable to and sent to the supplier *see International Factors* v. *Rodrigues* [1979] 1 All E.R. 17. In this case the director of the supplier company paid such a cheque into the supplier company's bank account; the defendant was held personally to be the primary tortfeasor and it was no defence that he had acted on behalf of the company. Furthermore, the contention that the factor could receive a second payment from the debtor and had not, therefore, suffered a loss was not considered to be a defence to the action.

assigned to the factor—such rights will include ownership of any returned goods;

(*h*) an undertaking by the supplier to provide proof of delivery of the goods or completion of the services which are the subject of any debt sold to the factor.

EQUITIES AFFECTING THE RIGHTS OF THE ASSIGNEE

All assignments are said to be "subject to equities"; the rights which the factor buys against the debtor are not better than the supplier has, and are thus subject to all the countervailing rights of the debtor as at the date when the assignment is completed. The notice of the assignment fixes the rights of the parties; thus if, after the debtor has notice of an assignment, a claim arises out of a contract which is independent of that in which the assigned debt arose, he cannot set off that claim against the factor's claim, even if the contract was made before notice of the assignment.[7] If, however, the set-off arises directly out of the same contract or transactions as the subject matter of the assignment, the debtor may set it up against the factor even though it did not accrue to him until after notice of the assignment. The extent of any such set-off is limited to the factor's own claim; although he is owner of the debt, he is not a party to the contract between the supplier and the debtor and so he incurs no positive liability to damages. The factor, as assignee, although subject to equities, is not subjected to them.

THE DEBTOR'S DEFENCES AND COUNTERCLAIM

Since the factor has purchased debts from the supplier for near their full value and has made available to the supplier a substantial part of the purchase price, the degree to which defences and counter-claims may be raised against his claims for recovery is of vital interest to him. He has the right to an indemnity from the supplier for losses from these causes, but his retention may be insufficient and the supplier may be insolvent. Indeed, the very incidence of such impediments to his recovery may cause the factor to withhold payments to the supplier which in normal circumstances are the supplier's only cash in-flow.

As notice of the assignment fixes the rights of the parties, the debtor is obliged to pay to the factor no more than he would

7. "Now an assignee of a chose in action ... takes subject to all rights of set-off and other defences which were available against the assignor subject only to this exception, that after notice of an assignment of a chose in action the debtor cannot by payment or otherwise do anything to take away or diminish the rights of the assignee as they stood at the time of the notice." per James LJ in *Roxburghe* v. *Cox* (1881) 17 Ch. D. 520.

have paid to the supplier but for the assignment, taking into account all events prior to the notice. Thus a credit note issued by a supplier which recognises an inherent defect in the goods or an event before the notice is a valid deduction by the debtor from the factor's claim.

It is generally accepted that, once the debtor has paid the factor in respect of an assigned debt, any counterclaim, whether arising from the contract to which the debt related or not, must be against the supplier. Thus, where the issue of a credit note by the supplier has the effect of creating a credit balance on the debtor's account in the factor's books (if the invoice to which it is related has already been settled), it is usually considered that the factor is not responsible in law. (As a matter of administrative convenience and to avoid arguments a factor would normally settle such a credit balance if asked by the debtor, and charge the supplier accordingly. At least one UK factor uses a form of factoring agreement which authorises the factor to make such payments to the customers and to debit the supplier's account.) If a customer paid the invoice in full and there were a defect in the goods which warranted a subsequent credit note from the supplier, he might be entitled to claim recovery of the amount paid as money paid under a mistake of fact. The point is not free from doubt and may never be decided; the amounts concerned are usually too small to warrant litigation.

CONTRACTUAL TERMS PROHIBITING ASSIGNMENTS

Difficulties may arise for the factor from contractual terms between a seller and a buyer prohibiting assignment of the benefit of the contract.[8] The general view of the law appears to have been that there was a difference between a contract term banning the assignment of the general rights of one party and a term which purported to make inalienable the fruits of the contract once the supplier had performed it to the full. It had been considered that whereas an assignment of the first kind, in breach of the contract, might be invalid, the second kind of prohibition "could no more operate to invalidate the assignment than it could interfere with the laws of gravitation."[9]

That view has now been upset. In *Helstan Securities* v. *Hertfordshire CC*[10] the contract provided, *inter alia*, that a road contractor for the Council should not assign the contract or any part thereof or any benefit or interest therein or thereunder without the written consent of the Council. It was held that the assignment of the amounts payable by the Council under the contract in breach of this

8. *See*, for example, Biscoe *Law and Practice of Credit Factoring*, p. 116.
9. *Shaw and Co.* v. *Moss Empire and Bastow* (1908) 25 T.L.R. 190, per Darling J.
10. [1978] 3 All E.R. 262.

condition was invalid. Although the judge in this instance was dealing only with the question whether the debtor was obliged to pay to the assignee and not with the relations between the assignor and assignee, a literal interpretation of the judgment indicates that a purported assignment in breach of such a contract term is wholly invalid. If this is so, and at present the law on this point is not entirely clear, then not only would the factor not be able to recover direct from the debtor in such a case but also the trust provisions in the factoring agreement might well be ineffective against a liquidator or receiver of an insolvent supplier.[11]

In any event, the factor's principal means of recovering the funds he lays out is his right to recover direct from the debtors, and the decision may seriously affect this right. In the *Helstan* case the judge considered that it was incumbent upon the purchaser of a debt to make inquiries as to the terms of the contract out of which the debt arose, but in the case of the continuing relationship of a factoring agreement under which a multitude of relatively small debts are purchased such inquiries are clearly not administratively possible. In order to protect himself a factor should look for such provisions in the case of exceptionally large debts, particularly where local authorities or government departments are the purchasers. However, it is considered that if a debtor, whose purchase contract includes such a ban, continues to make payments direct to him without protest, he will be entitled to rely on this as constituting a waiver of the prohibition, by way of estoppel by conduct. Factors now are more vigilant in watching for payments made to the assignor notwithstanding notice of assignment and in ascertaining the reasons for such mode of payment.

CONFLICTS BETWEEN ASSIGNEES

A supplier may sometimes enter into agreements with two separate organisations for the assignment of the same debt or series of debts. Quite apart from fraud this may happen by reason of negligence; a businessman may execute a document, without advice, in ignorance of its effect.

The general rule in a case of competition between two equitable assignees is that the first assignee to give notice to the debtor prevails, provided he took the assignment in good faith and for value and without notice of an earlier interest in the debt.[12] There is a reference to this rule in s. 137(1) of the Law of Property Act 1925

---

11. For a review of the *Helstan* case, *see* R. M. Goode, "Inalienable Rights?", *Modern Law Review*, Vol. 42, pp. 533 ff.
12. The rule in *Dearle* v. *Hall* (1828) 3 Russ. 1.

which would appear to accord it statutory recognition. Furthermore, contrary to the usual rule of priority between an equitable interest and a subsequent legal interest acquired for value and without notice of a prior encumbrance, the rule appears to apply even where the interest of the first to give notice is purely equitable and the later assignment is a legal assignment taken for value and without notice of the former.[13]

In the cases of competition between two assignees in respect of purely legal assignments it is doubtful if there can be an argument. By definition, both assignees must have given notice to the debtor, and if the second assignee gives notice first his is the first to become a legal assignment (provided all the other requirements are satisfied) and the supplier then has nothing more to assign (except subject to the first assignment).

CONFLICTS WITH CHARGEES, FIXED AND FLOATING

The position of a factor who purchases book debts which a supplier has already assigned by way of fixed charge is somewhat uncertain. It is clear that if the charge contained a restriction against dealings with the debts assigned and the factor had notice of such restriction, he would not get any title to the debt, and the rights of the fixed chargee would prevail, even as regards moneys advanced after receipt of notice of the assignment.[14] For this purpose notice of the charge is insufficient: the factor must have had notice of the restriction. In any event, the chargee, on receipt of notice of assignment from the factor, could rule off the supplier's account so as to defeat the operation of the rule in *Clayton*'s case.[15]

In the case of a floating charge the position is somewhat different. The essence of a floating charge is that it does not fasten on the property subject to the charge until crystallisation, and until then the chargor company is free to deal with its property in the ordinary course of business.[16] Modern forms of bank floating charge tend to include book debts within the scope of the fixed element of the charge.[16] Moreover, even if the debts are subject only to a floating

13. This is the consequence of the words "subject to equities having priority over the right of the assignee" in s. 136(1) of the Law of Property Act 1925, which sets out the requisites of a legal assignment.
14. *Siebe Gorman & Co.* v. *Barclays Bank*, (1978) *The Times*, 15th May. *See also* in *Swiss Bank Corporation* v. *Lloyds Bank* [1970] 2 All E.R. 853 "... the court will restrain a person from enforcing his contractual rights so as to cause a breach of another contract of which he had full knowledge when he entered into his own contract." per Browne-Wilkinson J; *Manchester Ship Canal Co.* v. *Manchester Racecourse Co.* [1901] 2 Ch. 37.
15. *Devaynes* v. *Noble* (1816) 1 Mer. 572. *See* Chapter Four.
16. *See* Chapter Seventeen.

charge, the form of charge may nevertheless contain restrictions against dealing with the debts, and if the factor had notice of such a restriction the chargee might well have priority. A factor should therefore search at the Companies Registry, and in particular see whether details of any such restriction are included in the registration of the floating charge. Moreover, as factors do not wish to be engaged in conflict with banks and other lenders, it is a matter of normal business prudence to ensure that such matters are clarified in advance by letters of waiver or priority agreements.

If a bank takes a floating charge from a supplier who has already entered into a factoring agreement of the type referred to above as the "equitable assignment method", the bank would have difficulty in establishing priority. First the floating charge would give the bank equitable rights only, and must therefore be subject to the prior equities of the factoring agreement. Secondly, if the supplier maintained its bank account with the chargee bank, and the only credits to its account were from the factor, the bank might be deemed to have notice of the factor's rights. If the other method is used, the factor's priority in relation to debts assigned after the charge is registered is more doubtful, but he should prevail in relation to debts assigned before the charge was registered, especially where notice of assignment has been given to the debtor concerned.

OTHER CONFLICTS

The other main source of difficulty arises from sellers who retain title to goods as in the *Romalpa* case.[17] That case was new, not because it confirmed the right of the seller who had reserved title to repossess goods still in the possession of the buyer, which had never been seriously disputed, but because it enabled the seller to trace his rights through the proceeds of the sale of goods to which he had reserved title, even where the money had already been received by the buyer. It is unclear whether the factor or the seller would prevail in a case where the seller has reserved title to the goods and claims title to the debts arising from the sale of such goods, and such debts have also been purchased by the factor. This is a complex and difficult question and there have been no reported cases.[18]

Although suppliers using terms with similar objectives have failed

17. *Aluminium Industrie Vaassen BV* v. *Romalpa Aluminium* [1976] 2 All E.R. 552.
18. For a full exposition of this difficult question of law *see* R.M. Goode, "The Right to Trace and its Impact on Commercial Transactions", *L.Q.R.* (1976), Vol. 92, pp. 547–60. For a contrary opinion *see* D.M. McLaughland, "Priorities—Equitable Tracing Rights and Assignments of Book Debts", *L.Q.R.* (1980), Vol. 96, pp. 90–100.

in two cases,[19] these cases were decided on their particular facts, one because of the form of words used and the other because the goods had been used in the manufacturing process and had thereby lost their identity.

Another difficulty may arise from the carrier's lien. The factor usually purchases the supplier's right to payment as soon as the goods have been placed in transit to the customer. The agreement usually provides that the supplier is obliged to offer or notify each debt as soon as he has performed all his obligations under his sale contract. It is common for the supplier to be responsible for arranging carriage of the goods and as the supplier will probably not have paid the carrier at the date when the ownership of the debts concerned is transferred to the factor, the supplier may often be technically in breach of his warranties.

If the supplier becomes insolvent, the carrier may rely on his lien on goods which are in transit, and so the factor will be unable to recover the debts from customers until he pays the carriers' charges, since otherwise the customers will not receive the goods. There is little that can be done about this, since it would usually be administratively impossible to ensure that debts were not offered or notified to the factor until the carrier had been paid for the goods in question. This will probably not be a serious problem in relation to sales within the United Kingdom, since the transit time will be short and the value of unpaid invoices relating to goods held by the carrier will usually be well within the factor's retention margin. If, however, the supplier is an exporter, the transport charges will be higher in relation to the value of the debts purchased and the risk would be more serious. The factor would therefore be well advised to make arrangements to ensure that the supplier keeps his payments to the carriers up to date.

Other claims by third parties to the debts which are the subject of a factoring agreement, such as an attachment of such a debt by a creditor of the supplier by way of garnishee order,[20] are rare. The debts under a factoring agreement vest in the factor very soon after they come into existence so that a would-be claimant, such as a garnishor, has little opportunity to act in time.

Consideration must, however, be given to a mercantile agent's common law lien on the proceeds of his sales of his principal's goods. The point does not appear to have been decided in England, but it may well be that a factor, who purchases from a supplier debts arising from sales through the supplier's mercantile agent, is

19. *Re Bond Worth* [1980] Ch. 228, and *Borden (UK)* v. *Scottish Timber Products* [1981] Ch. 25.
20. *See* Chapter Four.

susceptible to such a lien exercised by the agent in order to secure commission owing to him by the supplier.

A further possible conflict, as yet unresolved, may result from the purchase by a factor of debts arising from a supplier's sale of goods pledged to a bank or finance company and released to the supplier under a letter of trust whereby the proceeds of sale are to be held for the account of the pledgee.

In either of such cases, if the factor is aware of the arrangements, he would be well advised to obtain a letter of waiver, in the first case from the agent, and in the other from the pledgee.

BANKRUPTCY OF THE SUPPLIER

A general assignment of all existing or future book debts or any class thereof by a sole trader or partnership is void against a trustee in bankruptcy of the trader or the partners as regards debts unpaid at the commencement of the bankruptcy unless the assignment is registered as a bill of sale.[21] In view of the administrative impossibility of registering the assignments as bills of sale in the continuing arrangements of a factoring agreement, by which a myriad of relatively small debts arising from all the day-to-day sales of the firm may be assigned, it is not possible for a factor safely to use the type of agreement described as the "equitable assignment method" in the case of a sole trader or partnership.[22] The difficulty for the factor becomes more severe on account of the doctrine of relation back;[23] his supplier may well continue to operate the factoring agreement for several weeks after the commencement of bankruptcy and the factor may pay moneys for debts which do not vest in him.

However, assignments of specific debts or debts growing due under specified contracts are valid against the claims of a trustee in bankruptcy.[24] Therefore when dealing with a partnership or sole trader a factor may safely use the other method and take formal assignments of batches of specified debts; in the case of a large business the factor must, however, consider the question of stamp duty if it is likely that the value of any batch may exceed the exemption limit.[22]

Some writers have postulated that debts which are the subject of a factoring agreement entered into by a sole trader or partnership, as supplier, might be caught by the "reputed ownership" provisions of the Bankruptcy Act[25] and be claimed by a trustee in bankruptcy for

21. Bankruptcy Act 1914, s. 43(1). *See* Chapter Thirty.
22. *See* earlier in this chapter.
23. *See* Chapter Thirty.
24. Bankruptcy Act 1914, s. 43(1).
25. Ibid., s. 38(c). *See* Chapter Thirty.

the estate. Certainly trade debts are not excluded (as are other choses in action), but it is generally accepted that notice to the debtors of the assignments and of the existence of the arrangements generally would serve to take such debts out of the doctrine of reputed ownership.

LIQUIDATION OF COMPANIES

Neither the avoidance of a general assignment of book debts nor the "reputed ownership" provisions apply in the liquidation of a company. Thus a factor may with reasonable safety use either type of agreement.

However all dispositions of a company's property, including "things in action" made after the commencement of a winding up by the court, are void, unless otherwise ordered by the court.[26] In voluntary liquidation there is no comparable rule, but on the appointment of a liquidator the directors' powers cease. Furthermore, from the commencement of the winding up, the business may be carried on solely for the beneficial realisation of the assets. A liquidator has the right to disclaim an onerous contract[27] and it is unlikely that he would see any benefit in carrying on the factoring agreement.

These provisions pose no difficulties for the factor in the case of a creditors' voluntary liquidation, as the factor will normally have ample warning of the commencement of the winding up, if not by actual notice (as he is not a creditor), at least from the publication of the notice of the meeting at which the resolutions are to be passed to give effect to liquidation.

However, a factor can be seriously affected by a winding up by the court for the commencement of such a winding up (except where it is preceded by voluntary liquidation) is the date of the presentation of the petition on which the order is based.[28] Furthermore, the petition may be presented several weeks (or even months in the long vacation) before the hearing and it is not required that the notice of the petition be advertised until seven clear working days before the hearing.[29] Thus a factor may for several weeks pay the supplier for debts under offer, purporting to be assignments, or notified, when no assignments have taken place.

It may well be argued that, in the case of a factoring agreement which itself constituted an agreement by the supplier to sell and the factor to purchase all trade debts on their coming into existence

26. Companies Act 1948, s. 227.
27. Ibid., s. 323.
28. Ibid., s. 229(2).
29. *See* Chapter Twenty-Nine.

without further act by either party, the disposition of the debts which came into existence after the commencement of the winding up took place at the time of the execution of agreement.[30]

However, although there is a strong argument to support this view, it would be prudent for a factor to make his decisions on the assumption that all such dispositions are deemed to take place when the debts themselves come into existence.

A factoring agreement will normally provide for immediate termination upon notice in the event of a meeting of creditors or a petition for winding up. However, the circumstances may be such, even on publication of the notice of the petition, that it is apparent that the supplier company is not insolvent, that it is unlikely that an order will be made and that the business should be allowed to continue. In such an event, in order to protect the supplier's business and to allow the factoring agreement (which provides substantially all the supplier's cash flow) to continue, the supplier should be persuaded to make immediate application to the court for an order that the assignments under the factoring agreement will not be avoided if a winding-up order is made.

If, on the other hand, factoring is to cease then all that will be required is the non-avoidance of the assignments made between the presentation of the petition and the publication of the notice. It is doubtful if the supplier or, indeed, the court would be persuaded that such an order would be in the supplier's interest; therefore the factor will have to make such application after the liquidator has been appointed and it seems reasonable to suppose that in normal circumstances such an order would be made.

APPOINTMENT OF A RECEIVER BY A FLOATING CHARGEE

The position of the factor *vis à vis* the holder of such a charge has been dealt with. In most cases the factor would hold a letter of "waiver" from the chargee confirming the factor's right to enjoy the benefits of the assignments under the factoring agreement free from the charge. The factor, therefore, will in normal circumstances have little to fear as regards debts which have already vested in him before the appointment of a receiver. However, if the receiver is appointed with power to manage and decides to continue the business, it is important that a clear distinction be made between the rights of the

---

30. On the analogy of a floating charge in relation to which a disposition of the assets charged takes place on the appointment of a receiver, and such disposition after the commencement of a winding up has never been challenged, *see* W. J. Gough, *Company Charges*, pp. 407–8.

supplier under the contracts of sale from which the assigned debts arise—which will normally vest in the factor—and the rights relating to debts which come into existence after the receiver's appointment or which at that date have not been assigned. As such rights will include the ownership of any goods rejected by customers, it is important that arrangements should be made for the segregation of returned goods.

Such a debenture will constitute an incomplete assignment of the assets of the chargor company, and the assignment will become complete upon crystallisation.[31] Accordingly, upon the appointment of a receiver, the charge attaches to the company's assets and any debts created by subsequent sales will be subject to the charge and not assignable to the factor free from it. As regards debts which have been created on the appointment of the receiver but not offered to the factor (under a factoring agreement in which such offers are required), the receiver may refuse to honour the agreement and the factor's only remedy will be against the company for breach of contract; for any damages awarded he will be unsecured. However, under the type of agreement which in itself constitutes an equitable assignment of all existing and future debts, debts created before the receiver's appointment will vest in the factor, notwithstanding a failure by the company to notify either the factor by sending copy invoices, or the customers by notice on the original invoices.

If a receiver and manager wishes to carry on the business of a company, to which a factor has provided factoring services, he will need immediate finance; virtually all the cash flow of the company will have been coming from the factor and will on the receiver's appointment cease. In these circumstances it is often the case that the receiver will wish to continue the agreement. The factor will expect that the receiver, although continuing the agreement as agent for the company, should take personal responsibility for the obligations of the supplier in respect of debts assigned after his appointment, including, for example, recourse for goods or invoices not accepted by customers. In order to ensure the receiver's personal liability it is necessary to provide for the continuation by novation.[32] A clear line has to be drawn, a new current account opened and a clear distinction made in respect of debit or credit entries resulting from pre-receivership and post-receivership transactions.

If a winding-up order is made after the commencement of the receivership the receiver, ceasing to be agent of the company, may continue the agreement as principal.

31. Per Templeman LJ *Business Computers* v. *Anglo–African Leasing* [1977] 2 All E.R. 741.
32. Companies Act 1948, s. 369(2).

LENDING AGAINST SECURITY DISTINGUISHED

The distinction between the purchase of debts and payment of the purchase price by the assignee before they have been extinguished on the one hand, and the lending of money against a charge on book debts on the other, has long been recognised by the courts: "There are many ways of raising cash besides borrowing. One is by selling book debts . . ."[33]

However, in some circumstances there may be a fine line between an assignment by way of outright purchase of a book debt and an assignment by way of charge. In view of the provisions of s. 95 of the Companies Act 1948 it is necessary for the factor to keep this difference firmly in mind.[34] If the substance of the transaction is the lending of money against an assignment of specified book debts it would be caught by s. 95(2)(e), and if it is the lending of money against a general assignment of all existing and future book debts of a company it would be caught by s. 95(2)(c) on the analogy of the required registration as a bill of sale by a sole trader or partnership.

If the factor wishes to avoid the necessity for the transaction to be subject to registration, not only the factoring agreement, but also all internal and external conduct and communication by a factor and its staff, should be consistent with the out and out sale and purchase of debts.

---

33. *Chow Yoong Hong* v. *Choong Fah Rubber Manufactory* [1962] A.C. 209.
34. *See* Chapter Six.

CHAPTER TWENTY-SEVEN

Leasing

THE GROWTH AND DEVELOPMENT OF LEASING

From modest beginnings in the early 1960s, finance leasing has grown during the last twenty years to become a major source of finance for industry and the fastest expanding financial sector in the UK. There is no requirement to register the trade of leasing in the UK and, as a consequence, there are no comprehensive figures available for the total amount of leasing transacted or of the number of companies engaged in leasing in the UK. The most reliable figures available indicate that approximately £2,000 million of new leasing business was transacted in 1979, accounting for approximately 10 per cent of new capital investment by industry, and something of the order of 25 per cent of all external funds utilised by companies in the acquisition of plant, equipment and other fixed assets.

A number of factors have influenced the growth of leasing over the last twenty years, starting with the entry into the market in the 1960s of a number of finance houses and the easing of credit restrictions in 1969, when lending to separate leasing subsidiaries or associated companies was exempted from credit controls to ensure that adequate finance was available for the purchase of plant and equipment for industry. The real impetus came in 1972 with the introduction of 100 per cent first-year allowances for tax purposes and the entry into the market of the clearing banks which had access to the three key ingredients required to establish a successful leasing company, finance, taxable capacity and a strong customer base.

TAXATION

Although there is no separate legal framework for the supervision of leasing companies, the growth and development of leasing in the UK has been strongly influenced by UK corporation tax legislation.

Under the present tax legislation, 100 per cent allowances are given in the year in which capital expenditure is incurred on the provision of most items of machinery and plant.[1] These capital allowances are deducted in computing taxable profits, and any excess capital allowances over taxable profits creates a tax loss which may be carried back and set against taxable profits arising from the same trading activity during the previous three years or carried forward and set against future trading profits.[2] Alternatively, tax losses may be surrendered to other members of a group of companies, to be offset against the taxable profits of these other group companies, under the "group relief" provisions of the Taxes Acts.[3]

Leasing is regarded by the Inland Revenue as a trade for tax purposes, and the capital allowances and resulting tax losses generated by leasing companies from the purchase of plant and equipment are available for offset under the group relief provisions against taxable profits of other group companies. This provision is of particular relevance to financial groups, whose own capital expenditure is small in relation to their own taxable profits, and where the tax losses of the leasing subsidiary can be offset against group taxable profits.

Investment decisions by industry are obviously influenced by the after-tax cost of such investment and if, because of factors such as stock relief and heavy capital expenditure, the industrial investor is unable to set the full capital allowances off against taxable profits, the investment incentives are of little or no value to the purchaser of plant and equipment. The leasing company, therefore, purchases the plant and equipment and reflects the benefit of the tax savings in the lease rentals payable by the user. This cost benefit to the user of plant and equipment has been a significant factor in the growth of leasing since 1972.

MARKET SEGMENTATION

Lessors

There are virtually no barriers to entry into the leasing market and it is open to any corporate body or individual to establish the trade of leasing. Because of the availability of tax capacity and finance, the finance lease market has been dominated since the mid-1970s by the leasing subsidiaries of the clearing banks, which together accounted for approximately 75 per cent of all leased assets in 1978. Subsidiaries of other financial institutions, the merchant banks and American and other foreign banks accounted for the major part of the remaining market.

Although a number of manufacturing companies, such as ICL and

1. Finance Act 1971, s. 41.
2. Income and Corporation Taxes Act 1970, ss. 168–171 and 177.
3. Ibid., ss. 258–264.

IBM, have been established in the lease market for many years, as lessors of their own products, the latter part of the 1970s has seen the entry into the lease market of a large number of non-financial institutions, such as retail and manufacturing companies, insurance brokers, discount houses, and insurance companies, whch have seen leasing as a profitable diversification, particularly in view of the tax-saving advantage available under present tax legislation.

The majority of leasing companies offer a full range of leasing facilities in the market, with the clearing banks tending to concentrate on facilities in excess of £25,000. Most clearing banks are involved, either in their own name or in partnership with other clearing banks, in "big-ticket" lease transactions, a term used to describe large-value items, often of considerable complexity, such as oil refineries, chemical plants, ships, aircraft and drilling rigs. At the other end of the scale a number of the smaller independent leasing companies have identified a market for their services in what is known as the "small ticket" market where equipment costs may be anything between £1,000 and £20,000.

Other leasing companies have tended to specialise in particular equipment, such as computers, cars and office equipment, and other companies have specialised in a market sector such as agriculture. Frequently, these specialist leasing companies will combine with a manufacturer or supplier, either by way of a joint company or a loan support scheme, to provide a leasing facility to assist equipment sales.

Lessees

While leasing is generally available to all companies, irrespective of size, there is clear evidence that the leasing industry has tended to concentrate on the needs of medium and large firms, and central and local government authorities, possibly because of the better credit risk of these larger organisations. Since leasing is less acceptable to smaller companies as a form of finance, and the overheads incurred by leasing companies in penetrating this market are relatively high, in practice smaller companies usually resort to hire-purchase facilities or leasing facilities offered by specialised leasing companies operating in this small ticket market.

DEFINITION

Because there is no separate legal framework for the supervision of leasing there is no legal definition of a lease contract. Accordingly there is no one generally accepted definition of leasing in the UK, although the following definition, or perhaps more accurately "description", is widely used.

A lease is a contract between a lessor (the owner) and a lessee (the user) for the hire of a specific asset selected from a manufacturer or vendor of such assets by the lessee. The lessor retains ownership of the asset and the lessee has possession and use of the asset on payment of specified rentals over an agreed rental period. In the UK the lease contract does not confer on the lessee either the right or the obligation to acquire ownership of the asset either during the lease term or thereafter.

Within this general definition of a lease, a distinction must be drawn between a finance lease (also known as a full-pay-out lease) and an operating lease (also known as a true lease). Although classification of finance leases and operating leases can be difficult in practice, the distinction will become important in the future if, as expected, the Accounting Standards Committee of the Institute of Chartered Accountants in England and Wales introduce the proposed accounting standard on "Accounting for leases and hire purchase transactions in the accounts of lessee companies", which will require lessees to capitalise both lease assets and liabilities in their accounts. Following American precedent, it is expected that the accounting standard will identify leases as finance leases if they satisfy at least one of the following conditions.

(a) The lessee has the use of the asset for 75 per cent or more of the estimated economic life of the leased asset.

(b) The present value at the beginning of the lease term of the minimum (committed) rentals payable under the lease (exclusive of any amounts payable for insurance, maintenance and normal outgoings) is at least equivalent to 90 per cent of the cost of the leased asset net of any investment or other grants.

All leases which do not meet the above criteria are expected to be classified as operating leases.

In more general terms, a finance lease may be distinguished from an operating lease as follows.

Finance Lease	Operating Lease
The lessee is obliged to pay specified rentals over an agreed primary rental period sufficient in total to amortise the capital outlay of the lessor and to give the lessor his profit after deduction of interest costs and overheads.	The asset is not wholly amortised during the committed or non-cancellable period of the lease and the lessor does not rely for his profit on the rentals payable in this committed period.

Finance Lease	Operating Lease
The equipment is selected, from the manufacturer or supplier of such equipment, by the lessee and not the lessor, and accordingly primary responsibility for the fitness and condition of the equipment rests with the lessee.	The equipment is usually selected and purchased, or already owned, by the lessor and the lessor tends to assume a higher degree of responsibility for the equipment, frequently being responsible for replacing any defective equipment.
The lessee is usually responsible for maintenance and insurance of the equipment.	The lessor is frequently responsible for maintenance and insurance of the equipment.
The lessor's profit is not generally dependent on the residual value of the asset at the end of the lease term and it is common practice for the lessee to receive 95 per cent or more of the proceeds of sale of the equipment at the end of the primary lease period either as rebate of rentals paid or as commission for acting as the lessor's agent in arranging the sale of the equipment.	The lessor's profit is usually dependent to a significant extent on the residual value of the equipment which is realised by the lessor by selling or re-leasing the equipment. The lessee does not usually share in any proceeds of sale or disposal of the equipment.
The primary lease term usually anticipates the useful economic life of the asset and the lease term is rarely less than three years (or two years for cars).	The initial lease term covers only a part of the anticipated useful life of the asset and the committed lease period may be as short as twelve months
The primary lease period is usually followed by a secondary lease period at a nominal rental of between 1 to 5 per cent per annum of initial capital cost of the equipment.	The initial committed lease period is usually followed by a right to renew or extend the lease at rentals similar to those payable during the initial period.

OTHER FORMS OF LEASING

In addition to the difference between a finance lease and an operating lease, a distinction may be drawn between leasing and hiring (or rental) agreements. A hire agreement is essentially a short-term contract which enables the hirer to use an item of equipment for a specific purpose against payment of rental. Such contract may generally be terminated by the hirer on giving a relatively short period of notice. A hire agreement may most readily be identified by reference to the type of equipment involved and such agreements are commonly used in connection with plant hire, cars, commercial vehicles, aircraft and cranes.

Under a hire agreement, the owner usually accepts a much higher degree of responsibility for the fitness of the equipment supplied and will frequently provide maintenance, service, insurance and replacement equipment.

Contract hire, a term almost exclusively applied to cars and commercial vehicles, is a form of leasing developed by finance houses and motor dealers as a means of providing vehicles to users wishing to replace the vehicles at regular intervals of time, usually at the end of 12, 24 or 36 months. Maintenance and replacement vehicles are commonly included as part of the arrangement.

OWNERSHIP BY THE LESSOR

To the lessee, leasing is a means of financing the use rather than the purchase of an asset. The essential feature of leasing, which distinguishes it from other forms of instalment credit finance such as credit sale, conditional sale and hire purchase, is the separation of use from ownership. Unlike credit sale, conditional sale and hire purchase, which are essentially means of financing the purchase of an asset and where the user either has ownership from the start or has the option to acquire ownership of the asset, a lease contract must not provide that the lessee shall or may become owner of leased equipment, or the lessor's right to capital allowances will be lost.

The separation of use from ownership is fundamental not just to the form of the lease contract but to the taxation advantages which flow from ownership of equipment in the UK. As owner of the equipment the lessor is able to claim capital allowances for tax purposes and also any regional development grants payable in respect of equipment. It is the availability of these tax allowances and grants, the benefits of which are passed on to the lessee by way of reduced rentals, which has contributed to the growth of leasing.

However, notwithstanding the strict legal form of the lease contract, the lessee's position is similar to the position of someone who has borrowed money to buy an asset and a finance lease generally imposes on the lessee most of the responsibilities of ownership of an asset. The lessee selects the equipment and effectively undertakes all the risks of ownership in the use and operation of the equipment. The lessor looks to the lessee for full recovery of the initial capital outlay plus profit and, subject to compliance with the terms of the lease contract, the lessee has exclusive right to use the equipment during the contracted lease period. The lease contract rarely provides for any right of early termination on the part of the lessee, but in the event that early termination should occur the lessee is liable to pay to the lessor at least the outstanding book value of the asset in the accounts of the lessor. In addition some compensation for lost profit is generally required by the lessor.

In practice, one of two methods is commonly adopted in finance leases to enable the lessee to enjoy the benefit of the residual value of the equipment, without the lessee actually having an option or right to acquire the equipment, namely:

(a) the lease provides for a secondary rental period at a relatively nominal rental, and

(b) on sale or other disposal of the equipment, the lessee receives 95 per cent or more of the sale proceeds either by way of rebate of rentals paid or as a commission for acting as the lessor's agent for sale.

Lessee's obligations

The practical consequences of the above are that the lessee acquires a right to possession of the asset, which he has under his control and which he is obliged to maintain, and he has the obligation to pay rental for the asset while the lease continues. Lease commitments also have the effect of making lessees more highly geared than may be apparent from the lessee's accounts, and there is currently a strong school of thought which holds the view that a lease, which transfers to the lessee most of the benefits and risks incidental to the ownership of property, should be accounted for by the lessee as the acquisition of an asset and the incurring of the related obligations.

THE LESSOR'S CONTRACT WITH THE SUPPLIER

The lessor will contract with the supplier in a number of ways, including placing the order direct with the supplier, by appointing the lessee as agent, by an assignment or novation of an order already placed by the lessee but where title has not passed to the lessee, or, in some cases, by purchasing the goods from the lessee under a "sale and lease-back" arrangement. A "sale and lease-back" is only available where the goods have not been used by the lessee.

All the contractual arrangements between the lessor and the supplier involve potential problems in so far as the lessor is usually relatively remote from the supplier and generally relies completely on the lessee to agree the terms and conditions of the purchase agreement. However, in circumstances where there is no contractual arrangement between the lessor and the supplier, or where such contractual arrangements as do exist are incomplete, there is a risk that title to the goods will pass to the lessee and not the lessor, with the latter thereby losing the right to capital allowances. There is also a risk that because of an incomplete agency agreement or for some other reason the goods will have been used by the lessee before title is acquired by the lessor. This again will result in the loss of 100 per cent first year capital allowances.

THE LESSOR'S CONTRACT WITH THE LESSEE

There is no separate legal framework for the supervision of leasing companies in the UK and it is appropriate to treat finance lease agreements as distinguishable, under both commercial and fiscal law, from sales on deferred terms with reservation of title, such as conditional sales and hire-purchase.

A lease of equipment is classified under English law as a type of bailment, *locatio et conductio* (the hiring of a chattel for use), one of six classes of bailment established by Holt CJ, in *Coggs* v. *Bernard*.[4] Although the law of bailment is relevant to hire-purchase and the bailment aspect of hire-purchase case law might well have relevance to finance leases, there is virtually no case law in the UK concerned with finance leases as such. The terms and conditions of leasing contracts have not yet been tested and interpreted by the courts, although this may well change in the future as a result of the growth of the leasing industry and the influence of statutes such as the Consumer Credit Act 1974 and the Unfair Contract Terms Act 1977.

Subject to the ordinary rules of the law of contract, a lease agreement is not required to conform to any particular form, although the standard type of leasing agreement in general use in the UK specifies in considerable detail the terms and conditions for payment of rental and the rights and obligations of the contracting

4. (1703) 2 Ld. Raym. 909.

parties. Except in the case of consumer hire business, as defined in the Consumer Credit Act 1974, for which a licence to carry on business is required, and transactions subject to the Control of Hiring Order, there are no statutory restrictions on either lessors or lessees.

Implied terms and liability of the lessor

A lessee has no right or interest in leased equipment except as specified or implied under the leasing agreement. There is an implied warranty that the lessee may enjoy quiet possession for the period of the lease, and if there is any breach of this warranty and the lessee loses possession, the lessee may be able to treat the agreement as having been repudiated, and be discharged from performance of his obligations and entitled to claim damages against the lessor for breach of the warranty. Any provision in the lease agreement excluding or restricting the right to quiet possession is subject to a test of reasonableness under s. 7(4) of the Unfair Contract Terms Act, 1977.

At common law there may be implied into the lease agreement a term that the equipment will be fit for the purpose for which it is leased, though this is more likely to be the case under a hiring agreement as distinct from a lease, since in finance leases the equipment is almost invariably selected by the lessee and the lessor purchases the specific equipment at the request of the lessee. Both lease and pre-lease agreements between the lessor and the lessee usually contain clauses excluding the lessor from any liability in respect of the state, condition and performance of the goods, but the validity of such exclusion clauses would be subject to the "test of reasonableness" and void in any contract with a consumer, i.e. where the lessee is not contracting in the course of a business activity.

The lease agreement will also usually require an indemnity from the lessee for any injury caused by the equipment to any third party who seeks to hold the lessor responsible in some way. Apart from the "test of reasonableness" a lessor may no longer exclude or restrict liability for death or personal injury resulting from the lessor's negligence.[5] Exclusion clauses in the lease agreement do not directly protect the lessor from claims made by third parties as such third parties are not by definition a party to the lease contract containing the exclusion.

At the present time, lessors are regarded as suppliers of goods under the Health and Safety at Work, etc., Act 1974 and are subject to the obligations imposed by the Act. However, so far as is known, no action has been brought against lessors under the terms of the

5. Unfair Contract Terms Act 1977, s. 2.

Act and it is understood that exemption for finance lessors is under consideration.

Termination of the lease agreement

Termination of the lease agreement may occur:

(a) as a consequence of default by the lessee or lessor;
(b) by mutual agreement of the parties; or
(c) by expiry of the term of the leasing agreement.

The primary responsibility of the lessee is to observe the terms and conditions of the lease including the payment of rentals due under the lease agreement. Failure to pay rentals is the most common cause of lessee default, and lease agreements give the lessor the right to terminate the lease in the event of non-payment.

On termination the lessor will seek to recover at least the unamortised amount of the original investment in the leased assets. The relevant clause in the lease agreement will usually require the lessee to pay all rentals due to the date of termination plus all contracted future rentals which, but for the termination of the agreement, would have been payable under the terms of the agreement. It is usual for the future rentals payable to be discounted by an appropriate interest rate (frequently specified in the lease agreement) and any net proceeds of sale received in respect of the equipment are usually offset to the extent contemplated in the lease agreement against the amount payable by the lessee.

The extent to which a terminal payment by the lessee is enforceable by the lessor will depend on whether or not the required payment constitutes a penalty. If the sum payable on termination represents a genuine pre-estimate of the loss which the innocent party will suffer on a breach or default then the sum is not likely to be considered a penalty. If, however, the sum payable is not a genuine pre-estimate of the loss then the claim will succeed only to the extent of the loss suffered.[6]

When early termination occurs by mutual agreement of the parties, it is the generally held view that the terminal payment represents a commercial consideration for release from the obligations of the lease contract and therefore no penalty arises.[7]

If the lessor commits a breach of the terms of the agreement amounting to repudiation, it may be open to the lessee to accept the repudiation, return the equipment and sue for damages.

6. *Dunlop Pneumatic Tyre Company* v. *New Garage and Motor Company* [1915] A.C. 79.
7. *Associated Distributors* v. *Hall* [1938] 1 All E.R. 511; *Bridge* v. *Campbell Discount Company* [1962] 1 All E.R. 385.

THE LESSOR'S DISPOSAL OF THE EQUIPMENT AT THE END OF THE LEASE

On disposal of lease equipment the lessor is no longer in the position of a "remote" financier but moves towards the same position as any supplier of goods with the attendant responsibilities and potential liabilities. Apart from the legal risks there is also a potential tax problem if goods are sold at a significantly undervalued price, since the Inland Revenue might claim tax on a balancing charge based upon true market value rather than the sale value of the asset.

OTHER CONSIDERATIONS FOR THE LESSOR

In addition to the contractual risks outlined above there exists a remote possibility that the lessor may be sued in tort by third parties who are injured by the goods while they are on lease to the lessee. However, under present law and practice it would be difficult to construct a circumstance where the lessor owes a duty of care to a third party.

Finance leases are essentially concerned with moveable property and care must be exercised by the lessor to ensure that any item of leased equipment does not become affixed to land and buildings in such a way that it ceases to be a legal chattel and becomes part of the freehold property. The consequences of affixation are that the equipment may be claimed as a part of the real estate by the landlord or mortgagees and title to the equipment could thereby be lost by the lessor. To obtain some protection it is usual for the lessor to obtain a waiver from the lessee's landlord acknowledging the lessor's interest in the equipment and his right to remove it. The lease agreement also requires the lessee to notify the lessor before any charge is created over the property so that the necessary acknowledgment may be obtained from the proposed mortgagee.

Consumer hire agreements are regulated by the Consumer Credit Act 1974 and a licence issued by the Director General of Fair Trading is required by any leasing company transacting consumer hire business within the meaning defined in s. 15(1):

... an agreement made by a person with an individual (the "hirer") for the bailment or (in Scotland) the hiring of goods to the hirer, being an agreement which—(a) is not a hire-purchase agreement, and (b) is capable of subsisting for more than three months, and (c) does not require the hirer to make payments exceeding £5,000.

The Act does not distinguish between private and business use, and unincorporated businesses, partnerships and sole traders fall within the provisions of the Act. However, the Control of Hiring Order 1977, which came into operation on 1st June 1977, does recognise the distinction and so excludes from the controls all goods used for the purpose or in the course of a trade or business carried on by the hirer. Since 1973 the law has changed with great speed and, in addition to the legislation mentioned above, leasing companies have been affected, in one way or another, by such consumer protection legislation as the Supply of Goods (Implied Terms) Act 1973,[8] the Fair Trading Act 1973 and the Unfair Contract Terms Act 1977. It is not expected that the law will remain unchanged during the period of relatively long-term lease agreements and lessors will increasingly become aware of their potential responsibilities and liabilities in respect of leased assets.

LIKELY DEVELOPMENTS

It is not appropriate in this relatively brief summary of the law relating to leasing to examine in depth the present and future liabilities of lessors, but it is expected that if legislation continues to place responsibilities, both actual and potential, on lessors there will be a number of developments in the leasing industry including, *inter alia*:

(*a*) more detailed drafting of leasing arrangements with particular reference to the liabilities and responsibilities of the lessee in respect of the leased assets and, wherever possible, an extension of exclusion clauses relating to the liabilities of lessors;

(*b*) greater control over the length of secondary lease periods granted to lessees under the terms of lease agreements;

(*c*) detailed requirements on the part of the lessee in respect of insurance cover, particularly with reference to third party insurance and the level of such third party insurance; and

(*d*) possibly an increase in the level of rentals payable if lessors are obliged to insure in their own name against the risks referred to above.

INSURANCE

Under the terms of the lease agreement the lessee is usually required to accept full responsibility for any loss or damage to the equipment and of any third party claims arising in connection with the asset or the use thereof. As protection for both the lessor and the lessee, the lessee is normally required to arrange comprehensive

8. Now incorporated into the Sale of Goods Act 1979.

624   VI. CORPORATE FINANCE

insurance to cover such risks "as are normally insured against by prudent owners of similar equipment". If the equipment is specially dangerous lessors frequently require the lessee to take out third party insurance to protect the lessee and lessor against claims.

Because of the lessor's interest in the equipment, the insurance provisions of the lease agreement may require the lessee to effect the policy in the joint names of the lessor and the lessee, or at least for the interest of the lessor to be noted on the policy, and for any payments in respect of any claim under the policy to be made direct to the lessor or to be applied directly in or towards satisfaction of any third party liability claim.

Where the equipment is capable of repair, the insurance moneys are applied towards the expenditure incurred by the lessee in making good any damage. Where the goods are totally destroyed and the lease terminates, the insurance moneys are usually offset against the termination rental payment required by the lessor with most of any excess being paid to, or retained by, the lessee.

Although the lessor endeavours so far as possible to exclude the responsibilities of ownership both by exclusion clauses and indemnities given by the lessee, circumstances may arise in practice where the lessor remains at risk. These circumstances could include a failure of the lessee's insurance either wholly or in part, claims by third parties where for some reason the lessor is held liable, liability for defective equipment where negligence on the part of the lessor can be shown, damage to or caused by equipment during a period when the equipment is under the lessor's control and, perhaps potentially of greatest concern to lessors, liabilities which may arise following the sale or other disposal of leased equipment.

Prudent lessors are increasingly requiring, and increasing the scope of, third party and contingent liability insurance, and a sum of £100 million or more is not unusual for leased assets of potential high risk.

CHAPTER TWENTY-EIGHT

Hire-Purchase

THE NATURE OF HIRE-PURCHASE

Since 1958 when Midland Bank bought Forward Trust the clearing banks have shown an increasing interest in finance house business in general and hire-purchase in particular. All the major banks now have either wholly owned subsidiaries which are finance companies or a substantial interest in such companies. By this method the banks gain contact with a large number of people who do not maintain current accounts. It is therefore now apposite to consider the law relating to hire-purchase in a book devoted to banking in the widest sense.

Hire-purchase came to the forefront in England in the nineteenth century, first in relation to the boom in the sale of pianos to the middle classes in the 1840s; it was then spurred in the 1860s when the Singer Sewing Machine Company began selling its machines on hire with an option to purchase. In 1895 the volume of business was such that the Hire Traders Protection Association (now known as the Consumer Credit Trade Association) assisted one of its members to fight an action to the House of Lords in order to win the point that a hirer under a hire-purchase agreement was not a person who had agreed to buy goods within the meaning of the Factors Act 1889. This meant that if a hirer sold the goods he had on hire, he could not pass a good title to them even if the purchaser bought them in good faith.[1] This decision, together with the fact that subsequently hire-purchase was held not to be moneylending and, therefore, not controlled by the Moneylenders Acts 1900 to 1927, nor was it a bill of sale requiring registration under the Bills of Sale Acts 1878 and 1882, stimulated the growth of hire-purchase.

Unfortunately, the growth of hire-purchase business also brought with it serious abuses, principally in relation to the repossession of goods. Agreements could and would be terminated for the slightest default in payment when almost all the instalments had been paid, which meant that the financier or owner could then repossess the

1. *Helby* v. *Matthews* [1895] A.C. 471.

625

goods and dispose of them again at a profit. The Hire-Purchase Act 1938 was passed to control these abuses; it applied within certain financial limits and limited the owner's right of possession. At present the hire-purchase system is controlled by Part III of the Hire-Purchase Act 1964 which deals with title to motor vehicles, the Consumer Credit Act 1974, and by the Hire-Purchase and Credit Sale Agreements (Control) Order 1976 (as amended) which restricts the disposal, acquisition or possession of articles under certain types of hire-purchase agreement.

DEFINITION

At common law a hire-purchase agreement may be defined as an agreement under which an owner lets a chattel on hire and agrees that the hirer may either return those goods and terminate the hiring or alternatively purchase the goods upon the terms set out in the agreement. Basically, therefore, a common law hire-purchase agreement consists of a bailment of goods plus an option to purchase them.

A contract of hire-purchase is distinguishable from a contract of credit sale in that under a credit sale the property in the goods is transferred to the buyer at the time of the agreement. The latter is a sale of goods under which the purchase price or part of it is payable by instalments and is, therefore, governed by the Sale of goods Act 1979. Similarly, a hire-purchase agreement can be distinguished from a conditional sale agreement, since in the case of a conditional sale the buyer is in possession of the goods although they remain in the ownership of the seller, but the essential difference is that, unlike a hire-purchase agreement, where the hirer merely has an option to purchase the goods and also the right to return them, the buyer under a conditional sale agreement is under an obligation to purchase them and is unable to return them (subject, of course, to statutory rights).[2]

HIRE-PURCHASE AT COMMON LAW

Since the Consumer Credit Act 1974 is not a codifying statute, and some common law rules apply both to those agreements which fall within the Act and to those outside the Act, it is necessary to consider some of these common law principles as well as the statutory principles.

---

2. Consumer Credit Act 1974, s. 99. In this chapter, unless otherwise stated, all references to the Act and to sections are references to the Consumer Credit Act 1974.

A hire-purchase agreement does not need to be in any specific form. It may be under seal, in writing, or oral. The capacity of a person to enter into such an agreement is regulated by the general law of contract. Although at common law contracts of hire-purchase need not be in writing, it is very unusual today to find an oral contract. Generally, hire-purchase agreements are standard form documents prepared by finance companies and contain, so far as is possible, the totality of the terms of the agreement.

The usual procedure for the creation of a hire-purchase agreement is that a person seeking to obtain goods on credit will sign a hire-purchase agreement either at the premises of the seller of the goods or at the premises of a finance company. The signing of a hire-purchase agreement form generally constitutes an offer to the finance company by the hirer to enter into a contract of hire-purchase; that offer is accepted when the owner of the goods, usually a finance company, executes the document. Even then the contract is not yet completed because the acceptance of the offer must be communicated to the hirer and it is open to the hirer to withdraw his offer until such acceptance has been communicated. It must be noted that if a dealer negotiated the transaction with the hirer then that dealer will be the agent of the hirer for the purpose of receiving notice of withdrawal of the offer. If the hirer signs an agreement form in blank leaving the dealer to fill in certain details in accordance with an understanding between them and the dealer then fills in erroneous details, the hirer will be bound by any subsequent agreement unless the circumstances are such that he could successfully plead *non est factum*.

Duties of the owner

In the absence of any term in the agreement to the contrary, it is the duty of the owner to deliver the goods to the hirer and the hiring will commence when the goods are delivered to him. If the goods are not delivered the hirer is entitled to damages from the owner for breach of contract, but as a rule is not entitled to specific performance.

Section 8 of the Supply of Goods (Implied Terms) Act 1973 stipulates that there is an implied condition on the part of the person by whom the goods are bailed that he will have the right to sell the goods at the time when the property is to pass, i.e. usually when the hirer wishes to exercise his option to purchase. There are also implied warranties:

(*a*) that the goods are free, and will remain free until the time when the property is to pass, from any charge or encumbrance not disclosed or known to the person to whom the goods are bailed before the agreement is made;

(b) that the hirer will enjoy quiet possession of the goods except so far as it may be disturbed by any person entitled to the benefit of any charge or encumbrance so disclosed or known; and

(c) in relation to the disclosure of information concerning encumbrances and to the nature of the title to be transferred.

Any attempt to exclude the operation of this section is void.[3]

It has already been pointed out that many hire-purchase transactions are entered into at the premises of the dealer. When a hirer seeks to obtain goods and wishes to have instalment credit in order to pay for them, the dealer will sell the goods to the finance company and the finance company will enter into a hire-purchase agreement with the hirer. The original negotiations concerning the goods will almost always take place between the prospective hirer and the dealer. At common law the dealer is not an agent of the finance company in respect of the statements made by him to the hirer, and it is therefore unlikely that any warranties and representations made by the dealer to the prospective hirer are incorporated in the subsequent hire-purchase agreement. The hirer may, however, sue the dealer on such a warranty and recover damages for the breach of it.[4]

Section 56 of the Consumer Credit Act 1974 now stipulates that any representation (which has a very wide meaning) made by a dealer who is a negotiator in antecedent negotiations prior to the making of a regulated hire-purchase agreement is deemed to be made by him in the capacity of agent for the creditor as well as in his actual capacity.

Sections 9 to 11 of the Supply of Goods (Implied Terms) Act 1973 import into every hire-purchase agreement certain implied terms that the goods are merchantable and fit for their purpose and correspond with their description and sample. These terms are implied regardless of the amount of credit provided and of the fact that the debtor is not an individual, in contrast to the various protections given to hirers under the Consumer Credit Act 1974.

Breach of any of these implied terms entitles the hirer to treat the hire-purchase agreement as repudiated and sue for damages for any loss or damage (including consequential loss) which he may have suffered as a result of the breach. He can do this even if he has accepted the goods. Thus the hirer must return the goods but can claim the return of all moneys paid by him together with the cost

3. Unfair Contract Terms Act 1977, s. 6(1)(b).
4. *Brown* v. *Sheen and Richmond Car Sales* [1950] 1 All E.R. 1102; *Andrews* v. *Hopkinson* [1957] 1 Q.B. 229.

of any repairs to the goods, less a reduction for the use of the goods during the period they were in his possession. If, on the other hand, breach of the agreement only amounts to a breach of warranty, or if the hirer wishes to keep the goods rather than return them, he may do so but he can then only obtain damages amounting to the cost of putting the goods into a proper state of repair together with damages for the loss of use while the repair work is being done.

These sections cannot be excluded as against "a person dealing as a consumer"[5] and in other cases can be excluded and modified only to the extent that the exclusion or modification is reasonable.[6] "Consumer" here must not be confused with the concept of a consumer under the Consumer Credit Act 1974. For the purposes of the 1977 Act a hirer will be a person "dealing as a consumer" if the owner makes the contract in the course of a business, the hirer does not, and does not hold himself out as doing so, and the goods are of a type ordinarily supplied for private use or consumption.[7] The onus of proving that the hirer did not deal as a consumer lies on the party so contending. Schedule 2 to the 1977 Act sets out guidelines to the court as to what is reasonable.

Duties of the hirer

The hirer must accept delivery of the goods hired and if he refuses to do so then the owner may recover the balance of the hire-purchase price less:

(a) the value of the goods;

(b) a discount in respect of the earlier return to the owner of his capital outlay (even if the capital is not paid immediately); and

(c) any option-to-purchase fee.

Default in payment of rentals does not necessarily amount to the repudiation of the agreement. The default must be such as to evince an intention not to be bound by the agreement.[8] Unless this intention can be shown then the owner's remedy is to sue for arrears of hire only.

The hirer is under a duty to take reasonable care of the goods but is not responsible for fair wear and tear unless there is an express term in the contract to that effect.[9] Similarly, there is no duty on a hirer to insure the goods unless the contract so stipulates.

5. Unfair Contract Terms Act 1977, s. 6(2)(b).
6. Ibid., s. 6(3).
7. Unfair Contract Terms Act 1977, s. 12(1).
8. *Contrast Financings* v. *Baldock* [1963] 2 Q.B. 104, and *Yeoman Credit* v. *Waragowski* [1961] 1 W.L.R. 1124.
9. *Blakemore* v. *Bristol & Exeter Ry.* (1858) 8 E. & B. 1035.

Termination and breach

The most common method by which a hire-purchase agreement is brought to an end is by performance, i.e. payment of all the moneys due under the agreement and the exercise by the hirer of his option to purchase. However, by definition the hirer has a right to terminate the agreement and return the goods, such a right being dependent upon the terms of the actual contract itself. The terms of a hire-purchase agreement almost always allow the owner to terminate the agreement or the hiring under it, but such a right usually arises only in the event of the breach of the agreement by the hirer or in the event of some other event happening which would prejudice the owner's position, such as the bankruptcy of the hirer or distress being levied against the goods.

A hire-purchase agreement can also be terminated if one party to it repudiates the agreement and the repudiation is accepted by the other. What constitutes repudiation of an agreement will depend on the facts of each case but it is now clear that if the hirer merely fails to pay some instalments then that will not be a repudiation; to be a repudiation the hirer's default must go to the root of the contract.[8]

At common law it is not necessary for the owner to give the hirer notice of default before he terminates the agreement or the hiring, unless the hire-purchase agreement stipulates that he must. If no notice is given particular care must be taken by an owner not to waive his rights; he may well be deemed to have done so if, for example, he accepts arrears of hire.[10] It would seem to be prudent practice to confirm termination in writing.

The owner's remedies

Once an owner has the right to immediate possession of the goods he may re-take possession of them, e.g. upon the breach of the agreement by the hirer. Unless there is any statutory restriction the owner can exercise this right to repossession without any reference to the court, but unless he is given a licence to do so the owner cannot enter onto the land of the hirer or of a third party in order to re-take possession of the goods. Normally, therefore, in a standard form hire-purchase agreement a licence is granted by the hirer to enable the owner to do this.

If, however, the hirer refuses permission for the goods to be re-taken then the owner has to resort to the court to recover them by an action in conversion.[11] Instead of specific delivery of the goods

10. *Keith Prowse & Co.* v. *National Telephone Co.* [1894] 2 Ch. 147; *Reynolds* v. *General and Finance Facilities* (1963) 107 Sol. J. 889.
11. Under the Torts (Interference with Goods) Act 1977 detinue has been abolished and the remedies previously available in detinue are now available in conversion.

damages may be claimed and the measure of damages will be the owner's interest in the goods. Usually this is the unpaid balance of the hire-purchase price or the value of the goods, whichever is less.

The owner's remedies upon the termination of the hire-purchase agreement are not restricted merely to the repossession of the goods; he may retain all moneys that have been paid by the hirer up to termination and also, as appropriate, recover any instalments that were in arrear and damages for breach of contract.

The amount that an owner can recover by way of damages depends on whether the breach of contract by the hirer amounts to repudiation. In other words, did the hirer evince an intention no longer to be bound by the agreement? If there had been a repudiation which has been accepted by the owner then the measure of damages recoverable will probably be calculated by deducting from the hire-purchase price of the goods the sum of the moneys already paid by the hirer, the value or resale price of the goods repossessed, the amount of the option fee and a discount in respect of the theoretical accelerated payment to the owner of his capital outlay.

If, on the other hand, breach by the hirer does not amount to repudiation then at best the owner can recover only the arrears of instalments up to the termination of the hiring (and, if the agreement permits, interest on those instalments) and the costs of repossession. Damages may also be claimed for any other breach of the agreement which was committed before the termination, e.g. failure to repair the goods.

The considerable variation between damages for repudiation and otherwise has meant that most standard hire-purchase agreements include what is called a "minimum payment clause", under which the owner endeavours to quantify in advance the loss he is likely to suffer in the event of a termination of the agreement prior to its contractual date as a result of a breach by the hirer. Such clauses attract very close scrutiny by the courts and unless it can be shown that the clause is, in fact, a genuine pre-estimate of the owner's loss it is more than likely that such a clause will be held to be a penalty, and the owner will be left to seek damages at common law.

The whole question of minimum payment clauses was considered by the House of Lords in the leading case of *Bridge* v. *Campbell Discount Co.*[12] It would seem from an analysis of that case that for a minimum payment clause to be valid the amount claimed under it must be expressed (*a*) not as a proportion of the hire-purchase price but in some other way, e.g. as a proportion of the cash price; (*b*) it should increase rather than decrease as the hiring

12. [1962] A.C. 600.

continues, as it is meant to compensate the owner for the depreciation in the goods; (*c*) it should not give the owner more than he would have obtained under the original contract, after giving credit for the repossessed goods; and finally (*d*) it should take into account the particular nature and condition of the goods that have been hired.

It is, however, also clear that the court will not consider a minimum-payment clause as a penalty clause unless it operates as a result of a breach of the terms of the agreement. If the clause comes into operation, not as a result of a breach, but because of the exercise of a right, say, by the hirer under the agreement, then the clause will be enforceable.

THE SCOPE OF THE CONSUMER CREDIT ACT 1974

Definition
The 1974 Act extends the definition of hire-purchase; it is now defined as

... an agreement, other than a conditional sale agreement, under which (*a*) goods are bailed in return for periodical payments by the person to whom they are bailed, and (*b*) the property in the goods will pass to that person if the terms of the agreement are complied with and one or more of the following occurs: (*i*) the exercise of an option to purchase by that person; (*ii*) the doing of any other specified act by any party to the agreement; (*iii*) the happening of any other specified event.[13]

It will be noted that the traditional definition of hire-purchase, namely, bailment plus an option, has now been extended by sub-paragraphs (*ii*) and (*iii*), and the scope of the Act is defined by reference to the amount of the credit extended to the hirer.[14] The Act therefore goes on to define how the amount of the credit can be ascertained for a hire purchase agreement; it is the total price of the goods less the deposit (if any) and the "total charge for credit".[15] If the amount of the credit under the hire-purchase agreement is £5,000 or less and it is made with an individual then the hire-purchase agreement falls within the Act and is a "regulated agreement" within the meaning of the Act.[16]

The provisions of the Act relating to the licensing and control of consumer credit businesses and the regulation of consumer credit

13. Section 189(1).
14. In the Act he is always called the "debtor", s. 189(1).
15. Section 9(3).
16. Section 8(2) and (3).

agreements apply to the business of letting goods on hire-purchase and to hire-purchase agreements.[17]

Before a person may commence any business in so far as it comprises or relates to the provision of credit under regulated consumer credit agreements or the bailment of goods under regulated consumer hire agreements, he must obtain a licence from the Director General of Fair Trading under s. 21 of the Act. Licences are, therefore, not required by businesses (a) which provide credit only in excess of £5,000 or which bail goods to hirers only in circumstances where the hirer must pay in excess of £5,000 by way of rentals, (b) which provide credit or hire only to companies, or (c) which provide credit or hire only under exempt agreements. If a person trades without a licence, not only does he attract criminal sanctions but any regulated agreements he enters into are unenforceable, although it is possible to apply for such an agreement to be legitimised by an order of the Director General of Fair Trading.[18]

Who is a consumer?

The Act seeks to strengthen and extend the protection given to the consumer. It should be noted, however, that the expression "consumer" is not directly defined, but by implication from the definitions of "consumer credit" and "consumer hire" agreements a consumer is an individual who enters into a personal credit agreement under which the credit does not exceed £5,000.[19] An individual is defined as including "a partnership or other unincorporated body of persons not consisting entirely of bodies corporate" with the result that it is not only the domestic consumer who receives the protection of the Act, but also sole traders, partnerships and the like. In other words, the fact that the credit is required for business purposes is irrelevant; it is the legal status of the debtor and the amount of credit which provide the basic criteria for protection by the Act.

THE SCHEME OF THE 1974 ACT

There follows an outline of some of the more noteworthy provisions of the Act which are applicable to hire-purchase agreements. The Act regulates four main areas:

(a) the information to be available to a debtor before he enters into an agreement and the responsibility of the creditor for that information;

17. Part III.
18. Section 40.
19. Section 8.

(*b*) the formalities surrounding the making of the agreement itself;

(*c*) the conduct of the creditor and debtor during the currency of the hire-purchase agreement; and

(*d*) default and the right to repossess goods.

Information to debtors

All advertisements[20] of hire-purchase facilities fall within the controls imposed by the Act unless the advertiser can bring the advertisement within the exemptions in s. 43(3) of the Act or in the regulations themselves.[21] The most important exemptions are those where the credit must exceed £5,000 and no land security is required,[22] those where the credit is available only to a body corporate[23] and an advertisement which "expressly or by implication indicates clearly" that the credit is to be provided "for the purpose of a person's business" but does not indicate that the creditor is willing to provide those facilities for consumers.[24]

The regulations themselves are detailed and complex and a careful study of them is necessary before any advertisement is issued in respect of hire-purchase business. There is also the overriding principle contained in s. 46 that it is an offence to convey information in an advertisement which is "false or misleading" in a "material respect".

The principle behind the regulations governing the contents of advertisements is that the consumer when shopping around for credit is able to obtain at least a minimum amount of information or a point of contact with a creditor where he can get that information. Thus since an "intermediate credit advertisement" need not include all the fundamental information, such as an annual percentage rate of charge, the creditor must include in the advertisement his name and either an address or a telephone number to which requests for a quotation can be directed, and also an "indication" that information in writing may be obtained about the terms on which the advertiser is prepared to do business.[25]

The Consumer Credit (Quotations) Regulations 1980 (S.I. 1980 No. 55) govern the information which must be given in a quotation and should be studied in detail.

The regulations apply to "any request made to a trader or credit broker by . . . the customer, or by a person acting on his behalf which"

20. Defined in s. 189(1).
21. The Consumer Credit (Advertisements) Regulations 1980 S.I. 1980 No. 54 and the Consumer Credit (Exempt Advertisements) Order 1980 S.I. 1980 No. 53.
22. Section 43(3)(*a*).
23. Section 43(3)(*b*).
24. The Consumer Credit (Exempt Advertisements) Order 1980 S.I. 1980 No. 53.
25. Ibid., Regulation 7.

is for a written quotation and which is either made in writing or made orally in the presence and on the premises of the trader or credit broker or is in effect made in response to an intermediate advertisement. There are exceptions to these general rules, the most important of which are where a quotation has been given within the previous 28 days, or where there is a full credit advertisement conspicuously displayed on the premises where the request is made. There is also no requirement to give a quotation to a minor.[26]

ENTRY INTO CREDIT AGREEMENTS

A hire-purchase agreement will not be "properly executed" unless such information as is specified by regulation is disclosed to the prospective debtor in the prescribed manner before an agreement is made.[27]

Section 56(1) defines antecedent negotiations to mean any negotiations conducted by the creditor in relation to any regulated agreement[28] or, in respect of a hire-purchase agreement, negotiations conducted by the dealer in relation to the goods sold or proposed to be sold by the dealer to the creditor before forming the subject matter of a hire-purchase agreement.[29] The person by whom these negotiations are conducted is called in the Act a "negotiator", and the negotiator is deemed to have conducted the negotiations in the capacity of agent for the creditor as well as his actual capacity. The creditor, therefore, will be liable for express misrepresentations by the dealer and representations given by him may become terms of the regulated agreement. This liability cannot be excluded.[30] It should also be noted that the negotiations are deemed to begin when the negotiator and debtor first enter into negotiations, e.g. through an advertisement, so that it is possible for negotiations to become binding on a creditor even though they took place before the creditor has been selected by the debtor.[31]

The agreement

Section 60(1) of the Act requires the Secretary of State to make regulations as to the form and content of hire-purchase agreements and those regulations must contain such provisions as appear to him appropriate with a view to ensuring that the debtor is made aware of (a) the rights and duties conferred or imposed upon him by

26. Ibid., Regulation 2(1).
27. Section 55.
28. Section 56(1)(a).
29. Section 56(1)(b).
30. Section 56(3).
31. Section 56(4).

the agreement, (b) the amount and rate of the total charge for credit, (c) the protection and remedies available to him under the Act, and (d) any other matters which in the opinion of the Secretary of State it is desirable for him to know about in connection with the agreement. The Act goes on to stipulate that an agreement will not be properly executed unless the document containing all the prescribed terms and conforming to the regulations under s. 60(1) is signed in the prescribed manner by the debtor, and by or on behalf of the creditor. Provision is also made for the supply of copies of the agreement, particularly in relation to those agreement which must contain cancellation rights.[32]

Cancellable agreements

The debtor sometimes has the right to a "cooling-off period", i.e. a period during which he can reconsider whether he wishes to proceed with the transaction. This right is given to offset the "hard sell" techniques of some door-to-door salesmen.

Nearly every regulated agreement is cancellable if the antecedent negotions included oral representations made in the presence of the debtor by an individual acting as, or on behalf of, the negotiator, unless, in effect, the agreement is signed at the business premises of the creditor, any party to a "linked transaction"[33] or the negotiator.[34] Thus any agreement signed after purely postal negotiations will not be cancellable.

If the agreement is cancellable the Act lays down a cooling-off period to enable the debtor to decide whether or not he wishes to proceed with the transaction. The period begins with the signing of the agreement by the debtor and ends at the end of the fifth day following the day on which the debtor receives the second copy of the executed agreement[35] or a notice under s. 64(1)(b). The cooling-off period will be fourteen days where regulations have dispensed with service of a further notice.[36]

There are detailed provisions dealing with the repayment of moneys to the debtor which have already been paid by him and the obligations on the debtor to restore goods to the person from whom he acquired possession[37] and the return of goods which have been taken in part exchange, e.g. a car.[38] Basically the debtor is entitled

---

32. Section 63.
33. For the meaning of "linked transactions" see s. 19(1).
34. Also excluded are certain agreements secured on land to finance the purchase of land. See also ss. 74 and 82(4).
35. Section 63(2).
36. Section 68(b).
37. Section 70.
38. Section 73.

to have his goods back within ten days of the cancellation or a sum allowed in part exchange.[39]

Early settlements

At common law a debtor does not have the right to settle a hire-purchase contract before the expiration of the contractual period and obtain title to the goods. He now has this right[40] and the Secretary of State is empowered to make regulations for the allowance of a rebate of charges to a debtor under a regulated consumer credit agreement.[41]

DURING THE AGREEMENT

Creditor's duty to give notice before certain action

One of the main planks of consumer protection built into the 1974 Act is that a creditor cannot take any action against a debtor in order to accelerate, enforce or terminate an agreement unless he serves a notice on the debtor in a prescribed form. Thus a creditor, if he wishes to enforce a term of a regulated agreement which falls within the provisions of s. 76(2), cannot

(*a*) demand earlier repayment of any sum, or

(*b*) recover possession of any goods, or

(*c*) treat any right conferred on the debtor by the agreement as terminated, restricted or deferred,

unless he has given the debtor not less than seven days' notice. The notice has a dual purpose in that it gives notice of the creditor's intention and enables the debtor to apply to the court for a time order.[42]

It should be noted that notice under s. 76 cannot be used to terminate an agreement. If the creditor wishes to terminate the agreement and there has been no default on the part of the debtor then the creditor must serve the appropriate notice under s. 98 of the Act. As under s. 76, the period of notice under s. 98 is seven days and the notice must be in the prescribed form.[43]

Default

On the other hand if a creditor wishes to take action as a result of the debtor's default then he must follow the procedure laid down by

39. Section 73(2) and (7)(*b*).
40. Section 94(1).
41. Section 95.
42. Section 129(1)(*b*).
43. Section 98(3).

s. 87. If, therefore, a creditor wishes to terminate the agreement, or enforce it in any other manner detailed in s. 87(1), he must serve a notice of default in accordance with s. 88. Unlike the notices provided for under ss. 76 and 98 the default notice must specify the nature of the alleged breach and, if the breach is capable of remedy, what action is required to remedy it and the date before which the action is to be taken. If, however, the breach is not capable of remedy then the creditor must state the sum required to be paid as compensation for the breach and the date before which it is to be paid. The dates referred to in the notice must be not less than seven days after the date of service of the default notice. It follows from all this that the debtor is then given an opportunity to put right his breach. If he does remedy it, then the breach is treated as not having occurred.[44]

Finally, where the notice is served under any of the above sections a copy of the notice must also be served by the creditor on any surety.[45]

Restrictions on the recovery of goods

The 1974 Act continues the protection given to a debtor which was first given in 1938, namely, the protection against an unjustified "snatch back" of the goods the subject matter of the agreement. The 1974 Act, in fact, follows very much the principle of the 1938 and subsequent Hire-Purchase Acts by imposing restrictions on the right to recover possession of goods where the debtor is in breach of a regulated hire-purchase agreement and has paid or tendered to the creditor one-third or more of the total price of the goods. When this situation arises the goods are known as "protected goods".[46] Once the goods have become protected goods the creditor cannot recover possession of them except on the order of the court unless the debtor himself has terminated or terminates the agreement. This restriction will not apply to the recovery of protected goods from a person other than a debtor, nor is there any contravention of the Act if at the time of recovery of possession the debtor consents to it.[47]

If protected goods are recovered from the debtor in breach of s. 90, the regulated agreement terminates, the debtor is released from all liability under the agreement, and is entitled to recover all moneys paid by him under the agreement.[48] Any security or any linked transaction is also avoided.[49]

44. Section 89.
45. Section 111(1).
46. Section 90(7).
47. Section 173(3).
48. Section 91.
49. Section 106 and 113(3)(b).

Restriction on right of entry
As an additional safeguard to the debtor the Act provides that the creditor is not entitled to enter any premises in order to repossess goods. This prohibition applies even though the goods are not protected goods within the meaning of the Act. This means that any licence taken by the creditor in the agreement itself which authorises the creditor to go on any premises to recover the goods is void.[50]

Debtors' rights to terminate agreement
The debtor may want to bring the hire-purchase agreement to an end. First, he can do this by consenting to the creditor's repossessing the goods.[51] Secondly, the Act gives the debtor the right to terminate the agreement at any time before the final payment falls due. A debtor may exercise this right by giving notice to any person who is entitled or authorised to receive the rentals under the agreement.[52]

Obviously upon termination of the agreement in this way the creditor is entitled to his goods back and the Act also makes provision for a monetary payment to the creditor in a statutory attempt to give him compensation for the depreciation of the goods. Upon termination, the debtor becomes liable to pay to the creditor the amount, if any, by which one-half of the total price[53] exceeds the aggregate of the sums paid and the sums due in respect of the total price immediately before the termination.[54]

However, this sum may be reduced when the matter comes before a court and the court is satisfied that a lesser sum would be equal to the loss sustained by the creditor. Additionally, if the debtor had "contravened an obligation to take reasonable care of the goods", then the court can increase the payment referred to above in order to recompense the creditor for the contravention.[55]

JUDICIAL CONTROL
As under previous hire-purchase legislation, the County Court has exclusive jurisdiction to hear and determine any action by the creditor to enforce a regulated agreement or any security or linked transaction relating to such an agreement.[56]

50. Section 173(1).
51. Section 173(3).
52. Section 99.
53. Section 189(1).
54. Section 100(1).
55. Section 100(4).
56. Section 141.

Enforcement orders

The Act stipulates that failure to follow certain of the procedures laid down by it means that the creditor must go to the court to obtain an order to rectify that failure. The order sought is an enforcement order and is required in particular in relation to hire-purchase if the agreement was "improperly executed".[57] Upon an application for such an order the court is to dismiss the application if, but only if, it considers it just to do so, having regard to the prejudice caused to any person by the breach and the degree of culpability for it. The court is also to have regard to its powers to impose conditions, or to suspend an order under s. 135, or to amend any agreement or security under s. 136. Additionally, even if the court permits enforcement, it has power to reduce or discharge any sum payable by the debtor so as to compensate him for any prejudice he may have suffered. The court has no power to make an enforcement order if an agreement in proper form was not signed by the debtor.

Time orders

The court is empowered to make what is called a "time order" in three different situations:

(a) on an application by the creditor for an enforcement order;

(b) on an application specially made by the debtor after service on him of a default notice or a notice under s. 76(1) or 98(1) (where an agreement is for a specified period and the creditor wishes to enforce early repayment or terminate the agreement in the absence of default); or

(c) in an action brought by a creditor to enforce a hire-purchase agreement or any security to recover possession of the goods to which the hire-purchase agreement relates.[58]

The court has power to make a time order to deal with sums which, although not payable by the debtor at the time the order is made, would, if the agreement continued in full, become payable under it subsequently. The court can, for example, order not only that the debtor be allowed time to pay off the arrears of rentals by instalments commensurate with his means, but also that his obligation to pay future instalments of rentals be rescheduled in a similar manner. If such an order is made then the debtor is to be treated as a bailee of the goods under the terms of the agreement, notwithstanding the agreement being terminated.

57. Section 111.
58. Section 129.

Protection orders

The court has power upon application by the creditor under a regulated agreement to make such an order as it thinks fit for the protection of any property of the creditor from damage or depreciation pending the outcome of court proceedings. Such an order may restrict or prohibit the use of the property or give directions as to its custody.[59]

Return orders and transfer orders

The court has special power in relation to regulated hire purchase agreements. On an application for an enforcement order or a time order, or in an action for repossession, the court may make an order for return of the goods to the creditor (a return order). Such an order can be either unconditional or suspended.[60] There appears, therefore, nothing to stop the court's combining a time order, made under s. 129, with a suspended order, whereby the goods could be ordered to be returned to the creditor but suspended upon condition that the debtor pays the unpaid balance of the total price by such instalments and at such times as the court provides under a time order.

Alternatively, in circumstances similar to those outlined above, the court, instead of making a return order, could make a transfer order which would have the effect of returning part of the goods to the creditor and allowing part of the goods to be retained by the debtor. How the goods are apportioned under such an order is entirely in the hands of the court, subject always to the provisions of s. 133(2) and (3).

If the debtor does not return the goods which are the subject matter of a return order or a transfer order then the court may revoke the order relating to the goods and order the debtor to pay the unpaid portion of such of the total price as is referable to those goods.[61]

It should be noted also that s. 134 provides that where goods are comprised in a regulated hire-purchase agreement and the creditor proves either that the default notice itself contained a demand for delivery up, or that a separate request in writing had been served on the consumer before the action seeking the surrender of the goods, then for the purposes of the claim the possession by the debtor of the goods shall be "deemed to be adverse" to the creditor.

Finally, s. 136 provides that the court may, if it thinks just, include in any order a provision for amending any agreement or security in consequence of a term of the order.

59. Section 131.
60. Section 135.
61. Section 133(6).

Extortionate credit bargains

Sections 136 to 140 deal with "extortionate credit bargains" and empower a court to reopen transactions in order to do justice between the parties. When considering these provisions two points must be noted carefully. First, the phrase "credit agreement" is not confined to regulated agreements or even consumer credit agreements; it extends to any agreement between an individual and any other person by which the creditor provides the debtor with credit of any amount. Secondly, the power of the court is not confined to any examination of the whole "credit bargain", i.e. it includes any other transactions which are to be taken into account with the credit agreement itself.

A credit bargain will be extortionate if it requires the debtor or a relative of his to make payments (whether unconditionally or on certain contingencies) which are grossly exorbitant, or which otherwise grossly contravene ordinary principles of fair dealing.[62] The Act goes on to lay down a number of guidelines to assist the court in determining whether a bargain is extortionate having regard to the evidence which is adduced.[63] Thus the court will have to have regard to any evidence which is placed before it as to the rate of interest which was current when the bargain was made, the age, business capacity and health of the debtor, together with the financial pressure which he was under at the time of the contract, the degree of risk accepted by the creditor and so on.

If a debtor or any surety alleges that a credit bargain is extortionate it is for the creditor to prove to the contrary. An application for a credit agreement to be reopened may be made by the debtor or a surety, although no court proceedings have previously been instituted by the creditor. Such an application may be made to the High Court or the County Court. A hire-purchase agreement may also be reopened at the instance of the debtor or a surety in any proceedings to which the debtor or creditor are party, being proceedings to enforce a hire-purchase agreement.

In reopening a hire-purchase agreement the court may, for the purpose of relieving the debtor or a surety from payment of any sum in excess of that fairly due and reasonable, make any of the orders set out in s. 139(2). It is important to appreciate that in making such an order the court may place a burden on the creditor despite the fact that the "advantage unfairly enjoyed" was enjoyed by someone else, i.e. under a linked agreement.

---

62. Section 138.
63. Section 138(2) to (5).

PART VII

THE BANKER AND INSOLVENCY

CHAPTER TWENTY-NINE

Winding up

MODES OF WINDING UP

A company incorporated under the Companies Acts terminates its career when it is either "wound up", during which process it is said to be "in liquidation", or removed from the register as a defunct company under s. 353 of the Act.[1]

Winding up may be either by the court or voluntary;[2] voluntary winding up is further sub-divided into members' voluntary winding up and creditors' voluntary winding up.

Voluntary winding up is the more common[3] and is consistent with the general policy of the Companies Acts, namely that shareholders should manage their own affairs, including the winding up of their company. Nevertheless, winding up is a matter governed wholly by statute law and since the Act and the rules made under the Act deal primarily with compulsory winding up, and then specify how voluntary winding up differs from compulsory winding up, we will deal first with compulsory winding up.

COMPULSORY WINDING UP

Grounds for winding up

Section 222 of the Act sets out six grounds on which the court may order the winding up of a company.

1. In this chapter, references to "The Act" are to the Companies Act 1948, references to sections are to sections of that Act, and references to "the Rules" or to "Rules" are to the Companies (Winding-up) Rules 1949 and the Rules contained therein.

2. Section 211. There is, as this section notes, a third category. Where a company has passed a resolution for voluntary winding up the court may make an order that the voluntary winding up shall continue, but subject to the supervision of the court (s. 311). Such orders are very rare, there being only one in the five year period from 1972 to 1976. It is possible, but again very rare, for an order to be made for compulsory winding up after a resolution has been passed for voluntary winding up.

3. In 1975 roughly 75 per cent of all liquidations were voluntary (4,100 members' and 3,250 creditors' out of 10,000).

(*a*) The company has by special resolution resolved that the company be wound up by the court.

(*b*) The company fails to obtain a certificate under s. 4 of the 1980 Act within a year of registration. (This applies to public companies only).[4]

(*c*) The company does not commence its business within a year from its incorporation, or suspends its business for a whole year.

(*d*) The number of members is reduced below two.[5]

(*e*) The company is unable to pay its debts.

(*f*) The court is of the opinion that it is just and equitable that the company should be wound up.

By far the most usual is inability to pay its debts. Section 223 of the Act specifies three cases in which a company is deemed to be unable to pay its debts.

(*a*) A creditor for a debt in excess of £200[6] has served written demand on the company by leaving it at the registered office of the company and the company has for three weeks thereafter neglected to pay the sum or secure or compound for it to the reasonable satisfaction of the creditor.

(*b*) An execution or other process for a judgment, decree or order of any court in favour of a creditor is returned unsatisfied in whole or in part (there is a similar ground relating to Scottish companies).

(*c*) It is proved to the satisfaction of the court that the company is unable to pay its debts. In this case the court must take into account contingent and prospective liabilities of the company.

The third of these is much the most common. The fact that a company, after repeated demands, does not pay a debt properly due affords strong evidence that the company is unable to pay its debts. A creditor should never attempt to use this procedure if there is a bona fide dispute as to the debt claimed, since in such case the court will dismiss the petition on the grounds that a winding-up petition is not the right procedure for enforcing such a claim.[7] If, however, there is no doubt that the company is indebted to the creditor and the only dispute is as to the amount, the court will, provided the greater part of the debt is undoubtedly due, make a winding-up order without requiring the precise amount of the debt to be quantified. If a petition to wind up is presented in relation to a debt which is the subject of a bona fide dispute, the petitioner

4. This ground was introduced by the Companies Act 1980, Sched. 3, para. 27. There are transitional provisions concerning "old public companies".
5. Companies Act 1980, Sched. 4.
6. The figure was increased from £50 to £200 by the Insolvency Act 1976, Sched. 1.
7. *Re London and Paris Banking Corporation* (1874) L.R. 19 Eq. 444; *Re Lympne Investments* [1972] 1 W.L.R. 523.

runs the risk of being sued for damages for malicious prosecution. In an entirely straight-forward case, e.g. indebtedness to a bank on a loan or overdraft, or a sale of goods, where there is no dispute about either the fact or the amount of the debt, there is not strictly any need for either a 21-day notice or repeated demands. One unambiguous demand will suffice for the presentation of a petition three or four days later, provided the demand makes it clear that failure to pay immediately will result in the presentation of a petition.

The next most common ground is the "just and equitable" ground. Winding-up orders have been made on the following grounds:

(a) that the sub-stratum of the company (the main object for which the company was formed) has gone or become impracticable;[8]

(b) that the company was formed for the purposes of fraud;[9]

(c) that there is a complete deadlock;[10]

(d) that the articles provided for a winding up on the occurrence of an event which has occurred;[11]

(e) that the petitioner was excluded from all participation in the business;[12]

(f) in the case of a small private company, that the company was in substance a partnership and the facts would justify the dissolution of a partnership.[13]

Even in such cases, the court is reluctant to make a winding-up order if there is any other remedy for the petitioner; such as an order that the other shareholders should buy out the petitioner's shareholding.

Who may petition for a winding up

Section 224 provides that a petition may be presented by:

(a) the company;

(b) any creditor;

(c) any contributory;[14]

(d) the Official Receiver (if the company is already being wound up voluntarily or subject to the supervision of the court);

---

8. *Re German Date Coffee Co.* (1882) 20 Ch. D. 169, *Re Haven Gold Co.* (1882) 20 Ch. D. 151.

9. *Re T.E. Brinsmead & Sons* [1897] 1 Ch. 406.

10. *Re Yenidje Tobacco Co.* [1916] 2 Ch. 426.

11. *Re American Pioneer Leather Co.* [1918] 1 Ch. 556.

12. *Thompson* v. *Drysdale*, 1925 S.C. 311; *Re Lundie Brothers* [1965] 1 W.L.R. 1051.

13. *Re Yenidje Tobacco Co. supra*; *Re Davis & Collett* [1935] Ch. 693.

14. This term is defined below.

(*e*) the Department of Trade;[15]

(*f*) the Attorney General in the case of charitable companies;

(*g*) the Bank of England in the case of a company which is a recognised bank or a licensed institution.[16]

It is rare for a company to petition for its own winding up, since it has only to pass a special or extraordinary resolution to do so.[17] Nevertheless, where directors of a public company wished to put the company into immediate liquidation, and avoid at least the initial expense and the delay of convening an extraordinary general meeting, this course was sometimes followed. The authority for this was considered somewhat dubious,[18] and it has now been held to be quite improper for the directors to petition without the authority of a resolution of the company,[19] and petitions by a company for its own winding up will now presumably become even rarer.

Petitions by contributories are rare. Since the Act provides a procedure for members to bring about a voluntary winding up, there are restrictions on the ability of a contributory to bring about a compulsory winding up. Contributories must make out a special case, which would usually be founded on the "just and equitable" ground, and in any event no contributory is entitled to present a petition unless either the number of members is reduced below the statutory minimum or he was the original allotee of the shares in question (or some of them) or he has held them and has been the registered shareholder for at least six months during the immediately preceding 18 months, or they devolved on him through the death of a former holder. This prevents a petitioner buying a few shares in the company with a view to presenting a petition immediately. In any event, a court is unlikely to make a winding-up order on a contributory's petition unless he shows that it is at least probable that there will be a substantial surplus of assets for distribution amongst the shareholders, otherwise he has no tangible interest in the winding up.[20] It follows that the evidence to support such a petition must be such as to establish in detail the basis of the case for relief.

Where a company's affairs are being conducted in a manner

15. Section 35(1) of the 1967 Act and Insurance Companies Act 1974, s. 46.

16. Banking Act 1979, s. 18(1), on any of the grounds specified in that sub-section.

17. An insurance company which carries on long term business (*see* Insurance Companies Act 1974 for the definition of this) may not be wound up voluntarily; Insurance Companies Act 1974, s. 47.

18. On the ground that the directors have power in the usual form of article (e.g. Table A, No. 80) to manage the business of the company, this does not include power to wind the company up without the authority of a resolution of the company. *See* Buckley *Companies Acts* (14th Edn.); Halsbury *Laws of England* (4th Edn.), Vol. 7, para. 1002.

19. *Re Emmadart* [1979] 1 All E.R. 599.

20. *See Re Chesterfield Catering Co.* [1976] 3 All E.R. 294.

oppressive to some part of the members and the facts would justify the making of a winding-up order on the "just and equitable" ground, but to make such an order would unfairly prejudice such part of the members, the court has power to make such order as it thinks fit, whether for regulating the conduct of the company's affairs in future, or for the purchase of any members' shares by any other members, or otherwise.[21] Petitions for winding up are sometimes presented with a view to obtaining relief in the form of such an order.

Mere mismanagement by the directors is not of itself a ground for a shareholder petitioning. His remedy in that case is to convene a meeting of the company.

Creditors are the most frequent petitioners. More or less any creditor is entitled to present a petition, however the debt arises and in whatever right he holds it, and a petitioning creditor who cannot obtain payment of a sum presently payable has prima facie an absolute right to an order. The only bar would be if a majority in value of the creditors wished otherwise, and in such a case the court has a discretion to refuse an order.

Procedure

The petition must be in the prescribed form, stating details such as the date of incorporation of the company, its registered office, the amount of its nominal and paid up capital, etc. and the ground on which the petition is founded, such as, for example, that the company is indebted to the petitioner in a specified sum, that he has made application for payment but without success, that the company is unable to pay its debts and that in the circumstances it is just and equitable that the company be wound up.

The petition is presented at the office of the Registrar of the Companies Court, and he appoints the time and place at which the petition is to be heard.[22] The petitioner must attend before the Registrar, at the time fixed by the Registrar at least two days before the date for the hearing of the petition, to satisfy the Registrar that the petition has been duly advertised, that the prescribed affidavit verifying the statements in the petition ("the statutory affidavit") and the affidavit of service have been duly filed, and that the provisions of the Winding-Up Rules with regard to petitions have been duly complied with.[23] The Rules provide for the statutory affidavit in support (on a petition by the company or a creditor) to be brief, stating merely that the statements in the petition relating

21. Section 210.
22. Rule 27.
23. Rule 33.

to his own acts and deeds are true and that he believes the other statements to be true.[24] This is to avoid the filing of long affidavits which turn out to be unnecessary. Where a corporation is the petitioner, the affidavit is made by some person who has been concerned in the matter on behalf of the corporation.

The petition must be served on the company, unless it is presented by the company itself.[25] It must also be advertised once in the *London Gazette* at least seven clear days after it has been served on the company and at least seven clear days before the hearing.[26] The advertisement must be in the prescribed form and contain details stating where any person who intends to appear at the hearing, whether to support or oppose, must send notice of such intention to the petitioner or his solicitor.[27]

An affidavit in opposition may be filed; such affidavits must be filed within fourteen days of the date of the filing of the statutory affidavit,[28] but as the petitioner has no obligation to serve with the petition a copy of the evidence in support, this must be obtained from the petitioner or any solicitors acting for him.

On the hearing of the petition, the court may dismiss it, may adjourn conditionally or unconditionally, or may make an interim order, or may make any other order it deems just.[29]

In recent years the practice has grown of seeking repeated and lengthy unopposed adjournments. A Practice Note has now been issued to the effect that the courts will be reluctant to grant long and repeated adjournments unless there are cogent grounds for the application, and that four weeks from the date of the first hearing ought to suffice to enable the creditor to decide whether to press for a winding-up order or to rely on other arrangements, and to enable the company to decide whether or not to promote a moratorium or other scheme of arrangement.[30]

If the court orders a winding up, the commencement of the winding up dates back to the presentation of the petition.[31] This differs markedly from a voluntary winding up where the commencement

24. Rule 30.
25. Rule 30.
26. Rule 28 (as amended by the Companies (Winding-up) (Amendment) Rules 1979, S.I. 1979 No. 209). In each case the reference to seven days means week days (excluding Saturdays); Rules of the Supreme Court, Order 3, rule 2(5); *Re Display Multiples* [1967] 1 All E.R. 685.
27. Rule 28 (as amended by the Companies (Winding-up) (Amendment) Rules 1979) *supra*.
28. Rule 36 (as amended by the Companies (Winding-up) (Amendment) Rules 1979 *supra*).
29. Section 225.
30. [1977] All E.R. 64.
31. Section 229(2).

dates from the passing of the resolution;[32] if a winding-up order is made after a voluntary winding up has commenced, the winding up commences from the passing of the resolution.[33]

Effect of winding-up order

The effect of the winding-up order is to avoid all dispositions of the property of the company made after the commencement of the winding up (i.e. made between the presentation of the petition and the winding-up order) unless the court otherwise directs.[34] The effect of this is that the company is unable to deal with its assets, e.g. by sale or by creating a charge in favour of a lender, once a petition has been presented.[35] If any such transaction is proposed, an application should be made to the court for an order which protects the transaction from being avoided under this section. In such cases an affidavit is sworn by a person having conduct of the transaction in question, stating the nature of the transaction and why it is in the interests of the company and its creditors generally that the transaction should be effected whilst the petition is outstanding, and specifying the dispositions to be protected. If the court considers that the proposed transaction is in the interests of the company and its creditors generally, the court will make an order to the effect that if a winding-up order is made on the petition, the specified dispositions will not be avoided under s. 227.

A winding-up order operates as a notice of discharge of the employment of servants and other agents of the company,[36] and the directors are similarly dismissed and their powers to act on behalf of the company cease. The liquidator may continue to employ servants where he continues the business after a winding up,[37] and in such cases it is open to the liquidator and the employees to agree to waive the effect of the notice. However, in order to sustain a case of waiver of notice the facts would have to be clear.[38] In appropriate cases there may be agreement that the employees will continue under a new contract in similar terms to the old, but this cannot occur where the business of the company has ceased and an analogous business is carried on by the liquidator during arrangements for reconstruction. In such cases the position is similar to that

32. Section 280.
33. Section 229(1).
34. Section 227.
35. For the effect of this on the company's bank account *see* below in this chapter.
36. *Re General Rolling Stock Co., Chapman's case* (1866) L.R. 1 Eq. 346.
37. *Re English Joint Stock Bank, ex parte Harding* (1867) L.R. 3 Eq. 341.
38. *Re Oriental Bank Corpn., MacDowall's case* (1886) 32 Ch. D. 366.

of any employee who continues to serve, and is paid, for a short period after the time when notice expires.[39]

Every invoice or order for goods or business letter issued by or on behalf of the company or the liquidator after the winding-up order must contain a statement that the company is in liquidation.[40]

The winding-up order usually contains provision for payment of costs to the petitioning creditor, the company (if it appears), and contributories and creditors who reasonably support the petition. The costs are directed to be paid in the first instance (subject always to any mortgages) out of the company's assets.

Appointment and duties of liquidator

It is often necessary for the company's business to be managed in some way between the presentation of the petition and the hearing. In such cases it is usual for the petitioner to apply to the court for the appointment of the Official Receiver as provisional liquidator.[41] The company or any interested creditor or contributory may also apply, but preferably after consultation with the senior Official Receiver so as to ascertain whether he is willing to act. He will need some information as to assets, for if he is appointed he may have to appoint agents and incur fees. The Official Receiver becomes, by virtue of his office, provisional liquidator when the winding-up order is made.[42]

When a provisional liquidator has been appointed he may, in appropriate circumstances, apply for the appointment of a fit and proper person as special manager, to take all steps necessary for the preservation of the assets on terms that his fees shall be fixed by the court. In such cases the application will set out the powers it is intended that the special manager should have.[43]

Within one month of the winding-up order, the Official Receiver is required to summon separate meetings of the creditors and contributories for the purpose of determining whether they desire a liquidator of their own choosing in place of the Official Receiver and whether there should be a committee of inspection.[44] The result of the two meetings is then reported to the court.[45]

Where there are available assets, it is usual for a major creditor or creditors to vote for the nomination of a particular person as liquidator. Even in these cases, the court has a discretion,

39. *Re Oriental Bank Corpn., MacDowall's case, supra.*
40. Section 338.
41. Rule 32(1).
42. Section 239(*a*).
43. Section 263 and Rule 50.
44. Section 239(1) and Rule 121.
45. Rule 58.

but if a majority in number and value are in favour of a particular person, the court will usually appoint him liquidator in place of the Official Receiver, with or without a committee of inspection. In many cases, however, there will not even be sufficient assets to cover the costs and the remuneration of the liquidator, and in such cases the position of liquidator usually remains with the Official Receiver.[46]

Any vacancy in the office of a liquidator appointed by the court is filled by the court.[47] If more than one liquidator is appointed the court declares whether any act which is authorised or required to be done is to be done by all or any one or more of them.[48]

Sections 252 and 253 contain the procedure for determining whether or not there should be a committee of inspection, and if so, its composition. It is customary to appoint as members of the committee either creditors or their duly authorised representatives.

VOLUNTARY WINDING UP

Commencement
By far the most frequent form of winding up is voluntary winding up. Section 278 provides for winding up by resolution of the shareholders. This may be:

(a) if the company resolves by special resolution that the company be wound up voluntarily;

(b) if the company resolves by extraordinary resolution to the effect that it cannot by reason of its liabilities continue its business, and that it is desirable to wind up; or

(c) much the rarest case is where a company is by its articles formed for a fixed period or the articles provide for it to be dissolved on the occurrence of a specified event; when the period expires or the event occurs the company may pass an ordinary resolution for voluntary winding up.

The commencement of the winding up in the case of a voluntary winding up is the passing of the winding-up resolution.[49]

Members' voluntary winding up
If a company is solvent and in a position to pay its debts in full within twelve months, the winding up may be a members' winding

46. In 1976 the Official Receiver was liquidator in over 75 per cent of all compulsory liquidations.
47. Section 242(3).
48. Section 242(4).
49. Section 280.

up. To qualify for a members' voluntary winding up, the directors, or a majority of them if there are more than two directors, must make a statutory declaration to the effect that they have made a full inquiry into the affairs of the company and that, having done so, they have formed the opinion that the company will be able to pay its debts in full within a specified period not exceeding twelve months from the commencement of the winding up. This declaration must be made within the five weeks immediately preceding the passing of the winding-up resolution, or on the same day, but before it is passed, and must be filed at the Companies Registry within fifteen days of the day on which the resolution is passed. It must also embody a statement of the company's assets and liabilities as at the latest practicable date before the making of the declaration.[50]

Such a declaration should only be made with the greatest of caution and after very careful consideration of all the liabilities and the realisable value of the assets, since if any director makes a declaration under this section without having reasonable grounds, he may be prosecuted and, if convicted, either fined or convicted or both. Moreover, if a company is wound up in pursuance of a resolution passed after the making of such a declaration and the company's debts are not paid or provided for in full within the specified period, it is presumed until the contrary is shown that the directors did not have reasonable grounds for their opinion.[51]

The essential difference between a members', or solvent, winding up and creditors', or insolvent, winding up, is that control rests in the former with the members and in the latter with the creditors.

In a members' voluntary winding up, the company in general meeting appoints one or more liquidators and on the appointment of a liquidator all the powers of the directors cease except so far as the company in general meeting or the liquidator sanctions the continuance of those powers.[52] There is power to fill any vacancy in the office of liquidator, whether the vacancy arises by death, resignation or otherwise. This power is exercisable subject to any arrangements with the creditors of the company.[53]

If in a members' voluntary winding up the liquidator forms the opinion that the company will not be able to pay its debts in full within the period stated in the declaration, he must summon a meeting of creditors and lay before the meeting the statement of the assets and liabilities of the company.[54] The liquidation then

50. Section 283(1) and (2) as amended by the Companies Act 1981, s. 105(1).
51. Section 283(3).
52. Section 285.
53. Section 285.
54. Section 288.

continues in most respects as a creditors' voluntary winding up,[55] but in this case the creditors have no say in the appointment of the liquidator, and there is no provision for the appointment of a committee of inspection.

The liquidator is bound to summon a general meeting of the company at the end of the first year from the commencement of the winding up and at the end of each succeeding year, and as soon as the affairs of the company are fully wound up he prepares an account and calls a general meeting of the company to lay such account before the company. The meeting is called by advertisement in the *London Gazette*, and within a week after the meeting the liquidator must file a copy of the account at the Companies Registry and send in a return of the holding of the meeting.[56]

Creditors' voluntary winding up
If no such statutory declaration is made, the winding up will be a creditors' voluntary winding up.[57] In such a case, a meeting of the creditors of the company is convened, either for the day on which the meeting of members to pass the extraordinary resolution is convened, or for the following day, and the notices of the meeting of creditors must be sent simultaneously with the sending of the notices of the meeting of members.[58]

Special and extraordinary resolutions are resolutions passed by a majority of 75 per cent or more of the votes cast, where the notice convening the meeting specifies that they were to be proposed as special or extraordinary resolutions as the case may be. A special resolution requires 21 days' notice, but no particular period of notice is required for an extraordinary resolution, unless otherwise specified in the articles. Since the minimum period of notice for any general meeting is fourteen days, it is usual for a meeting convened to pass an extraordinary resolution to be convened on not less than fourteen days' notice. Any resolution can, of course, be passed with less than the statutory minimum period of notice if the requisite number of members agree (usually a majority in number holding at least 95 per cent of the voting rights),[59] but a minimum of seven days' notice is now required in any event.[59A]

The creditors' meeting is normally convened to follow immediately after the members' meeting, and in view of the need to send notice of the meeting to all creditors, it is usual for the meeting to be

55. *See* below.
56. Sections 289 and 290.
57. Section 283(4).
58. Section 293.
59. Sections 133(3) and 141(2).
59A. Companies Act 1981 s. 106(1).

convened on somewhat more than fourteen days' notice. If it is essential to act quickly, and sufficient members consent to short notice, it may be possible to put the company into liquidation immediately and to convene a creditors' meeting some weeks later to confirm the appointment of the liquidator or appoint another.[60] This artificial procedure is technically a breach of s. 293 of the Act, under which the creditors' meeting is required to be held on the same day as or the day following the members' meeting, but so far as is known default fines have never been imposed in such cases.

Notice of the creditors' meeting is to be advertised once in the *London Gazette* and at least once in two local newspapers circulating in the district where the company has its registered office or principal place of business.[61] At the meeting the directors of the company must cause a full statement of the position of the company's affairs, together with a list of the creditors and the estimated amount of their claims, to be laid before the creditors. The directors choose one of their number to preside at the creditors' meeting and it is his duty to attend and preside at the meeting.[62]

The company and the creditors may each nominate a person (or more than one person) to be liquidator. The person(s) appointed by the members will be the liquidator unless a majority in number and in value of the creditors appoint some other person(s), in which case the person(s) so appointed by the creditors will be the liquidator.[68]

The company has the right to appoint a committee of inspection, but in practice the committee is usually appointed by the creditors; it usually consists of not more than five persons.[64] The general function of the committee of inspection is to assist the conduct of the liquidation, and the liquidation is actually conducted by the liquidator subject to the general directions of the committee of inspection. Thus, he would obtain their sanction before compromising any action, and in any other matters where a policy decision is required, he should obtain their approval. The committee of inspection may fix the remuneration of the liquidator. If there is no such committee the creditors fix the remuneration. On the appointment of the liquidator all the powers of the directors cease except so far as the committee of inspection (or the creditors, if there is no committee) sanction their continuance. If a vacancy occurs in the office of liquidator the creditors may fill the vacancy.[65]

60. *See Re Centrebind* [1966] 3 All E.R. 889.
61. Section 293(2).
62. Section 293(3).
63. Section 294, Rule 134, and *Re Caston Cushioning* [1955] 1 All E.R. 508.
64. Section 295.
65. Section 297.

The liquidator is required to summon meetings of the company and of the creditors at the end of the first year from the commencement of the winding up and at the end of each succeeding year, and he lays before the meetings a general account of his acts and dealings during the preceding year. The difference here from a members' voluntary winding up is that in a creditors' voluntary winding up, meetings of creditors must be held as well as meetings of members.[66]

A meeting may not act (except for the election of a chairman, proving debts, and adjournment of the meeting) unless there are present or represented at least three creditors entitled to vote, or all the creditors entitled to vote if less than three. If within half an hour a quorum is not present, the meeting must be adjourned to the same day in the following week at the same time and place or to such other day, time and place as the chairman may appoint, between 7 and 21 days from the day from which the meeting was adjourned.[67] A resolution is deemed to be passed when a majority in number and value of the creditors present personally or by proxy and voting on the resolution have voted in favour.[68]

Effect of commencement of voluntary winding up

Unlike a compulsory winding up, where the order operates as a dismissal of the company's employees,[69] a resolution for voluntary winding up does not of itself constitute a dismissal of the employees of the company, but the circumstances of the company may mean that a voluntary winding up involves a termination of the employment or constitutes a repudiation by the company of an agreement, e.g. to appoint an agent for a long period of years.[70] In another case[71] in a members' winding up, it was held that the circumstances of that case were such that liquidation did not dissolve an employee's contract with the company. It depends on the circumstances of each case. Liquidation does not of itself amount to a termination or breach, but may, coupled with other circumstances, amount to such a breach as would entitle the other party to decline to perform, or to claim damages for breach.

Whether the liquidator is entitled to assign contracts will depend upon the circumstances. Cases involving personal performance by the company may be incapable of being assigned.

66. Section 299.
67. Rule 138.
68. Rule 134.
69. *Re General Rolling Stock Co., Chapman's case* (1866) L.R. 1 Eq. 346.
70. See *Midland Counties District Bank* v. *Attwood* [1905] 1 Ch. 357; *Fowks* v. *Commercial Timber Co.* [1930] 2 K.B. 1.
71. *Gerard* v. *Worth of Paris* [1936] 2 All E.R. 905.

POWERS OF LIQUIDATOR

The general duties of the liquidator are to take possession of and protect the assets, and make out the appropriate lists of contributories[72] and creditors, to have disputed cases adjudicated upon, to realise the assets, subject to the control of the committee of inspection in certain matters, and to apply the proceeds in payment of the company's debts and liabilities in the prescribed order of priority. Any surplus is divided amongst the contributories according to their rights and interests in the company under the articles, unless the memorandum of association provides that any income and property of the company are to be applied solely towards the promotion of its objects and that no portion thereof must be transferred to the members of the company. Before making any distribution to contributories the liquidator must make every attempt to satisfy himself that all creditors have been paid. In an insolvent liquidation the sums paid to creditors are usually referred to as "dividends".

The property of the company does not vest in the liquidator, unless the court makes an order vesting it in him,[73] and any proceedings are normally taken by the liquidator in the name of the company. (Sometimes they have to be taken by the liquidator in his own name, e.g. to invalidate a charge which, if not registered, is void against the liquidator.)[74] Thus all conveyances and contracts should be in the name of the company, not the liquidator personally, and deeds will be sealed with the seal of the company, not the liquidator's own seal, though the company's seal will be affixed in the presence of the liquidator rather than of the directors.

Section 245 states a number of specific powers of the liquidator in a compulsory winding up. Some require the sanction of either the court or the committee of inspection; in this category come bringing or defending any action or other legal proceeding, carrying on the business of the company so far as is necessary for the beneficial winding up, the appointment of solicitors, the payment of any class of creditors in full, making any compromise or arrangement with creditors and compromising any claims by the company against third parties, or other questions relating to or affecting the assets or the winding up of the company. Others may be exercised without this consent, such as selling the property of the company, executing deeds and using the company's seal, proving as a creditor against other companies or persons, drawing cheques, bills of exchange or promissory notes in the name of the company, raising money on the

72. This term is defined below.
73. Section 244.
74. *Independent Automatic Sales* v. *Knowles & Foster* [1962] 3 All E.R. 27.

security of the assets of the company and appointing agents to do any business which he is unable to do himself.

In a compulsory winding up, the liquidator must pay all moneys received into the Insolvency Services Account at the Bank of England, unless the Department of Trade authorises him to have an account at such other bank as the committee of inspection may select.[75]

In a voluntary winding up, the liquidator may, without the sanction of the court, exercise all the powers given by the Act to a liquidator in a compulsory winding up. Whilst the liquidator can appoint an agent to do any business which he cannot do himself, he cannot delegate his powers generally, and joint liquidators cannot delegate their powers generally to one of themselves, even if they all concur in making the delegation. If more than one liquidator is appointed, any power given by the Act to all of them may, if they so determine at the time of their appointment, be exercised by such one or all of them as they so determine, or in default of such determination, by any number not less than two.[76] If one of two liquidators dies, the survivor cannot act until a new liquidator is appointed.[77]

In a voluntary winding up, the liquidator has power, without the sanction of the court, to carry on the business of the company, but *only so far as it may be necessary for the beneficial winding up.* If the liquidator proposes to carry on business for any considerable length of time, he should obtain the approval of either the court or the company in a solvent liquidation, or the committee of inspection or the creditors in the case of an insolvent winding up. If application is made to the court, the court usually limits the period to three or six months. Debts and liabilities incurred in properly carrying on the business, including the liquidator's remuneration, rank in priority to the unsecured debts and liabilities of the company. The liquidator should be careful to contract in the name of the company, not in his own name.

Neither the liquidator nor any member of the committee of inspection is allowed to make any direct or indirect personal profit out of any transaction carried out by the liquidator.

COSTS, EXPENSES AND LIQUIDATOR'S REMUNERATION

In a compulsory winding up, the court may make an order as to the

---

75. Section 248(1) as amended by the Insolvency Act 1976, s. 3. *See also* Chapter Thirty for the corresponding provisions in bankruptcy.
76. Section 303(3).
77. *Re Metropolitan Bank and Jones* (1876) 2 Ch. 366.

payment out of the assets of the costs, charges and expenses incurred in the winding up in such order of priority as the court thinks just.[78] In a voluntary winding up, all costs, charges and expenses properly incurred in the winding up, including the remuneration of the liquidator, are payable out of the assets of the company in priority to all other claims.[79] Thus the general rule is that the assets of the company are to be applied (subject, of course, to any mortgages on the assets) first in paying the costs and expenses of the winding up, and then in paying the liquidator's remuneration. The costs and expenses of the winding up include liabilities to tax, even if incurred in the course of a receivership.[80]

A solicitor's claim for costs incurred before the winding up is an unsecured claim in the liquidation; the court has jurisdiction to make an order for taxation of the costs. If a solicitor has a valid lien on a document belonging to a company before the winding up, the lien will not be defeated by the winding up, but he may be required to deliver up documents acquired in the course of the winding up. Costs incurred in connection with the meetings for voluntary liquidation and the expense of advertising are not costs, charges and expenses incurred in the winding up, but when an order for compulsory winding up is made, the costs of the company on the petition are usually ordered to be taxed and paid out of the assets.

The costs of the solicitor employed by the liquidator are part of the costs, charges and expenses properly incurred in the winding up, and these, together with the remuneration of the liquidator, are payable out of the assets in priority to all other claims.[81] This priority does not confer priority over mortgagees or others holding a specific charge on assets, except so far as the liquidator has incurred costs in realising or preserving securities of which the mortgagees have had the benefit.

DEBTS AND CLAIMS AND PROOF OF DEBTS

Section 316 provides that all debts payable on a contingency and all claims against the company, present or future, certain or contingent, ascertained or sounding only in damages, are to be admitted to proof against the company. In the case of an insolvent company, the rules

78. Section 267.
79. Section 309.
80. *Re Beni-Felkai Mining Company* [1934] Ch. 406; [1933] All E.R. Rep. 693; *Re Barleycorn Enterprises* [1970] 2 All E.R. 155.
81. Section 209, in a voluntary winding up; in a compulsory winding up, the court fixes the order or priority as it thinks just (s. 267) and it normally follows the same order as in a voluntary winding up.

concerning the respective rights of secured and unsecured creditors, debts provable and the valuation of certain assets and liabilities applicable in bankruptcy apply to the winding up of a company.[82]

As soon as possible after his appointment, the liquidator should fix a day by which creditors are to prove their debts or claims and to establish any title to priority under s. 319. He should advertise a notice to creditors to send in their claims in such newspaper as he considers convenient. It is advisable to advertise in newspapers circulating in the district where the company carried on business, and in the *London Gazette*. Rule 106 provides for at least fourteen days' notice. In addition to advertising, the liquidator must send a similar notice to the last known address or place of abode of each creditor shown in the company's books, and of every person who, to the knowledge of the liquidator, claims to be an ordinary or preferential creditor and whose claim the liquidator has not admitted. Notice should also be given to persons whose claims are contingent only, persons who the liquidator knows claim to be creditors and persons who the liquidator knows may have claims or might wish to claim to be creditors.

The practice in voluntary liquidation has for some time been for the liquidator to ask for claims only in the first instance with an intimation that, if required by subsequent notice, the debts will be proved formally. In a compulsory winding up debts formerly had to be proved by affidavit. The Winding-Up Rules now provide that the Official Receiver or the liquidator, if one has been appointed, may require an affidavit verifying the debt, but unless he does a debt may be proved by an unsworn claim.[83]

A creditor may prove for a debt not payable at the date of the winding-up order or resolution as if it were presently payable, and may receive dividends equally with the other creditors, but he must make a deduction for interest at the rate of 5 per cent per annum from the declaration of a dividend to the time when the debt would have become payable according to the terms on which it was contracted.[84]

The liquidator is required to examine every proof of debt and claim to priority, and the grounds, and in writing either admit or reject it in whole or in part, or require further evidence.[85] The liquidator must make certain that all debts are properly due before he admits them, and must put forward any available defences. If he improperly admits a claim, he may be ordered personally to refund

82. Section 317.
83. Companies (Winding-up) (Amendment No. 2) Rules 1977, S.I. 1977 No. 1395.
84. Rule 101.
85. Rule 107.

the money paid in respect of that claim, together with interest. If the liquidator is not absolutely certain as to the admissibility of a claim, he should call for formal proof by affidavit and, on receipt, if necessary, give notice of rejection to the creditor, stating the grounds of the rejection.

A creditor or contributory dissatisfied with the decision of the liquidator in respect of a proof may apply to the court for the decision to be reversed or varied.[86] He is not entitled to bring an action against the company; his remedy is to apply to the court.[87] In a compulsory winding up, notice of any such application must be given within 21 days from the date of service of notice of rejection, but this time limit does not apply in a voluntary winding up. Even if a creditor does not take active steps to re-assert his claim, the liquidator will not be safe in distributing the assets without applying to the court unless the creditor withdraws his claim. Rule 106, which provides a mechanism for the liquidator to give notice to creditors to prove or be excluded, does not state that if a creditor does not prove, he is in fact excluded. The liquidator may apply to the court to fix a time within which creditors must prove or else be excluded from the benefit of any distribution made before their debts are proved,[88] and if a liquidator wishes definitely to exclude creditors who neglect to prove, he must obtain an order to that effect.[89]

A liquidator must not pay debts which have become statute-barred by the time of the commencement of the winding up, though he may do so if the company is solvent and all the contributories approve.[90] In a compulsory winding up, time ceases to run against the creditor when the winding-up order is made, since after the winding-up order no action can be commenced against the company except with the leave of the court.[91]

The bankruptcy rule against double proof also applies in the winding up of companies. If, therefore, a creditor who has a guarantee of the company's debt and has proved and received dividends in the winding up, is then paid the balance of the debt by the guarantor under the guarantee, the guarantor cannot prove for the same debt. To do so would be to allow a double proof.[92]

86. Rule 108.
87. *Craven* v. *Blackpool Greyhound Stadium and Racecourse* [1936] 3 All E.R. 513.
88. Section 264.
89. Sections 264 and 307.
90. *Re Fleetwood etc. Syndicate* [1915] 1 Ch. 486.
91. *Re General Rolling Stock Co., Joint Stock Discount Co.'s claim* (1872) 7 Ch. App. 646.
92. *Re Moss, ex parte Hallett* [1905] 2 K.B. 307.

If the creditor has not proved, the guarantor may prove even if he has not yet paid the principal debt,[93] but he may not do so if there is a possibility of double proof.[94]

INTEREST

Where a debt carries interest, interest is provable only up to the commencement of the winding up, unless there is a surplus of assets over liabilities.[95] Secured creditors may, of course, look to their security for payment of the interest, and if the liquidator elects to redeem the security, he can do so only on payment of the principal and interest (including interest incurred after the commencement of the winding up) if the security is sufficient to cover the interest.[96] However, if the creditor has exhausted his security and the debt is still unsatisfied, he cannot apply the proceeds of the security first in payment of interest accrued subsequent to the winding up. If he proves at all, his proof must be limited to principal and interest at the commencement of the winding up, less the proceeds of sale of the security.

Where a creditor is proving for a debt which includes interest, he is, for dividend purposes, restricted in the first instance to interest at the rate of 5 per cent per annum, until all other debts have been paid.[97] From a banker's point of view, this means that on a fixed loan account where the interest has not been paid, he is restricted to interest at 5 per cent per annum for the period from the last interest payment until the commencement of the liquidation. On a running account, where there have been both debits and credits in the three years before the commencement of the liquidation, payments in may have to be apportioned as between interest at the contractual rate and principal in the proportions which interest and principal bear to each other.

Interest at the rate of 5 per cent per annum is then calculated on the daily principal balances thrown up by such allocations, and if that interest figure exceeds the amounts so allocated to interest, the excess ranks for dividends and the remaining interest is postponed. If interest at 5 per cent per annum is less than the amount so credited, the whole of the remaining interest is postponed for dividend

93. *Re Herepath & Delmar, ex parte Delmar* (1890) T.L.R. 280.
94. *Re Parrott, ex parte Whittaker* (1891) 63 L.T. 777.
95. *Re Humber Ironworks Co., Warrant Finance Co.'s case* (1869) 4 Ch. App. 643.
96. *Re Humber Ironworks Co., Warrant Finance Co.'s case* (*No. 2*) (1869) 5 Ch. App. 88.
97. Bankruptcy Act 1914, s. 66(1).

purposes.[98] In making the apportionment calculations, interest will be charged on different figures from the figures used in the bank statements because it will be charged on the revised figures, not on the debit balance on the account while it was a "live" account.

If a payment is made which, on ordinary accounting principles, would be treated as interest, it is counted as interest and not apportioned, e.g. a payment in, on or very shortly after the due date for interest, of the exact amount of the interest. However, as the apportionment rule applies notwithstanding any agreement to the contrary, where a loan is repaid by equal instalments comprising mixed interest and principal, each payment must be apportioned on the principles mentioned above. In determining what interest is unpaid, interest should not be treated as having been paid merely because it is debited to the account.

Secured creditors, if they wish to prove at all, are subject to the same restrictions. A secured creditor may look to his security alone, but if he wishes to prove at all, his proof must, for interest purposes, be calculated in the same way as an unsecured creditor's, and realisations must be apportioned in the same manner. He cannot apply realisations first to interest at the full contractual rate, and any balance to principal, and then claim dividends on the shortfall of principal.

Under Rule 100, if a debt is overdue at the commencement of the winding up and is payable by virtue of a written instrument at a certain time, the creditor may prove for interest from that time up to the commencement of the winding up at the rate of 4 per cent per annum, even if the instrument does not provide for interest. If it is not payable under a written instrument, he may prove for interest from the time when a demand in writing has been made giving notice that interest will be claimed from the date of demand until payment.

THE COMPANY'S BANKING ACCOUNT

As soon as the banker receives notice of the commencement of a winding up, whether voluntary or compulsory, he should immediately suspend all operations on the account. Apart from direct notice to the bank, various advertisements are required in the *London Gazette* and sometimes in one or more local newspapers. The bank is likely to discover the fact from one of these sources even if it does not receive express notice of the meeting as a creditor (if the company's account is overdrawn).

In the case of a voluntary winding up, cheques paid before notice

98. Bankruptcy Act 1914, s. 66(2).

of the winding up first came to the banker's knowledge would probably be allowed. The position is, however, different in the case of a compulsory winding up, since any disposition of the company's property made after the commencement of the winding up is void, unless the court otherwise orders, and it will be recalled that the commencement of the winding up is in this case the date of the presentation of the petition.[99]

Great care should therefore be exercised when dealing with a company in financial difficulties. It is likely that the court would sanction the payment of cheques made by the banker between the presentation of the petition and the date when the banker received notice of this. Even after such notice, it appears that a banker may, if and to the extent that the company's account is in credit (which must be rare in the case of petitions for winding up by the court), pay to the company, against the receipt of an authorised official, amounts standing to the company's credit, because payment to a company of a debt owing to it is not a "disposition" of the company's property.[100]

Cheques in favour of third parties, however, should be treated with great caution. One of the clearing banks allows a company to continue to operate its account, provided that the cheques are drawn in the ordinary course of business, on the ground that if a liquidator challenged the payments, they would be sanctioned by the court as being for the benefit of the creditors of the company. It does, however, seem hard to understand why a bank should be willing to incur this risk, since if this results in any pre-liquidation creditors being paid in full, the bank may have to make good the loss incurred by the creditors generally.[101] There is a recognised procedure under which the company may apply to the court for an order which could include sanction for the payment of cheques. The court has jurisdiction to make such an order between the presentation and the hearing of the petition.[102] and in recent years this procedure has become more frequent.[103] Otherwise a banker should decline to pay cheques until the petition has been heard, returning them in the meantime marked "Refer to drawer; winding-up petition presented".

LANDLORDS

Where rent due from a company is in arrears, the landlord is neither a secured nor a preferential creditor, but he has a right of

99. Section 229(2).
100. *Mersey Steel and Iron Co.* v. *Naylor* (1884) 9 App. Cas. 434.
101. *Re Gray's Inn Constructions Co.* [1980] 1 All E.R. 814.
102. *Re A.I. Levy (Holdings) Limited* [1964] Ch. 19; [1963] 2 All E.R. 556.
103. On average there was about one per week in 1978.

distress.[104] In a compulsory winding up, if a landlord or other person has distrained on goods or effects of the company during the three months immediately before the winding-up order, the preferential creditors under s. 319 have a first charge on the goods or effects so distrained on or the proceeds of sale, but if any money is paid under such charge, the landlord or other person has the same rights of priority as the preferential creditor to whom the payment is made.[105] In a voluntary winding up, if a landlord levies distress before the resolution to wind up, such distress will usually be allowed to proceed unless there are special reasons rendering this course inequitable, even if the distress is not completed by sale before the commencement of the winding up.

If the liquidator retains possession of the premises for the purpose of carrying on the company's business, or keeps the property in order to sell, the liquidator must pay rent accruing after the commencement of the liquidation in full, even if he does not subsequently assign.

If the lease contains a provision for re-entry on non-payment of rent, a landlord may retake possession without bringing an action for recovery of the property if he can do so peaceably, but if he does the liquidator can, on payment of the arrears, apply to the court for relief against forfeiture, provided that he does so within six months of resumption of possession by the landlord.[106]

The landlord may also, if the lease contains a power of re-entry (i.e. a power for the landlord to forfeit the lease for non-payment of rent or breach of some other covenant or on liquidation of the lessee), apply to the court for liberty to re-enter. If so, the court will grant him liberty to do so without his having to bring an action for the rent, and if the lease is of greater value than the rent due, this will in effect compel payment of the rent. Section 146(10) of the Law of Property Act 1925, however, restricts the right of the landlord to exercise this right of re-entry and gives the tenant a right to apply for relief within one year from the commencement of the liquidation. Moreover, any underlessee (including a mortgagee) is entitled to apply for relief, and this will normally be granted if the underlessee or mortgagee accepts liability for all the obligations, including the rent, under the lease. Thus landlords rarely apply for liberty to re-enter where there is a mortgagee who is paying the rent, or if the liquidator himself is continuing to pay the rent.[107]

104. *See* Chapter Fifteen.
105. Section 319(7).
106. *Howard* v. *Fanshawe* [1895] 2 Ch. 581. *See also* Chapter Fifteen.
107. There are some exceptional cases to which s. 146(10) does not apply, the main exceptions being agricultural land and licensed premises, or any case where the personal qualifications of the tenant are important. In these cases there is no right to relief under s. 146 if re-entry is sought on the grounds of the insolvency alone.

If the landlord is willing, the lease may be determined and he may be allowed to prove for the loss sustained by him.

Disclaimer

If the assets of the company include property, such as land, burdened with onerous covenants, shares or other assets with liabilities attached to them, unprofitable contracts, or other property which is either unsaleable or not readily saleable but which will require the expenditure of money to keep the asset in being, the liquidator may apply to the court for leave to disclaim the property.[108] This happens most frequently with leases, but may apply to other sorts of property. He may apply even if he has endeavoured to sell or take possession of the property, provided he makes such application within twelve months after the commencement of the winding up, or such extended period as may be allowed by the court. This time limit may be further extended if the property does not come to the knowledge of the liquidator within one month after the commencement of the winding up; he will then be given twelve months from the date when he becomes aware of the property. Before or on granting leave to disclaim, the court may require notices to be given to persons interested, and may impose terms.

Persons interested in the property may not be willing to wait for twelve months from the commencement of the liquidation. The section gives them the right to apply in writing to the liquidator requiring him to decide whether he will or will not disclaim. The liquidator must then give notice to the applicant within 28 days after receipt of the notice saying that he intends to apply to the court for leave to disclaim. If he does not give such notice, he is barred from applying for disclaimer and in the case of contracts he is deemed to have adopted the contract.[109]

If the court does allow the liquidator to disclaim, the disclaimer operates to determine, as from the date of disclaimer, the rights, interest and liabilities of the company and all title of the company to the property concerned. It does not, however, affect the rights or liabilities of any other person, except so far as is necessary for the purpose of releasing the company and the property concerned from liability.[110]

A disclaimer of a lease immediately gives the landlord the right to claim damages for all loss. This will include a capital sum representing the rent for the whole of the unexpired portion of the lease, together with any costs incurred in reletting. The landlord

108. Section 323.
109. Section 323(4).
110. Section 323(2).

will, however, be subject to the general duty to mitigate his loss, and must make a reasonable endeavour to relet the property. If he succeeds in reletting, he will only be entitled to damages for loss of rent for the period during which the property remained unlet, the costs of reletting, and any other actual loss; if he is able to let at an increased rent, this will further mitigate his loss.

Where property is subject to a mortgage, an underlessee or mortgagee may apply to the court for an order vesting the property in him, provided that he undertakes liability for all the obligations to which the company was subject in respect of the property at the commencement of the winding up.

SECURED CREDITORS

A secured creditor is a creditor who has some mortgage, charge or lien on the company's property. He has various options:

(*a*) he may rest on his security and not prove;

(*b*) he may realise his security and prove for the deficiency;

(*c*) he may value his security and prove for the deficiency after deduction of the assessed value, in which case the liquidator may redeem at the value so assessed plus 20 per cent;[111]

(*d*) he may surrender his security and prove for the whole debt.

If a creditor values his security, he cannot prove for more than the balance even if the security realises less than his valuation. However, to prevent him from valuing his security at too low a figure, he risks redemption of the security at 120 per cent of his valuation. He may revise the valuation at any time before being required to give it up, but if so, he will not have the benefit of the 20 per cent addition if he is required to give it up. Thus it is rare for a creditor to value his security.

A creditor is not entitled to vote in respect of any unliquidated or contingent debt or any debt the value of which is not ascertained, nor can a creditor vote in respect of any debt on or secured by a current bill of exchange or promissory note held by him unless he is willing to treat the liability to him thereon of every person who is liable thereon antecedently to the company, and against whom a receiving order in bankruptcy has not been made, as a security in his hands and to estimate its value and to deduct it from his proof.[112] This applies for the purpose of voting only and not for the purposes of dividend.

111. Rule 142.
112. Rule 140.

For the purpose of voting a secured creditor must, unless he surrenders his security, lodge with the liquidator (or if there is no liquidator, at the registered office of the company before the meeting) a statement giving particulars of his security; he is entitled to vote in respect of the balance (if any) due to him after deducting the value at which he assesses his security.[113] If he votes in respect of his whole debt, he is deemed to have surrendered his security unless the court on application is satisfied that the omission to value the security has arisen from inadvertence.[114] For this reason secured creditors usually abstain from voting.

It used to be thought that a secured creditor, or a receiver, could no longer exercise the power of sale and sell in the name of the mortgagor company if the morgagor company went into liquidation. This view has now been shown to be incorrect by two cases in 1977 concerning the powers of a receiver after the company had gone into liquidation.[115] In each case the company in liquidation was a "secondary bank" where a receiver and manager of the bank company had been appointed by debentureholders, and the cases concerned the sale of property mortgaged to the bank in exericse of the power of sale vested in the bank under the mortgage. Although the power of the receiver to bind the company and to pledge the company's credit ceases on liquidation, his power to hold and dispose of the company's property, and to use the company's name for that purpose, continues, and the agency conferred by the attorney clause in favour of the debentureholder (and/or the receiver appointed by the debentureholder) survives liquidation on two grounds: (a) an agency coupled with an interest is irrevocable, and (b) s. 4 of the Powers of Attorney Act 1971 preserves such powers. Thus the debentureholder and the receiver are still entitled, at least so far as may be necessary to give effect to the power of sale, to act and sell in the name of the company. A receiver is also entitled to be indemnified out of the mortgaged assets for any liability he incurs in the course of realising the company's property.

PREFERENTIAL DEBTS

The priority of the various debts is governed by s. 319 which provides that certain debts have priority to all others. The most important of these are:

113. Rule 144.
114. Rule 141.
115. In *Re Satis House, Sowman* v. *David Samuel Trust* [1978] 1 W.L.R. 22 and *Barrows and others* v. *Chief Land Registrar and another* (1977) *The Times*, 20th October (the G.T. Whyte & Co. case). *See* Chapter Seventeen.

(*a*) the following rates and taxes:

(*i*) all local rates due from the company at the relevant date and having become due and payable within the twelve months immediately preceding that date;

(*ii*) all corporation tax and other taxes assessed on the company up to the 5th April next before that date, but not exceeding in the whole one year's assessment;

(*iii*) any purchase tax due at the relevant date and having become due within twelve months before that date;

(*b*) all wages or salary (whether or not earned wholly or in part by way of commission) of any clerk or servant for services rendered to the company during the four months next before the relevant date, but not exceeding £800[116] per person, together with all accrued holiday remuneration becoming payable on account of the termination of the employment—"wages or salary for services rendered" includes holiday pay and sick pay, and the reference to "any clerk or servant" includes executive directors, but not non-executive directors;

(*c*) employed earners' social security contributions payable by the company as employer becoming due during the twelve months immediately preceding the relevant date.

The basic list set out in s. 319 has been amended over the years. Thus the taxes in question now include car tax[117] and development land tax[118] and certain betting duties rank as preferential,[119] while wages and salaries now includes amounts in respect of various rights under the Employment Protection (Consolidation) Act 1978,[120] namely guarantee payments,[121] remuneration on suspension on medical grounds,[122] payment for time off[123] and remuneration under a protective award.[124]

If any person advances money to the company for the purpose of paying wages or accrued holiday remuneration which would have been preferential if they had not been paid, the person advancing the money for such purpose has the same priority as the employee

116. The figure was increased from £200 to £800 by the Insolvency Act 1976, Sched. 1. It is not clear whether this figure is a gross figure or whether it is net of PAYE and other deductions.
117. Finance Act 1972, Sched. 7, para. 18.
118. Development Land Tax Act 1976, s. 42.
119. Betting and Gaming Duties Act 1972, ss. 1, 6, 13 and 17.
120. Employment Protection (Consolidation) Act 1978, s. 121.
121. Ibid., s. 12.
122. Ibid., s. 19.
123. For trade union activities or to look for new work or make arrangements for training: Employment Protection (Consolidation) Act 1978, ss. 27(3) and 31(3).
124. Employment Protection Act 1975, s. 101.

would have had if the wages or salary or accrued holiday remuneration had not been paid.[125]

The preferential debts rank equally amongst themselves, and if the assets are insufficient they abate in equal proportions. These debts also have priority over the claims of floating chargees, but if a debentureholder has both a fixed and a floating charge, it is only his right to assets subject to the floating charge which ranks after the preferential claims; his claim to assets subject to a fixed charge ranks before the preferential creditors.[126]

The relevant date is normally the date of the winding-up order in the case of a compulsory winding up, or the date of the passing of the resolution for winding up in a voluntary winding up.[127]

AVOIDANCE OF CERTAIN TRANSACTIONS

Fraudulent preference

Section 320 provides that any conveyance, mortgage, delivery of goods, payment, execution or other act relating to property made or done by or against a company within six months before the commencement of the winding up which would be deemed a fraudulent preference in an individual bankruptcy is to be deemed a fraudulent preference of creditors in the winding up of a company.

The essence of a fraudulent preference under the bankruptcy rules is a conveyance, mortgage or other transfer or payment with the dominant intention of preferring one creditor over another. "Fraudulent" does not mean fraud in the criminal sense of fraud. It is used in the purely technical sense of preferring one creditor and giving him a priority over the general run of creditors.[128]

If the payment or transfer or mortgage is made under pressure from the creditor concerned, or where the dominant intention of the company is not to confer an advantage on the creditor but to benefit the company by keeping on good terms with the creditor (e.g. a banker from whom they expect to receive either further time to pay or further advances) this will not be a fraudulent preference.[129]

If the company promises to create a mortgage this may either be expressed so as to give a present equitable right to security, or constitute an agreement that in some future circumstances a security

125. Section 319(4).
126. Section 319(5).
127. *See* s. 319(8)(*d*) for the full definition.
128. *Re Patrick & Lyon* [1933] Ch. 786.
129. *Re F.L.E. Holdings* [1967] 3 All E.R. 553.

will be created. The former requires registration;[130] the latter, which does not confer any present security, does not. If a promise of the former kind is given, but the creditor in order to avoid injuring the borrower's credit does not actually take the security, that is a transparent attempt to avoid the requirements of s. 95 and any security when executed may well constitute a fraudulent preference.[131]

The intention in question is that of the debtor, and the courts will draw whatever inferences are proper from the facts. If the creditor makes an advance against a promise to create security on request, the court will readily infer, in the absence of other circumstances, that the intention of the parties was to give the creditor the right to be preferred on request. If so, the agreement is fraudulent and unenforceable, and if a charge is subsequently executed at his request that will be void as a fraudulent preference. However, if the creation of the charge is part of a wider arrangement, the intention of the debtor is to be ascertained from the arrangement as a whole, and here the promise is only one factor.[132] If there is an existing equitable charge created by deposit of deeds and the company is obliged under the terms of the memorandum of deposit to execute a legal charge on request, such a legal charge will not be a fraudulent preference, but the original equitable charge is registrable under s. 95 (as is the later legal charge if and when executed).

If the creditor concerned has already issued a writ and agrees to discontinue the proceedings upon payment of the debt or the creation of a charge, that will not in general be a fraudulent preference, unless perhaps there were other creditors in the same position who were not so paid or granted a charge. If a particular debt is paid not so as to prefer that creditor, but so as to secure the release of a guarantor, that may constitute a fraudulent preference of the guarantor and the amount paid can in such case be recovered from the guarantor.[133]

Avoidance of floating charges

Section 322 provides a further ground under which a floating charge may be set aside. Under that section, if a floating charge is created on the undertaking or property of the company within twelve months of the commencement of the winding up, the floating charge is invalid, except to the amount of any cash paid to the company at the time of or subsequently to the creation of, and in consideration

130. Under s. 95; *see* Chapter Seventeen.
131. *Re Jackson & Bassford* [1906] 2 Ch. 467.
132. *Re Eric Holmes (Property) Limited* [1965] Ch. 1052.
133. *Re Conley, ex parte the Trustee* v. *Barclays Bank*; *Re Conley, ex parte the Trustee* v. *Lloyds Bank* [1938] 2 All E.R. 127.

of, the charge unless it is proved that the company was solvent immediately after the creation of the charge.

This section applies only to floating charges. If the same document creates both a fixed charge on some assets, and a floating charge on the remainder of the assets, it is only the floating charge which will be void under this section (though of course the fixed charge may be void under the fraudulent preference provisions of s. 320).[134]

Executions and attachments

Section 325 provides that if a judgment has been obtained against a company and an execution, garnishee, or attachment is threatened or has been put into operation, notice should immediately be given to the judgment creditor and to any debtor whose debt may be garnisheed and to the sheriff, bailiff or other persons levying execution that a meeting to wind up voluntarily has been called. The notice should be delivered by hand or by registered post, and in the case of judgment creditors express notice should also be given to the sheriff or county court bailiff, and should be delivered by hand or sent by registered post to the address of the under-sheriff or the office of the county court bailiff as the case may be. Further notice should be given after the resolution to wind up has been passed. A creditor is not entitled to retain the benefit of an execution, garnishee or attachment of a company's assets against the liquidator, unless the same is completed before the commencement of the winding up. An execution against goods is completed by seizure and sale, an attachment or garnishee of a debt is completed by receipt of the debt and an execution against land is completed by seizure or, in the case of an equitable interest in land, by the appointment of a receiver.[135]

The liquidator's rights may be set aside by the court in favour of the creditor to such extent and subject to such terms as the court may think fit.[136]

SET-OFF

The banker's implied right of set-off is discussed in Chapter Four. In the winding up of an insolvent company, however, the bankruptcy rules with regard to set-off apply, except in the case of amounts due from contributories as such.[137]

---

134. This topic is discussed in greater detail in Chapter Seventeen.
135. Section 325(2).
136. Section 325(1)(c).
137. See Chapter Thirty.

Thus a banker is entitled to set off a credit balance on the company's account against its contingent liability on bills discounted. If at the commencement of the winding up a company has a debit balance on current account, and credit balances on one or more dividend accounts representing unclaimed dividends, the credit balances are available for set-off against the overdraft, since these balances are not considered to be impressed with a trust in favour of the holders of the dividend warrants.[138] Any amounts not required for set-off in this way should be paid to the liquidator, and not to the holders of the outstanding warrants who will rank as unsecured creditors, or if debentureholders appoint a receiver under a floating charge, the balances should be paid to the receiver.[139] If, however, the moneys are provided by a third party for the payment of a dividend, and put into a separate dividend account, the banker may not be able to retain these moneys and set them off against debit balances if the company goes into liquidation before the dividend is paid, since in these circumstances there will probably be a resulting trust in favour of the persons providing the moneys entitling him to repayment.[140]

Set-off applies to the Crown and this tends to have unfortunate consequences for liquidators, since the Crown, in the form of HM Customs and Excise, is frequently a debtor in the liquidation of a company in respect of an overpayment of VAT for one period, or the company may be a supplier to some government department; HM Customs and Excise will not repay the excess, and the government department concerned will not pay for the supplies, until satisfied that the company is not indebted to any other government department in any respect, and since such debts to the Crown could include not only taxes but also liability in respect of redundancy payments made by the Department of Employment, it may well delay the administration of the estate.

CONTRIBUTORIES AND CALLS

If the shares in a company are not all fully paid before the commencement of the liquidation, it will be necessary for the liquidator to prepare lists of contributories. In the case of an insolvent company, this will be with a view to making calls in order to discharge the company's liabilities so far as possible, and in a solvent winding up, it may be necessary to make calls on partly paid share-

138. *Q.B.P.*, No. 81.
139. *Q.B.P.*, No 82.
140. *Barclays Bank* v. *Quistclose Investments* [1968] 3 All E.R. 651.

holders for the purpose of adjusting the rights between them and the holders of fully paid shares.

The term "contributory" means every person liable to contribute to the assets of a company in the event of its being wound up,[141] and for some purposes the word "contributories" is used synonymously with "members". A holder of fully paid shares is a contributory for the purpose of adjustment of rights between fully paid and partly paid shareholders, but his name should not be placed upon the list of contributories unless there is likely to be a surplus of assets for the contributories.

Every present and past member is, subject to certain qualifications, liable to contribute to the assets of the company in a winding up an amount sufficient to pay its liabilities and the expenses of the winding up and for the adjustment of the rights of the contributories among themselves.[142]

The main qualifications are that a past member is not liable to contribute if he has ceased to be a member for one year or more before the commencement of the winding up[143] and, in the case of a company limited by shares, no contribution is required from any member in excess of the amount (if any) unpaid on the shares in respect of which he is liable as a present or past member.[144] In addition, past members are not liable to contribute in respect of any debt or liability contracted after they ceased to be members,[145] and past members are not liable to contribute unless it appears to the court that the existing members are unable to satisfy the contributions required to be made by them.[146]

In a voluntary winding up, after settling the lists of contributories, the liquidator should make such calls upon the contributories whose shares are not fully paid as may be necessary for paying the debts of the company and the costs of the winding up. It may also be necessary to make calls in order to adjust the rights of members between themselves, where some shareholders have paid more on their shares than others.

The liability of a contributory is not affected by the company's articles or any separate contract for deferred payment in respect of any shares. The liquidator is not bound by any agreement made between the members and the company for deferred payment, and can immediately call up any sum unpaid on the shares earlier

141. Section 213.
142. Section 212(1).
143. Section 212(1)(*a*).
144. Section 212(1)(*d*).
145. Section 212(1)(*b*).
146. Section 212(1)(*c*).

than the articles or any prospectus would have permitted the directors to do.[147]

OFFENCES BEFORE OR DURING WINDING UP

Where a company is being wound up, certain acts or omissions before or during the winding up are offences. Any person who is a past or present officer of the company must disclose to the liquidator all information concerning any property of the company, real or personal, and how and to whom and for what consideration it has been disposed of, and must deliver up to the liquidator, or as he directs, any property of the company and any books or papers of the company in his custody or under his control, and must not conceal any debt due to or from the company or fraudulently remove any part of the property of the company. Non-compliance with any of these is an offence, as are a number of other acts, such as preventing the production of any books or papers affecting or relating to the property or affairs of the company, making omissions in any statements or failure to give information to the liquidator, or destroying, mutilating, altering or falsifying books.[148] So are certain frauds before the winding up, such as fraudulently inducing any person to give credit to the company, or causing the company to make any gift, transfer or charge with intent to defraud creditors.[149] The liquidator may also take proceedings for misfeasance, breach of trust, or misapplication of or retaining any money or property of the company, against any past or present director, manager or liquidator.[150]

There is a further offence of carrying on the business of the company with intent to defraud creditors or for any fraudulent purpose.[151] If directors, or indeed any other person who is knowingly a party to carrying on the business in the manner concerned, cause or permit the company to continue to incur liabilities at a time when there is no reasonable prospect of meeting those liabilities, that constitutes fraudulent trading, and the person or persons concerned may be liable under the section. This could apply to a banker, accountant, or other professional, or any person supervising or exercising *de facto* control over the running of the company's business.

As a general rule, where directors become aware that a company will not be able to meet its liabilities in full, they are obliged to wind

147. *Re Cordova Union Gold Co.* (1891) 2 Ch. 580.
148. Sections 328 and 329.
149. Section 330.
150. Section 333.
151. Section 332.

the company up unless they genuinely believe that, if they continue the business, they will be able either to pay all the creditors, both the previous creditors and the new creditors, in full, or at least to pay creditors a greater dividend than they would if they closed down the business immediately. In the latter case, great care must be taken to see that new creditors do not suffer, and so arrangements should be made for them to be paid in full. It is sometimes possible to continue the business if the liabilities are knowingly underwritten by a person who will agree to defer payment until all the other creditors have been paid in full. In any other case, it is advisable to convene a meeting of creditors to lay the facts before the creditors. In such cases it may be possible to propose a scheme, whether formal or informal, to the creditors, and if they all agree, then provided that there was no material non-disclosure, the directors will not be guilty of fraudulent trading if the liabilities are not met in full. The scheme might provide for a moratorium for a fixed or an indefinite period, or for all the creditors to accept a proportion only of their debts.

For directors to escape liability under the section it is not necessary for the creditors actually to be paid in full, provided that the directors are able to establish that at the time when they continued to incur new credit, they had a reasonable prospect of paying off the creditors, or at least of paying them more by continuing the business than if it had ceased.

If the court finds that any person was knowingly a party to fraudulent trading, the court may order that he shall be personally liable, without any limitation of liability, for all or any debts or liabilities of the company as the court may direct. There must, however, be evidence to justify a finding of fraud, meaning in this case actual dishonesty (unlike fraudulent preference which is a mere technical offence). One single transaction, such as the acceptance of a deposit by an insolvent company when its directors know that it cannot supply goods contracted to be supplied or repay the deposit, may be sufficient to constitute fraudulent trading.[152]

RECEIVERS

In a voluntary winding up the liquidator does not, subject to a few exceptions, displace a receiver whether the receiver was appointed by the court or by debentureholders or by a mortgagee, and if assets are in the hands of the liquidator he will have to give up possession to any receiver who has been regularly appointed when called upon

152. *Re Gerald Cooper Chemicals* [1978] Ch. 262.

to do so, though he will have a claim on the assets which come into his hands for the costs incurred in the winding up, including tax on any capital gains made on sale of the assets in the winding up.[153]

Complications may arise between a receiver and a liquidator in the exercise of their respective powers. The receiver has power to take possession of assets charged by the security under which he is appointed and he usually has a power of sale. A receiver appointed by a mortgagee under s. 101 of the Law of Property Act 1925 is a receiver of income only, and has no power of sale unless the mortgage expressly confers one. The mortgagee does, however, have a power of sale. A receiver appointed under an express power contained in a debenture usually has an express power of sale, and if so the liquidator cannot interfere with the power if properly exercised.

The appointment of a voluntary liquidator will not affect the right of a receiver and manager appointed by the court to continue carrying on business under his order, the company's power in this respect being in abeyance during the continuance of the order. A receiver appointed by debentureholders is usually empowered under the terms of the debenture to carry on business as the agent of the company, and as the power of the company to carry on business ceases from the commencement of the winding up, the power of carrying on the business to the extent mentioned above is vested in the liquidator. Since, therefore, the company cannot carry on business itself, the receiver cannot do so as agent of the company.

The receiver can, however, do so in his own name; he is then personally liable on all contracts entered into by him, whether before or after the commencement of the liquidation, except in so far as the contract otherwise provides, but is entitled to an indemnity out of the assets.

A liquidator should not attempt to oust a receiver, lawfully appointed, from conduct of the business against his will without an order of the court.

GENERAL

Any arrangement entered into between a company which is about to be, or is in the course of being, wound up and its creditors will be binding on the company if sanctioned by an extraordinary resolution (i.e. 75 per cent majority) and on the creditors if agreed to by 75 per cent in number and value of the creditors. Dissentient creditors

---

153. *Re Barleycorn Enterprises* [1970] 2 All E.R. 155. *See* further Chapter Seventeen.

have the right to appeal to the court, which may amend, vary or confirm the agreement as it thinks just.[154]

As soon as the affairs of the company are wound up, the liquidator prepares an account and summons meetings of the company and the creditors. The meetings are advertised in the *London Gazette* and the liquidator must file at the Companies Registry a return of the holding of the meeting(s) and a copy of the account.[155]

Where a company has passed a resolution for winding up and, owing to a sudden or unexpected change in circumstances, it is decided not to proceed with the winding up, the winding up has nevertheless commenced and cannot be determined without application to the court, even if no other steps have been taken in the liquidation.

DEFUNCT COMPANIES

The Registrar has power to strike a defunct company off the register.[156] The procedure is that he sends a letter to the company through the post inquiring whether the company is carrying on business or in operation.[157] If he does not receive any reply within a month, he sends a letter by registered post within fourteen days after the expiration of that month, stating that, if an answer is not received to the second letter within one month, a notice will be published in the *Gazette* with a view to striking the name of the company off the Register.[158] Unless a satisfactory reply is received to that letter, he then publishes a notice in the *Gazette*, and sends a notice to the company through the post, stating that at the expiration of three months from the date of the notice, unless cause is shown to the contrary the name of the company will be struck off, and the company will be dissolved.[159]

If the company or any member or creditor feels aggrieved by the company having been struck off the register, the court may on an application made by the company or a member or creditor within 20 years from the publication of the notice in the *London Gazette*, and if it is satisfied that the company was at the time of the striking off carrying on business or in operation, or otherwise that it is just that the company be restored to the register, order the name of the company to be restored, and when an office copy of the order is filed

154. Section 306.
155. Section 300.
156. Section 353.
157. Section 353(1).
158. Section 353(2).
159. Section 353(3).

at the Companies Registry, the company will be deemed to have continued in existence as if it had never been struck off.[160]

Where a company is dissolved, all property and rights whatsoever vested in or held on trust for the company immediately before its dissolution are deemed to be *bona vacantia* and vest in the Crown.[161].

160. Section 353(6).
161. Section 354.

CHAPTER THIRTY

Bankruptcy

DEFINITION AND GENERAL EFFECT OF BANKRUPTCY

A bankrupt is a person who, after committing a statutory act of bankruptcy, has been deprived of the possession and control of his property by a decree of a court competent to exercise jurisdiction in such matters. A person may be insolvent simply by being unable to pay his debts as they fall due, but no person, however insolvent, is a bankrupt until so adjudicated by the Court. Any person, whether in trade or not, may be made bankrupt, with the exception of minors (including minor partners)[1] and persons incapable by reason of mental disorder.[2] Even minors and the mentally incapable may be made bankrupt in some circumstances. When a person is made bankrupt his property is put under the control of the Official Receiver or a trustee in bankruptcy, who, after discharging all liabilities and all expenses incurred in winding up the estate, shares out the remainder of the property *pro rata* among the creditors. If there is a surplus after all the creditors have been paid in full, it is returned to the bankrupt.

Bankruptcy procedure is governed by the Bankruptcy Act 1914 as amended by the Insolvency Act 1976. When a debtor commits one or more of the statutory acts of bankruptcy,[3] and a bankruptcy petition is presented by a creditor or by the debtor himself, the court may make a receiving order for the protection of the debtor's estate.[4] The receiving order does not divest the debtor of his property,[5] though the Official Receiver has some powers over it. Only when the debtor is adjudicated bankrupt does his property vest in a "fit person" appointed to act as a trustee in bankruptcy.[6] The trustee's control of the debtor's property is retrospective, and relates back

1. *See* under "Minors" in Chapter Five.
2. *See* Chapter Five.
3. Bankruptcy Act 1914, s. 1(1); *see* below. In this chapter, references to the Act, to section numbers and to Schedules are references to the Bankruptcy Act 1914. References to the Rules are to the Bankruptcy Rules 1952.
4. Section 3.
5. *Rhodes* v. *Dawson* (1886) 16 Q.B.D. 548.
6. Sections 18 and 19.

to the time of the act upon which the petition is grounded or, if
more than one act of bankruptcy has been committed, then the time
of the first act of bankruptcy proved to have been committed by
the bankrupt within the three months prior to the date of the
petition.[7]

ACTS OF BANKRUPTCY

The following are the statutory acts of bankruptcy, with a few notes
in explanation. Except for the final one, they are all set out in s.
1(1) of the 1914 Act.

(*a*) "If in England or elsewhere he makes a conveyance or assignment of his property to a trustee or trustees for the benefit of his
creditors generally."

A conveyance or assignment to one or more creditors, not being
all the creditors, cannot be construed as an act of bankruptcy under
this heading (though it might come under (*b*) or (*c*) below[8]), nor
can an assignment for the benefit of a particular class of creditors,
e.g. the *trade* creditors to the exclusion of the *private* creditors.

A creditor has usually three months in which to present his
petition,[9] but where the debtor has made an assignment of the whole,
or substantially the whole, of his property to a trustee for the benefit
of his creditors generally, the period may be reduced to one month.
The trustee may send to any creditor, by prepaid registered post,
a notice in writing of the execution of the deed, and of the filing,
of the certificate of creditors' assents to the deed of arrangement.[10]
The trustee's notice, sent on Form 14, states that after the expiration
of one month from the date of posting the notice, the creditor will
not be entitled to present a bankruptcy petition founded on the
execution of the deed or on any other act connected with the proceedings preliminary to the execution of the deed. This notice from
the trustee binds a non-assenting creditor unless the deed of assignment becomes void. Such a deed is void if not duly registered and
if not assented to within the prescribed time by a majority in number
and value of the creditors.[11]

(*b*) "If in England or elsewhere he makes a fraudulent conveyance,
gift, delivery or transfer of his property, or any part thereof."

Any conveyance is fraudulent if it is intended to defeat or delay

7. Section 37.
8. *Re Phillips, ex parte Barton* [1900] 2 Q.B. 329.
9. Section 4(*c*).
10. Deeds of Arrangement Act 1914, s. 24(1).
11. Ibid., s. 3(1).

creditors.[12] The assignment of the whole or substantially the whole of the debtor's property as security for a past debt is fraudulent, and is an act of bankruptcy under this clause. However, an assignment, partly in consideration of a past debt and partly in consideration of fresh advances, is not of itself fraudulent. For example, if the fresh advances were made bona fide to enable him to continue his business, it would not be fraudulent, but if it is shown that the real intention of the creditor in making the fresh advances was to obtain security for the past debt, then it is fraudulent.[13] If the debtor sells the whole of his property, that is not of itself an act of bankruptcy, for by doing this he is merely exchanging one kind of property for another kind of property,[14] but if after selling he absconds with the money, then it is an act of bankruptcy, but in such a case the buyer is protected if he acted in good faith and without knowledge.[15]

(c) "If in England or elsewhere he makes any conveyance or transfer of his property or any part thereof, or creates any charge thereon, which would under this or any other Act be void as a fraudulent preference if he were adjudged bankrupt."

A preference to be fraudulent must be made by a person when insolvent, and it must be voluntary and made with the dominant (though not necessarily the sole) intention of favouring some particular creditor. If a creditor, not knowing at the time that the debtor is about to become bankrupt, presses the debtor, and forces him to pay by threatening him with an action, the preference will not be fraudulent. If, however, the debtor says to the creditor "I am going to file my petition next week", and thereupon the creditor forces him to pay the debt, then the preference is a fraudulent one for the creditor, through the debtor's confession, has knowledge that by getting the money he is being preferred over the other creditors. In every case the burden of proving that the preference is fraudulent lies upon the trustee in bankruptcy.

Section 44(1) defines fraudulent preference as follows:
Every conveyance or transfer of property and every payment made ... by any person unable to pay his debts as they become due ... with a view of giving such creditor, or any surety or guarantor for the debt due to such creditor, a preference over the other creditors, shall, if the person making ... the same is adjudged bankrupt on a bankruptcy

12. Law of Property Act 1925, s. 172.
13. *Ex parte Johnson, re Chapman* [1884] 26 Ch. D. 338; *Ex parte King* [1876] 2 Ch. D. 256; *Ex parte Wilkinson* [1882] 22 Ch. D. 788; *Administrator-General of Jamaica* v. *Lascelles, de Mercado & Co.* [1894] A.C. 135.
14. *Baxter* v. *Pritchard* [1834] 1 A. & E. 456; *Rose* v. *Haycock* [1834] 1 A. & E. 460; *Lee* v. *Hart* [1856] 11 Ex. 880.
15. Section 45.

petition presented within six[16] months after the date of making ...
the same, be deemed fraudulent and void as against the trustee in the
bankruptcy.[17]

A banker may be innocently involved in a fraudulent preference.
In *Re Conley, ex parte the Trustee* v. *Barclays Bank*, and *The Same*
v. *Lloyds Bank*,[18] securities had been pledged by relatives of the
borrower under the banks' usual forms of charge which did not
involve any personal liability. Later, the borrower got into financial
difficulties but was able to obtain sufficient funds to repay his overdrafts and get the securities released. Within three months he was
made bankrupt and his trustees claimed successfully that the relatives
were "sureties or guarantors" for the purposes of the section and
that the payments made by the bankrupt to the banks could be
avoided as fraudulent preferences.

In liquidations, persons fraudulently preferred in this manner have
rights against sureties,[19] and these provisions now apply to bankruptcies.[20]

(*d*) "If with intent to defeat or delay his creditors he does any
of the following things, namely, departs out of England, or being
out of England remains out of England, or departs from his dwelling-
house, or otherwise absents himself, or begins to keep house."

The acts mentioned in this sub-section must, if they are to be acts
of bankruptcy, be done with the purpose of delaying or avoiding
creditors. It is a question of fact whether the debtor by absenting
himself had any such intention or not, and the burden of proof is
on the petitioning creditor.[21] If, for example, the debtor is in bad
health and goes abroad or to a resort to recuperate, or if he goes on
a business journey, he is not necessarily delaying or defeating his
creditors, but if before going away he makes no provision for meeting
bills he has accepted, the inference generally speaking would be that
his intention was to avoid payment. Moreover, if he vacates his usual
place of business without notifying his change of address to his
creditors, it is an act of bankruptcy.

A debtor is said to keep house when he has issued orders that
he will not see any creditors who may call, and a creditor upon calling
is denied admittance.[22] If, however, the creditor calls at an un-

16. The period was increased from three to six months by the Companies Act 1947,
s. 115.
17. Section 44(1).
18. [1938] 2 All E.R. 127.
19. Companies Act 1948, s. 321.
20. Companies Act 1947, s. 115.
21. *Ex parte Coates, re Skelton* (1877) 5 Ch. D. 979.
22. *Fisher* v. *Boucher* (1830) 10 B. & C. 705.

reasonable hour and is refused admittance, that would not be accepted as evidence that the debtor was keeping house.[23]

(e) "If execution has been levied by seizure of his goods under process in any action in any court, or in any civil proceeding in the high court, and the goods have been either sold or held by the sheriff for twenty-one days; provided that, where an interpleader summons has been taken out in regard to the goods seized, the time elapsing between the date at which such summons is taken out and the date at which the proceedings on such summons are finally disposed of, settled or abandoned, shall not be taken into accout in calculating such period of twenty-one days."

This act of bankruptcy occurs if the sheriff either sells the goods or holds them for 21 days, not counting the day of seizure, except where an interpleader summons has been taken out.[24] After the expiration of the 21 days, the act of bankruptcy is complete, and any petition based on it must be presented within three months of that date. An execution levied by seizure and sale of the goods of a debtor is not invalid by reason only of its being an act of bankruptcy, and in all cases a person who purchases the goods in good faith under a sale by the sheriff acquires a good title to them against the trustee in bankruptcy.[25]

(f) "If he files in the court a declaration of his inability to pay his debts or presents a bankruptcy petition against himself."

(g) "If a creditor has obtained a final judgment or final order against him for any amount, and, execution thereon not having been stayed, has served on him in England, or, by leave of the court, elsewhere, a bankruptcy notice under this Act, and he does not within ten[26] days after service of the notice in case the service is effected in England, and in case the service is effected elsewhere, then within the time limited in that behalf by the order giving leave to effect the service, either comply with the requirements of the notice or satisfy the court that he has a counter-claim, set-off or cross-demand which equals or exceeds the amount of the judgment debt or sum ordered to be paid, and which he could not set up in the action in which the judgment was obtained, or the proceedings in which the order was obtained. For the purposes of this paragraph and of s. 2 of this Act, any person who is, for the time being, entitled to enforce a final judgment or final order, shall be deemed to

23. *See Smith* v. *Currie* (1813) 3 Camp. 349.
24. The sheriff takes out an interpleader summons when two or more adverse parties claim goods in his possession in order that the claimants may interplead, i.e. fight out their claims in a court of law.
25. Bankruptcy Act 1914, s. 40(3).
26. The period was increased from seven to ten days by the Insolvency Act 1976, s. 4.

be a creditor who has obtained a final judgment or final order."

Any creditor may, within the statutory three months, serve on the debtor a bankruptcy notice founded on this act of bankruptcy. The judgment on which it is based must be a final judgment. The judgment debt, or sum ordered to be paid, must amount to not less than £200.[27] The debtor is given ten days after the service of the notice to pay or give satisfactory security for the judgment debt or sum ordered to be paid, or within the same time must enter a counter-claim equal or greater in amount. If he does not do any of these things, he has committed an act of bankruptcy on which a petition may be based.

(h) "If the debtor gives notice to any of his creditors that he has suspended, or that he is about to suspend, payment of his debts."

The absence of definition as to what amounts to notice has created considerable difficulty. From the decisions it is clear that no special form of words is necessary. The notice may be oral or written,[28] or by means of a circular, or transmitted by the debtor's agent to the creditor's agent. The crucial point is that it must be so expressed that the creditor who hears or reads it must be in no doubt that the debtor has suspended or is about to suspend payment.[29] Even the offer by the debtor of a composition does not necessarily bring him within the sub-section, but if, when making the offer, he leads his creditors to believe that suspension of payment is the alternative to acceptance, then he does come within the sub-section.

(i) To the acts of bankruptcy mentioned above there has now been added the making of an administration order by the County Court under s. 148(1) of the County Courts Act 1959. This additional act of bankruptcy was first created by s. 21 of the Administration of Justice Act 1965.

An administration order may be made under s. 148 where a debtor is unable to pay forthwith the amount of a County Court judgment, and alleges that his total indebtedness, inclusive of that judgment, does not exceed £5,000. The order provides for the administration of his estate, and may provide for payment of his debts by instalments or otherwise, and either in full or to such extent as the court considers practicable under the circumstances of the case, and subject to any conditions as to his future earnings or income which the court may think just. Until amended by s. 20(4) of the Administration

27. Bankruptcy Act 1914, s. 4(1)(a); the figure was increased from £50 to £200 by the Insolvency Act 1976, Sched. 1.

28. *Ex parte Nickoll, re Walker* (1884) 13 Q.B.D. 469.

29. *See* for examples: *Re Morgan, ex parte Turner* (1895) 2 Mans. 508; *Re Simonson, ex parte Ball* [1894] 1 Q.B. 433; *Crook* v. *Morley* [1891] A.C. 316; *Re Selwood, ex parte Dash* (1894) 1 Mans. 66; *Re Dagnall* [1896] 2 Q.B. 407; *Re Wolstenholme* (1885) 2 Mor. 213; *Re Miller* [1901] 1 K.B. 51; *Re a Debtor* [1929] 1 Ch. 362.

of Justice Act 1965, such an order acted as a stay of, *inter alia*, bankruptcy proceedings *pending* in a County Court. Creditors whose debts were notified to the court by the debtor or were scheduled to the order had no remedy against the person or property of the debtor except with the leave of that County Court. Now, however, where a person fails to make any payment which he is required to make by virtue of an administration order, the appropriate court may, if it thinks fit, revoke the administration order and make a receiving order against that person; where a receiving order is made under s. 20 the debtor is deemed to have committed an act of bankruptcy at the time when the receiving order is made. The provisions of the Bankruptcy Act 1914[30] apply as if for references to the presentation of a petition, there were substituted references to the making of the receiving order.[31]

The appropriate court means either (*a*) if the County Court administering the estate of a person in question under the order has bankruptcy jurisdiction, that court, or (*b*) in any other case, a County Court having bankruptcy jurisdiction to which the matter has been referred by the court in paragraph (*a*) above. The powers of the High Court under s. 11 may be exercised by the registrars in bankruptcy of the appropriate court.

Those are the acts of bankruptcy. The banker's difficulty is not that he does not know what are the acts of bankruptcy, but that he cannot often be certain that his customer has actually committed one of these acts. Since he may have to answer to the trustee in bankruptcy for any dealings with his customer from the time of notice of the relevant act of bankruptcy, certainty is of the utmost importance to the banker. Information does not always come from the customer himself. It may be conveyed in the form of hints and rumours of impending disaster. If the banker takes notice of the information, coming to him (as it often does) in roundabout ways, and refuses to honour his customer's cheques payable to third parties, he may, should the information prove false or exaggerated, have to defend an action for damages to credit or for libel.[32] If on the other hand he does not consider the information conveyed to him is sufficient to constitute an act of bankruptcy, and bankruptcy does in fact occur within three months, he may have to refund to the trustee all such payments made after receipt of the notice. "It has been held that information by a stranger that he has filed a petition against a man is a notice of an act of bankruptcy, though the

---

30. Except Part VII (Bankruptcy Offences), ss. 154–166.
31. Insolvency Act 1976, s. 11.
32. *See* Chapter Four.

informant did not actually say on what alleged act of bankruptcy the petition was based."[33]

In cases like the foregoing, when the information does not come direct from the customer, the banker should if possible get in touch with him before paying or dishonouring his cheques. It should not be forgotten that in cases where the transaction is protected by the sections of the 1914 Act only if the person concerned had no notice, actual or constructive, the onus of proving absence of notice lies upon the person benefiting.

THE BANKRUPTCY PETITION

The petition may be presented by a single creditor, or by two or more creditors acting jointly, or by the debtor himself.[34] If the debtor himself presents the petition, he must allege that he is unable to pay his debts. If a creditor or creditors present a petition the following conditions are essential to make it valid.

(a) The debt owing (or the aggregate of the debts where there are joint petitioning creditors) must not be less than £200,[35] or if the petitioning creditor is a secured creditor, the balance of the debt must not be less than £200 after deducting the value of the security.

(b) The debt must be a liquidated sum (i.e. a clear or agreed-upon sum) payable either immediately or at some certain future date.

(c) The act of bankruptcy upon which the petition is founded must have occurred within the three months preceding the presentation of the petition.

(d) The debtor must be domiciled in, or within a year before the presentation have ordinarily resided in, or have had a dwellinghouse or place of business in, England.

A creditor who has taken a bill (for £200 or over) for a debt may present a petition, if the acceptor has committed an act of bankruptcy, even though the bill has not matured, since the giving of the bill suspends the cause of action on the original debt, and the act of bankruptcy puts an end to the suspension and determines the period of credit.[36]

A receiving order cannot be made against any corporation, partnership, association or company registered under the Companies Acts.[37] These corporate bodies are wound up under those Acts.

---

33. Gilbart Lectures 1912.
34. Sections 3 and 4.
35. The figure was increased from £50 to £200 by the Insolvency Act 1976, Sched. 1.
36. *Re Raatz, ex parte Raatz* [1897] 2 Q.B. 80.
37. Section 126.

Ordinary partnerships and limited partnerships are not affected by this provision. Any foreigner is now subject to the bankruptcy laws equally with British citizens, if at the time when any act of bankruptcy was done or suffered by him he was:

(a) personally present in England; or

(b) ordinarily resident or had a place of residence in England; or

(c) carrying on business in England, personally, or by means of an agent or manager; or

(d) a member of a firm or partnership which carried on business in England.[38]

If a foreigner, although having a place of business here, is resident abroad, he is beyond the jurisdiction of the English courts, but he can be adjudicated bankrupt here and his property in this country seized and administered. A bankruptcy petition cannot be presented against a deceased person, but an insolvent estate is to be administered in accordance with the rules in bankruptcy, subject to the priority of the funeral, testamentary and administration expenses.[39] The effect of bankruptcy upon partnerships, joint and other accounts, is dealt with under the appropriate headings in Chapters Five and Six.

If the debtor is in the London Bankruptcy District, or is not resident in England, or his place of business or residence cannot be ascertained, the place of presentation of the petition is the High Court of Justice. In any other case the petition must be presented at the County Court for the district in which the debtor has resided, or carried on business, for the greater part of the six months preceding the presentation of the petition.[40] Where the debtor has both private and business addresses, preference is to be given to the latter.[41] The person presenting the petition must pay the stamp duty and costs and lodge a deposit,[42] but he is entitled to the repayment of these items out of the assets in the priority stated in Rule 115.

Under the Land Charges Act 1972, every petition in bankruptcy, and every receiving order should be registered at the Land Charges Registry, the former in the register of pending actions, and the latter in that of writs and orders affecting land, whether or not it is known to affect land.[43] If it is not so registered, a purchaser of the legal estate in the land, in good faith, for money or money's worth and without notice of an available act of bankruptcy, is protected against

38. Section 1(2).
39. Administration of Estates Act 1925, s. 34.
40. Section 98.
41. Rule 145.
42. Rule 146.
43. Land Charges Act 1972, ss. 5, 6(1).

the title of the trustee in bankruptcy.[44] If necessary, registration must be renewed every five years.[45] In the case of registered land, a creditors' notice must be entered in the register, followed by a bankruptcy inhibition when the receiving order has been registered.[46]

Accordingly, when the petition is filed, the Registrar is required to send notice of the petition to the Chief Land Registrar with a request that it be registered in the register of pending actions.[47] When the receiving order is made the Registrar sends two copies to the Official Receiver who is obliged to send notice of the order to the Chief Land Registrar with a request that it be registered in the register of writs and orders affecting land.[48]

The above regulations emphasise the need to search before completing a purchase, or advancing under a mortgage.

The effect of making a receiving order is that an Official Receiver (appointed by and under the direction of the Department of Trade) becomes the receiver of the debtor's property. Thereafter no creditor, except as directed by the Act, has any remedies against the person or property of the debtor.[49] The power of secured creditors to realise or otherwise deal with their securities is not affected,[50] but no secured creditor may receive more than 100p in the pound,[51] any surplus being handed over by him to the Official Receiver.

The Official Receiver or trustee is entitled to request a banker to pay over any balance standing to the credit of the bankrupt customer and to deliver any property or securities held for safe custody. He is also entitled to any information he requires about the account and banking transactions of the bankrupt, but not of course to any information concerning any other customer.

After a receiving order has been made the debtor must draw up and submit to the Official Receiver a statement of affairs in the prescribed form, giving full particulars of his assets, debts and liabilities, creditors and securities held by them.[52] Not later than fourteen days after the making of the receiving order (unless a later day is fixed for some special reason) there must be a general meeting of creditors[53] which decides whether any proposal for a composition

44. Land Charges Act 1972, ss. 5(8), 6(5).
45. Ibid., s. 8.
46. Land Registration Act 1925, ss. 59, 61.
47. Rule 147.
48. Rules 177 and 178.
49. Section 7(1).
50. Section 7(2).
51. Schedule 2, para. 18.
52. Section 14(1).
53. Schedule 1, para. 1.

or scheme of arrangement shall be accepted, or whether the debtor shall be made bankrupt.[54]

Every creditor whose debt has been admitted as provable in bankruptcy, except in respect of any unliquidated or contingent debt, or any debt the value of which is not ascertained, is entitled to vote at the meeting either in person or by proxy.[55] If a secured creditor wishes to vote he must assess the value of his security, and may vote for the balance (if any) of the debt after deducting the value of his security, but if he elects to surrender his security he may vote in respect of the whole debt. If he votes in respect of the whole debt, he is deemed to have surrendered his security unless the court is satisfied that the omission to value the security has arisen from inadvertence.[56] The Official Receiver or trustee has the power, within 28 days of a secured creditor's voting, to buy him out for the benefit of the creditors generally, at the proof value plus 20 per cent. The creditor also has some right of amending his estimated value, but if he does so he loses the 20 per cent increase should the trustee require the security to be given up.[57] If at this first meeting of creditors (or at any adjournment thereof) they do not adopt a scheme or accept a composition satisfactory to the court, the debtor is adjudicated bankrupt.[58]

Notice of all receiving orders and adjudication orders must be advertised in the *London Gazette* and in a local newspaper,[59] and such notice is deemed to be sufficient notice to all persons concerned. Registration of receiving orders under the Land Charges Act 1972 has already been dealt with.[60]

It should be noted that a receiving order commences from the first moment of the day on which it is made. For example, if a banker pays the debtor's cheques in the morning and a receiving order is made in the afternoon of the same day, he gets no protection, and is responsible to the trustee in bankruptcy for the amounts paid. Another serious danger arises from the fact that frequently a considerable delay elapses before a receiving order is advertised. The banker gets no protection whatever should he have dealings with the debtor after the date of the receiving order, and in ignorance of the making of it. This danger may be further increased if the advertisement of the receiving order is postponed by order of the court.

---

54. Section 13(1).
55. Schedule 1, paras. 8, 9.
56. Schedule 1, para. 10.
57. Schedule 1, para. 12.
58. Section 18.
59. Sections 11 and 18.
60. *See* earlier in this chapter.

In the case of *In re Wigzell, ex parte Hart*,[61] the advertisement of a receiving order was postponed pending an appeal by the debtor, who in the meantime paid into and drew out of his account. A month later the appeal was heard and dismissed, and the receiving order was later advertised. Even though the banker was entirely ignorant of the making of the receiving order, or even of an available act of bankruptcy, it was held by the Court of Appeal that the banker was responsible for all sums paid in, and could not take credit for any sums drawn out.

In an attempt to alleviate the position, s. 4 of the Bankruptcy (Amendment) Act 1926 provides that:

> Where any money or property of a bankrupt has, on or after the date of the receiving order but before notice thereof has been gazetted in the prescribed manner, been paid or transferred by a person having possession of it to some other person, and the payment or transfer is under the provisions of the principal Act void as against the trustee in the bankruptcy, then, if the person by whom the payment or transfer was made proves that when it was made he had not had notice of the receiving order, any right of recovery which the trustee may have against him in respect of the money or property shall not be enforced by any legal proceedings except where and in so far as the court is satisfied that it is not reasonably practicable for the trustee to recover in respect of the money or property or of some part thereof from the person to whom it was paid or transferred.

It was hoped that it would protect bankers in such cases as that of the *Wigzell* case. The section does at least put the onus on the trustee as the attacking party, but the burden may be fairly easy to discharge. It is probable, as the authors of Williams and Muir Hunter on *Bankruptcy*[62] say, that "except in unusual cases an abortive demand by the trustee for payment from the transferee would be sufficient to satisfy the court that it is not 'reasonably practicable' to recover from him unless the transferor, for whose benefit the section exists, is prepared to give the trustee an indemnity against the costs of proceeding against the transferee." In practice it is understood that the Department of Trade will often, on request, ascertain the financial standing of the person paid and undertake to proceed against him, if given an indemnity for costs. This has been known to achieve the desired effect. It will not, however, protect a banker against payments made in the interval between the time when the receiving order is gazetted and when the *London Gazette* can reach him.[63]

---

61. [1921] 2 K.B. 835.
62. (19th Edn.), p. 366.
63. The date of gazetting is the date on which the *London Gazette* appears in London, irrespective of when it actually reaches other parts of England and Wales.

COMPOSITIONS AND ARRANGEMENTS
(UNDER BANKRUPTCY)

Where a debtor intends to make a proposal for a composition in satisfaction of his debts, or a proposal for a scheme of arrangement of his affairs, he must, within four days of submitting his statement of affairs or within such time thereafter as the Official Receiver may fix, lodge with the Official Receiver a proposal in writing, signed by him, embodying the terms of the composition or scheme and setting out particulars of any sureties or securities proposed.[64] A copy of this proposal and a report thereon is sent to each creditor, and if, at the meeting that follows, a majority in number and three-fourths in value of all the creditors who have proved resolve to accept the proposal, the same, when approved by the court, is binding on all the creditors.[65] The court, whose approval is essential, will not assent to any scheme, unless it provides reasonable security for the payment of not less than 25p in the pound on all unsecured debts provable against the debtor's estate.[66]

Acceptance of the composition or scheme involves discharge of the receiving order. The debtor (or the trustee appointed under the scheme) is then put into possession of his property and thereby released, subject to the provisions of the composition or scheme, from all debts from which a discharge in bankruptcy would have released him.[67] The court may annul any scheme which in practice, owing to legal or other difficulties, fails to be workable, or if the debtor defaults in payment of any instalment, and may adjudge the debtor bankrupt. This will not affect the validity of any sale, disposition or payment duly made, or thing duly done under or in pursuance of the composition or scheme.[68] A banker, therefore, is protected if he pays a credit balance to a trustee appointed to carry out a scheme or composition authorised by the court.

The above provisions apply to compositions or deeds of arrangement made after a receiving order has been made. The rules of bankruptcy do not apply to deeds of arrangement or compositions made before a receiving order is made.[69]

THE DEBTOR'S PROPERTY

Where a receiving order is made against a debtor, and no approved

64. Section 16(1).
65. Section 16(13).
66. Section 16(10).
67. Rule 209.
68. Section 16(16).
69. *See* "Deeds of arrangement" below.

composition or scheme is made and accepted within the time prescribed by the court, the debtor is made bankrupt and his property becomes divisible among his creditors and vests in his trustee.[70] A committee of inspection is appointed by the creditors to superintend the administration of the estate by the trustee. The Act uses the word "superintend" but this is really a misnomer because the actual powers of the committee are limited and the trustee has substantial powers without needing to refer to the committee.[71]

The debtor's property under the control of the trustee comprises:[72]

(a) all property belonging to the bankrupt at the commencement of the bankruptcy, or that may be acquired by or devolve upon him before his discharge;

(b) all goods which, at the commencement of the bankruptcy, were in the possession, order or disposition of the bankrupt in his trade or business, by the consent and permission of the true owner, in such circumstances as he is the reputed owner thereof, provided that things in action, other than debts due or growing due to the bankrupt in the course of his trade or business, shall not be deemed to be goods within the meaning of this section. But the trustee shall not have any control over property held by the bankrupt in trust for any other person.

The trustee has the right to exercise all powers in respect of property which might have been exercised by the debtor himself.[72]

The trustee must pay all moneys received into the Insolvency Services Account at the Bank of England.[73] The Department of Trade may give permission for accounts to be opened with local banks,[74] but only if some administrative advantage will accrue to the creditors; the fact that it will earn interest is not a reason, as interest earned on the account at the Bank of England is applicable to defray the costs of the Department.[75]

RELATION BACK

The title of the trustee to the debtor's property is deemed to relate back and commence, not from the date of his appointment, but from the time of the commission of the act of bankruptcy on which the receiving order was made, or, if more than one act has been com-

70. Section 18(1).
71. Section 20(1).
72. Section 38.
73. Section 89, as amended by the Insolvency Services Act 1976, s. 3.
74. Section 89(2)(a).
75. Re Walker decd. (in bankruptcy) [1974] 1 All E.R. 551.

mitted, the commission of the first act of bankruptcy committed within the three months preceding the date of presentation of the bankruptcy petition.[76] This doctrine of "relation back" as it is called, would have serious consequences for every creditor who had dealings with the bankrupt after the commission of the act of bankruptcy, were it not that by ss. 45 and 46 the effects of the doctrine are mitigated in certain directions.

The transactions protected by s. 45 include:

(a) any payment by the bankrupt to any of his creditors;

(b) any payment or delivery to the bankrupt;

(c) any conveyance or assignment by the bankrupt for valuable consideration;

(d) any contract, dealing or transaction by or with the bankrupt for valuable consideration;

provided in all these cases that the payment, delivery, conveyance, etc., took place before the date of the receiving order and that the person claiming the benefit of the section was unaware that the debtor had committed an available act of bankruptcy.

Section 46 allows certain payments of money or delivery of property to the debtor or to his assignee before the date of the receiving order, provided that the person making such payment or delivery was unaware that a bankruptcy petition had been presented against the debtor. Moreover, the payment or delivery must have been made bona fide, and in the ordinary course of business. It will be noted that s. 46 says nothing about notice of an act of bankruptcy. This is important, because it relieves the persons who are affected by this section from having to decide whether or not some act that the debtor has committed was or was not an act of bankruptcy within the meaning of the Act.

The wording of s. 46 raises the question whether a banker is protected in paying cheques drawn on his credit balance by the debtor in favour of third parties. He is undoubtedly protected in paying cheques payable to and personally presented by the debtor himself. The section says that the payment must be made "to a person subsequently adjudged bankrupt, or to a person claiming by assignment from him." Since a cheque is not an assignment of the funds in the banker's hands,[77] it has been contended that a payee or holder of the cheque cannot be considered as a person claiming by assignment. If that is so, then the banker must fall back on s. 45 of the Bankruptcy Act. Some writers say that the wording of this section

76. Section 37(1).
77. Bills of Exchange Act 1882, s. 53(1).

does protect the banker provided that he had no notice of an act of bankruptcy, but Paget[78] is of the opinion that neither s. 45 nor s. 46 protects the banker in respect of cheques payable to third parties, and that consequently a banker who pays such cheques after the commission of an act of bankruptcy, to which the trustee's title relates back, may be liable to the trustee for all such sums, even though the banker was unaware that a statutory act of bankruptcy had been committed. The contrary view has been argued and is supported by the decision in *Re Dalton*,[79] but in view of the confused position and to avoid any risk, it is advisable for the banker to follow the procedure indicated below.

PROCEDURE ON NOTICE OF ACT OF BANKRUPTCY

On receipt of notice of an act of bankruptcy, it has not been necessary since the Bankruptcy Act 1914 for the banker to stop all operations on the debtor's account. Until the receiving order is actually made, the customer is entitled (save in two cases indicated below) to draw out his credit balance personally by cheques payable to himself.[80] Such transactions are covered by s. 46, provided that they are done in the ordinary course of business, are otherwise bona fide, and are carried out before a receiving order is made and without knowledge of the presentation of a bankruptcy petition. For the reason stated in the preceding paragraph, the banker should only pay cheques made payable to the customer himself, and not those made payable to third parties. These should be returned marked "Refer to drawer".

There is, however, some element of risk in dishonouring cheques in this way, since wrongful dishonour will involve libel. It was formerly thought that the marking "Refer to drawer" was neutral, and meant only something like, "We are not paying: go back to the drawer and ask him to pay." It has now been held, however, that "Refer to drawer" is capable of being defamatory,[81] and in a New Zealand case even "Present again" was held to be capable of bearing a defamatory meaning.[82] Nor will the defence of qualified privilege avail the bank, since a mistake by the bank which appears to make a communication on their part necessary cannot create an occasion of qualified privilege. The occasion must be there irrespective of the mistake.[83]

---

78. (8th Edn.), pp. 93–8.
79. [1962] 2 All E.R. 499; [1963] Ch. 336.
80. *See* above.
81. *Jayson* v. *Midland Bank* [1968] 1 Lloyd's Rep. 409. *See* Chapter Four.
82. *Baker* v. *Australia and New Zealand Bank* [1958] N.Z.L.R. 907.
83. *Davidson* v. *Barclays Bank* (1940) 56 T.L.R. 343.

To put matters upon a proper footing, the banker should, immediately on receipt of notice of an act of bankruptcy, advise his customer that he intends to pay only those cheques made payable to and presented personally by the customer himself.

As regards property acquired by the bankrupt after adjudication, a banker is required to pay and deliver to the trustee all money and securities in his possession or power which he is not by law entitled to retain as against the bankrupt or the trustee.[84] Therefore, when a customer who has a credit balance is adjudicated bankrupt, the banker should inform the trustee or the Department of Trade of the fact by registered post, unless the account is a trust account, or held by the bankrupt in a fiduciary capacity.

Section 46 (which covers the period between an available act of bankruptcy and the receiving order) protects the banker when the customer draws against his credit balance, but it does not appear to cover the feeding of the account by the collection of cheques, the proceeds of which are subsequently drawn out by the customer. Owing to the doctrine of relation back, cheques paid in for collection do not belong to the customer but to the trustee in bankruptcy when he is appointed. If therefore it is necessary to collect such cheques, the proceeds should be credited to a suspense account where the money can remain until it is known definitely whether or not the customer is to be made bankrupt. If the debtor's account is overdrawn, the banker cannot of course after notice of an act of bankruptcy apply any cheques for collection in reduction of the overdraft.

There are two acts of bankruptcy which immediately stop the customer's account, namely, the execution of a deed of assignment which involves holding any credit balance at the disposal of the assigneee, and the presentation of a petition by the customer against himself, which, though classed as an act of bankruptcy, operates in the same way as a petition presented by a creditor, knowledge of which at once stops all operations on the account.

Section 46 would entitle the banker to deliver securities or articles deposited for safe custody to the customer, but not to third parties, under similar circumstances as for a credit balance.

In *Re Clark (a bankrupt), ex parte the Trustee* v. *Texaco*,[85] the trustee in bankruptcy claimed against a petrol company, which had at all material times no knowledge of the bankruptcy proceedings, for the recovery under ss. 18(1), 37(1) and 38(2)(a) of sums paid by the bankrupt for three deliveries of petrol supplied for the benefit of his estate after a receiving order was made and before adjudication.

---

84. Section 48(6).
85. [1975] 1 All E.R. 453.

The judge held that the trustee was not entitled to recover the sums paid since (*a*) the assets of the debtor's estate had been enriched by the conversion of an overdraft into a credit balance during the relevant period at the expense of the petrol company in consequence of the transactions of which the payments formed part, (*b*) the petrol company would not be entitled to submit a proof of debt in respect of the petrol delivered, and (*c*) in all the circumstances it could not be regarded as fair to allow the estate to take the whole benefit of the sale price of the petrol whilst repudiating all obligation to pay for it, as to do so would enable the trustee to extract funds from the third party which did not form part of the assets of the bankrupt's estate at the commencement of the bankruptcy.

All the debtor's property, whether belonging to him at the time of his bankruptcy or acquired by him afterwards and before his discharge, is divisible among his creditors. However, the two kinds of property are treated differently. The former kind, subject to the provisions of ss. 45 and 46, vests in the trustee immediately after the adjudication order. In regard to the latter kind (called "after-acquired property"), the rule is[86] that until the trustee intervenes all transactions by a bankrupt after his adjudication with any person dealing with him bona fide and for value, in respect of this after-acquired property, are valid against the trustee. This section applies to both real and personal property. Wages earned by the bankrupt, after adjudication, by his own personal labour, do not pass to the trustee, at least such part of the personal earnings as is deemed necessary for the support of himself and his family.[87]

REPUTED OWNERSHIP

From s. 38, already mentioned, it follows that not only property of which the debtor is the true owner, but also property of which he is the reputed owner passes to the trustee. "Reputed ownership" was defined by Lord Selborne in *Ex parte Watkins*:[88]

> The doctrine of reputed ownership does not require any investigation into the actual state of knowledge or belief, either of all creditors or of particular creditors; and still less of the outside world, who are not creditors at all, as to the position of particular goods. It is enough for the doctrine if those goods are in such a situation as to convey to the minds of those who know their situation the reputation of ownership; that reputation arising by the legitimate exercise of reason and judgment on the knowledge of those facts

86. Section 47(1).
87. *Re Roberts* [1900] 1 Q.B. 122: "The necessity is the limit of the exception" per Lindley MR at p. 128. *See also* "Account with undischarged bankrupt" below.
88. (1873) L.R. 8 Ch. 520.

which are capable of being generally known to those who choose to make inquiry on the subject.

Nearly every kind of possession is some evidence of ownership, and in almost all cases where goods in the possession of the bankrupt have been held not to be within this clause, the reason has been not that the possession afforded no evidence, or insufficient evidence, of reputed ownership, but that the facts negatived the consent of the true owner.

For goods which do not belong to the bankrupt to pass to the trustee under this section, three requirements are necessary:

(a) the goods must be in the possession, order or disposition of the bankrupt in his trade or business;

(b) they must be there under such circumstances that he is the reputed owner thereof; and

(c) both of the above must be with the consent of the true owner.

"Goods" are defined as including chattels personal, but they do not include chattels real, fixtures,[89] heirlooms[90] or growing crops.[91] They do, however, include all personal estate in the shape of stock, bonds, notes, money, plate, furniture, etc. (except chattels real and heirlooms). The doctrine applies only to goods in the possession of the bankrupt in his trade or business, which means in the ordinary course of his business.[92] It does not apply to goods not ordinarily used for business purposes, or kept at the bankrupt's home if he does not carry on his business from his home. With the spread of the use of limited liability companies for business activities this doctrine is of less importance now than it was in the nineteenth century.

Debts due or growing due to the bankrupt in the course of his trade or business are included, but other things in action are not.

The expression "things in action" (more commonly "choses in action") has been defined in various ways. Literally the expression means things recoverable by suit or action at law, or personal rights of property which can only be claimed or enforced by action, as opposed to things of which one can take physical possession. It does not include a right of action, such as, for instance, a right to recover damages for breach of contract, or a legal right to recover damages in tort, but such rights would not come within the scope of the section anyway.

---

89. *Horn* v. *Baker* (1808) 9 East. 215.
90. *Shaftesbury* v. *Russell* (1823) 1 B. & C. 666.
91. *Cooper* v. *Woolfitt* (1857) 2 H. & N. 122.
92. *Colonial Bank* v. *Whinney* (1886) 30 Ch. D. 261 at pp. 274 and 281; reversed by the House of Lords but on other grounds: (1886) 11 App. Cas. 426. *See also Lamb* v. *Wright & Co.* [1924] 1 K.B. 857, and *Sharman* v. *Mason* [1899] 2 Q.B. 679.

Farming stock subject to an agricultural charge is not within the scope of reputed ownership;[93] it would probably be excluded anyway by trade custom.

As to the second requirement, where an established custom or course of trade is proved, whereby traders have in their possession goods of which they are not the owners, the doctrine will be excluded because the existence of the custom would both prevent any reputation of ownership arising from the bankrupt's possession of the goods and negative any consent to the reputation of ownership.[94]

In *Ex parte Turquand*,[95] a case concerning hotel furniture, Lord Selborne stated:

> When the existence of a custom notorious in a particular trade or business is proved, the effect of which is that everyone who knows the custom knows the articles to which it is applicable, and which are in the place in which that trade or business is carried on, may or may not be the property of the person who is carrying on the trade or business, may or may not be held by him for other purposes, then the doctrine of reputed ownership is absolutely excluded as to all articles which are within the scope of the custom.

This would apply even to goods in the warehouse of a third person to the order of the bankrupt, or to bankrupts who are agents for sale and describe themselves on their business premises as "merchants and manufacturers' agents", since creditors would have sufficient notice to exclude reputed ownership.[96] Moreover, when goods are in a place where they might or might not be there by reason of the custom, it is irrelevant that they were not in fact there by reason of the custom. It is the notoriety of the custom which excludes the reputation, and so makes the clause inapplicable.

If, for example, a building contract provides for materials delivered to the site to pass into the ownership of the employer, but because of congestion on the site the employer allows the builder to store them in the builder's own yard, the doctrine of reputed ownership will apply and defeat the employer's title to those materials. However, materials on the building site itself are not within the reputed ownership of the builder, since it would be expected that some of the materials on the site might belong to the builder and some to the employer.

Goods in the matrimonial home which belong to one spouse and goods in the possession of a firm and belonging to the firm, are not, if the other spouse or partner becomes bankrupt, within the reputed ownership clause, not only because the bankrupt is not in

93. Agricultural Credits Act 1928, s. 8(4).
94. *Ex parte Watkins* (1873) L.R. 8 Ch. 520.
95. (1885) 14 Q.B.D. 636.
96. *Ex parte Bright* (1879) 10 Ch. D. 566.

possession, or not in sole possession, but also because the reputation of ownership is absent, the situation of the goods being consistent with their being the property of either spouse or of all the partners.

The third essential is that the true owner should consent both to the possession, etc. of the bankrupt and to the reputation of ownership.[97] The true owner must have consented to a state of things from which he must have known, if he had considered the matter, that the inference of ownership must arise, and must have consented to the use of the goods in the bankrupt's trade or business.

If the goods are taken out of the possession, etc. of the bankrupt by the true owner after, but without notice of, an act of bankruptcy but before the receiving order, this will constitute a dealing protected by s. 45. A mere invitation by the true owner to take possession, or an event entitling him to take possession, would not prevent the goods from being, with his consent, in the reputed ownership of the bankrupt: if, however, a bona fide demand for possession of the goods is made by the owner and is actually communicated to the bankrupt, even if it did not reach him until after he had committed an act of bankruptcy, this will show that the goods no longer remain with his consent and permission in the possession, order and disposition of the bankrupt.[98]

Consent to possession by the bankrupt under circumstances not naturally justifying such possession is of itself strong evidence of consent to reputation of ownership, since a man is held to intend the natural consequences of his own act. Where goods are not in the custody of the bankrupt, but are held by a third party to his order, and the true owner fails to give notice to the agent, this will be strong evidence of his consent to the reputed ownership of the bankrupt.[99]

In the case of trade debts, it seems that the fact that no notice has been given to the debtor, where there is an opportunity of giving such notice, is conclusive evidence of the consent of the true owner to the debt remaining in the reputed ownership of the bankrupt.[100] Registration of a bill of sale does not on its own exclude reputed ownership.[101]

Bills, promissory notes and any other negotiable instruments are examples of things in action, as are debentures and life assurance

97. *Load* v. *Green* (1846) 15 M. & W. 216; *Smith* v. *Hudson* (1865) 34 L.J.Q.B. 145; *Re Watson & Co.* [1904] 2 K.B. 753.
98. *Ex parte Wright* (1876) 3 Ch. D. 70.
99. *Ex parte Stewart* (1865) 34 L.J. Bank. 6; *Knowles* v. *Horsfall* (1821) 5 B. & A. 134.
100. *Ryall* v. *Rolle* (1749) 1 Ves. 348; *Edwards* v. *Martin* (1865) L.R. 1 Eq. 121.
101. *Re Ginger* [1897] 2 Q.B. 461, approved in *Hollinshead & another* v. *P. & H. Egan* [1913] A.C. 564.

policies, and they are therefore not within the section. Thus, any banker who has a mortgage on such things in action need not give notice to the company in order to protect himself against the trustee in bankruptcy. Even so, in the case of debentures and other things in action which are not negotiable instruments, notice is highly desirable so as to prevent future equities or rights of set-off arising as between the bankrupt and the company which would be binding against the banker. In the case of an assignment of trade book debts, quite apart from the question of rights of set-off, failure to give notice of the assignment to the debtor will as a general rule be taken to mean that the assignee has consented to the debts remaining in the order and disposition of the bankrupt, and in such cases the assignee will not be protected.

A general assignment of book debts is void against the trustee as regards any debts which have not been paid at the commencement of the bankruptcy, unless the assignment has been registered as if it were a bill of sale given otherwise than by way of security for the payment of money.[102] This, however, does not render void any assignment of book debts due at the date of the assignment from specified debtors, or of debts growing due under specified contracts, or any assignment of book debts included in a transfer of a business made bona fide and for value, or in any assignment of assets for the benefit of creditors generally. "Assignment" here includes assignment by way of security and other charges on book debts.[103] Notice should be served on the debtors in order to take the debts out of the "order and disposition" of the bankrupt.

DEBTS PROVABLE

A creditor may prove for all debts and liabilities, present or future, certain or contingent, to which the debtor was subject at the date of the receiving order, or to which he may be subject before his discharge by reason of any obligations incurred before the date of the receiving order.[104] The trustee must estimate the value of any contingent liability, but if the creditor disagrees with his estimate, the creditor has the right of appeal to the court.[105] A creditor cannot prove for a debt or liability contracted by the debtor after notice of any act of bankruptcy has been received by the creditor, or contracted after a receiving order has been made.[106]

If there have been mutual dealings between the bankrupt and a

102. Section 43(1).
103. Section 43(2).
104. Section 30.
105. Section 30(4).
106. Section 30(2).

creditor proving for a debt, an account must be taken of what is due from one party to the other in respect of such mutual dealings, and the balance will be provable, or paid, as the case may be.[107] However, the creditor cannot claim the benefit of any set-off against the debtor's property in respect of a debt incurred after notice of an available act of bankruptcy.

A debtor is released from any other liability on all debts provable in bankruptcy,[108] except in certain cases where a bankrupt will not be discharged save by the written consent of the Treasury or by an order of the court.[109]

PREFERENTIAL CREDITORS

There are certain debts and liabilities which must be paid in priority to all others.[110] Among these are parochial and local rates, income and other taxes, wages and salaries up to four months with a maximum of £800[111] for each clerk, servant, workman or labourer, and others. It is not established whether this figure of £800 is gross, or net of PAYE and other deductions. The list of the preferential payments has been extended over the years in keeping with the spirit of the section.[112]

SECURED CREDITORS

A banker "holding a mortgage charge or lien on the property of the debtor, or any part thereof, as a security for a debt due to him from the debtor" is a secured creditor,[113] and as a secured creditor he may:

(a) rely on his security and not prove;
(b) realise the security and prove for the balance;
(c) surrender the security and prove for the whole debt; or
(d) assess the value of the security and prove for the balance.[114]

He cannot rank for dividend unless he elects to assess the value, and he is entitled to receive a dividend only in respect of the balance, after deducting the value so assessed.[115] Moreover in this event the trustee may at any time redeem the security at the assessed value,

---

107. Section 31. *See* below.
108. Section 28(2).
109. Section 28(1).
110. Section 33.
111. The figure was increased from £200 by the Insolvency Act 1976, Sched. 1.
112. *See* Chapter Twenty-Nine.
113. Section 167.
114. Schedule 2, paras. 10–12.
115. Schedule 2, para. 10.

or if dissatisfied with the assessed value may require the security to be offered for sale.[116] The banker may at any time by notice in writing require the trustee to elect whether he will or will not exercise his power of redeeming the security or requiring it to be sold. If the trustee does not within six months signify in writing his intention to exercise the power, then he loses his right to exercise that power, and the equity of redemption and any other interest vests in the banker, the amount of his debt being reduced by the assessed value of the security.[117]

Where a banker has assessed the value of his security, he may at any time amend his valuation and proof on showing to the satisfaction of the trustee, or the court, that the valuation and proof were made bona fide on a mistaken valuation, or that the security has diminished or increased in value since its previous valuation. In these circumstances, the secured creditor must forthwith repay any surplus dividend he may have received in excess of that appropriate to the amended valuation, or, as the case may be, is entitled to be paid out of any moneys available for further dividends any amount he has not received by reason of the inaccuracy of the original valuation, but he cannot disturb the distribution of any dividend declared before the date of amendment.[118] For example, suppose the debt is £1,000; if the banker has assessed the value of his security as £600 for dividend purposes, he may receive dividends in respect of £400. If he then sells the security for £650, he must repay any dividends received on £50. If he sells it for only £450, he is entitled to dividends on £150 at the rate at which dividends have already been paid, as well as to future dividends on £550, but if the undistributed assets are insufficient to pay him even a dividend on £150, he cannot upset past distributions.

If a valued security is subsequently sold, the net amount realised is substituted for any previous valuation, and treated as an amended valuation.[119] It is advisable for the banker to consult the trustee before dealing in any way with the bankrupt's securities.

Where a policy of life assurance is taken as security, the banker cannot prove for the value of future premiums, even though the bankrupt, in the memorandum of deposit, covenanted to pay the future premiums, for there cannot be two proofs in respect of one debt, even if there are separate contracts in respect of the same debt.[120]

---

116. Schedule 2, paras. 13(1) and (2). (In this case he is not entitled to the extra 20 per cent; contrast Sched. 1, para. 12, which refers to voting.)
117. Schedule 2, para. 13(3).
118. Schedule 2, paras. 14–15.
119. Schedule 2, para. 16.
120. *Deering* v. *Bank of Ireland* (1886) 12 App. Cas. 20; *see also Re Moss, ex parte Hallett* [1905] 2 K.B. 307; [1904–7] All E.R. Rep. 713.

Security belonging to and deposited by a third party to secure an account need not be valued, for this is not "the property of the bankrupt"[121] but the property of the third party, and can be treated as collateral security. The banker, therefore, can claim on the bankrupt's estate for the full amount of the debt, and after receiving a dividend fall back on the collateral security to make up any deficit. The proceeds of any collateral security realised by the banker while the bankrupt's estate is being administered should be placed to a suspense account pending final settlement of the estate. These remarks apply to security belonging to and deposited by an individual partner to secure his firm's account and to a guarantee or other security given by a third party to secure the bankrupt's account.

Every memorandum of deposit or guarantee taken by a banker should contain a clause renouncing in favour of the banker the depositor's right of proof against the principal debtor's estate.[122] A guarantor may (provided the creditor himself does not) prove for his contingent liability in respect of a debt which he has not paid, and in the same way a banker can prove in a bankrupt guarantor's estate in respect of the contingent liability.

Where property in the name of a bankrupt and a third party (often a wife or father) is charged to secure a debt due from the bankrupt, the rule seems to be that each party's share in the property is regarded as charged for a corresponding share of the debt; where the interests in the property are equal, each will be security for half the debt. In such cases where the debt is equal to, or slightly below, half of the value of the property, the solvent party will be entitled to acquire the bankrupt's share for a nominal, or for a low consideration, subject of course to the mortgage.[123] Where the security is realised by the creditor and the creditor wishes to prove against the bankrupt's estate, he must (in cases where the interests are equal) regard half of the debt as secured, and may only prove for half the balance.[124]

INTEREST

Bankruptcy breaks the relationship of banker and customer. Consequently the banker is unable to charge compound interest after the date of the receiving order, and can only prove for interest up to the date of the order, or, where there is a deed of assignment, up to the date of the deed. Where a debt has been proved, and the

121. Section 38.
122. *See* Chapter Fourteen.
123. *Re Rushton (a bankrupt), ex parte National Westminster Bank* v. *Official Receiver* [1971] 2 All E.R. 937.
124. *Re a Debtor (No. 24 of 1971), ex parte Marley* v. *Trustee of the property of the Debtor* [1976] 2 All E.R. 1010.

debt includes interest, such interest must for the purposes of dividend be calculated at a rate not exceeding 5 per cent per annum, without prejudice to the right of a creditor to receive out of the estate any higher rate of interest to which he may be entitled after all the debts proved in the estate have been paid in full.[125]

From a banker's point of view, this means that on a fixed loan account, he is restricted to interest at 5 per cent per annum for the period from the last interest payment until the commencement of the bankruptcy. On a running account, where there have been both debits and credits in the three years before the commencement of the bankruptcy, interest which has been debited to the account is not treated as having been paid simply because it has been debited. Payments in must be allocated between principal and interest in the proportions interest at the contractual rate (as so debited) bears to principal.[126] For this purpose interest is calculated at the contractual rate on the principal balances thrown up by such calculations, and if interest at the rate of 5 per cent per annum exceeds the amounts credited as interest in such calculations, the excess ranks for dividends and the balance is postponed, but if it is less than the amounts so allocated, the whole of the remaining interest is postponed for dividend purposes.

PROOF OF DEBTS

Where the Official Receiver so requires, a debt is proved by delivering or sending to him through the post in a prepaid letter an affidavit veryifying the debt. Otherwise an unsworn claim to the debt will suffice.[127]

The general practice is that an affidavit will not be required and the claim (proof of debt) is only required to be signed by the creditor or a person authorised to sign on his behalf. It is no longer required to be stamped.

The proof of debt must be made on the regulation Form 60,[128] and must state the amount of the debt, when contracted, particulars of securities held (if any), and in the case of bills the dates on which they were drawn and due to be paid and the names of the drawers and acceptors. The proof of the debt should specify the vouchers (if any) by which the claim can be substantiated.[129] A proof intended

---

125. Section 66(1).
126. Section 66(2). These apportionments are required to be made "notwithstanding any agreement to the contrary". For further discussion of this topic, *see* under "Interest" in Chapter Twenty-Nine.
127. Schedule 2, para. 2, as amended by the Insolvency Act 1976, s. 5.
128. Rule 7 and Appendix 1.
129. Schedule 2, para. 4.

to be used at the first meeting of creditors must be lodged with the Official Receiver not later than the time appointed for the meeting.[130]

PROOF ON BILLS OF EXCHANGE

If a banker holds bills indorsed by the bankrupt as security for an overdraft, he is not, so far as regards the bills, a secured creditor bound to value them in his proof, though he must name them. The banker therefore can prove against the estate for the whole of the overdraft, and when the bills become due can claim against the other parties to the bills, provided that in the aggregate he does not receive more than 100p in the pound. However, if the bankrupt has not indorsed the bills he has deposited with the banker as security, the property in the bills remains in the bankrupt, the banker having a lien or charge on them – that is to say, he is a secured creditor and must value them in his proof.

If bills have been given by the debtor to the creditor as security for a debt, the creditor can only prove for the actual amount of the debt still remaining due, even if the amount of the bills is greater; so also if the bill was received by the creditor in pursuance of a guarantee given by the bankrupt. If a bill held by the banker as security for the account of the drawer is an accommodation bill, he can on the bankruptcy of the acceptor prove for the whole amount of the bill, even though it exceeds in amount the balance of the account, but he cannot retain more than is due to him in respect of the overdraft granted to the party accommodated.[131]

If the banker has discounted bills for a customer who has become bankrupt, he may prove against the customer's estate for the amount of the bills, but if any of them is paid in full on maturity by the acceptors he must either deduct the amount so paid from his proof or else refund the proper amount from any dividend paid.[132] If both drawer and acceptor of such bills become bankrupt, the discounting banker can prove against each estate for the whole amount of the discounted bills, but he cannot receive more than 100p in the pound.[133] If he receives a dividend from one estate before sending in his proof against any other estate, or if any dividend has been

130. Schedule 1, para. 8.
131. *Ex parte Schofield* (1879) 12 Ch. D. 337; *Ex parte Bagshaw* (1879) 13 Ch. D. 304; *Ex parte Bloxham* (1802) 6 Ves. 600; *Re Willats, ex parte Reader* (1819) Buck. 381.
132. *Re Moulson, ex parte Burn* (1814) 2 Rose. 55.
133. *Ex parte Lee* (1721) 1 P. Wms. 782.

declared,[134] he can only prove for the balance after deducting the dividend received.[135]

The holder of a bill is simply a creditor, not a secured creditor. In certain circumstances, however, the holder may be entitled to securities specifically deposited as security for payment by one party liable on the bill with another party liable on the same bill. This can only happen when the one party has specifically lodged the securities with the other party as cover for the bill, and when both parties to the bill have become bankrupt. For example, where the drawer of the bill gets another party to accept it by depositing some of his property as security. This rule is known as the rule in *Ex parte Waring*.[136] It only applies if both parties become bankrupt, and the holder would therefore have a double right of proof.

Any bill of exchange, promissory note, or other negotiable instrument or security on which proof has been made must be exhibited to the trustee before payment of any dividend thereon.[137] If the bill or other instrument has been lost, the court may order that the loss shall not be set up, provided that a satisfactory indemnity is given by the party claiming on the lost instrument.[138]

A banker is entitled to retain either the whole or a part of a bankrupt customer's credit balance in order to meet the contingent liability on bills discounted for the customer, since a contingent liability on a bill is a provable debt, and is there subject to a set-off.[139]

Where the banker is a holder for the value of a bill which is dishonoured on maturity, the banker must give notice of dishonour to the drawer and each indorser, since any drawer or indorser to whom such notice is not given is discharged.[140] If the drawer or indorser is bankrupt, notice may be given either to the party himself or to his trustee.[141] Delay in giving notice of dishonour is excused, and notice is dispensed with, if any of the statutory causes of delay applies.[142]

If in such circumstances it is the acceptor who fails, and the banker becomes a party to a deed of assignment without the knowledge and consent of the drawer or indorser, the latter will be discharged from all liability, unless the deed of assignment contained a

134. *Ex parte Leers* (1802) 6 Ves. 644; *Re Stein, ex parte Royal Bank of Scotland* (1815) 2 Rose. 197.
135. *Cooper* v. *Pepys* (1741) 1 Atk. 107; *Ex parte Rushforth* (1805) 10 Ves. 409.
136. *Re Brickwood, ex parte Waring, Re Bracken, ex parte Inglis* (1815) 19 Ves. 345.
137. Rule 271.
138. Bills of Exchange Act 1882, s. 70.
139. Sections 30 and 31; *see* below.
140. Bills of Exchange Act 1882, s. 48. *See* Chapter Nine.
141. Bills of Exchange Act 1882, s. 49(10).
142. Bills of Exchange Act 1882, s. 50.

clause expressly reserving the banker's rights against the other parties.[143]

SET-OFF

Set-off is governed by s. 31 of the Bankruptcy Act which applies where there have been mutual credits, mutual debits or other mutual dealings between the debtor and any other person proving or claiming to prove. Section 31 requires that the sum due from the one party shall be set off against the sum due from the other and only the balance is claimed. Set-off is compulsory and it is not possible to exclude it by agreement.[144] It is not necessary that the sum should be presently due for set-off to apply, but the claims on each side must be such as to result in pecuniary liabilities.[145]

The law was examined in some detail by the Court of Appeal in *Rolls Razor v. Cox*[146] where the company's salesmen claimed a set-off in respect of their unpaid or withheld remuneration against (*a*) moneys received by them from the sale by them of the company's goods, (*b*) goods in their possession but unsold at the date of the winding up, and (*c*) goods to be used by them for the purpose of effecting such sale or installing the goods. It was held that set-off applied in all three classes.

The crucial date is, in bankruptcy, the date of the receiving order and, in liquidation, the commencement of the winding up.[147] A liability under a contract made before the receiving order, but which only arose or could only be quantified after the date of the receiving order may be set off.[148] However, there is no set-off if at the relevant date there is no "debt" due from one party to the other, but only a wholly contingent liability. Thus if a guarantor has not been called upon to pay or has not paid, there is no set-off in respect of the guarantee liability,[148] even if the guarantor subsequently discharges the guarantee liability.[149] Suppose, for example, that A is a creditor of B for goods sold and delivered to B, and B, who has guaranteed A's bank overdraft, becomes bankrupt. B's trustee is entitled on paying off A's overdraft (he may, for example, wish to obtain the release of securities charged by B) to pursue A for the

143. *Oriental Financial Corporation* v. *Overend, Gurney & Co.* (1871) 7 Ch. App. 142; *see also* Chapter Fourteen.
144. *Halesowen Presswork and Assemblies* v. *National Westminster Bank* [1972] 1 All E.R. 641.
145. *Rose* v. *Hart* (1818) 8 Taunt. 499.
146. [1967] 1 Q.B. 552.
147. *Re Daintrey, ex parte Mant* [1900] 1 Q.B. 546.
148. *Re Fenton, ex parte Fenton Textile Association* [1931] 1 Ch. 85.
149. *Re Waite (Re a Debtor (66 of 1955), ex parte Debtor* v. *Trustee of Waite)* [1956] 2 All E.R. 94.

amount paid to A's bank and to petition for his bankruptcy. A is not entitled to set off the debt due to him from B, even though if A became bankrupt, the question of set-off would arise in A's bankruptcy.[149]

If one follows this principle through, and looks at the position from the banker's point of view, it would appear that if the banker has not made demand on a guarantor, or if the guarantor has not become actually liable to pay the banker, when the receiving order is made, there is no set-off as between the guarantee liability and any credit balance the guarantor may have. Thus if a guarantor has backed his guarantee liability by a cash deposit without creating a charge on the deposit, there would not necessarily be a set-off as between the guarantee liability and the cash deposit, unless steps were taken to ensure that on the bankruptcy of the depositor the guarantee liability became immediately due. (This is a problem which does not arise where a borrower himself makes a cash deposit, since on the bankruptcy of the depositor set-off would apply anyway as between the deposit and the loan, even if neither deposit nor loan had matured.)

Set-off applies to any pecuniary liability; for example, rent due from a tenant to a bankrupt landlord may be set off against the tenant's claim for damages for misrepresentation by the landlord.[150] Moreover, since set-off extends to everything which may be proved, it covers not only breaches of contract but also breaches of obligations arising out of the contract, such as misrepresentation (for which damages may now be awarded even in the absence of fraud).[151]

Money given for a specific purpose which is not being carried out cannot be set off. Thus if money is paid to a solicitor on account of future costs which, because of the supervening bankruptcy, never became payable, the money could not be set off by the solicitor against a debt for costs previously incurred, nor, if there was a balance after satisfying such costs, could the balance be set off.[152]

In *Re City Equitable Fire Insurance Co (No. 2)*,[153] a reinsurance treaty provided that the insurance company could retain and accumulate a proportion of all premiums credited to the re-insurers as a deposit to secure the due performance of the re-insurers' obligations; so long as the agreement continued, the deposit was to be maintained at a certain level, and any balance after satisfying any obligation in respect of which the insurers defaulted, was to bear

150. *Kitchen's Trustee* v. *Madders* [1950] Ch. 134.
151. *Jack* v. *Kipping* (1882) 9 Q.B.D. 113; *Peat* v. *Jones & Co.* (1881) 8 Q.B.D. 147.
152. *Re Pollitt* [1893] 1 Q.B. 455.
153. [1930] 2 Ch. 293.

interest in favour of the re-insurers. When the re-insurers went into liquidation, it was held that interest was one of a number of mutual credits or debits which could be set off, but that the deposit was money handed over for a specific purpose and therefore had to be repaid in full without set-off.

Differences in the nature of the claims, such as, for example, that one arises under a deed and the other under a simple contract, or that one is legal and the other equitable, are immaterial.[154] Where a banker has both a preferential debt (in respect of advances for the payment of wages) and an unsecured claim, the credit balance would be applied first in discharge of the preferential debt.[155] The debts must, however, be between the same parties and in the same right,[156] and therefore a joint debt cannot be set off against a separate debt, nor a debt from three partners against a debt due to two.[157] Nor can a debt due to an executor *qua* executor be set off against a debt due from him personally.[158] A debt due to or from the trustee, arising in his management of the estate in bankruptcy, cannot be set off against a debt due from or to the bankrupt before the bankruptcy[159] (except where the set-off is claimed in respect of the same contract which gave rise after the bankruptcy to the debt which the trustee is seeking to enforce).[160]

There can be no set-off by a contributory against calls on shares made by a company,[161] unless the contributory is bankrupt,[162] nor can any debt be assigned to an assignee after notice of an available act of bankruptcy (or after the commencement of the liquidation) so as to give the assignee a right of set-off.[163] However, if a person is liable, such as, for example, an indorser upon a negotiable instrument which he is compelled to take up, the ruling in respect of notice does not apply and he is entitled to set off what he has paid against any claim by the trustee against him.[164] Furthermore a guarantor paying off his principal's debt after bankruptcy of the principal may

154. *Ex parte Law* (1846) De Gex. 378; *Mathieson's Trustee* v. *Burrup Mathieson & Co.* [1927] 1 Ch. 562.
155. *Re E.J. Morel (1934) Ltd.* [1962] Ch. 21.
156. *West* v. *Pryce* (1825) 2 Bing. 455.
157. *Ex parte Ross* (1817) Buck. 125; *Staniforth* v. *Fellowes* (1814) 1 Marshall 184; *Ex parte Twogood* (1805) 11 Ves. 517.
158. *Bishop* v. *Church* (1748) 3 Atk. 691.
159. *Ince Hall Rolling Mills Co.* v. *Douglas Forge & Co.* (1882) 8 Q.B.D. 179.
160. *Mangles* v. *Dixon* (1852) 3 H.L.C. 702.
161. *Re Whitehouse & Co.* (1878) 9 Ch. 595; *Re Overend, Gurney & Co., Grissell's case* (1866) 1 Ch. App. 528.
162. *Re Duckworth* (1867) 2 Ch. App. 578; *Re Anglo-Greek Steam Navigation and Trading Co., Carralli and Haggard's Claim* (1869) 4 Ch. App. 174.
163. *De Mattos* v. *Saunders* (1872) L.R. 7 C.P. 570; *Re Asphaltic Wood Pavement Co., Lee and Chapman's case* (1885) 30 Ch. D. 216.
164. *Macarty* v. *Barrow* (1733) 2 Stra. 949; *Collins* v. *Jones* (1830) 10 B. & C. 777.

set off any securities held by the creditor to which such payment may entitle him, so long as the whole debt is extinguished and the creditor no longer has a right of proof.[165]

Set-off applies to the Crown,[166] and if, for example, HM Customs and Excise is a debtor of the estate in respect of an overpayment of VAT for one period, repayment might be delayed until HM Customs and Excise was satisfied that no other department was a creditor. This could in some cases delay the administration of the estate.[167]

AVOIDANCE OF VOLUNTARY SETTLEMENTS

Under Section 42(1) any voluntary settlement of property is void against the trustee if the settlor becomes bankrupt at any subsequent time within two years after the date of the settlement. If he becomes bankrupt at any subsequent time within ten years of the date of the settlement, it is void against the trustee unless the parties claiming under the settlement can prove that the settlor was, at the time of making the settlement, able to pay his debts without the aid of the property comprised in the settlement.

For this purpose "becomes bankrupt" means commits an available act of bankruptcy,[168] so that the period of two or ten years runs back from the commencement of the bankruptcy.

Section 42 covers settlements or gifts of any property. A voluntary settlement made by a person who does not become bankrupt within ten years of making it is not affected by these provisions, but may nevertheless be set aside as having been made with intent to defraud creditors.[169] Settlements made before and in consideration of marriage and settlements in favour of a purchaser or mortgagee taking in good faith and for valuable consideration are excluded from the section. Consideration in this section means "consideration moving to the debtor, which replaces the property extracted from his creditors."[170] The mere assumption by the "purchaser" of the debtor's liability under a mortgage of some property which he was receiving from the debtor would not amount to consideration for this purpose, though it might be consideration for other purposes.

"Void" in fact means voidable, as the settlement is not avoided from its date, but only from the date when the trustee's title arises;

165. *Jones* v. *Mossop* (1844) 3 Hare. 568; *Re Fenton* [1931] 1 Ch. 85, and *Re Fenton (No. 2)* [1932] 1 Ch. 178.
166. *See Re D.H. Curtis (Builders)* [1978] Ch. 162.
167. *See* Chapter Twenty-Nine.
168. *Fawcett* v. *Fearn* (1844) 6 Q.B. 20; *Re Reis* [1904] 1 K.B. 451.
169. Law of Property Act 1925, s. 172.
170. *Re a Debtor (803 of 1961)* [1965] 1 W.L.R. 1498.

anyone who claims under the settlement as a purchaser for valuable consideration without notice has a good title.[171] A purchaser for value from the donee under such a settlement, without notice of an act of bankruptcy committed by the settlor, is nevertheless entitled to hold the property, even though the purchase is subsequent to the act of bankruptcy to which the trustee's title relates back.[172]

If a settlement is avoided, it is avoided completely and does not enable the trustee to obtain priority over encumbrances created subsequently by the settlor, or permit the trustee to disregard other events preventing the settlor from having the free disposition of his property.[173] It is, however, avoided only so far as is necessary to satisfy the debts and costs of the bankruptcy; the title to any surplus of the settled property is unaffected.[174]

The reference to good faith here appears to mean the absence of dishonesty and of any conscious attempt to defraud any other person[175] rather than a reference to a duty owed to the general body of creditors.[176]

It is not certain whether proof that at some time after the date of settlement the settlor was solvent would, in the absence of any evidence to the contrary, be prima facie evidence that he was solvent at the time of the settlement, but it seems that it would at least be admissible evidence. In determining whether a trader was able to pay all his debts at the time of the settlement without the aid of the property comprised in the settlement, the value of the implements of his trade and of the goodwill of his business must be excluded if he was intending to continue the business, since he must be able to pay his debts in the ordinary course of his business if he was proposing to continue it.[177]

ACCOUNT WITH UNDISCHARGED BANKRUPT

Section 47(1)1 provides that:

All transactions by a bankrupt with any person dealing with him bona fide and for value, in respect of property, whether real or personal, acquired by the bankrupt after the adjudication, shall, if completed before any intervention by the trustee, be valid against the trustee ... For the purposes of this sub-section, the receipt of any money, security or negotiable

171. *Re Brall* [1893] 2 Q.B. 381; *Re Vansittart* [1893] 2 Q.B. 377.
172. *Re Hart* [1912] 3 K.B. 6.
173. *Sanguinetti* v. *Stuckey's Banking Co.* [1895] 1 Ch. 176; *Re Farnham* [1895] 2 Ch. 799.
174. *Re Sims* (1896) 3 Mans. 340.
175. *See*, for example, *Re a Debtor (803 of 1961)* [1965] 1 W.L.R. 1498.
176. As in s. 46; *see*, for example, *Re Dalton* [1963] Ch. 336.
177. *Ex parte Russell* (1882) 19 Ch. D. 588.

instrument from or by the order or direction of a bankrupt by his banker, and any payment and any delivery of any security or negotiable instrument made to or by the order or direction of a bankrupt by his banker, shall be deemed to be a transaction by the bankrupt with such banker dealing with him for value.

This section only applies to after-acquired property, i.e. property acquired after ajudication, but not, it would appear, to property acquired between the date of the act of bankruptcy and the date of the adjudication. Furthermore, it is clear that provided the property dealt with comes within the section, a banker's dealings with it (until the trustee intervenes) are protected. However, in spite of the protection afforded by this section, the risk of opening an account with an undischarged bankrupt is a very real one, for how is the banker to know what is after-acquired property and what is not? If it is proved not to be after-acquired property or personal earnings, he may be held liable to refund it to the trustee.[178]

There is another difficulty in regard to an undischarged bankrupt's account, for

Where a banker has ascertained that a person having an account with him is an undischarged bankrupt, then, unless the banker is satisfied that the account is on behalf of some other person (e.g. a trust account) it is his duty forthwith to inform the trustee in bankruptcy or the Department of Trade of the existence of the account, and thereafter he must not make any payments out of the account, except under an order of the court or in accordance with instructions from the trustee in the bankruptcy, unless by the expiration of one month from the date of giving the information no instructions have been received from the trustee.[179]

Since it is a statutory obligation on the part of a banker to stop all payments out of the account upon discovering that his customer is an undischarged bankrupt, the banker cannot be liable in damages for dishonouring his customer's cheques immediately after the discovery. The statutory notice to the trustee or Department of Trade should be sent by registered post in order to prove delivery, if necessary. The banker should also advise his customer that he has sent the statutory notice.

Before opening an account with the wife or other nominee of an undischarged bankrupt, who is continuing the business formerly carried on by the bankrupt, the banker should give notice to the trustee and obtain his written consent, otherwise he may be called upon to refund to the trustee all moneys paid out. If the wife's account does not purport to be in connection with her husband's

178. *See also* "The debtor's property" above.
179. Section 47(2).

business, the banker should satisfy himself beyond doubt that it is concerned only with her separate property. An undischarged bankrupt is guilty of an offence if he engages in any trade or business under a name other than that under which he was adjudicated bankrupt, without disclosing to all persons with whom he enters into any business transaction the name under which he was adjudicated bankrupt.[180]

An undischarged bankrupt is prohibited from acting as a director of, or directly or indirectly taking part in or being concerned in the management of, any company, unless he has obtained the leave of the court.[181] If, therefore, a director of any of the banker's customer companies is known to be in financial difficulties, the banker should be on the alert and, if the director is adjudicated bankrupt, the banker should see that he no longer takes part in the management of the company unless he has leave to do so.

It may be added that a banker should not pay open cheques drawn in favour of and presented by a person known to be an undischarged bankrupt. Such a payment would not be "payment in due course", which means payment in good faith and without notice of any defect in the title of the presenter. The paying banker in such circumstances would not be able to debit his customer, and would be responsible to the trustee in bankruptcy should it be proved that the money belonged to the bankrupt's estate and that it had been misappropriated by him. The cheque should be returned to the payee in such a way as to protect the credit of the drawer by use of some such words as "Title of payee requires confirmation".[182] If the banker does not know of the bankruptcy, he would be paying the cheque to the holder in good faith and without notice of the holder's defective title, and would thus obtain a good discharge and be entitled to debit his customer's account.[183]

DEEDS OF ARRANGEMENT COMPARED WITH BANKRUPTCY

By means of a deed of arrangement, a debtor may assign all his property to a trustee for the benefit of his creditors generally, in consideration of their releasing him from the debts he owes to them, the trustee under the deed being directed to realise the estate and distribute the proceeds among the creditors *pro rata*. By thus assigning his property the debtor commits an act of bankruptcy, but that

180. Section 155(b); R. v. Doubleday (1964) 49 Cr. App. R. 62.
181. Companies Act 1948, s. 187.
182. Q.B.P., No. 148.
183. Bills of Exchange Act 1882, s. 59.

does not necessarily make him a bankrupt. Before that can happen a bankruptcy petition must be presented against him by a duly qualified creditor or creditors within three months of the commission of the act. If therefore all the creditors agree to accept the deed of arrangement, the costly and slow-moving official proceedings in bankruptcy may be avoided. However, if a cantankerous or dissatisfied creditor or combination of creditors for £200 or over objects to the private arrangements, then the estate may be forced into bankruptcy.[184]

It is necessary to emphasise the fact that these private arrangements are not compositions or schemes under the Bankruptcy Act; they are arrangements made between debtors and their creditors quite outside the provisions of the Act and are regulated by another Act, the Deeds of Arrangement Act 1914. The object of such private arrangements is to avoid the publicity and expense unavoidable in bankruptcy proceedings. They have another advantage from the debtor's point of view, namely that none of the disabilities of an undischarged bankrupt attach either to the debtor or to those dealing with him.

The creditors also stand to benefit by such an arrangement, inasmuch as the debtor's estate can usually be wound up more quickly and less expensively than by official proceedings in bankruptcy. There is also less chance under this arrangement of a forced realisation of assets. The two main disadvantages of a private arrangement as compared with bankruptcy proceedings are first, that it is of no effect unless all the creditors agree to it—one dissentient claiming for £200 or over can wreck the whole scheme, unless the assenting creditors decide to pay him out in full—and secondly, there is no public examination under oath, and the absence of penalty for concealment of available assets makes the chance of this kind of fraud happening greater than it would be in the publicity of the bankruptcy court and in face of the stringent regulations of the Act. The bankruptcy law also provides effective punishment for such serious offences as indulgence in gambling or in hazardous speculation, which are the proximate causes of so many bankruptcies.

The chief disadvantage of bankruptcy proceedings as compared with a private arrangement is the less speedy, less profitable and more costly realisation of the assets.

LEGAL REQUIREMENTS

A deed of arrangement is void unless registered with the Registrar

184. *See* under "Acts of Bankruptcy" above.

of Bills of Sale under the Act within seven clear days of its execution.[185] It will also become void unless, before or within 21 days after it has been registered, or within such extended time as the court may allow, it has received the assent of a majority in number and value of the creditors.[186] The assent of a creditor must be established by his executing the deed or by sending to the trustee his written consent attested by a witness.[187] In calculating a majority in number and value of the creditors, a creditor holding security upon the debtor's property shall be reckoned as a creditor only for the balance (if any) due to him after deducting the value of his security.[188] Creditors for sums not exceeding £10 are reckoned in the majority in value but not in number.[188]

A deed of arrangement is only binding on those that assent to it, but a trustee may serve on any creditor who has not assented a written notice of the execution of the deed and the filing of the certificate of creditors' assents, with the intimation that the creditor will not, after one month from the service of the notice, be entitled to present a bankruptcy petition against the debtor founded on the execution of the deed or any other act connected with the proceedings preliminary to the execution of the deed.[189] Unless the deed becomes void, the trustee's written notice is binding upon the dissenting creditor. If bankruptcy intervenes, the deed becomes void.

When such a deed becomes void, the fact that a creditor has assented to the deed does not disentitle him to present a bankruptcy petition founded on the execution of the deed as an act of bankruptcy.[190] When a deed becomes void the trustee must give notice of the avoidance to every creditor, and file a copy of the notice with the Registrar of Bills of Sale.[191]

When a banker receives notice of a deed of arrangement and the deed relates to the customer's property generally, or if it specifically mentions the banking account, then he must not permit any further payments from the account. Before paying over any credit balance or parting with any of the debtor's property to the trustee, the banker should see the deed, satisfy himself that it has been duly registered and that it has received the necessary assents, and that it has not become void for any reason. The discharge of the trustee will be good provided a receiving order has not been made and

185. Deeds of Arrangement Act 1914, s. 2.
186. Ibid., s. 3(1).
187. Ibid., s. 3(3).
188. Ibid., s. 3(5).
189. Ibid., s. 24(1).
190. Ibid., s. 24(2).
191. Ibid., s. 20.

provided the banker has not had notice of the presentation of a bankruptcy petition.[192]

The banking account of the trustee or assignee of the estate must be opened in the name of the debtor's estate.[193] It is desirable to treat such an account as a paying-in one only until the period during which a bankruptcy petition may be presented has elapsed. The actions of the trustee are controlled by the provisions of the deed of his appointment. Unless he has already done so, the banker should see this deed and satisfy himself as to its due registration and its continuing validity, before allowing withdrawals.

Any deed of arrangement affecting land should be registered in the register of deeds of arrangement affecting land, in the name of the debtor, and re-registered every five years if necessary to preserve its effect.[194] Unless so registered, a deed of arrangement is void against a purchaser of any land comprised therein.[195]

COMPOSITION WITH CREDITORS

Another method by which a debtor may avoid bankruptcy proceedings is to call his creditors together privately and offer them a composition, i.e. so much in the pound, in full satisfaction of the moneys owing to them. It is usually arranged that the composition shall be payable by instalments upon agreed dates. Sometimes the debtor is asked to provide sureties who will guarantee the due payment of the instalments. The agreement may be under seal or under hand. An agreement not under seal to pay so much in the pound is not of itself an act of bankruptcy, but as, when carrying out the arrangement, the debtor may make statements which can be construed as an act of bankruptcy, the banker should act with great caution in regard to all operations on the debtor's account. If the debtor defaults in the payment of the instalments when due, the creditors have the power to take bankruptcy proceedings.

The same rules and requirements relating to avoidance and registration apply to such compositions.[196]

192. Bankruptcy Act 1914, s. 46.
193. Deeds of Arrangement Act 1914, s. 11(4).
194. Land Charges Act 1972, s. 8.
195. Ibid., s. 7(2).
196. Deeds of Arrangement Act 1914, s. 1(2)(b).

APPENDIXES

Specimen Forms

1. MISCELLANEOUS

REQUEST FOR PAYMENT OF INTEREST OR DIVIDENDS

To: The Secretary or Registrar

Date .... 19 ......

....

....

Insert name and address of Company

Please forward, until further notice, all Interest and Dividends that may from time to time become due on any Stocks or Shares now standing, or which may hereafter stand in my (our) name(s) or in the name(s) of the survivor(s) of us in the Company's books to:—

....

....

....

Full name and address of the Bank, Firm or Person to whom Interest and Dividends are to be sent

or, where payment is made to a Bank, to such other Branch of that Bank as the Bank may from time to time request. Your compliance with this request shall discharge the Company's liability in respect of such interest or dividends.

(1) *Signature* ....

Name in full ....
(BLOCK CAPITALS)

Address ....

....

This form must be signed by ALL *the Registered Holders, Executors or Administrators as the case may be*

Any change of
address may be
notified by
quoting former
and present
address

(2) *Signature* ....

Name in full ....
(BLOCK CAPITALS)

Address ....

....

(3) *Signature* ....

Name in full ....
(BLOCK CAPITALS)

Address ....

....

(4) *Signature* ....

Name in full ....
(BLOCK CAPITALS)

Address ....

....

NOTE (i) Directions to credit a particular account MUST
be given to the Bank direct and NOT INCLUDED
in this form.

(ii) Where the stock is in the name of a deceased
Holder, instructions signed by Executor(s) or
Administrator(s) should indicate the name of the
deceased.

Where the instructions are in favour of a Bank, this form
should be sent to the Bank branch concerned for the insertion of the following details:—

Bank's Reference Numbers and Details:—

(1) Sorting Code No. ....

(2) Name of Bank and
Title of Branch ....

(3) Account Number (if any) ....

STAMP OF BANK BRANCH (*use Stamp No.* 287)

MANDATE OR AUTHORITY FOR SOCIETY OR CLUB

To the.. Bank, PLC.

Copy of Resolutions passed by the[1] .... of the[2] .... at their meeting held on the .... day of .... 19 ......

[1] Committee or other Governing Body.

[2] Full name of the Club, or Society.

(1) "That the.................. Bank, PLC, be and are hereby appointed Bankers to the[3] ....
....

[3] Club or Society.

(2) "That the bank be authorised and requested to pay all cheques signed and all bills, notes and other negotiable instruments drawn, accepted, and made on behalf of the[3] .... by any[4] .... or more of them, and to debit the same to the account whether such account be in credit or otherwise.

[4] Here insert smallest number allowed to sign.

(3) "That cheques, bills, notes, and other negotiable instruments payable to the[3] .... may be indorsed for the[3] .... by any one or more of the persons mentioned in the Resolution No. 2 or by the Secretary of the[3] .... for the time being.

(4) "That all changes that may take place from time to time in those authorised to sign by virtue of these resolutions be advised by letter to the Bank signed by the Chairman for the time being."

(5) "That a copy of these Resolutions,[5] (under the Common Seal and) signed by the Chairman, be handed to the Bank, together with specimens of the necessary signatures, and that these Resolutions shall remain in force until the receipt by the Bank of a copy of a Resolution rescinding the same."

[5] Strike out words in brackets in cases where there is no seal.

I certify that the Resolutions, of which the above are copies, were duly passed at a meeting of the[1] .... held on the ...... day of .... 19......

..............Chairman.

Countersigned.

..............Secretary.

Dated this .... day of .... 19 ....
The following are the signatures of the persons mentioned in the above Resolutions—

....

....

....

LETTER CONCERNING APPOINTMENT OF BANKERS BY COMPANY

To　　　　BANK PLC

_____

_____

_____19

Dear Sirs,

_____ Public Limited Company.
　　　　(Registered Office_____).

　　　My Directors request you to open an account with the above-mentioned Company, and I hand you herewith:—

(3) This Certificate is not required in the case of a private company.

1. Certificate of Incorporation (for inspection and return).
2. Copy of the Memorandum and Articles of Association.
3. Certificate of Registrar of Companies, that the company is entitled to commence business (for inspection and return).
4. Certified copy of a resolution of the Board of Directors regulating the conduct of the Account, together with specimens of the signatures of the authorised signatories.

　　　　Yours faithfully,
　　　　　　　　_____Secretary.
　　　　_____Public Limited Company.

RESOLUTION FOR APPOINTMENT OF BANKERS

At a Meeting of the Board of Directors of _____
_____Public Limited Company, whose Registered
Office is at _____
held the _____ day of _____ 19____

IT WAS RESOLVED:—

1. "That   Bank PLC be appointed by the bankers of the company and that they be and are hereby authorised and requested to:—

(1) Honour and comply with all cheques, drafts, bills, promissory notes, acceptances, negotiable instruments and orders expressed to be drawn, accepted, made or given on behalf of the company at any time or times whether the banking account or accounts of the company are overdrawn by any payment or in relation thereto or are in credit or otherwise;

(2) Accept and comply with all agreements, indemnities and counter-indemnities in connection with the issue of letters of credit, drafts, telegraphic transfers, purchase and sale of foreign currencies;

(3) Act on any deposit or hypothecation of securities and documents of title belonging to the company and on any request for the withdrawal of the same;

(4) Act on any instructions relating to the accounts, affairs or transactions of the company generally, provided they are signed by _____

and countersigned by_____

2. That the Bank be and they are hereby authorised to treat all bills, promissory notes and acceptances as being indorsed on behalf of the company and to discount or otherwise deal with the same provided they purport to be signed by _____

_____

_____

3. That a list of the names and specimen signatures of the persons at present authorised to sign under this resolution be furnished to the Bank and that they be advised by letter signed by the chairman for the time being of all changes that may take place in the same from time to time; that a copy of this resolution be furnished to the Bank; and that it remain in force until the receipt by the Bank of a copy of a resolution rescinding the same."

We hereby certify the above to be a true copy from the Minutes.

_____ Chairman.

_____ Secretary.

Date _____ 19____

SPECIMEN SIGNATURES
will sign

_____	,,	_____
_____	,,	_____
_____	,,	_____
_____	,,	_____
_____	,,	_____
_____	,,	_____

SECURITIES REGISTER

Name_____   Other Liabilities Yes/No (Delete which is inapplicable)   **SECURITIES**

Date of Lodgement	Form Number Date By Whom Given Stamping	Formalities Completed Security Certificate Number	Description of Security	Debtor's Initial	Valuation	A or E with Date	Control & Information card marked	Discharge	Date	Checker's Initial

Securities (continued)

Name_____

Date of Lodgement	Form Number Date By Whom Given Stamping	Formalities Completed Security Certificate Number	Description of Security	Debtor's Initial	Valuation	A or E with Date	Control & Information card marked	Discharge	Date	Checker's Initial

2. SECURITY FORMS

GUARANTEE

To: ... Bank PLC

1. In consideration of your granting or continuing to grant to ...
of (hereinafter called "the Principal") time credit or other accom-

modation for so long as you shall think fit we ... of ... (hereinafter called "the Guarantor") hereby guarantee to you the due payment and discharge of and undertake on your demand in writing to pay to you and discharge

    (*a*) all sums of money and liabilities advanced or paid by you to or for or on account of the Principal or incurred by the Principal to you and

    (*b*) all other sums of money and liabilities which now are or shall at any time be due or owing or incurred or payable and unpaid by the Principal to you or for which the Principal may be or become liable to you anywhere

in either case upon any current or other banking account or upon any discount account or otherwise and whether alone or jointly with any person and whether actually or contingently and in whatever name style or form and whether as principal or surety or otherwise including or together with interest commission and other charges including legal costs charges and expenses (on a full indemnity basis) occasioned by or incidental to this or any other security held by or offered to you for the same indebtedness or by or to the enforcement or preservation of this security or which you may incur in enforcing or obtaining payment of any sums of money due to you from the Principal either alone or jointly as aforesaid or in attempting so to do/Provided nevertheless that the total amount recoverable from the Guarantor hereunder shall not exceed the sum of £... together with a further sum for all such interest (whether or not any of such interest has been capitalised and as well after as before any demand or judgment obtained hereunder) and other costs charges and expenses as aforesaid/

2. You shall be at liberty without thereby affecting your rights against the Guarantor hereunder at any time to determine enlarge or vary any credit to the Principal to vary exchange abstain from perfecting or release any other securities held or to be held by you for or on account of the moneys intended to be hereby secured or any part thereof to renew bills and promissory notes in any manner and to compound with give time for payment to accept compositions from and make any other arrangements with the Principal or any obligants on bills notes or other securities held or to be held by you for or on behalf of the Principal

3. This guarantee shall not be considered as satisfied or discharged by any intermediate payment or satisfaction of the whole or any part of any sum or sums of money owing as aforesaid but shall

constitute and be a continuing guarantee and extend to cover any sum or sums which shall for the time being constitute the balance due from the Principal to you on any such account or for any such matter or thing as hereinbefore mentioned

4. This guarantee shall be in addition to and shall not prejudice or affect and shall not be in any way prejudiced or affected by any collateral or other security now or hereafter held or judgment or order obtained by you for all or any part of the moneys hereby guaranteed nor shall such collateral or other security judgment or order or any lien to which you may be otherwise entitled or the liability of any person or persons not parties hereto for all or any part of the moneys hereby secured be in anywise prejudiced or affected by this present guarantee In particular it shall not be necessary for you to resort to or seek to enforce any security or personal guarantee or liability whether of the Principal or any other person or persons before claiming payment from the Guarantor You shall have full power at your discretion to give time for payment to or make any other arrangement with any such person or persons without prejudice to this present guarantee or any liability hereunder All moneys received by you from the Guarantor or the Principal or any person or persons liable to pay the same may be applied by you to any account or item of account or to any transaction to which the same may be applicable

5. This guarantee shall remain in full force and the Guarantor hereby so undertakes notwithstanding the full discharge of the sums secured by this guarantee or the release of any security held therefor if such discharge or release shall have been given or made on the faith of any assurance security or payment which is avoided under any statute relating to bankruptcy or winding up or is otherwise avoided in any manner and any discharge or release shall be conditional upon no assurance security or payment being avoided

6. The Guarantor hereby agrees that the said sums of money and liabilities shall be paid to you and discharged strictly in accordance with the terms and provisions of any agreement(s) express or implied which has/have been or may hereafter be made or entered into by the Principal in reference thereto regardless of any law regulation or decree or other legal provision now or hereafter in effect which might in any manner affect any of the terms or provisions of any such agreement(s) or your rights with respect thereto as against the Principal or cause or permit to be invoked any alteration in the time amount or manner of payment by the Principal of any of the sums

covered by this guarantee and in particular but without prejudice to the generality of the foregoing the Guarantor hereby further agrees as a separate and independent stipulation that any sum(s) of money intended to be the subject of this guarantee which may not be legally recoverable from the Principal by reason of any defect informality or insufficiency in the borrowing powers of the Principal or in the exercise thereof or any legal limitation disability incapacity on or of the Principal or of any other fact or circumstances whatsoever and whether or not known to you shall nevertheless be recoverable from the Guarantor as sole or principal debtor in respect thereof and shall be repaid to you by the Guarantor on demand and the Guarantor agrees to indemnify you and keep you indemnified against any loss you may suffer or incur by reason of any of the matters referred to in this clause

7. Notwithstanding the death bankruptcy or liquidation of the Principal this guarantee shall apply to all sums due to you from the Principal or which would have been due to you from the Principal if the death had taken place or the bankruptcy or liquidation had begun at the time of receipt by you of notice thereof

8. This present guarantee shall be construed and take effect as a guarantee of the whole and every part of the principal moneys and interest due or owing and unpaid as aforesaid and accordingly the Guarantor is not to be entitled as against you to any right of proof in the bankruptcy or insolvency of the Principal or other right of a surety discharging his liability in respect of the principal debt unless and until the whole of such principal moneys and interest shall have first been completely discharged and satisfied And further for the purpose of enabling you to sue the Principal to prove against the Principal's estate for the whole of the moneys due or owing and unpaid as aforesaid or to preserve intact the liability of any other party you may at any time place and keep for such time as you may think prudent any moneys received recovered or realised hereunder to the credit either of the Guarantor or such other person(s) or transaction(s) (if any) as you shall think fit without any intermediate obligation on your part to apply the same or any part thereof in or towards the discharge of the moneys due or owing and unpaid as aforesaid or any intermediate right on the part of the Guarantor to sue the Principal or prove against the estate of the Principal in competition with or so as to diminish any dividend or other advantage that would or might come to you or to treat the liability of the Principal as diminished

9. If the Guarantor shall have taken or shall hereafter take any security from the Principal in respect of the liability of the Guarantor under this guarantee such security shall stand as a security for you and shall forthwith be deposited with or transferred to you

10. This is a continuing guarantee and shall remain in full force and effect until six months from the date when written notice shall have been received by you from the Guarantor or the personal representatives of the Guarantor to discontinue it but so that the liability of the Guarantor or the personal representatives of the Guarantor shall continue to exist to the extent of all such sums of money and liabilities outstanding at the close of the day fixed for discontinuance (including liabilities not yet accrued at the close of the day fixed for discontinuance together with interest costs commission discount and other bankers' charges as aforesaid) until payment in full is received by you and shall be binding on the Guarantor and the personal representatives of the Guarantor and shall enure to the benefit of any be enforceable by you and your successors transferees and assigns and it is understood and agreed that none of its terms or provisions may be waived altered modified or amended except in writing duly signed for you and on your behalf In the event of this guarantee being determined it shall be lawful for you to continue any account with the Principal notwithstanding such determination and the liability of the Guarantor for the amount due from the Principal at the date when this guarantee is so determined shall remain notwithstanding any subsequent payment into or out of the account by or on behalf of the Principal

11. If this guarantee is executed by two or more parties they shall be jointly and severally liable hereunder and the word "Guarantor" wherever used herein shall be construed to refer to each of such parties separately in the same manner and with the same effect as if each of them had signed separate guarantees and in any such case this guarantee shall not be revoked or impaired as to any one or more of such parties by the death incapacity or liquidation or insolvency of any of the others. You shall be at liberty to release or discharge any one or more of such parties from liability under this guarantee or to accept any composition from or make any other arrangements with any of such parties without thereby releasing or discharging any other party hereto or otherwise prejudicing or affecting your rights and remedies against any such other party

12. The Guarantor hereby agrees that any certificate signed by any of your officers or executives or any person duly authorised on your behalf shall be conclusive evidence of the amount of all sums for

the time being due or owing to you from the Principal and the nature and character of such sums

13. Except as otherwise specified herein any notice (which expression shall where the context so permits include any request demand or other communication) to or upon any of the parties hereto shall be deemed to have been duly served if in writing either delivered to the party to whom it is addressed or sent by post (whether ordinary prepaid or registered or recorded delivery) addressed to such party at its address as stated hereon or at such other address as it may specify by notice in writing to the other party or parties or in the case of a company to its registered office Any notice sent by post shall be deemed to have been served on the day following that on which the envelope containing the same is posted and in proving such service it shall in the case of ordinary prepaid post be sufficient to prove that the envelope containing the same was properly addressed and either delivered to a Post Office or put into a Post Office letter box All references herein to writing shall be construed as including communications by telex telegram or cable and in such case it shall be sufficient if the communication is addressed to the party to whom it is addressed at its then current official telex number or telegram or cable address or if more than one such number or address any of them Any such telex telegram or cable shall be deemed to have been served at the time of sending and in proving such service it shall be sufficient to produce a sender's copy of such telex telegram or cable showing such number or address Any notice must be signed personally by the party serving it (or if by a company on behalf of the sender by a duly authorised director) or in your case by any of your officers or executives or any person duly authorised on your behalf provided that any notice by telex telegram or cable need not bear any manuscript signature In the case of the death of the Guarantor or any person who is a Guarantor hereunder and until the Bank receives notice in writing of the grant of probate of the will or of administration of the estate of such deceased Guarantor any notice or demand by the Bank sent or delivered as aforesaid addressed to such deceased Guarantor or his personal representatives at the address of such deceased Guarantor last known to the Bank or stated hereon shall for all purposes of this Guarantee be deemed a sufficient notice or demand by the Bank to the Guarantor and the personal representatives of such deceased Guarantor and shall be as effectual as if such deceased Guarantor were still living

14. This guarantee shall be construed in accordance with and governed in all respects by English law

15. The Guarantor hereby agrees to submit to the jurisdiction of the English Courts

16. This guarantee is and will remain your property

DATED this ... day of ... 19 ...

CHARGE BY WAY OF LEGAL MORTGAGE

THIS CHARGE made the   day of   19— BE-TWEEN ... PLC whose registered office is at ... (hereinafter called "the Company") of the one part and ... PLC whose registered office is at ... (hereinafter called "the Bank") of the other part

WITNESSETH as follows:—

1. The Company hereby covenants with the Bank to pay to the Bank immediately upon the same becoming due to the Bank and discharge

(*a*) all moneys and liabilities advanced or paid by the Bank to or for or on account of the Company or incurred by the Company to the Bank and

(*b*) all other sums of money and liabilities which now are or at any time hereafter may be due and owing or incurred by the Company to the Bank or for which the Company may be or become liable to the Bank

in either case on any current or other account or in any manner whatever and whether in pursuance of the Facility Letter or otherwise (and whether alone or jointly with any other person and in whatever style or name and whether as principal or surety or otherwise) including or together with commission banking or other charges costs and expenses (on a full indemnity basis) and interest (computed on a day-to-day basis) on all such sums moneys or liabilities from the time or the respective times of the same being advanced or incurred until payment (as well after as before any demand and/or judgment) at the rate or rates/corresponding to the effective rate or rates of interest payable by the Company in respect of bills discounted in force at the date of the said moneys or liabilities being incurred or at such other rate or rates as may be/ agreed from time to time between the Bank and the Company.

2. The Company will pay interest at the rate aforesaid on moneys so due (whether under this Deed or under any judgment which may

be recovered therefor and as well after as before any demand) quarterly on the days in March June September and December in each year which are for the time being and are from time to time notified by the Bank to the Company as being the Bank's usual days for the payment of interest or are otherwise agreed as being the days for payment of interest on any such moneys and such interest shall (but without prejudice to the obligation of the Company to pay the same punctually) be compounded with quarterly rests on the said dates in the event of its not being punctually paid.

3. As security for the payment and discharge of all sums covenanted to be paid to the Bank hereunder and all other moneys intended to be hereby secured (including any expenses and charges arising out of or in connection with the acts or matters referred to in Clause 10 hereof) the Company as beneficial owner hereby charges in favour of the Bank by way of legal mortgage the property referred to in the Schedule hereto (hereinafter called "the Property" which expression shall where the context so permits include each and every or any part thereof) and so that the charge hereby created shall be a continuing security

4. PROVISO FOR REDEMPTION
PROVIDED ALWAYS that if the Company shall pay to the Bank and discharge all moneys and liabilities hereby covenanted to be paid and all other moneys intended to be hereby secured the Bank will at the request and cost of the Company discharge this security

5. RESTRICTIONS AFFECTING THE PROPERTY

(*a*) (*i*) The statutory power of leasing entering into agreements for leases and accepting surrenders of leases shall not during the continuance of this security be exercisable by the Company without the prior consent of the Bank nor without such consent as aforesaid shall the Company grant or agree to grant any lease or tenancy of any freehold or leasehold land comprised in the Property which if granted would be valid as between the Company and the lessee or tenant but not binding on the Bank but it shall not be necessary to express such consent in any lease agreement or surrender.

(*ii*) The statutory powers of the Bank as mortgagee while in possession to grant leases and/or enter into agreements for leases or surrender of leases and/or accept surrenders of leases of the Property shall not apply to this security but the Bank shall have absolute and unrestricted power to grant leases and/or enter into agreements for leases or surrender of leases and/or accept surrenders of leases of the Property on any terms and conditions and at any rent as the Bank shall in its absolute discretion think fit (including but without prejudice to the generality of the foregoing the grant of leases and/or agreements for leases and/or the acceptance of surrenders of leases and/or the entry into agreements to surrender leases at or paying a fine or premium as the case may be and in the case of a surrender or agreement to surrender without any obligation to grant any new leases of any of the premises comprised in the surrendered lease) to the intent that the Bank shall be entitled to exercise enjoy and enforce any rights and privileges appertaining to the grant of any leases or agreement for leases or surrender of leases and the acceptance of any surrender of leases of the Property or any part thereof as if the Bank were the sole and absolute unencumbered beneficial owner of the Property.

(*iii*) The Company will not without the consent in writing of the Bank use or permit to be used for any other purpose other than as (high class) self-contained flats or maisonettes or as private residences limited in the case of each self-contained flat, maisonette or private residence to a single residence any part of the Property which if now occupied is, or if now unoccupied was when last occupied, used for the purposes of residential occupation.

(*iv*) Except in the case of leases of residential premises granted at a fine or premium for a term exceeding 21 years from the date of the lease the Company will not without prior consent of the Bank such consent not to be unreasonably withheld (grant to any tenant of the Property any licence to assign or underlet the premises comprised in that tenancy or any part thereof unless under the terms of the lease or agreement between the Company and the lessee or tenant such consent is not to be unreasonably withheld, and the Company will immediately notify the Bank in writing the terms of any assignment or underletting in respect of which this does not prohibit the Company from granting a licence without such consent, provided that nothing in this sub-Clause shall require the Company to require any tenant under a lease of residential premises granted at a fine or premium for a term exceeding 21 years from the date of the lease to covenant not to assign or underlet the premises comprised in such lease or any part thereof without the prior consent in writing of the Company.

(*v*) The Company will use its best endeavours to enforce against any lessee or tenant of the Property any or all the covenants in the lease or tenancy agreement concerned forthwith upon being requested in writing by the Bank so to do.

(*b*) During the continuance of this security no person or persons shall be registered under the Land Registration Acts 1925 to 1971 or any Act amending or re-enacting the same as proprietor of any freehold or leasehold land comprised in the Property or any part thereof without the consent in writing of the Bank and the costs incurred by the Bank in lodging from time to time a restriction against dealings or a caution against registration of the said land (as the case may be) shall be deemed to be costs properly incurred by it hereunder

(c) The Company will during the continuance of this security duly observe and perform all restrictive and other covenants and stipulations affecting any freehold or leasehold land comprised in the Property including in the case of leasehold land the terms covenants conditions restrictions and stipulations contained in the lease under which the Company holds such land (and will keep the Bank indemnified in respect of all actions proceedings costs claims and demands whatsoever occasioned by any breach of such covenants or stipulations.

(d) The Company will within ten days of the receipt of notice of the same by the Company give full particulars to the Bank of any notice order direction designation resolution or proposal having specific application to the Property or to the area in which it is situate given or made by any Planning Authority or other public body or authority or any other statutory power or by planning authority under or by virtue of any legislation for the time being in force on the subject of town and country planning or any orders regulations and directions issued under virtue of such Acts (hereinafter collectively referred to as "the Planning Acts") or the Community Land Act 1975 or the Development Land Tax Act 1976 or any subsequent or amended or other Acts in so far as the same relate to the Property and if so required by the Bank will also without delay and at the cost of the Company take all reasonable or necessary steps to comply with any such notice or order and will also at the request of the Bank but at the cost of the Company make or join with the Bank in making such objection or representation against or in respect of any proposal for such a notice or order as the Bank shall deem expedient

(e) The Company will not make any further application for planning permission in respect of the Property nor do or cause or suffer to be done anything thereon or with reference thereto which may be grounds for the compulsory acquisition thereof under the Community Land Act 1975 or any statutory modification thereof for the time being in force and any regulations or order made thereunder

(f) The Company will not at any time during the continuance of this security make or suffer to be made any structural alterations in or additions to any building on the Property or carry out or suffer to be carried out on the Property any development as defined in the Planning Acts or make or suffer to be made any material change in the use thereof without the prior consent in writing of the Bank such consent not to be unreasonably withheld. Such consent shall not be deemed to have been unreasonably withheld if given subject to the condition that any plans specifications or contracts with architects builders or other contractors shall be approved by the Bank in writing before any relevant works are commenced.

(*g*) The Company will not do or omit or suffer to be done or omitted any act matter or thing in on or respecting any freehold or leasehold land comprised in the Property required to be done or omitted by the Planning Acts or the Defective Premises Act 1972 or any other Acts or statutory provisions of such Acts or any of them and will at all times hereafter indemnify and keep indemnified the Bank against all actions proceedings costs expenses claims and demands whatsoever in respect of any such act matter or thing contravening the provisions of the Planning Acts or any of them as aforesaid.

(*h*) The Company will not pull down remove or permit or suffer to be pulled down or removed any building erection or structure on the Property and for the time being comprised in or subject to this security or (except in connection with the renewal or replacement thereof) any fixtures and fittings not will erect or make or suffer to be erected or made on the Property any building erection alteration or improvement or make or suffer to be made any material change or addition whatsoever in or to the use of the Property

6. REPAIRS, INSURANCE AND CONDUCT OF BUSINESS

(*a*) During the continuance of this security the Company shall

(*i*) keep all buildings and erections on the Property and all Plant Machinery fixtures fittings implements utensils and other effects used thereon for the purpose of or in connection with the business of the Company and every part thereof in a good state of repair and in good working order and condition

(*ii*) permit the Bank and any person authorised by the Bank to enter upon any freehold or leasehold land comprised in the Property at all reasonable hours during the daytime to view the state and condition of the same and to give or leave at the premises concerned notice in writing of all matters there found which in the absolute discretion of the Bank constitute defects decays or wants of reparation

(*iii*) forthwith after service of any such notice well and substantially repair and make good all such defects decays and wants of reparation

   (*iv*) (1) insure and keep insured to the full insurable value thereof in an office to be approved by and in the name of the Bank such of the Property as is insurable against loss or damage by fire and such other risks and contingencies as are in accordance with sound commercial practice and in such respective amounts as the Bank may from time to time require and shall produce to the Bank the receipts for the current premiums within seven days after their becoming due and payable failing which the Bank may at the expense of the Company effect or renew any such insurance as to the Bank shall seem fit /PROVIDED THAT in the case of any leasehold land forming part of the Property the Bank will (subject to production from time to time on demand and in any event within fourteen days of each occasion on which a payment falls to be made of satisfactory evidence of compliance therewith) accept compliance with the provisions as to insurance contained in the lease under which such part of the Property is held as being due compliance with the provisions of this sub-Clause/

   (2) at all times during the continuance of this security duly and promptly effect and maintain in such office as aforesaid and in such amounts as shall be approved by the Bank all such insurances against risks and liabilities to employees or third parties and contingencies arising under any Act or at Common Law or in any other manner whatsoever as the Bank shall from time to time direct

   (*v*) indemnify the Bank against all costs charges and expenses incurred by the Bank in exercising any of its powers expressly or impliedly hereby conferred and will pay interest at the rate or rates aforesaid on each such sum from the time when each sum is paid by the Bank for or in connection with any such matter or thing as aforesaid

   (*vi*) pay into the Company's account with the Bank all moneys which it may receive in respect of the book debts and other debts hereby charged and shall not without the prior consent of the Bank in writing purport to charge or assign the same in favour of any other person and shall if called upon to do so by the Bank execute a legal assignment of such book debts and other debts to the Bank

   (*vii*) carry on and conduct its business in a proper and efficient manner and not make any substantial alteration in the nature of that business.

(*b*) Unless otherwise agreed in writing by the Bank all moneys to be received by virtue of any such insurance as aforesaid shall so far as they are in respect of any part of the Property be deemed part of the Property and shall be paid to the Bank and shall if the Company so requests and the Bank thinks fit be applied in making good or in recouping expenditure incurred in making good any loss or damage which may so arise to the Property

7. POWERS AND RIGHTS OF THE BANK

(a) This security shall constitute and be a continuing security to the Bank notwithstanding any settlement of account the reduction or repayment of the amount for the time being owing or any other matter or thing whatsoever

(b) The security hereby created is in addition to any other security or securities which the Bank may now or from time to time hold or take from or on account of the Company

(c) The Company will forthwith on being required from time to time by notice in writing by the Bank so to do at the cost and expense of the Company execute sign and do all documents deeds and things which shall be necessary to create a formal charge by way of legal mortgage in favour of the Bank of all or such parts as shall be specified in the said notice of the freehold and leasehold property then vested in the Company to secure further the payment of all moneys and interest as aforesaid intended to be hereby secured

(d) The Company will deposit with the Bank and the Bank during the continuance of this security shall be entitled to hold all deeds and documents of title relating to the Property (and the insurance policies thereof)

8. EVENTS OF DEFAULT

The moneys hereby secured shall become immediately payable without demand and the statutory power of sale shall be exercisable at any time, notwithstanding the provisions of Section 103 of the Law of Property Act 1925 (which section shall not apply to this security or any sale made by virtue hereof) upon the happening of any of the following events:

(a) if the Company makes default for more than seven days in the payment of any money which may have become due to the Bank;

(b) if any distress execution sequestration or other process is levied or enforced upon the Property and is not paid out within seven days;

(c) if the Company is unable to pay its debts whether within the meaning of Section 223 of the Companies Act 1948 or any statutory modification or re-enactment thereof for the time being in force or otherwise;

(*d*) if the Company certifies that it is unable to pay its debts as and when they fall due;

(*e*) if there is any breach of the terms and conditions of this deed;

(*f*) if the Property or any substantial part thereof becomes subject to an order for compulsory acquisition by or on behalf of any local or other authority;

(*g*) if a petition is presented or an effective resolution passed for winding up the Company otherwise than for the purpose of reconstruction or amalgamation on terms previously approved in writing by the Bank;

(*h*) if the Company convenes a meeting of or proposes or enters into any arrangement with its creditors;

(*i*) if the Company stops payment or ceases to carry on its business or substantially the whole thereof or threatens to cease to carry on the same;

(*j*) if an encumbrancer takes possession or a receiver is appointed of the Property;

(*k*) if the Company makes default in payment of any hire-purchase payment for any equipment used in its business; or

(*l*) if any notice is served upon the Company pursuant to Section 146 of the Law of Property Act 1925 with a view to re-entry on or forfeiture of any leasehold premises of the Company and the Company fails to comply with the same

9. APPOINTMENT OF RECEIVER

At any time after the moneys hereby secured shall have become immediately payable or upon the happening of any of the events specified in Clause 8 hereof the Bank may in writing under the hand of any duly authorised officer of the Bank from time to time appoint any person to be a Receiver of the Property or any part thereof and may in writing under the hand of a duly authorised officer of the Bank from time to time remove any Receiver so appointed and appoint another in his stead.

10. POWERS OF RECEIVER

(*a*) (*i*) If when the power of sale conferred on mortgagees by the Law of Property Act 1925 shall become exercisable in accordance with the provisions hereof there shall be any building works or other development on the Property which shall in the opinion of the Bank remain unfinished it shall be lawful for the Bank or any Receiver appointed by the Bank to enter upon and take possession of the Property and of all buildings erections and fixtures whatsoever therein and to complete the said development in such manner as the Bank or the Receiver shall think fit for the purposes aforesaid the Bank or such Receiver as aforesaid shall be at liberty to employ contractors builders workmen and others and purchase all proper materials as the Bank or the Receiver may think fit.

(*ii*) The Bank or such Receiver shall be entitled but not bound to give instructions to contractors architects quantity surveyors and all other persons who in respect of the said development shall have entered into contracts for personal services to be rendered to the Company or to any of those persons requiring them (as the case may be) to complete or to supervise the completion of the said development in accordance with their obligations to the Company.

(*iii*) The Bank or such Receiver as aforesaid shall also be entitled to require the Company's solicitors upon payment of their proper charges to hand over all deeds documents and papers in their possession which the Bank or such Receiver may require to enable the Bank or the Receiver to complete the said development.

(*b*) A RECEIVER so appointed shall be a receiver and manager and entitled to exercise all the powers conferred on a Receiver by the Law of Property Act 1925 and by way of addition to and without limiting those powers such Receiver shall have power in addition to the rights and liberties set out in sub-Clause (*a*) of this Clause;

(*i*) to take possession of collect and get in the property in respect of which he is appointed or any part thereof and for that purpose to take any proceedings in the name of the Company or otherwise as may seem expedient;

(*ii*) to carry on or manage or concur in carrying on or managing the business of the Company and for that purpose to raise money on the security of any part of the Property in priority to this security or otherwise;

(*iii*) to sell or concur in selling let or concur in letting and to accept surrenders of leases of any part of the Property in such manner and generally on such terms and conditions as he thinks fit and to carry any such sale letting or surrender into effect by conveying leasing letting or accepting surrenders in the name of or on behalf of the Company or otherwise Any such sale may be for cash debentures or other obligations shares stock or other valuable consideration and may be payable in a lump sum or by instalments spread over such period as the Bank shall think fit and so that any consideration or part thereof received in a form other than cash shall *ipso facto* forthwith on receipt be and become charged with the payment of all moneys due hereunder as though it had been included in the charge created by Clause 3 hereof and formed part of the property hereby charged; Plant machinery and other fixtures may be severed and sold separately from the premises containing them without the consent of the Company being obtained thereto;

(*iv*) to take any indemnity from the Company from and against all actions claims expenses demands and liabilities whether arising out of contract or out of tort or out of breach of statutory obligation or in any other way incurred by him or by any manager agent officer servant or workman for whose debt default or miscarriage he may be answerable for anything done or omitted to be done in the exercise or purported exercise of his powers under this security or under any appointment duly made under the provisions hereof and if he thinks fit but without prejudice to the foregoing to effect with any insurance company or office or underwriters any policy or policies of insurance either in lieu or in satisfaction of or in addition to such indemnity from the Company;

(*v*) to make any arrangements or compromise which he shall think expedient in the interest of the Bank;

(*vi*) to make and effect all such repairs improvements and insurances as he shall think fit and renew such of the plant machinery and any other effects of the Company whatsoever as shall be worn out lost or otherwise become unserviceable;

(*vii*) to appoint managers accountants servants workmen and agents for the aforesaid purposes upon such terms as to remuneration or otherwise as he may determine;

(*viii*) to do all such other acts and things as may be considered to be incidental or conducive to any of the matters and powers aforesaid which he may or can lawfully do as agent for the Company;

(*ix*) to borrow money either from the Bank or from such other source as he may deem desirable and the Bank may approve on the security of the Property either in priority to the security hereby created or subject thereto as he may deem fit;

(*x*) to obtain all Planning Permissions building regulation approvals and other permissions consents or licences for the development of the Property and any other property which it may in the opinion of the Bank or the Receiver be necessary or desirable to develop in conjunction with the Property and to effect and/or carry out any development building or other works as he shall in his absolute discretion think fit;

(*xi*) to employ for the purposes aforesaid Solicitors Architects Surveyors Quantity Surveyors Estate Agents contractors builders and workmen and others and purchase all proper materials as he shall in his absolute discretion think fit;

(*xii*) the full and unrestricted rights and powers of dealing with the Property of a sole and absolute unencumbered owner beneficially entitled thereto and all moneys costs and expenses expended and incurred in relation thereto shall be added to and form part of the moneys hereby secured.

(c) All moneys received by the Receiver shall be applied by him for the following purposes subject to the claims of secured and unsecured creditors (if any) ranking in priority to this Deed and in the following order

(i) in payment of all costs charges and expenses of and incidental to the appointment of the Receiver and the exercise of all or any of the powers aforesaid and of all outgoings properly paid by him;

(ii) in payment of remuneration to the Receiver at such rate as may be agreed between him and the person by whom the appointment is made;

(iii) in or towards payment to the Bank of all moneys payment of which is hereby secured;

(iv) any surplus shall be paid to the Company/(without prejudice to any question as to how such surplus should be dealt with as between the Company and the Guaranteeing Subsidiaries)/

(d) Any such Receiver shall so far as the law allows be deemed to be agent of the Company for all purposes and the Company will be solely responsible for his acts defaults and remuneration and the Bank shall not be under any liability for his remuneration or otherwise.

(e) The Bank shall not nor shall any Receiver or Receivers appointed hereunder be liable to account as mortgagee or mortgagees in possession in respect of the Property or any part thereof or be liable for any loss upon realisation or for any neglect or default of any nature whatsoever in connection with the Property for which a mortgagee in possession might as such be liable and all costs charges and expenses incurred by the Bank or any Receiver or Receivers appointed hereunder (including the costs of any proceedings to enforce the security hereby given) shall be paid by the Company on a full indemnity basis and so be charged on the Property.

(f) The foregoing powers of appointment of and powers of a receiver shall be in addition to and not to the prejudice of statutory and other powers of the Bank under the Law of Property Act 1925 or otherwise and so that such powers shall be and remain exercisable by the Bank in respect of any part of the Property in respect of which no appointment of a receiver by the Bank shall from time to time be subsisting and that notwithstanding that an appointment under the powers of Clause 9 hereof shall have subsisted and been withdrawn in respect of that part of the Property or shall be subsisting in respect of any other part of the Property.

11. POWER OF BANK TO ACT IN DEFAULT OF ACTION BY COMPANY

(*a*) If the Company shall make default under any of the covenants relating to the Property or any part thereof or in repairing or keeping in repair the Property the Bank shall be at liberty to enter on the Property and perform or cause to be performed every obligation imposed on the Company and effect such work or repairs as the Bank may in its absolute discretion consider necessary and in case of default of the Company in insuring or keeping insured or procuring to be kept insured any of the Property in the manner set out in this deed the Bank shall be at liberty to insure and keep insured the Property for the amounts hereinbefore set out or for such other sums as it may in its absolute discretion think fit.

(*b*) In the event of the Company failing to comply with any requirement of any competent authority made under or by virtue of the Planning Acts the Bank may in so far as the same may be necessary to comply with such requirement enter upon the Property and execute any works and do anything thereon necessary to ensure such compliance upon giving the Company seven days' previous notice in writing of its intention so to do.

(*c*) The Company will indemnify the Bank against all costs charges and expenses incurred by the Bank in exercising any of its powers under this Clause with interest as provided by Clause 6(*a*)(*v*) hereof and all sums paid by the Bank and interest thereon shall be treated as part of the moneys due to the Bank under Clause 1 hereof and shall accordingly be charged upon the Property.

(*d*) The Company hereby irrevocably appoints the Bank and its substitutes for the time being to be its attorneys to apply for and procure on its behalf any licences permissions or other things from any competent authority necessary for the execution of the repairs and other works hereby authorised to be executed by the Bank on the default of the Company.

(*e*) All expenses incurred by the Bank in securing the said licences permissions and other things shall be treated as part of the cost of the said repairs.

12. POWER OF ATTORNEY

The Company hereby irrevocably appoints the Bank and any receiver appointed by the Bank jointly and also severally the Attorney and Attorneys of the Company for the Company and in its name and on its behalf and as its act and deed or otherwise to seal and deliver and otherwise perfect any deed assurance agreement instrument or act which the Bank may in its absolute discretion consider necessary or proper for any of the purposes of this security

13. CONSOLIDATION

The restriction on the right of consolidating mortgages contained in Section 93 of the Law of Property Act 1925 shall not apply to this security

14. SET-OFF

It is agreed that in addition to any right of set-off or other similar right to which the Bank may be entitled in law, the Bank may at any time and without notice to the Company combine and consolidate all or any of the accounts between the Company and the Bank and/or set-off any moneys whatsoever and whether on current account or deposit account and whether in sterling or in any other currency which the Bank may at any time hold for the account of the Company against any liabilities whatsoever whether in sterling or in any other currency which may be due or accruing due to the Bank from the Company whether such liabilities are or may be joint or several or primary or contingent

15. NOTICES

The provisions of Section 196 of the Law of Property Act 1925 as amended by the provisions of the Recorded Delivery Service Act 1962 with respect to notices required or authorised by this Act to be served on mortgagors shall apply to any notice required or authorised by or under this deed to be served on or given to the Company or the Bank

16. FINANCIAL INFORMATION

During the continuance of this security the Company shall furnish to the Bank yearly or oftener if required at the Company's expense a Balance Sheet Profit and Loss Account and Trading Accounts showing the true position of the Company's affairs at a date no more than six months earlier and certified by the auditor for the time being of the Company and also from time to time such other information respecting the affairs of the Company as the Bank may reasonably require

17. OTHER CHARGES

(*a*) The Company hereby warrants to the Bank that except as aforesaid there are not now and will not during the continuance of this security without the prior written consent of the Bank first had and obtained be any other mortgages charges liens pledges or encumbrances on the Property.

(*b*) In the event of any action proceedings or steps being taken to exercise or enforce any powers or remedies conferred by any prior mortgage charge or encumbrance against the Property the Bank may redeem such mortgage charge or encumbrance or procure the transfer thereof to itself and may settle and pass the accounts of the prior mortgagee chargee or encumbrancer and any accounts so settled and passed shall be conclusive and binding on the Company and all principal moneys interest costs charges and expenses of and incidental to such redemption and transfer shall be paid by the Company to the Bank on demand with interest thereon at the rate or rates aforesaid from the time or respective times of the same having been paid or incurred and until payment the Property shall stand charged with the amount so to be paid with interest at the rate aforesaid

18. COSTS
All the costs charges and expenses of the Bank in connection with the Facility Letter including the costs charges and expenses incurred in the preparation and execution of the Facility letter and this security and the carrying of the same into effect and the operation of the same (including any VAT or other relevant tax in respect of any of the same) shall be paid by the Company on a full indemnity basis and in default shall be charged on the Property on the terms and conditions herein contained

19. RESTRICTION AGAINST DISPOSITIONS
In the case of any part of the Property consisting of land for the time being registered at HM Land Registry the Company and the Bank hereby jointly apply to the Chief Land Registrar to enter a restriction in the Proprietorship Register of the relevant title in the following terms:

Except under an order of the Registrar no dealing by the proprietor of the property comprised in this title or made in exercise of the power of sale under any charge subsequent to the charge hereby created is to be registered without the consent of the proprietor for the time being of the charge hereby created

20. DEFINITIONS
In this deed:

(a) the expression "the Bank" shall where the context so admits include the successors in title and assigns of the Bank and

(b) where this deed is executed by two or more persons as the Company the expression "the Company" shall wherever the context so permits be construed as referring to them jointly and to each and every or any of them separately and covenants on the part of the

Company herein contained shall be deemed to be joint and several covenants by each of them and

(*c*) the expression "the Facility Letter" shall mean /the letter dated ... addressed by the Bank to the Company and accepted by the Company/ or the Agreement dated ... and made between the Bank and the Company/ and shall, where the context so admits include any amendments thereto agreed from time to time between the Bank and the Company and any letter or letters or agreement or agreements replacing the same (in either case whether before or after the date hereof) and

(*d*) the Clause headings are for convenience only and shall not affect the construction

IN WITNESS whereof the Company has caused its Common Seal to be hereunto affixed the day and year first before written

THE SCHEDULE above referred to

THE COMMON SEAL of ... ⎫
PLC was hereunto affixed ⎬
in the presence of: ⎭

Director

Secretary

OR

SIGNED SEALED and DELIVERED ⎫
by the said ... ⎬
in the presence of: ⎭

RECEIPT ON DISCHARGE OF CHARGE BY WAY OF LEGAL MORTGAGE

We ... Bank PLC of ... hereby acknowledge that we have this ... day of ... 19... received the sum of £... representing the whole of the moneys secured by the within written Legal Charge the payment having been made by ... of ...

THE COMMON SEAL of ... ⎫
BANK PLC was hereto ⎬
affixed in the presence of: ⎭

Director

Secretary

MEMORANDUM OF DEPOSIT OF TITLE DEEDS

MEMORANDUM that:

1. The documents of title of the property known as ... (hereinafter called "the Property") have this day been deposited by ... of ... (hereinafter called "the Borrower" which expression shall where the context so admits include his successors in title and assigns) with ... BANK PLC whose registered office is at ... (hereinafter called "the Bank" which expression shall where the context so admits include its successors in title and assigns) to the intent that the said property may be equitably charged with the payment to the Bank on demand and discharge of

(*a*) all sums of money and liabilities advanced or paid by the Bank to or for or on account of the Borrower or incurred by the Borrower to the Bank and

(*b*) all other sums of money and liabilities which now are or at any time hereafter may be due and owing or incurred by the Borrower to the Bank or for which the Borrower may be or become liable to the Bank anywhere

in either case on any current or other account or in any manner whatever (and whether alone or jointly with any person and in whatever style or name and whether as principal or surety or otherwise) together with commission banking charges costs and expenses (on a full indemnity basis) and interest on all sums from the time or respective times of the same being advanced or incurred until repayment (as well after as before any judgment) at the rate or rates from time to time agreed between the Bank and the Borrower and such interest shall be computed on a day to day basis and shall be payable quarterly on the Bank's usual days for the payment of interest and shall be compounded with quarterly rests on the said dates in the event of its not being punctually paid

2. The Borrower undertakes to execute at his own cost when called upon a proper charge by way of legal mortgage in favour of the Bank of the Property to secure all moneys for the time being owing to the Bank on this security with compound interest at the aforesaid rate such charge by way of legal mortgage to be in such form and to contain such covenants and conditions as the Bank shall require including provisions excluding Section 93 (relating to consolidation) and Section 99(1) (relating to mortgagors' powers of leasing) of the Law of Property Act 1925 which sections shall not apply to the security

3. (*a*) During the continuance of this security the Borrower shall

(*i*) keep all buildings and erections on the Property and all Plant Machinery fixtures fittings implements utensils and other effects used thereon for the purpose of or in connection with the business of the Borrower and every part thereof in a good state of repair and in good working order and condition

(*ii*) insure and keep insured to the full insurable value thereof in an office to be approved by and in the name of the Bank such of the Property as is insurable against loss or damage by fire and such other risks and contingencies as are in accordance with sound commercial practice and in such respective amounts as the Bank may from time to time require and shall produce to the Bank the receipts for the current premiums within seven days after their becoming due and payable failing which the Bank may at the expense of the Borrower effect or renew any such insurance as to the Bank shall seem fit PROVIDED THAT in the case of any leasehold land forming part of the Property the Bank will (subject to production from time to time on demand and in any event within fourteen days of each occasion on which a payment falls to be made of satisfactory evidence of compliance therewith) accept compliance with the provisions as to insurance contained in the lease under which such part of the Property is held as being due compliance with the provisions of this sub-clause

(*b*) If the Borrower shall make default under any of the covenants relating to the Property or any part thereof or in repairing or keeping in repair the Property the Bank shall be at liberty to enter on the Property and perform or cause to be performed every obligation imposed on the Borrower and effect such works or repairs as the Bank may in its absolute discretion consider necessary and in case of default of the Borrower in insuring or keeping insured or procuring to be kept insured any of the Property in the manner set out in this deed the Bank shall be at liberty to insure and keep insured the Property for the amounts hereinbefore set out or for such other sums as it may in its absolute discretion think fit

4. The Borrower will during the continuance of this security duly observe and perform all restrictive and other covenants and stipulations affecting any freehold or leasehold land comprised in the Property (including in the case of leasehold land the terms covenants conditions restrictions and stipulations contained in the lease under which the Borrower holds such land) and will keep the Bank indemnified in respect of all actions proceedings costs claims and demands whatsoever occasioned by any breach of any such covenants or stipulations.

5. The security hereby created is in addition to any other security or securities which the Bank may now or from time to time hold or take from the Borrower and shall constitute and be a continuing security to the Bank notwithstanding any settlement of account the reduction or repayment of the amount for the time being owing or any other matter or thing whatsoever

6. The moneys hereby secured shall become immediately payable and the statutory power of sale shall be exercisable at any time notwithstanding the provisions of Section 103 of the Law of Property Act 1925 (which section shall not apply to the security or any sale made by virtue hereof) upon the happening of any of the following events:

(a) if the Borrower makes default for more than seven days in the payment of any money which may have become due to the Bank;

(b) if the Property or any substantial part thereof is compulsorily acquired by or by order of any local or other authority;

(c) if an encumbrancer takes possession or a receiver is appointed of the Property or any part thereof

(d) if the Borrower being an individual dies or has a receiving order made against him or being a company goes into liquidation whether voluntary or compulsory;

(e) if any notice is served on the Borrower pursuant to Section 146 of the Law of Property Act 1925 with a view to re-entry on or forfeiture of the Property and the Borrower shall fail to comply with the same

7. The Borrower hereby warrants to the Bank that there are not now and will not during the continuance of this security without the prior written consent of the Bank first had and obtained be any prior mortgages charges liens pledges or encumbrances on the Property

8. The Borrower hereby agrees and declares that this security shall be construed and take effect as a security for the whole and every part of the moneys owing and to become owing as aforesaid and shall be independent of and in addition to and shall not be in any way prejudiced or affected by and shall not prejudice or affect any collateral or other security now or hereafter held by the Bank or the liability of any person firm or company for all or any part of the moneys owing and to become owing as aforesaid

9. The Borrower hereby irrevocably appoints the Bank and any receiver appointed by the Bank jointly and also severally the Attorney

and Attorneys of the Borrower for the Borrower and in his name and on his behalf and as his act and deed or otherwise to seal and deliver and otherwise perfect any deed assurance agreement instrument or act which the Bank may in its absolute discretion consider necessary or proper for any of the purposes of this security

10. It is agreed that in addition to any right of set-off or other similar right to which the Bank may be entitled in law, the Bank may at any time and without notice to the Borrower combine and consolidate all or any of the accounts between the Borrower and the Bank and/or set-off any moneys whatsoever and whether on current account or deposit account and whether in sterling or in any other currency which the Bank may at any time hold for the account of the Borrower against any liabilities whatsoever whether in sterling or in any other currency which may be due or accruing due to the Bank from the Borrower whether such liabilities are or may be joint or several or primary or contingent.

11. Any notice or demand hereunder shall be deemed to have been sufficiently given if sent by prepaid post letter to the address in the United Kingdom last known to the Bank or stated hereon of the person to whom or to whose personal representatives such notice is given or, if the Borrower is a company, to the address hereon or to the registered office of the company, and shall be assumed to have reached the addressee in the course of post. In the case of the death of any person a party hereto and until receipt by the Bank of a notice in writing of the grant of probate of the will or administration of the estate of the deceased, any notice or demand by the Bank sent by post as aforesaid addressed to the deceased or to his personal representatives at the address of the deceased in the United Kingdom last known to the Bank or stated hereon shall for all purposes be deemed a sufficient notice or demand by the Bank to the deceased and his personal representatives and shall be as effectual as if the deceased were still living

12. Where this Memorandum is executed by two or more persons, the expression "the Borrower" shall wherever the context so permits be construed as referring to them jointly and to each and every or any of them separately and covenants on the part of the Borrower herein contained shall be deemed to be joint and several covenants by each of them

IN WITNESS whereof the Borrower has /hereunto set his hand and seal/ /caused its Common Seal to be hereunto affixed/ this ... day of ... 19...

SIGNED SEALED and DELIVERED ⎫
by the said ... ⎬
in the presence of: ⎭

OR

THE COMMON SEAL of ⎫
PLC was hereunto affixed ⎬
in the presence of: ⎭

Director

Secretary

MEMORANDUM OF DEPOSIT OF SHARES BY A CUSTOMER TO SECURE HIS OWN LIABILITY

To: ... Bank PLC

1. In consideration of your giving me time credit banking facilities or other accommodation howsoever made or given I the undersigned ... of ... hereby charge in your favour the securities of mine short particulars of which are set out in the Schedule hereto and any other securities or property for the time being representing all or any of the same or acquired in respect thereof and all accretions to the same (all such securities being hereinafter called "the mortgaged securities") as security for the payment and discharge on demand of

(*a*) all moneys and liabilities advanced or paid to you to or for me or on my account or incurred by me to you and

(*b*) all other sums of money and liabilities which now are or shall at any time be due or owing or incurred by me to you or for which I may be or become liable to you anywhere

in either case upon any current or other banking account or upon any discount account or otherwise and whether alone or jointly with any other person and whether as principal or surety or otherwise or for cheques notes or bills drawn accepted or indorsed by me or for advances made to me or for my accommodation or benefit and whether actually or contingently and in whatever name style or firm or for any other matter or thing whatsoever including discount commission and other bankers charges including (but without prejudice to the generality of the foregoing and to the intent that you shall be afforded a full complete and unlimited indemnity against all costs charges and expenses paid or incurred by you notwithstanding any rule of law or equity to the contrary) all costs charges and expenses which you may pay or incur in stamping perfecting or enforcing this security and in the negotiation for and preparation and signing of these presents or in obtaining payment or discharge of such moneys or liabilities or any part thereof or in realising the mortgaged securities or any part thereof and whether arising directly or indirectly in respect of this security or of any other security held by you for the same indebtedness together with interest (computed on a day-to-day basis) on all such moneys and liabilities from the time or respective times of the same being advanced or incurred until payment (as well after as before any demand therefor or any judgment recovered in respect thereof) at the rate or rates agreed from time to time between you and me such interest to be compounded with quarterly rests in the event of its not being punctually paid on the due dates.

2. Without prejudice to the generality of the security hereby constituted it is hereby declared that this charge is made to secure the said current or other account or accounts and further advances by you to me to the intent that it shall constitute a continuing security for all sums which shall on the execution hereof or at any time hereafter be or become owing by me to you in any manner whatsoever.

3. At any time after default by me in payment on demand of all moneys hereby secured or on default by me in respect of any obligation by me to you or in case of my becoming bankrupt or insolvent or going into liquidation or making or attempting to make any composition or arrangement with my creditors you may without notice to me sell the mortgaged securities or any of them in such manner and upon such terms and for such consideration (whether payable or deliverable immediately or by instalments) as you may think fit without liability for any loss howsoever in connection with such sale and you may apply the net proceeds of sale and any moneys for the time being in your hands in or towards discharge of the moneys and liabilities aforesaid and I undertake to pay you forthwith any difference between such net proceeds and moneys so applied and the moneys hereby secured.

4. All dividends interest bonuses accretions benefits and advantages accruing in respect of the mortgaged securities shall be included in the security hereby constituted but you shall not incur any liability in respect of calls instalments or other payments.

5. You or your nominees may exercise at your or their discretion (in my name at any time whether before or after the power of sale hereunder has arisen and without any further consent or authority of my part) in respect of the mortgaged securities any voting rights and all the powers given to trustees by subsections (3) and (4) of Section 10 of the Trustee Act 1925 as amended by Section 9 of the Trustee Investments Act 1961 in respect of securities or property subject to a trust and all powers or rights which may be exercised by the person or persons in whose name or names the securities are registered under the terms hereof or otherwise.

6. PROVIDED ALWAYS AND IT IS HEREBY FURTHER AGREED that:

(*a*) This security shall not be considered as satisfied or discharged by any intermediate payment or satisfaction of the whole or any part of any sum or sums of money owing as aforesaid but shall constitute and be a continuing security and extend to cover any sum or sums of money which shall for the time being constitute the balance due from me to you on any such account or for any such matter or thing as hereinbefore mentioned.

(*b*) This security shall be in addition to and shall not prejudice or affect and shall not be in anywise prejudiced or affected by any collateral or other security now or hereafter held or judgment or order obtained by you for all or any part of the moneys hereby secured nor shall such collateral or other security judgment or order or any lien to which you may be otherwise entitled (including any security charge or lien prior to the date of these presents on the mortgaged securities) or the liability of any person or persons not parties hereto for all or any part of the moneys hereby secured be in anywise prejudiced or affected by this security. In particular that it shall not be necessary for you to resort to or seek to enforce any other security or personal guarantee or liability of any other person. And also that you shall have full power at your discretion to give time for payment to or make any other arrangement with any other person or persons without prejudice to my liability hereunder. And that all moneys received by you from me or any person or persons liable to pay the same may be applied to you to any account or item of account or any transaction to which the same may be applicable.

(*c*) In addition to any right of set-off or other similar right to which you may be entitled in law you may at any time and without notice to me combine and consolidate all or any of the accounts between me and you and/or set off any moneys whatsoever and whether on current account or deposit account and whether in sterling or in any other currency which you may at any time hold for my account against any liabilities whatsoever including any liability under this memorandum whether in sterling or in any other currency which may be due or accruing due to you from me whether such liabilities are or may be joint or several or primary or contingent.

7. IT IS HEREBY DECLARED AND AGREED that:

(*a*) The restriction on consolidation of mortages contained in Sub-section (1) of Section 93 of the Law of Property Act 1925 shall not apply to this security.

(*b*) A certificate by any of your officers or executives or any person duly authorised on your behalf as to the money and liabilities for the time being due owing or incurred by me to you shall be conclusive evidence against me in any proceedings.

8. I hereby engage myself and my assigns at any time during the continuance of this security upon demand and at my/their own cost to execute and do all transfers and things requisite for vesting the legal title to the mortgaged securities or any accretions or additions thereto in you or in your nominees or in any purchasers under any exercise of the power of sale herein contained.

9. This security shall be available for your successors or assigns.

10. I hereby covenant that during the continuance of the security hereby constituted there shall not be any increase in either the authorised or the issued share capital of the company or any of the companies mentioned in the schedule hereto.

11. Except as otherwise specified herein any notice (which expression shall where the context so permits include any request demand or other communication) to or upon any of the parties hereto shall be deemed to have been duly served if in writing either delivered to the party to whom it is addressed or sent by post (whether ordinary prepaid or registered or recorded delivery) addressed to such party at its address as stated hereon or at such other address as it may specify by notice in writing to the other party or parties or in the case of a company to its registered office. Any notice sent by post shall be deemed to have been served on the day following that on which the envelope containing the same is posted and in proving such service it shall in the case of ordinary prepaid post be sufficient to prove that the envelope containing the same was

properly addressed and either delivered to a Post Office or put into a Post Office letter box. All references herein to writing shall be construed as including communications by telex telegram or cable and in such case it shall be sufficient if the communication is addressed to the party to whom it is addressed at its then current official telex number or telegram or cable address or if more than one such number or address any of them. Any such telex telegram or cable shall be deemed to have been served at the time of sending and in proving such service it shall be sufficient to produce a sender's copy of such telex telegram or cable showing such number or address. Any notice must be signed personally by the party serving it (or if by a company on behalf of the sender by a duly authorised director) or in your case by any of your officers or executives or any person duly authorised on your behalf provided that any notice by telex telegram or cable need not bear any manuscript signature. In the case of the death of any person who is a party hereto and until you receive notice in writing of the grant of probate of the will or letters of administration of the estate of such deceased person any notice served by you as aforesaid addressed to such deceased person at his address or number as aforesaid last known to you or stated hereon shall for all purposes of this document be deemed a sufficient notice by you to such deceased person and his personal representatives and shall be as effectual as if such deceased person were still living.

12. This Memorandum shall be governed by and construed in accordance with English law.

13. It is hereby agreed that my total liability hereunder shall not exceed the net proceeds of sale of the mortgaged securities.

THE SCHEDULE

All the issued share capital of ... PLC.

DATED the ... day of ... 19...

DEBENTURE (FLOATING CHARGE)

THIS CHARGE made the   day of   19
BETWEEN ... PLC whose registered office is at ... (hereinafter called "the Company") of the one part and ... PLC whose registered office is at ... (hereinafter called "the Bank") of the other part

STOCK TRANSFER FORM

STOCK TRANSFER FORM

Section 1

	Certificate lodged with the Registrar
Consideration Money £	(For completion by the Registrar/Stock Exchange)
Full name of Undertaking.	
Full description of security.	

Number or amount of Shares, Stock or other security and, in figures column only, number and denomination of units, if any.	Words	Figures
		(units of)

Name(s) of registered holder(s) should be given in full: the address should be given where there is only one holder.	in the name(s) of
If the transfer is not made by the registered holder(s) insert also the name(s) and capacity (*e.g.* Executor(s)), of the person(s) making the transfer.	

Delete words in italics except for stock exchange transactions. Bodies corporate should execute under their common seal.	I/We hereby transfer the above security out of the name(s) aforesaid to the person(s) named below *or to the several persons named in Parts 2 of Brokers Transfer Forms relating to the above security:*	Stamp of Selling Broker(s) or, for transactions which are not stock exchange transactions, of Agent(s), if any, acting for the Transferor(s)
	Signature(s) of transferor(s)	
	1.................. 3.................. 2.................. 4	Date..............

Full name(s), full postal address(es) (including County or, if applicable, Postal District number) of the person(s) to whom the security is transferred. Please state title, if any, or whether Mr., Mrs. or Miss Please complete in typewriting or in Block Capitals.	

I/We request that such entries be made in the register as are necessary to give effect to this transfer.

Stamp of Buying Broker(s) (if any).	Stamp or name and address of person lodging this form (if other than the Buying Broker(s))

WITNESSETH as follows:

Same as charge by way of legal mortgage of land but substitute the following for Clause 3:

3. (*a*) As security for the payment and discharge of all sums covenanted to be paid to the Bank hereunder and all other moneys intended to be hereby secured (including any expenses and charges arising out of or in connection with the acts or matters referred to in Clause 10 hereof) the Company as beneficial owner hereby charges in favour of the Bank by way of floating charge all its undertaking and other property and assets whatsoever and wheresoever both present and future including its uncalled capital for the time being and so that the charge hereby created shall be a continuing security. The property and assets hereby charged are hereinafter collectively known as "the Property" which expression shall where the context so permits include each and every part or any part thereof

(*b*) The Company shall not except with the prior written consent of the Bank have power to part with sell or dispose of the whole or any substantial part of its undertaking property or assets except by way of sale in the ordinary course of its business and for the purpose of carrying on the same or to create or permit to subsist any mortgage charge lien pledge or other security ranking in priority to or *pari passu* with the floating charge hereby created

MORTGAGE OF INSURANCE POLICY

THIS MORTGAGE is made the   day of   One thousand nine hundred and eighty ...

BETWEEN:

1. ... of ... (hereinafter called "the Assignor"); and
2. ... whose registered office is at ... (hereinafter called "the Bank")

WHEREAS the Assignor is entitled to the policy or policies of insurance particulars of which are contained in the Schedule hereto (hereinafter called "the Policy" which expression shall where the context so permits include each and every such policy)

NOW THIS DEED WITNESSETH as follows:—

1. The assignor hereby covenants with the Bank that he will pay to the Bank immediately upon the same becoming due to the Bank and discharge

(*a*) all moneys and liabilities advanced or paid by the Bank to or for or on account of the Assignor or incurred by the Assignor to the Bank and

(*b*) all other sums of money and liabilities which now are or at any time hereafter may be due and owing or incurred by the Assignor to the Bank or for which the Assignor may be or become liable to the Bank

in either case on any current or other account or in any manner whatever (and whether alone or jointly with any other person and in whatever style or name and whether as principal or surety or otherwise) including or together with commission banking or other charges costs expenses (on a full indemnity basis) and interest (computed on a day-to-day basis) on all such sums moneys or liabilities from the time or the respective times of the same being advance or incurred until payment (as well after as before any demand and/or judgment) at the rate or rates agreed from time to time between the Bank and the Assignor

2. The Assignor as beneficial owner hereby assigns unto the Bank the Policy and all moneys (including profits and bonuses already accrued or hereafter to accrue) which shall become payable thereunder and the benefit of all powers and remedies for enforcing the same TO HOLD the same and the moneys hereby assigned unto the Bank absolutely subject to the proviso for redemption hereinafter contained

3. The Assignor hereby covenants with the Bank as follows:—

(*a*) That the Policy is valid and that nothing shall be done or suffered whereby the Bank may be prevented from receiving the moneys payable thereunder or any part thereof

(*b*) That if the Policy shall become voidable or void the Assignor will forthwith at his own sole cost do all such things as may be necessary for keeping the same on foot (if only voidable) or for effecting or for enabling the Bank to effect (as it is hereby authorised to do) a new policy or new policies on the life of the insured (if it shall become void) for such sum or sums as would have been payable under the void policy if the life insured had ceased immediately before the same became void such policy or policies to be effected in the name of the Bank or in such other name or names and in such insurance company as it may direct

(*c*) That every such new policy and the moneys to be assured thereby shall be subject to this security and to the powers and provisions herein contained or implied by statute and applicable hereto as fully to all intents as the Policy

(*d*) That the Assignor will during the continuance of this security punctually pay all premiums for keeping on foot the Policy or any such new and substituted policy or policies as aforesaid within one week after the same shall from time to time fall due and will deliver the receipts for every such payment to the Bank forthwith

(*e*) That if the Assignor shall at any time make default in payment of any of the said premiums it shall be lawful for the Bank to pay the same or convert the Policy into a paid up policy and retain it subject to the provisions hereof or to surrender the Policy

(*f*) That any sums so paid or expended by the Bank in effecting any new policy or policies in place of any Policy which may become void and any sums paid by it in respect of premiums shall be added to the moneys hereby covenanted to be paid and bear interest accordingly at the rate aforesaid from the time or respective times of payment and be charged upon the Policy and upon every new policy effected under this Clause in the same manner as if such moneys had orginally formed part of the moneys hereby covenanted to be paid

4. This is to be a continuing security notwithstanding any settlement of account, the reduction or repayment of the amount for the time being owing or any other matter or thing whatsoever, and it is to be in addition and without prejudice to any other securities or guarantees which the Bank may now or from time to time hold or take from the Assignor or on his account or in respect of the moneys hereby secured

5. Provided always and it is hereby declared as follows that if the Assignor shall on the same becoming due pay to the Bank all sums hereby covenanted to be paid the Bank will at any time thereafter at the request and cost of the Assignor re-assign the Policy to the Assignor or as he shall direct or otherwise discharge this security

6. In this deed the expression "the Bank" shall where the context so admits include the successors in title and assigns of the Bank

IN WITNESS whereof these presents have been executed the day and year first before written

THE SCHEDULE before referred to

Name of
Insurance Company   :

Policy No.
and Date   :

Life Insured   :

            Sum Insured:

  Maturing:

SIGNED SEALED and DELIVERED ⎫
by the said ...   ⎬
in the presence of: ⎭

REQUEST FOR GUARANTEE AND COUNTER-INDEMNITY

To: ... Bank PLC

Dear Sirs,

We hereby request and authorise you to give a guarantee on our behalf to ... in the form of the draft a copy of which is annexed hereto and has been initialled for the purpose of identification and, in consideration of your giving such guarantee, we hereby undertake to and agree with you as follows:

(*a*) We will indemnify you and keep you indemnified against any liability you may incur by reason of or on account of your giving such guarantee, including any actions proceedings costs claims and demands in connection therewith;

(*b*) We will forthwith upon demand pay to you and you may immediately debit our account with you with the amount of any payments that may be made by you to ... under or in pursuance of the said guarantee together with interest at the rate of ... per cent on any amount so paid by you or so debited to our account (or on so much thereof as shall for the time being remain outstanding) from the date on which it is so paid or debited until actual payment by us to you;

(*c*) Any request made upon you by ... for payment of any sum of money shall be sufficient authority to you for making any such payment.

Yours faithfully,

10. FORM NO. 47

THE COMPANIES ACTS 1948 TO 1976

Form No. 47

Particulars of a mortgage or charge

Pursuant to section 95 of the Companies Act 1948

Please do not write in this binding margin

Please complete legibly, preferably in black type, or bold block lettering

* delete if inappropriate

For official use

Company number

Name of company

Limited *

Date and description of the instrument creating or evidencing the mortgage or charge (note 2)

Amount due or owing on the mortgage or charge

Names, addresses and descriptions of the mortgagees or persons entitled to the charge

Presentor's name, address and reference (if any) :

For official use

Mortgage section

Post room

Time critical reference

page 1

[P.T.O.

Short particulars of all the property mortgaged or charged

Particulars as to commission, allowance or discount (note 3)

Signed _____ Date _____

Designation of position in relation to the company_____

Notes

1   The original instrument creating the charge, together with this form, must be delivered to the
Registrar of Companies within 21 days after the date of creation of the charge (Section 95 (1)). If
the property is situated and the charge was created outside the United Kingdom delivery to the
Registrar must be effected within 21 days after the date on which the copy instrument could in due
course of post, and if posted with due diligence, have been received in the United Kingdom
(section 95 (3)). A certified copy of the instrument creating the charge will only be accepted where
the property charged and the charge so created are both outside the United Kingdom (section 95 (3))
and in such cases the copy must be verified or certified to be a true copy under the seal of the
Company or under the hand of some person interested therein otherwise than on behalf of the
company.

2   A description of the instrument, eg, "Trust Deed", "Debenture", "Mortgage" or "legal charge", etc,
as the case may be, should be given.

3   In this section there should be inserted the amount or rate per cent. of the commission, allowance or
discount (if any) paid or made either directly or indirectly by the company to any person in
consideration of his subscribing or agreeing to subscribe, whether absolutely or conditionally, or
procuring or agreeing to procure subscriptions, whether absolute or conditional for any of the
debentures included in this return. The rate of interest payable under the terms of the debentures
should not be entered.

3. DOCUMENTS RELATING TO GOODS
BILL OF LADING[1]

BILL OF LADING*

TO BE USED WITH CHARTER-PARTIES
CODE NAME: "CONGENBILL"
EDITION 1978
ADOPTED BY
THE BALTIC AND INTERNATIONAL
MARITIME CONFERENCE (BIMCO)

Conditions of Carriage.

(1) All terms and conditions, liberties and exceptions of the Charter Party, dated as overleaf, are herewith incorporated. The Carrier shall in no case be responsible for loss of or damage to cargo arisen prior to loading and after discharging.

(2) General Paramount Clause.
The Hague Rules contained in the International Convention for the Unification of certain rules relating to Bills of Lading, dated Brussels the 25th August 1924 as enacted in the country of shipment shall apply to this contract. When no such enactment is in force in the country of shipment, the corresponding legislation of the country of destination shall apply, but in respect of shipments to which no such enactments are compulsorily applicable, the terms of the said Convention shall apply.

Trades where Hague-Visby Rules apply.
In trades where the International Brussels Convention 1924 as amended by the Protocol signed at Brussels on February 23rd 1968 – the Hague-Visby Rules – apply compulsorily, the provisions of the respective legislation shall be considered incorporated in this Bill of Lading. The Carrier takes all reservations possible under such applicable legislation, relating to the period before loading and after discharging and while the goods are in the charge of another Carrier, and to deck cargo and live animals.

(3) General Average.
General Average shall be adjusted, stated and settled according to York-Antwerp Rules 1974, in London unless another place is agreed in the Charter.

Cargo's contribution to General Average shall be paid to the Carrier even when such average is the result of a fault, neglect or error of the Master, Pilot or Crew. The Charterers, Shippers and Consignees expressly renounce the Netherlands Commercial Code, Art. 700, and the Belgian Commercial Code, Part II, Art. 148.

(4) New Jason Clause.
In the event of accident, danger, damage or disaster before or after the commencement of the voyage, resulting from any cause whatsoever, whether due to negligence or not, for which, or for the consequence of which, the Carrier is not responsible, by statute, contract or otherwise, the goods, Shippers, Consignees or owners of the goods shall contribute with the Carrier in general average to the payment of any sacrifices, losses or expenses of a general average nature that may be made or incurred and shall pay salvage and special charges incurred in respect of the goods.

If a salving ship is owned or operated by the Carrier, salvage shall be paid for as fully as if the said salving ship or ships belonged to strangers. Such deposit as the Carrier or his agents may deem sufficient to cover the estimated contribution of the goods and any salvage and special charges thereon shall, if required, be made by the goods, Shippers, Consignees or owners of the goods to the Carrier before delivery.

(5) Both-to-Blame Collision Clause.
If the Vessel comes into collision with another ship as a result of the negligence of the other ship and any act, neglect or default of the Master, Mariner, Pilot or the servants of the Carrier in the navigation or in the management of the Vessel, the owners of the cargo carried hereunder will indemnify the Carrier against all loss or liability to the other or non-carrying ship or her Owners in so far as such loss or liability represents loss of, or damage to, or any claim whatsoever of the owners of said cargo, paid or payable by the other or non-carrying ship or her Owners to the owners of said cargo and set-off, recouped or recovered by the other or non-carrying ship or her Owners as part of their claim against the carrying Vessel or Carrier. The foregoing provisions shall also apply where the Owners, operators or those in charge of any ship or ships or objects other than, or in addition to, the colliding ships or objects are at fault in respect of a collision or contact.

For particulars of cargo, freight, destination, etc., see overleaf.

*This is the 1978 edition, code-named "Congenbill", adopted by the Baltic and International Maritime Conference for use with charterparties, and reproduced with their permission.

---

[1] This is the 1978 edition, code-named "Congenbill", adopted by the Baltic and International Maritime Conference for use with charterparties, and reproduced with their permission.

CODE NAME: "CONGENBILL". EDITION 1978

Page 2

Shipper

BILL OF LADING
TO BE USED WITH CHARTER-PARTIES

B/L No.

Reference No.

Consignee

Notify address

Vessel | **Port of loading**

Port of discharge

Shipper's description of goods | **Gross weight**

(of which   on deck at Shipper's risk; the Carrier not being responsible for loss or damage howsoever arising)

Freight payable as per
CHARTER-PARTY dated ....

FREIGHT ADVANCE.
Received on account of freight:

....

Time used for loading .... days .... hours.

SHIPPED at the Port of Loading in apparent good order and condition on board the Vessel for carriage to the Port of Discharge or so near thereto as she may safely get the goods specified above.

Weight, measure, quality, quantity, condition, contents and value unknown.

IN WITNESS whereof the Master or Agent of the said Vessel has signed the number of Bills of Lading indicated below all of this tenor and date, any one of which being accomplished the others shall be void.

FOR CONDITIONS OF CARRIAGE SEE OVERLEAF

Freight payable at | Place and date of issue

Number of original Bs/L | Signature

DOCK WARRANT

DOCK WARRANT

No...... ....Docks, Co.
19....

Warrant for............imported in the ship............Master
..........., from...........entered by...........on the...........
deliverable to......or assigns by indorsement hereon. Rent commences
on the..........and all other charges from the date hereof.
Rate Charged.

MARK.	NUMBERS.	WEIGHT.	
		GROSS.	TARE.

Ledger No...... Folio.......
..........., Clerk.
...................., Warrant Clerk.

WAREHOUSE-KEEPER'S CERTIFICATE

WAREHOUSE-KEEPER'S CERTIFICATE

No......
Not transferable.
MESSRS. ....
We hold at your disposal in our warehouse as per conditions on back
hereof........................ ex S.S. ....
....
Warehouse keepers.
(Conditions as to issue of delivery orders, payment of rent, etc.,
indorsed.)

DELIVERY ORDER

DELIVERY ORDER

London,
No...... ....19......
Please deliver to................the undernoted goods, entered by
.... on................in the ship............... Captain
.......................from....................... Charges from
....................to be paid...................
Mark.
No......
Contents.

GENERAL LETTER OF HYPOTHECATION

General Letter of Hypothecation

To: BANK LIMITED

In consideration of your making loans or advances to me/us or incurring liability on my our behalf by way of acceptance or discount of bills of exchange or in respect of documentary credits or collections or otherwise in any way whatsoever, I/we hereby agree with you as follows to the intent that the provisions hereinafter set out shall apply on a continuing basis to all such transactions:—

(1) All bills of exchange, promissory notes and negotiable instruments of any description, all bills of lading, dock warrants, delivery orders, warehouse warrants and receipts, policies and certificates of insurance and all other documents of title to or documents relating to goods, and all goods thereby represented or to which such documents relate, which are now or may at any time hereafter be in your possession or deposited with you or your agents or representatives or lodged with you or transferred to you or your nominees by me/us or on my/our account by me/us or by others in my/our name or for my/our account (whether deposited for safe custody, collection, security or for any specific purpose or generally and whether in England or elsewhere) shall be a security for the due payment to you of all sums (including interest, commission, charges and expenses, and the satisfaction of all liabilities, whether present or maturing in the future, absolute or contingent) for which I am/we are now or I/we may at any time hereafter be indebted or liable to you on any account or in any manner whatever, and whether on an individual, joint or partnership account and in whatever name, style or firm.

(2) This security shall be a continuing security, notwithstanding any intermediate settlement of account, for the payment of all liabilities of mine/ours to you and shall be in addition to, and without prejudice to, any other securities which you may now or hereafter hold for my/our account.

(3) You are at liberty, without notice to me/us and without my/our consent, to dispose, by sale or otherwise, of the said goods or any of them in such manner and at such time or times as you may deem fit and to apply the proceeds thereof as you may think fit and I/we undertake on request by you to execute all such documents as you may require to vest the same in you or your nominees or transferees. In the event that the proceeds of sale thereof shall be insufficient to cover the whole of my/our liabilities to you, I/we undertake to pay to you forthwith on demand any balance which may then be due.

(4) I/We undertake to keep all the said goods insured against fire and all other usual risks in such amount as you may specify and, in the case of damage or loss, to recover the proceeds and apply them in accordance with your directions. You shall nevertheless be at liberty yourselves to insure the said goods against whatever risk and for whatever amount, whenever you may think fit, and to charge me/us with the cost thereof.

(5) I/We undertake to reimburse to you on demand, and authorise you at your discretion without any demand, to debit my/our account or any of my/our accounts with all charges, costs and expenses incurred in warehousing, storing, insuring or realising all or any of the said goods or other securities as well as any charges, costs and expenses which may be incurred by your agents or correspondents in connection therewith.

(6) I/We agree that you are not in any circumstances to be held responsible for any detention, loss or deterioration of any of the said goods or any damage thereto or for the quantity, quality, condition, delivery or insurance thereof or the correctness, validity, sufficiency or genuineness of any of the documents relative thereto from time to time deposited with you or your agents or representatives as aforesaid, or for any delay or omission which may occur in connection with the acceptance or payment of any drafts drawn on the buyers of any of such goods.

(7) I/We undertake to maintain such margin of security over liabilities as you shall from time to time stipulate, either by payment to you of cash or, if so agreed by you, by the deposit of additional collateral approved by you.

*Delete if only one party.

(8) *Any liability of ours to you arising hereunder shall be our joint and several responsibility.

(9) This letter shall be governed by and construed in accordance with the laws of England.

Dated this   day of   19

TRUST RECEIPT

TRUST RECEIPT

TO: Bank Limited

We acknowledge that we have received from you, upon and subject to the terms and conditions set out below, the undermentioned documents of title relating to the undermentioned goods, pledged to you upon the terms of a memorandum/letter of hypothecation dated   , which we hereby confirm and declare to continue.

We agree that we have received the said documents and will hold the same and the goods and all the proceeds of any sale thereof as trustees for you; and that we hold the said documents and will deal with the same only for the following purpose and on the following terms:—

*Delete
whichever
is not
appropriate.

*(1) **In order to obtain delivery of and to warehouse the goods.** The goods will be warehoused in your name and we will hand to you the warrants forthwith on receipt. We undertake to keep the goods duly covered by insurance as provided in the said memorandum/letter of hypothecation and in case of loss to pay the insurance moneys immediately and specifically to you.

*(2) **In order to deliver the goods to the buyer(s) named below.** We agree to pay to you immediately and specifically on receipt the whole proceeds of sale (whatever form the proceeds may take) without any deduction. We confirm that we are not indebted to the buyer(s).

We undertake that this transaction shall be kept separate from all other transactions and that the documents, goods and proceeds shall be kept separate and distinct from any other documents, goods or proceeds relating to or arising from any other transaction.

We undertake to deliver to you immediately upon your request at any time (whether or not the purpose set out above shall have been completed) the said documents and/or any other documents received in exchange or substitution for the said documents; and to comply promptly and fully with any instructions which you may give as to the manner of dealing with the goods or any of the goods or the removal of the same to, or storage of the same at, any place.

DOCK WARRANT

Description of Documents.	Description of Goods.	Vessel.	Name(s) of Buyer(s)	Invoice Price.

Indorsements

1. Misspelling
If the name of the holder is misspelt on the cheque, his indorsement will be irregular unless he follows the misspelling exactly when he indorses the cheque. He may add his proper signature, but this is not essential.

2. First names and initials
If the name of the holder is preceded by his first name, as by the words "Pay John Smith", his indorsement will be regular if he indorses the cheque "John Smith" or "J. Smith". Similarly, if the name of the holder is preceded by his initials, as by the words "Pay J. Smith", his indorsement will be regular if he indorses the cheque "J. Smith" or "John Smith".

3. Surnames alone
If the name of the holder is given by such words as "Pay Smith" or "Pay Mr Smith", his indorsement will be irregular unless he gives his initials or his first name as well as his surname when he indorses the cheque. There is one exception to this rule: a peer of the realm may sign his name by his surname alone and may therefore indorse a cheque by his surname alone.

4. Wife's name
If the name of the holder is given by such words as "Pay Mrs Smith", her indorsement will be regular if it is given by such words as "Alice Smith", or "A. Smith". If, however, the name of the holder is given by such words as "Pay Mrs John Smith", her indorsement will only be regular if it is given by words such as "Alice Smith, wife of J. Smith" or "A. Smith, widow of the late John Smith". If the name of the holder is given by such words as "Pay Alice Brown" and the holder subsequently marries, the holder should indorse the cheque by words such as "Alice Smith nee Brown".

5. Courtesy titles

If the name of the holder is given by such words as "Pay Mr J. Smith" or "Pay J. Smith, Esq" or "Pay Capt J. Smith" or "Pay Dr Smith", his indorsement will be irregular if it contains the courtesy title. However, the indorsement will be regular if it is given by words such as "J. Smith" or "John Smith". It will also be regular if it is given by words such as "J. Smith, MD" or "J. Smith, Capt." This is because the expressions added in these cases are not to be regarded as courtesy titles, but merely as descriptions of the indorser. An indorsement which included a courtesy title would be regular if it was made in a country where such indorsements were regarded as being regular.

6. Trustees and personal representatives

If the name of the holder is given by words such as "Pay Trustees of John Smith", the holder's indorsement will be regular if all the trustees indorse the cheque, using words such as "H. Jones, A. Brown, Trustees for John Smith". If trustees delegate authority to one of their number, the delegee can make a regular indorsement, using word such as "For self and co-trustee(s) of John Smith, H. Jones". However an indorsement by the delegee would be irregular if it was made by such words as "H. Jones, Trustee for John Smith", because the holder was described as "Trustees" and the indorsement would appear to suggest a single trustee. If the name of the holder is given by words such as "Pay John Smith", an indorsement by such words as "H. Jones, Trustee for John Smith" would be irregular.

Exactly the same rules apply to indorsements by personal representatives.

7. Joint names

If the name of the holder is given by words such as "Pay J. Smith, H. Jones", the holder's indorsement will be irregular unless it is made by both holders or by one holder, using words which indicate that he is acting as the agent of the other holder. If the name of the holder is given by words such as "Pay J. Smith and another", the holder's indorsement will be regular if it is made by words such as "For self and another J. Smith". However, the holder's indorsement will be irregular if it is made by words such as "J. Smith", or if it is made by words such as "J. Smith, H. Brown" even if H. Brown is the "another" referred to as the co-holder of the cheque.

8. Partnerships

If the name of the holder is given by words such as "Pay Messrs

Smith & Co", the holder's indorsement will be regular if it is given by words such as "Smith & Co"; but will be irregular if given by words such as "J. Smith & Co." If the name of the holder is given by words such as "Pay Smith, Jones & Co", the holder's indorsement will be regular if it is given by words such as "Smith, Jones & Co". It will also be regular if it is given by words such as "Smith, Jones & Co, H. Brown, Partner"; but it will not be regular if the word "Partner" is omitted.

If the name of the holder is given by words such as "Pay Messrs Smith", the holder's indorsement will be regular if it is given by words such as "Smiths", "Smith & Smith", "Smith & Son", "J. Smith & Sons", "J. & J. Smith", "J. Smith, S. Smith", or "Smith Bros." All these indorsements will be regular because all mean "Messrs Smith". But an indorsement by such words as "Smith & Co" would not be regular because a firm called "Smith & Co" could indicate persons whose name would not fit the description "Messrs Smith".

If the name of the holder is given by words such as "Pay Smith Bros", the holder's indorsement will be irregular if it is given by such words as "J. Smith, S. Smith", but would be regular if given by such words as "J. Smith, S. Smith, Brothers".

9. Companies

If the name of the holder is given by such words as "Pay John Smith & Co Ltd", the holder's indorsement will be regular if given by such words as "*per pro.* John Smith & Co Ltd, H. Jones, Secretary" or "*per pro.* John Smith & Co Ltd, H. Jones" or "John Smith & Co Ltd, H. Jones, Secretary". In other words, the indorsement will be regular if there are words such as "*per pro.*" or "Secretary", showing that the indorser has authority to sign on behalf of the holder.

It therefore follows that the holder's indorsement would be irregular if made by words such as "John Smith & Co Ltd" or "John Smith & Co Ltd, H. Jones". An indorsement would also be irregular if the indorser himself described himself as occupying any position other than the position of director, company secretary or manager of the company. There are two exceptions to this rule: an indorsement made by a person who described himself as receiver for debentureholders or as liquidator would be regular provided that the drawee knew of the appointment of the receiver or liquidator.

An indorsement will be irregular if the name of the holder is not followed exactly even if the name of the holder is misspelt. Thus, if a cheque was drawn "Pay J. Smith & Co Ltd", an indorsement which contained the words "Pay John Smith & Co. Ltd." would be irregular even if "John Smith & Co Ltd" was the correct name of the company.

10. Officials

If the name of the holder is given by words such as "Pay John Smith, Treasurer of the Blanktown Association", the holder's indorsement would be regular if it was made by words such as *"per pro.* the Blanktown Union, J. Smith", but it would be irregular if it was made by words such as "J. Smith" or by words such as "Treasurer of the Blanktown Association".

11. Foreign characters

If the name of the holder is given in Latin characters, the holder's indorsement will be irregular if it is given in foreign characters, such as Greek or Arabic characters, unless the drawee is satisfied that the foreign characters "represent the equivalent of the name of the person whose indorsement is necessary". A translation of the characters certified by a notary would be acceptable. The Council of the Institute of Bankers has suggested that the cost of procuring the translation should be borne by the holder whose indorsement has been called into question or by his banker who presents the cheque for payment to the drawee. The same rules would presumably apply if the name of the holder was given in foreign characters and the indorsement was made either in foreign characters or in Latin characters

12. Agents

If the name of the holder is given by words such as "H. Brown per J. Smith", Smith is the agent of Brown. If Brown indorses the cheque, the indorsement will be irregular. If Smith indorses the cheque, the indorsement will be regular provided that Smith makes clear that he is indorsing as the agent of Brown.

Bibliography

BOOKS

Anson. *The Law of Contract.* 25th Edn. London: Oxford University Press, 1979.

Buckley. *The Companies Acts.* 14th Edn. London: Butterworths, 1981.

Byles. *Bills of Exchange.* 24th Edn. London: Sweet & Maxwell, 1979.

Chalmers. *Sale of Goods.* 18th Edn. London: Butterworths, 1981.

Cheshire & Fifoot. *Law of Contract.* 10th Edn. London: Butterworths, 1981.

Chorley and Smart. *Leading Cases on the Law of Banking.* 4th Edn. London: Sweet & Maxwell, 1977.

Crystal and Nicholson. *A Handbook of Bankruptcy Law and Practice.* 3rd Edn. London: Oyez Longman, 1979.

Gore-Brown. *Handbook on the Formation, Management and Winding Winding-up of Joint Stock Companies.* 43rd Edn. Jordan & Sons, 1977 (Supplement 1981).

Gower. *Company Law.* 4th Edn. London: Stevens & Sons, 1979 (Supplement 1981).

Gutteridge and Megrah. *The Law of Bankers' Commercial Credits.* 6th Edn. Europa Publications, 1979.

Holden. *The History of Negotiable Instruments in English Law.* The Athlone Press, 1955.

Holden. *The Law and Practice of Banking.* Vol. 1. *Banker and Customer.* 2nd Edn. Pitmans, 1974. Vol. 2. *Securities for Bankers' Advances.* 6th Edn. Pitmans, 1980.

Institute of Bankers. *Legal Decisions Affecting Bankers.* Annual Volumes 1900–1968.

Institute of Bankers. *Questions on Banking Practice.* 11th Edn. 1978.

James. *Introduction to English Law.* 10th Edn. London: Butterworths, 1979.

Lindley. *The Law of Partnership.* 14th Edn. London: Sweet & Maxwell, 1979.

Lowe. *Commercial Law.* 5th Edn. London: Sweet & Maxwell, 1976.

Mather. *Banker and Customer Relationship and Accounts of Personal Customers*. Waterlows, 5th Edn. 1977.

Megarry. *Manual of the Law of Real Property*. 5th Edn. London: Sweet & Maxwell, 1975.

Paget. *Law of Banking*. 8th Edn. London: Butterworths, 1972.

Palmer. *Company Law*. London: Steven & Sons, 1981.

Perry. *A Dictionary of Banking*. Macdonald & Evans, 1979.

Sergeant and Sims. *Stamp Duties and Capital Duty*. 7th Edn. London: Butterworths, 1977; Cumulative Supplement, 1980.

Smart. *Cases on the Law of Banking 1977–1980*. London: Sweet & Maxwell, Institute of Bankers, 1981.

Stevens and Borrie. *Elements of Mercantile Law*. 17th Edn. London: Butterworths, 1978.

Williams and Muir Hunter. *The Law and Practice in Bankruptcy*. 19th Edn. London: Stevens & Sons, 1979.

Winfield & Jolowicz. *On Tort*. 11th Edn. London: Sweet & Maxwell, 1979.

PERIODICALS

The Banker. Published monthly by Banker, Minster House, Arthur Street, London, EC4.

Bankers' Magazine. Published monthly by Waterlow & Sons, Holywell House, Worship Street, London, EC2.

Journal of the Institute of Bankers. Published alternate months by Institute of Bankers, 10 Lombard Street, London, EC3.

Index

mortgage—*cont.*
 leasehold, 362–3, 395–6
 legal, 293, 362–3
  deposit of title deeds, specimen
   memorandum, 743–7
 loan interest, 31
 to minor, 78–9
 occupation of property and, 361
 particulars of, specimen form, 757–8
 by partner, 131
 in partner's bankruptcy, 136
 priority order, 366–8, 373–4
 proof of title for, 350
 puisne, 354
 rates on, 388–9
 redemption, 369–71
 registered land, 406–8
 right to insure, 383–4
 right to sell, 376–9
 running account on, 372–3
 second, 372–4, 384–5, 409–11, 517
  and subsequent, 363, 368
 sub-mortgages, 410
 tacking on, 371–2, 373, 384
 taxes on, 390
 transfer of, 386, 387–8
 trust property, 359–60
 under seal, 365
 unregistered, 407
mortgagee
 first, entitlement to deeds, 363
 power of attorney, 366
 rights of, 371–84, 408
  appointment of receiver, 379–80
  consolidation, 382–3
  foreclosure, 380–1
  grant of leases, 381
  insurance, 383–4
  possession, 375–6
  sale, 366, 376–9
  suing, 374–5
  in winding up, 666
mortgages (*see also* charge; life policies;
  property; unit trusts)
 chattels, enforcement of, 521–2
 goods, 480
 insurance policy, specimen form, 753–756
 interests under trusts, 475–7
 matrimonial home, 342–3, 355–6, 360–361, 399–400
 overdraft, 416
 parol, 480
 ship, 491–3

stocks and shares, 415–22
 equitable, 418–21, 423–4
 stop notice, 420
 legal, 415–18
  advantages of, 421–4
  disadvantages of, 424–5
Mortgagors
 bankrupt, 379
 in breach of obligation, 373–4
 company in liquidation, 667
 joint, 391
  in enforcement action, 518–19
 redemption rights of, 369–71
Motor vehicles, contract hire of (*see also*
  cars), 6, 278, 667
multinational banks, 7

National Girobank, 7, 248–50
National Savings, 414
 Bank, 204, 257
 Certificates, 414
 Contracts, 257, 423n.
 Stock Register, 257, 414
negative pledge, 576
negligence, 188–9
 banker's draft, 245
 bills of exchange, 213
 breach of trust, 87
 cheque drawn by partner, 133
 collecting banker's, 184, 189–94
 company director's account, 117
 contributory, 194
 creditor's, 201
 incorrect indorsement, 188–90
 investment advice, 55
 loans to companies, 125
 paying banker's, 176
 safe custody, 57
 taking up references, 62–5
negotiable instrument, 152, 446
 title by estoppel, 432–3
negotiation credit, 539 (Fig. 9), 543
Northern Bank, 4
Northern Ireland, 111, 127
nostro accounts, 527

Official Receiver, 645, 650–1, 679, 691
 information for, from banker, 688
operating lease, 615–16
order to a banker, 140
overdraft, 171, 175, 277–8, 285, 291
 advertisements, 286
 after notice of act of Bankruptcy, 695
 appropriation of payments in case of, 46

Details of other Macdonald & Evans
Publications on related subjects can be found
in the FREE Macdonald & Evans Business
Studies catalogue available from Department
BP1, Macdonald & Evans Ltd., Estover Road,
Plymouth PL6 7PZ